PYTHON

IN A NUTSHELL

Second Edition

Alex Martelli

Beijing • Cambridge • Farnham • Köln • Paris • Sebastopol • Taipei • Tokyo

Python in a Nutshell, Second Edition
by Alex Martelli

Copyright © 2006, 2003 O'Reilly Media, Inc. All rights reserved.
Printed in the United States of America.

Published by O'Reilly Media, Inc., 1005 Gravenstein Highway North, Sebastopol, CA 95472.

O'Reilly books may be purchased for educational, business, or sales promotional use. Online editions are also available for most titles (*safari.oreilly.com*). For more information, contact our corporate/institutional sales department: (800) 998-9938 or *corporate@oreilly.com*.

Editor:	Mary T. O'Brien	**Cover Designer:**	Emma Colby
Production Editor:	Matt Hutchinson	**Interior Designer:**	Brett Kerr
Copyeditor:	Linley Dolby	**Cover Illustrator:**	Karen Montgomery
Proofreader:	Matt Hutchinson	**Illustrators:**	Robert Romano and Jessamyn
Indexer:	Johnna Dinse		Read

Printing History:

March 2003:	First Edition.
July 2006:	Second Edition.

RepKover™ This book uses RepKover™, a durable and flexible lay-flat binding.

ISBN-10: 0-596-10046-9
ISBN-13: 978-0596-10046-9

[M]   [11]06]

Table of Contents

Preface ix

Part I. Getting Started with Python

1. **Introduction to Python** **3**
   The Python Language   3
   The Python Standard Library and Extension Modules   5
   Python Implementations   5
   Python Development and Versions   8
   Python Resources   9

2. **Installation** **14**
   Installing Python from Source Code   14
   Installing Python from Binaries   18
   Installing Jython   20
   Installing IronPython   21

3. **The Python Interpreter** **22**
   The python Program   22
   Python Development Environments   26
   Running Python Programs   28
   The jython Interpreter   29
   The IronPython Interpreter   30

Part II. Core Python Language and Built-ins

4. The Python Language **33**
Lexical Structure   33
Data Types   38
Variables and Other References   46
Expressions and Operators   50
Numeric Operations   52
Sequence Operations   53
Set Operations   58
Dictionary Operations   59
The print Statement   61
Control Flow Statements   62
Functions   70

5. Object-Oriented Python **81**
Classes and Instances   82
Special Methods   104
Decorators   115
Metaclasses   116

6. Exceptions **121**
The try Statement   121
Exception Propagation   126
The raise Statement   128
Exception Objects   129
Custom Exception Classes   132
Error-Checking Strategies   134

7. Modules **139**
Module Objects   139
Module Loading   144
Packages   149
The Distribution Utilities (distutils)   150

8. Core Built-ins **153**
Built-in Types   154
Built-in Functions   158
The sys Module   168
The copy Module   172
The collections Module   173

The functional Module   175
The bisect Module   176
The heapq Module   177
The UserDict Module   178
The optparse Module   179
The itertools Module   183

9. **Strings and Regular Expressions** **186**
Methods of String Objects   186
The string Module   191
String Formatting   193
The pprint Module   197
The repr Module   198
Unicode   198
Regular Expressions and the re Module   201

Part III. Python Library and Extension Modules

10. **File and Text Operations** **215**
Other Chapters That Also Deal with Files   215
Organization of This Chapter   215
File Objects   216
Auxiliary Modules for File I/O   224
The StringIO and cStringIO Modules   229
Compressed Files   230
The os Module   240
Filesystem Operations   241
Text Input and Output   256
Richer-Text I/O   258
Interactive Command Sessions   265
Internationalization   269

11. **Persistence and Databases** **277**
Serialization   278
DBM Modules   285
Berkeley DB Interfacing   288
The Python Database API (DBAPI) 2.0   292

12. Time Operations **302**
The time Module   302
The datetime Module   306
The pytz Module   313
The dateutil Module   313
The sched Module   316
The calendar Module   317
The mx.DateTime Module   319

13. Controlling Execution **328**
Dynamic Execution and the exec Statement   328
Internal Types   331
Garbage Collection   332
Termination Functions   337
Site and User Customization   338

14. Threads and Processes **340**
Threads in Python   341
The thread Module   341
The Queue Module   342
The threading Module   344
Threaded Program Architecture   350
Process Environment   353
Running Other Programs   354
The mmap Module   360

15. Numeric Processing **365**
The math and cmath Modules   365
The operator Module   368
Random and Pseudorandom Numbers   370
The decimal Module   372
The gmpy Module   373

16. Array Processing **375**
The array Module   375
Extensions for Numeric Array Computation   377
The Numeric Package   378
Array Objects   378
Universal Functions (ufuncs)   399
Auxiliary Numeric Modules   403

17. Tkinter GUIs **405**
Tkinter Fundamentals   406
Widget Fundamentals   408
Commonly Used Simple Widgets   415
Container Widgets   420
Menus   423
The Text Widget   426
The Canvas Widget   436
Layout Management   442
Tkinter Events   446

18. Testing, Debugging, and Optimizing **451**
Testing   452
Debugging   461
The warnings Module   471
Optimization   474

Part IV. Network and Web Programming

19. Client-Side Network Protocol Modules **493**
URL Access   493
Email Protocols   503
The HTTP and FTP Protocols   506
Network News   511
Telnet   515
Distributed Computing   516
Other Protocols   519

20. Sockets and Server-Side Network Protocol Modules **520**
The socket Module   521
The SocketServer Module   528
Event-Driven Socket Programs   533

21. CGI Scripting and Alternatives **545**
CGI in Python   546
Cookies   553
Other Server-Side Approaches   557

22. MIME and Network Encodings **561**
Encoding Binary Data as Text 561
MIME and Email Format Handling 564

23. Structured Text: HTML **575**
The sgmllib Module 576
The htmllib Module 580
The HTMLParser Module 583
The BeautifulSoup Extension 585
Generating HTML 586

24. Structured Text: XML **591**
An Overview of XML Parsing 592
Parsing XML with SAX 593
Parsing XML with DOM 599
Changing and Generating XML 606

Part V. Extending and Embedding

25. Extending and Embedding Classic Python **613**
Extending Python with Python's C API 614
Extending Python Without Python's C API 645
Embedding Python 647
Pyrex 650

26. Extending and Embedding Jython **655**
Importing Java Packages in Jython 656
Embedding Jython in Java 659
Compiling Python into Java 662

27. Distributing Extensions and Programs **666**
Python's distutils 666
py2exe 675
py2app 676
cx_Freeze 676
PyInstaller 676

Index **677**

Preface

The Python programming language manages to reconcile many apparent contradictions: it's both elegant and pragmatic, it's both simple and powerful, it's very high-level yet doesn't get in your way when you need to fiddle with bits and bytes, it's suitable for programming novices and great for experts, too.

This book is aimed at programmers with some previous exposure to Python, as well as experienced programmers coming to Python for the first time from other programming languages. The book is a quick reference to Python itself, the most commonly used parts of its vast standard library, and some of the most popular and useful third-party modules and packages, covering a wide range of application areas, including web and network programming, GUIs, XML handling, database interactions, and high-speed numeric computing. The book focuses on Python's cross-platform capabilities and covers the basics of extending Python and embedding it in other applications, using either C or Java™.

How This Book Is Organized

This book has five parts, as follows.

Part I, Getting Started with Python

Chapter 1, *Introduction to Python*
> Covers the general characteristics of the Python language and its implementations, and discusses where to get help and information.

Chapter 2, *Installation*
> Explains how to obtain and install Python on your computer(s).

Chapter 3, *The Python Interpreter*
> Covers the Python interpreter program, its command-line options, and how it is used to run Python programs and in interactive sessions. The chapter also

mentions text editors that are particularly suitable for editing Python programs and auxiliary programs for thoroughly checking your Python sources, and examines some full-fledged integrated development environments, including IDLE, which comes free with standard Python.

Part II, Core Python Language and Built-ins

Chapter 4, *The Python Language*
Covers Python syntax, built-in data types, expressions, statements, and how to write and call functions.

Chapter 5, *Object-Oriented Python*
Explains object-oriented programming in Python.

Chapter 6, *Exceptions*
Covers how to deal with errors and abnormal conditions in Python programs.

Chapter 7, *Modules*
Covers how Python lets you group code into modules and packages, how to define and import modules, and how to install third-party Python extensions that are packaged in standard Python ways.

Chapter 8, *Core Built-ins*
Refers to built-in data types and functions, and some of the most fundamental modules in the standard Python library (roughly, modules supplying functionality that, in some other languages, is built into the language itself).

Chapter 9, *Strings and Regular Expressions*
Covers Python's powerful string-processing facilities, including Unicode strings and regular expressions.

Part III, Python Library and Extension Modules

Chapter 10, *File and Text Operations*
Explains how to deal with files and text processing using built-in Python file objects, many modules from Python's standard library, and platform-specific extensions for rich text I/O. The chapter also covers issues of internationalization and localization, and the specific task of defining interactive text-mode command sessions with Python.

Chapter 11, *Persistence and Databases*
Introduces Python's serialization and persistence mechanisms, as well as Python's interfaces to DBM databases, the Berkeley Database, and relational (SQL-based) databases.

Chapter 12, *Time Operations*
Covers how to deal with times and dates in Python, using the standard library and popular extensions.

Chapter 13, *Controlling Execution*
Explains how to achieve advanced execution control in Python, including execution of dynamically generated code and control of garbage-collection operations. The chapter also covers some Python internal types, and the

specific issue of registering "clean-up" functions to be executed at program-termination time.

Chapter 14, *Threads and Processes*
Covers Python's functionality for concurrent execution, both via multiple threads running within one process and via multiple processes running on a single machine. The chapter also covers how to access the process's environment, and how to access files via memory-mapping mechanisms.

Chapter 15, *Numeric Processing*
Shows Python's features for numeric computations, both in standard library modules and in third-party extension packages; in particular, the chapter covers how to use decimal floating-point numbers instead of the default binary floating-point numbers. The chapter also covers how to get and use pseudorandom and truly random numbers.

Chapter 16, *Array Processing*
Covers built-in and extension packages for array handling, focusing on the traditional Numeric third-party extension, and mentions other, more recently developed alternatives.

Chapter 17, *Tkinter GUIs*
Explains how to develop graphical user interfaces in Python with the Tkinter package included with the standard Python distribution, and briefly mentions other alternative Python GUI frameworks.

Chapter 18, *Testing, Debugging, and Optimizing*
Deals with Python tools and approaches that help ensure your programs are correct (i.e., that your programs do what they're meant to do), find and correct errors in your programs, and check and enhance your programs' performance. The chapter also covers the concept of "warning" and the Python library module that deals with it.

Part IV, Network and Web Programming

Chapter 19, *Client-Side Network Protocol Modules*
Covers many modules in Python's standard library that help you write network client programs, particularly by dealing with various network protocols from the client side and handling URLs.

Chapter 20, *Sockets and Server-Side Network Protocol Modules*
Explains Python's interfaces to low-level network mechanisms (sockets), standard Python library modules that help you write network server programs, and asynchronous (event-driven) network programming with standard modules and the powerful Twisted extension.

Chapter 21, *CGI Scripting and Alternatives*
Covers the basics of CGI programming, how to perform CGI programming in Python with standard Python library modules, and how use "cookies" to deal with session-state in HTTP server-side programming. The chapter also mentions many alternatives to CGI programming for server-side web programming through popular Python extensions.

Chapter 22, *MIME and Network Encodings*
> Shows how to process email and other network-structured and encoded documents in Python.

Chapter 23, *Structured Text: HTML*
> Covers Python library modules that let you process and generate HTML documents.

Chapter 24, *Structured Text: XML*
> Covers Python library modules and popular extensions that let you process, modify, and generate XML documents.

Part V, Extending and Embedding

Chapter 25, *Extending and Embedding Classic Python*
> Shows how to code Python extension modules using C and other classic compiled languages, how to embed Python in applications coded in such languages, and alternative ways to extend Python and access existing C, C++, and Fortran libraries.

Chapter 26, *Extending and Embedding Jython*
> Shows how to use Java classes from the Jython implementation of Python, and how to embed Jython in applications coded in Java.

Chapter 27, *Distributing Extensions and Programs*
> Covers the tools that let you package Python extensions, modules, and applications for distribution.

Conventions Used in This Book

The following conventions are used throughout this book.

Reference Conventions

In the function/method reference entries, when feasible, each optional parameter is shown with a default value using the Python syntax *name=value*. Built-in functions need not accept named parameters, so parameter names are not significant. Some optional parameters are best explained in terms of their presence or absence, rather than through default values. In such cases, I indicate that a parameter is optional by enclosing it in brackets ([ ]). When more than one argument is optional, the brackets are nested.

Typographic Conventions

Italic
> Used for filenames, program names, URLs, and to introduce new terms. Also used for Unix commands and their options.

Constant width
> Used for all code examples, as well as for all items that appear in code, including keywords, methods, functions, classes, and modules.

Constant width italic
> Used to show text that can be replaced with user-supplied values in code examples.

Constant width bold
> Used for commands that must be typed on the command line, and occasionally for emphasis in code examples or to indicate code output.

Using Code Examples

This book is here to help you get your job done. In general, you may use the code in this book in your programs and documentation. You do not need to contact the publisher for permission unless you're reproducing a significant portion of the code. For example, writing a program that uses several chunks of code from this book does not require permission. Selling or distributing a CD-ROM of examples from O'Reilly books *does* require permission. Answering a question by citing this book and quoting example code does not require permission. Incorporating a significant amount of example code from this book into your product's documentation *does* require permission.

We appreciate, but do not require, attribution. An attribution usually includes the title, author, publisher, and ISBN. For example: "*Python in a Nutshell*, Second Edition, by Alex Martelli. Copyright 2006 O'Reilly Media, Inc., 0-596-10046-9."

How to Contact Us

I have tested and verified the information in this book to the best of my ability, but you may find that features have changed (or even that I have made mistakes!). Please let the publisher know about any errors you find, as well as your suggestions for future editions, by writing to:

> O'Reilly Media, Inc.
> 1005 Gravenstein Highway North
> Sebastopol, CA 95472
> 800-928-9938 (in the United States or Canada)
> 707-829-0515 (international or local)
> 707-829-0104 (fax)

There is a web page for this book, which lists errata, examples, and any additional information. You can access this page at:

> *http://www.oreilly.com/catalog/pythonian2*

To ask technical questions or comment on the book, send email to:

> *bookquestions@oreilly.com*

For more information about books, conferences, resource centers, and the O'Reilly Network, see the O'Reilly web site at:

> *http://www.oreilly.com*

Safari® Enabled

 When you see a Safari® Enabled icon on the cover of your favorite technology book, that means the book is available online through the O'Reilly Network Safari Bookshelf.

Safari offers a solution that's better than e-books: it's a virtual library that lets you easily search thousands of top tech books, cut and paste code samples, download chapters, and find quick answers when you need the most accurate, current information. Try it for free at *http://safari.oreilly.com*.

Acknowledgments

My heartfelt thanks to everybody who helped me out on this book, both in the first edition and in its current second edition. Many Python beginners, practitioners, and experts have read drafts of parts of the book and have offered feedback to help me make the book clear, precise, accurate, and readable. Out of all of them, for the quality and quantity of their feedback and other help, I must single out for special thanks my colleagues at Google, especially Neal Norwitz and Mohsin Ahmed.

The first edition received indispensable help from Python experts in specific areas (Aahz on threading, Itamar Shtull-Trauring on Twisted, Mike Orr on Cheetah, Eric Jones and Paul Dubois on Numeric, and Tim Peters on threading, testing, and optimization), a wonderful group of technical reviewers (Fred Drake, Magnus Lie Hetland, Steve Holden, and Sue Giller), and the book's editor, Paula Ferguson. The second edition benefited from the efforts of editors Jonathan Gennick and Mary O'Brien, and technical reviewers Ryan Alexander, Jeffery Collins, and Mary Gardiner. I owe special thanks to the wonderful folks in the O'Reilly Tools Group, who (both directly and personally, and through the helpful tools they developed) helped me through several difficult technical problems.

As always, even though they're back in my native Italy and my career with Google has taken me to California, my thoughts go to my family: my children Flavia and Lucio, my sister Elisabetta, and my father Lanfranco.

But the one, incredible individual to which my heart gushes out in gratitude, and more than gratitude, is my wife, Anna Martelli Ravenscroft, my co-author in the second edition of the *Python Cookbook*, a fellow Python Software Foundation member, and the harshest, most wonderful technical reviewer any author could possibly dream of. Besides her innumerable direct contributions to this book, Anna managed to create for me, out of thin air, enough peace, quiet, and free time over the last year (despite my wonderful and challenging responsibilities as Uber Tech Lead for Google) to make this book possible. Truly, this is her book at least as much as it is mine.

Getting Started with Python

Introduction to Python

Python is a general-purpose programming language. It has been around for quite a while: Guido van Rossum, Python's creator, started developing Python back in 1990. This stable and mature language is very high-level, dynamic, object-oriented, and cross-platform—all characteristics that are very attractive to developers. Python runs on all major hardware platforms and operating systems, so it doesn't constrain your platform choices.

Python offers high productivity for all phases of the software life cycle: analysis, design, prototyping, coding, testing, debugging, tuning, documentation, deployment, and, of course, maintenance. Python's popularity has seen steady, unflagging growth over the years. Today, familiarity with Python is an advantage for every programmer, as Python has infiltrated every niche and has useful roles to play as a part of *any* software solution.

Python provides a unique mix of elegance, simplicity, practicality, and power. You'll quickly become productive with Python, thanks to its consistency and regularity, its rich standard library, and the many third-party modules that are readily available for it. Python is easy to learn, so it is quite suitable if you are new to programming, yet at the same time, it is powerful enough for the most sophisticated expert.

The Python Language

The Python language, while not minimalist, is rather spare for good pragmatic reasons. Once a language offers one good way to express a design idea, adding other ways has only modest benefits, while the cost in terms of language complexity grows more than linearly with the number of features. A complicated language is harder to learn and master (and implement efficiently and without bugs) than a simpler one. Any complications and quirks in a language hamper productivity in software maintenance, particularly in large projects, where many developers cooperate and often maintain code originally written by others.

Python is simple, but not simplistic. It adheres to the idea that if a language behaves a certain way in some contexts, it should ideally work similarly in all contexts. Python also follows the principle that a language should not have "convenient" shortcuts, special cases, ad hoc exceptions, overly subtle distinctions, or mysterious and tricky under-the-covers optimizations. A good language, like any other designed artifact, must balance such general principles with taste, common sense, and a high degree of practicality.

Python is a general-purpose programming language, so Python's traits are useful in just about any area of software development. There is no area where Python cannot be part of an optimal solution. "Part" is an important word here; while many developers find that Python fills all of their needs, Python does not have to stand alone. Python programs can easily cooperate with a variety of other software components, making it an ideal language for gluing together components written in other languages.

Python is a very-high-level language (VHLL). This means that Python uses a higher level of abstraction, conceptually farther from the underlying machine, than do classic compiled languages such as C, C++, and Fortran, which are traditionally called high-level languages. Python is also simpler, faster to process, and more regular than classic high-level languages. This affords high programmer productivity and makes Python an attractive development tool. Good compilers for classic compiled languages can often generate binary machine code that runs much faster than Python code. However, in most cases, the performance of Python-coded applications proves sufficient. When it doesn't, you can apply the optimization techniques covered in "Optimization" on page 474 to enhance your program's performance while keeping the benefits of high programming productivity.

Newer languages such as Java and C# are slightly higher-level (farther from the machine) than classic ones such as C and Fortran, and share some characteristics of classic languages (such as the need to use declarations) as well as some of VHLLs like Python (such as the use of portable bytecode as the compilation target in typical implementations, and garbage collection to relieve programmers from the need to manage memory). If you find you are productive with Java or C# than with C or Fortran, try Python (possibly in the Jython or IronPython implementations, covered in "Python Implementations" on page 5) and become even *more* productive.

In terms of language level, Python is comparable to other powerful VHLLs like Perl or Ruby. The advantages of simplicity and regularity, however, remain on Python's side.

Python is an object-oriented programming language, but it lets you develop code using both object-oriented and traditional procedural styles, and a touch of the functional programming style, too, mixing and matching as your application requires. Python's object-oriented features are like those of C++, although they are much simpler to use.

The Python Standard Library and Extension Modules

There is more to Python programming than just the Python language: the standard Python library and other extension modules are almost as important for effective Python use as the language itself. The Python standard library supplies many well-designed, solid, 100 percent pure Python modules for convenient reuse. It includes modules for such tasks as representing data, string and text processing, interacting with the operating system and filesystem, and web programming. Because these modules are written in Python, they work on all platforms supported by Python.

Extension modules, from the standard library or from elsewhere, let Python code access functionality supplied by the underlying operating system or other software components such as graphical user interfaces (GUIs), databases, and networks. Extensions also afford maximal speed in computationally intensive tasks such as XML parsing and numeric array computations. Extension modules that are not coded in Python, however, do not necessarily enjoy the same cross-platform portability as pure Python code.

You can write special-purpose extension modules in lower-level languages to achieve maximum performance for small, computationally intensive parts that you originally prototyped in Python. You can also use tools such as SWIG to wrap existing C/C++ libraries into Python extension modules, as we'll see in "Extending Python Without Python's C API" on page 645. Finally, you can embed Python in applications coded in other languages, exposing existing application functionality to Python scripts via dedicated Python extension modules.

This book documents many modules, both from the standard library and from other sources, in areas such as client- and server-side network programming, GUIs, numerical array processing, databases, manipulation of text and binary files, and interaction with the operating system.

Python Implementations

Python currently has three production-quality implementations, known as CPython, Jython, and IronPython, and several other experimental implementations, such as PyPy. This book primarily addresses CPython, the most widely used implementation, which I refer to as just Python for simplicity. However, the distinction between a language and its implementations is an important one.

CPython

Classic Python (a.k.a. CPython, often just called Python) is the fastest, most up-to-date, most solid and complete implementation of Python. Therefore, it can be considered the "reference implementation" of the language. CPython is a compiler, interpreter, and set of built-in and optional extension modules, all coded in standard C. CPython can be used on any platform where the C compiler complies with the ISO/IEC 9899:1990 standard (i.e., all modern, popular platforms). In Chapter 2, I'll explain how to download and install CPython. All of this book, except Chapter 26 and a few sections explicitly marked otherwise, applies to CPython, since CPython is the most widely used version of Python.

Jython

Jython is a Python implementation for any Java Virtual Machine (JVM) compliant with Java 1.2 or better. Such JVMs are available for all popular, modern platforms. With Jython, you can use all Java libraries and frameworks. For optimal use of Jython, you need some familiarity with fundamental Java classes. You do not have to code in Java, but documentation and examples for existing Java classes are couched in Java terms, so you need a nodding acquaintance with Java to read and understand them. You also need to use Java supporting tools for tasks such as manipulating *.jar* files and signing applets. This book deals with Python, not with Java. For Jython usage, you should complement this book with *Jython Essentials*, by Noel Rappin and Samuele Pedroni (O'Reilly), possibly *Java in a Nutshell*, by David Flanagan (O'Reilly), and, if needed, some of the many other Java resources available.

IronPython

IronPython is a Python implementation for the Microsoft-designed Common Language Runtime (CLR), most commonly known as .NET. With IronPython, you can use all CLR libraries and frameworks. In addition to Microsoft's own implementation, a cross-platform implementation of the CLR (known as Mono) works with other, non-Microsoft operating systems, as well as with Windows. For optimal use of IronPython, you need some familiarity with fundamental CLR libraries. You do not have to code in C#, but documentation and examples for existing CLR libraries are often couched in C# terms, so you need a nodding acquaintance with C# to read and understand them. You also need to use CLR supporting tools for tasks such as making CLR assemblies. This book deals with Python, not with the CLR. For IronPython usage, you should complement this book with IronPython's own online documentation, and, if needed, some of the many other resources available about .NET, the CLR, C#, Mono, and so on.

Choosing Between CPython, Jython, and IronPython

If your platform is able to run CPython, Jython, and IronPython, how do you choose among them? First of all, don't choose; download and install them all. They coexist without problems, and they're free. Having them all on your machine costs only some download time and a little extra disk space.

The primary difference between the implementations is the environment in which they run and the libraries and frameworks they can use. If you need to work in a JVM environment, then Jython is an excellent choice. If you need to work in a CLR environment, you can take advantage of IronPython. If you're mainly working in a traditional environment, then CPython is an excellent fit. If you don't have a strong preference for one or the other, then you should start with the standard CPython reference implementation.

In other words, when you're just experimenting, learning, and trying things out, you will most often use CPython, since it's faster. To develop and deploy, your best choice depends on the extension modules you want to use and how you want to distribute your programs. CPython applications are often faster, particularly if they can use suitable extension modules, such as Numeric (covered in Chapter 16). CPython is more mature: it has been around longer, while Jython, and especially IronPython, are newer and less field-proven. The development of CPython versions tends to proceed faster than that of Jython and IronPython versions: at the time of writing, for example, the current language level supported is 2.2 for Jython, 2.4 for IronPython, and 2.4 rapidly progressing towards 2.5 for CPython (2.5 should be out by the time you read this).

However, as you'll see in Chapter 26, Jython can use any Java class as an extension module, whether the class comes from a standard Java library, a third-party library, or a library you develop yourself. Similarly, IronPython can use any CLR class, whether from the standard CLR libraries, or coded in C#, Visual Basic .NET, or other CLR-compliant languages. A Jython-coded application is a 100 percent pure Java application, with all of Java's deployment advantages and issues, and runs on any target machine having a suitable JVM. Packaging opportunities are also identical to Java's. Similarly, an IronPython-coded application is entirely compliant with .NET's specifications.

Jython, IronPython, and CPython are all good, faithful implementations of Python, and are reasonably close in terms of usability and performance. Since each of the JVM and CLR platforms carries a lot of baggage, but also supplies large amounts of useful libraries, frameworks, and tools, any of the implementations may enjoy decisive practical advantages in a specific deployment scenario. It is wise to become familiar with the strengths and weaknesses of each, and then choose optimally for each development task.

PyPy and Other Experimental Versions

There are several interesting implementations of Python that are not yet suitable for production use at the time of this writing, but may well be worth looking into for intrinsic interest and high future potential. Two such experimental implementations that are being actively worked on are Pirate (*http://pirate.tangentcode.com*), a Python implementation on top of the Parrot virtual machine, which also supports Perl 6 and other VHLs, and PyPy (*http://codespeak.net/pypy/*), a fast and flexible implementation of Python coded in Python itself, which is able to target several lower-level languages and virtual machines using advanced techniques such as type inferencing.

Licensing and Price Issues

CPython is covered by the CNRI Open Source GPL-Compatible License, allowing free use of Python for both commercial and free-software development (*http://www.python.org/2.4.2/license.html*). Jython's and IronPython's licenses are similarly liberal. Anything you download from the main Python, Jython, and IronPython sites will not cost you a penny. These licenses do not constrain what licensing and pricing conditions you can use for software you develop using the tools, libraries, and documentation they cover.

However, not everything Python-related is totally free from licensing costs or hassles. Many third-party Python sources, tools, and extension modules that you can freely download have liberal licenses, similar to that of Python itself. Others, however, are covered by the GNU Public License (GPL) or Lesser GPL (LGPL), constraining the licensing conditions you are allowed to place on derived works. Some commercially developed modules and tools may require you to pay a fee, either unconditionally or if you use them for profit.

There is no substitute for careful examination of licensing conditions and prices. Before you invest time and energy into any software component, check that you can live with its license. Often, especially in a corporate environment, such legal matters may involve consulting lawyers. Modules and tools covered in this book, unless I explicitly say otherwise, can be taken to be, at the time of this writing, freely downloadable, open source, and covered by a liberal license akin to Python's. However, I claim no legal expertise, and licenses can change over time, so double-checking is always prudent.

Python Development and Versions

Python is developed, maintained, and released by a team of core developers headed by Guido van Rossum, Python's inventor, architect, and Benevolent Dictator For Life (BDFL). This title means that Guido has the final say on what becomes part of the Python language and standard libraries. Python's intellectual property is vested in the Python Software Foundation (PSF), a nonprofit corporation devoted to promoting Python, with dozens of individual members (nominated for their contributions to Python, and including all of the Python core team) and corporate sponsors. Most PSF members have commit privileges to Python's SVN repositories (*http://svn.python.org/projects/*), and most Python SVN committers are members of the PSF.

Proposed changes to Python are detailed in public documents called Python Enhancement Proposals (PEPs), debated (and sometimes advisorily voted on) by Python developers and the wider Python community, and finally approved or rejected by Guido, who takes debates and votes into account but is not bound by them. Many hundreds of people actively contribute to Python development through PEPs, discussion, bug reports, and proposed patches to Python sources, libraries, and documentation.

The Python core team releases minor versions of Python (2.*x*, for growing values of *x*), currently at a pace of about once every year or two. Python 2.2 was released in December 2001, 2.3 in July 2003, and 2.4 in November 2004. Python 2.5 is scheduled to be released in the summer of 2006 (at the time of this writing, the first alpha release of 2.5 has just appeared). Each minor release adds features that make Python more powerful and simpler to use, but also takes care to maintain backward compatibility. One day there will be a Python 3.0 release, which will be allowed to break backward compatibility to some extent in order to remove some redundant "legacy" features and simplify the language even further. However, that release is still years in the future, and no specific schedules for it currently exist; the current state of Guido's ideas about Python 3.0 can be studied at *http://python.org/peps/pep-3000.html*.

Each minor release 2.*x* starts with alpha releases, tagged as 2.*x*a0, 2.*x*a1, and so on. After the alphas comes at least one beta release, 2.*x*b1, and after the betas, at least one release candidate, 2.*x*rc1. By the time the final release of 2.*x* comes out, it is always solid, reliable, and well tested on all major platforms. Any Python programmer can help ensure this by downloading alphas, betas, and release candidates, trying them out extensively, and filing bug reports for any problem that might emerge.

Once a minor release is out, part of the attention of the core team switches to the next minor release. However, a minor release normally gets successive point releases (i.e., 2.*x*.1, 2.*x*.2, and so on) that add no functionality but can fix errors, port Python to new platforms, enhance documentation, and add optimizations and tools.

This book focuses on Python 2.4 (and all its point releases), the most stable and widespread release at the time of this writing. I also cover, or at least mention, the changes that are scheduled to appear in Python 2.5, and I document which parts of the language and libraries were first introduced in 2.4 and thus cannot be used with the previous 2.3 release. Whenever I say that a feature is "in 2.4," I mean 2.4 and all following versions (in other words, with this phrasing I mean to include Python 2.5 but to exclude 2.3), unless I immediately continue by explaining some difference that is specific to 2.5.

At the time of this writing, the released version of Jython supports only Python 2.2 (and some, but not all, of Python 2.3), but not the full specifications of Python 2.4. IronPython 1.0 supports Python 2.4.

This book does not address older versions of Python, such as 1.5.2, 2.0, 2.1, 2.2; such versions are over four years old and should not be used for any new development. However, you might have to worry about such legacy versions if they are embedded in some application you need to script. Fortunately, Python's backward compatibility is quite good: current versions of Python are able to properly process just about any valid Python program that was written for Python 1.5.2 or later. You can find code and documentation for all old releases of Python at *http://python.org/doc/versions.html*.

Python Resources

The richest of all Python resources is the Internet. The best starting point is Python's site, *http://www.python.org*, which is full of interesting links to explore. *http://www.jython.org* is a must if you have any interest in Jython. For IronPython, at the time of writing the most relevant site is *http://workspaces.gotdotnet.com/ironpython*, but the IronPython team's near-future plans include reviving the site *http://ironpython.com*; by the time you read this, *http://ironpython.com* should be back in its role as the primary IronPython web site.

Documentation

Python, Jython, and IronPython come with good documentation. The manuals are available in many formats, suitable for viewing, searching, and printing. You can browse the manuals on the Web at *http://www.python.org/doc/current/*. You can find links to the various formats you can download at *http://www.python.org/doc/current/download.html*, and *http://www.python.org/doc/* has links to a large variety of documents. For Jython, *http://www.jython.org/docs/* has links to Jython-specific documents as well as general Python ones. The Python FAQ (Frequently Asked Questions) document is at *http://www.python.org/doc/FAQ.html*, and the Jython-specific FAQ document is at *http://www.jython.org/cgi-bin/faqw.py?req=index*.

Most Python documentation (including this book) assumes some software development knowledge. However, Python is quite suitable for first-time programmers, so there are exceptions to this rule. A few good introductory online texts for nonprogrammers are:

- Josh Cogliati's "Non-Programmers Tutorial For Python," available at *http://www.honors.montana.edu/~jjc/easytut/easytut/*
- Alan Gauld's "Learning to Program," available at *http://www.freenetpages.co.uk/hp/alan.gauld/*
- Allen Downey and Jeffrey Elkner's "How to Think Like a Computer Scientist (Python Version)," available at *http://www.ibiblio.org/obp/thinkCSpy/*

Newsgroups and Mailing Lists

The URL *http://www.python.org/community/lists/* has links to Python-related mailing lists and newsgroups. Always use plain-text format, *not* HTML, in any message you send to mailing lists or newsgroups.

The Usenet newsgroup for Python discussions is *comp.lang.python*. The newsgroup is also available as a mailing list. To subscribe, send a message whose body is the word "subscribe" to *python-list-request@python.org*. "Dr. Dobb's Python URL!," an interesting weekly collection of the most notable news and Python resources, is regularly posted to *comp.lang.python*. All issues, in reverse chronological order (most recent first), can be found by visiting the URL:

> *http://groups.google.com/groups?q=+Python-URL!+group%3Acomp.lang.python&start=0&scoring=d&*

A somewhat similar daily list of Python news can be found at *http://www.pythonware.com/daily/*.

Python-related announcements are posted to *comp.lang.python.announce*. To subscribe to its mailing-list equivalent, send a message whose body is the word "subscribe" to *python-announce-list-request@python.org*. To subscribe to Jython's mailing list, visit *http://lists.sf.net/lists/listinfo/jython-users*. To ask for individual help with Python, email your question to *python-help@python.org*. For questions and discussions about using Python to teach or learn programming, write to *tutor@python.org*.

Special-Interest Groups

Discussions on some specialized subjects related to Python take place on the mailing lists of Python Special Interest Groups (SIGs). The page at *http://www.python.org/ sigs/* has a list of active SIGs and pointers to general and specific information about them. Over a dozen SIGs are active at the time of this writing. Here are a few examples:

http://www.python.org/sigs/c++-sig/
    Bindings between C++ and Python

http://www.python.org/sigs/i18n-sig/
    Internationalization and localization of Python programs

http://www.python.org/sigs/image-sig/
    Image processing in Python

Python Business Forum

The Python Business Forum (PBF), at *http://www.python-in-business.org/*, is an international society of companies that base their businesses on Python. The PBF's site offers interesting information about some of the many business uses of Python.

Python Journal

The Python Journal, *http://pythonjournal.cognizor.com/*, is a free online publication that focuses on Python, how to use it, and its applications.

Extension Modules and Python Sources

A good starting point to explore the world of available Python extensions and sources is the Python Cheese Shop, *http://www.python.org/pypi*, which currently contains more than 1,200 packages with descriptions and pointers. Another good one is "The Vaults of Parnassus," available at *http://www.vex.net/parnassus/*, which has over 2,000 classified and commented links. By following these links, you can find and download most freely available Python modules and tools.

The standard Python source distribution contains excellent Python source code in the standard library and in the Demos and Tools directories, as well as C source for the many built-in extension modules. Even if you have no interest in building Python from source, I suggest you download and unpack the Python source distribution for study purposes.

Many Python modules and tools covered in this book also have dedicated sites. References to these sites are included in the appropriate chapters in this book.

The Python Cookbook

ActiveState's web site *http://www.activestate.com/ASPN/Python/Cookbook* hosts a living collection of Python recipes. Each recipe contains Python code, comments, and discussion, contributed by volunteers and enriched by readers, under the editorial supervision of David Ascher. All code is covered by a license similar to Python's. Everyone is invited to participate as author and reader in this community endeavor. Hundreds of recipes from the site—edited, commented, and grouped into chapters with introductions by Python experts—are published by O'Reilly as the *Python Cookbook*, edited by Alex Martelli, Anna Martelli Ravenscroft, and David Ascher.

Books and Magazines

Although the Net is a rich source of information, books and magazines still have their place (if you and I didn't agree on this, I wouldn't have written this book, and you wouldn't be reading it). At the time of this writing, the only magazine entirely devoted to Python is *Py* (for up-to-date information, visit *http://www.pyzine.com/*).

Books about Python and Jython are numerous. Here are a few that I recommend, although many of them cover older versions of the language rather than current ones:

- If you are just starting to learn Python (but have some previous programming experience), *Learning Python*, by Mark Lutz and David Ascher (O'Reilly), will serve you well. It sticks to the basics of Python's language and core libraries, covering clearly and in depth each of the subjects it touches.

- *Python Web Programming*, by Steve Holden (New Riders), teaches the basics of both Python and many other technologies that can help you build dynamic web sites, including TCP/IP, HTTP, HTML, XML, and relational databases. The book offers substantial examples, including a complete database-backed site.

- *Dive Into Python*, by Mark Pilgrim (APress), teaches by example in a fast-paced and thorough way that is very suitable for people who are already expert programmers in other languages. You can also freely download the book, in any of several formats, from *http://diveintopython.org/*.

- *Beginning Python: From Novice to Professional*, by Magnus Lie Hetland (APress), teaches both by thorough explanations and by fully developing 10 complete programs in various application areas.

- *Python Programming on Win32*, by Mark Hammond and Andy Robinson (O'Reilly), is indispensable for optimal Python use on Windows. The book details platform-specific extensions to Python for COM, ActiveScripting, Win32 API calls, and integration with Windows applications. The current edition uses Python's old 1.5.2 version, but everything also applies to Python's current version.

- *Jython Essentials*, by Samuele Pedroni and Noel Rappin (O'Reilly), is a rich and concise book on Jython, suitable if you already have some Java knowledge. For effective Jython use, I also suggest *Java in a Nutshell*, by David Flanagan (O'Reilly).

- *Python Essential Reference*, by David Beazley (New Riders), is a complete reference to the Python language and its standard libraries.

- *Python Standard Library*, by Fredrik Lundh (O'Reilly), offers terse and usable coverage of all modules in the standard Python library, with over 300 well-commented scripts to show how you can use each module. The amount and quality of examples stands out as the book's outstanding feature.

- For a very concise summary reference and reminder of Python's essentials, check out *Python Pocket Reference*, also by Mark Lutz (O'Reilly).

2

Installation

You can install Python, in classic (CPython), JVM (Jython), and .NET (IronPython) versions, on most platforms. With a suitable development system (C for CPython, Java for Jython, .NET for IronPython), you can install Python from its source code distribution. On popular platforms, you also have the alternative of installing from pre-built binary distributions. If your platform comes with a pre-installed version of Python, you may still want to install another richer or better updated one: if you do, I recommend you do *not* remove nor overwrite your platform's original version—rather, install the other version "side by side" with the first one. In this way, you can be sure you are not going to disturb any other software that is installed as part of your platform: such software might well rely on the exact Python version that came with the platform itself.

Installing CPython from a binary distribution is faster, saves you substantial work on some platforms, and is the only possibility if you have no suitable C compiler. Installing from sources gives you more control and flexibility and is the only possibility if you can't find a suitable pre-built binary distribution for your platform. Even if you install from binaries, I recommend you also download the source distribution because it includes examples and demos that may be missing from pre-built binary packages.

Installing Python from Source Code

To install CPython from source code, you need a platform with an ISO-compliant C compiler and ancillary tools such as *make*. On Windows, the normal way to build Python is with Microsoft Visual Studio (version 7.1, a.k.a. VS2003, for Python 2.4 and 2.5).

To download Python source code, visit *http://www.python.org* and follow the link labeled Download. The latest version at the time of this writing is:

> *http://www.python.org/ftp/python/2.4.3/Python-2.4.3.tgz*

The *.tgz* file extension is equivalent to *.tar.gz* (i.e., a *tar* archive of files, compressed by the powerful and popular *gzip* compressor). You can also get a version with an extension of *.tar.bz2* instead of *.tgz*, compressed with the even more powerful *bzip2* compressor, if you're able to deal with Bzip-2 compression (most popular utilities can nowadays).

To download sources for Python 2.5, see *http://www.python.org/download/ releases/2.5/*. At the same URL, you will also find Python 2.5 documentation and binary releases. At the time of this writing, the first alpha release of 2.5 had just appeared, but by the time you read this book the final release of 2.5 is likely to be available.

Windows

On Windows, installing Python from source code can be a chore unless you are already familiar with Microsoft Visual Studio and also used to working at the Windows command line (i.e., in the text-oriented windows known as MS-DOS Prompt or Command Prompt, depending on your version of Windows).

If the following instructions give you trouble, I suggest you skip ahead to "Installing Python from Binaries" on page 18. It may be a good idea to do an installation from binaries anyway, even if you also install from source code. This way, if you notice anything strange while using the version you installed from source code, you can double-check with the installation from binaries. If the strangeness goes away, it must be due to some quirk in your installation from source code, and then you know you must double-check the latter.

In the following sections, for clarity, I assume you have made a new directory named *C:\Py* and downloaded *Python-2.4.3.tgz* there. Of course, you can choose to name and place the directory as it best suits you.

Uncompressing and unpacking the Python source code

You can uncompress and unpack a *.tgz* file with programs *tar* and *gunzip*. If you do not have *tar* and *gunzip*, you can download the collection of utilities *ftp://ftp.object-central.com/winutils.zip* into *C:\Py*. If you do not have other ways to unpack a ZIP file, download *ftp://ftp.th-soft.com/UNZIP.EXE* into *C:\Py*. Open an MS-DOS Prompt window and give the following commands:

```
C:\> My Documents> cd \Py
C:\Py> unzip winutils
    [unzip lists the files it is unpacking - omitted here]
C:\Py> gunzip Python-2.4.3.tgz
C:\Py> tar xvf Python-2.4.3.tar
    [tar lists the files it is unpacking - omitted here]
C:\Py>
```

Many commercial programs, such as WinZip (*http://www.winzip.com*) and Power-Archiver (*http://www.powerarchiver.com*), can also uncompress and unpack *.tgz* archives (and *.tar.bz2* ones too). Whether via *gunzip* and *tar*, a commercial program, or some other program, you now have a directory *C:\Py\Python-2.4.3*, the root of a tree that contains the entire standard Python distribution in source form.

Building the Python source code with Microsoft Visual Studio 2003

Open the workspace file *C:\Py\Python-2.4.3\PCbuild\pcbuild.dsw* with Microsoft Visual Studio—for example, by starting Windows Explorer, going to directory *C:\Py\Python-2.4.3\PCbuild*, and double-clicking on file *pcbuild.dsw*.

Choose Build → Set Active Configuration → python Win32 Release, and then choose Build → Build python.exe. Visual Studio builds projects *pythoncore* and *python*, making files *python24.dll* and *python.exe* in *C:\Py\Python-2.4.3\PCbuild*. You can also build other subprojects (for example, with Build → Batch Build...). To build subprojects *_tkinter*, *bsddb*, *pyexpat*, and *zlib*, you first need to download other open source packages and install them in the *C:\Py* directory. Follow the instructions in *C:\Py\Python-2.4.3\PCbuild\readme.txt* to build every Python package that is in the distribution.

Building Python for debugging

You can also, optionally, build the debug versions, as well as the release versions, of the Python packages.

With Visual Studio, an executable (*.exe*) built for release can interoperate fully only with dynamic load libraries (DLLs) also built for release, while an executable built for debugging interoperates fully only with DLLs also built for debugging. Trying to mix and match can cause program crashes and assorted strangeness. To help you avoid accidentally mixing parts built for release with others built for debugging, the Python workspace appends a *_d* to the name of debugging executables and DLLs. For example, when you build for debugging, project *pythoncore* produces *python24_d.dll* and project *python* produces *python24_d.exe*.

What makes the debugging and release Visual Studio builds incompatible is the choice of C runtime library. Executables and DLLs can fully interoperate only by using the same C runtime library, and the runtime library must in turn be a DLL. You can tweak Project → Settings → C/C++ → Code Generation → Use run-time library, setting all projects to use Multithreaded DLL (*MSVCRT.DLL*) (also remove the _DEBUG definition in C/C++ → Code Generation → Preprocessor). I recommend you follow this approach only if you are highly experienced with Microsoft Visual Studio and have special, advanced requirements. Otherwise, resign yourself to keeping two separate and distinct release and debugging "worlds"; this is, by far, the simplest approach on Windows.

Installing after the build

python24.dll (or *python24_d.dll* if you want to run a debug-mode *python_d.exe*) must be in a directory from which Windows loads DLLs when needed. Suitable directories depend on your version of Windows; for example, *c:\windows\system* is one possibility. If you don't copy *python24.dll* to such a suitable directory, you can run Python only when the current directory is the directory in which *python24.dll* resides.

Similarly, *python.exe* must be in a directory in which Windows looks for executables, normally a directory listed in the Windows environment variable named PATH. How to set PATH and other environment variables depends on your version of

Windows, as mentioned in "Environment Variables" on page 22. Python can locate other files, such as the standard library modules, according to various strategies. *C:\Py\Python-2.4.3\PC\readme.txt* documents the various possibilities.

Building Python for Cygwin

Python 2.4 is also available as a part of the free Cygwin Unix-like environment for Windows (see *http://cygwin.com/* for more information). Cygwin runs on top of Windows. However, Cygwin is quite similar to Linux and other free Unix-like environments in many respects. In particular, Cygwin uses the popular, free *gcc* C/C++ compiler and associated tools such as *make*. Building Python from source code on Cygwin is therefore similar to building from source code on Unix-like environments, even though Cygwin runs on Windows.

Unix-Like Platforms

On Unix-like platforms, installing Python from source code is generally simple. In the following sections, for clarity, I assume you have created a new directory named *~/Py* and downloaded *Python-2.4.3.tgz* there. Of course, you can choose to name and place the directory as it best suits you.

Uncompressing and unpacking the Python source code

You can uncompress and unpack a *.tgz* file with programs *tar* and *gunzip*. If you have the popular GNU version of *tar*, you can just type the following at a shell prompt:

```
$ cd ~/Py
$ tar xzf Python-2.4.3.tgz
```

Similarly, if you choose to download the substantially smaller *.tar.bz2* file instead, again with the GNU version of *tar*, you could unpack it with the command:

```
$ tar xjf Python-2.4.3.tar.bz2
```

With either unpacking procedure, you now have a directory *~/Py/Python-2.4.3*, the root of a tree that contains the entire standard Python distribution in source form.

Configuring, building, and testing

You will find detailed notes in file *~/Py/Python-2.4.3/README* under the heading "Build instructions," and I strongly suggest reading those notes. In the simplest case, however, all you need to get started may be to give the following commands at a shell prompt:

```
$ cd ~/Py/Python-2.4.3
$ ./configure
    [configure writes much information - snipped here]
$ make
    [make takes quite a while, and emits much information]
```

If you run *make* without first running *./configure*, *make* implicitly runs *./configure* for you. When *make* finishes, you should test that the Python you have just built works as expected, as follows:

```
$ make test
    [takes quite a while, emits much information]
```

Most likely, *make test* will confirm that your build is working, but also inform you that some tests have been skipped because optional modules were missing.

Some of the modules are platform-specific (e.g., some work only on machines running SGI's Irix operating system), so you should not worry about them if your machine just doesn't support them. However, other modules are skipped during the build procedure because they depend on other open source packages that may not be installed on your machine. For example, module _tkinter—needed to run the Tkinter GUI package covered in Chapter 17, and also needed to run the IDLE integrated development environment, which comes with Python—can be built only if *./configure* is able to find an installation of Tcl/Tk 8.0 or later on your machine. See *~/Py/Python-2.4.3/README* for more details and specific caveats about many different Unix and Unix-like platforms.

Building from source code lets you tweak your configuration in several useful ways. For example, you can build Python in a special way that will help you track down memory leaks if you develop C-coded Python extensions, covered in "Building and Installing C-Coded Python Extensions" on page 614. Again, *~/Py/ Python-2.4.3/README* is a good source of information about the configuration options you can use.

Installing after the build

By default, *./configure* prepares Python for installation in */usr/local/bin* and */usr/ local/lib*. You can change these settings by running *./configure* with option *--prefix* before running *make*. For example, if you want a private installation of Python in subdirectory *py24* of your home directory, run:

```
$ cd ~/Py/Python-2.4.3
$ ./configure --prefix=~/py24
```

and continue with *make* as in the previous section. Once you're done building and testing Python, to perform the actual installation of all files, run:

```
$ make install
```

The user running *make install* must have write permissions on the target directories. Depending on your choice of target directories and the permissions set on those directories, you may therefore need to *su* to *root*, *bin*, or some other special user when you run *make install*. A common idiom for this purpose is *sudo make install*: if *sudo* prompts for a password, enter your current user's password, not *root*'s.

Installing Python from Binaries

If your platform is popular and current, you may find pre-built and packaged binary versions of Python ready for installation. Binary packages are typically self-installing, either directly as executable programs, or via appropriate system tools, such as the RedHat Package Manager (RPM) on Linux and the Microsoft Installer (MSI) on Windows. Once you have downloaded a package, install it by running the program and interactively choosing installation parameters, such as the directory where Python is to be installed.

To download Python binaries, visit *http://www.python.org* and follow the link labeled Download. At the time of this writing, the binary installers directly available from the main Python site are a Windows Installer (MSI) package:

> *http://www.python.org/ftp/python/2.4.3/Python-2.4.3.msi*

and a Mac OS X Disk Image (*.dmg*) package suitable for Mac OS X 10.3.9 and later on either a PowerPC or Intel processor ("Universal" format):

> *http://www.python.org/ftp/python/2.4.3/Universal-MacPython-2.4.3.dmg*

Many third parties supply free binary Python installers for other platforms. For Linux distributions, see *http://rpmfind.net* if your distribution is RPM-based (RedHat, Fedora, Mandriva, SUSE, etc.) or *http://www.debian.org* for Debian and Ubuntu. The site *http://www.python.org/download/* provides links to binary distributions for OS/2, Amiga, RISC OS, QNX, VxWorks, IBM AS/400, Sony PlayStation 2, Sharp Zaurus, and Windows CE (also known as "Pocket PC"). Older Python versions, starting from 1.5.2, are also usable and functional, though not as powerful and polished as the current Python 2.4.3. The download page provides links to 1.5.2 and other installers for older or less popular platforms (MS-DOS, Windows 3.1, Psion, BeOS, etc.).

To get Python for Nokia Series 60 cellphones, see *http://www.forum.nokia.com/ python*.

ActivePython (*http://www.activestate.com/Products/ActivePython*) is a binary package of Python 2.4, with several third-party extensions included, available for AIX, HP-UX, Linux (x86 processors only), Mac OS X, Solaris (SPARC, x64, and x86 processors), and Windows (all versions from Windows 95 to Windows XP and Windows Server 2003).

Enthought (*http://www.enthought.com/python/*) offers a large, rich binary distribution containing Python itself (at the time of writing, the stable release contained Python 2.3) and a huge wealth of pre-built, tested, and integrated add-on packages and tools that are particularly suitable for (but not limited to) scientific computing. At the time of writing, Enthought is available only as a self-installing EXE file for Windows, but there are plans to develop a similar packaging for Mac OS X, informally known as MacEnthon.

Apple Macintosh

Apple's Mac OS X, 10.3 ("Panther") and later, comes with Python 2.3 (text-mode only). Nevertheless, I heartily recommend you install the latest version and enhancements by following the instructions and links at *http://www.python.org/ download/releases/2.4.3/*; due to Apple's release cycles, the Python version included with Mac OS is generally somewhat out of date, and lacks some functionality, such as `bsddb` and `readline`. Python's latest version installs in addition to, not instead of, Apple's supplied one; Apple uses its own version of Python and proprietary extensions to implement some of the software distributed as a part of Mac OS X, and it's unwise to risk disturbing that version.

Installing Jython

To install Jython, you need a Java Virtual Machine (JVM) that complies with Java 1.1 or higher. See *http://www.jython.org/platform.html* for advice on JVMs for your platform.

To download Jython, visit *http://www.jython.org* and follow the link labeled Download. The latest version, which at the time of this writing (supporting some Python 2.3 features, as well as all of Python 2.2) is:

http://prdownloads.sf.net/jython/jython-22.class

In the following section, for clarity, I assume you have created a new directory named *C:\Jy* and downloaded *jython-22.class* there. Of course, you can choose to name and place the directory as it best suits you. On Unix-like platforms, in particular, the directory name will probably be something like *~/Jy*.

The Jython installer *.class* file is a self-installing program. Open an MS-DOS Prompt window (or a shell prompt on a Unix-like platform), change directory to *C:\Jy*, and run your Java interpreter on the Jython installer. Make sure to include directory *C:\Jy* in the Java CLASSPATH. With most releases of Sun's Java Development Kit (JDK), for example, you can run:

```
C:\Jy> java -cp . jython-22
```

This runs a GUI installer that lets you choose destination directory and options. If you want to avoid the GUI, you can use the *-o* switch on the command line. The switch lets you specify the installation directory and options on the command line. For example:

```
C:\Jy> java -cp . jython-22 -o C:\Jython-2.2 demo lib source
```

installs Jython, with all optional components (demos, libraries, and source code), in directory *C:\Jython-2.2*. The Jython installation builds two small, useful command files. One, run as *jython* (named *jython.bat* on Windows), runs the interpreter. The other, run as *jythonc*, compiles Python source into JVM byte-code. You can add the Jython installation directory to your PATH or copy these command files into any directory on your PATH.

You may want to use Jython with different JDKs on the same machine. For example, while JDK 1.5 is best for most development, you may also need to use JDK 1.1 occasionally in order to compile applets that can run on browsers that support only Java 1.1. In such cases, you could share a single Jython installation among multiple JVMs. However, to avoid confusion and accidents, I suggest you perform separate installations from the same Jython download on each JVM you want to support. Suppose, for example, that you have JDK 1.5 installed in *C:\Jdk15* and JDK 1.1 installed in *C:\Jdk11*. In this case, you could use the commands:

```
C:\Jy> \Jdk15\java -cp . jython-22 -o C:\Jy22-15 demo lib source
C:\Jy> \Jdk11\java -cp . jython-22 -o C:\Jy22-11 demo lib source
```

With these installations, you could then choose to work off *C:\Jy22-15* most of the time (e.g., by placing it in your PATH) and *cd* to *C:\Jy22-11* when you specifically need to compile applets with JDK 1.1.

Installing IronPython

To install IronPython, you need to have a current Common Language Runtime (CLR) implementation installed on your machine. Both the latest version of Mono (see *http://www.mono-project.com/Main_Page*), and Microsoft .NET Framework 2.0, work fine with IronPython. To download IronPython, visit *http://workspaces.gotdotnet.com/ironpython* (or *http://ironpython.com*, which will eventually become IronPython's main site, but is still out of date at the time of this writing) and follow download instructions on that page. The latest version at the time of this writing is 1.0. The same site also provides up-to-date installation instructions. I cannot provide such instructions in this book because they are still in flux at the time of this writing.

3

The Python Interpreter

To develop software systems in Python, you write text files that contain Python source code and documentation. You can use any text editor, including those in Integrated Development Environments (IDEs). You then process the source files with the Python compiler and interpreter. You can do this directly, implicitly inside an IDE, or via another program that embeds Python. The Python interpreter also lets you execute Python code interactively, as do IDEs.

The python Program

The Python interpreter program is run as *python* (it's named *python.exe* on Windows). *python* includes both the interpreter itself and the Python compiler, which is implicitly invoked, as needed, on imported modules. Depending on your system, the program may have to be in a directory listed in your PATH environment variable. Alternatively, as with any other program, you can give a complete pathname to it at a command (shell) prompt, or in the shell script (or *.BAT* file, shortcut target, etc.) that runs it.* On Windows, you can also use Start → Programs → Python 2.4 → Python (command line).

Environment Variables

Besides PATH, other environment variables affect the *python* program. Some environment variables have the same effects as options passed to *python* on the command line, as documented in the next section. A few environment variables provide settings not available via command-line options:

PYTHONHOME

> The Python installation directory. A *lib* subdirectory, containing the standard Python library modules, should exist under this directory. On Unix-like

---

* This may involve using quotes if the pathname contains spaces—again, this depends on your operating system.

systems, the standard library modules should be in subdirectory *lib/python-2.3* for Python 2.3, *lib/python-2.4* for Python 2.4, and so on.

PYTHONPATH

A list of directories separated by colons on Unix-like systems and by semicolons on Windows. Modules are imported from these directories. This list extends the initial value for Python's sys.path variable. Modules, importing, and the sys.path variable are covered in Chapter 7.

PYTHONSTARTUP

The name of a Python source file that is automatically executed each time an interactive interpreter session starts. No such file is run if this variable is not set or if it is set to the path of a file that is not found. The PYTHONSTARTUP file is not used when you run a Python script; it is used only when you start an interactive session.

How you set and examine environment variables depends on your operating system: shell commands, persistent startup shell files (e.g., *AUTOEXEC.BAT* on Windows), or other approaches (e.g., Start → Settings → Control Panel → Classic View → System → Advanced → Environment on Windows XP). Some Python versions for Windows also look for this information in the Registry, in addition to the environment. On Macintosh systems, the Python interpreter can be started as in other Unix-like systems, but there are also other options, including a MacPython-specific IDE. For more information about Python on the Mac, see *http://www.python.org/doc/current/mac/mac.html*.

Command-Line Syntax and Options

The Python interpreter command-line syntax can be summarized as follows:

[*path*]python {*options*} [-c *command* | -m *module* | *file* | -] {*arguments*}

Here, brackets ([]) enclose something that is optional, braces ({}) enclose items of which 0 or more may be present, and vertical bars (|) mean a choice among alternatives.

Options are case-sensitive short strings, starting with a hyphen, that ask *python* for a nondefault behavior. Unlike most Windows programs, *python* accepts only options that start with a hyphen (-), not with a slash. Python consistently uses a slash (/) for file paths, as in Unix. The most useful options are listed in Table 3-1. Each option's description gives the environment variable (if any) that, when set to any value, requests the same behavior.

Table 3-1. Python frequently used command-line options

Option	Meaning (and equivalent environment variable)
-c	Specifies Python statements as part of the command line
-E	Ignores all environment variables
-h	Prints a full list of options and summary help, then terminates
-i	Ensures an interactive session, no matter what (PYTHONINSPECT)
-m	Specifies a Python module to run as the main script
-O	Optimizes generated bytecode (PYTHONOPTIMIZE)

Table 3-1. Python frequently used command-line options (continued)

Option	Meaning (and equivalent environment variable)
-OO	Like *-O*, but also removes documentation strings from the bytecode
-Q arg	Controls the behavior of division operator / on integers
-S	Omits the implicit import site on startup (covered in "The site and sitecustomize Modules" on page 338)
-t	Warns about inconsistent usage of tabs and blank spaces
-tt	Like *-t*, but raises an error rather than a warning
-u	Uses unbuffered binary files for standard output and standard error (PYTHONUNBUFFERED)
-v	Verbosely traces module import and cleanup actions (PYTHONVERBOSE)
-V	Prints the Python version number, then terminates
-W arg	Adds an entry to the warnings filter (covered in "Filters" on page 472)
-x	Excludes (skips) the first line of the main script's source

Use *-i* when you want to get an interactive session immediately after running some script, with variables still intact and available for inspection. You do not need *-i* for normal interactive sessions, although it does no harm. *-t* and *-tt* ensure that your tabs and spaces in Python sources are used consistently (see "Lines and Indentation" on page 33 for more information about whitespace usage in Python).

-O and *-OO* yield small savings of time and space in bytecode generated for modules you import, and specifically turn assert statements into no-operations, as covered in "The assert Statement" on page 138. With *-OO*, documentation strings will not be available. *-Q* determines the behavior of division operator / used between two integer operands (division is covered in "Division" on page 52). *-W* adds an entry to the warnings filter (warnings are covered in "The warnings Module" on page 471).

-u uses binary mode for standard output (and standard error). Some platforms, mostly Windows, distinguish binary and text modes. Binary mode is needed to emit binary data to standard output, as in some Common Gateway Interface (CGI) scripts. *-u* also ensures that output is performed immediately, rather than buffered to enhance performance. This is needed when delays due to buffering could cause problems, as in some Unix pipelines.

After the options, if any, comes an indication of which Python program is to be run. A file path is that of a Python source or bytecode file to run, complete with file extension, if any. On any platform, you may use a slash (/) as the separator between components in this path. On Windows only, you may alternatively use a backslash (\). Instead of a file path, you can use *-c command* to execute a Python code string *command*. *command* normally contains spaces, so you need quotes around it to satisfy your operating system's shell or command-line processor. Some shells (e.g., *bash*) let you enter multiple lines as a single argument so that *command* can be a series of Python statements. Other shells (e.g., Windows shells) limit you to a single line; *command* can then be one or more simple statements separated by semicolons (;), as discussed in "Statements" on page 37. In Python 2.4, another way to specify which Python program is to be run is to use *-m module*. This option tells

Python to load and run a module named *module* from some directory that is part of Python's sys.path.

A hyphen, or the lack of any token in this position, tells the interpreter to read program source from standard input—normally, an interactive session. You need an explicit hyphen only if arguments follow. *arguments* are arbitrary strings; the Python application being run can access the strings as items of the list sys.argv.

For example, on a standard Windows installation of Python 2.4, you can enter the following at an MS-DOS Prompt (or Command Prompt) to have Python emit the current date and time:

```
C:\> c:\python24\python -c "import time; print time.asctime( )"
```

On a default installation of Python from sources, performed on Cygwin, Linux, OpenBSD, or other Unix-like systems, you can enter the following at a shell prompt to start an interactive session with verbose tracing of import and cleanup:

```
$ /usr/local/bin/python -v
```

In each case, you can start the command with just *python* (you do not have to specify the full path to the Python executable) if the directory of the Python executable is in your PATH environment variable.

Interactive Sessions

When you run *python* without a script argument, *python* enters an interactive session and prompts you to enter Python statements or expressions. Interactive sessions are useful to explore, check things out, and use Python as a powerful, extensible interactive calculator.

When you enter a complete statement, Python executes it. When you enter a complete expression, Python evaluates it. If the expression has a result, Python outputs a string representing the result and assigns the result to the variable named _ (a single underscore) so that you can easily use that result in another expression. The prompt string is >>> when Python expects a statement or expression and ... when a statement or expression has been started but not completed. For example, Python prompts you with ... when you have opened a parenthesis on a previous line and have not closed it yet.

An interactive session is terminated by end-of-file on standard input (Ctrl-Z on Windows, Ctrl-D on Unix-like systems). The statement raise SystemExit also ends the session, as does a call to sys.exit( ), either interactively or in code being run (SystemExit and Python exception handling are covered in Chapter 6).

Line-editing and history facilities depend in part on how Python was built: if the optional readline module was included, the features of the GNU readline library are available. Windows NT, 2000, and XP have a simple but usable history facility for interactive text-mode programs like *python*. Windows 95, 98, and ME don't. You can use other line-editing and history facilities by installing the Alternative Read-Line package for Windows (*http://newcenturycomputers.net/projects/readline.html*) or pyrepl for Unix (*http://starship.python.net/crew/mwh/hacks/pyrepl.html*).

In addition to the built-in Python interactive environment, and those offered as part of richer development environments covered in the next section, you can freely download other alternative, powerful interactive environments. The most popular one is IPython, *http://ipython.scipy.org/*, which offers a wealth of features.

Python Development Environments

The Python interpreter's built-in interactive mode is the simplest development environment for Python. It is a bit primitive, but it is lightweight, has a small footprint, and starts fast. Together with an appropriate text editor (as discussed in "Free Text Editors with Python Support" on page 27), and line-editing and history facilities, the interactive interpreter (or, alternatively, IPython) offers a usable and popular development environment. However, there are a number of other development environments that you can also use.

IDLE

Python's Integrated DeveLopment Environment (IDLE) comes with the standard Python distribution. IDLE is a cross-platform, 100 percent pure Python application based on Tkinter (see Chapter 17). IDLE offers a Python shell similar to interactive Python interpreter sessions but richer in functionality. It also includes a text editor optimized to edit Python source code, an integrated interactive debugger, and several specialized browsers/viewers.

Other Free Cross-Platform Python IDEs

IDLE is mature, stable, easy to use, and fairly rich in functionality. Promising new Python IDEs that share IDLE's free and cross-platform nature are emerging. Red Hat's Source Navigator (*http://sources.redhat.com/sourcenav/*) supports many languages. It runs on Linux, Solaris, HPUX, and Windows. Boa Constructor (*http://boa-constructor.sf.net/*) is Python-only and still beta-level, but well worth trying out. Boa Constructor includes a GUI builder for the wxWindows cross-platform GUI toolkit.

eric3 (*http://www.die-offenbachs.de/detlev/eric3.html*) is a full-featured IDE for Python and Ruby, based on the PyQt 3.1 cross-platform GUI toolkit.

The popular cross-platform, cross-language modular IDE Eclipse has plug-ins that support CPython and Jython; see *http://pydev.sourceforge.net/* for more information.

Another new but very popular cross-platform Python editor and IDE is SPE, "Stani's Python Editor" (*http://stani.be/python/spe/blog/*).

Platform-Specific Free Python IDEs

Python is cross-platform, and this book focuses on cross-platform tools and components. However, Python also provides good platform-specific facilities, including IDEs, on many platforms it supports. On Windows, in particular, ActivePython includes the PythonWin IDE. PythonWin is also available as a free add-on to the standard Python distribution for Windows, part of Mark Hammond's win32all extensions (see *http://starship.python.net/crew/mhammond*).

Commercial Python IDEs

Several companies sell commercial Python IDEs, both cross-platform and platform-specific. You must pay for them if you use them for commercial development and, in most cases, even if you develop free software. However, they offer support contracts and rich arrays of tools. If you have funding for software tool purchases, it is worth looking at these in detail and trying out their free demos or evaluations. Most of these tools work on Linux and Windows.

Archaeopterix sells an excellent Python IDE, Wing, that is particularly note-worthy for its powerful source-browsing and remote-debugging facilities (*http://wingware.com/*). theKompany sells a Python IDE, BlackAdder, that also includes a GUI builder for the PyQt GUI toolkit (*http://www.thekompany.com/products/blackadder*).

ActiveState (*http://www.activestate.com*) sells Komodo, which is built on top of Mozilla (*http://www.mozilla.org*) and includes remote debugging capabilities.

Free Text Editors with Python Support

You can edit Python source code with any text editor, even simplistic ones such as Notepad on Windows or *ed* on Linux. Powerful free editors also support Python, with extra features such as syntax-based colorization and automatic indentation. Cross-platform editors let you work in uniform ways on different platforms. Good programmers' text editors also let you run, from within the editor, tools of your choice on the source code you're editing. An up-to-date list of editors for Python can always be found at *http://wiki.python.org/moin/PythonEditors*.

The best of the best for sheer editing power is the classic Emacs (*http://www.emacs.org*, and *http://www.python.org/emacs* for Python-specific add-ons). However, Emacs is not the easiest editor to learn, nor is it lightweight. My personal favorite is another classic, *vim* (*http://www.vim.org*), the modern, improved version of the traditional Unix editor *vi*, not *quite* as powerful as Emacs but still well worth considering. *vim* is fast, lightweight, Python-programmable, and runs everywhere in both text-mode and GUI versions. *vim*, like *vi*, has a modal design, which lets you use normal keys for cursor movement and text changes when in command mode. Some love this as an ergonomic trait, mini-mizing finger travel. Others find it confusing and detest it. Newer editors challenge the classic ones. SciTE (*http://www.scintilla.org*) builds on the Scintilla programming language editor component. FTE (*http://fte.sf.net*) is also worth trying.

Other advanced free editors with Python syntax support are platform-specific. On Windows, try SynEdit (*http://www.mkidesign.com/syneditinfo.html*). On Unix-like systems, try Glimmer (*http://glimmer.sf.net*) and Cooledit (*http://freshmeat.net/projects/cooledit/*), which, like *vim*, also offers Python programmability, but without *vim*'s modal architecture. On Mac OS X, TextWrangler (*http://www.barebones.com/products/textwrangler/index.shtml*) is quite powerful and supports Python well. SubEthaEdit (*http://www.codingmonkeys.de/subethaedit/*), free for noncommercial use and sold (quite cheaply) for commercial uses, is uniquely featured and optimized to let multiple programmers cooperate by editing the same files, simultaneously, on different Macs on the same LAN.

A vast summary of editors (free and nonfree) that are particularly suitable for Python, including IDEs, can be found at *http://wiki.python.org/moin/PythonEditors*.

Tools for Checking Python Programs

The Python compiler does not check programs and modules thoroughly: the compiler checks only the code's syntax. If you want more thorough checking of your Python code, there are several tools you may download and install for the purpose. PyChecker, available at *http://pychecker.sourceforge.net/*, is simple to install and use: it relies on the normal Python compiler to turn Python source into bytecode, then imports the bytecode and checks all code for many kinds of errors and anomalies. Pyflakes, available at *http://divmod.org/projects/pyflakes*, is faster than PyChecker, although not quite as thorough, and does not import the modules it's checking, which may make its use safer. PyLint, available at *http://www.logilab.org/projects/pylint*, is very powerful and highly configurable. PyLint is not quite as lightweight and easy to install as PyChecker or Pyflakes, since it requires some other packages freely downloadable from Logilab; however, PyLint amply repays the effort by being able to check many kinds of stylistic aspects in a highly configurable way based on customizable configuration files.

Running Python Programs

Whatever tools you use to produce your Python application, you can see your application as a set of Python source files, which are normal text files. A *script* is a file that you can run directly. A *module* is a file that you can import (as covered in Chapter 7) to provide functionality to other files or to interactive sessions. A Python file can be both a module and a script, exposing functionality when imported, but is also suitable for being run directly. A useful and widespread convention is that Python files that are primarily intended to be imported as modules, when run directly, should execute some simple self-test operations, as covered in "Testing" on page 452.

The Python interpreter automatically compiles Python source files as needed. Python source files normally have extension *.py*. Python saves the compiled byte-code file for each module in the same directory as the module's source, with the same basename and extension *.pyc* (or *.pyo* if Python is run with option -O). Python does not save the compiled bytecode form of a script when you run the script directly; rather, Python recompiles the script each time you run it. Python saves bytecode files only for modules you import. It automatically rebuilds each module's bytecode file whenever necessary—for example, when you edit the module's source. Eventually, for deployment, you may package Python modules using tools covered in Chapter 27.

You can run Python code interactively with the Python interpreter or an IDE. Normally, however, you initiate execution by running a top-level script. To run a script, give its path as an argument to *python*, as covered earlier in "The python Program" on page 22. Depending on your operating system, you can invoke *python* directly from a shell script or in a command file. On Unix-like systems, you can make a Python script directly executable by setting the file's permission bits x and r and beginning the script with a so-called *shebang* line, which is a first line such as:

```
#!/usr/bin/env python {options}
```

or some other line starting with #! followed by a path to the *python* interpreter program.

On Windows, you can associate file extensions *.py*, *.pyc*, and *.pyo* with the Python interpreter in the Windows Registry. Most Python versions for Windows perform this association when installed. You can then run Python scripts with the usual Windows mechanisms, such as double-clicking on their icons. On Windows, when you run a Python script by double-clicking on the script's icon, Windows automatically closes the text-mode console associated with the script as soon as the script terminates. If you want the console to linger, to allow the user to read the script's output on the screen, you need to ensure the script doesn't terminate too soon. For example, use the following as the script's last statement:

```
raw_input('Press Enter to terminate')
```

This is not necessary when you run the script from a preexisting console (also known as a Command Prompt window).

On Windows, you can also use extension *.pyw* and interpreter program *pythonw.exe* instead of *.py* and *python.exe*. The *w* variants run Python without a text-mode console, and thus without standard input and output. These variants are appropriate for scripts that rely on GUIs or run invisibly in the background. Use them only when a program is fully debugged, to keep standard output and error available for information, warnings, and error messages during development. On the Mac, you need to use interpreter program *pythonw*, rather than *python*, when you want to run a script that needs to access any GUI toolkit, rather than just text-mode interaction.

Applications coded in other languages may embed Python, which controls the execution of Python code for their own purposes. We examine this subject further in "Embedding Python" on page 647.

The jython Interpreter

The *jython* interpreter built during installation (see "Installing Jython" on page 20) is run similarly to the *python* program:

```
[path]jython {options} [ -j jar | -c command | file | - ] {arguments}
```

-j jar tells *jython* that the main script to run is *__run__.py* in the *.jar* file. Options *-i*, *-S*, and *-v* are the same as for *python*. *--help* is like *python*'s *-h*, and *--version* is like *python*'s *--V*. Instead of environment variables, *jython* uses a text file named *registry* in the installation directory to record properties with structured names. Property python.path, for example, is the Jython equivalent of Python's environment variable PYTHONPATH. You can also set properties with *jython* command-line options in the form *-D name=value*.

The IronPython Interpreter

IronPython may be run similarly to the *python* program:

    *[path]*IronPythonConsole *{options}* [-c *command* | *file* | -] *{arguments}*

Unfortunately, details are still in flux at the time of this writing, so I cannot provide them in this book. See *http://ironpython.com* for up-to-date information.

II

Core Python Language and Built-ins

4

The Python Language

This chapter is a quick guide to the Python language. To learn Python from scratch, I suggest you start with *Learning Python*, by Mark Lutz and David Ascher (O'Reilly). If you already know other programming languages and just want to learn the specific differences of Python, this chapter is for you. However, I'm not trying to teach Python here, so we're going to cover a lot of ground at a pretty fast pace. I focus on teaching the rules, and only secondarily on pointing out best practices and recommended style; for a standard Python style guide, see *http:// python.org/doc/peps/pep-0008/*.

Lexical Structure

The lexical structure of a programming language is the set of basic rules that govern how you write programs in that language. It is the lowest-level syntax of the language and specifies such things as what variable names look like and which characters denote comments. Each Python source file, like any other text file, is a sequence of characters. You can also usefully consider it as a sequence of lines, tokens, or statements. These different lexical views complement and reinforce each other. Python is very particular about program layout, especially with regard to lines and indentation, so you'll want to pay attention to this information if you are coming to Python from another language.

Lines and Indentation

A Python program is composed of a sequence of *logical lines*, each made up of one or more *physical lines*. Each physical line may end with a comment. A hash sign (#) that is not inside a string literal begins a comment. All characters after the # and up to the physical line end are part of the comment, and the Python interpreter ignores them. A line containing only whitespace, possibly with a comment, is known as a *blank line*, and Python totally ignores it. In an interactive interpreter session, you must enter an empty physical line (without any whitespace or comment) to terminate a multiline statement.

In Python, the end of a physical line marks the end of most statements. Unlike in other languages, you don't normally terminate Python statements with a delimiter, such as a semicolon (;). When a statement is too long to fit on a single physical line, you can join two adjacent physical lines into a logical line by ensuring that the first physical line has no comment and ends with a backslash (\). However, Python automatically joins adjacent physical lines into one logical line if an open parenthesis ((), bracket ([), or brace ({) has not yet been closed, and taking advantage of this mechanism, generally produces more readable code instead of explicitly inserting backslashes at physical line ends. Triple-quoted string literals can also span physical lines. Physical lines after the first one in a logical line are known as *continuation lines*. The indentation issues covered next do not apply to continuation lines but only to the first physical line of each logical line.

Python uses indentation to express the block structure of a program. Unlike other languages, Python does not use braces, or other begin/end delimiters, around blocks of statements; indentation is the only way to denote such blocks. Each logical line in a Python program is *indented* by the whitespace on its left. A block is a contiguous sequence of logical lines, all indented by the same amount; a logical line with less indentation ends the block. All statements in a block must have the same indentation, as must all clauses in a compound statement. The first statement in a source file must have no indentation (i.e., must not begin with any whitespace). Statements that you type at the interactive interpreter primary prompt >>> (covered in "Interactive Sessions" on page 25) must also have no indentation.

Python logically replaces each tab by up to eight spaces, so that the next character after the tab falls into logical column 9, 17, 25, etc. Standard Python style is to use four spaces (*never* tabs) per indentation level. Don't mix spaces and tabs for indentation, since different tools (e.g., editors, email systems, printers) treat tabs differently. The -*t* and -*tt* options to the Python interpreter (covered in "Command-Line Syntax and Options" on page 23) ensure against inconsistent tab and space usage in Python source code. I recommend you configure your favorite text editor to expand tabs to spaces, so that all Python source code you write always contains just spaces, not tabs. This way, you know that all tools, including Python itself, are going to be perfectly consistent in handling indentation in your Python source files. Optimal Python style is to indent by exactly four spaces.

Character Sets

Normally, a Python source file must be entirely made up of characters from the ASCII set (character codes between 0 and 127). However, you may choose to tell Python that in a certain source file you are using a character set that is a superset of ASCII. In this case, Python allows that specific source file to contain characters outside the ASCII set, but only in comments and string literals. To accomplish this, start your source file with a comment whose form must be as rigid as the following:

```
# -*- coding: utf-8 -*-
```

Between the coding: and the -*-, write the name of a codec known to Python, such as utf-8 or iso-8859-1. Note that this *coding directive* comment is taken as such only if it is at the start of a source file (possibly after the "shebang line" covered in "Running Python Programs" on page 28), and that the *only* effect of a coding directive is to let you use non-ASCII characters in string literals and comments.

Tokens

Python breaks each logical line into a sequence of elementary lexical components known as *tokens*. Each token corresponds to a substring of the logical line. The normal token types are *identifiers*, *keywords*, *operators*, *delimiters*, and *literals*, as covered in the following sections. You may freely use whitespace between tokens to separate them. Some whitespace separation is necessary between logically adjacent identifiers or keywords; otherwise, Python would parse them as a single, longer identifier. For example, printx is a single identifier; to write the keyword print followed by the identifier x, you need to insert some whitespace (e.g., print x).

Identifiers

An *identifier* is a name used to identify a variable, function, class, module, or other object. An identifier starts with a letter (A to Z or a to z) or an underscore (_) followed by zero or more letters, underscores, and digits (0 to 9). Case is significant in Python: lowercase and uppercase letters are distinct. Python does not allow punctuation characters such as @, $, and % within identifiers.

Normal Python style is to start class names with an uppercase letter and all other identifiers with a lowercase letter. Starting an identifier with a single leading underscore indicates by convention that the identifier is meant to be private. Starting an identifier with two leading underscores indicates a strongly private identifier; if the identifier also ends with two trailing underscores, the identifier is a language-defined special name. The identifier _ (a single underscore) is special in interactive interpreter sessions: the interpreter binds _ to the result of the last expression statement it has evaluated interactively, if any.

Keywords

Python has 30 keywords, which are identifiers that Python reserves for special syntactic uses. Keywords contain lowercase letters only. You cannot use keywords as regular identifiers. Some keywords begin simple statements or clauses of compound statements, while other keywords are operators. All the keywords are covered in detail in this book, either in this chapter, or in Chapters 5, 6, and 7. The keywords in Python are:

and	del	for	is	raise
assert	elif	from	lambda	return
break	else	global	not	try
class	except	if	or	while
continue	exec	import	pass	with (2.5)
def	finally	in	print	yield

The identifier with is a new keyword starting with Python 2.5 (up to Python 2.4, it is a completely normal identifier). The identifier as, which is not, strictly speaking, a keyword, is used as a pseudokeyword as part of some statements (specifically, the statements from, import, and, in Python 2.5, with). In Python 2.5, using with or as as normal identifiers produces warnings. To enable with usage as a keyword (and therefore to enable the new with statement) in Python 2.5, begin your source file with the statement:

```
from __future__ import with_statement
```

This "import from the future" enables use of the with statement in this module.

Operators

Python uses nonalphanumeric characters and character combinations as operators. Python recognizes the following operators, which are covered in detail in "Expressions and Operators" on page 50:

+	-	*	/	%	**	//	<<	>>	&
|	^	~	<	<=	>	>=	<>	!=	==

Delimiters

Python uses the following symbols and symbol combinations as delimiters in expressions, lists, dictionaries, various aspects of statements, and strings, among other purposes:

(	)	[	]	{	}
,	:	.	`	=	;
+=	-=	*=	/=	//=	%=
&=	|=	^=	>>=	<<=	**=

The period (.) can also appear in floating-point literals (e.g., 2.3) and imaginary literals (e.g., 2.3j). The last two rows list the augmented assignment operators, which lexically are delimiters but also perform an operation. I discuss the syntax for the various delimiters when I introduce the objects or statements with which they are used.

The following characters have special meanings as part of other tokens:

```
'          "        #        \
```

The characters $ and ?, all control characters except whitespace, and all characters with ISO codes above 126 (i.e., non-ASCII characters, such as accented letters) can never be part of the text of a Python program, except in comments or string literals (to use non-ASCII characters in comments or string literals, you must start your Python source file with a "coding directive," as covered in "Character Sets" on page 34). This also applies to the character @ in Python 2.3; however, in Python 2.4, @ indicates *decorators*, as covered in "Decorators" on page 115.

Literals

A *literal* is a number or string that appears directly in a program. The following are all literals in Python:

```
42              # Integer literal
3.14            # Floating-point literal
1.0j            # Imaginary literal
'hello'         # String literal
"world"         # Another string literal
"""Good
night"""        # Triple-quoted string literal
```

Using literals and delimiters, you can create data values of some other fundamental types:

```
[ 42, 3.14, 'hello' ]    # List
( 100, 200, 300 )        # Tuple
{ 'x':42, 'y':3.14 }     # Dictionary
```

The syntax for literals and other fundamental-type data values is covered in detail in "Data Types" on page 38, when I discuss the various data types Python supports.

Statements

You can consider a Python source file as a sequence of simple and compound statements. Unlike other languages, Python has no declarations or other top-level syntax elements, just statements.

Simple statements

A *simple statement* is one that contains no other statements. A simple statement lies entirely within a logical line. As in other languages, you may place more than one simple statement on a single logical line, with a semicolon (;) as the separator. However, one statement per line is the usual Python style, and makes programs more readable.

Any *expression* can stand on its own as a simple statement (I'll discuss expressions in detail in "Expressions and Operators" on page 50). The interactive interpreter shows the result of an expression statement you enter at the prompt (>>>) and binds the result to a variable named _ (a single underscore). Apart from interactive sessions, expression statements are useful only to call functions (and other *callables*) that have side effects (e.g., ones that perform output, change global variables, or raise exceptions).

An *assignment* is a simple statement that assigns values to variables, as I'll discuss in "Assignment Statements" on page 47. Unlike in some other languages, an assignment in Python is a statement and can never be part of an expression.

Compound statements

A *compound statement* contains one or more other statements and controls their execution. A compound statement has one or more *clauses*, aligned at the same indentation. Each clause has a *header* starting with a keyword and ending with a colon (:), followed by a *body*, which is a sequence of one or more statements. When the body contains multiple statements, also known as a *block*, these statements should be placed on separate logical lines after the header line, indented four spaces rightward. The block lexically ends when the indentation returns to that of the clause header (or further left from there, to the indentation of some enclosing compound statement). Alternatively, the body can be a single simple statement, following the : on the same logical line as the header. The body may also consist of several simple statements on the same line with semicolons between them, but, as I've already indicated, this is not good style.

Data Types

The operation of a Python program hinges on the data it handles. All data values in Python are objects, and each object, or value, has a *type*. An object's type determines which operations the object supports, or, in other words, which operations you can perform on the data value. The type also determines the object's attributes and items (if any) and whether the object can be altered. An object that can be altered is known as a *mutable object*, while one that cannot be altered is an *immutable object*. I cover object attributes and items in detail in "Object attributes and items" on page 46.

The built-in type(*obj*) accepts any object as its argument and returns the type object that is the type of *obj*. Built-in function isinstance(*obj, type*) returns True if object *obj* has type *type* (or any subclass thereof); otherwise, it returns False.

Python has built-in types for fundamental data types such as numbers, strings, tuples, lists, and dictionaries, as covered in the following sections. You can also create user-defined types, known as *classes*, as discussed in "Classes and Instances" on page 82.

Numbers

The built-in number objects in Python support integers (plain and long), floating-point numbers, and complex numbers. In Python 2.4, the standard library also offers decimal floating-point numbers, covered in "The decimal Module" on page 372. All numbers in Python are immutable objects, meaning that when you perform any operation on a number object, you always produce a new number object. Operations on numbers, also known as arithmetic operations, are covered in "Numeric Operations" on page 52.

Note that numeric literals do not include a sign: a leading + or -, if present, is a separate operator, as discussed in "Arithmetic Operations" on page 52.

Integer numbers

Integer literals can be decimal, octal, or hexadecimal. A decimal literal is represented by a sequence of digits in which the first digit is nonzero. To denote an octal literal, use 0 followed by a sequence of octal digits (0 to 7). To indicate a hexadecimal literal, use 0x followed by a sequence of hexadecimal digits (0 to 9 and A to F, in either upper- or lowercase). For example:

```
1, 23, 3493           # Decimal integers
01, 027, 06645        # Octal integers
0x1, 0x17, 0xDA5      # Hexadecimal integers
```

In practice, you don't need to worry about the distinction between plain and long integers in modern Python, since operating on plain integers produces results that are long integers when needed (i.e., when the result would not fit within the range of plain integers). However, you may choose to terminate any kind of integer literal with a letter L (or l) to explicitly denote a long integer. For instance:

```
1L, 23L, 99999333493L       # Long decimal integers
01L, 027L, 013510331316165L # Long octal integers
0x1L, 0x17L, 0x17486CBC75L  # Long hexadecimal integers
```

Use uppercase L here, not lowercase l, which might look like the digit 1. The difference between long and plain integers is one of implementation. A long integer has no predefined size limit; it may be as large as memory allows. A plain integer takes up just a few bytes of memory and its minimum and maximum values are dictated by machine architecture. sys.maxint is the largest positive plain integer available, while -sys.maxint-1 is the largest negative one. On 32-bit machines, sys.maxint is 2147483647.

Floating-point numbers

A floating-point literal is represented by a sequence of decimal digits that includes a decimal point (.), an exponent part (an e or E, optionally followed by + or -, followed by one or more digits), or both. The leading character of a floating-point literal cannot be e or E; it may be any digit or a period (.). For example:

```
0., 0.0, .0, 1., 1.0, 1e0, 1.e0, 1.0e0
```

A Python floating-point value corresponds to a C double and shares its limits of range and precision, typically 53 bits of precision on modern platforms. (Python offers no way to find out the exact range and precision of floating-point values on your platform.)

Complex numbers

A complex number is made up of two floating-point values, one each for the real and imaginary parts. You can access the parts of a complex object z as read-only attributes z.real and z.imag. You can specify an imaginary literal as a floating-point or decimal literal followed by a j or J:

```
0j, 0.j, 0.0j, .0j, 1j, 1.j, 1.0j, 1e0j, 1.e0j, 1.0e0j
```

The j at the end of the literal indicates the square root of -1, as commonly used in electrical engineering (some other disciplines use i for this purpose, but Python has chosen j). There are no other complex literals. To denote any constant complex number, add or subtract a floating-point (or integer) literal and an imaginary one. For example, to denote the complex number that equals one, use expressions like 1+0j or 1.0+0.0j.

Sequences

A *sequence* is an ordered container of items, indexed by nonnegative integers. Python provides built-in sequence types known as strings (plain and Unicode), tuples, and lists. Library and extension modules provide other sequence types, and you can write yet others yourself (as discussed in "Sequences" on page 109). You can manipulate sequences in a variety of ways, as discussed in "Sequence Operations" on page 53.

Iterables

A Python concept that generalizes the idea of "sequence" is that of *iterables*, covered in "The for Statement" on page 64 and "Iterators" on page 65. All sequences are iterable: whenever I say that you can use an iterable, you can, in particular, use a sequence (for example, a list).

Also, when I say that you can use an iterable, I mean, in general, a *bounded* iterable, which is an iterable that eventually stops yielding items. All sequences are bounded. Iterables, in general, can be unbounded, but if you try to use an unbounded iterable without special precautions, you could easily produce a program that never terminates, or one that exhausts all available memory.

Strings

A built-in string object (plain or Unicode) is a sequence of characters used to store and represent text-based information (plain strings are also sometimes used to store and represent arbitrary sequences of binary bytes). Strings in Python are *immutable*, meaning that when you perform an operation on strings, you always produce a new string object, rather than mutating an existing string. String objects provide many methods, as discussed in detail in "Methods of String Objects" on page 186.

A string literal can be quoted or triple-quoted. A quoted string is a sequence of zero or more characters enclosed in matching quotes, single (') or double ("). For example:

```
'This is a literal string'
"This is another string"
```

The two different kinds of quotes function identically; having both allows you to include one kind of quote inside of a string specified with the other kind without needing to escape them with the backslash character (\):

```
'I\'m a Python fanatic'        # a quote can be escaped
"I'm a Python fanatic"         # this way is more readable
```

All other things being equal, using single quotes to denote string literals is a more common Python style. To have a string literal span multiple physical lines, you can use a backslash as the last character of a line to indicate that the next line is a continuation:

```
"A not very long string\
that spans two lines"          # comment not allowed on previous line
```

To make the string output on two lines, you can embed a newline in the string:

```
"A not very long string\n\
that prints on two lines"      # comment not allowed on previous line
```

A better approach is to use a triple-quoted string, which is enclosed by matching triplets of quote characters (''' or """):

```
"""An even bigger
string that spans
three lines"""                 # comments not allowed on previous lines
```

In a triple-quoted string literal, line breaks in the literal are preserved as newline characters in the resulting string object.

The only character that cannot be part of a triple-quoted string is an unescaped backslash, while a quoted string cannot contain unescaped backslashes, nor line ends, nor the quote character that encloses it. The backslash character starts an escape sequence, which lets you introduce any character in either kind of string. Python's string escape sequences are listed in Table 4-1.

Table 4-1. String escape sequences

Sequence	Meaning	ASCII/ISO code
\<newline>	End of line is ignored	None
\\	Backslash	0x5c
\'	Single quote	0x27
\"	Double quote	0x22
\a	Bell	0x07
\b	Backspace	0x08
\f	Form feed	0x0c
\n	Newline	0x0a
\r	Carriage return	0x0d
\t	Tab	0x09
\v	Vertical tab	0x0b
\DDD	Octal value DDD	As given
\xXX	Hexadecimal value XX	As given
\other	Any other character	0x5c + as given

A variant of a string literal is a *raw string*. The syntax is the same as for quoted or triple-quoted string literals, except that an r or R immediately precedes the leading quote. In raw strings, escape sequences are not interpreted as in Table 4-1, but are literally copied into the string, including backslashes and newline characters. Raw string syntax is handy for strings that include many backslashes, as in regular expressions (see "Pattern-String Syntax" on page 201). A raw string cannot end with an odd number of backslashes; the last one would be taken as escaping the terminating quote.

Unicode string literals have the same syntax as other string literals, with a u or U immediately before the leading quote. Unicode string literals can use \u followed by four hex digits to denote Unicode characters and can include the escape sequences listed in Table 4-1. Unicode literals can also include the escape sequence \N{*name*}, where *name* is a standard Unicode name, as listed at *http://www.unicode.org/charts/*. For example, \N{Copyright Sign} indicates a Unicode copyright sign character (©). Raw Unicode string literals start with ur, not ru. Note that raw strings are *not* a different type from ordinary strings: raw strings are just an alternative syntax for literals of the usual two string types, plain (a.k.a. byte strings) and Unicode.

Multiple string literals of any kind (quoted, triple-quoted, raw, Unicode) can be adjacent, with optional whitespace in between. The compiler concatenates such adjacent string literals into a single string object. If any literal in the concatenation is Unicode, the whole result is Unicode. Writing a long string literal in this way lets you present it readably across multiple physical lines and gives you an opportunity to insert comments about parts of the string. For example:

```
marypop = ('supercalifragilistic'   # Open paren -> logical line continues
           'expialidocious')         # Indentation ignored in continuation
```

The string assigned to marypop is a single word of 34 characters.

Tuples

A *tuple* is an immutable ordered sequence of items. The items of a tuple are arbitrary objects and may be of different types. To specify a tuple, use a series of expressions (the *items* of the tuple) separated by commas (,). You may optionally place a redundant comma after the last item. You may group tuple items within parentheses, but the parentheses are necessary only where the commas would otherwise have another meaning (e.g., in function calls), or to denote empty or nested tuples. A tuple with exactly two items is often known as a *pair*. To create a tuple of one item (often known as a *singleton*), add a comma to the end of the expression. To denote an empty tuple, use an empty pair of parentheses. Here are some tuples, all enclosed in the optional parentheses:

```
(100, 200, 300)        # Tuple with three items
(3.14,)                # Tuple with one item
()                     # Empty tuple (parentheses NOT optional!)
```

You can also call the built-in type tuple to create a tuple. For example:

```
tuple('wow')
```

This builds a tuple equal to:

```
('w', 'o', 'w')
```

`tuple( )` without arguments creates and returns an empty tuple. When *x* is iterable, `tuple(x)` returns a tuple whose items are the same as the items in *x*.

Lists

A *list* is a mutable ordered sequence of items. The items of a list are arbitrary objects and may be of different types. To specify a list, use a series of expressions (the *items* of the list) separated by commas (,) and within brackets ([ ]). You may optionally place a redundant comma after the last item. To denote an empty list, use an empty pair of brackets. Here are some example lists:

```
[42, 3.14, 'hello']     # List with three items
[100]                   # List with one item
[]                      # Empty list
```

You can also call the built-in type `list` to create a list. For example:

```
list('wow')
```

This builds a list equal to:

```
['w', 'o', 'w']
```

`list( )` without arguments creates and returns an empty list. When *x* is iterable, `list(x)` creates and returns a new list whose items are the same as the items in *x*. You can also build lists with list comprehensions, as discussed in "List comprehensions" on page 67.

Sets

Python 2.4 introduces two built-in set types, `set` and `frozenset`, to represent arbitrarily ordered collections of unique items. These types are equivalent to classes `Set` and `ImmutableSet` found in standard library module `sets`, which also exists in Python 2.3. To ensure that your module uses the best available sets, in any release of Python from 2.3 onwards, place the following code at the start of your module:

```
try:
  set
except NameError:
  from sets import Set as set, ImmutableSet as frozenset
```

Items in a set may be of different types, but they must be *hashable* (see `hash` on page 162). Instances of type `set` are mutable, and therefore not hashable; instances of type `frozenset` are immutable and hashable. So you can't have a set whose items are sets, but you can have a set (or frozenset) whose items are frozensets. Sets and frozensets are *not* ordered.

To create a set, call the built-in type `set` with no argument (this means an empty set) or one argument that is iterable (this means a set whose items are the items of the iterable).

Dictionaries

A *mapping* is an arbitrary collection of objects indexed by nearly arbitrary values called *keys*. Mappings are mutable and, unlike sequences, are *not* ordered.

Python provides a single built-in mapping type, the dictionary type. Library and extension modules provide other mapping types, and you can write others yourself (as discussed in "Mappings" on page 110). Keys in a dictionary may be of different types, but they must be *hashable* (see hash on page 162). Values in a dictionary are arbitrary objects and may be of different types. An *item* in a dictionary is a key/value pair. You can think of a dictionary as an associative array (known in other languages as a "map," "hash table," or "hash").

To specify a dictionary, you can use a series of pairs of expressions (the pairs are the items of the dictionary) separated by commas (,) within braces ({}). You may optionally place a redundant comma after the last item. Each item in a dictionary is written as *key:value*, where *key* is an expression giving the item's key and *value* is an expression giving the item's value. If a key appears more than once in a dictionary literal, only one of the items with that key is kept in the resulting dictionary object—dictionaries do not allow duplicate keys. To denote an empty dictionary, use an empty pair of braces. Here are some dictionaries:

```
{'x':42, 'y':3.14, 'z':7 }    # Dictionary with three items and string keys
{1:2, 3:4 }                   # Dictionary with two items and integer keys
{}                            # Empty dictionary
```

You can also call the built-in type dict to create a dictionary in a way that, while less concise, can sometimes be more readable. For example, the dictionaries in this last snippet can also, equivalently, be written as, respectively:

```
dict(x=42, y=3.14, z=7)       # Dictionary with three items and string keys
dict([[1, 2], [3, 4]])        # Dictionary with two items and integer keys
dict()                        # Empty dictionary
```

dict() without arguments creates and returns an empty dictionary. When the argument *x* to dict is a mapping, dict returns a new dictionary object with the same keys and values as *x*. When *x* is iterable, the items in *x* must be pairs, and dict(*x*) returns a dictionary whose items (key/value pairs) are the same as the items in *x*. If a key appears more than once in *x*, only the *last* item with that key is kept in the resulting dictionary.

When you call dict, in addition to or instead of the positional argument *x* you may pass *named arguments*, each with the syntax *name=value*, where *name* is an identifier to use as an item's key and *value* is an expression giving the item's value. When you call dict and pass both a positional argument and one or more named arguments, if a key appears both in the positional argument and as a named argument, Python associates to that key the value given with the named argument (i.e., the named argument "wins").

You can also create a dictionary by calling dict.fromkeys. The first argument is an iterable whose items become the keys of the dictionary; the second argument is the value that corresponds to each key (all keys initially have the same corresponding value). If you omit the second argument, the value corresponding to each key is None. For example:

```
dict.fromkeys('hello', 2)    # same as {'h':2, 'e':2, 'l':2, 'o':2}
dict.fromkeys([1, 2, 3])     # same as {1:None, 2:None, 3:None}
```

None

The built-in None denotes a null object. None has no methods or other attributes. You can use None as a placeholder when you need a reference but you don't care what object you refer to, or when you need to indicate that no object is there. Functions return None as their result unless they have specific return statements coded to return other values.

Callables

In Python, callable types are those whose instances support the function call operation (see "Calling Functions" on page 73). Functions are callable. Python provides several built-in functions (see "Built-in Functions" on page 158) and supports user-defined functions (see "The def Statement" on page 70). Generators are also callable (see "Generators" on page 78).

Types are also callable, as we already saw for the dict, list, and tuple built-in types. (See "Built-in Types" on page 154 for a complete list of built-in types.) As we'll discuss in "Python Classes" on page 82, class objects (user-defined types) are also callable. Calling a type normally creates and returns a new instance of that type.

Other callables are *methods*, which are functions bound to class attributes and instances of classes that supply a special method named __call__.

Boolean Values

Every data value in Python can be taken as a truth value: true or false. Any nonzero number or nonempty container (e.g., string, tuple, list, set, or dictionary) is true. 0 (of any numeric type), None, and empty containers are false. Be careful about using a floating-point number as a truth value: such use is equivalent to comparing the number for exact equality with zero, and floating point numbers should almost never be compared for exact equality!

Built-in type bool is a subclass of int. The only two values of type bool are True and False, which have string representations of 'True' and 'False', but also numerical values of 1 and 0, respectively. Several built-in functions return bool results, as do comparison operators. You can call bool(x) with any x as the argument. The result is True if x is true and False if x is false. Good Python style is not to use such calls when they are redundant: *always* write if x:, *never* if bool(x):, if x==True:, if bool(x)==True, and so on.

Variables and Other References

A Python program accesses data values through references. A *reference* is a name that refers to the location in memory of a value (object). References take the form of variables, attributes, and items. In Python, a variable or other reference has no intrinsic type. The object to which a reference is bound at a given time always has a type, but a given reference may be bound to objects of various types during the program's execution.

Variables

In Python there are no declarations. The existence of a variable begins with a statement that *binds* the variable, or, in other words, sets a name to hold a reference to some object. You can also *unbind* a variable, resetting the name so it no longer holds a reference. Assignment statements are the most common way to bind variables and other references. The del statement unbinds references.

Binding a reference that was already bound is also known as *rebinding* it. Whenever I mention binding in this book, I implicitly include rebinding except where I explicitly exclude it. Rebinding or unbinding a reference has no effect on the object to which the reference was bound, except that an object disappears when nothing refers to it. The automatic cleanup of objects bereft of references is known as *garbage collection*.

You can name a variable with any identifier except the 30 that are reserved as Python's keywords (see "Keywords" on page 35). A variable can be global or local. A *global variable* is an attribute of a module object (Chapter 7 covers modules). A *local variable* lives in a function's local namespace (see "Namespaces" on page 76).

Object attributes and items

The main distinction between the attributes and items of an object is in the syntax you use to access them. An *attribute* of an object is denoted by a reference to the object, followed by a period (.), followed by an identifier known as the *attribute name* (for example, x.y refers to one of the attributes of the object bound to name x, specifically that attribute which is named y).

An *item* of an object is denoted by a reference to the object, followed by an expression within brackets ([ ]). The expression in brackets is known as the item's *index* or *key*, and the object is known as the item's *container* (for example, x[y] refers to the item at the key or index bound to name y, within the container object bound to name x).

Attributes that are callable are also known as *methods*. Python draws no strong distinctions between callable and noncallable attributes, as some other languages do. All rules about attributes also apply to callable attributes (methods).

Accessing nonexistent references

A common programming error is trying to access a reference that does not exist. For example, a variable may be unbound, or an attribute name or item index may not be valid for the object to which you apply it. The Python compiler, when it analyzes and compiles source code, diagnoses only syntax errors. Compilation does not diagnose semantic errors, such as trying to access an unbound attribute, item, or variable. Python diagnoses semantic errors only when the errant code executes, i.e., *at runtime*. When an operation is a Python semantic error, attempting it raises an exception (see Chapter 6). Accessing a nonexistent variable, attribute, or item, just like any other semantic error, raises an exception.

Assignment Statements

Assignment statements can be plain or augmented. Plain assignment to a variable (e.g., `name=value`) is how you create a new variable or rebind an existing variable to a new value. Plain assignment to an object attribute (e.g., `x.attr=value`) is a request to object *x* to create or rebind attribute `attr`. Plain assignment to an item in a container (e.g., `x[k]=value`) is a request to container *x* to create or rebind the item with index *k*.

Augmented assignment (e.g., `name+=value`) cannot, per se, create new references. Augmented assignment can rebind a variable, ask an object to rebind one of its existing attributes or items, or request the target object to modify itself (an object may, of course, create whatever it wants in response to such requests). When you make a request to an object, it is up to the object to decide whether to honor the request or raise an exception.

Plain assignment

A plain assignment statement in the simplest form has the syntax:

```
target = expression
```

The target is also known as the lefthand side (LHS), and the expression is the righthand side (RHS). When the assignment executes, Python evaluates the RHS expression, then binds the expression's value to the LHS target. The binding does not depend on the type of the value. In particular, Python draws no strong distinction between callable and noncallable objects, as some other languages do, so you can bind functions, methods, types, and other callables to variables, just as you can numbers, strings, lists, and so on.

Details of the binding do depend on the kind of target, however. The target in an assignment may be an identifier, an attribute reference, an indexing, or a slicing:

An identifier
    Is a variable's name. Assignment to an identifier binds the variable with this name.

An attribute reference
    Has the syntax `obj.name`. *obj* is an arbitrary expression, and *name* is an identifier, known as an *attribute name* of the object. Assignment to an attribute reference asks object *obj* to bind its attribute named *name*.

An indexing

Has the syntax *obj*[*expr*]. *obj* and *expr* are arbitrary expressions. Assignment to an indexing asks container *obj* to bind its item indicated by the value of *expr*, also known as the index or key of the item in the container.

A slicing

Has the syntax *obj*[*start*:*stop*] or *obj*[*start*:*stop*:*stride*]. *obj*, *start*, *stop*, and *stride* are arbitrary expressions. *start*, *stop*, and *stride* are all optional (i.e., *obj*[:*stop*:] and *obj*[:*stop*] are also syntactically correct slicings, equivalent to *obj*[None:*stop*:None]). Assignment to a slicing asks container *obj* to bind or unbind some of its items. Assigning to a slicing such as *obj*[*start*:*stop*:*stride*] is equivalent to assigning to the indexing *obj*[slice(*start*, *stop*, *stride*)], where slice is a Python built-in type (see slice on page 156) whose instances represent slices.

I'll come back to indexing and slicing targets when I discuss operations on lists, in "Modifying a list" on page 56, and on dictionaries, in "Indexing a Dictionary" on page 60.

When the target of the assignment is an identifier, the assignment statement specifies the binding of a variable. This is never disallowed: when you request it, it takes place. In all other cases, the assignment statement specifies a request to an object to bind one or more of its attributes or items. An object may refuse to create or rebind some (or all) attributes or items, raising an exception if you attempt a disallowed creation or rebinding (see also _ _setattr_ _ on page 108 and _ _setitem_ _ on page 112).

You can give multiple targets and equals signs (=) in a plain assignment. For example:

```
a = b = c = 0
```

binds variables a, b, and c to the same value, 0. Each time the statement executes, the RHS expression is evaluated just once, no matter how many targets are part of the statement. Each target then gets bound to the single object returned by the expression, just as if several simple assignments executed one after the other.

The target in a plain assignment can list two or more references separated by commas, optionally enclosed in parentheses or brackets. For example:

```
a, b, c = x
```

This statement requires x to be an iterable with exactly three items, and binds a to the first item, b to the second, and c to the third. This kind of assignment is known as an *unpacking assignment*. The RHS expression must be an iterable with exactly as many items as there are references in the target; otherwise, Python raises an exception. Each reference in the target gets bound to the corresponding item in the RHS. An unpacking assignment can also be used to swap references:

```
a, b = b, a
```

This assignment statement rebinds name *a* to what name *b* was bound to, and vice versa.

Augmented assignment

An augmented assignment differs from a plain assignment in that, instead of an equals sign (=) between the target and the expression, it uses an *augmented operator*, which is a binary operator followed by =. The augmented operators are +=, -=, *=, /=, //=, %=, **=, |=, >>=, <<=, &=, and ^=. An augmented assignment can have only one target on the LHS; augmented assignment doesn't support multiple targets.

In an augmented assignment, just as in a plain one, Python first evaluates the RHS expression. Then, if the LHS refers to an object that has a special method for the appropriate *in-place* version of the operator, Python calls the method with the RHS value as its argument. It is up to the method to modify the LHS object appropriately and return the modified object ("Special Methods" on page 104 covers special methods). If the LHS object has no appropriate in-place special method, Python applies the corresponding binary operator to the LHS and RHS objects, then rebinds the target reference to the operator's result. For example, x+=y is like x=x.__iadd__(y) when x has special method __iadd__. Otherwise, x+=y is like x=x+y.

Augmented assignment never creates its target reference; the target must already be bound when augmented assignment executes. Augmented assignment can rebind the target reference to a new object or modify the same object to which the target reference was already bound. Plain assignment, in contrast, can create or rebind the LHS target reference, but it never modifies the object, if any, to which the target reference was previously bound. The distinction between objects and references to objects is crucial here. For example, x=x+y does not modify the object to which name x was originally bound. Rather, it rebinds the name x to refer to a new object. x+=y, in contrast, modifies the object to which the name x is bound when that object has special method __iadd__; otherwise, x+=y rebinds the name x to a new object, just like x=x+y.

del Statements

Despite its name, a del statement does not delete objects; rather, it unbinds references. Object deletion may automatically follow as a consequence, by garbage collection, when no more references to an object exist.

A del statement consists of the keyword del, followed by one or more target references separated by commas (,). Each target can be a variable, attribute reference, indexing, or slicing, just like for assignment statements, and must be bound at the time del executes. When a del target is an identifier, the del statement means to unbind the variable. If the identifier was bound, unbinding it is never disallowed; when requested, it takes place.

In all other cases, the del statement specifies a request to an object to unbind one or more of its attributes or items. An object may refuse to unbind some (or all) attributes or items, raising an exception if you attempt a disallowed unbinding (see also __delattr__ on page 106 and __delitem__ on page 112). Unbinding a slicing normally has the same effect as assigning an empty sequence to that slice, but it is up to the container object to implement this equivalence.

Expressions and Operators

An *expression* is a phrase of code that Python evaluates to produce a value. The simplest expressions are literals and identifiers. You build other expressions by joining subexpressions with the operators and/or delimiters in Table 4-2. This table lists operators in decreasing order of precedence, higher precedence before lower. Operators listed together have the same precedence. The third column lists the associativity of the operator: L (left-to-right), R (right-to-left), or NA (nonassociative).

Table 4-2. Operator precedence in expressions

Operator	Description	Associativity
`` `expr,...` ``	String conversion	NA
`{key:expr,...}`	Dictionary creation	NA
`[expr,...]`	List creation	NA
`(expr,...)`	Tuple creation or just parentheses	NA
`f(expr,...)`	Function call	L
`x[index:index]`	Slicing	L
`x[index]`	Indexing	L
`x.attr`	Attribute reference	L
`x**y`	Exponentiation (*x* to *y*th power)	R
`~x`	Bitwise NOT	NA
`+x,-x`	Unary plus and minus	NA
`x*y,x/y,x//y,x%y`	Multiplication, division, truncating division, remainder	L
`x+y,x-y`	Addition, subtraction	L
`x<<y,x>>y`	Left-shift, right-shift	L
`x&y`	Bitwise AND	L
`x^y`	Bitwise XOR	L
`x|y`	Bitwise OR	L
`x<y,x<=y,x>y,x>=y,x<>y,` `x!=y,x==y`	Comparisons (less than, less than or equal, greater than, greater than or equal, inequality, equality) [a]	NA
`x is y,x is not y`	Identity tests	NA
`x in y,x not in y`	Membership tests	NA
`not x`	Boolean NOT	NA
`x and y`	Boolean AND	L
`x or y`	Boolean OR	L
`lambda arg,...: expr`	Anonymous simple function	NA

[a] `<>` and `!=` are alternate forms of the same operator. `!=` is the preferred version; `<>` is obsolete.

In Table 4-2, *expr*, *key*, *f*, *index*, *x*, and *y* indicate any expression, while *attr* and *arg* indicate any identifier. The notation `,...` means commas join zero or more repetitions, except for string conversion, where you need one or more repetitions.

A trailing comma is allowed and innocuous in all such cases, except for string conversion, where it's forbidden. The string conversion operator, with its quirky behavior, is not recommended; use built-in function repr (covered in repr on page 166) instead.

Comparison Chaining

You can *chain* comparisons, implying a logical and. For example:

```
a < b <= c < d
```

has the same meaning as:

```
a < b and b <= c and c < d
```

The chained form is more readable and evaluates each subexpression once at the most.

Short-Circuiting Operators

Operators and and or *short-circuit* their operands' evaluation: the righthand operand evaluates only if its value is needed to get the truth value of the entire and or or operation.

In other words, x and y first evaluates x. If x is false, the result is x; otherwise, the result is y. Similarly, x or y first evaluates x. If x is true, the result is x; otherwise, the result is y.

and and or don't force their results to be True or False, but rather return one or the other of their operands. This lets you use these operators more generally, not just in Boolean contexts. and and or, because of their short-circuiting semantics, differ from all other operators, which fully evaluate all operands before performing the operation. and and or let the left operand act as a *guard* for the right operand.

The Python 2.5 ternary operator

Python 2.5 introduces another short-circuiting operator, the ternary operator if/else:

```
whentrue if condition else whenfalse
```

Each of *whentrue*, *whenfalse*, and *condition* is an arbitrary expression. *condition* evaluates first. If *condition* is true, the result is *whentrue*; otherwise, the result is *whenfalse*. Only one of the two subexpressions *whentrue* and *whenfalse* evaluates, depending on the truth value of *condition*.

The order of the three subexpressions in this new ternary operator may be a bit confusing. Also, a recommended style is to always place parentheses around the whole expression.

Numeric Operations

Python supplies the usual numeric operations, as we've just seen in Table 4-2. Numbers are immutable objects: when you perform numeric operations on number objects, you always produce a new number object and never modify existing ones. You can access the parts of a complex object z as read-only attributes z.real and z.imag. Trying to rebind these attributes on a complex object raises an exception.

A number's optional + or - sign, and the + that joins a floating-point literal to an imaginary one to make a complex number, are not part of the literals' syntax. They are ordinary operators, subject to normal operator precedence rules (see Table 4-2). For example, -2**2 evaluates to -4: exponentiation has higher precedence than unary minus, so the whole expression parses as -(2**2), not as (-2)**2.

Numeric Conversions

You can perform arithmetic operations and comparisons between any two numbers of Python built-in types. If the operands' types differ, *coercion* applies: Python converts the operand with the "smaller" type to the "larger" type. The types, in order from smallest to largest, are integers, long integers, floating-point numbers, and complex numbers.

You can request an explicit conversion by passing a noncomplex numeric argument to any of the built-in number types: int, long, float, and complex. int and long drop their argument's fractional part, if any (e.g., int(9.8) is 9). You can also call complex with two numeric arguments, giving real and imaginary parts. You cannot convert a complex to another numeric type in this way, because there is no single unambiguous way to convert a complex number into, e.g., a float.

Each built-in numeric type can also take a string argument with the syntax of an appropriate numeric literal, with small extensions: the argument string may have leading and/or trailing whitespace, may start with a sign, and, for complex numbers, may sum or subtract a real part and an imaginary one. int and long can also be called with two arguments: the first one a string to convert, and the second the *radix*, an integer between 2 and 36 to use as the base for the conversion (e.g., int('101', 2) returns 5, the value of '101' in base 2).

Arithmetic Operations

Python arithmetic operations behave in rather obvious ways, with the possible exception of division and exponentiation.

Division

If the right operand of /, //, or % is 0, Python raises a runtime exception. The // operator performs truncating division, which means it returns an integer result (converted to the same type as the wider operand) and ignores the remainder, if any. When both operands are integers (plain or long), the / operator behaves like // if the switch -*Qold* was used on the Python command line (-*Qold* is the default in Python 2.3, 2.4, and 2.5). Otherwise, / performs true division, returning a floating-point result (or a complex result if either operand is a complex number). To have / perform true division on integer operands in Python 2.3, 2.4, or 2.5, use the switch -Qnew on the Python command line, or begin your source file with the statement:

```
from __future__ import division
```

This statement ensures that operator / (within the module that starts with this statement only) works without truncation on operands of any type.

To ensure that the behavior of division does *not* depend on the -Q switch, and on the exact version of Python you're using, always use // when you want truncating division. When you do not want truncation, use /, but also ensure that at least one operand is *not* an integer. For example, instead of using just a/b, code 1.*a/b to avoid making any assumption on the types of a and b. To check whether your program has version dependencies in its use of division, use the switch -Qwarn on the Python command line to get runtime warnings about all uses of / on integer operands.

The built-in divmod function takes two numeric arguments and returns a pair whose items are the quotient and remainder, so you don't have to use both // for the quotient and % for the remainder.

Exponentiation

The exponentiation ("raise to power") operation, $a**b$, raises an exception if a is less than zero and b is a floating-point value with a nonzero fractional part. The built-in pow(a, b) function returns the same result as $a**b$. With three arguments, pow(a, b, c) returns the same result as $(a**b)\%c$ but faster.

Comparisons

All objects, including numbers, can be compared for equality (==) and inequality (!=). Comparisons requiring order (<, <=, >, >=) may be used between any two numbers, unless either operand is complex, in which case they raise runtime exceptions. All these operators return Boolean values (True or False).

Bitwise Operations on Integers

Integers and long integers can be taken as strings of bits and used with the bitwise operations shown in Table 4-2. Bitwise operators have lower priority than arithmetic operators. Positive integers are conceptually extended by an infinite string of 0 bits on the left. Negative integers are represented in two's complement notation, and therefore are conceptually extended by an infinite string of 1 bits on the left.

Sequence Operations

Python supports a variety of operations applicable to all sequences, including strings, lists, and tuples. Some sequence operations apply to all containers (including, for example, sets and dictionaries, which are not sequences), and some apply to all iterables (meaning "any object on which you can loop," as covered in "Iterables" on page 40; all containers, be they sequences or otherwise, are iterable, and so are many objects that are not containers, such as files, covered in "File Objects" on page 216, and generators, covered in "Generators" on page 78). In the following, I use the terms *sequence*, *container*, and *iterable*, quite precisely and specifically, to indicate exactly which operations apply to each category.

Sequences in General

Sequences are containers with items that are accessible by indexing or slicing. The built-in len function takes any container as an argument and returns the number of items in the container. The built-in min and max functions take one argument, a nonempty iterable whose items are comparable, and return the smallest and largest items, respectively. You can also call min and max with multiple arguments, in which case they return the smallest and largest arguments, respectively. The built-in sum function takes one argument, an iterable whose items are numbers, and returns the sum of the numbers.

Sequence conversions

There is no implicit conversion between different sequence types, except that plain strings are converted to Unicode strings if needed. (String conversion is covered in detail in "Unicode" on page 198.) You can call the built-ins tuple and list with a single argument (any iterable) to get a new instance of the type you're calling, with the same items (in the same order) as in the argument.

Concatenation and repetition

You can concatenate sequences of the same type with the + operator. You can multiply a sequence S by an integer n with the * operator. S*n or n*S is the concatenation of n copies of S. When n<=0, S*n is an empty sequence of the same type as S.

Membership testing

The x in S operator tests to check whether object x equals any item in the sequence (or other kind of container or iterable) S. It returns True if it does and False if it doesn't. The x not in S operator is just like not (x in S). In the specific case of strings, though, x in S is more widely applicable; in this case, the operator tests whether x equals any *substring* of string S, not just any single *character*.

Indexing a sequence

The nth item of a sequence S is denoted by an *indexing*: S[n]. Indexing is zero-based (S's first item is S[0]). If S has L items, the index n may be 0, 1...up to and including L-1, but no larger. n may also be -1, -2...down to and including -L, but no smaller. A negative n indicates the same item in S as L+n does. In other words, S[-1], like S[L-1], is the last element of S, S[-2] is the next-to-last one, and so on. For example:

```
x = [1, 2, 3, 4]
x[1]                # 2
x[-1]               # 4
```

Using an index >=L or <-L raises an exception. Assigning to an item with an invalid index also raises an exception. You can add one or more elements to a list, but to do so you assign to a slice, not an item, as I'll discuss shortly.

Slicing a sequence

To indicate a subsequence of S, you can use a *slicing*, with the syntax S[i:j], where i and j are integers. S[i:j] is the subsequence of S from the ith item, included, to the jth item, excluded. In Python, ranges always include the lower bound and exclude the upper bound. A slice is an empty subsequence if j is less than or equal to i, or if i is greater than or equal to L, the length of S. You can omit i if it is equal to 0, so that the slice begins from the start of S. You can omit j if it is greater than or equal to L, so that the slice extends all the way to the end of S. You can even omit both indices, to mean a copy of the entire sequence: S[:]. Either or both indices may be less than 0. A negative index indicates the same spot in S as L+n, just like in indexing. An index greater than or equal to L means the end of S, while a negative index less than or equal to -L means the start of S. Here are some examples:

```
x = [1, 2, 3, 4]
x[1:3]            # [2, 3]
x[1:]             # [2, 3, 4]
x[:2]             # [1, 2]
```

Slicing can also use the extended syntax S[i:j:k]. k is the *stride* of the slice, or the distance between successive indices. S[i:j] is equivalent to S[i:j:1], S[::2] is the subsequence of S that includes all items that have an even index in S, and S[::-1] has the same items as S, but in reverse order.

Strings

String objects are immutable, so attempting to rebind or delete an item or slice of a string raises an exception. The items of a string object (corresponding to each of the characters in the string) are themselves strings, each of length 1. The slices of a string object are also strings. String objects have several methods, which are covered in "Methods of String Objects" on page 186.

Tuples

Tuple objects are immutable, so attempting to rebind or delete an item or slice of a tuple raises an exception. The items of a tuple are arbitrary objects and may be of different types. The slices of a tuple are also tuples. Tuples have no normal (nonspecial) methods, only some of the special methods covered in "Special Methods" on page 104.

Lists

List objects are mutable, so you may rebind or delete items and slices of a list. The items of a list are arbitrary objects and may be of different types. The slices of a list are lists.

Modifying a list

You can modify a list by assigning to an indexing. For instance:

```
x = [1, 2, 3, 4]
x[1] = 42                       # x is now [1, 42, 3, 4]
```

Another way to modify a list object L is to use a slice of L as the target (LHS) of an assignment statement. The RHS of the assignment must then be an iterable. If the LHS slice is in extended form, then the RHS must have just as many items as the number of items in the LHS slice. However, if the LHS slice is in normal (nonextended) form, then the LHS slice and the RHS may each be of any length; assigning to a (nonextended) slice of a list can add or remove list items. For example:

```
x = [1, 2, 3, 4]
x[1:3] = [22, 33, 44]    # x is now [1, 22, 33, 44, 4]
x[1:4] = [8, 9]          # x is now [1, 8, 9, 4]
```

Here are some important special cases of assignment to slices:

- Using the empty list [] as the RHS expression removes the target slice from L. In other words, L[i:j]=[] has the same effect as del L[i:j].

- Using an empty slice of L as the LHS target inserts the items of the RHS at the appropriate spot in L. In other words, L[i:i]=['a','b'] inserts the items 'a' and 'b' before the item that was at index i in L before the assignment.

- Using a slice that covers the entire list object, L[:], as the LHS target totally replaces the contents of L.

You can delete an item or a slice from a list with del. For instance:

```
x = [1, 2, 3, 4, 5]
del x[1]                        # x is now [1, 3, 4, 5]
del x[::2]                      # x is now [3, 5]
```

In-place operations on a list

List objects define in-place versions of the + and * operators, which you can use via augmented assignment statements. The augmented assignment statement L+=L1 has the effect of adding the items of iterable L1 to the end of L. L*=n has the effect of adding n-1 copies of L to the end of L; if n<=0, L*=n empties the contents of L, like L[:]=[].

List methods

List objects provide several methods, as shown in Table 4-3. *Nonmutating methods* return a result without altering the object to which they apply, while *mutating methods* may alter the object to which they apply. Many of the mutating methods behave like assignments to appropriate slices of the list. In Table 4-3, L indicates any list object, i any valid index in L, s any iterable, and x any object.

Table 4-3. List object methods

Method	Description
Nonmutating methods	
L.count(x)	Returns the number of items of L that are equal to x.
L.index(x)	Returns the index of the first occurrence of an item in L that is equal to x, or raises an exception if L has no such item.
Mutating methods	
L.append(x)	Appends item x to the end of L ; e.g., L[len(L):]=[x].
L.extend(s)	Appends all the items of iterable s to the end of L; e.g., L[len(L):]=s.
L.insert(i, x)	Inserts item x in L before the item at index i, moving following items of L (if any) "rightward" to make space (increases len(L) by one, does not replace any item, does not raise exceptions: acts just like L[i:i]=[x]).
L.remove(x)	Removes from L the first occurrence of an item in L that is equal to x, or raises an exception if L has no such item.
L.pop([i])	Returns the value of the item at index i and removes it from L; if i is omitted, removes and returns the last item; raises an exception if L is empty or i is an invalid index in L.
L.reverse()	Reverses, in place, the items of L.
L.sort([f]) (2.3)	Sorts, in place, the items of L, comparing items pairwise via function f; if f is omitted, comparison is via the built-in function cmp. For more details, see "Sorting a list" on page 57.
L.sort(cmp=cmp, key=None, reverse=False)(2.4)	Sorts, in-place, the items of L, comparing items pairwise via the function passed as *cmp* (by default, the built-in function cmp). When argument *key* is not None, what gets compared for each item x is *key*(x), not x itself. For more details, see "Sorting a list" on page 57.

All mutating methods of list objects, except pop, return None.

Sorting a list

A list's method sort causes the list to be sorted in-place (its items are reordered to place them in increasing order) in a way that is guaranteed to be stable (elements that compare equal are not exchanged). In practice, sort is extremely fast, often *preternaturally* fast, as it can exploit any order or reverse order that may be present in any sublist (the advanced algorithm sort uses, known as *timsort* to honor its developer, Tim Peters, is technically a "non-recursive adaptive stable natural mergesort/binary insertion sort hybrid").

In Python 2.3, a list's sort method takes one optional argument. If present, the argument must be a function that, when called with any two list items as arguments, returns -1, 0, or 1, depending on whether the first item is to be considered less than, equal to, or greater than the second item for sorting purposes. Passing the argument slows down the sort, although it makes it easy to sort small lists in flexible ways. The decorate-sort-undecorate idiom, covered in "Searching and sorting" on page 485 is faster, at least as flexible, and often less error-prone than passing an argument to sort.

In Python 2.4, the sort method takes three optional arguments, which may be passed with either positional or named-argument syntax. Argument *cmp* plays just the same role as the only (unnamed) optional argument in Python 2.3. Argument *key*, if not None, must be a function that can be called with any list item as its only argument. In this case, to compare any two items *x* and *y*, Python uses cmp(key(x),key(y)) rather than cmp(x,y) (in practice, this is implemented in the same way as the decorate-sort-undecorate idiom presented in "Searching and sorting" on page 485, and can be even faster). Argument *reverse*, if True, causes the result of each comparison to be reversed; this is not the same thing as reversing *L* after sorting because the sort is stable (elements that compare equal are never exchanged) whether argument *reverse* is true or false.

Python 2.4 also provides a new built-in function sorted (covered in sorted on page 167) to produce a sorted list from any input iterable. sorted accepts the same input arguments as a list's method sort. Moreover, Python 2.4 adds to module operator (covered in "The operator Module" on page 368) two new higher-order functions, attrgetter and itemgetter, which produce functions particularly suitable for the *key=* optional argument of lists' method sort and the new built-in function sorted. In Python 2.5, an identical *key=* optional argument has also been added to built-in functions min and max, and to functions nsmallest and nlargest in standard library module heapq, covered in "The heapq Module" on page 177.

Set Operations

Python provides a variety of operations applicable to sets. Since sets are containers, the built-in len function can take a set as its single argument and return the number of items in the set object. A set is iterable, so you can pass it to any function or method that takes an iterable argument. In this case, the items of the set are iterated upon, in some arbitrary order. For example, for any set *S*, min(*S*) returns the smallest item in *S*.

Set Membership

The *k* in *S* operator checks whether object *k* is one of the items of set *S*. It returns True if it is and False if it isn't. Similarly, *k* not in *S* is just like not (*k* in *S*).

Set Methods

Set objects provide several methods, as shown in Table 4-4. Nonmutating methods return a result without altering the object to which they apply and can also be called on instances of type frozenset, while mutating methods may alter the object to which they apply and can be called only on instances of type set. In Table 4-4, *S* and *S1* indicate any set object, and *x* any hashable object.

Table 4-4. Set object methods

Method	Description
Nonmutating methods	
S.copy( )	Returns a shallow copy of the set (a copy whose items are the same objects as S's, not copies thereof)
S.difference(S1)	Returns the set of all items of S that aren't in S1

Table 4-4. Set object methods (continued)

Method	Description
S.intersection(S1)	Returns the set of all items of S that are also in S1
S.issubset(S1)	Returns True if all items of S are also in S1; otherwise, returns False
S.issuperset(S1)	Returns True if all items of S1 are also in S; otherwise, returns False (like S1.issubset(S))
S.symmetric_difference(S1)	Returns the set of all items that are in either S or S1, but not in both sets
S.union(S1)	Returns the set of all items that are in S, S1, or in both sets
Mutating methods	
S.add(x)	Adds x as an item to S; no effect if x was already an item in S
S.clear( )	Removes all items from S, leaving S empty
S.discard(x)	Removes x as an item of S; no effect if x was not an item of S
S.pop( )	Removes and returns an arbitrary item of S
S.remove(x)	Removes x as an item of S; raises a KeyError exception if x is not an item of S

All mutating methods of set objects, except pop, return None.

The pop method can be used for destructive iteration on a set, consuming little extra memory. The memory savings make pop usable for a loop on a huge set, when what you want is to "consume" the set in the course of the loop.

Sets also have mutating methods named difference_update, intersection_update, symmetric_difference_update, and update (corresponding to nonmutating method union). Each such mutating method performs the same operation as the corresponding nonmutating method, but it performs the operation in place, altering the set on which you call it, and returns None. These four nonmutating methods are also accessible with operator syntax: respectively, S-S1, S&S1, S^S1, and S|S1; the corresponding mutating methods are also accessible with augmented assignment syntax: respectively, S-=S1, S&=S1, S^=S1, and S|=S1. When you use operator or augmented assignment syntax, both operands must be sets or frozensets; however, when you call the named methods, argument S1 can be any iterable with hashable items, and the semantics are just the same as if the argument you passed was set(S1).

Dictionary Operations

Python provides a variety of operations applicable to dictionaries. Since dictionaries are containers, the built-in len function can take a dictionary as its single argument and return the number of items (key/value pairs) in the dictionary object. A dictionary is iterable, so you can pass it to any function or method that takes an iterable argument. In this case, only the keys of the dictionary are iterated upon, in some arbitrary order. For example, for any dictionary D, min(D) returns the smallest key in D.

Dictionary Membership

The k in D operator checks whether object k is one of the keys of the dictionary D. It returns True if it is and False if it isn't. k not in D is just like not (k in D).

Indexing a Dictionary

The value in a dictionary D that is currently associated with key k is denoted by an indexing: D[k]. Indexing with a key that is not present in the dictionary raises an exception. For example:

```
d = { 'x':42, 'y':3.14, 'z':7 }
d['x']                        # 42
d['z']                        # 7
d['a']                        # raises KeyError exception
```

Plain assignment to a dictionary indexed with a key that is not yet in the dictionary (e.g., D[newkey]=value) is a valid operation and adds the key and value as a new item in the dictionary. For instance:

```
d = { 'x':42, 'y':3.14}
d['a'] = 16                   # d is now {'x':42, 'y':3.14,'a':16}
```

The del statement, in the form del D[k], removes from the dictionary the item whose key is k. If k is not a key in dictionary D, del D[k] raises an exception.

Dictionary Methods

Dictionary objects provide several methods, as shown in Table 4-5. Nonmutating methods return a result without altering the object to which they apply, while mutating methods may alter the object to which they apply. In Table 4-5, D and D1 indicate any dictionary object, k any hashable object, and x any object.

Table 4-5. Dictionary object methods

Method	Description
Nonmutating methods	
D.copy()	Returns a shallow copy of the dictionary (a copy whose items are the same objects as D's, not copies thereof)
D.has_key(k)	Returns True if k is a key in D; otherwise, returns False, just like k in D
D.items()	Returns a new list with all items (key/value pairs) in D
D.keys()	Returns a new list with all keys in D
D.values()	Returns a new list with all values in D
D.iteritems()	Returns an iterator on all items (key/value pairs) in D
D.iterkeys()	Returns an iterator on all keys in D
D.itervalues()	Returns an iterator on all values in D
D.get(k[, x])	Returns D[k] if k is a key in D; otherwise, returns x (or None, if x is not given)
Mutating methods	
D.clear()	Removes all items from D, leaving D empty
D.update(D1)	For each k in D1, sets D[k] equal to D1[k]
D.setdefault(k[, x])	Returns D[k] if k is a key in D; otherwise, sets D[k] equal to x and returns x

Table 4-5. Dictionary object methods (continued)

Method	Description
D.pop(k[,x])	Removes and returns D[k] if k is a key in D; otherwise, returns x (or raises an exception if x is not given)
D.popitem( )	Removes and returns an arbitrary item (key/value pair)

The items, keys, and values methods return their resulting lists in arbitrary order. If you call more than one of these methods without any intervening change to the dictionary, however, the order of the results is the same for all. The iteritems, iterkeys, and itervalues methods return iterators equivalent to these lists (iterators are discussed in "Iterators" on page 65). An iterator consumes less memory than a list, but you must never modify the set of keys in a dictionary (i.e., you must never add nor remove keys) while iterating on any of that dictionary's iterators. Iterating on the lists returned by items, keys, or values carries no such constraint. Iterating directly on a dictionary D is exactly like iterating on D.iterkeys( ).

The popitem method can be used for destructive iteration on a dictionary. Both items and popitem return dictionary items as key/value pairs, but using popitem consumes less memory, as it does not rely on a separate list of items. The memory savings make the idiom usable for a loop on a huge dictionary, when what you want is to "consume" the dictionary in the course of the loop.

The setdefault method returns the same result as get, but if k is not a key in D, setdefault also has the side effect of binding D[k] to the value x. Similarly, the pop method returns the same result as get, but if k is a key in D, pop also has the side effect of removing D[k] (when x is not specified, and k is not a key in D, get returns None, but pop raises an exception).

In Python 2.4, the update method can also accept an iterable of key/value pairs as an alternative argument instead of a mapping, and can accept keyword arguments instead of or in addition to its only positional argument; the semantics are the same as for passing such arguments when calling the built-in dict type, as covered in "Dictionaries" on page 44.

The print Statement

A print statement is denoted by the keyword print followed by zero or more expressions separated by commas. print is a handy, simple way to output values in text form, mostly for debugging purposes. print outputs each expression x as a string that's just like the result of calling str(x) (covered in str on page 157). print implicitly outputs a space between expressions, and implicitly outputs \n after the last expression, unless the last expression is followed by a trailing comma (,). Here are some examples of print statements:

```
letter = 'c'
print "give me a", letter, "..."        # prints: give me a c ...
answer = 42
print "the answer is:", answer          # prints: the answer is: 42
```

The destination of print's output is the file or file-like object that is the value of the stdout attribute of the sys module (covered in "The sys Module" on page 168). If you want to direct the output from a certain print statement to a specific file object f (which must be open for writing), you can use the special syntax:

```
print >>f, rest of print statement
```

(if f is None, the destination is sys.stdout, just as it would be without the >>f). You can also use the write or writelines methods of file objects, as covered in "Attributes and Methods of File Objects" on page 218. However, print is very simple to use, and simplicity is important in the common case where all you need are the simple output strategies that print supplies—in particular, this is often the case for the kind of simple output statements you may temporarily add to a program for debugging purposes. "The print Statement" on page 256 has more advice and examples concerning the use of print.

Control Flow Statements

A program's *control flow* is the order in which the program's code executes. The control flow of a Python program is regulated by conditional statements, loops, and function calls. (This section covers the if statement and for and while loops; functions are covered in "Functions" on page 70.) Raising and handling exceptions also affects control flow; exceptions are covered in Chapter 6.

The if Statement

Often, you need to execute some statements only if some condition holds, or choose statements to execute depending on several mutually exclusive conditions. The Python compound statement if, comprising if, elif, and else clauses, lets you conditionally execute blocks of statements. Here's the syntax for the if statement:

```
if expression:
    statement(s)
elif expression:
    statement(s)
elif expression:
    statement(s)
...
else:
    statement(s)
```

The elif and else clauses are optional. Note that, unlike some languages, Python does not have a switch statement. Use if, elif, and else for all conditional processing.

Here's a typical if statement with all three kinds of clauses:

```
if x < 0: print "x is negative"
elif x % 2: print "x is positive and odd"
else: print "x is even and non-negative"
```

When there are multiple statements in a clause (i.e., the clause controls a block of statements), the statements are placed on separate logical lines after the line containing the clause's keyword (known as the *header line* of the clause), indented rightward from the header line. The block terminates when the indentation returns to that of the clause header (or further left from there). When there is just a single simple statement, as here, it can follow the : on the same logical line as the header, but it can also be on a separate logical line, immediately after the header line and indented rightward from it. Most Python programmers prefer the separate-line style, with four-space indents for the guarded statements. Such a style is considered more general and more readable.

```
if x < 0:
    print "x is negative"
elif x % 2:
    print "x is positive and odd"
else:
    print "x is even and non-negative"
```

You can use any Python expression as the condition in an if or elif clause. Using an expression this way is known as using it "in a Boolean context." In a Boolean context, any value is taken as either true or false. As mentioned earlier, any nonzero number or nonempty container (string, tuple, list, dictionary, set) evaluates as true; zero (of any numeric type), None, and empty containers evaluate as false. When you want to test a value x in a Boolean context, use the following coding style:

```
if x:
```

This is the clearest and most Pythonic form. Do *not* use any of the following:

```
if x is True:
if x == True:
if bool(x):
```

There is a crucial difference between saying that an expression *returns* True (meaning the expression returns the value 1 with the bool type) and saying that an expression *evaluates as* true (meaning the expression returns any result that is true in a Boolean context). When testing an expression, you care about the latter condition, not the former.

If the expression for the if clause evaluates as true, the statements following the if clause execute, and the entire if statement ends. Otherwise, Python evaluates the expressions for each elif clause, in order. The statements following the first elif clause whose condition evaluates as true, if any, execute, and the entire if statement ends. Otherwise, if an else clause exists, the statements following it execute.

The while Statement

The while statement in Python supports repeated execution of a statement or block of statements that are controlled by a conditional expression. Here's the syntax for the while statement:

```
while expression:
    statement(s)
```

A while statement can also include an else clause, covered in "The else Clause on Loop Statements" on page 69, and break and continue statements, covered in "The break Statement" on page 68 and "The continue Statement" on page 68.

Here's a typical while statement:

```
count = 0
while x > 0:
    x = x // 2              # truncating division
    count += 1
print "The approximate log2 is", count
```

First, Python evaluates *expression*, which is known as the *loop condition*. If the condition is false, the while statement ends. If the loop condition is satisfied, the statement or statements that make up the *loop body* execute. When the loop body finishes executing, Python evaluates the loop condition again to check whether another iteration should execute. This process continues until the loop condition is false, at which point the while statement ends.

The loop body should contain code that eventually makes the loop condition false; otherwise, the loop will never end (unless an exception is raised or the loop body executes a break statement). A loop that is in a function's body also ends if a return statement executes in the loop body, since the whole function ends in this case.

The for Statement

The for statement in Python supports repeated execution of a statement, or block of statements, controlled by an iterable expression. Here's the syntax for the for statement:

```
for target in iterable:
    statement(s)
```

The in keyword is part of the syntax of the for statement and is distinct from the in operator, which tests membership. A for statement can also include an else clause, covered in "The else Clause on Loop Statements" on page 69, and break and continue statements, covered in "The break Statement" on page 68 and "The continue Statement" on page 68.

Here's a typical for statement:

```
for letter in "ciao":
    print "give me a", letter, "..."
```

iterable may be any Python expression suitable as an argument to built-in function iter, which returns an iterator object (explained in detail in the next section). In particular, any sequence is iterable. *target* is normally an identifier that names the *control variable* of the loop; the for statement successively rebinds this variable to each item of the iterator, in order. The statement or statements that make up the *loop body* execute once for each item in *iterable* (unless the loop ends because an exception is raised or a break or return statement executes). Note that, since the loop body may contain a break statement to terminate the loop, this is one case in which you may want to use an *unbounded* iterable—one that, per se, would never cease yielding items.

You can also have a target with multiple identifiers, as with an unpacking assignment. In this case, the iterator's items must then be iterables, each with exactly as many items as there are identifiers in the target. For example, when *d* is a dictionary, this is a typical way to loop on the items (key/value pairs) in *d*:

```
for key, value in d.items( ):
    if not key or not value:        # keep only true keys and values
        del d[key]
```

The items method returns a list of key/value pairs, so we can use a for loop with two identifiers in the target to unpack each item into key and value.

When an iterator has a mutable underlying object, you must not alter that object during a for loop on it. For example, the previous example cannot use iteritems instead of items. iteritems returns an iterator whose underlying object is d, so the loop body cannot mutate d (by executing del d[key]). items returns a list so that d is not the underlying object of the iterator; therefore, the loop body can mutate d. Specifically:

- When looping on a list, do not insert, append, or delete items (rebinding an item at an existing index is OK).
- When looping on a dictionary, do not add or delete items (rebinding the value for an existing key is OK).
- When looping on a set, do not add or delete items (no alteration is permitted).

The control variable may be rebound in the loop body but is rebound again to the next item in the iterator at the next iteration of the loop. The loop body does not execute at all if the iterator yields no items. In this case, the control variable is not bound or rebound in any way by the for statement. If the iterator yields at least one item, however, when the loop statement terminates, the control variable remains bound to the last value to which the loop statement has bound it. The following code is therefore correct, as long as someseq is not empty:

```
for x in someseq:
    process(x)
print "Last item processed was", x
```

Iterators

An *iterator* is an object *i* such that you can call *i*.next( ) with no arguments. *i*.next( ) returns the next item of iterator *i* or, when iterator *i* has no more items, raises a StopIteration exception. When you write a class (see "Classes and Instances" on page 82), you can allow instances of the class to be iterators by defining such a method next. Most iterators are built by implicit or explicit calls to built-in function iter, covered in iter on page 163. Calling a generator also returns an iterator, as we'll discuss in "Generators" on page 78.

The for statement implicitly calls iter to get an iterator. The following statement:

```
for x in c:
    statement(s)
```

is exactly equivalent to:

```
_temporary_iterator = iter(c)
while True:
    try: x = _temporary_iterator.next()
    except StopIteration: break
    statement(s)
```

where _temporary_iterator is some arbitrary name that is not used elsewhere in the current scope.

Thus, if iter(c) returns an iterator i such that i.next() never raises StopIteration (an *unbounded iterator*), the loop for x in c never terminates (unless the statements in the loop body include suitable break or return statements, or raise or propagate exceptions). iter(c), in turn, calls special method c.__iter__() to obtain and return an iterator on c. I'll talk more about the special method __iter__ in __iter__ on page 112.

Many of the best ways to build and manipulate iterators are found in standard library module itertools, covered in "The itertools Module" on page 183.

range and xrange

Looping over a sequence of integers is a common task, so Python provides built-in functions range and xrange to generate and return integer sequences. The simplest way to loop *n* times in Python is:

```
for i in xrange(n):
    statement(s)
```

range(x) returns a list whose items are consecutive integers from 0 (included) up to x (excluded). range(x, y) returns a list whose items are consecutive integers from x (included) up to y (excluded). The result is the empty list if x is greater than or equal to y. range(x, y, step) returns a list of integers from x (included) up to y (excluded), such that the difference between each two adjacent items in the list is step. If step is less than 0, range counts down from x to y. range returns the empty list when x is greater than or equal to y and step is greater than 0, or when x is less than or equal to y and step is less than 0. When step equals 0, range raises an exception.

While range returns a normal list object, usable for all purposes, xrange returns a special-purpose object, specifically intended for use in iterations like the for statement shown previously (unfortunately, to keep backward compatibility with old versions of Python, xrange does not return an iterator, as would be natural in today's Python; however, you can easily obtain such an iterator, if you need one, by calling iter(xrange(...))). The special-purpose object xrange returns consumes less memory (for wide ranges, *much* less memory) than the list object range returns, but the overhead of looping on the special-purpose object is slightly higher than that of looping on a list. Apart from performance and memory consumption issues, you can use range wherever you could use xrange, but not vice versa. For example:

```
>>> print range(1, 5)
[1, 2, 3, 4]
>>> print xrange(1, 5)
xrange(1, 5)
```

Here, `range` returns a perfectly ordinary list, which displays quite normally, but `xrange` returns a special-purpose object, which displays in its own special way.

List comprehensions

A common use of a `for` loop is to inspect each item in an iterable and build a new list by appending the results of an expression computed on some or all of the items. The expression form known as a *list comprehension* lets you code this common idiom concisely and directly. Since a list comprehension is an expression (rather than a block of statements), you can use it wherever you need an expression (e.g., as an argument in a function call, in a `return` statement, or as a subexpression for some other expression).

A list comprehension has the following syntax:

```
[ expression for target in iterable lc-clauses ]
```

target and *iterable* are the same as in a regular `for` statement. You must enclose the *expression* in parentheses if it indicates a tuple.

lc-clauses is a series of zero or more clauses, each with one of the following forms:

```
for target in iterable
if expression
```

target and *iterable* in each `for` clause of a list comprehension have the same syntax and meaning as those in a regular `for` statement, and the *expression* in each `if` clause of a list comprehension has the same syntax and meaning as the *expression* in a regular `if` statement.

A list comprehension is equivalent to a `for` loop that builds the same list by repeated calls to the resulting list's `append` method. For example (assigning the list comprehension result to a variable for clarity):

```
result1 = [x+1 for x in some_sequence]
```

is the same as the `for` loop:

```
result2 = []
for x in some_sequence:
    result2.append(x+1)
```

Here's a list comprehension that uses an `if` clause:

```
result3 = [x+1 for x in some_sequence if x>23]
```

This list comprehension is the same as a `for` loop that contains an `if` statement:

```
result4 = []
for x in some_sequence:
    if x>23:
        result4.append(x+1)
```

And here's a list comprehension that uses a `for` clause:

```
result5 = [x+y for x in alist for y in another]
```

This is the same as a for loop with another for loop nested inside:

```
result6 = []
for x in alist:
    for y in another:
        result6.append(x+y)
```

As these examples show, the order of for and if in a list comprehension is the same as in the equivalent loop, but in the list comprehension, the nesting remains implicit.

The break Statement

The break statement is allowed only inside a loop body. When break executes, the loop terminates. If a loop is nested inside other loops, a break in it terminates only the innermost nested loop. In practical use, a break statement is usually inside some clause of an if statement in the loop body so that break executes conditionally.

One common use of break is in the implementation of a loop that decides whether it should keep looping only in the middle of each loop iteration:

```
while True:                         # this loop can never terminate naturally
    x = get_next()
    y = preprocess(x)
    if not keep_looping(x, y): break
    process(x, y)
```

The continue Statement

The continue statement is allowed only inside a loop body. When continue executes, the current iteration of the loop body terminates, and execution continues with the next iteration of the loop. In practical use, a continue statement is usually inside some clause of an if statement in the loop body so that continue executes conditionally.

Sometimes, a continue statement can take the place of nested if statements within a loop. For example:

```
for x in some_container:
    if not seems_ok(x): continue
    lowbound, highbound = bounds_to_test()
    if x<lowbound or x>=highbound: continue
    if final_check(x):
        do_processing(x)
```

This equivalent code does conditional processing without continue:

```
for x in some_container:
    if seems_ok(x):
        lowbound, highbound = bounds_to_test()
        if lowbound <= x < highbound:
            if final_check(x):
                do_processing(x)
```

Both versions function identically, so which one you use is a matter of personal preference and style.

The else Clause on Loop Statements

while and for statements may optionally have a trailing else clause. The state-ment or block under that else executes when the loop terminates *naturally* (at the end of the for iterator, or when the while loop condition becomes false), but not when the loop terminates *prematurely* (via break, return, or an exception). When a loop contains one or more break statements, you often need to check whether the loop terminates naturally or prematurely. You can use an else clause on the loop for this purpose:

```
for x in some_container:
    if is_ok(x): break          # item x is satisfactory, terminate loop
else:
    print "Warning: no satisfactory item was found in container"
    x = None
```

The pass Statement

The body of a Python compound statement cannot be empty; it must always contain at least one statement. You can use a pass statement, which performs no action, as a placeholder when a statement is syntactically required but you have nothing to do. Here's an example of using pass in a conditional statement as a part of somewhat convoluted logic to test mutually exclusive conditions:

```
if condition1(x):
    process1(x)
elif x>23 or condition2(x) and x<5:
    pass                        # nothing to be done in this case
elif condition3(x):
    process3(x)
else:
    process_default(x)
```

Note that, as the body of an otherwise empty def or class statement, you may use a docstring, covered in "Docstrings" on page 72; if you do write a docstring, then you do not need to also add a pass statement, although you are still allowed to do so if you wish.

The try and raise Statements

Python supports exception handling with the try statement, which includes try, except, finally, and else clauses. A program can explicitly raise an exception with the raise statement. As I discuss in detail in "Exception Propagation" on page 126, when an exception is raised, normal control flow of the program stops, and Python looks for a suitable exception handler.

The with Statement

In Python 2.5, a with statement has been added as a more readable alternative to the try/finally statement. I discuss it in detail in "The with statement" on page 125.

Functions

Most statements in a typical Python program are grouped and organized into functions (code in a function body may be faster than at a module's top level, as covered in "Avoiding exec and from...import *" on page 486, so there are excellent practical reasons to put most of your code into functions). A *function* is a group of statements that execute upon request. Python provides many built-in functions and allows programmers to define their own functions. A request to execute a function is known as a *function call*. When you call a function, you can pass arguments that specify data upon which the function performs its computation. In Python, a function always returns a result value, either None or a value that represents the results of the computation. Functions defined within class statements are also known as *methods*. Issues specific to methods are covered in "Bound and Unbound Methods" on page 91; the general coverage of functions in this section, however, also applies to methods.

In Python, functions are objects (values) that are handled like other objects. Thus, you can pass a function as an argument in a call to another function. Similarly, a function can return another function as the result of a call. A function, just like any other object, can be bound to a variable, an item in a container, or an attribute of an object. Functions can also be keys into a dictionary. For example, if you need to quickly find a function's inverse given the function, you could define a dictionary whose keys and values are functions and then make the dictionary bidirectional. Here's a small example of this idea, using some functions from module math, covered in "The math and cmath Modules" on page 365:

```
inverse = {sin:asin, cos:acos, tan:atan, log:exp}
for f in inverse.keys( ): inverse[inverse[f]] = f
```

The fact that functions are ordinary objects in Python is often expressed by saying that functions are *first-class* objects.

The def Statement

The def statement is the most common way to define a function. def is a single-clause compound statement with the following syntax:

```
def function-name(parameters):
    statement(s)
```

function-name is an identifier. It is a variable that gets bound (or rebound) to the function object when def executes.

parameters is an optional list of identifiers, known as *formal parameters* or just parameters, that get bound to the values supplied as arguments when the function is called. In the simplest case, a function doesn't have any formal parameters, which means the function doesn't take any arguments when it is called. In this case, the function definition has empty parentheses after *function-name*.

When a function does take arguments, *parameters* contains one or more identifiers, separated by commas (,). In this case, each call to the function supplies values, known as *arguments*, corresponding to the parameters listed in the function definition. The parameters are local variables of the function (as we'll discuss

---

later in this section), and each call to the function binds these local variables to the corresponding values that the caller supplies as arguments.

The nonempty sequence of statements, known as the *function body*, does not execute when the def statement executes. Rather, the function body executes later, each time the function is called. The function body can contain zero or more occurrences of the return statement, as we'll discuss shortly.

Here's an example of a simple function that returns a value that is twice the value passed to it each time it's called:

```
def double(x):
    return x*2
```

Parameters

Formal parameters that are just identifiers indicate *mandatory parameters*. Each call to the function must supply a corresponding value (argument) for each mandatory parameter.

In the comma-separated list of parameters, zero or more mandatory parameters may be followed by zero or more *optional parameters*, where each optional parameter has the syntax:

identifier=expression

The def statement evaluates each such *expression* and saves a reference to the expression's value, known as the *default value* for the parameter, among the attributes of the function object. When a function call does not supply an argument corresponding to an optional parameter, the call binds the parameter's identifier to its default value for that execution of the function. Note that each default value gets computed when the def statement evaluates, *not* when the resulting function gets called. In particular, this means that the *same* object, the default value, gets bound to the optional parameter whenever the caller does not supply a corresponding argument. This can be tricky when the default value is a mutable object and the function body alters the parameter. For example:

```
def f(x, y=[]):
    y.append(x)
    return y
print f(23)              # prints: [23]
prinf f(42)             # prints: [23, 42]
```

The second print statement prints [23, 42] because the first call to f altered the default value of y, originally an empty list [ ], by appending 23 to it. If you want y to be bound to a new empty list object each time f is called with a single argument, use the following style instead:

```
def f(x, y=None):
    if y is None: y = []
    y.append(x)
    return y
print f(23)              # prints: [23]
prinf f(42)             # prints: [42]
```

At the end of the parameters, you may optionally use either or both of the special forms *identifier1* and **identifier2*. If both forms are present, the form with two asterisks must be last. *identifier1* specifies that any call to the function may supply any number of extra positional arguments, while **identifier2* specifies that any call to the function may supply any number of extra named arguments (positional and named arguments are covered in "Calling Functions" on page 73). Every call to the function binds *identifier1* to a tuple whose items are the extra positional arguments (or the empty tuple, if there are none). Similarly, *identifier2* gets bound to a dictionary whose items are the names and values of the extra named arguments (or the empty dictionary, if there are none). Here's a function that accepts any number of positional arguments and returns their sum:

```
def sum_args(*numbers):
    return sum(numbers)
print sum_args(23, 42)              # prints: 65
```

The number of parameters of a function, together with the parameters' names, the number of mandatory parameters, and the information on whether (at the end of the parameters) either or both of the single- and double-asterisk special forms are present, collectively form a specification known as the function's *signature*. A function's signature defines the ways in which you can call the function.

Attributes of Function Objects

The def statement sets some attributes of a function object. The attribute func_name, also accessible as _ _name_ _, refers to the identifier string given as the function name in the def statement. In Python 2.3, this is a read-only attribute (trying to rebind or unbind it raises a runtime exception); in Python 2.4, you may rebind the attribute to any string value, but trying to unbind it raises an exception. The attribute func_defaults, which you may freely rebind or unbind, refers to the tuple of default values for the optional parameters (or the empty tuple, if the function has no optional parameters).

Docstrings

Another function attribute is the *documentation string*, also known as the *docstring*. You may use or rebind a function's docstring attribute as either func_doc or _ _doc_ _. If the first statement in the function body is a string literal, the compiler binds that string as the function's docstring attribute. A similar rule applies to classes (see "Class documentation strings" on page 85) and modules (see "Module documentation strings" on page 142). Docstrings most often span multiple physical lines, so you normally specify them in triple-quoted string literal form. For example:

```
def sum_args(*numbers):
    '''Accept arbitrary numerical arguments and return their sum.
    The arguments are zero or more numbers.  The result is their sum.'''
    return sum(numbers)
```

Documentation strings should be part of any Python code you write. They play a role similar to that of comments in any programming language, but their applicability is wider, since they remain available at runtime. Development environments

---

and tools can use docstrings from function, class, and module objects to remind the programmer how to use those objects. The doctest module (covered in "The doctest Module" on page 454) makes it easy to check that sample code present in docstrings is accurate and correct.

To make your docstrings as useful as possible, you should respect a few simple conventions. The first line of a docstring should be a concise summary of the function's purpose, starting with an uppercase letter and ending with a period. It should not mention the function's name, unless the name happens to be a natural-language word that comes naturally as part of a good, concise summary of the function's operation. If the docstring is multiline, the second line should be empty, and the following lines should form one or more paragraphs, separated by empty lines, describing the function's parameters, preconditions, return value, and side effects (if any). Further explanations, bibliographical references, and usage examples (which you should check with doctest) can optionally follow toward the end of the docstring.

Other attributes of function objects

In addition to its predefined attributes, a function object may have other arbitrary attributes. To create an attribute of a function object, bind a value to the appropriate attribute reference in an assignment statement after the def statement executes. For example, a function could count how many times it gets called:

```
def counter():
    counter.count += 1
    return counter.count
counter.count = 0
```

Note that this is *not* common usage. More often, when you want to group together some state (data) and some behavior (code), you should use the object-oriented mechanisms covered in Chapter 5. However, the ability to associate arbitrary attributes with a function can sometimes come in handy.

The return Statement

The return statement in Python is allowed only inside a function body and can optionally be followed by an expression. When return executes, the function terminates, and the value of the expression is the function's result. A function returns None if it terminates by reaching the end of its body or by executing a return statement that has no expression (or, of course, by executing return None).

As a matter of style, you should *never* write a return statement without an expression at the end of a function body. If some return statements in a function have an expression, all return statements should have an expression. return None should only be written explicitly to meet this style requirement. Python does not enforce these stylistic conventions, but your code will be clearer and more readable if you follow them.

Calling Functions

A function call is an expression with the following syntax:

```
function-object(arguments)
```

function-object may be any reference to a function (or other callable) object; most often, it's the function's name. The parentheses denote the function-call operation itself. *arguments*, in the simplest case, is a series of zero or more expressions separated by commas (,), giving values for the function's corresponding parameters. When the function call executes, the parameters are bound to the argument values, the function body executes, and the value of the function-call expression is whatever the function returns.

Note that just *mentioning* a function (or other callable object) does *not* call it. To *call* a function (or other object) without arguments, you must use ( ) after the function's name.

The semantics of argument passing

In traditional terms, all argument passing in Python is *by value*. For example, if you pass a variable as an argument, Python passes to the function the object (value) to which the variable currently refers, not "the variable itself." Thus, a function cannot rebind the caller's variables. However, if you pass a mutable object as an argument, the function may request changes to that object because Python passes the object itself, not a copy. Rebinding a variable and mutating an object are totally disjoint concepts. For example:

```
def f(x, y):
    x = 23
    y.append(42)
a = 77
b = [99]
f(a, b)
print a, b              # prints: 77 [99, 42]
```

The print statement shows that a is still bound to 77. Function f's rebinding of its parameter x to 23 has no effect on f's caller, nor, in particular, on the binding of the caller's variable that happened to be used to pass 77 as the parameter's value. However, the print statement also shows that b is now bound to [99, 42]. b is still bound to the same list object as before the call, but that object has mutated, as f has appended 42 to that list object. In either case, f has not altered the caller's bindings, nor can f alter the number 77, since numbers are immutable. However, f can alter a list object, since list objects are mutable. In this example, f mutates the list object that the caller passes to f as the second argument by calling the object's append method.

Kinds of arguments

Arguments that are just expressions are known as *positional arguments*. Each positional argument supplies the value for the parameter that corresponds to it by position (order) in the function definition.

In a function call, zero or more positional arguments may be followed by zero or more *named arguments*, each with the following syntax:

```
identifier=expression
```

The *identifier* must be one of the parameter names used in the def statement for the function. The *expression* supplies the value for the parameter of that name. Most built-in functions do not accept named arguments, you must call such functions with positional arguments only. However, all normal functions coded in Python accept named as well as positional arguments, so you may call them in different ways.

A function call must supply, via a positional or a named argument, exactly one value for each mandatory parameter, and zero or one value for each optional parameter. For example:

```
def divide(divisor, dividend):
    return dividend // divisor
print divide(12, 94)                        # prints: 7
print divide(dividend=94, divisor=12)       # prints: 7
```

As you can see, the two calls to divide are equivalent. You can pass named arguments for readability purposes whenever you think that identifying the role of each argument and controlling the order of arguments enhances your code's clarity.

A common use of named arguments is to bind some optional parameters to specific values, while letting other optional parameters take default values:

```
def f(middle, begin='init', end='finis'):
    return begin+middle+end
print f('tini', end='')                     # prints: inittini
```

Thanks to named argument end='', the caller can specify a value, the empty string '', for f's third parameter, end, and still let f's second parameter, begin, use its default value, the string 'init'.

At the end of the arguments in a function call, you may optionally use either or both of the special forms *seq and **dct. If both forms are present, the form with two asterisks must be last. *seq passes the items of seq to the function as positional arguments (after the normal positional arguments, if any, that the call gives with the usual syntax). seq may be any iterable. **dct passes the items of dct to the function as named arguments, where dct must be a dictionary whose keys are all strings. Each item's key is a parameter name, and the item's value is the argument's value.

Sometimes you want to pass an argument of the form *seq or **dct when the parameters use similar forms, as described earlier in "Parameters" on page 71. For example, using the function sum_args defined in that section (and shown again here), you may want to print the sum of all the values in dictionary *d*. This is easy with *seq:

```
def sum_args(*numbers):
    return sum(numbers)
print sum_args(*d.values())
```

(Of course, in this case, print sum(d.values()) would be simpler and more direct!)

However, you may also pass arguments of the form *seq or **dct when calling a function that does not use the corresponding forms in its parameters. In that case, of course, you must ensure that iterable *seq* has the right number of items, or, respectively, that dictionary *dct* uses the right names as its keys; otherwise, the call operation raises an exception.

Namespaces

A function's parameters, plus any variables that are bound (by assignment or by other binding statements, such as def) in the function body, make up the function's *local namespace*, also known as *local scope*. Each of these variables is known as a *local variable* of the function.

Variables that are not local are known as *global variables* (in the absence of nested function definitions, which we'll discuss shortly). Global variables are attributes of the module object, as covered in "Attributes of module objects" on page 140. Whenever a function's local variable has the same name as a global variable, that name, within the function body, refers to the local variable, not the global one. We express this by saying that the local variable *hides* the global variable of the same name throughout the function body.

The global statement

By default, any variable that is bound within a function body is a local variable of the function. If a function needs to rebind some global variables, the first statement of the function must be:

```
global identifiers
```

where *identifiers* is one or more identifiers separated by commas (,). The identifiers listed in a global statement refer to the global variables (i.e., attributes of the module object) that the function needs to rebind. For example, the function counter that we saw in "Other attributes of function objects" on page 73 could be implemented using global and a global variable, rather than an attribute of the function object:

```
_count = 0
def counter( ):
    global _count
    _count += 1
    return _count
```

Without the global statement, the counter function would raise an UnboundLocal-Error exception because _count would then be an uninitialized (unbound) local variable. While the global statement enables this kind of programming, this style is often inelegant and unadvisable. As I mentioned earlier, when you want to group together some state and some behavior, the object-oriented mechanisms covered in Chapter 5 are usually best.

Don't use global if the function body just *uses* a global variable (including mutating the object bound to that variable if the object is mutable). Use a global statement only if the function body *rebinds* a global variable (generally by assigning to the variable's name). As a matter of style, don't use global unless it's strictly necessary, as its presence will cause readers of your program to assume the statement is there for some useful purpose. In particular, never use `global` except as the first statement in a function body.

Nested functions and nested scopes

A `def` statement within a function body defines a *nested function*, and the function whose body includes the `def` is known as an *outer function* to the nested one. Code in a nested function's body may access (but not rebind) local variables of an outer function, also known as *free variables* of the nested function.

The simplest way to let a nested function access a value is often not to rely on nested scopes, but rather to explicitly pass that value as one of the function's arguments. If necessary, the argument's value can be bound when the nested function is defined by using the value as the default for an optional argument. For example:

```
def percent1(a, b, c):
    def pc(x, total=a+b+c): return (x*100.0) / total
    print "Percentages are:", pc(a), pc(b), pc(c)
```

Here's the same functionality using nested scopes:

```
def percent2(a, b, c):
    def pc(x): return (x*100.0) / (a+b+c)
    print "Percentages are:", pc(a), pc(b), pc(c)
```

In this specific case, percent1 has a tiny advantage: the computation of *a+b+c* happens only once, while percent2's inner function pc repeats the computation three times. However, if the outer function rebinds its local variables between calls to the nested function, repeating the computation can be necessary. It's therefore advisable to be aware of both approaches, and choose the most appropriate one case by case.

A nested function that accesses values from outer local variables is also known as a *closure*. The following example shows how to build a closure:

```
def make_adder(augend):
    def add(addend):
        return addend+augend
    return add
```

Closures are an exception to the general rule that the object-oriented mechanisms covered in Chapter 5 are the best way to bundle together data and code. When you need specifically to construct callable objects, with some parameters fixed at object construction time, closures can be simpler and more effective than classes. For example, the result of make_adder(7) is a function that accepts a single argument and adds 7 to that argument. An outer function that returns a closure is a "factory" for members of a family of functions distinguished by some parameters, such as the value of argument *augend* in the previous example, and may often help you avoid code duplication.

lambda Expressions

If a function body is a single return *expression* statement, you may choose to replace the function with the special lambda expression form:

    lambda *parameters*: *expression*

A lambda expression is the anonymous equivalent of a normal function whose body is a single return statement. Note that the lambda syntax does not use the return keyword. You can use a lambda expression wherever you could use a reference to a function. lambda can sometimes be handy when you want to use a simple function as an argument or return value. Here's an example that uses a lambda expression as an argument to the built-in filter function (covered in filter on page 161):

```
aList = [1, 2, 3, 4, 5, 6, 7, 8, 9]
low = 3
high = 7
filter(lambda x, l=low, h=high: h>x>l, aList)     # returns: [4, 5, 6]
```

As an alternative, you can always use a local def statement that gives the function object a name. You can then use this name as the argument or return value. Here's the same filter example using a local def statement:

```
aList = [1, 2, 3, 4, 5, 6, 7, 8, 9]
low = 3
high = 7
def within_bounds(value, l=low, h=high):
    return h>value>l
filter(within_bounds, aList)                      # returns: [4, 5, 6]
```

While lambda can occasionally be useful, many Python users prefer def, which is more general, and may make your code more readable if you choose a reasonable name for the function.

Generators

When the body of a function contains one or more occurrences of the keyword yield, the function is known as a *generator*. When you call a generator, the function body does not execute. Instead, calling the generator returns a special iterator object that wraps the function body, its local variables (including its parameters), and the current point of execution, which is initially the start of the function.

When the next method of this iterator object is called, the function body executes up to the next yield statement, which takes the form:

    yield *expression*

When a yield statement executes, the function execution is "frozen," with current point of execution and local variables intact, and the expression following yield is returned as the result of the next method. When next is called again, execution of the function body resumes where it left off, again up to the next yield statement. If the function body ends, or executes a return statement, the iterator raises a StopIteration exception to indicate that the iteration is finished. return statements in a generator cannot contain expressions.

A generator is a very handy way to build an iterator. Since the most common way to use an iterator is to loop on it with a for statement, you typically call a generator like this:

```
for avariable in somegenerator(arguments):
```

For example, say that you want a sequence of numbers counting up from 1 to N and then down to 1 again. A generator can help:

```
def updown(N):
    for x in xrange(1, N): yield x
    for x in xrange(N, 0, -1): yield x
for i in updown(3): print i                    # prints: 1 2 3 2 1
```

Here is a generator that works somewhat like the built-in xrange function, but returns a sequence of floating-point values instead of a sequence of integers:

```
def frange(start, stop, step=1.0):
    while start < stop:
        yield start
        start += step
```

This frange example is only *somewhat* like xrange because, for simplicity, it makes arguments start and stop mandatory, and silently assumes step is positive.

Generators are more flexible than functions that returns lists. A generator may build an *unbounded* iterator, meaning one that returns an infinite stream of results (to use only in loops that terminate by other means, e.g., via a break statement). Further, a generator-built iterator performs *lazy evaluation*: the iterator computes each successive item only when and if needed, just in time, while the equivalent function does all computations in advance and may require large amounts of memory to hold the results list. Therefore, if all you need is the ability to iterate on a computed sequence, it is often best to compute the sequence in a generator rather than in a function that returns a list. If the caller needs a list of all the items produced by some bounded generator G(*arguments*), the caller can simply use the following code:

```
resulting_list = list(G(arguments))
```

Generator expressions

Python 2.4 introduces an even simpler way to code particularly simple generators: *generator expressions*, commonly known as *genexps*. The syntax of a genexp is just like that of a list comprehension (as covered in "List comprehensions" on page 67) except that a genexp is enclosed in parentheses (( )) instead of brackets ([ ]); the semantics of a genexp are the same as those of the corresponding list comprehension, except that a genexp produces an iterator yielding one item at a time, while a list comprehension produces a list of all results in memory (therefore, using a genexp, when appropriate, saves memory). For example, to sum the squares of all single-digit integers, in any modern Python, you can code sum([x*x for x in xrange(10)]); in Python 2.4, you can express this functionality even better, coding it as sum(x*x for x in xrange(10)) (just the same, but omitting the brackets), and obtain exactly the same result while consuming less memory. Note that the parentheses that indicate the function call also "do double duty" and enclose the genexp (no need for extra parentheses).

Generators in Python 2.5

In Python 2.5, generators are further enhanced, with the possibility of receiving a value (or an exception) back from the caller as each yield executes. These advanced features allow generators in 2.5 to implement full-fledged co-routines, as explained at *http://www.python.org/peps/pep-0342.html*. The main change is that, in 2.5, yield is not a statement, but an expression, so it has a value. When a generator is resumed by calling its method next, the corresponding yield's value is None. To pass a value *x* into some generator *g* (so that *g* receives *x* as the value of the yield on which it's suspended), instead of calling *g*.next( ), the caller calls *g*.send(*x*) (calling *g*.send(None) is just like calling *g*.next( )). Also, a bare yield without arguments, in Python 2.5, becomes legal, and equivalent to yield None.

Other Python 2.5 enhancements to generators have to do with exceptions, and are covered in "Generator enhancements" on page 126.

Recursion

Python supports recursion (i.e., a Python function can call itself), but there is a limit to how deep the recursion can be. By default, Python interrupts recursion and raises a RecursionLimitExceeded exception (covered in "Standard Exception Classes" on page 130) when it detects that the stack of recursive calls has gone over a depth of 1,000. You can change the recursion limit with function setrecursionlimit of module sys, covered in setrecursionlimit on page 171.

However, changing the recursion limit does not give you unlimited recursion; the absolute maximum limit depends on the platform on which your program is running, particularly on the underlying operating system and C runtime library, but it's typically a few thousand levels. If recursive calls get too deep, your program crashes. Such runaway recursion, after a call to setrecursionlimit that exceeds the platform's capabilities, is one of the very few ways a Python program can crash—really crash, hard, without the usual safety net of Python's exception mechanisms. Therefore, be wary of trying to fix a program that is getting RecursionLimitExceeded exceptions by raising the recursion limit too high with setrecursionlimit. Most often, you'd be better advised to look for ways to remove the recursion or, more specifically, limit the depth of recursion that your program needs.

Readers who are familiar with Lisp, Scheme, or functional-programming languages must in particular be aware that Python does *not* implement the optimization of "tail-call elimination," which is so important in these languages. In Python, any call, recursive or not, has the same cost in terms of both time and memory space, dependent only on the number of arguments: the cost does not change, whether the call is a "tail-call" (meaning that the call is the last operation that the caller executes) or any other, nontail call.

5

Object-Oriented Python

Python is an object-oriented programming language. Unlike some other object-oriented languages, Python doesn't force you to use the object-oriented paradigm exclusively. Python also supports procedural programming with modules and functions, so you can select the most suitable programming paradigm for each part of your program. Generally, the object-oriented paradigm is suitable when you want to group state (data) and behavior (code) together in handy packets of functionality. It's also useful when you want to use some of Python's object-oriented mechanisms covered in this chapter, such as inheritance or special methods. The procedural paradigm, based on modules and functions, may be simpler, and thus more suitable when you don't need any of the benefits of object-oriented programming. With Python, you can mix and match the two paradigms.

Python today is in transition between two slightly different object models. This chapter mainly describes the *new-style*, or *new object model*, which is simpler, more regular, more powerful, and the one I recommend you *always* use; whenever I speak of classes or instances, without explicitly specifying otherwise, I mean new-style classes or instances. However, for backward compatibility, the default object model in all Python 2.*x* versions, for every value of *x*, is the *legacy object model*, also known as the *classic* or *old-style* object model; the new-style object model will become the default (and the legacy one will disappear) in a few years, when Python 3.0 comes out. Therefore, in each section, after describing how the new-style object model works, this chapter covers the small differences between the new and legacy object models, and discusses how to use both object models with Python 2.*x*. Finally, the chapter covers *special methods*, in "Special Methods" on page 104, and then two advanced concepts known as *decorators*, in "Decorators" on page 115, and *metaclasses*, in "Metaclasses" on page 116.

Classes and Instances

If you're already familiar with object-oriented programming in other languages such as C++ or Java, then you probably have a good intuitive grasp of classes and instances: a *class* is a user-defined type, which you can *instantiate* to obtain *instances*, meaning objects of that type. Python supports these concepts through its class and instance objects.

Python Classes

A *class* is a Python object with several characteristics:

- You can call a class object as if it were a function. The call returns another object, known as an *instance* of the class; the class is also known as the *type* of the instance.

- A class has arbitrarily named attributes that you can bind and reference.

- The values of class attributes can be *descriptors* (including functions), covered in "Descriptors" on page 85, or normal data objects.

- Class attributes bound to functions are also known as *methods* of the class.

- A method can have a special Python-defined name with two leading and two trailing underscores. Python implicitly invokes such *special methods*, if a class supplies them, when various kinds of operations take place on instances of that class.

- A class can *inherit* from other classes, meaning it delegates to other class objects the lookup of attributes that are not found in the class itself.

An instance of a class is a Python object with arbitrarily named attributes that you can bind and reference. An instance object implicitly delegates to its class the lookup of attributes not found in the instance itself. The class, in turn, may delegate the lookup to the classes from which it inherits, if any.

In Python, classes are objects (values) and are handled like other objects. Thus, you can pass a class as an argument in a call to a function. Similarly, a function can return a class as the result of a call. A class, just like any other object, can be bound to a variable (local or global), an item in a container, or an attribute of an object. Classes can also be keys into a dictionary. The fact that classes are ordinary objects in Python is often expressed by saying that classes are *first-class* objects.

The class Statement

The class statement is the most common way to create a class object. class is a single-clause compound statement with the following syntax:

```
class classname(base-classes):
    statement(s)
```

classname is an identifier. It is a variable that gets bound (or rebound) to the class object after the class statement finishes executing.

---

base-classes is a comma-delimited series of expressions whose values must be class objects. These classes are known by different names in different programming languages; you can, depending on your choice, call them the *bases*, *superclasses*, or *parents* of the class being created. The class being created can be said to *inherit* from, *derive* from, *extend*, or *subclass* its base classes, depending on what programming language you are familiar with. This class is also known as a *direct subclass* or *descendant* of its base classes.

Syntactically, *base-classes* is optional: to indicate that you're creating a class without bases, you can omit *base-classes* (and the parentheses around it), placing the colon right after the classname (in Python 2.5, you may also use empty parentheses between the classname and the colon, with the same meaning). However, a class without bases, for reasons of backward compatibility, is an old-style one (unless you define the _ _metaclass_ _ attribute, covered in "How Python Determines a Class's Metaclass" on page 117). To create a new-style class C without any "true" bases, code class C(*object*):; since every type subclasses the built-in object, specifying *object* as the value of base-classes just means that class C is new-style rather than old-style. If your class has ancestors that are all old-style and does not define the _ _metaclass_ _ attribute, then your class is old-style; otherwise, a class with bases is always new-style (even if some bases are new-style and some are old-style).

The subclass relationship between classes is transitive: if *C1* subclasses *C2*, and *C2* subclasses *C3*, then *C1* subclasses *C3*. Built-in function issubclass(*C1*, *C2*) accepts two arguments that are class objects: it returns True if *C1* subclasses *C2*; otherwise, it returns False. Any class is considered a subclass of itself; therefore, issubclass(*C*, *C*) returns True for any class *C*. The way in which the base classes of a class affect the functionality of the class is covered in "Inheritance" on page 94.

The nonempty sequence of statements that follows the class statement is known as the *class body*. A class body executes immediately as part of the class statement's execution. Until the body finishes executing, the new class object does not yet exist and the *classname* identifier is not yet bound (or rebound). "How a Metaclass Creates a Class" on page 118 provides more details about what happens when a class statement executes.

Finally, note that the class statement does not immediately create any instance of the new class but rather defines the set of attributes that will be shared by all instances when you later create instances by calling the class.

The Class Body

The body of a class is where you normally specify the attributes of the class; these attributes can be descriptor objects (including functions) or normal data objects of any type (an attribute of a class can also be another class—so, for example, you can have a class statement "nested" inside another class statement).

Attributes of class objects

You normally specify an attribute of a class object by binding a value to an identifier within the class body. For example:

```
class C1(object):
    x = 23
print C1.x                                  # prints: 23
```

Class object C1 has an attribute named x, bound to the value 23, and C1.x refers to that attribute.

You can also bind or unbind class attributes outside the class body. For example:

```
class C2(object): pass
C2.x = 23
print C2.x                                  # prints: 23
```

However, your program is more readable if you bind, and thus create, class attributes with statements inside the class body. Any class attributes are implicitly shared by all instances of the class when those instances are created, as we'll discuss shortly.

The class statement implicitly sets some class attributes. Attribute __name__ is the *classname* identifier string used in the class statement. Attribute __bases__ is the tuple of class objects given as the base classes in the class statement. For example, using the class C1 we just created:

```
    print C1.__name__, C1.__bases__         # prints: C1, (<type 'object'>,)
```

A class also has an attribute __dict__, which is the dictionary object that the class uses to hold all of its other attributes. For any class object C, any object x, and any identifier S (except __name__, __bases__, and __dict__), C.S=x is equivalent to C.__dict__['S']=x. For example, again referring to the class C1 we just created:

```
C1.y = 45
C1.__dict__['z'] = 67
print C1.x, C1.y, C1.z                      # prints: 23, 45, 67
```

There is no difference between class attributes created in the class body, outside the body by assigning an attribute, or outside the body by explicitly binding an entry in C.__dict__.

In statements that are directly in a class's body, references to attributes of the class must use a simple name, not a fully qualified name. For example:

```
class C3(object):
    x = 23
    y = x + 22                              # must use just x, not C3.x
```

However, in statements that are in methods defined in a class body, references to attributes of the class must use a fully qualified name, not a simple name. For example:

```
class C4(object):
    x = 23
    def amethod(self):
        print C4.x                          # must use C4.x, not just x
```

Note that attribute references (i.e., an expression like C.5) have semantics richer than those of attribute bindings. I cover these references in detail in "Attribute Reference Basics" on page 89.

Function definitions in a class body

Most class bodies include def statements, since functions (called methods in this context) are important attributes for most class objects. A def statement in a class body obeys the rules presented in "Functions" on page 70. In addition, a method defined in a class body always has a mandatory first parameter, conventionally named self, that refers to the instance on which you call the method. The self parameter plays a special role in method calls, as covered in "Bound and Unbound Methods" on page 91.

Here's an example of a class that includes a method definition:

```
class C5(object):
    def hello(self):
        print "Hello"
```

A class can define a variety of special methods (methods with names that have two leading and two trailing underscores) relating to specific operations on its instances. I discuss special methods in detail in "Special Methods" on page 104.

Class-private variables

When a statement in a class body (or in a method in the body) uses an identifier starting with two underscores (but not ending with underscores), such as __ident, the Python compiler implicitly changes the identifier into _classname__ident, where classname is the name of the class. This lets a class use "private" names for attributes, methods, global variables, and other purposes, reducing the risk of accidentally duplicating names used elsewhere.

By convention, all identifiers starting with a single underscore are meant to be private to the scope that binds them, whether that scope is or isn't a class. The Python compiler does not enforce this privacy convention; it's up to Python programmers to respect it.

Class documentation strings

If the first statement in the class body is a string literal, the compiler binds that string as the documentation string attribute for the class. This attribute is named __doc__ and is known as the *docstring* of the class. See "Docstrings" on page 72 for more information on docstrings.

Descriptors

A *descriptor* is any new-style object whose class supplies a special method named __get__. Descriptors that are class attributes control the semantics of accessing and setting attributes on instances of that class. Roughly speaking, when you access an instance attribute, Python obtains the attribute's value by calling __get__ on the corresponding descriptor, if any. For more details, see "Attribute Reference Basics" on page 89.

Overriding and nonoverriding descriptors

If a descriptor's class also supplies a special method named __set__, then the descriptor is known as an *overriding descriptor* (or, by an older and slightly confusing terminology, a *data descriptor*); if the descriptor's class supplies only __get__, and not __set__, then the descriptor is known as a *nonoverriding* (or *nondata*) *descriptor*. For example, the class of function objects supplies __get__, but not __set__; therefore, function objects are nonoverriding descriptors. Roughly speaking, when you assign a value to an instance attribute with a corresponding descriptor that is overriding, Python sets the attribute value by calling __set__ on the descriptor. For more details, see "Attributes of instance objects" on page 87.

Old-style classes can have descriptors, but descriptors in old-style classes always work as if they were nonoverriding ones (their __set__ method, if any, is ignored).

Instances

To create an instance of a class, call the class object as if it were a function. Each call returns a new instance whose type is that class:

```
anInstance = C5( )
```

You can call built-in function isinstance(I, C) with a class object as argument C. isinstance returns True if object I is an instance of class C or any subclass of C. Otherwise, isinstance returns False.

__init__

When a class defines or inherits a method named __init__, calling the class object implicitly executes __init__ on the new instance to perform any needed instance-specific initialization. Arguments passed in the call must correspond to the parameters of __init__, except for parameter self. For example, consider the following class:

```
class C6(object):
    def __init__(self, n):
        self.x = n
```

Here's how you can create an instance of the C6 class:

```
anotherInstance = C6(42)
```

As shown in the C6 class, the __init__ method typically contains statements that bind instance attributes. An __init__ method must not return a value; otherwise, Python raises a TypeError exception.

The main purpose of __init__ is to bind, and thus create, the attributes of a newly created instance. You may also bind or unbind instance attributes outside __init__, as you'll see shortly. However, your code will be more readable if you initially bind all attributes of a class instance with statements in the __init__ method.

When __init__ is absent, you must call the class without arguments, and the newly generated instance has no instance-specific attributes.

Attributes of instance objects

Once you have created an instance, you can access its attributes (data and methods) using the dot (.) operator. For example:

```
anInstance.hello( )                      # prints: Hello
print anotherInstance.x                  # prints: 42
```

Attribute references such as these have fairly rich semantics in Python and are covered in detail in "Attribute Reference Basics" on page 89.

You can give an instance object an arbitrary attribute by binding a value to an attribute reference. For example:

```
class C7: pass
z = C7( )
z.x = 23
print z.x                                # prints: 23
```

Instance object z now has an attribute named x, bound to the value 23, and z.x refers to that attribute. Note that the __setattr__ special method, if present, intercepts every attempt to bind an attribute. (__setattr__ is covered in __setattr__ on page 108.) Moreover, if you attempt to bind, on a new-style instance, an attribute whose name corresponds to an overriding descriptor in the instance's class, the descriptor's __set__ method intercepts the attempt. In this case, the statement z.x=23 executes type(z).x.__set__(z, 23) (old-style instances ignore the overriding nature of descriptors found in their classes, i.e., they never call their __set__ methods).

Creating an instance implicitly sets two instance attributes. For any instance z, z.__class__ is the class object to which z belongs, and z.__dict__ is the dictionary that z uses to hold its other attributes. For example, for the instance z we just created:

```
print z.__class__.__name__, z.__dict__      # prints: C7, {'x':23}
```

You may rebind (but not unbind) either or both of these attributes, but this is rarely necessary. A new-style instance's __class__ may be rebound only to a new-style class, and a legacy instance's __class__ may be rebound only to a legacy class.

For any instance z, any object x, and any identifier S (except __class__ and __dict__), z.S=x is equivalent to z.__dict__['S']=x (unless a __setattr__ special method, or an overriding descriptor's __set__ special method, intercept the binding attempt). For example, again referring to the z we just created:

```
z.y = 45
z.__dict__['z'] = 67
print z.x, z.y, z.z                      # prints: 23, 45, 67
```

There is no difference between instance attributes created in __init__ by assigning to attributes or by explicitly binding an entry in z.__dict__.

The factory-function idiom

A common task is to create instances of different classes depending on some condition, or to avoid creating a new instance if an existing one is available for reuse. A common misconception is that such needs might be met by having __init__ return a particular object, but such an approach is absolutely unfeasible: Python raises an exception when __init__ returns any value other than None. The best way to implement flexible object creation is by using an ordinary function rather than calling the class object directly. A function used in this role is known as a *factory function*.

Calling a factory function is a flexible approach: a function may return an existing reusable instance, or create a new instance by calling whatever class is appropriate. Say you have two almost interchangeable classes (SpecialCase and NormalCase) and want to flexibly generate instances of either one of them, depending on an argument. The following appropriateCase factory function allows you to do just that (the role of the self parameter is covered in "Bound and Unbound Methods" on page 91):

```
class SpecialCase(object):
    def amethod(self): print "special"
class NormalCase(object):
    def amethod(self): print "normal"
def appropriateCase(isnormal=True):
    if isnormal: return NormalCase()
    else: return SpecialCase()
aninstance = appropriateCase(isnormal=False)
aninstance.amethod()                    # prints "special", as desired
```

__new__

Each new-style class has (or inherits) a static method named __new__ (static methods are covered in "Static methods" on page 99). When you call C(*args,**kwds) to create a new instance of class C, Python first calls C.__new__(C,*args,**kwds). Python uses __new__'s return value x as the newly created instance. Then, Python calls C.__init__(x,*args,**kwds), but only when x is indeed an instance of C or any of its subclasses (otherwise, x's state remains as __new__ had left it). Thus, for example, the statement x=C(23) is equivalent to:

```
x = C.__new__(C, 23)
if isinstance(x, C): type(x).__init__(x, 23)
```

object.__new__ creates a new, uninitialized instance of the class it receives as its first argument. It ignores other arguments if that class has an __init__ method, but it raises an exception if it receives other arguments beyond the first, and the class that's the first argument does not have an __init__ method. When you override __new__ within a class body, you do not need to add __new__=staticmethod(__new__), as you normally would: Python recognizes the name __new__ and treats it specially in this context. In those rare cases in which you rebind C.__new__ later, outside the body of class C, you do need to use C.__new__=staticmethod(*whatever*).

__new__ has most of the flexibility of a factory function, as covered in "The factory-function idiom" on page 88. __new__ may choose to return an existing instance or make a new one, as appropriate. When __new__ does need to create a new instance, it most often delegates creation by calling object.__new__ or the __new__ method of another superclass of C. The following example shows how to override static method __new__ in order to implement a version of the Singleton design pattern:

```
class Singleton(object):
    _singletons = {}
    def __new__(cls, *args, **kwds):
        if cls not in cls._singletons:
            cls._singletons[cls] = super(Singleton, cls).__new__(cls)
        return cls._singletons[cls]
```

(Built-in super is covered in "Cooperative superclass method calling" on page 97.) Any subclass of Singleton (that does not further override __new__) has exactly one instance. If the subclass defines an __init__ method, the subclass must ensure its __init__ is safe when called repeatedly (at each creation request) on the one and only class instance.

Old-style classes do not have a __new__ method.

Attribute Reference Basics

An *attribute reference* is an expression of the form *x.name*, where *x* is any expression and *name* is an identifier called the *attribute name*. Many kinds of Python objects have attributes, but an attribute reference has special rich semantics when *x* refers to a class or instance. Remember that methods are attributes too, so everything I say about attributes in general also applies to attributes that are callable (i.e., methods).

Say that x is an instance of class C, which inherits from base class B. Both classes and the instance have several attributes (data and methods), as follows:

```
class B(object):
    a = 23
    b = 45
    def f(self): print "method f in class B"
    def g(self): print "method g in class B"
class C(B):
    b = 67
    c = 89
    d = 123
    def g(self): print "method g in class C"
    def h(self): print "method h in class C"
x = C()
x.d = 77
x.e = 88
```

A few attribute names are special. For example, C.__name__ is the string 'C' and the class name. C.__bases__ is the tuple (B,), the tuple of C's base classes. x.__class__ is the class C, the class to which x belongs. When you refer to an attribute with one of these special names, the attribute reference looks directly into a dedicated slot in the class or instance object and fetches the value it finds there. You cannot unbind these attributes. Rebinding them is allowed, so you can change the name or base classes of a class, or the class of an instance, on the fly, but this advanced technique is rarely necessary.

Both class C and instance x each have one other special attribute: a dictionary named __dict__. All other attributes of a class or instance, except for the few special ones, are held as items in the __dict__ attribute of the class or instance.

Getting an attribute from a class

When you use the syntax C.*name* to refer to an attribute on a class object C, the lookup proceeds in two steps:

1. When '*name*' is a key in C.__dict__, C.*name* fetches the value v from C.__dict__['*name*']. Then, if v is a descriptor (i.e., type(v) supplies a method named __get__), the value of C.*name* is the result of calling type(v).__get__(v, None, C). Otherwise, the value of C.*name* is v.

2. Otherwise, C.*name* delegates the lookup to C's base classes, meaning it loops on C's ancestor classes and tries the *name* lookup on each (in "method resolution order," as covered in "Method resolution order" on page 94).

Getting an attribute from an instance

When you use the syntax x.*name* to refer to an attribute of instance x of class C, the lookup proceeds in three steps:

1. When '*name*' is found in C (or in one of C's ancestor classes) as the name of an overriding descriptor v (i.e., type(v) supplies methods __get__ and __set__), the value of C.*name* is the result of calling type(v).__get__(v, x, C). (This step doesn't apply to old-style instances).

2. Otherwise, when '*name*' is a key in x.__dict__, x.*name* fetches and returns the value at x.__dict__['*name*'].

3. Otherwise, x.*name* delegates the lookup to x's class (according to the same two-step lookup used for C.*name*, as just detailed). If a descriptor v is found, the overall result of the attribute lookup is, again, type(v).__get__(v, x, C); if a nondescriptor value v is found, the overall result of the attribute lookup is v.

When these lookup steps do not find an attribute, Python raises an AttributeError exception. However, for lookups of x.*name*, if C defines or inherits special method __getattr__, Python calls C.__getattr__(x,'*name*') rather than raising the exception (it's then up to __getattr__ to either return a suitable value or raise the appropriate exception, normally AttributeError).

Consider the following attribute references:

```
print x.e, x.d, x.c, x.b, x.a          # prints: 88, 77, 89, 67, 23
```

x.e and x.d succeed in step 2 of the instance lookup process, since no descriptors are involved, and 'e' and 'd' are both keys in x.__dict__. Therefore, the lookups go no further, but rather return 88 and 77. The other three references must proceed to step 3 of the instance process and look in x.__class__ (i.e., C). x.c and x.b succeed in step 1 of the class lookup process, since 'c' and 'b' are both keys in C.__dict__. Therefore, the lookups go no further but rather return 89 and 67.

x.a gets all the way to step 2 of the class process, looking in C.__bases__[0] (i.e., B). 'a' is a key in B.__dict__; therefore, x.a finally succeeds and returns 23.

Setting an attribute

Note that the attribute lookup steps happen in this way only when you refer to an attribute, not when you bind an attribute. When you bind (on either a class or an instance) an attribute whose name is not special (unless a __setattr__ method, or the __set__ method of an overriding descriptor, intercepts the binding of an instance attribute), you affect only the __dict__ entry for the attribute (in the class or instance, respectively). In other words, in the case of attribute binding, there is no lookup procedure involved, except for the check for overriding descriptors.

Bound and Unbound Methods

Method __get__ of a function object returns an *unbound method object* or a *bound method object* that wraps the function. The key difference between unbound and bound methods is that an unbound method is not associated with a particular instance while a bound method is.

In the code in the previous section, attributes f, g, and h are functions; therefore, an attribute reference to any one of them returns a method object that wraps the respective function. Consider the following:

```
print x.h, x.g, x.f, C.h, C.g, C.f
```

This statement outputs three bound methods represented by strings like:

```
<bound method C.h of <__main__.C object at 0x8156d5c>>
```

and then three unbound ones represented by strings like:

```
<unbound method C.h>
```

We get bound methods when the attribute reference is on instance x, and unbound methods when the attribute reference is on class C.

Because a bound method is already associated with a specific instance, you call the method as follows:

```
x.h( )                    # prints: method h in class C
```

The key thing to notice here is that you don't pass the method's first argument, self, by the usual argument-passing syntax. Rather, a bound method of instance x implicitly binds the self parameter to object x. Thus, the body of the method can access the instance's attributes as attributes of self, even though we don't pass an explicit argument to the method.

An unbound method, however, is not associated with a specific instance, so you must specify an appropriate instance as the first argument when you invoke an unbound method. For example:

```
C.h(x)                    # prints: method h in class C
```

You call unbound methods far less frequently than bound methods. The main use for unbound methods is for accessing overridden methods, as discussed in

"Inheritance" on page 94; moreover, even for that task, it's generally better to use the super built-in covered in "Cooperative superclass method calling" on page 97.

Unbound method details

As we've just discussed, when an attribute reference on a class refers to a function, a reference to that attribute returns an unbound method that wraps the function. An unbound method has three attributes in addition to those of the function object it wraps: im_class is the class object supplying the method, im_func is the wrapped function, and im_self is always None. These attributes are all read-only, meaning that trying to rebind or unbind any of them raises an exception.

You can call an unbound method just as you would call its im_func function, but the first argument in any call must be an instance of im_class or a descendant. In other words, a call to an unbound method must have at least one argument, which corresponds to the wrapped function's first formal parameter (conventionally named self).

Bound method details

When an attribute reference on an instance, in the course of the lookup, finds a function object that's an attribute in the instance's class, the lookup calls the function's _ _get_ _ method to obtain the attribute's value. The call, in this case, creates and returns a *bound method* that wraps the function.

Note that when the attribute reference's lookup finds a function object in x._ _dict_ _, the attribute reference operation does *not* create a bound method because in such cases the function is not treated as a descriptor, and the function's _ _get_ _ method does not get called; rather, the function object itself is the attribute's value. Similarly, no bound method is created for callables that are not ordinary functions, such as built-in (as opposed to Python-coded) functions, since they are not descriptors.

A bound method is similar to an unbound method in that it has three read-only attributes in addition to those of the function object it wraps. Like in an unbound method, im_class is the class object that supplies the method, and im_func is the wrapped function. However, in a bound method object, attribute im_self refers to x, the instance from which the method was obtained.

A bound method is used like its im_func function, but calls to a bound method do not explicitly supply an argument corresponding to the first formal parameter (conventionally named self). When you call a bound method, the bound method passes im_self as the first argument to im_func before other arguments (if any) given at the point of call.

Let's follow in excruciating low-level detail the conceptual steps involved in a method call with the normal syntax x.*name*(*arg*). In the following context:

```
def f(a, b): ...          # a function f with two arguments
```

```
class C(object):
    name = f
x = C( )
```

x is an instance object of class C, *name* is an identifier that names a method of *x*'s (an attribute of C whose value is a function, in this case function f), and *arg* is any expression. Python first checks if `'name'` is the attribute name in C of an overriding descriptor, but it isn't—functions are descriptors, because their class defines method `__get__`, but not overriding ones, because their class does not define method `__set__`. Python next checks if `'name'` is a key in `x.__dict__`, but it isn't. So Python finds *name* in C (everything would work in just the same way if *name* was found, by inheritance, in one of C's `__bases__`). Python notices that the attribute's value, function object *f*, is a descriptor. Therefore, Python calls *f*.`__get__`(*x*, *C*), which creates a bound method object with `im_func` set to f, `im_class` set to C, and `im_self` set to *x*. Then Python calls this bound method object, with *arg* as the only actual argument. The bound method inserts `im_self` (i.e., *x*) as the first actual argument, and *arg* becomes the second one, in a call to the bound method's `im_func` (i.e., function f). The overall effect is just like calling:

```
x.__class__.__dict__['name'](x, arg)
```

When a bound method's function body executes, it has no special namespace relationship to either its `self` object or any class. Variables referenced are local or global, just as for any other function, as covered in "Namespaces" on page 76. Variables do not implicitly indicate attributes in `self`, nor do they indicate attributes in any class object. When the method needs to refer to, bind, or unbind an attribute of its `self` object, it does so by standard attribute-reference syntax (e.g., `self.name`). The lack of implicit scoping may take some getting used to (since Python differs in this respect from many other object-oriented languages), but it results in clarity, simplicity, and the removal of potential ambiguities.

Bound method objects are first-class objects, and you can use them wherever you can use a callable object. Since a bound method holds references to the function it wraps, and to the `self` object on which it executes, it's a powerful and flexible alternative to a closure (covered in "Nested functions and nested scopes" on page 77). An instance object whose class supplies special method `__call__` (covered in `__call__` on page 105) offers another viable alternative. Each of these constructs lets you bundle some behavior (code) and some state (data) into a single callable object. Closures are simplest, but limited in their applicability. Here's the closure from "Nested functions and nested scopes" on page 77:

```
def make_adder_as_closure(augend):
    def add(addend, _augend=augend): return addend+_augend
    return add
```

Bound methods and callable instances are richer and more flexible than closures. Here's how to implement the same functionality with a bound method:

```
def make_adder_as_bound_method(augend):
    class Adder(object):
        def __init__(self, augend): self.augend = augend
        def add(self, addend): return addend+self.augend
    return Adder(augend).add
```

Here's how to implement it with a callable instance (an instance whose class supplies special method __call__):

```
def make_adder_as_callable_instance(augend):
    class Adder(object):
        def __init__(self, augend): self.augend = augend
        def __call__(self, addend): return addend+self.augend
    return Adder(augend)
```

From the viewpoint of the code that calls the functions, all of these factory functions are interchangeable, since all of them return callable objects that are polymorphic (i.e., usable in the same ways). In terms of implementation, the closure is simplest; the bound method and the callable instance use more flexible, general, and powerful mechanisms, but there is really no need for that extra power in this simple example.

Inheritance

When you use an attribute reference *C.name* on a class object *C*, and *'name'* is not a key in *C.__dict__*, the lookup implicitly proceeds on each class object that is in *C.__bases__* in a specific order (which for historical reasons is known as the *method resolution order*, or MRO, even though it's used for all attributes, not just methods). *C*'s base classes may in turn have their own bases. The lookup checks direct and indirect ancestors, one by one, in MRO, stopping when *'name'* is found.

Method resolution order

The lookup of an attribute name in a class essentially occurs by visiting ancestor classes in left-to-right, depth-first order. However, in the presence of multiple inheritance (which makes the inheritance graph a general Directed Acyclic Graph rather than specifically a tree), this simple approach might lead to some ancestor class being visited twice. In such cases, the resolution order is clarified by leaving in the lookup sequence only the *rightmost* occurrence of any given class. This last, crucial simplification is not part of the specifications for the legacy object model, making multiple inheritance hard to use correctly and effectively within that object model. The new-style object model is vastly superior in this regard.

The problem with purely left-right, depth-first search, in situations of multiple inheritance, can be easily demonstrated with an example based on old-style classes:

```
class Base1:
    def amethod(self): print "Base1"
class Base2(Base1): pass
class Base3:
    def amethod(self): print "Base3"
class Derived(Base2, Base3): pass
aninstance = Derived()
aninstance.amethod()                    # prints: "Base1"
```

In this case, the lookup for amethod starts in Derived. When it isn't found there, lookup proceeds to Base2. Since the attribute isn't found in Base2, the legacy-style lookup then proceeds to Base2's ancestor, Base1, where the attribute is found. Therefore, the legacy-style lookup stops at this point and never considers Base3, where it would also find an attribute with the same name. The new-style MRO solves this problem by removing the leftmost occurrence of Base1 from the search so that the occurrence of amethod in Base3 is found instead.

Figure 5-1 shows the legacy and new-style MROs for the case of this kind of "diamond-shaped" inheritance graph.

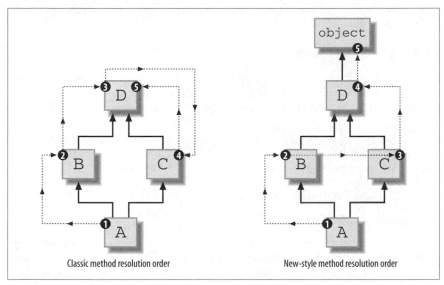

Figure 5-1. Legacy and new-style MRO

Each new-style class and built-in type has a special read-only class attribute called __mro__, which is the tuple of types used for method resolution, in order. You can reference __mro__ only on classes, not on instances, and, since __mro__ is a read-only attribute, you cannot rebind or unbind it. For a detailed and highly technical explanation of all aspects of Python's MRO, you may want to study a paper by Michele Simionato, "The Python 2.3 Method Resolution Order," at *http://www.python.org/2.3/mro.html*.

Overriding attributes

As we've just seen, the search for an attribute proceeds along the MRO (typically up the inheritance tree) and stops as soon as the attribute is found. Descendant classes are always examined before their ancestors so that, when a subclass defines an attribute with the same name as one in a superclass, the search finds the definition in the subclass and stops there. This is known as the subclass *overriding* the definition in the superclass. Consider the following:

```
class B(object):
    a = 23
    b = 45
    def f(self): print "method f in class B"
```

```
        def g(self): print "method g in class B"
    class C(B):
        b = 67
        c = 89
        d = 123
        def g(self): print "method g in class C"
        def h(self): print "method h in class C"
```

In this code, class C overrides attributes b and g of its superclass B. Note that, unlike in some other languages, in Python you may override data attributes just as easily as callable attributes (methods).

Delegating to superclass methods

When a subclass C overrides a method f of its superclass B, the body of C.f often wants to delegate some part of its operation to the superclass's implementation of the method. This can sometimes be done using an unbound method, as follows:

```
    class Base(object):
        def greet(self, name): print "Welcome ", name
    class Sub(Base):
        def greet(self, name):
            print "Well Met and",
            Base.greet(self, name)
    x = Sub()
    x.greet('Alex')
```

The delegation to the superclass, in the body of Sub.greet, uses an unbound method obtained by attribute reference Base.greet on the superclass, and therefore passes all attributes normally, including self. Delegating to a superclass implementation is the most frequent use of unbound methods.

One common use of delegation occurs with special method __init__. When Python creates an instance, the __init__ methods of base classes are not automatically invoked, as they are in some other object-oriented languages. Thus, it is up to a subclass to perform the proper initialization by using delegation if necessary. For example:

```
    class Base(object):
        def __init__(self):
            self.anattribute = 23
    class Derived(Base):
        def __init__(self):
            Base.__init__(self)
            self.anotherattribute = 45
```

If the __init__ method of class Derived didn't explicitly call that of class Base, instances of Derived would miss that portion of their initialization, and thus such instances would lack attribute anattribute.

Cooperative superclass method calling

Calling the superclass's version of a method with unbound method syntax, however, is quite problematic in cases of multiple inheritance with diamond-shaped graphs. Consider the following definitions:

```
class A(object):
    def met(self):
        print 'A.met'
class B(A):
    def met(self):
        print 'B.met'
        A.met(self)
class C(A):
    def met(self):
        print 'C.met'
        A.met(self)
class D(B,C):
    def met(self):
        print 'D.met'
        B.met(self)
        C.met(self)
```

In this code, when we call D( ).met( ), A.met ends up being called twice. How can we ensure that each ancestor's implementation of the method is called once, and only once? The solution is to use built-in type super. super(*aclass, obj*), which returns a special superobject of object *obj*. When we look up an attribute (e.g., a method) in this superobject, the lookup begins *after* class *aclass* in *obj*'s MRO. We can therefore rewrite the previous code as:

```
class A(object):
    def met(self):
        print 'A.met'
class B(A):
    def met(self):
        print 'B.met'
        super(B,self).met( )
class C(A):
    def met(self):
        print 'C.met'
        super(C,self).met( )
class D(B,C):
    def met(self):
        print 'D.met'
        super(D,self).met( )
```

Now, D( ).met( ) results in exactly one call to each class's version of met. If you get into the habit of always coding superclass calls with super, your classes will fit smoothly even in complicated inheritance structures. There are no ill effects whatsoever if the inheritance structure instead turns out to be simple, as long, of course, as you're only using the new-style object model, as I recommend.

The only situation in which you may prefer to use the rougher approach of calling a superclass method through the unbound-method technique is when the various classes have different and incompatible signatures for the same method—an unpleasant situation in many respects, but, if you do have to deal with it, the unbound-method technique may sometimes be the least of evils. Proper use of multiple inheritance will be seriously hampered—but then, even the most fundamental properties of OOP, such as polymorphism between base and subclass instances, are seriously impaired when corresponding methods have different and incompatible signatures.

"Deleting" class attributes

Inheritance and overriding provide a simple and effective way to add or modify class attributes (particularly methods) noninvasively (i.e., without modifying the class in which the attributes are defined) by adding or overriding the attributes in subclasses. However, inheritance does not offer a way to delete (hide) base classes' attributes noninvasively. If the subclass simply fails to define (override) an attribute, Python finds the base class's definition. If you need to perform such deletion, possibilities include:

- Override the method and raise an exception in the method's body.
- Eschew inheritance, hold the attributes elsewhere than in the subclass's __dict__, and define __getattr__ for selective delegation.
- Use the new-style object model and override __getattribute__ to similar effect.

The last of these techniques is demonstrated in "__getattribute__" on page 102.

The Built-in object Type

The built-in object type is the ancestor of all built-in types and new-style classes. The object type defines some special methods (documented in "Special Methods" on page 104) that implement the default semantics of objects:

__new__
__init__
> You can create a direct instance of object by calling object() without any arguments. The call implicitly uses object.__new__ and object.__init__ to make and return an instance object without attributes (and without even a __dict__ in which to hold attributes). Such an instance object may be useful as a "sentinel," guaranteed to compare unequal to any other distinct object.

__delattr__
__getattribute__
__setattr__
> By default, an object handles attribute references (as covered in "Attribute Reference Basics" on page 89) using these methods of object.

__hash__
__repr__
__str__
> Any object can be passed to functions hash and repr and to type str.

A subclass of object may override any of these methods and/or add others.

Class-Level Methods

Python supplies two built-in nonoverriding descriptors types, which give a class two distinct kinds of "class-level methods."

Static methods

A *static method* is a method that you can call on a class, or on any instance of the class, without the special behavior and constraints of ordinary methods, bound and unbound, with regard to the first parameter. A static method may have any signature; it may have no parameters, and the first parameter, if any, plays no special role. You can think of a static method as an ordinary function that you're able to call normally, despite the fact that it happens to be bound to a class attribute. While it is never necessary to define static methods (you can always define a normal function instead), some programmers consider them to be an elegant alternative when a function's purpose is tightly bound to some specific class.

To build a static method, call built-in type staticmethod and bind its result to a class attribute. Like all binding of class attributes, this is normally done in the body of the class, but you may also choose to perform it elsewhere. The only argument to staticmethod is the function to invoke when Python calls the static method. The following example shows how to define and call a static method:

```
class AClass(object):
    def astatic(): print 'a static method'
    astatic = staticmethod(astatic)
anInstance = AClass()
AClass.astatic()                    # prints: a static method
anInstance.astatic()                # prints: a static method
```

This example uses the same name for the function passed to staticmethod and for the attribute bound to staticmethod's result. This style is not mandatory, but it's a good idea, and I recommend you always use it. Python 2.4 offers a special, simplified syntax to support this style, covered in "Decorators" on page 115.

Class methods

A *class method* is a method you can call on a class or on any instance of the class. Python binds the method's first parameter to the class on which you call the method, or the class of the instance on which you call the method; it does not bind it to the instance, as for normal bound methods. There is no equivalent of unbound methods for class methods. The first parameter of a class method is conventionally named cls. While it is never necessary to define class methods (you could always alternatively define a normal function that takes the class object as its first parameter), some programmers consider them to be an elegant alternative to such functions.

To build a class method, call built-in type classmethod and bind its result to a class attribute. Like all binding of class attributes, this is normally done in the body of the class, but you may also choose to perform it elsewhere. The only argument to classmethod is the function to invoke when Python calls the class method. Here's how you can define and call a class method:

```
class ABase(object):
    def aclassmet(cls): print 'a class method for', cls.__name__
    aclassmet = classmethod(aclassmet)
class ADeriv(ABase): pass
bInstance = ABase( )
dInstance = ADeriv( )
ABase.aclassmet( )              # prints: a class method for ABase
bInstance.aclassmet( )          # prints: a class method for ABase
ADeriv.aclassmet( )             # prints: a class method for ADeriv
dInstance.aclassmet( )          # prints: a class method for ADeriv
```

This example uses the same name for the function passed to classmethod and for the attribute bound to classmethod's result. This style is not mandatory, but it's a good idea, and I recommend that you always use it. Python 2.4 offers a special, simplified syntax to support this style, covered in "Decorators" on page 115.

Properties

Python supplies a built-in overriding descriptor type, which you may use to give a class's instances *properties*.

A property is an instance attribute with special functionality. You reference, bind, or unbind the attribute with the normal syntax (e.g., print x.prop, x.prop=23, del x.prop). However, rather than following the usual semantics for attribute reference, binding, and unbinding, these accesses call on instance x the methods that you specify as arguments to the built-in type property. Here's how you define a read-only property:

```
class Rectangle(object):
    def __init__(self, width, height):
        self.width = width
        self.height = height
    def getArea(self):
        return self.width * self.height
    area = property(getArea, doc='area of the rectangle')
```

Each instance r of class Rectangle has a synthetic read-only attribute r.area, computed on the fly in method r.getArea( ) by multiplying the sides of the rectangle. The docstring Rectangle.area.__doc__ is 'area of the rectangle'. Attribute r.area is read-only (attempts to rebind or unbind it fail) because we specify only a get method in the call to property, no set or del methods.

Properties perform tasks similar to those of special methods __getattr__, __setattr__, and __delattr__ (covered in "General-Purpose Special Methods" on page 104), but in a faster and simpler way. You build a property by calling built-in type property and binding its result to a class attribute. Like all binding of class attributes, this is normally done in the body of the class, but you may also choose to perform it elsewhere. Within the body of a class C, use the following syntax:

```
attrib = property(fget=None, fset=None, fdel=None, doc=None)
```

When x is an instance of C and you reference *x.attrib*, Python calls on x the method you passed as argument *fget* to the property constructor, without arguments. When you assign *x.attrib = value*, Python calls the method you passed as argument *fset*, with *value* as the only argument. When you execute del *x.attrib*, Python calls the method you passed as argument *fdel*, without arguments. Python uses the argument you passed as *doc* as the docstring of the attribute. All parameters to property are optional. When an argument is missing, the corresponding operation is forbidden (Python raises an exception when some code attempts that operation). For example, in the Rectangle example, we made property area read-only, because we passed an argument only for parameter *fget*, and not for parameters *fset* and *fdel*.

Why properties are important

The crucial importance of properties is that their existence makes it perfectly safe and indeed advisable for you to expose public data attributes as part of your class's public interface. If it ever becomes necessary, in future versions of your class or other classes that need to be polymorphic to it, to have some code executed when the attribute is referenced, rebound, or unbound, you know you will be able to change the plain attribute into a property and get the desired effect without any impact on any other code that uses your class (a.k.a. "client code"). This lets you avoid goofy idioms, such as *accessor* and *mutator* methods, required by OO languages that lack properties or equivalent machinery. For example, client code can simply use natural idioms such as:

```
someInstance.widgetCounter += 1
```

rather than being forced into contorted nests of accessors and mutators such as:

```
someInstance.setWidgetCounter(someInstance.getWidgetCounter( ) + 1)
```

If at any time you're tempted to code methods whose natural names are something like *getThis* or *setThat*, consider wrapping those methods into properties, for clarity.

Properties and inheritance

Properties are inherited normally, just like any other attribute. However, there's a little trap for the unwary: the methods called upon to access a property are those that are defined in the class in which the property itself is defined, without intrinsic use of further overriding that may happen in subclasses. For example:

```
class B(object):
  def f(self): return 23
  g = property(f)
class C(B):
  def f(self): return 42
c = C( )
print c.g                    # prints 23, not 42
```

The access to property *c.g* calls *B.f*, not *C.f* as you might intuitively expect. The reason is quite simple: the property is created by passing the *function object f* (and is created at the time when the class statement for B executes, so the function object in question is the one also known as *B.f*). The fact that the *name f* is later redefined in subclass *C* is therefore quite irrelevant, since the property performs no lookup for that name, but rather uses the function object it was passed at creation time. If you need to work around this issue, you can always do it with one extra level of indirection:

```
class B(object):
  def f(self): return 23
  def _f_getter(self): return self.f()
  g = property(_f_getter)
class C(B):
  def f(self): return 42
c = C()
print c.g                  # prints 42, as expected
```

Here, the function object held by the property is *B._f_getter*, which in turn does perform a lookup for name *f* (since it calls self.f()); therefore, the overriding of f has the expected effect.

_ _slots_ _

Normally, each instance object *x* of any class *C* has a dictionary *x.__dict__* that Python uses to let you bind arbitrary attributes on *x*. To save a little memory (at the cost of letting *x* have only a predefined set of attribute names), you can define in a new-style class *C* a class attribute named _ _slots_ _, a sequence (normally a tuple) of strings (normally identifiers). When a new-style class *C* has an attribute _ _slots_ _, a direct instance *x* of class *C* has no *x.__dict__*, and any attempt to bind on *x* any attribute whose name is not in *C.__slots__* raises an exception. Using _ _slots_ _ lets you reduce memory consumption for small instance objects that can do without the powerful and convenient ability to have arbitrarily named attributes. _ _slots_ _ is worth adding only to classes that can have so many instances that saving a few tens of bytes per instance is important—typically classes that can have millions, not mere thousands, of instances alive at the same time. Unlike most other class attributes, _ _slots_ _ works as I've just described only if some statement in the class body binds it as a class attribute. Any later alteration, rebinding, or unbinding of _ _slots_ _ has no effect, nor does inheriting _ _slots_ _ from a base class. Here's how to add _ _slots_ _ to the Rectangle class defined earlier to get smaller (though less flexible) instances:

```
class OptimizedRectangle(Rectangle):
    __slots__ = 'width', 'height'
```

We do not need to define a slot for the area property. _ _slots_ _ does not constrain properties, only ordinary instance attributes, which are the attributes that would reside in the instance's _ _dict_ _ if _ _slots_ _ wasn't defined.

_ _getattribute_ _

All references to instance attributes for new-style instances proceed through special method _ _getattribute_ _. This method is supplied by base class object, where it implements all the details of object attribute reference semantics documented in "Attribute Reference Basics" on page 89. However, you may override _ _getattribute_ _ for special purposes, such as hiding inherited class attributes (e.g., methods) for your subclass's instances. The following example shows one way to implement a list without append in the new-style object model:

```
class listNoAppend(list):
    def __getattribute__(self, name):
        if name == 'append': raise AttributeError, name
        return list.__getattribute__(self, name)
```

An instance x of class listNoAppend is almost indistinguishable from a built-in list object, except that performance is substantially worse, and any reference to x.append raises an exception.

Per-Instance Methods

Both the legacy and new-style object models allow an instance to have instance-specific bindings for all attributes, including callable attributes (methods). For a method, just like for any other attribute (except those bound to overriding descriptors in new-style classes), an instance-specific binding hides a class-level binding: attribute lookup does not consider the class when it finds a binding directly in the instance. In both object models, an instance-specific binding for a callable attribute does not perform any of the transformations detailed in "Bound and Unbound Methods" on page 91. In other words, the attribute reference returns exactly the same callable object that was earlier bound directly to the instance attribute.

Legacy and new-style object models do differ on the effects of per-instance bindings of the special methods that Python invokes implicitly as a result of various operations, as covered in "Special Methods" on page 104. In the classic object model, an instance may usefully override a special method, and Python uses the per-instance binding even when invoking the method implicitly. In the new-style object model, implicit use of special methods always relies on the class-level binding of the special method, if any. The following code shows this difference between the legacy and new-style object models:

```
def fakeGetItem(idx): return idx
class Classic: pass
c = Classic()
c.__getitem__ = fakeGetItem
print c[23]                    # prints: 23
class NewStyle(object): pass
n = NewStyle()
n.__getitem__ = fakeGetItem
print n[23]                    # results in:
# Traceback (most recent call last):
#   File "<stdin>", line 1, in ?
# TypeError: unindexable object
```

The semantics of the classic object model in this regard are sometimes handy for tricky and somewhat obscure purposes. However, the new-style object model's approach is more general, and it regularizes and simplifies the relationship between classes and metaclasses, covered in "Metaclasses" on page 116.

Inheritance from Built-in Types

A new-style class can inherit from a built-in type. However, a class may directly or indirectly subclass multiple built-in types only if those types are specifically designed to allow this level of mutual compatibility. Python does not support unconstrained inheritance from multiple arbitrary built-in types. Normally, a new-style class only subclasses at most one substantial built-in type—this means at most one built-in type in addition to `object`, which is the superclass of all built-in types and new-style classes and imposes no constraints on multiple inheritance. For example:

```
class noway(dict, list): pass
```

raises a `TypeError` exception, with a detailed explanation of "Error when calling the metaclass bases: multiple bases have instance lay-out conflict." If you ever see such error messages, it means that you're trying to inherit, directly or indirectly, from multiple built-in types that are not specifically designed to cooperate at such a deep level.

Special Methods

A class may define or inherit special methods (i.e., methods whose names begin and end with double underscores). Each special method relates to a specific operation. Python implicitly invokes a special method whenever you perform the related operation on an instance object. In most cases, the method's return value is the operation's result, and attempting an operation when its related method is not present raises an exception. Throughout this section, I will point out the cases in which these general rules do not apply. In the following, *x* is the instance of class *C* on which you perform the operation, and *y* is the other operand, if any. The formal argument `self` of each method also refers to instance object *x*. Whenever, in the following sections, I mention calls to *x*.`__name__`(...), keep in mind that, for new-style classes, the exact call happening is rather, pedantically speaking, *x*.`__class__`.`__name__`(*x*, ...).

General-Purpose Special Methods

Some special methods relate to general-purpose operations. A class that defines or inherits these methods allows its instances to control such operations. These operations can be divided into the following categories:

Initialization and finalization
  A class can control its instances' initialization (a frequent need) via special methods `__new__` (new-style classes only) and `__init__`, and/or their finalization (a rare need) via `__del__`.

Representation as string
  A class can control how Python represents its instances as strings via special methods `__repr__`, `__str__`, and `__unicode__`.

Comparison, hashing, and use in a Boolean context
  A class can control how its instances compare with other objects (methods `__lt__`, `__le__`, `__gt__`, `__ge__`, `__eq__`, `__ne__`, and `__cmp__`), how

dictionaries use them as keys and sets as members (__hash__), and whether they evaluate to true or false in Boolean contexts (__nonzero__).

Attribute reference, binding, and unbinding
A class can control access to its instances' attributes (reference, binding, unbinding) via special methods __getattribute__ (new-style classes only), __getattr__, __setattr__, and __delattr__.

Callable instances
An instance is callable, just like a function object, if its class has the special method __call__.

The rest of this section documents the general-purpose special methods.

__call__   __call__(self[,*args*...])

When you call x([*args*...]), Python translates the operation into a call to x.__call__([*args*...]). The parameters for the call operation are the same as for the __call__ method, minus the first. The first parameter, conventionally called self, refers to x, and Python supplies it implicitly and automatically, just as in any other call to a bound method.

__cmp__   __cmp__(self,*other*)

Any comparison operator, when its specific special method (__lt__, __gt__, etc.) is absent or returns NotImplemented, calls x.__cmp__(*y*) instead, as do built-in functions requiring comparisons, such as cmp(x, y), max(x, y), and the sort method of list objects. __cmp__ should return -1 if x is less than y, 0 if x is equal to y, or 1 if x is greater than y. When __cmp__ is also absent, order comparisons (<, <=, >, >=) raise exceptions. Equality comparisons (==, !=), in this case, become identity checks: x==y evaluates id(x)==id(y) (i.e., x is y).

__del__   __del__(self)

Just before x disappears because of garbage collection, Python calls x.__del__() to let x finalize itself. If __del__ is absent, Python performs no special finalization upon garbage-collecting x (this is the usual case, as very few classes need to define __del__). Python ignores the return value of __del__. Python performs no implicit call to __del__ methods of class C's superclasses. C.__del__ must explicitly perform any needed finalization.

For example, when class C has a base class B to finalize, the code in C.__del__ must call B.__del__(self) (or better, for new-style classes, super(C, self).__del__()). __del__ is generally not the best approach when you need timely and guaranteed finalization. For such needs, use the try/finally statement covered in "try/finally" (or, even better, in Python 2.5, the new with statement, covered in "The with statement" on page 125).

Object-Oriented

Instances of classes defining __del__ cannot participate in cyclic-garbage collection, covered in "Garbage Collection" on page 332. Therefore, you should be particularly careful to avoid reference loops involving such instances, and define __del__ only when there is no reasonable alternative.

__delattr__   __delattr__(self, *name*)

At every request to unbind attribute *x.y* (typically, a del statement del *x.y*), Python calls *x*.__delattr__('*y*'). All the considerations discussed later for __setattr__ also apply to __delattr__. Python ignores the return value of __delattr__. If __delattr__ is absent, Python usually translates del *x.y* into del *x*.__dict__['*y*'].

__eq__,   __eq__(self, *other*) __ge__(self, *other*) __gt__(self, *other*)
__ge__,   __le__(self, *other*) __lt__(self, *other*) __ne__(self, *other*)
__gt__,
__le__,   Comparisons *x==y*, *x>=y*, *x>y*, *x<=y*, *x<y*, and *x!=y*, respectively, call
__lt__,   the special methods listed here, which should return False or True.
__ne__   Each method may return NotImplemented to tell Python to handle
                     the comparison in alternative ways (e.g., Python may then try *y>x*
                     in lieu of *x<y*).

__getattr__   __getattr__(self, *name*)

When attribute *x.y* is accessed but not found by the usual steps (i.e., where AttributeError would normally be raised), Python calls *x*.__getattr__('*y*') instead. Python does not call __getattr__ for attributes found by normal means (i.e., as keys in *x*.__dict__ or via *x*.__class__). If you want Python to call __getattr__ on every attribute reference, keep the attributes elsewhere (e.g., in another dictionary referenced by an attribute with a private name), or else write a new-style class and override __getattribute__ instead. __getattr__ should raise AttributeError if it cannot find *y*.

__get-   __getattribute__(self, *name*)
attribute__
                     At every request to access attribute *x.y*, if *x* is an instance of new-style class *C*, Python calls *x*.__getattribute__('*y*'), which must obtain and return the attribute value or else raise AttributeError. The normal semantics of attribute access (using *x*.__dict__, *C*.__slots__, *C*'s class attributes, *x*.__getattr__) are all due to object.__getattribute__.

                     If class *C* overrides __getattribute__, it must implement all of the attribute access semantics it wants to offer. Most often, the most convenient way to implement attribute access semantics is by delegating (e.g., calling object.__getattribute__(self, ...) as part of the operation of your override of __getattribute__). Note that when a class overrides _ _getattribute_ _, attribute accesses on instances of the class become slow, since the overriding code is called on every such attribute access.

_ _hash_ _

_ _hash_ _(self)

The hash(x) built-in function call, and the use of x as a dictionary key (such as D[x], where D is a dictionary) or a set member, call x._ _hash_ _( ). _ _hash_ _ must return a 32-bit int such that x==y implies hash(x)==hash(y), and must always return the same value for a given object.

When _ _hash_ _ is absent, hash(x), and the use of x as a dictionary key or a set member, call id(x) instead, as long as _ _cmp_ _ and _ _eq_ _ are also absent.

Any x such that hash(x) returns a result, rather than raising an exception, is known as a *hashable object*. When _ _hash_ _ is absent, but _ _cmp_ _ or _ _eq_ _ is present, hash(x), and the use of x as a dictionary key, raise an exception. In this case, x is not hashable and cannot be a dictionary key.

You normally define _ _hash_ _ only for immutable objects that also define _ _cmp_ _ and/or _ _eq_ _. Note that if there exists any y such that x==y, even if y is of a different type, and both x and y are hashable, you *must* ensure that hash(x)==hash(y).

_ _init_ _

_ _init_ _(self[,*args*...])

When a call C([*args*...]) creates instance x of class C, Python calls x._ _init_ _([*args*...]) to let x initialize itself. If _ _init_ _ is absent, you must call class C without arguments, C( ), and x has no instance-specific attributes upon creation. Strictly speaking, _ _init_ _ is never absent for a new-style class C, since such a class inherits _ _init_ _ from object unless it redefines it; however, even in this case, you must still call class C without arguments, C( ), and the resulting instance has no instance-specific attributes upon creation.

_ _init_ _ must return None. Python performs no implicit call to _ _init_ _ methods of class C's superclasses. C._ _init_ _ must explicitly perform any needed initialization. For example, when class C has a base class B to initialize without arguments, the code in C._ _init_ _ must explicitly call B._ _init_ _(self) (or better, for new-style classes, super(C, self)._ _init_ _( )).

_ _new_ _

_ _new_ _(cls[,*args*...])

When you call C([*args*...]) and C is a new-style class, Python obtains the new instance x that you are creating by invoking C._ _new_ _(C,[*args*...]). _ _new_ _ is a static method that every new-style class has (often simply inheriting it from object) and it can return any value x. In other words, _ _new_ _ is not constrained to return a new instance of C, although normally it's expected to do so. If, and only if, the value x that __new__ returns is indeed an instance of C (whether a new or previously existing one), Python continues after calling __new__ by implicitly calling __init__ on x (with the same [args...] that were originally passed to __new__).

Since you could perform most kinds of initialization on new instances in either special method, __init__ or __new__, you may wonder where it's best to place them. The answer is simple: put every kind of initialization in __init__ only, unless you have some specific, advanced reason to put some in __new__ instead. This will make your life much simpler in all kinds of situations, due to the fact that __init__ is an instance method while __new__ is a rather specialized static method.

__nonzero__   __nonzero__(self)

When evaluating x as true or false (see "Boolean Values" on page 45)—for example, on a call to bool(x)—Python calls x.__nonzero__(), which should return True or False. When __nonzero__ is not present, Python calls __len__ instead, and takes x as false when x.__len__() returns 0 (so, to check if a container is nonempty, avoid coding if len(container)>0:; just code if container: instead). When neither __nonzero__ nor __len__ is present, Python always considers x true.

__repr__   __repr__(self)

The repr(x) built-in function call, the `x` expression form, and the interactive interpreter (when x is the result of an expression statement) call x.__repr__() to obtain an "official," complete string representation of x. If __repr__ is absent, Python uses a default string representation. __repr__ should return a string with unambiguous information on x. Ideally, when feasible, the string should be an expression such that eval(repr(x))==x.

__setattr__   __setattr__(self, name, value)

At every request to bind attribute x.y (typically, an assignment statement x.y=value), Python calls x.__setattr__('y', value). Python always calls __setattr__ for *any* attribute binding on x—a major difference from __getattr__ (__setattr__ is closer to new-style classes' __getattribute__ in this sense). To avoid recursion, when x.__setattr__ binds x's attributes, it must modify x.__dict__ directly (e.g., via x.__dict__[name]=value); even better, for a new-style class, __setattr__ can delegate the setting to the superclass (by calling super(C, x).__setattr__('y', value)). Python ignores the return value of __setattr__. If __setattr__ is absent, Python usually translates x.y=z into x.__dict__['y']=z.

__str__	__str__(self)

The str(x) built-in type and the print x statement call x.__str__() to obtain an informal, concise string representation of x. If __str__ is absent, Python calls x.__repr__ instead. __str__ should return a conveniently human-readable string, even if it entails some approximation.

__unicode__	__unicode__(self)

The unicode(x) built-in type call invokes x.__unicode__(), if present, in preference to x.__str__(). If a class supplies both special methods __unicode__ and __str__, the two should return equivalent strings (of Unicode and plain-string type, respectively).

Special Methods for Containers

An instance can be a *container* (either a sequence or a mapping, but not both, as they are mutually exclusive concepts). For maximum usefulness, containers should provide not just special methods __getitem__, __setitem__, __delitem__, __len__, __contains__, and __iter__, but also a few nonspecial methods, as discussed in the following sections.

Sequences

In each item-access special method, a sequence that has L items should accept any integer *key* such that -L<=*key*<L. For compatibility with built-in sequences, a negative index *key*, 0>*key*>=-L should be equivalent to *key*+L. When *key* has an invalid type, the method should raise TypeError. When *key* is a value of a valid type, but out of range, the method should raise IndexError. For container classes that do not define __iter__, the for statement relies on these requirements, as do built-in functions that take iterable arguments. Every item-access special method of sequence should also accept as its index argument an instance of the built-in type slice whose start, step, and stop attributes are ints or None. The *slicing* syntax relies on this requirement, as covered in "Container slicing" on page 110.

A sequence should also allow concatenation (with another sequence of the same type) by + and repetition by * (multiplication by an integer). A sequence should therefore have special methods __add__, __mul__, __radd__, and __rmul__, covered in "Special Methods for Numeric Objects" on page 113. A sequence should be meaningfully comparable to another sequence of the same type, implementing *lexicographic* comparison like lists and tuples do. Mutable sequences should also have __iadd__ and __imul__, and the nonspecial methods covered in "List methods" on page 56: append, count, index, insert, extend, pop, remove, reverse, and sort, with the same signatures and semantics as the corresponding methods of lists. An immutable sequence should be hashable if all of its items are.

A sequence type may constrain its items in some ways (for example, by accepting only string items), but that is not mandatory.

Mappings

A mapping's item-access special methods should raise KeyError, rather than IndexError, when they receive an invalid *key* argument value of a valid type. Any mapping should define the nonspecial methods covered in "Dictionary Methods" on page 60: copy, get, has_key, items, keys, values, iteritems, iterkeys, and itervalues. Special method __iter__ should be equivalent to iterkeys. A mapping should be meaningfully comparable to another mapping of the same type. A mutable mapping should also define methods clear, popitem, setdefault, and update, while an immutable mapping should be hashable if all of its items are. A mapping type may constrain its keys in some ways (for example, by accepting only hashable keys, or, even more specifically, accepting, say, only string keys), but that is not mandatory.

Sets

Sets can be seen as rather peculiar kinds of containers—containers that are neither sequences nor mappings and cannot be indexed, but do have a length (number of elements) and are iterable. Sets also support many operators (&, |, ^, -, as well as membership tests and comparisons) and equivalent nonspecial methods (intersection, union, and so on). If you implement a set-like container, it should be polymorphic to Python built-in sets, covered in "Sets" on page 43. An immutable set-like type should be hashable if all of its elements are. A set-like type may constrain its elements in some ways (for example, by accepting only hashable elements, or, even more specifically, accepting, say, only integer elements), but that is not mandatory.

Container slicing

When you reference, bind, or unbind a slicing such as x[i:j] or x[i:j:k] on a container x, Python calls x's applicable item-access special method, passing as *key* an object of a built-in type called a *slice object*. A slice object has attributes start, stop, and step. Each attribute is None if the corresponding value is omitted in the slice syntax. For example, del x[:3] calls x.__delitem__(y), and y is a slice object such that y.stop is 3, y.start is None, and y.step is None. It is up to container object x to appropriately interpret the slice object argument passed to x's special methods. Method indices of slice objects can help: call it with your container's length as its only argument, and it returns a tuple of three nonnegative indices suitable as start, stop, and step for a loop indexing each item in the slice. A common idiom in a sequence class's __getitem__ special method, to fully support slicing, might be:

```
def __getitem__(self, index):
  # recursively specialcase slicing
  if isinstance(index, slice):
    return self.__class__(self[x]
                          for x in xrange(*self.indices(len(self))))
  # check index, dealing with negative indices too
```

```
if not isinstance(index, int): raise TypeError
if index<0: index+=len(self)
if not (0<=index<len(self)): raise IndexError
# index is now a correct int, within range(len(self))
...rest of __getitem__, dealing with single-item access by int index...
```

This idiom uses Python 2.4 generator-expression (genexp) syntax and assumes that your class's __init__ method can be called with an iterable argument to create a suitable new instance of the class.

Some built-in types, such as list and tuple, define (for reasons of backward compatibility) now-deprecated special methods __getslice__, __setslice__, and __delslice__. For an instance x of such a type, slicing x with only one colon, as in x[i:j], calls a slice-specific special method. Slicing x with two colons, as in x[i:j:k], calls an item-access special method with a slice object argument. For example:

```
class C:
    def __getslice__(self, i, j): print 'getslice', i, j
    def __getitem__(self, index): print 'getitem', index
x = C()
x[12:34]
x[56:78:9]
```

The first slicing calls x.__getslice__(12,34), while the second calls x.__getitem__(slice(56,78,9)). It's best to avoid this complication by simply *not* defining the slice-specific special methods in your classes; however, you may need to override these methods if your class subclasses list or tuple and you want to provide special functionality when an instance of your class is sliced with just one colon.

Container methods

Special methods __getitem__, __setitem__, __delitem__, __iter__, __len__, and __contains__ expose container functionality.

__contains__   __contains__(self,item)

The Boolean test y in x calls x.__contains__(y). When x is a sequence, __contains__ should return True when y equals the value of an item in the sequence. When x is a mapping, __contains__ should return True when y equals the value of a key in the mapping. Otherwise, __contains__ should return False. If __contains__ is absent, Python performs y in x as follows, taking time proportional to len(x):

```
for z in x:
    if y==z: return True
return False
```

__delitem__   __delitem__(self,*key*)

For a request to unbind an item or slice of *x* (typically del *x*[*key*]), Python calls *x*.__delitem__(*key*). A container *x* should have __delitem__ only if *x* is mutable so that items (and possibly slices) can be removed.

__getitem__   __getitem__(self,*key*)

When *x*[*key*] is accessed (i.e., when container *x* is indexed or sliced), Python calls *x*.__getitem__(*key*). All (non-set-like) containers should have __getitem__.

__iter__   __iter__(self)

For a request to loop on all items of *x* (typically for *item* in *x*), Python calls *x*.__iter__() to obtain an iterator on *x*. The built-in function iter(*x*) also calls *x*.__iter__(). When __iter__ is absent and *x* is a sequence, iter(*x*) synthesizes and returns an iterator object that wraps *x* and returns *x*[0], *x*[1], and so on until one of these indexings raises IndexError to indicate the end of the sequence. However, it is best to ensure that all of the container classes you code have __iter__.

__len__   __len__(self)

The len(*x*) built-in function call, and other built-in functions that need to know how many items are in container *x*, call *x*.__len__(). __len__ should return an int, the number of items in *x*. Python also calls *x*.__len__() to evaluate *x* in a Boolean context, when __nonzero__ is absent. Absent __nonzero__, a container is taken as false if and only if the container is empty (i.e., the container's length is 0). All containers should have __len__, unless it's exceedingly expensive for the container to determine how many items it currently contains.

__setitem__   __setitem__(self,*key*,*value*)

For a request to bind an item or slice of *x* (typically an assignment *x*[*key*]=*value*), Python calls *x*.__setitem__(*key*,*value*). A container *x* should have __setitem__ only if *x* is mutable so that items, and possibly slices, can be added and/or rebound.

Special Methods for Numeric Objects

An instance may support numeric operations by means of many special methods. Some classes that are not numbers also support some of the following special methods in order to overload operators such as + and *. For example, sequences should have special methods __add__, __mul__, __radd__, and __rmul__, as mentioned in "Sequences" on page 109.

__abs__, __invert__, __neg__, __pos__	__abs__(self) __invert__(self) __neg__(self) __pos__(self) Unary operators abs(x), ~x, -x, and +x, respectively, call these methods.
__add__, __div__, __floordiv__, __mod__, __mul__, __sub__, __truediv__	__add__(self,*other*) __div__(self,*other*) __floordiv__(self,*other*) __mod__(self,*other*) __mul__(self,*other*) __sub__(self,*other*) __truediv__(self,*other*) Operators x+y, x/y, x//y, x%y, x*y, x-y, and x/y, respectively, call these methods. The operator / calls __truediv__, if present, instead of __div__, in the situations where division is nontruncating, as covered in "Arithmetic Operations" on page 52.
__and__, __lshift__, __or__, __rshift__, __xor__	__and__(self,*other*) __lshift__(self,*other*) __or__(self,*other*) __rshift__(self,*other*) __xor__(self,*other*) Operators x&y, x<<y, x|y, x>>y, and x^y, respectively, call these methods.
__coerce__	__coerce__(self,*other*) For any numeric operation with two operands x and y, Python invokes x.__coerce__(y). __coerce__ should return a pair with x and y converted to acceptable types. __coerce__ returns None when it cannot perform the conversion. In such cases, Python calls y.__coerce__(x). This special method is now deprecated; your classes should not implement it, but instead deal with whatever types they can accept directly in the special methods of the relevant numeric operations. However, if a class does supply __coerce__, Python still calls it for backward compatibility.
__complex__, __float__, __int__, __long__	__complex__(self) __float__(self) __int__(self) __long__(self) Built-in types complex(x), float(x), int(x), and long(x), respectively, call these methods.

__divmod__	__divmod__(self,*other*)
	Built-in function divmod(*x*,*y*) calls *x*.__divmod__(*y*). __divmod__ should return a pair (*quotient*,*remainder*) equal to (*x*//*y*,*x*%*y*).

__hex__, **__oct__**	__hex__(self) __oct__(self)
	Built-in function hex(*x*) calls *x*.__hex__( ). Built-in function oct(*x*) calls *x*.__oct__( ). Each of these special methods should return a string representing the value of *x*, in base 16 and 8, respectively.

__iadd__, **__idiv__,** **__ifloordiv__,** **__imod__,** **__imul__,** **__isub__,** **__itruediv__**	__iadd__(self,*other*) __idiv__(self,*other*) __ifloordiv__(self,*other*) __imod__(self,*other*) __imul__(self,*other*) __isub__(self,*other*) __itruediv__(self,*other*)
	The augmented assignments *x*+=*y*, *x*/=*y*, *x*//=*y*, *x*%=*y*, *x**=*y*, *x*-=*y*, and *x*/=*y*, respectively, call these methods. Each method should modify *x* in place and return self. Define these methods when *x* is mutable (i.e., when *x* can change in place).

__iand__, **__ilshift__,** **__ior__,** **__irshift__,** **__ixor__**	__iand__(self,*other*) __ilshift__(self,*other*) __ior__(self,*other*) __irshift__(self,*other*) __ixor__(self,*other*)
	Augmented assignments *x*&=*y*, *x*<<=*y*, *x*|=*y*, *x*>>=*y*, and *x*^=*y*, respectively, call these methods. Each method should modify *x* in place and return self.

__index__	__index__(self)
	Python 2.5 only. Like __int__ but meant to be supplied only by types that are alternative implementations of integers (in other words, all of the type's instances can be exactly mapped into integers). For example, out of all built-in types, only int and long supply __index__; float and str don't, although they do supply __int__. Sequence indexing and slicing, in Python 2.5, internally use __index__ to get the needed integer indices (while up to Python 2.4, they demanded instances of types int or long exclusively). Through the new special method __index__, Python 2.5 offers better support for alternative implementations of integers supplied by user code or third-party extensions, such as gmpy, covered in "The gmpy Module" on page 373.

__ipow__	__ipow__(self,*other*)
	Augmented assignment *x***=*y* calls *x*.__ipow__(*y*). __ipow__ should modify *x* in place and return self.

__pow__	`__pow__(self,other[,modulo])`
	$x**y$ and $pow(x,y)$ both call $x.\_\_pow\_\_(y)$, while $pow(x,y,z)$ calls $x.\_\_pow\_\_(y,z)$. $x.\_\_pow\_\_(y,z)$ should return a value equal to the expression $x.\_\_pow\_\_(y)\%z$.

__radd__, **__rdiv__**, **__rmod__**, **__rmul__**, **__rsub__**	`__radd__(self,other)` `__rdiv__(self,other)`
	`__rmod__(self,other)` `__rmul__(self,other)`
	`__rsub__(self,other)`

	Operators $y+x$, y/x, $y\%x$, $y*x$, and $y-x$, respectively, call these methods when y doesn't have a needed method `__add__`, `__div__`, and so on.

__rand__, **__rlshift__**, **__ror__**, **__rrshift__**, **__rxor__**	`__rand__(self,other)` `__rlshift__(self,other)`
	`__ror__(self,other)` `__rrshift__(self,other)`
	`__rxor__(self,other)`

	Operators $y\&x$, $y<<x$, $y|x$, $y>>x$, and $y\^{}x$, respectively, call these methods when y doesn't have a needed method `__and__`, `__lshift__`, and so on.
__rdivmod__	`__rdivmod__(self,other)`
	Built-in function $divmod(y,x)$ calls $x.\_\_rdivmod\_\_(y)$ when y doesn't have `__divmod__`. `__rdivmod__` should return a pair (*remainder,quotient*).
__rpow__	`__rpow__(self,other)`
	$y**x$ and $pow(y,x)$ call $x.\_\_rpow\_\_(y)$ when y doesn't have `__pow__`. There is no three-argument form in this case.

Decorators

Due to the existence of descriptor types such as staticmethod and classmethod, covered in "Class-Level Methods" on page 99, which take as their argument a function object, Python somewhat frequently uses, within class bodies, idioms such as:

```
def f(cls, ...):
    ...definition of f snipped...
f = classmethod(f)
```

Having the call to classmethod occur textually after the def statement may decrease code readability because, while reading f's definition, the reader of the code is not yet aware that f is destined to become a class method rather than an ordinary instance method. The code would be more readable if the mention of classmethod could be placed right *before*, rather than *after*, the def. Python 2.4 allows such placement, through the new syntax form known as *decoration*:

```
@classmethod
def f(cls, ...):
    ...definition of f snipped...
```

The @classmethod decoration must be immediately followed by a def statement and means that *f*=classmethod(*f*) executes right after the def statement (for whatever name *f* the def defines). More generally, @*expression* evaluates the expression (which must be a name, possibly qualified, or a call) and binds the result to an internal temporary name (say, _ _*aux*); any such decoration must be immediately followed by a def statement and means that *f*=_ _*aux*(*f*) executes right after the def statement (for whatever name *f* the def defines). The object bound to _ _*aux* is known as a *decorator*, and it's said to *decorate* function *f*.

Decoration affords a handy shorthand for some higher-order functions (and other callables that work similarly to higher-order functions). You may apply decoration to any def statement, not just to def statements occurring in class bodies. You may also code custom decorators, which are just higher-order functions, accepting a function object as an argument and returning a function object as the result. For example, here is a decorator that does not modify the function it decorates, but rather emits the function's docstring to standard output at function-definition time:

```
def showdoc(f):
    if f.__doc__:
        print '%s: %s' % (f.__name__, f.__doc__)
    else:
        print '%s: No docstring!' % f.__name__
    return f

@showdoc
def f1(): "a docstring"
# emits: f1: a docstring

@showdoc
def f2(): pass
# emits: f2: No docstring!
```

Metaclasses

Any object, even a class object, has a type. In Python, types and classes are also first-class objects. The type of a class object is also known as the class's *metaclass*.* An object's behavior is mostly determined by the type of the object. This also holds for classes: a class's behavior is mostly determined by the class's metaclass.

---

* Strictly speaking, the type of a class *C* could be said to be the metaclass only of instances of *C* rather than of *C* itself, but this exceedingly subtle terminological distinction is rarely, if ever, observed in practice.

Metaclasses are an advanced subject, and you may want to skip the rest of this section on first reading. However, fully grasping metaclasses can help you obtain a deeper understanding of Python, and occasionally it can be useful to define your own custom metaclasses.

The distinction between legacy and new-style classes relies on the fact that each class's behavior is determined by its metaclass. In other words, the reason legacy classes behave differently from new-style classes is that legacy and new-style classes are objects of different types (metaclasses):

```
class Classic: pass
class Newstyle(object): pass
print type(Classic)                 # prints: <type 'class'>
print type(Newstyle)                # prints: <type 'type'>
```

The type of Classic is object types.ClassType from standard module types, while the type of Newstyle is built-in object type. type is also the metaclass of all Python built-in types, including itself (i.e., print type(type) also prints <type 'type'>).

How Python Determines a Class's Metaclass

To execute a class statement, Python first collects the base classes into a tuple *t* (an empty one if there are no base classes) and executes the class body in a temporary dictionary *d*. Then, Python determines the metaclass *M* to use for the new class object *C* that the class statement is creating.

When '__metaclass__' is a key in *d*, *M* is *d*['__metaclass__']. Thus, you can explicitly control class *C*'s metaclass by binding the attribute __metaclass__ in *C*'s class body. Otherwise, when *t* is nonempty (i.e., when *C* has one or more base classes), *M* is the leafmost metaclass among all of the metaclasses of *C*'s bases.* This is why inheriting from object indicates that *C* is a new-style class. Since type(object) is type, a class *C* that inherits from object (or some other built-in type) gets the same metaclass as object (i.e., type(*C*), *C*'s metaclass, is also type). Thus, being a new-style class is synonymous with having type as the metaclass.

When *C* has no base classes, but the current module has a global variable __metaclass__, *M* is the value of that global variable. This lets you make classes without base classes default to new-style classes, rather than legacy classes, throughout a module. Just place the following statement toward the start of the module body:

```
__metaclass__ = type
```

Failing all of these, *M* defaults to types.ClassType. This last "default of defaults" clause is why classes without base classes are legacy by default, when __metaclass__ is not bound in the class body or as a global variable of the module.

---

* if *C*'s bases' metaclasses do not form an inheritance lattice including its lower bound—i.e., if there is no leafmost metaclass—Python raises an exception diagnosing this metatype conflict.

How a Metaclass Creates a Class

Having determined M, Python calls M with three arguments: the class name (a string), the tuple of base classes t, and the dictionary d. The call returns the class object C, which Python then binds to the class name, completing the execution of the class statement. Note that this is in fact an instantiation of type M, so the call to M executes M.__init__(C, namestring, t, d), where C is the return value of M.__new__(M, namestring, t, d), just as in any other similar instantiation of a new-style class.

After class object C is created, the relationship between class C and its type (type(C), normally M) is the same as that between any object and its type. For example, when you call the class object C (to create an instance of C), M.__call__ executes with class object C as the first actual argument.

Note the benefit of the new-style approach described in "Per-Instance Methods" on page 103. Calling C to instantiate it must execute the metaclass's M.__call__, whether or not C has a per-instance attribute (method) __call__ (i.e., independently of whether *instances* of C are or aren't callable). This requirement is simply incompatible with the legacy object model, where per-instance methods override per-class ones—even for implicitly called special methods. The new-style approach avoids having to make the relationship between a class and its metaclass an ad hoc special case. Avoiding ad hoc special cases is a key to Python's power: Python has few, simple, general rules, and applies them consistently.

Defining and using your own metaclasses

It's easy to define custom metaclasses: inherit from type and override some of its methods. You can also perform most of these tasks with __new__, __init__, __getattribute__, and so on without involving metaclasses. However, a custom metaclass can be faster, since special processing is done only at class creation time, which is a rare operation. A custom metaclass lets you define a whole category of classes in a framework that magically acquires whatever interesting behavior you've coded, quite independently of what special methods the classes may choose to define. Moreover, some behavior of class objects can be customized only in metaclasses. The following example shows how to use a metaclass to change the string format of class objects:

```python
class MyMeta(type):
    def __str__(cls): return "Beautiful class '%s'"%cls.__name__
class MyClass:
    __metaclass__ = MyMeta
x = MyClass()
print type(x)        # emits: Beautiful class 'MyClass'
```

Strictly speaking, classes that instantiate such a custom metaclass are neither classic nor new-style: the semantics of classes and of their instances are entirely defined by their metaclass. In practice, custom metaclasses almost invariably subclass built-in type. Therefore, the semantics of the classes that instantiate such custom metaclasses are best thought of as variations on the semantics of new-style classes.

A substantial custom metaclass example

Suppose that, programming in Python, we miss C's struct type: an object that is just a bunch of data attributes with fixed names. Python lets us easily define an appropriate generic Bunch class, apart from the fixed names:

```
class Bunch(object):
    def __init__(self, **fields): self.__dict__ = fields
p = Bunch(x=2.3, y=4.5)
print p                       # prints: <__main__.Bunch object at 0x00AE8B10>
```

However, a custom metaclass lets us exploit the fact that the attribute names are fixed at class creation time. The code shown in Example 5-1 defines a metaclass, metaMetaBunch, and a class, MetaBunch, that let us write code like the following:

```
class Point(MetaBunch):
    """ A point has x and y coordinates, defaulting to 0.0, and a color,
        defaulting to 'gray' -- and nothing more, except what Python and
        the metaclass conspire to add, such as __init__ and __repr__
    """
    x = 0.0
    y = 0.0
    color = 'gray'
# example uses of class Point
q = Point()
print q                       # prints: Point()
p = Point(x=1.2, y=3.4)
print p                       # prints: Point(y=3.399999999, x=1.2)
```

In this code, the print statements print readable string representations of our Point instances. Point instances are quite memory-lean, and their performance is basically the same as for instances of the simple class Bunch in the previous example (there is no extra overhead due to special methods getting called implicitly). Note that Example 5-1 is quite substantial, and following all its details requires understanding aspects of Python covered later in this book, such as strings (Chapter 9) and module warnings ("The warnings Module" on page 471). The identifier mcl used in Example 5-1 stands for "metaclass," a use that is clearer in this special advanced case than the more habitual case of cls standing for "class."

Example 5-1. The metaMetaBunch metaclass

```
import warnings
class metaMetaBunch(type):
    """
    metaclass for new and improved "Bunch": implicitly defines __slots__,
    __init__ and __repr__ from variables bound in class scope.
    A class statement for an instance of metaMetaBunch (i.e., for a class
    whose metaclass is metaMetaBunch) must define only class-scope data
    attributes (and possibly special methods, but NOT __init__ and
    __repr__!).  metaMetaBunch removes the data attributes from class
    scope, snuggles them instead as items in a class-scope dict named
    __dflts__, and puts in the class a __slots__ with those attributes'
    names, an __init__ that takes as optional keyword arguments each of
    them (using the values in __dflts__ as defaults for missing ones), and
```

Example 5-1. The metaMetaBunch metaclass (continued)

a __repr__ that shows the repr of each attribute that differs from its
default value (the output of __repr__ can be passed to __eval__ to
make an equal instance, as per the usual convention in the matter, if
each of the non-default-valued attributes respects the convention too)
"""

```
def __new__(mcl, classname, bases, classdict):
    """ Everything needs to be done in __new__, since type.__new__ is
        where __slots__ are taken into account.
    """
    # define as local functions the __init__ and __repr__ that we'll
    # use in the new class
    def __init__(self, **kw):
        """ Simplistic __init__: first set all attributes to default
            values, then override those explicitly passed in kw.
        """
        for k in self.__dflts__: setattr(self, k, self.__dflts__[k])
        for k in kw: setattr(self, k, kw[k])
    def __repr__(self):
        """ Clever __repr__: show only attributes that differ from the
            respective default values, for compactness.
        """
        rep = ['%s=%r' % (k, getattr(self, k)) for k in self.__dflts__
                if getattr(self, k) != self.__dflts__[k]
              ]
        return '%s(%s)' % (classname, ', '.join(rep))
    # build the newdict that we'll use as class-dict for the new class
    newdict = { '__slots__':[ ], '__dflts__':{ },
        '__init__':__init__, '__repr__':__repr__, }
    for k in classdict:
        if k.startswith('__') and k.endswith('__'):
            # special methods: copy to newdict, warn about conflicts
            if k in newdict:
                warnings.warn("Can't set attr %r in bunch-class %r"
                    % (k, classname))
            else:
                newdict[k] = classdict[k]
        else:
            # class variables, store name in __slots__, and name and
            # value as an item in __dflts__
            newdict['__slots__'].append(k)
            newdict['__dflts__'][k] = classdict[k]
    # finally delegate the rest of the work to type.__new__
    return super(metaMetaBunch, mcl).__new__(
            mcl, classname, bases, newdict)
class MetaBunch(object):
    """ For convenience: inheriting from MetaBunch can be used to get
        the new metaclass (same as defining __metaclass__ yourself).
    """
    __metaclass__ = metaMetaBunch
```

6

Exceptions

Python uses exceptions to communicate errors and anomalies. An *exception* is an object that indicates an error or anomalous condition. When Python detects an error, it *raises* an exception—that is, Python signals the occurrence of an anomalous condition by passing an exception object to the exception-propagation mechanism. Your code can explicitly raise an exception by executing a raise statement.

Handling an exception means receiving the exception object from the propagation mechanism and performing whatever actions are needed to deal with the anomalous situation. If a program does not handle an exception, the program terminates with an error traceback message. However, a program can handle exceptions and keep running despite errors or other abnormal conditions.

Python also uses exceptions to indicate some special situations that are not errors, and are not even abnormal. For example, as covered in "Iterators" on page 65, an iterator's next method raises the exception StopIteration when the iterator has no more items. This is not an error, and it is not even an anomaly since most iterators run out of items eventually. The optimal strategies for checking and handling errors and other special situations in Python are therefore different from what might be best in other languages, and I cover such considerations in "Error-Checking Strategies" on page 134. This chapter also covers the logging module of the Python standard library, in "Logging Errors" on page 136, and the assert Python statement, in "The assert Statement" on page 138.

The try Statement

The try statement provides Python's exception-handling mechanism. It is a compound statement that can take one of two different forms:

- A try clause followed by one or more except clauses (and optionally an else clause)
- A try clause followed by exactly one finally clause

In Python 2.5, a try statement can have except clauses (and optionally an else clause) followed by a finally clause; however, in all previous versions of Python, the two forms cannot be merged, so I present them separately in the following. See "The try/except/finally statement" on page 124 for this small 2.5 enhancement to try statement syntax.

try/except

Here's the syntax for the try/except form of the try statement:

```
try:
    statement(s)
except [expression [, target]]:
    statement(s)
[else:
    statement(s)]
```

This form of the try statement has one or more except clauses, as well as an optional else clause.

The body of each except clause is known as an *exception handler*. The code executes if the *expression* in the except clause matches an exception object propagating from the try clause. *expression* is a class or tuple of classes, and matches any instance of one of those classes or any of their subclasses. The optional *target* is an identifier that names a variable that Python binds to the exception object just before the exception handler executes. A handler can also obtain the current exception object by calling the exc_info function of module sys (covered in exc_info on page 168).

Here is an example of the try/except form of the try statement:

```
try: 1/0
except ZeroDivisionError: print "caught divide-by-0 attempt"
```

If a try statement has several except clauses, the exception-propagation mechanism tests the except clauses in order; the first except clause whose expression matches the exception object is used as the handler. Thus, you must always list handlers for specific cases before you list handlers for more general cases. If you list a general case first, the more specific except clauses that follow will never enter the picture.

The last except clause may lack an expression. This clause handles any exception that reaches it during propagation. Such unconditional handling is a rare need, but it does occur, generally in wrapper functions that must perform some extra task before re-raising an exception, as we'll discuss in "The raise Statement" on page 128. Beware of using a "bare except" (an except clause without an expression) unless you're re-raising the exception in it: such sloppy style can make bugs very hard to find, since the bare except is generally over-broad and can easily mask coding errors and other kinds of bugs.

Exception propagation terminates when it finds a handler whose expression matches the exception object. Thus, if a try statement is nested in the try clause of another try statement, a handler established by the inner try is reached first

---

during propagation and, therefore, is the one that handles the exception, if it matches the expression. For example:

```
try:
    try: 1/0
    except: print "caught an exception"
except ZeroDivisionError:
    print "caught divide-by-0 attempt"
# prints: caught an exception
```

In this case, it does not matter that the handler established by clause except ZeroDivisionError: in the outer try clause is more specific and appropriate than the catch-all except: in the inner try clause. The outer try does not even enter into the picture because the exception doesn't propagate out of the inner try. For more on propagation, see "Exception Propagation" on page 126.

The optional else clause of try/except executes only when the try clause terminates normally. In other words, the else clause does not execute when an exception propagates from the try clause, or when the try clause exits with a break, continue, or return statement. The handlers established by try/except cover only the try clause, not the else clause. The else clause is useful to avoid accidentally handling unexpected exceptions. For example:

```
print repr(value), "is ",
try:
    value + 0
except TypeError:
    # not a number, maybe a string, Unicode, UserString...?
    try:
        value + ''
    except TypeError:
        print "neither a number nor a string"
    else:
        print "a string or string-like value"
else:
    print "some kind of number"
```

try/finally

Here's the syntax for the try/finally form of the try statement:

```
try:
    statement(s)
finally:
    statement(s)
```

This form has exactly one finally clause and cannot have an else clause.

The finally clause establishes what is known as a *clean-up handler*. The code always executes after the try clause terminates in any way. When an exception propagates from the try clause, the try clause terminates, the clean-up handler executes, and the exception keeps propagating. When no exception occurs, the clean-up handler executes anyway, whether the try clause reaches its end or exits by executing a break, continue, or return statement.

Clean-up handlers established with try/finally offer a robust and explicit way to specify finalization code that must always execute, no matter what, to ensure consistency of program state and/or external entities (e.g., files, databases, network connections). Here is an example of the try/finally form of the try statement:

```
f = open(someFile, "w")
try:
    do_something_with_file(f)
finally:
    f.close()
```

Note that the try/finally form is distinct from the try/except form: a try statement cannot have both except and finally clauses, unless you're using Python 2.5. If you need both exception handlers and a clean-up handler, and your code must run under Python 2.3 or 2.4, nest a try statement in the try clause of another try statement to define execution order explicitly and unambiguously.

A finally clause cannot directly contain a continue statement, but it may contain a break or return statement. Such usage, however, makes your program less clear, as exception propagation stops when such a break or return executes. Most programmers would not normally expect propagation to be stopped in a finally clause, so this usage may confuse people who are reading your code. In Python 2.3 and 2.4, a try/finally statement cannot contain a yield statement (in 2.5, it can).

Python 2.5 Exception-Related Enhancements

Besides allowing a try statement to have both except clauses and a finally clause, Python 2.5 introduces a new with statement, which nicely wraps many cases of try/except into one concise and handy syntax. Python 2.5 also includes enhancements to generators that make them more useful with the new with statement and with exceptions in general.

The try/except/finally statement

A Python 2.5–only try/except/finally statement, such as:

```
try:
    ...guarded clause...
except ...expression...:
    ...exception handler code...
finally:
    ...clean-up code...
```

is equivalent to the statement (which you can write in 2.5 or any previous version):

```
try:
    try:
        ...guarded clause...
    except ...expression...:
        ...exception handler code...
finally:
    ...clean-up code...
```

You can also have multiple except clauses, and optionally an else clause, before the terminating finally clause. In all variations, the effect is always like the above—i.e., just like nesting a try/except statement, with all the except clauses and the else clause if any, into a containing try/finally statement.

The with statement

The with statement is new in Python 2.5. To use this statement in a given module in Python 2.5, you must turn with into a keyword by placing the following instruction at the start of the module:

```
from __future__ import with_statement
```

In Python 2.6 and later, with will always be a keyword, and the above statement will be unnecessary (although accepted and innocuous).

with has the following syntax:

```
with expression [as varname]
    statement(s)
```

The semantics of with are defined as being equivalent to:

```
_normal_exit = True
_temporary = expression
varname = _temporary.__enter__()
try:
    statement(s)
except:
    _normal_exit = False
    if not _temporary.__exit__(*sys.exc_info()):
        raise
    # exception does not propagate if __exit__ returns a true value
finally:
    if _normal_exit:
        _temporary.__exit__(None, None, None)
```

where _temporary and _normal_exit are arbitrary internal names that are not used elsewhere in the current scope. If you omit the optional as varname part of the with clause, Python still calls _temporary.__enter__(), but doesn't bind the result to any name, and still calls _temporary.__exit__() at block termination.

The new with statement embodies the well-known C++ idiom "resource acquisition is initialization": you need only write classes with the two new special methods __enter__ (callable without arguments) and __exit__ (callable with three arguments; all None if the body completes without propagating exceptions, otherwise the type, value, and traceback of the exception) to have the same guaranteed finalization behavior as typical *ctor/dtor* pairs have for auto variables in C++ (with the added ability to finalize differently depending on what exception, if any, propagates, as well as optionally blocking a propagating exception by returning a true value from __exit__).

For example, here is one way, with Python 2.5, to wrap the opening of a file in order to ensure the file is closed when you're done:

```
class opened(object):
    def __init__(self, filename, mode='r'):
```

```
        self.f = open(filename, mode)
    def __enter__(self):
        return self.f
    def __exit__(self, etyp, einst, etb):
        self.f.close()
# to be used as:
with opened('foo.txt') as f:
    ...statements using open file object f...
```

This example code is not particularly useful, since in Python 2.5 built-in file objects already supply the needed methods __enter__ and __exit__; the example's purpose is a purely illustrative one.

An even simpler way to build such wrappers is most likely going to be supplied by the new contextlib module of the standard Python library: the module is scheduled to contain a decorator (probably to be called contextmanager) that turns a generator function into a factory of such wrappers, as well as wrapper functions closing (to call some object's close method upon __exit__) and nested (to nest multiple such wrappers for use in a single with statement).

Many more examples and detailed discussion can be found in PEP 343 at *http:// www.python.org/peps/pep-0343.html*.

Generator enhancements

In Python 2.5, yield statements are allowed inside try/finally statements (in previous versions, this combination was not allowed). Moreover, generator objects now have two other new methods, throw and close (in addition to the other new method send mentioned in "Generators in Python 2.5" on page 80). Given a generator object *g*, built by calling a generator function, the throw method's syntax is:

> g.throw(*exc_type, exc_value=None, exc_traceback=None*]

When the generator's caller calls *g*.throw, the effect is just as if a raise statement with the same arguments was executed at the spot of the yield at which generator *g* is suspended. Method close has no arguments; when the generator's caller calls *g*.close(), the effect is just like calling *g*.throw(GeneratorExit). GeneratorExit is a built-in exception class, new in 2.5, which inherits directly from Exception. A generator's close method should re-raise (or propagate) the GeneratorExit exception, or, equivalently, raise StopIteration, after doing whatever clean-up operations the generator may need. Generators now also have a destructor (special method __del__) that is exactly equivalent to method close.

For many more details on Python 2.5's generator enhancements, and examples of how they can be used (for example, to use generators for implementing co-routines), see PEP 342 at *http://www.python.org/peps/pep-0342.html*.

Exception Propagation

When an exception is raised, the exception-propagation mechanism takes control. The normal control flow of the program stops, and Python looks for a suitable exception handler. Python's try statement establishes exception handlers via its

---

except clauses. The handlers deal with exceptions raised in the body of the try clause, as well as exceptions propagating from any of the functions called by that code, directly or indirectly. If an exception is raised within a try clause that has an applicable except handler, the try clause terminates and the handler executes. When the handler finishes, execution continues with the statement after the try statement.

If the statement raising the exception is not within a try clause that has an applicable handler, the function containing the statement terminates, and the exception propagates "upward" along the stack of function calls to the statement that called the function. If the call to the terminated function is within a try clause that has an applicable handler, that try clause terminates, and the handler executes. Otherwise, the function containing the call terminates, and the propagation process repeats, *unwinding* the stack of function calls until an applicable handler is found.

If Python cannot find any applicable handler, by default the program prints an error message to the standard error stream (the file *sys.stderr*). The error message includes a traceback that gives details about functions terminated during propagation. You can change Python's default error-reporting behavior by setting sys.excepthook (covered in excepthook on page 168). After error reporting, Python goes back to the interactive session, if any, or terminates if no interactive session is active. When the exception class is SystemExit, termination is silent, and ends the interactive session, if any.

Here are some functions that you can use to see exception propagation at work:

```
def f( ):
    print "in f, before 1/0"
    1/0                          # raises a ZeroDivisionError exception
    print "in f, after 1/0"

def g( ):
    print "in g, before f( )"
    f( )
    print "in g, after f( )"

def h( ):
    print "in h, before g( )"
    try:
        g( )
        print "in h, after g( )"
    except ZeroDivisionError:
        print "ZD exception caught"
    print "function h ends"
```

Calling the h function has the following results:

```
>>> h( )
in h, before g( )
in g, before f( )
in f, before 1/0
ZD exception caught
function h ends
```

Function h establishes a try statement and calls function g within the try clause. g, in turn, calls f, which performs a division by 0, raising an exception of class ZeroDivisionError. The exception propagates all the way back to the except clause in h. Functions f and g terminate during the exception propagation phase, which is why neither of their "after" messages is printed. The execution of h's try clause also terminates during the exception-propagation phase, so its "after" message isn't printed either. Execution continues after the handler, at the end of h's try/except block.

The raise Statement

You can use the raise statement to raise an exception explicitly. raise is a simple statement with the following syntax:

```
raise [expression1[, expression2]]
```

Only an exception handler (or a function that a handler calls, directly or indirectly) can use raise without any expressions. A plain raise statement re-raises the same exception object that the handler received. The handler terminates, and the exception propagation mechanism keeps searching for other applicable handlers. Using raise without expressions is useful when a handler discovers that it is unable to handle an exception it receives, or can handle the exception only partially, so the exception should keep propagating to allow handlers up the call stack to perform handling and clean-up.

When only *expression1* is present, it can be a *legacy-style* instance object or class object (Python 2.5 changes this rule in order to allow new-style classes, as long as they inherit from the new built-in new-style class BaseException and instances of BaseException). In this case, if *expression1* is an instance object, Python raises that instance. When *expression1* is a class object, raise instantiates the class without arguments and raises the resulting instance. When both expressions are present, *expression1* must be a legacy-style class object. raise instantiates the class, with *expression2* as the argument (or multiple arguments if *expression2* is a tuple), and raises the resulting instance. Note that the raise statement is the only construct remaining in Python 2.3 and 2.4, where only legacy classes and instances, *not* new-style ones, are allowed. In Python 2.5, on the other hand, built-in exception classes are all new-style, although, for backward compatibility, legacy classes will also still be allowed in a raise statement in all Python 2.*x* versions, and removed only in Python 3.0.

Here's an example of a typical use of the raise statement:

```
def crossProduct(seq1, seq2):
    if not seq1 or not seq2:
        raise ValueError, "Sequence arguments must be non-empty"
    return [(x1, x2) for x1 in seq1 for x2 in seq2]
```

The crossProduct function returns a list of all pairs with one item from each of its sequence arguments, but first it tests both arguments. If either argument is empty, the function raises ValueError rather than just returning an empty list as the list comprehension would normally do. Note that there is no need for crossProduct to test if seq1 and seq2 are iterable: if either isn't, the list comprehension itself will raise the appropriate exception, presumably a TypeError. Once an exception is raised, be it by Python itself or with an explicit raise statement in your code, it's up to the caller to either handle it (with a suitable try/except statement) or let it propagate further up the call stack.

Use the raise statement only to raise additional exceptions for cases that would normally be okay but that your specifications define to be errors. Do not use raise to duplicate the same error-checking that Python already, implicitly, does on your behalf.

Exception Objects

Exceptions are instances of subclasses of the built-in, legacy-style Exception class.[*] An instance of any subclass of Exception has an attribute args, the tuple of arguments used to create the instance. args holds error-specific information, usable for diagnostic or recovery purposes. In Python 2.5, class Exception is new-style, since it inherits from the new built-in new-style class BaseException; this, in turn, makes all built-in exception classes new-style in Python 2.5. For detailed explanations of how the standard exception hierarchy changes in 2.5, and how things will move further in 3.0, see *http://python.org/doc/peps/pep-0352/*.

The Hierarchy of Standard Exceptions

All exceptions that Python itself raises are instances of subclasses of Exception. The inheritance structure of exception classes is important, as it determines which except clauses handle which exceptions. In Python 2.5, however, classes KeyboardInterrupt and SystemExit inherit directly from the new class BaseException and are not subclasses of Exception: the new arrangement makes it more likely that a general handler clause coded as except Exception: does what's intended, since you rarely want to catch KeyboardInterrupt and SystemExit (exception handlers are covered in "try/except" on page 122).

In Python 2.3 and 2.4, the SystemExit, StopIteration, and Warning classes inherit directly from Exception. Instances of SystemExit are normally raised by the exit function in module sys (covered in exit on page 169). StopIteration is used in the iteration protocol, covered in "Iterators" on page 65. Warning is covered in "The warnings Module" on page 471. Other standard exceptions derive from StandardError, a direct subclass of Exception. In Python 2.5, class GeneratorExit, covered in "Generator enhancements" on page 126, also inherits directly from Exception, while the rest of the standard exception hierarchy is like the one in 2.3 and 2.4, covered in the following.

Three subclasses of StandardError, like StandardError itself and Exception, are never instantiated directly (at least, not by Python itself). Their purpose is to make it easier for you to specify except clauses that handle a broad range of related errors. These three abstract subclasses of StandardError are:

[*] For backward compatibility, Python also lets you use strings, or instances of any legacy class, as exception objects, but such usage risks future incompatibility and gives no benefits.

ArithmeticError
    The base class for exceptions due to arithmetic errors (i.e., OverflowError, ZeroDivisionError, FloatingPointError)

LookupError
    The base class for exceptions that a container raises when it receives an invalid key or index (i.e., IndexError, KeyError)

EnvironmentError
    The base class for exceptions due to external causes (i.e., IOError, OSError, WindowsError)

```
Exception
    SystemExit
    StandardError
        AssertionError, AttributeError, ImportError,
        KeyboardInterrupt, MemoryError,
        NotImplementedError, SystemError, TypeError,
        UnicodeError, ValueError
        NameError
            UnboundLocalError
        SyntaxError
            IndentationError
        ArithmeticError
            FloatingPointError, OverflowError, ZeroDivisionError
        LookupError
            IndexError, KeyError
        EnvironmentError
            IOError
            OSError
                WindowsError
    StopIteration
    Warning
```

Standard Exception Classes

Common runtime errors raise exceptions of the following classes:

AssertionError
    An assert statement failed.

AttributeError
    An attribute reference or assignment failed.

FloatingPointError
    A floating-point operation failed. Derived from ArithmeticError.

IOError
    An I/O operation failed (e.g., the disk was full, a file was not found, or needed permissions were missing). Derived from EnvironmentError.

ImportError
    An import statement (covered in "The import Statement" on page 140) cannot find the module to import or cannot find a name specifically requested from the module.

IndentationError

> The parser encountered a syntax error due to incorrect indentation. Derived from SyntaxError.

IndexError

> An integer used to index a sequence is out of range (using a noninteger as a sequence index raises TypeError). Derived from LookupError.

KeyError

> A key used to index a mapping is not in the mapping. Derived from LookupError.

KeyboardInterrupt

> The user pressed the interrupt key (Ctrl-C, Ctrl-Break, or Delete, depending on the platform).

MemoryError

> An operation ran out of memory.

NameError

> A variable was referenced, but its name was not bound.

NotImplementedError

> Raised by abstract base classes to indicate that a concrete subclass must override a method.

OSError

> Raised by functions in module os (covered in "The os Module" on page 240 and "Running Other Programs with the os Module" on page 354) to indicate platform-dependent errors. Derived from EnvironmentError.

OverflowError

> The result of an operation on an integer is too large to fit into an integer (operator << did not raise this exception; rather, it dropped excess bits). Derived from ArithmeticError. Dates back to Python 2.1; in today's Python versions, too-large integer results implicitly become long integers, without raising exceptions. This standard exception remained a built-in for backward compatibility (to support existing code that raises or tries to catch it). Do *not* use in any new code.

SyntaxError

> The parser encountered a syntax error.

SystemError

> An internal error within Python itself or some extension module. You should report this to the authors and maintainers of Python, or of the extension in question, with all possible details to allow them to reproduce the problem.

TypeError

> An operation or function was applied to an object of an inappropriate type.

UnboundLocalError

> A reference was made to a local variable, but no value is currently bound to that local variable. Derived from NameError.

UnicodeError
    An error occurred while converting Unicode to a string or vice versa.

ValueError
    An operation or function was applied to an object that has a correct type but an inappropriate value, and nothing more specific (e.g., KeyError) applies.

WindowsError
    Raised by functions in module os (covered in "The os Module" on page 240 and "Running Other Programs with the os Module" on page 354) to indicate Windows-specific errors. Derived from OsError.

ZeroDivisionError
    A divisor (the righthand operand of a /, //, or % operator, or the second argument to built-in function divmod) is 0. Derived from ArithmeticError.

Custom Exception Classes

You can subclass any of the standard exception classes in order to define your own exception class. Often, such a subclass adds nothing more than a docstring:

```
class InvalidAttribute(AttributeError):
    "Used to indicate attributes that could never be valid"
```

As covered in "The pass Statement" on page 69, you don't need a pass statement to make up the body of this class; the docstring (which you should always write) is quite sufficient to keep Python happy. Best style for such "empty" classes, just like for "empty" functions, is to have a docstring and no pass.

Given the semantics of try/except, raising a custom exception class such as InvalidAttribute is almost the same as raising its standard exception superclass, AttributeError. Any except clause that can handle AttributeError can handle InvalidAttribute just as well. In addition, client code that knows specifically about your InvalidAttribute custom exception class can handle it specifically, without having to handle all other cases of AttributeError if it is not prepared for those. For example:

```
class SomeFunkyClass(object):
    "much hypothetical functionality snipped"
    def __getattr__(self, name):
        "this __getattr__ only clarifies the kind of attribute error"
        if name.startswith('_'):
            raise InvalidAttribute, "Unknown private attribute "+name
        else:
            raise AttributeError, "Unknown attribute "+name
```

Now client code can be more selective in its handlers. For example:

```
s = SomeFunkyClass()
try:
    value = getattr(s, thename)
except InvalidAttribute, err:
    warnings.warn(str(err))
    value = None
# other cases of AttributeError just propagate, as they're unexpected
```

It's an excellent idea to define, and raise, custom exception classes in your modules rather than plain standard exceptions: by using custom exceptions, you make it easier for all callers of your module's code to handle exceptions that come from your module separately from others.

A special case of custom exception class that you may sometimes find useful is one that wraps another exception and adds further information. To gather information about a pending exception, you can use the exc_info function from module sys (covered in exc_info on page 168). Given this, your custom exception class could be defined as follows:

```
import sys
class CustomException(Exception):
    "Wrap arbitrary pending exception, if any, in addition to other info"
    def __init__(self, *args):
        Exception.__init__(self, *args)
        self.wrapped_exc = sys.exc_info()
```

You would then typically use this class in a wrapper function such as:

```
def call_wrapped(callable, *args, **kwds):
    try: return callable(*args, **kwds)
    except: raise CustomException, "Wrapped function propagated exception"
```

Custom Exceptions and Multiple Inheritance

A particularly effective approach to custom exceptions (one that is, however, not often used in Python practice) is to multiply inherit exception classes from your module's special custom exception class and a standard exception class, as in the following snippet:

```
class CustomAttributeError(CustomException, AttributeError): pass
```

Now when your code raises an instance of CustomAttributeError, that exception can be caught by calling code that's designed to catch all cases of AttributeError as well as by code that's designed to catch all exceptions raised by your module. Whenever you must decide whether to raise a specific standard exception, such as AttributeError, or a custom exception class you define in your module, consider this multiple-inheritance approach, which gives you the best of both worlds. Make sure you clearly document this aspect of your module; since the technique I just described is not widely used, users of your module will not expect it unless you clearly and explicitly document what you are doing.

Other Exceptions Used in the Standard Library

Many modules in Python's standard library define their own exception classes, which are equivalent to the custom exception classes that your own modules can define. Typically, all functions in such standard library modules may raise exception of such classes, in addition to exceptions in the standard hierarchy covered in "Standard Exception Classes" on page 130. For example, module socket supplies class socket.error, which is directly derived from built-in class Exception, and several subclasses of error named sslerror, timeout, gaierror, and herror; all functions and methods in module socket, besides standard exceptions, may raise exceptions of class socket.error and subclasses thereof. I cover the main cases of such exception classes, in the rest of this book, in correspondence to the standard library modules that supply them.

Error-Checking Strategies

Most programming languages that support exceptions are geared to raise exceptions only in rare cases. Python's emphasis is different. In Python, exceptions are considered appropriate whenever they make a program simpler and more robust, even if that means that exceptions are raised rather frequently.

LBYL Versus EAFP

A common idiom in other languages, sometimes known as "look before you leap" (LBYL), is to check in advance, before attempting an operation, for all circumstances that might make the operation invalid. This approach is not ideal for several reasons:

- The checks may diminish the readability and clarity of the common, mainstream cases where everything is okay.
- The work needed for checking may duplicate a substantial part of the work done in the operation itself.
- The programmer might easily err by omitting some needed check.
- The situation might change between the moment the checks are performed and the moment the operation is attempted.

The preferred idiom in Python is generally to attempt the operation in a try clause and handle the exceptions that may result in except clauses. This idiom is known as "it's easier to ask forgiveness than permission" (EAFP), a motto widely credited to Admiral Grace Murray Hopper, co-inventor of COBOL, and that shares none of the defects of LBYL. Here is a function written using the LBYL idiom:

```
def safe_divide_1(x, y):
    if y==0:
        print "Divide-by-0 attempt detected"
        return None
    else:
        return x/y
```

With LBYL, the checks come first, and the mainstream case is somewhat hidden at the end of the function. Here is the equivalent function written using the EAFP idiom:

```
def safe_divide_2(x, y):
    try:
        return x/y
    except ZeroDivisionError:
        print "Divide-by-0 attempt detected"
        return None
```

With EAFP, the mainstream case is up front in a try clause, and the anomalies are handled in an except clause.

Proper usage of EAFP

EAFP is most often the preferable error-handling strategy, but it is not a panacea. In particular, you must be careful not to cast too wide a net, catching errors that you did not expect and therefore did not mean to catch. The following is a typical case of such a risk (built-in function getattr is covered in getattr on page 162):

```
def trycalling(obj, attrib, default, *args, **kwds):
    try: return getattr(obj, attrib)(*args, **kwds)
    except AttributeError: return default
```

The intention of function trycalling is to try calling a method named attrib on object obj, but to return default if obj has no method thus named. However, the function as coded does not do *just* that: it also mistakenly hides any error case where AttributeError is raised inside the implementation of the sought-after method, silently returning default in those cases. This may easily hide bugs in other code. To do exactly what is intended, the function must take a little bit more care:

```
def trycalling(obj, attrib, default, *args, **kwds):
    try: method = getattr(obj, attrib)
    except AttributeError: return default
    else: return method(*args, **kwds)
```

This implementation of trycalling separates the getattr call, placed in the try clause and therefore watched over by the handler in the except clause, from the call of the method, placed in the else clause and therefore free to propagate any exceptions it may need to. Using EAFP in the most effective way involves frequent use of the else clause on try/except statements.

Handling Errors in Large Programs

In large programs, it is especially easy to err by making your try/except statements too wide, particularly once you have convinced yourself of the power of EAFP as a general error-checking strategy. A try/except combination is too wide when it catches too many different errors, or an error that can occur in too many different places. The latter is a problem if you need to distinguish exactly what happened and where, and the information in the traceback is not sufficient to pinpoint such details (or you discard some or all of the information in the traceback). For effective error handling, you have to keep a clear distinction between errors and anomalies that you expect (and thus know exactly how to handle) and unexpected errors and anomalies that indicate a bug in your program.

Some errors and anomalies are not really erroneous, and perhaps not even all that anomalous: they are just special cases, perhaps rare but nevertheless quite expected, which you choose to handle via EAFP rather than via LBYL to avoid LBYL's many intrinsic defects. In such cases, you should just handle the anomaly, usually without even logging or reporting it. Be very careful, under these circumstances, to keep the relevant try/except constructs as narrow as feasible. Use a small try clause that contains a small amount of code that doesn't call too many other functions and very specific exception-class tuples in the except clauses.

Errors and anomalies that depend on user input or other external conditions not under your control are always expected, to some extent, precisely because you have no control over their underlying causes. In such cases, you should concentrate your effort on handling the anomaly gracefully, normally reporting and logging its exact nature and details, and generally keep your program running with undamaged internal and persistent state. The breadth of try/except clauses under such circumstances should also be reasonably narrow, although this is not quite as crucial as when you use EAFP to structure your handling of not-really-erroneous special cases.

Lastly, entirely unexpected errors and anomalies indicate bugs in your program's design or coding. In most cases, the best strategy regarding such errors is to avoid try/except and just let the program terminate with error and traceback messages. (You might want to log such information and/or display it more suitably with an application-specific hook in sys.excepthook, as we'll discuss shortly.) In the unlikely case that your program must keep running at all costs, even under the direst circumstances, try/except statements that are quite wide may be appropriate, with the try clause guarding function calls that exercise vast swaths of program functionality and broad except clauses.

In the case of a long-running program, make sure that all details of the anomaly or error are logged to some persistent place for later study (and that some indication of the problem gets displayed, too, so that you know such later study is necessary). The key is making sure that the program's persistent state can be reverted to some undamaged, internally consistent point. The techniques that enable long-running programs to survive some of their own bugs are known as *checkpointing* and *transactional behavior*, but I do not cover them further in this book.

Logging Errors

When Python propagates an exception all the way to the top of the stack without finding an applicable handler, the interpreter normally prints an error traceback to the standard error stream of the process (sys.stderr) before terminating the program. You can rebind sys.stderr to any file-like object usable for output in order to divert this information to a destination more suitable for your purposes.

When you want to change the amount and kind of information output on such occasions, rebinding sys.stderr is not sufficient. In such cases, you can assign your own function to sys.excepthook, and Python will call it before terminating the program due to an unhandled exception. In your exception-reporting function, you can output whatever information you think will help you diagnose and debug the problem and direct that information to whatever destinations you please. For example, you might use module traceback (covered in "The traceback Module" on page 466) to help you format stack traces. When your exception-reporting function terminates, so does your program.

The logging module

The Python standard library offers the rich and powerful logging package to let you organize the logging of messages from your applications in systematic and flexible ways. You might organize a whole hierarchy of Logger classes and subclasses, coupled with instances of Handler (and subclasses thereof), possibly with instances of class Filter inserted to fine-tune criteria determining what messages get logged in which ways, and the messages that do get emitted are formatted by instances of the Formatter class—indeed, the messages themselves are instances of the LogRecord class. The logging package even includes a dynamic configuration facility, whereby logging-configuration files may be dynamically set by reading them from on-disk files or even by receiving them on a dedicated socket in a specialized thread.

While the logging package sports a frighteningly complex and powerful architecture, suitable for implementing highly sophisticated logging strategies and policies that may be needed in vast and complicated programming systems, in many applications you may get away with using a tiny subset of the package through some simple functions supplied by the logging module itself. First of all, import logging. Then, emit your message by passing it as a string to any of the functions debug, info, warning, error, or critical, in increasing order of severity. If the string you pass contains format specifiers such as %s (as covered in "String Formatting" on page 193) then after the string, you must pass as further arguments all the values to be formatted in that string. For example, don't call:

```
logging.debug('foo is %r' % foo)
```

which performs the formatting operation whether it's needed or not; rather, call:

```
logging.debug('foo is %r', foo)
```

which performs formatting if and only if that's necessary (i.e., if and only if calling debug is going to result in logging output, depending on the current threshold level).

By default, the threshold level is WARNING, meaning that any of the functions warning, error, or critical results in logging output, but the functions debug and info don't. To change the threshold level at any time, call logging.getLogger().setLevel, passing as the only argument one of the corresponding constants supplied by module logging: DEBUG, INFO, WARNING, ERROR, or CRITICAL. For example, once you call:

```
logging.getLogger().setLevel(logging.DEBUG)
```

all of the functions from debug to critical will result in logging output until you change level again; if later you call:

```
logging.getLogger().setLevel(logging.ERROR)
```

then only the functions error and critical will result in logging output (debug, info, and warning will not result in logging output); this condition, too, will persist only until you change level again, and so forth.

By default, logging output is to your process's standard error stream (sys.stderr, as covered in stdin, stdout, stderr on page 171) and uses a rather simplistic format (for example, it does not include a timestamp on each line it outputs). You can control these settings by instantiating an appropriate handler instance, with a suitable formatter instance, and creating and setting a new logger instance to hold it. In the simple, common case in which you just want to set these logging parameters once and for all, after which they persist throughout the run of your program, the simplest approach is to call the logging.basicConfig function, which lets you set up things quite simply via named parameters. Only the very first call to logging.basicConfig has any effect, and only if you call it before any of the functions debug, info, and so on. Therefore, the most reasonable use is to call logging.basicConfig at the very start of your program. For example, a common idiom at the start of a program is something like:

```
import logging
logging.basicConfig(format='%(asctime)s %(levelname)8s %(message)s',
                    filename='/tmp/logfile.txt', filemode='w')
```

This setting emits all logging messages to a file and formats them nicely with a precise human-readable timestamp, followed by the severity level right-aligned in an eight-character field, followed by the message proper.

For excruciatingly large amounts of detailed information on the logging package and all the wonders you can perform with it, be sure to consult Python's rich online information about it at *http://docs.python.org/lib/module-logging.html*.

The assert Statement

The assert statement allows you to introduce debugging code into a program. assert is a simple statement with the following syntax:

```
assert condition[,expression]
```

When you run Python with the optimize flag (-*O*, as covered in "Command-Line Syntax and Options" on page 23), assert is a null operation: the compiler generates no code for it. Otherwise, assert evaluates *condition*. If *condition* is satisfied, assert does nothing. If *condition* is not satisfied, assert instantiates AssertionError with *expression* as the argument (or without arguments, if there is no *expression*) and raises the resulting instance.

assert statements are an effective way to document your program. When you want to state that a significant condition *C* is known to hold at a certain point in a program's execution, assert *C* is better than a comment that just states *C*. The advantage of assert is that, when the condition does *not* in fact hold, assert immediately alerts you to the problem by raising AssertionError.

The _ _debug_ _ built-in variable

When you run Python without option -*O*, the _ _debug_ _ built-in variable is True. When you run Python with option -*O*, _ _debug_ _ is False. Also, with option -*O*, the compiler generates no code for any if statement whose condition is _ _debug_ _.

To exploit this optimization, surround the definitions of functions that you call only in assert statements with if _ _debug_ _:. This technique makes compiled code smaller and faster when Python is run with -*O*, and enhances program clarity by showing that those functions exist only to perform sanity checks.

7

Modules

A typical Python program is made up of several source files. Each source file corresponds to a *module*, grouping program code and data for reuse. Modules are normally independent of each other so that other programs can reuse the specific modules they need. A module explicitly establishes dependencies upon another module by using import or from statements. In some other programming languages, global variables can provide a hidden conduit for coupling between modules. In Python, however, global variables are not global to all modules, but rather attributes of a single module object. Thus, Python modules communicate in explicit and maintainable ways.

Python also supports *extensions*, which are components written in other languages, such as C, C++, Java, or C#, for use with Python. Extensions are seen as modules by the Python code that uses them (known as *client code*). From the client code viewpoint, it does not matter whether a module is 100 percent pure Python or an extension. You can always start by coding a module in Python. Later, should you need better performance, you can recode some modules in lower-level languages without changing the client code that uses the modules. Chapters 25 and 26 discuss writing extensions in C and Java.

This chapter discusses module creation and loading. It also covers grouping modules into *packages*, which are modules that contain other modules, in a hierarchical, tree-like structure. Finally, the chapter discusses using Python's distribution utilities (distutils) to prepare packages for distribution and to install distributed packages.

Module Objects

A module is a Python object with arbitrarily named attributes that you can bind and reference. The Python code for a module named *aname* normally resides in a file named *aname.py*, as covered in "Module Loading" on page 144.

In Python, modules are objects (values) and are handled like other objects. Thus, you can pass a module as an argument in a call to a function. Similarly, a function can return a module as the result of a call. A module, just like any other object, can be bound to a variable, an item in a container, or an attribute of an object. For example, the sys.modules dictionary, covered in "Module Loading" on page 144, holds module objects as its values. The fact that modules are ordinary objects in Python is often expressed by saying that modules are *first-class* objects.

The import Statement

You can use any Python source file as a module by executing an import statement in some other Python source file. import has the following syntax:

```
import modname [as varname][,...]
```

The import keyword is followed by one or more module specifiers, separated by commas. In the simplest, most common case, a module specifier is just *modname*, an identifier—a variable that Python binds to the module object when the import statement finishes. In this case, Python looks for the module of the same name to satisfy the import request. For example:

```
import MyModule
```

looks for the module named MyModule and binds the variable named MyModule in the current scope to the module object. *modname* can also be a sequence of identifiers separated by dots (.) to name a module in a package, as covered in "Packages" on page 149.

When as *varname* is part of a module specifier, Python looks for a module named *modname* but then binds the module object as variable *varname*. For example:

```
import MyModule as Alias
```

looks for the module named MyModule and binds the module object to variable Alias in the current scope. *varname* is always a simple identifier.

Module body

The body of a module is the sequence of statements in the module's source file. There is no special syntax required to indicate that a source file is a module; any valid Python source file can be used as a module. A module's body executes immediately the first time the module is imported in a given run of a program. During execution of the body, the module object already exists, and an entry in sys.modules is already bound to the module object, getting gradually populated as the module's body executes.

Attributes of module objects

An import statement creates a new namespace containing all the attributes of the module. To access an attribute in this namespace, use the name of the module as a prefix:

```
import MyModule
a = MyModule.f( )
```

or:

```
import MyModule as Alias
a = Alias.f( )
```

Attributes of a module object are normally bound by statements in the module body. When a statement in the body binds a variable (a global variable), what gets bound is an attribute of the module object. The normal purpose of a module body is exactly that of creating the module's attributes: def statements create and bind functions, class statements create and bind classes, and assignment statements can bind attributes of any type.

You can also bind and unbind module attributes outside the body (i.e., in other modules), generally using attribute reference syntax M.*name* (where M is any expression whose value is the module, and identifier *name* is the attribute name). For clarity, however, it's usually best to limit yourself to binding module attributes in the module's own body.

The import statement implicitly sets some module attributes as soon as it creates the module object, before the module's body executes. The __dict__ attribute is the dictionary object that the module uses as the namespace for its attributes. Unlike all other attributes of the module, __dict__ is not available to code in the module as a global variable. All other attributes in the module are entries in the module's __dict__ and are available to code in the modules as global variables. Attribute __name__ is the module's name, and attribute __file__ is the filename from which the module was loaded.

For any module object M, any object x, and any identifier string S (except __dict__), binding M.S=x is equivalent to binding M.__dict__['S']=x. An attribute reference such as M.S is also substantially equivalent to M.__dict__['S']. The only difference is that when 'S' is not a key in M.__dict__, accessing M.__dict__['S'] raises KeyError, while accessing M.S raises AttributeError. Module attributes are also available to all code in the module's body as global variables. In other words, within the module body, S used as a global variable is equivalent to M.S (i.e., M.__dict__['S']) for both binding and reference.

Python built-ins

Python supplies several built-in objects (covered in Chapter 8). All built-in objects are attributes of a preloaded module named __builtin__. When Python loads a module, the module automatically gets an extra attribute named __builtins__, which refers either to module __builtin__ or to __builtin__'s dictionary. Python may choose either, so don't rely on __builtins__. If you need to access module __builtin__ directly (a rare need), use an import __builtin__ statement. Note the difference between the name of the attribute and the name of the module: the attribute has an extra s. When a global variable is not found in the current module, Python looks for the identifier in the current module's __builtins__ before raising NameError.

The lookup is the only mechanism that Python uses to let your code access built-ins. The built-ins' names are not reserved, nor are they hardwired in Python itself. Since the access mechanism is simple and documented, your own code can use the mechanism directly (but do so in moderation, or your program's clarity and simplicity will suffer). Thus, you can add your own built-ins or substitute your functions for the normal built-in ones. The following example shows how you can wrap a built-in function with your own function (see "Module Loading" on page 144 for information about __import__ and "The reload Function" on page 146 for information about reload):

```
# reload takes a module object; let's make it accept a string as well
import __builtin__
_reload = __builtin__.reload                 # save the original built-in
def reload(mod_or_name):
    if isinstance(mod_or_name, str):         # if argument is a string
        mod_or_name = __import__(mod_or_name) # get the module instead
    return _reload(mod_or_name)              # invoke the real built-in
__builtin__.reload = reload                  # override built-in w/wrapper
```

Module documentation strings

If the first statement in the module body is a string literal, the compiler binds that string as the module's documentation string attribute, named __doc__. Documentation strings are also called *docstrings* and are covered in "Docstrings" on page 72.

Module-private variables

No variable of a module is truly private. However, by convention, starting an identifier with a single underscore (_), such as _secret, indicates that the identifier is meant to be private. In other words, the leading underscore communicates to client-code programmers that they should not access the identifier directly.

Development environments and other tools rely on the leading-underscore naming convention to discern which attributes of a module are public (i.e., part of the module's interface) and which are private (i.e., to be used only within the module). It is good programming practice to distinguish between private and public attributes, by starting the private ones with _, for clarity and to get maximum benefit from tools.

It is particularly important to respect the convention when you write client code that uses modules written by others. In other words, avoid using any attributes in such modules whose names start with _. Future releases of the modules will no doubt maintain their public interface but are quite likely to change private implementation details, and private attributes are meant exactly for such implementation details.

The from Statement

Python's from statement lets you import specific attributes from a module into the current namespace. from has two syntax variants:

```
from modname import attrname [as varname][,...]
from modname import *
```

A from statement specifies a module name, followed by one or more attribute specifiers separated by commas. In the simplest and most common case, an

---

attribute specifier is just an identifier *attrname*, which is a variable that Python binds to the attribute of the same name in the module named *modname*. For example:

```
from MyModule import f
```

modname can also be a sequence of identifiers separated by dots (.) that names a module within a package, as covered in "Packages" on page 149.

When as *varname* is part of an attribute specifier, Python gets from the module the value of attribute *attrname* but then binds it to variable *varname*. For example:

```
from MyModule import f as foo
```

attrname and *varname* are always simple identifiers.

Since Python 2.4, you may optionally enclose in parentheses all the attribute specifiers that follow the keyword import in a from statement. This is sometimes useful when you have many attribute specifiers in order to split the single logical line of the from statement into multiple logical lines more elegantly than by using backslashes (\):

```
from some_module_with_a_long_name import (another_name, and_another,
                                           one_more, and_yet_another)
```

The from ... import * statement

Code that is directly inside a module body (not in the body of a function or class) may use an asterisk (*) in a from statement:

```
from MyModule import *
```

The * requests that all attributes of module *modname* be bound as global variables in the importing module. When module *modname* has an attribute named __all__, the attribute's value is the list of the attributes that are bound by this type of from statement. Otherwise, this type of from statement binds all attributes of *modname* except those beginning with underscores. Since from M import * may bind an arbitrary set of global variables, it can often have unforeseen and undesired side effects, such as hiding built-ins and rebinding variables you still need. Use the * form of from very sparingly, if at all, and only from modules that are explicitly documented as supporting such usage. Most likely, your programs will be better if you *never* use this form.

from versus import

In general, the import statement is most often a better choice than the from statement. Think of the from statement, and most particularly from M import *, as conveniences meant only for occasional use in interactive Python sessions. If you always access module M with the statement import M and always access M's attributes with explicit syntax M.A, your code will be slightly less concise but far clearer and more readable. One good use of from is to import specific modules from a package, as we'll discuss in "Packages" on page 149. But in the vast majority of cases, import is better than from.

Module Loading

Module-loading operations rely on attributes of the built-in sys module (covered in "The sys Module" on page 168). The module-loading process described in this section is carried out by built-in function __import__. Your code can call __import__ directly, with the module name string as an argument. __import__ returns the module object or raises ImportError if the import fails.

To import a module named M, __import__ first checks dictionary sys.modules, using string M as the key. When key M is in the dictionary, __import__ returns the corresponding value as the requested module object. Otherwise, __import__ binds sys.modules[M] to a new empty module object with a __name__ of M, then looks for the right way to initialize (load) the module, as covered in "Searching the Filesystem for a Module" on page 144.

Thanks to this mechanism, the relatively slow loading operation takes place only the first time a module is imported in a given run of the program. When a module is imported again, the module is not reloaded, since __import__ rapidly finds and returns the module's entry in sys.modules. Thus, all imports of a given module after the first one are very fast: they're just dictionary lookups. (To *force* a reload, see "The reload Function" on page 146.)

Built-in Modules

When a module is loaded, __import__ first checks whether the module is built-in. Built-in modules are listed in tuple sys.builtin_module_names, but rebinding that tuple does not affect module loading. When Python loads a built-in module, as when it loads any other extension, Python calls the module's initialization function. The search for built-in modules also looks for modules in platform-specific locations, such as resource forks and frameworks on the Mac, and the Registry in Windows.

Searching the Filesystem for a Module

If module M is not built-in, __import__ looks for M's code as a file on the filesystem. __import__ looks at the strings, which are the items of list sys.path, in order. Each item is the path of a directory, or the path of an archive file in the popular ZIP format. sys.path is initialized at program startup, using environment variable PYTHONPATH (covered in "Environment Variables" on page 22), if present. The first item in sys.path is always the directory from which the main program (script) is loaded. An empty string in sys.path indicates the current directory.

Your code can mutate or rebind sys.path, and such changes affect which directories and ZIP archives __import__ searches to load modules. Changing sys.path does *not* affect modules that are already loaded (and thus already recorded in sys.modules) when you change sys.path.

If a text file with extension *.pth* is found in the *PYTHONHOME* directory at startup, the file's contents are added to sys.path, one item per line. *.pth* files can contain blank lines and comment lines starting with the character #; Python ignores any such lines. *.pth* files can also contain import statements, which Python executes before your program starts to execute, but no other kinds of statements.

When looking for the file for module *M* in each directory and ZIP archive along sys.path, Python considers the following extensions in the order listed:

1. *.pyd* and *.dll* (Windows) or *.so* (most Unix-like platforms), which indicate Python extension modules. (Some Unix dialects use different extensions; e.g., *.sl* is the extension used on HP-UX.) On most platforms, extensions cannot be loaded from a ZIP archive—only pure source or bytecode-compiled Python modules can.

2. *.py*, which indicates pure Python source modules.

3. *.pyc* (or *.pyo*, if Python is run with option -O), which indicates bytecode-compiled Python modules.

One last path at which Python looks for the file for module *M* is *M/__init__.py*, meaning a file named *__init__.py* in a directory named *M*, as covered in "Packages" on page 149.

Upon finding source file *M.py*, Python compiles it to *M.pyc* (or *M.pyo*), unless the bytecode file is already present, is newer than *M.py*, and was compiled by the same version of Python. If *M.py* is compiled from a writable directory, Python saves the bytecode file to the filesystem in the same directory so that future runs will not needlessly recompile. When the bytecode file is newer than the source file (based on an internal timestamp in the bytecode file, not on trusting the date as recorded in the filesystem), Python does not recompile the module.

Once Python has the bytecode file, either from having constructed it by compilation or by reading it from the filesystem, Python executes the module body to initialize the module object. If the module is an extension, Python calls the module's initialization function.

The Main Program

Execution of a Python application normally starts with a top-level script (also known as the *main program*), as explained in "The python Program" on page 22. The main program executes like any other module being loaded, except that Python keeps the bytecode in memory without saving it to disk. The module name for the main program is always __main__, both as the __name__ global variable (module attribute) and as the key in sys.modules. You should not normally import the same *.py* file that is in use as the main program. If you do, the module is loaded again, and the module body is executed once more from the top in a separate module object with a different __name__.

Code in a Python module can test whether the module is being used as the main program by checking if global variable __name__ equals '__main__'. The idiom:

```
if __name__=='__main__':
```

is often used to guard some code so that it executes only when the module is run as the main program. If a module is designed only to be imported, it should normally execute unit tests when it is run as the main program, as covered in "Unit Testing and System Testing" on page 452.

The reload Function

Python loads a module only the first time you import the module during a program run. When you develop interactively, you need to make sure your modules are reloaded each time you edit them (some development environments provide automatic reloading).

To reload a module, pass the module object (*not* the module name) as the only argument to built-in function reload. reload(M) ensures the reloaded version of M is used by client code that relies on import M and accesses attributes with the syntax M.A. However, reload(M) has no effect on other existing references bound to previous values of M's attributes (e.g., with a from statement). In other words, already bound variables remain bound as they were, unaffected by reload. reload's inability to rebind such variables is a further incentive to avoid from in favor of import.

reload is not recursive: when you reload a module M, this does not imply that other modules imported by M get reloaded in turn. You must specifically arrange to reload, by explicit calls to the reload function, each and every module you have modified.

Circular Imports

Python lets you specify circular imports. For example, you can write a module a.py that contains import b, while module b.py contains import a. In practice, you are typically better off avoiding circular imports, since circular dependencies are always fragile and hard to manage. If you decide to use a circular import for some reason, you need to understand how circular imports work in order to avoid errors in your code.

Say that the main script executes import a. As discussed earlier, this import statement creates a new empty module object as sys.modules['a'], and then the body of module a starts executing. When a executes import b, this creates a new empty module object as sys.modules['b'], and then the body of module b starts executing. The execution of a's module body suspends until b's module body finishes.

Now, when b executes import a, the import statement finds sys.modules['a'] already defined, and therefore binds global variable a in module b to the module object for module a. Since the execution of a's module body is currently suspended, module a may be only partly populated at this time. If the code in b's module body immediately tries to access some attribute of module a that is not yet bound, an error results.

If you do insist on keeping a circular import in some case, you must carefully manage the order in which each module defines its own globals, imports other modules, and accesses globals of other modules. You can have greater control on the sequence in which things happen by grouping your statements into functions, and calling those functions in a controlled order, rather than just relying on sequential execution of top-level statements in module bodies. However, removing circular dependencies is almost always easier than ensuring bomb-proof ordering while keeping such circular dependencies. Since circular dependencies are also bad for other reasons, I recommend striving to remove them.

sys.modules Entries

The built-in __import__ function never binds anything other than a module object as a value in sys.modules. However, if __import__ finds an entry that is already in sys.modules, it returns that value, whatever type of object it may be. The import and from statements rely on the __import__ function, so they too can end up using objects that are not modules. This lack of type-checking is an advanced feature that was introduced several Python versions ago (very old versions of Python used to type-check, allowing only module objects as values in sys.modules). The feature lets you set class instances as entries in sys.modules, in order to exploit features such as __getattr__ and __setattr__ special methods, covered in "General-Purpose Special Methods" on page 104. This advanced technique lets you import module-like objects whose attributes can be computed on the fly. Here's a toy-like example:

```
class TT(object):
    def __getattr__(self, name): return 23
import sys
sys.modules[__name__] = TT()
```

When you import this code as a module, you get a module-like object (which in fact is an instance of this class *TT*) that appears to have any attribute name you try to get from it; all attribute names correspond to the integer value 23.

Custom Importers

An advanced, rarely needed functionality that Python offers is the ability to change the semantics or some or all import and from statements.

Rebinding __import__

You can rebind the __import__ attribute of module __builtin__ to your own custom importer function—for example, one built with the generic built-in-wrapping technique shown in "Python built-ins" on page 141. Such a rebinding influences all import and from statements that execute after the rebinding and thus has possibly undesired global impacts. A custom importer built by rebinding __import__ must implement the same interface as the built-in __import__, and, in particular, it is responsible for supporting the correct use of sys.modules. While rebinding __import__ may initially look like an attractive approach, in most cases where custom importers are necessary, you will be better off implementing them via *import hooks* instead.

Import hooks

Python offers rich support for selectively changing the details of imports, including standard library modules imp and ihooks. Custom importers are an advanced and rarely used technique, and yet some applications may need them for all sorts of purposes, including the import of code from archive files in formats that differ from ZIP files, from databases, from network servers, and so on. The most suitable approach for such highly advanced needs is to record *importer factory* callables as items in attributes meta_path and/or path_hooks of module sys, as detailed at *http://www.python.org/peps/pep-0302.html*. This approach is also the one that Python uses to hook up standard library module zipimport in order to allow seamless importing of modules from ZIP files, as previously mentioned. A full study of the details of PEP 302 is indispensable for any substantial use of sys.path_hooks and friends, but here's a simple, toy-level example that may help you understand the possibilities it offers, should you ever need them.

Suppose that while developing a first outline of some program, you want to be able to use import statements for modules that you haven't written yet, getting just warning messages (and empty modules) as a consequence. You can easily obtain such functionality (leaving aside the complexities connected with packages and dealing with simple modules only) by coding a custom importer module as follows:

```
import sys, new
class ImporterAndLoader(object):
    '''importer and loader functionality is usually in a single class'''
    fake_path = '!dummy!'
    def __init__(self, path):
        '''we only handle our own fake-path marker'''
        if path != self.fake_path: raise ImportError
    def find_module(self, fullname):
        '''we don't even try to handle any qualified module-name'''
        if '.' in fullname: return None
        return self
    def load_module(self, fullname):
        # emit some kind of warning messages
        print 'NOTE: module %r not written yet' % fullname
        # make new empty module, put it in sys.modules too
        mod = sys.modules[fullname] = new.module(fullname)
        # minimally populate new module and then return it
        mod.__file__ = 'dummy<%s>' % fullname
        mod.__loader__ = self
        return mod
# add the class to the hook and its fake-path marker to the path
sys.path_hooks.append(ImporterAndLoader)
sys.path.append(ImporterAndLoader.fake_path)

if __name__ == '__main__':      # self-test when run as main script
    import missing_module        # importing a simple missing module
    print sys.modules.get('missing_module')  #...should succeed
    # check that we don't deal with importing from packages
    try: import missing_module.sub_module
    except ImportError:
    else: print 'Unexpected:', sys.modules.get('missing_module.sub_module')
```

Packages

A *package* is a module that contains other modules. Some or all of the modules in a package may be subpackages, resulting in a hierarchical tree-like structure. A package named P resides in a subdirectory, also called P, of some directory in sys.path. Packages can also live in ZIP files; in the following, I explain the case in which the package lives on the filesystem, since the case in which a package lives in a ZIP file is strictly analogous, relying on the hierarchical filesystem-like structure inside the ZIP file.

The module-body of P is in the file P/_ _init_ _.py. You must have a file named P/_ _init_ _.py, even if it's empty (representing an empty module-body) in order to indicate to Python that directory P is indeed a package. The module-body of a package is loaded when you first import the package (or any of the package's modules) and behaves in all respects like any other Python module. The other .py files in directory P are the modules of package P. Subdirectories of P containing _ _init_ _.py files are subpackages of P. (In Python 2.5, all subdirectories of P are subpackages of P, whether such subdirectories contain _ _init_ _.py files or not.) Nesting can continue to any depth.

You can import a module named M in package P as P.M. More dots let you navigate a hierarchical package structure. (A package's module-body is always loaded *before* any module in the package is loaded.) If you use the syntax import P.M, variable P is bound to the module object of package P, and attribute M of object P is bound to module P.M. If you use the syntax import P.M as V, variable V is bound directly to module P.M.

Using from P import M to import a specific module M from package P is a perfectly acceptable practice: the from statement is specifically okay in this case.

A module M in a package P can import any other module X of P with the statement import X. Python searches the module's own package directory before searching the items in sys.path. However, this applies only to sibling modules, not to ancestors or other more complicated relationships. The simplest, cleanest way to share objects (such as functions or constants) among modules in a package P is to group the shared objects in a file named P/Common.py. Then you can import Common from every module in the package that needs to access the objects, and then refer to the objects as Common.f, Common.K, and so on.

Special attributes of package objects

A package P's _ _file_ _ attribute is the string that is the path of P's module-body—that is, the path of the file P/_ _init_ _.py.

A package P's module-body—that is, the Python source that is in the file P/_ _init_ _.py—can optionally set a global variable named _ _all_ _ (just like any other module can) to control what happens if some other module executes the statement from P import *. In particular, if _ _all_ _ is not set, from P import * does not import P's modules, but only other names that are set in P's module-body. However, in any case, using from P import *is *not* recommended usage.

A package *P*'s __path__ attribute is the list of strings that are the paths to the directories from which *P*'s modules and subpackages are loaded. Initially, Python sets __path__ to a list with a single element: the path of the directory containing the file *__init__.py* that is the module-body of the package. However, your code can modify this list to affect all future searches for modules and subpackages of this package. This advanced technique is rarely necessary, but it can occasionally be useful when you want to place a package's modules in several disjoint directories.

Absolute Versus Relative Imports

In Python 2.5, if you start a module with:

```
from __future__ import absolute_import
```

then the rules change: import *X* means a normal ("absolute") import of a module from somewhere in sys.path; to get a relative import, meaning an import of a module from within the current package, code from . import *X* instead. With this feature, you can also code richer and more complex relative imports, although getting too fancy could easily damage your code's clarity. These rules will become the default in some future version of Python; see *http://www.python.org/doc/peps/ pep-0328/* for more details, including the best current forecast for the schedule of these changes.

The Distribution Utilities (distutils)

Python modules, extensions, and applications can be packaged and distributed in several forms:

Compressed archive files
　　Generally *.zip* for Windows and *.tar.gz* (a.k.a. *.tgz*) for Unix-based systems, but both forms are portable

Self-unpacking or self-installing executables
　　Normally *.exe* for Windows

Self-contained, ready-to-run executables that require no installation
　　For example, *.exe* for Windows, ZIP archives with a short script prefix on Unix, *.app* for the Mac, and so on

Platform-specific installers
　　For example, *.msi* on Windows, *.rpm* and *.srpm* on most Linux distributions, and *.deb* on Debian GNU/Linux and Ubuntu

Python Eggs
　　A very popular third-party extension, covered in "Python Eggs" on page 151

When you distribute a package as a self-installing executable or platform-specific installer, a user can then install the package simply by running the installer. How to run such an installer program depends on the platform, but it no longer matters which language the program was written in. How to build self-contained, ready-to run executables for various platforms is covered in Chapter 27.

When you distribute a package as an archive file or as an executable that unpacks but does not install itself, it does matter that the package was coded in Python. In this case, the user must first unpack the archive file into some appropriate directory, say *C:\Temp\MyPack* on a Windows machine or *~/MyPack* on a Unix-like machine. Among the extracted files there should be a script, conventionally named *setup.py*, which uses the Python facility known as the *distribution utilities* (standard library package distutils). The distributed package is then almost as easy to install as a self-installing executable would be. The user opens a command-prompt window and changes to the directory into which the archive is unpacked. Then the user runs, for example:

```
C:\Temp\MyPack> python setup.py install
```

The *setup.py* script, run with this *install* command, installs the package as a part of the user's Python installation, according to the options specified in the setup script by the package's author (of course, the user needs appropriate permissions to write into the directories of the Python installations, so permission-raising commands such as *su* or *sudo* may be needed). distutils, by default, provides tracing information when the user runs *setup.py*. Option *--quiet*, placed right before the *install* command, hides most details (the user still sees error messages, if any). The following command gives detailed help on distutils:

```
C:\> python setup.py --help
```

When you are installing a package prepared with distutils, you can, if you wish, exert detailed control over how distutils performs installations. You can record installation options in a text file with extension *.cfg*, called a *config* file, so that distutils applies your favorite installation options by default. Such customization can be done on a system-wide basis for a single user, or even for a single package installation. For example, if you want an installation with minimal amounts of output to be your system-wide default, create the following text file named *pydistutils.cfg*:

```
[global]
quiet=1
```

Put this file in the same directory in which the distutils package resides. On a typical Python 2.4 installation on Windows, for example, the file is *C:\Python24\ Lib\distutils\pydistutils.cfg*. "Python's distutils" on page 666 provides more information on using distutils to prepare modules, packages, extensions, and applications for distribution.

Python Eggs

A new emerging standard for distributing Python packages is *Python Eggs*, ZIP files that optionally include structured metadata as well as Python code, and sporting a file extension of *.egg*. Among the many endearing characteristics of Eggs is the fact that sufficiently simple Eggs need no real "installation" procedure: just place an *.egg* file anywhere along your Python sys.path, and your Python code can immediately start using that package. Despite this simplicity, the fact that Eggs can contain rich metadata also offers many other exciting possibilities.

Unfortunately, Eggs have not made it into the Python 2.5 release, for reasons of mere timing (Eggs were still under development at the time of the cut-off date for new features to be accepted into Python 2.5). Nevertheless, you can use Eggs with all Python releases from 2.3 onward by downloading and running a single Python script from *http://peak.telecommunity.com/DevCenter/EasyInstall*. I highly recommend Eggs as an excellent way to distribute your Python packages; besides their other advantages, Eggs also come with a package of powerful tools for setup and installations, setuptools, to complement distutils, covered in "Python's distutils" on page 666. Read all about Eggs and setuptools at *http://peak.telecommunity.com/DevCenter/PythonEggs*.

8

Core Built-ins

The term *built-in* has more than one meaning in Python. In most contexts, a *built-in* means an object directly accessible to Python code without an import statement. "Python built-ins" on page 141 shows the mechanism that Python uses to allow this direct access. Built-in types in Python include numbers, sequences, dictionaries, sets, functions (covered in Chapter 4), classes (covered in "Python Classes" on page 82), standard exception classes (covered in "Exception Objects" on page 129), and modules (covered in "Module Objects" on page 139). The built-in file object is covered in "File Objects" on page 216, and "Internal Types" on page 331 covers some built-in types intrinsic to Python's internal operation. This chapter provides additional coverage of the core built-in types (in "Built-in Types" on page 154) and covers built-in functions available in module __builtin__ (in "Built-in Functions" on page 158).

As I mentioned in "Python built-ins" on page 141, some modules are known as "built-in" because they are an integral part of the Python standard library (even though it takes an import statement to access them), as distinguished from separate, optional add-on modules, also called Python *extensions*. This chapter documents some *core* built-in modules, essentially those that offer functionality that, in some other languages, is built into the languages themselves: namely, modules sys in "The sys Module" on page 168, copy in "The copy Module" on page 172, collections in "The collections Module" on page 173, functional (2.5 only) in "The functional Module" on page 175, bisect in "The bisect Module" on page 176, heapq in "The heapq Module" on page 177, UserDict in "The UserDict Module" on page 178, optparse in "The optparse Module" on page 179, and itertools in "The itertools Module" on page 183. Chapter 9 covers some string-related core built-in modules (string in "The string Module" on page 191, codecs in "The codecs Module" on page 199, unicodedata in "The unicodedata Module" on page 200, and re in "Regular Expressions and the re Module" on page 201). Parts III and IV cover many other modules found in Python's standard library.

Built-in Types

This section documents Python's core built-in types, such as int, float, dict, and many others. More details about many of these types, and about operations on their instances, are found throughout Chapter 4. In the rest of this section, by "number" I mean, specifically, "noncomplex number."

basestring   basestring

Noninstantiable (*abstract*) common basetype of types str and unicode. Used mostly to ascertain whether some object *x* is a string (either plain or Unicode) by testing isinstance(*x*, basestring).

bool   bool(*x*)

Returns False if argument *x* evaluates as false; returns True if argument *x* evaluates as true. (See also "Boolean Values" on page 45.) bool is a subclass of int, and built-in names False and True refer to the only two instances of type bool. These instances are also integer numbers, equal to 0 and 1, respectively, but str(True) is 'True', and str(False) is 'False'.

buffer   buffer(*obj*,*offset*=0,*size*=-1)

Returns a read-only buffer object that refers to a compact slice of *obj*'s data, starting at the given *offset* and with the given *size* (all the way to the end of *obj*'s data, if *size*<0, or if *obj*'s data is too short to provide *size* bytes after the *offset*). *obj* must be of a type that supports the buffer call interface, such as a string or array.

classmethod   classmethod(*function*)

Returns a class method object. In practice, you call this built-in type only within a class body, and, most often, in Python 2.4, you use it as a decorator. See "Class methods" on page 99.

complex   complex(*real*,*imag*=0)

Converts any number, or a suitable string, to a complex number. *imag* may be present only when *real* is a number and is the imaginary part of the resulting complex number. See also "Complex numbers" on page 40.

dict   dict(*x*={ })

Returns a new dictionary object with the same items as argument *x*. (Dictionaries are covered in "Dictionaries" on page 44.) When *x* is a dictionary, dict(*x*) returns a copy of *x*, like *x*.copy( ) does.

Alternatively, x can be an iterable whose items are pairs (iterables with two items each). In this case, dict(x) returns a dictionary whose keys are the first items of each pair in x, while the values are the corresponding second items. In other words, when x is a sequence, c=dict(x) has the same effect as the following:

```
c = {}
for key, value in x: c[key] = value
```

You can also call dict with named arguments in addition to, or instead of, positional argument x. Each named argument becomes an additional item in the resulting dictionary, with the name as the key, possibly overwriting an item coming from x.

---

enumerate   enumerate(*iterable*)

Returns a new iterator object whose items are pairs. For each such pair, the second item is the corresponding item in *iterable*, while the first item is an integer: 0, 1, 2.... For example, the following snippet loops on a list L of integers, halving each even value:

```
for i,num in enumerate(L):
    if num % 2 == 0:
        L[i] = num // 2
```

---

file, open   file(*path*,*mode*='r',*bufsize*=-1)
                 open(*filename*,*mode*='r',*bufsize*=-1)

Opens or creates a file and returns a new file object. See "File Objects" on page 216.

---

float   float(*x*)

Converts any number, or a suitable string, to a floating-point number. See "Floating-point numbers" on page 39.

---

frozenset   frozenset(*seq*=[ ])

Returns a new frozen (immutable) set object with the same items as the iterable object *seq*. When *seq* is a frozen set, frozenset(*seq*) returns *seq* itself, like *seq*.copy( ) does. See "Set Operations" on page 58.

---

int   int(*x*[,*radix*])

Converts any number, or a suitable string, to an int. When x is a number, int truncates toward 0, dropping any fractional part. *radix* may be present only when x is a string. *radix* is the conversion base, between 2 and 36, with 10 as the default. *radix* can be explicitly passed as 0: the base is then 8, 10, or 16, depending on the form of string *x*, just like for integer literals, as covered in "Integer numbers" on page 39.

list

list(*seq*=[ ])

Returns a new list object with the same items as the iterable object *seq*, in the same order. When *seq* is a list, list(*seq*) returns a copy of *seq*, like *seq*[:] does. See "Lists" on page 43.

long

long(*x*[,*radix*])

Converts any number, or a suitable string, to a long. The rules regarding the *radix* argument are exactly the same as for int. See "Integer numbers" on page 39.

object

object( )

Returns a new instance of the most fundamental type. Such direct instances of type object have no functionality, so the only practical reason to create one is to obtain a "sentinel" object, i.e., one guaranteed to compare unequal to any distinct object.

property

property(*fget*=None,*fset*=None,*fdel*=None,*doc*=None)

Returns a property descriptor. In practice, you call this built-in type only within a class body. See "Properties" on page 100.

reversed

reversed(*seq*)

Returns a new iterator object whose items are the items of sequence *seq* (which must be a proper sequence, not just any iterable) in reverse order.

set

set(*seq*=[ ])

Returns a new mutable set object with the same items as the iterable object *seq*. When *seq* is a set, set(*seq*) returns a copy of *seq*, like *seq*.copy( ) does. See "Sets" on page 43.

slice

slice([*start*,]*stop*[,*step*])

Returns a slice object with read-only attributes start, stop, and step bound to the respective argument values, each defaulting to None when missing. Such a slice is essentially meant to signify the same set of indices as range(*start*,*stop*,*step*). Slicing syntax *obj*[*start*:*stop*:*step*] passes such a slice object as the argument to the __getitem__, __setitem__, or __delitem__ method of object *obj*, as appropriate. It is up to *obj* to interpret the slice objects that its methods receive. See also "Container slicing" on page 110.

---

staticmethod
staticmethod(*function*)

Returns a static method object. In practice, you call this built-in type only within a class body, and, most often, in Python 2.4, you use it as a decorator. See "Static methods" on page 99.

---

str
str(*obj*)

Returns a concise and readable string representation of *obj*. If *obj* is a string, str returns *obj*. See also repr on page 166 and __str__ on page 109.

---

super
super(*cls*,*obj*)

Returns a super-object of object *obj* (which must be an instance of class *cls* or a subclass of *cls*) suitable for calling superclass methods. In practice, you call this built-in type only within a method's code. See "Cooperative superclass method calling" on page 97.

---

tuple
tuple(*seq*)

Returns a tuple with the same items as the iterable object *seq* in the same order. When *seq* is a tuple, tuple returns *seq* itself, like *seq*[:] does. See "Tuples" on page 42.

---

type
type(*obj*)

Returns the type object that is the type of *obj* (i.e., the most-derived, a.k.a. *leafmost*, type object of which *obj* is an instance). All legacy instance objects have the same type (InstanceType), even when they are instances of different classes: use isinstance (covered in "isinstance") to check whether an instance belongs to a particular class. In the new-style object model, however, type(*x*) is *x*.__class__ for any *x*.

Checking type(*x*) for equality or identity to some other type object is known as *type-checking*. Type-checking is hardly ever appropriate in production Python code because it interferes with polymorphism. The normal idiom in Python is to try to use *x* as if it were of the type you expect, handling any problems with a try/except statement, as discussed in "Error-Checking Strategies" on page 134. When you just *have* to type-check, typically for debugging purposes, use isinstance instead. isinstance(*x*,*atype*) is a lesser evil than type(*x*) is *atype*, since at least it accepts an *x* that is an instance of any subclass of *atype*, not just a direct instance of *atype* itself.

unicode   unicode(*string*[,*codec*[,*errors*]])

Returns the Unicode string object obtained by decoding *string*. *codec* names the codec to use. If *codec* is missing, unicode uses the default codec (generally 'ascii'). *errors*, if present, is a string that specifies how to handle decoding errors. See also "Unicode" on page 198, particularly for information about codecs and *errors*, and __unicode__ on page 109.

xrange   xrange([*start*,]*stop*[,*step*=1])

Returns a read-only sequence object whose items are integers in arithmetic progression. The arguments are the same as for range, covered in "range". While range creates and returns a normal list object, xrange returns a sequence object of a special type, mostly meant to be used in a for statement (you can index that object, but you cannot slice it). xrange consumes less memory than range for this specific, frequent use, in which all you need to do is loop on an arithmetic progression. However, xrange has a slightly higher overhead than range for the loop itself. Overall, performance differences between xrange and range are normally small and not worth worrying about.

Built-in Functions

This section documents the Python functions available in module __builtin__ in alphabetical order. Note that the names of these built-ins are *not* reserved words. Thus, your program can bind for its own purposes, in local or global scope, an identifier that has the same name as a built-in function. Names bound in local or global scope have priority over names bound in built-in scope, so local and global names hide built-in ones. You can also rebind names in built-in scope, as covered in "Python built-ins" on page 141. Be very careful, however, to avoid accidentally hiding built-ins that your code might need. It's tempting to use, for your own variables, natural names such as file, input, list, filter, but *don't do it*: these are all names of built-in Python types or functions, and, unless you get into the habit of *never* shadowing such built-in names with your own, you'll end up with some mysterious bug in your code sooner or later due to such hiding.

Like most built-in functions and types, the functions documented in this section cannot normally be called with named arguments, only with positional ones; in the following, I specifically mention any case in which this limitation does not hold.

| __import__ | __import__(module_name[,globals[,locals[,fromlist]]]) |

Loads the module named by string *module_name* and returns the resulting module object. *globals*, which defaults to the result of globals(), and *locals*, which defaults to the result of locals() (both covered in this section), are dictionaries that __import__ treats as read-only and uses only to get context for package-relative imports, covered in "Packages" on page 149. *fromlist* defaults to an empty list, but can be a list of strings that name the module attributes to be imported in a from statement. See "Module Loading" on page 144 for more details on module loading.

In practice, when you call __import__, you generally pass only the first argument, except in the rare and dubious case in which you use __import__ for a package-relative import. Should you replace the built-in __import__ function with your own, in order to provide special import functionality, you may unfortunately have to take parameters *globals*, *locals*, and *fromlist* into account.

| abs | abs(x) |

Returns the absolute value of number *x*. When *x* is complex, abs returns the square root of *x*.imag**2+*x*.real**2 (also known as the *magnitude* of the complex number). Otherwise, abs returns -*x* if *x* is less than 0, or *x* if *x* is greater than or equal to 0. See also __abs__, __invert__, __neg__, __pos__ on page 113.

| all | all(seq) |

seq is any iterable. all returns False if any item of *seq* is false; otherwise (including the case in which *seq* is empty), all returns True. **Python 2.5 only**. Like operators and and or, covered in "Short-Circuiting Operators" on page 51, all stops evaluating, and returns a result as soon as the answer is known; in the case of all, this means that evaluation stops as soon as a false item is reached but proceeds throughout *seq* if all of *seq*'s items are true. Here is a typical toy example of the use of all:

```
if all(x>0 for x in numbers):
    print "all of the numbers are positive"
else:
    print "some of the numbers are not positive"
```

| any | any(seq) |

seq is any iterable. any returns True if any item of *seq* is true; otherwise (including the case in which *seq* is empty), any returns False. **Python 2.5 only**. Like operators and and or, covered in "Short-Circuiting Operators" on page 51, any stops evaluating, and returns a result, as soon as the answer is known; in the case of any, this means that evaluation stops as soon as a true item is reached but

Core Built-ins

proceeds throughout *seq* if all of *seq*'s items are false. Here is a typical toy example of the use of any:

```
if any(x<0 for x in numbers):
    print "some of the numbers are negative"
else:
    print "none of the numbers are negative"
```

callable callable(*obj*)

Returns True if *obj* can be called, otherwise False. An object can be called if it is a function, method, class, type, or an instance with a __call__ method. See also __call__ on page 105.

chr chr(*code*)

Returns a string of length 1, a single character corresponding to integer *code* in the ASCII/ISO encoding. See also ord on page 165 and unichr on page 167.

cmp cmp(*x,y*)

Returns 0 when *x* equals *y*, -1 when *x* is less than *y*, or 1 when *x* is greater than *y*. See also __cmp__ on page 105.

coerce coerce(*x,y*)

Returns a pair whose two items are numbers *x* and *y* converted to a common type. See "Numeric Conversions" on page 52.

compile compile(*string,filename,kind*)

Compiles a string and returns a code object usable by exec or eval. compile raises SyntaxError when *string* is not syntactically valid Python. When *string* is a multiline compound statement, the last character must be '\n'. *kind* must be 'eval' when *string* is an expression and the result is meant for eval; otherwise, *kind* must be 'exec'. *filename* must be a string, and is used only in error messages (if and when errors occur). See also eval on page 161 and "Compile and Code Objects" on page 329.

delattr delattr(*obj,name*)

Removes attribute *name* from *obj*. delattr(*obj*,'*ident*') is like del *obj.ident*. If *obj* has an attribute named *name* just because its class has it (as is normally the case, for example, with methods of *obj*), you cannot delete that attribute from *obj* itself. You may be able to delete that attribute from the class, depending on what the metaclass allows.

If you can delete that class attribute, *obj* would cease to have the attribute, and so would every other object of that class.

dir	dir([*obj*])

Called without arguments, dir( ) returns a sorted list of all variable names that are bound in the current scope. dir(*obj*) returns a sorted list of all names of attributes of *obj*, including ones coming from *obj*'s type or by inheritance. See also vars on page 167.

divmod	divmod(*dividend,divisor*)

Divides two numbers and returns a pair whose items are the quotient and remainder. See also __divmod__ on page 114.

eval	eval(*expr,*[*globals*[,*locals*]])

Returns the result of an expression. *expr* may be a code object ready for evaluation or a string. In the case of a string, eval gets a code object by calling compile(*expr, 'string', 'eval'*). eval evaluates the code object as an expression, using the *globals* and *locals* dictionaries as namespaces. When both arguments are missing, eval uses the current namespace. eval cannot execute statements; it can only evaluate expressions. See also "Expressions" on page 329.

execfile	execfile(*filename,*[*globals*[,*locals*]])

execfile is a shortcut for the following statement:

    exec open(*filename*).read( ) in *globals, locals*

See "Dynamic Execution and the exec Statement" on page 328.

filter	filter(*func,seq*)

Constructs a list from those elements of *seq* for which *func* is true. *func* can be any callable object that accepts a single argument or None. *seq* can be any iterable object. When *func* is callable, filter calls *func* on each item of *seq* and returns the list of items for which *func*'s result is true, just like the following string comprehension:

    [*item* for *item* in *seq* if *func*(*item*)]

When *seq* is a string or tuple, filter's result is also a string or tuple rather than a list. When *func* is None, filter tests for true items, just like:

    [*item* for *item* in *seq* if *item*]

Core Built-ins

getattr   getattr(*obj*,*name*[,*default*])

Returns *obj*'s attribute named by string *name*. getattr(*obj*, '*ident*') is like *obj.ident*. When *default* is present and *name* is not found in *obj*, getattr returns *default* instead of raising AttributeError. See also "Attribute Reference Basics" on page 89.

globals   globals( )

Returns the _ _dict_ _ of the calling module (i.e., the dictionary used as the global namespace at the point of call). See also locals on page 164.

hasattr   hasattr(*obj*,*name*)

Returns False if *obj* has no attribute *name* (i.e., if getattr(*obj*,*name*) raises AttributeError). Otherwise, hasattr returns True. See also "Attribute Reference Basics" on page 89.

hash   hash(*obj*)

Returns the hash value for *obj*. *obj* can be a dictionary key, or an item in a set, only if *obj* can be hashed. All numbers that compare equal have the same hash value, even if they are of different types. If the type of *obj* does not define equality comparison, hash(*obj*) normally returns id(*obj*). See also_ _hash_ _ on page 107.

hex   hex(*x*)

Converts integer *x* to hexadecimal string representation. See also _ _hex_ _, _ _oct_ _ on page 114.

id   id(*obj*)

Returns the integer value that denotes the identity of *obj*. The id of *obj* is unique and constant during *obj*'s lifetime but may be reused at any later time after *obj* is garbage-collected. When a type or class does not define equality comparison, Python uses id to compare and hash instances. For any objects *x* and *y*, the identity check *x* is *y* has the same result as id(*x*)==id(*y*).

input   input(*prompt*='')

input(*prompt*) is a shortcut for eval(raw_input(*prompt*)). In other words, input prompts the user for a line of input, evaluates the resulting string as an expression, and returns the expression's result. The implicit eval may raise SyntaxError or other exceptions. input is rather user-unfriendly and inappropriate for most programs, but it can be handy for small experiments and your own small exploratory scripts. See also eval on page 161 and raw_input on page 165.

intern

intern(*string*)

Ensures that *string* is held in a table of interned strings and returns *string* itself or a copy. Interned strings may compare for equality slightly faster than other strings because you can use operator is instead of operator == for such comparisons. However, garbage collection can never recover the memory used for interned strings, so interning too many strings might slow down your program by making it take up too much memory. I do not cover the concept of interned strings elsewhere in this book.

isinstance

isinstance(*obj*,*cls*)

Returns True when *obj* is an instance of class *cls* (or any subclass of *cls*), or when *cls* is a type object and *obj* is an object of that type. Otherwise, it returns False. *cls* can also be a tuple whose items are classes or types. In this case, isinstance returns True if *obj* is an instance of any of the items of tuple *cls*; otherwise, isinstance returns False.

issubclass

issubclass(*cls1*,*cls2*)

Returns True if *cls1* is a direct or indirect subclass of *cls2*; otherwise, returns False. *cls1* and *cls2* must be types or classes.

iter

iter(*obj*)
iter(*func*,*sentinel*)

Creates and returns an *iterator*, which is an object with a next method that you can call repeatedly to get one item at a time (see "Iterators" on page 65). When called with one argument, iter(*obj*) normally returns *obj*.__iter__( ). When *obj* is a sequence without a special method __iter__, iter(*obj*) is equivalent to the following generator:

```
def iterSequence(obj):
    i = 0
    while 1:
        try: yield obj[i]
        except IndexError: raise StopIteration
        i += 1
```

See also "Sequences" on page 40 and __iter__ on page 112.

When called with two arguments, the first argument must be callable without arguments, and iter(*func,sentinel*) is equivalent to the following generator:

```
def iterSentinel(func, sentinel):
    while 1:
        item = func( )
        if item == sentinel: raise StopIteration
        yield item
```

As discussed in "The for Statement" on page 64, the statement for *x* in *obj* is exactly equivalent to for *x* in iter(*obj*); therefore, do *not* call iter in such a for statement because it would be redundant, and therefore bad Python style. iter is *idempotent*. In other words, when *x* is an iterator, iter(*x*) is *x*, as long as *x*'s class supplies an __iter__ method whose body is just return self, as an iterator's class should.

---

len   len(*container*)

Returns the number of items in *container*, which may be a sequence, a mapping, or a set. See also __len__ on page 112.

---

locals   locals( )

Returns a dictionary that represents the current local namespace. Treat the returned dictionary as read-only; trying to modify it may affect the values of local variables and might even raise an exception. See also globals on page 162 and vars on page 167.

---

map   map(*func,seq,*seqs*)

Applies *func* to every item of *seq* and returns a list of the results. When map is called with *n+1* arguments, the first one, *func*, can be any callable object that accepts *n* arguments or None. The remaining arguments to map must be iterable. When *func* is callable, map repeatedly calls *func* with *n* arguments (one corresponding item from each iterable) and returns the list of results. For example, map(*func, seq*) is like:

[*func(item)* for *item* in *seq*]

When *func* is None, map returns a list of tuples, each with *n* items (one item from each iterable); this is similar to "zip." When the iterable objects have different lengths, however, map conceptually pads the shorter ones with None, while zip conceptually truncates the longer ones.

---

max   max(*s,*args*)

Returns the largest item in the only argument *s* (*s* must then be iterable) or the largest of multiple arguments. In Python 2.5, you

---

can also call max with one positional argument and a named argument key= with the same semantics as for function sorted, covered in sorted on page 167.

min min(s,*args)

Returns the smallest item in the only argument s (s must then be iterable) or the smallest of multiple arguments. In Python 2.5, you can also call min with one positional argument and a named argument key= with the same semantics as for function sorted, covered in sorted on page 167.

oct oct(x)

Converts integer x to an octal string representation. See also __hex__, __oct__ on page 114.

ord ord(ch)

Returns the ASCII/ISO integer code between 0 and 255 (inclusive) for the single-character string ch. When ch is Unicode, ord returns an integer code between 0 and 65534 (inclusive). See also chr on page 160 and unichr on page 167.

pow pow(x,y[,z])

When z is present, pow(x,y,z) returns x**y%z. When z is missing, pow(x,y) returns x**y. See also __pow__ on page 115.

range range([start,]stop[,step=1])

Returns a list of integers in arithmetic progression:
    [start, start+step, start+2*step, ...]
When start is missing, it defaults to 0. When step is missing, it defaults to 1. When step is 0, range raises ValueError. When step is greater than 0, the last item is the largest start+i*step strictly less than stop. When step is less than 0, the last item is the smallest start+i*step strictly greater than stop. The result is an empty list when start is greater than or equal to stop and step is greater than 0, or when start is less than or equal to stop and step is less than 0. Otherwise, the first item of the result list is always start. See also xrange on page 158.

raw_input raw_input(prompt='')

Writes prompt to standard output, reads a line from standard input, and returns the line (without \n) as a string. When at end-of-file, raw_input raises EOFError. See also input on page 162.

reduce   reduce(*func*,*seq*[,*init*])

Applies *func* to the items of *seq*, from left to right, to reduce the
iterable to a single value. *func* must be callable with two arguments. reduce calls *func* on the first two items of *seq*, then on the
result of the first call and the third item, and so on. reduce returns
the result of the last such call. When *init* is present, it is used
before *seq*'s first item, if any. When *init* is missing, *seq* must be
nonempty. When *init* is missing and *seq* has only one item, reduce
returns *seq*[0]. Similarly, when *init* is present and *seq* is empty,
reduce returns *init*. reduce is thus roughly equivalent to:

```
def reduce_equivalent(func,seq,init=None):
    seq = iter(seq)
    if init is None: init = seq.next()
    for item in seq: init = func(init,item)
    return init
```

An example use of reduce is to compute the product of a sequence
of numbers:

```
thesum = reduce(operator.mul, seq, 1)
```

reload   reload(*module*)

Reloads and reinitializes module object *module*, and returns *module*.
See "The reload Function" on page 146.

repr   repr(*obj*)

Returns a complete and unambiguous string representation of *obj*.
When feasible, repr returns a string that you can pass to eval in
order to create a new object with the same value as *obj*. See also str
on page 273 and _ _repr_ _ on page 108.

round   round(*x*,*n*=0)

Returns a float whose value is number *x* rounded to *n* digits after
the decimal point (i.e., the multiple of 10**-*n* that is closest to *x*).
When two such multiples are equally close to *x*, round returns the
one that is farther from 0. Since today's computers represent
floating-point numbers in binary, not in decimal, most of round's
results are not exact. See "The decimal Module" on page 372.

setattr   setattr(*obj*,*name*,*value*)

Binds *obj*'s attribute *name* to *value*. setattr(*obj*,'*ident*',*val*) is like
obj.*ident*=*val*. See also "Object attributes and items" on page 46
and "Setting an attribute" on page 91.

sorted	sorted(*seq*,*cmp*=None,*key*=None,*reverse*=False)

Returns a list with the same items as iterable *seq*, in sorted order. Same as:

```
def sorted(seq,cmp=None,key=None,reverse=False):
    result = list(seq)
    result.sort(cmp,key,reverse)
    return result
```

See "Sorting a list" on page 57 for the meaning of the arguments; sorted is one of the few built-in functions that's callable with named arguments. New in Python 2.4.

sum	sum(*seq*,*start*=0)

Returns the sum of the items of iterable *seq* (which should be numbers and, in particular, cannot be strings) plus the value of *start*. When *seq* has no items, returns *start*. To "sum" (concatenate) a sequence of strings, use ''.join(*seqofstrs*), as covered in join on page 188 and "Building up a string from pieces" on page 484.

unichr	unichr(*code*)

Returns a Unicode string whose single character corresponds to *code*, where *code* is an integer between 0 and 65535 (inclusive). See also str on page 157 and ord on page 165.

vars	vars([*obj*])

When called with no argument, vars() returns a dictionary that represents all variables that are bound in the current scope (exactly like locals, covered in "locals"). This dictionary should be treated as read-only. vars(*obj*) returns a dictionary that represents all attributes currently bound in *obj*, as covered in dir on page 161. This dictionary may be modifiable, depending on the type of *obj*.

zip	zip(*seq*,**seqs*)

Returns a list of tuples, where the *n*th tuple contains the *n*th element from each of the argument sequences. zip must be called with at least one argument, and all arguments must be iterable. If the iterables have different lengths, zip returns a list as long as the shortest iterable, ignoring trailing items in the other iterable objects. See also map on page 164.

Core Built-ins

The sys Module

The attributes of the sys module are bound to data and functions that provide information on the state of the Python interpreter or affect the interpreter directly. This section documents the most frequently used attributes of sys, in alphabetical order.

argv	The list of command-line arguments passed to the main script. argv[0] is the name or full path of the main script, or '-c' if the -c option was used. See "The optparse Module" on page 179 for a good way to use sys.argv.

displayhook   displayhook(*value*)

In interactive sessions, the Python interpreter calls displayhook, passing it the result of each expression statement entered. The default displayhook does nothing if *value* is None; otherwise, it preserves and displays *value*:

```
if value is not None:
    __builtin__._ = value
    print repr(value)
```

You can rebind sys.displayhook in order to change interactive behavior. The original value is available as sys.__displayhook__.

excepthook   excepthook(*type*,*value*,*traceback*)

When an exception is not caught by any handler, and thus propagates all the way up the call stack, Python calls excepthook, passing it the exception class, exception object, and traceback object, as covered in "Exception Propagation" on page 126. The default excepthook displays the error and traceback. You can rebind sys. excepthook to change what is displayed for uncaught exceptions (just before Python returns to the interactive loop or terminates). The original value is available as sys.__excepthook__.

exc_info   exc_info( )

If the current thread is handling an exception, exc_info returns a tuple whose three items are the class, object, and traceback for the exception. If the current thread is not handling any exception, exc_info returns (None,None,None). A traceback object indirectly holds references to all variables of all functions that propagated the exception. Thus, if you hold a reference to the traceback object (for example, indirectly, by binding a variable to the whole tuple that exc_info returns), Python must retain in memory data that might otherwise be garbage-collected; so make sure that any binding to the traceback object is of short duration. To ensure that the binding gets removed, you can use a try/finally statement (discussed in "try/finally" on page 123). To print information from a traceback object, see "The traceback Module" on page 466.

exit

exit(*arg*=0)

Raises a SystemExit exception, which normally terminates execution after executing cleanup handlers installed by try/finally statements. If *arg* is an integer, Python uses *arg* as the program's exit code: 0 indicates successful termination, while any other value indicates unsuccessful termination of the program. Most platforms require exit codes to be between 0 and 127. If *arg* is not an integer, Python prints *arg* to sys.stderr, and the exit code of the program is 1 (i.e., a generic unsuccessful termination code).

getdefaulten-coding

getdefaultencoding( )

Returns the name of the default codec used to encode and decode Unicode and string objects (normally 'ascii'). Unicode, codecs, encoding, and decoding are covered in "Unicode" on page 198.

getrefcount

getrefcount(*object*)

Returns the reference count of *object*. Reference counts are covered in "Garbage Collection" on page 332.

getrecursionlimit

getrecursionlimit( )

Returns the current limit on the depth of Python's call stack. See also "Recursion" on page 80 and setrecursionlimit on page 171.

_getframe

_getframe(*depth*=0)

Returns a frame object from the call stack. When *depth* is 0, the result is the frame of _getframe's caller. When *depth* is 1, the result is the frame of the caller's caller, and so forth. The leading _ in _getframe's name is a reminder that it's a private system function to be used only for internal specialized purposes. Debugging, covered in "Debugging" on page 461, is a typical, good reason to use _getframe.

maxint

The largest int in this version of Python (at least 2**31, that is, 2147483647). Negative ints can go down to -maxint-1, due to 2's complement notation.

modules

A dictionary whose items are the names and module objects for all loaded modules. See "Module Loading" on page 144 for more information on sys.modules.

path

A list of strings that specifies the directories and ZIP files that Python searches when looking for a module to load. See "Searching the Filesystem for a Module" on page 144 for more information on sys.path.

platform

A string that names the platform on which this program is running. Typical values are brief operating system names, such as 'sunos5', 'linux2', and 'win32'.

ps1, ps2

ps1 and ps2 specify the primary and secondary interpreter prompt strings, initially '>>> ' and '... ', respectively. These attributes exist only in interactive interpreter sessions. If you bind either attribute to a nonstring object *x*, Python prompts by calling str(*x*) on the object each time a prompt is output. This feature lets you create dynamic prompting by coding a class that defines __str__ and assigning an instance of that class to sys.ps1 and/or sys.ps2. For example, to get numbered prompts:

```
>>> import sys
>>> class Ps1(object):
...     def __init__(self):
...         self.p = 0
...     def __str__(self):
...         self.p += 1
...         return '[%d]>>> ' % self.p
...
>>> class Ps2(object):
...     def __str__(self):
...         return '[%d]... ' % sys.ps1.p
...
>>> sys.ps1 = Ps1( ); sys.ps2 = Ps2( )
[1]>>> (2 +
[1]... 2)
4
[2]>>>
```

setdefaultenco-ding

setdefaultencoding(*name*)

Sets the default codec used to encode and decode Unicode and string objects (normally 'ascii'). setdefaultencoding is meant to be called only from *sitecustomize.py* at program startup; the site module then removes this attribute from sys. You can call reload(sys) to make this attribute available again, but this is not a good programming practice. Unicode, codecs, encoding, and decoding are covered in "Unicode" on page 198. The site and sitecustomize modules are covered in "The site and sitecustomize Modules" on page 338.

setprofile	setprofile(*profilefunc*)
	Sets a global profile function, a callable object that Python then calls at each function entry and return. Profiling is covered in "Profiling" on page 480.
setrecursionlimit	setrecursionlimit(*limit*)
	Sets the limit on the depth of Python's call stack (the default is 1000). The limit prevents runaway recursion from crashing Python. Raising the limit may be necessary for programs that rely on deep recursion, but most platforms cannot support very large limits on call-stack depth. More usefully, *lowering* the limit may help you check, during testing and debugging, that your program is gracefully degrading, rather than abruptly crashing, under situations of almost-runaway recursion. See also "Recursion" on page 80 and getrecursionlimit on page 169.
settrace	settrace(*tracefunc*)
	Sets a global trace function, a callable object that Python then calls as each logical source line executes. settrace is meant to be used for implementing tools such as profilers, coverage analyzers, and debuggers. I do not cover tracing further in this book.
stdin, stdout, stderr	stdin, stdout, and stderr are predefined file objects that correspond to Python's standard input, output, and error streams. You can rebind stdout and stderr to file-like objects (objects that supply a write method that accepts a string argument) to redirect the destination of output and error messages. You can rebind stdin to a file-like object open for reading (one that supplies a readline method returning a string) to redirect the source from which built-in functions raw_input and input read. The original values are available as __stdin__, __stdout__, and __stderr__. File objects are covered in "File Objects" on page 216.
tracebacklimit	The maximum number of levels of traceback displayed for unhandled exceptions. By default, this attribute is not set (i.e., there is no limit). When sys.tracebacklimit is <=0, Python suppresses traceback and prints only the exception type and value.
version	A string that describes the Python version, build number and date, and C compiler used. version[:3] is '2.3' for Python 2.3, '2.4' for Python 2.4, and so on.

Core Built-ins

The copy Module

As discussed in "Assignment Statements" on page 47, assignment in Python does not copy the righthand side object being assigned. Rather, assignment adds a reference to the righthand side object. When you want a copy of object *x*, you can ask *x* for a copy of itself, or you can ask *x*'s type to make a new instance copied from *x*. If *x* is a list, list(*x*) returns a copy of *x*, as does *x*[:]. If *x* is a dictionary, dict(*x*) and *x*.copy() return a copy of *x*. If *x* is a set, set(*x*) and *x*.copy() return a copy of *x*. In each of these cases, my strong personal preference is for the uniform and readable idiom of calling the type, but there is no consensus on this style issue in the community of Python experts.

The copy module supplies a copy function to create and returns a copy of many types of objects. Normal copies, such as list(*x*) for a list *x* and copy.copy(*x*), are also known as *shallow* copies: when *x* has references to other objects (as items or attributes), a normal (shallow) copy of *x* has distinct references to the same objects. Sometimes, however, you need a *deep* copy, where referenced objects are copied recursively; fortunately, this requirement is rare, because a deep copy can take a lot of memory and time. Module copy supplies a deepcopy(*x*) function to create and return a deep copy.

---

copy   copy(*x*)

Creates and returns a shallow copy of *x*, for *x* of many types (copies of several types, such as modules, classes, files, frames, and other internal types, are, however, not supported). If *x* is immutable, copy.copy(*x*) may return *x* itself as an optimization. A class can customize the way copy.copy copies its instances by having a special method __copy__(self) that returns a new object, a copy of self.

---

deepcopy   deepcopy(*x*,[*memo*])

Makes a deep copy of *x* and returns it. Deep copying implies a recursive walk over a directed (not necessarily acyclic) graph of references. A special precaution is needed to preserve the graph's shape: when references to the same object are met more than once during the walk, distinct copies must not be made. Rather, references to the same copied object must be used. Consider the following simple example:

```
sublist = [1,2]
original = [sublist, sublist]
thecopy = copy.deepcopy(original)
```

original[0] is original[1] is True (i.e., the two items of list original refer to the same object). This is an important property of original and therefore must be preserved in anything that claims to be a copy of it. The semantics of copy.deepcopy are defined to ensure that thecopy[0] is thecopy[1] is also True in this case. In other words, the shapes of the graphs of references of original and

---

thecopy are the same. Avoiding repeated copying has an important beneficial side effect: it prevents infinite loops that would otherwise occur when the graph of references has cycles.

copy.deepcopy accepts a second, optional argument *memo*, which is a dictionary that maps the id( ) of objects already copied to the new objects that are their copies. *memo* is passed by all recursive calls of deepcopy to itself, and you may also explicitly pass it (normally as an originally empty dictionary) if you need to maintain such a correspondence map between the identities of originals and copies of objects.

A class can customize the way copy.deepcopy copies its instances by having a special method __deepcopy__(self, *memo*) that returns a new object, a deep copy of self. When __deepcopy__ needs to deep copy some referenced object *subobject*, it must do so by calling copy.deepcopy(*subobject, memo*). When a class has no special method __deepcopy__, copy.deepcopy on an instance of that class also tries to call special methods __getinitargs__, __getnewargs__, __getstate__, and __setstate__, which are covered in "Pickling instances" on page 282.

The collections Module

The collections module (introduced in Python 2.4) is intended to eventually supply several interesting types that are collections (i.e., containers).

deque

In Python 2.4, the collections module supplies only one type, deque, whose instances are "double-ended queues" (i.e., sequence-like containers suitable for additions and removals at both ends). Call deque with a single argument, any iterable, to obtain a new deque instance whose items are those of the iterable in the same order, or call deque without arguments to obtain a new empty deque instance. A deque instance *d* is a mutable sequence and thus can be indexed and iterated on (however, *d* cannot be sliced, only indexed one item at a time, whether for access, rebinding, or deletion). A deque instance *d* supplies the following methods.

append	*d*.append(*item*)
	Appends *item* at the right (end) of *d*.
appendleft	*d*.appendleft(*item*)
	Appends *item* at the left (start) of *d*.

clear	*d*.clear( )
	Removes all items from *d*.
extend	*d*.extend(*iterable*)
	Appends all items of *iterable* at the right (end) of *d*.
extendleft	*d*.extendleft(*item*)
	Appends all items of *iterable* at the left (start) of *d*.
pop	*d*.pop( )
	Removes and returns the last (rightmost) item from *d*. If *d* is empty, raises IndexError.
popleft	*d*.popleft( )
	Removes and returns the first (leftmost) item from *d*. If *d* is empty, raises IndexError.
rotate	*d*.rotate(*n*=1)
	Rotates *d* *n* steps to the right (if *n*<0, rotates left).

defaultdict

In Python 2.5, the collections module also supplies type defaultdict. defaultdict subclasses dict and adds one per-instance attribute, named default_factory. When an instance *d* of defaultdict has None as the value of *d*.default_factory, *d* behaves exactly like a normal dictionary. Otherwise, *d*.default_factory must be callable without arguments, and *d* behaves like a normal dictionary except when *d* is indexed with a key *k* that is not in *d*. In this specific case, the indexing *d*[*k*] calls *d*.default_factory( ), *assigns* the result as the value of *d*[*k*], and returns the result. In other words, type defaultdict behaves like the following Python-coded class:

```
class defaultdict(dict):
    def __init__(self, default_factory, *a, **k):
        dict.__init__(self, *a, **k)
        self.default_factory = default_factory
    def __getitem__(self, key):
        if key not in self and self.default_factory is not None:
            self[key] = self.default_factory()
        return dict.__getitem__(self, key)
```

As this Python equivalent implies, to instantiate defaultdict you pass it an extra first argument (before any other arguments, positional and/or named, if any, to be passed on to plain dict). That extra first argument becomes the initial value of default_factory. Other behavior of defaultdict is also essentially as implied by this Python equivalent (with the exception of str and repr, which return strings that are different from those they would return for a plain dict). You can read and rebind default_factory, other methods such as get and pop are not affected, all behavior related to the set of keys (method keys, iteration, membership test via operator in, etc.) reflects exactly the keys that are currently in the container (whether you put them there explicitly, or implicitly via indexing calling default_factory), and so forth.

A typical use of a defaultdict is as a *bag* (also known as a *multiset*), a dictionary-like object that keeps a count that corresponds to each key; for such a use, the natural choice for default_factory is int, since calling int( ) returns 0 (the correct count for a key that is not yet in the bag). For example:

```
import collections, operator

def sorted_histogram(seq):
    d = collections.defaultdict(int)
    for item in seq: d[item] += 1
    return sorted(d.iteritems, key=operator.itemgetter(1), reverse=True)
```

Called with any iterable whose items are hashable, this *sorted_histogram* function returns a list of pairs, each of the form (*item,count*), giving all distinct items in the iterable, each associated with its number of occurrences, sorted in reverse order of counts (items seen most often come first). Another typical use of defaultdict is to set default_factory to list, to make a mapping from keys to lists of values:

```
def multi_dict(items):
    d = collections.defaultdict(list)
    for key, value in items: d[key].append(value)
    return d
```

Called with any iterable whose items are pairs of the form (*key,value*), with all keys being hashable, this *multi_dict* function returns a mapping that associates each key to the lists of values that accompanied it in the iterable (if you want a pure dict result, change the last statement into return dict(d); but this is generally not necessary).

The functional Module

The functional module (introduced in Python 2.5) is intended to eventually supply several interesting functions and types to support functional programming in Python. At the time of writing, there is debate about renaming the module to functools, or perhaps introducing a separate functools module, to hold higher-order functions not strictly connected to the idioms of functional programming (in particular, built-in decorators). However, again at the time of writing, only one function has been definitively accepted for inclusion in the functional module.

partial   partial(*func*,**a*,***k*)

func is any callable. partial returns another callable *p* that is just like *func*, but with some positional and/or named parameters already bound to the values given in *a* and *k*. In other words, *p* is a *partial application* of *func*, often also known (with debatable correctness, but colorfully) as a *currying* of *func* to the given arguments (named in honor of mathematician Haskell Curry). For example, say that we have a list of numbers L and want to clip the negative ones to 0. In Python 2.5, one way to do it is:

    L = map(functional.partial(max, 0), L)

as an alternative to the lambda-using snippet:

    L = map(lambda x: max(0, x), L)

and the list-comprehension:

    L = [max(0, x) for x in L]

functional.partial really comes into its own in situations that require callbacks, such as event-driven programming for GUIs (covered in Chapter 17) and networking applications (covered in "Event-Driven Socket Programs" on page 533).

The bisect Module

The bisect module uses a bisection algorithm to keep a list in sorted order as items are inserted. bisect's operation is faster than calling a list's sort method after each insertion. This section documents the main functions supplied by bisect.

bisect   bisect(*seq*,*item*,*lo*=0,*hi*=None)

Returns the index *i* into *seq* where *item* should be inserted to keep *seq* sorted. In other words, *i* is such that each item in *seq*[:*i*] is less than or equal to *item*, and each item in *seq*[*i*:] is greater than *item*. *seq* must be a sorted sequence. For any sorted sequence *seq*, *seq*[bisect(*seq*,*y*)-1]==*y* is equivalent to *y* in *seq*, but is faster if len(*seq*) is large. You may pass optional arguments *lo* and *hi* to operate on the slice *seq*[*lo*:*hi*].

insort   insort(*seq*,*item*,*lo*=0,*hi*=None)

Like *seq*.insert(bisect(*seq*,*item*),*item*). In other words, *seq* must be a sorted mutable sequence (usually a sorted list), and insort modifies *seq* by inserting *item* at the right spot so that *seq* remains sorted. You may pass optional arguments *lo* and *hi* to operate on the slice *seq[lo:hi]*.

Module bisect also supplies functions bisect_left, bisect_right, insort_left, and insort_right for explicit control of search and insertion strategies into sequences that contain duplicates. bisect is a synonym for bisect_right, and insort is a synonym for insort_right.

The heapq Module

The heapq module uses *heap* algorithms to keep a list in "nearly sorted" order as items are inserted and extracted. heapq's operation is faster than either calling a list's sort method after each insertion or using bisect, and, for many purposes, (such as implementing "priority queues") the nearly sorted order supported by heapq may be just as useful as a fully sorted order. Module heapq supplies the following functions.

heapify	heapify(*alist*)
	Permutes *alist* as needed to make it satisfy the *heap condition*: for any *i*>=0, *alist[i]*<=*alist[2*i+1]* and *alist[i]*<=*alist[2*i+2]*(if all the indices in question are <len(*alist*)). Note that if a list satisfies the heap condition, the list's first item is the smallest (or equal-smallest) one. A sorted list satisfies the heap condition, but there are many other permutations of a list that satisfy the heap condition without requiring the list to be fully sorted. heapify runs in O(len(*alist*)) time.
heappop	heappop(*alist*)
	Removes and returns the smallest (first) item of *alist*, a list that satisfies the heap condition, and permutes some of the remaining items of *alist* to ensure the heap condition is still satisfied after the removal. heappop runs in O(len(*alist*)) time.
heappush	heappush(*alist,item*)
	Inserts the *item* in *alist*, a list that satisfies the heap condition, and permutes some items of *alist* to ensure the heap condition is still satisfied after the insertion. heappush runs in O(log(len(*alist*))) time.

heapreplace	heapreplace(*alist*,*item*)

Logically equivalent to heappop followed by heappush, similar to:

```
def heapreplace(alist, item):
    try: return heappop(alist)
    finally: heappush(alist, item)
```

heapreplace runs in O(log(len(*alist*))) time and is generally faster than the logically equivalent function just shown.

nlargest	nlargest(*n*,*seq*)

Returns a reverse-sorted list with the *n* largest items of iterable *seq* (less than *n* if *seq* has less than *n* items); like sorted(*seq*, reverse=True)[:*n*] but faster. In Python 2.5, you may also specify a key= argument, like you can for sorted.

nsmallest	nsmallest(*n*,*seq*)

Returns a sorted list with the *n* smallest items of iterable *seq* (less than *n* if *seq* has less than *n* items); like sorted(*seq*)[:*n*] but faster. In Python 2.5, you may also specify a key= argument, like you can for sorted.

The UserDict Module

The main content of the UserDict module of Python's standard library (analogous to those of now semi-obsolete modules UserList and UserString) used to be classes that emulated the behavior of standard built-in container types. Their usefulness used to be that, in the legacy object model, you could not inherit from built-in types, and what we now call the legacy object model used to be the only object model available in Python. Nowadays, you can simply subclass built-in types such as list and dict, so there isn't much point in emulating the built-in types by Python-coded classes. However, the UserDict module does contain one class that is still extremely useful.

Implementing the full interface defined as a "mapping" (i.e., the interface of a dictionary) takes a lot of programming because dictionaries have so many useful and convenient methods. The UserDict module supplies one class, DictMixin, that makes it easy for you to code classes that offer the complete mapping interface while coding a minimal number of methods: your class just needs to inherit (possibly multiply inherit) from UserDict.DictMixin. At a minimum, your class must define methods __getitem__, keys, and copy; if instances of your class are meant to be mutable, then your class must also define methods __setitem__ and __delitem__.

Optionally, for efficiency, you may also choose to define methods __contains__, __iter__, and/or iteritems; if you don't define such methods, your DictMixin superclass defines them on your behalf, but the versions you get by inheritance from DictMixin are probably substantially less efficient than ones you could define yourself on the basis of your knowledge of your class's specific concrete structure (the many other methods of the mapping interface, on the other hand, tend to get reasonably efficient implementations even just by inheritance from DictMixin, so there is generally no particular need to define them in your own class).

The optparse Module

The optparse module offers rich, powerful ways to parse the command-line *options* (a.k.a. *flags*) that the user passed upon starting your programs (by using syntax elements such as *-x* or *--foo=bar* on the command line, after your program name and before other program arguments). Instantiate (without arguments) the OptionParser class supplied by the module, populate the instance so it knows about your program's options (by calls to its add_option method), and finally call the instance's parse_args method to handle your program's command line, dealing with each option appropriately and returning the collection of option values and a list of nonoption arguments.

optparse supports many advanced ways to customize and fine-tune your program's option-parsing behavior. In most cases, you can accept optparse's reasonable defaults and use it effectively with just the two methods of class OptionParser that I cover here (omitting many advanced options of these methods, which you do not normally need). For all of the powerful and complex details, consult Python's online docs.

An OptionParser instance *p* supplies the following methods.

add_option	`p.add_option(opt_str,*opt_strs,**kw)`

The positional arguments specify the *option strings*, i.e., the strings that the user passes as part of your program's command line to set this option. Each argument can be a short-form option string (a string starting with a single dash [hyphen] followed by a single letter or digit) or a long-form option string (a string starting with two dashes followed by an identifier that may also contain dashes). You normally pass exactly one short-form and one long-form option string, but it's also okay to pass multiple "synonyms," or just short forms, or just long forms.

The named (optional) arguments (*kw*) are where the action is... literally, too, because the most important argument is the named one, action, with a default value of 'store', which specifies that the value associated with the option string gets bound as an attribute of the options-object, which method parse_args returns.

'store' implies that if the user who starts your program supplies this option at all, then the user must also supply a value associated with this option. If the user does not pass the option at all, the associated attribute of the options-object gets set to None. To use a different default value, include in the call to add_option a named argument such as default='foo' (this uses 'foo' as the default value for the attribute). If the user does pass the option, it must be followed by a value to associate with it. The value can be the immediately following command-line argument, or can be juxtaposed to the option string as part of the same argument—just concatenated, for a short-form option string, or concatenated with an = in between for a long-form option string. Otherwise, parse_args will emit an error message and raise a SystemExit exception.

The name of the option-object's attribute associated with an option is the identifier in its first long-form option string (with dashes, if any, replaced by underscores), or the single letter in the first short-form option string if the option has no long form. To use a different name for the attribute, include in the call to add_option a named argument such as dest='foo' (this uses name 'foo' for the attribute associated to this option).

An option's value is normally a string, but you can include in the call to add_option a named argument such as type='int' (meaning that the value associated with this option must be a decimal representation of an integer and is stored as an int). Acceptable values for named argument type are string, int, long, choice, float, and complex. When you pass type='choice', you must also pass another named argument, choices=..., whose value is a list of strings among which the user must choose one as the value associated with this option (if the user passes this option).

Other useful values of action do not require (nor allow) the user to pass a value associated with the option. 'store_const' stores a constant value in the attribute associated with this option (if the user passes the option at all); when you pass action='store_const', you must also pass another named argument const=..., whose value is the constant to store in the attribute. As a convenience, action can also be 'store_true' or 'store_false', equivalent to 'store_const' with const=True or False, respectively. action='count' increments (by 1 each time the user passes the option) the attribute associated with the option, which is intrinsically an integer with an initial value of 0.

Summarizing, the most frequently used named arguments to add_option are:

action
> Action to take when the user passes this option; can be 'store', 'store_const', 'store_true', 'store_false', 'count', or one of several advanced possibilities we did not cover, such as 'callback', 'append', 'help', 'version'.

choices
> List of strings allowed as the option's value, when action='store' and type='choice'.

const
> Constant to store when the user passes this option, when action='store_const'.

default
> Value to store when the user does not pass this option (default is None).

dest
> Name of the attribute associated with this option (default is the identifier of the first long-form option string, or the letter of the first short-form option string when there are no long-form option strings).

help
> Text to emit to explain this option if the user passes option '-h' or '–help'.

type
> Type of the value associated with this option can be 'string', 'int', 'long', 'choice', 'float', or 'complex'.

optparse also allows many highly advanced customization possibilities, including the ability to add other possible actions and types, but I do not cover them in this book.

parse_args   *p*.parse_args(*args*=sys.argv[1:])

Parses the list of strings that you pass as *args* (by default, the command-line arguments of your programs) and returns a pair *options,arguments*. *options* is an options-object with attributes set according to your program's available options and the list of arguments that parse_args just parsed; *arguments* is a (possibly empty) list of the strings that are the non-option-related arguments among those in *args*.

If parse_args finds any parsing errors (including unknown options, no value associated to an option that needs one, some value associated to an option that does not take one, invalid types, etc.), parse_args writes an error message to sys.stderr and raises SystemExit. If parse_args finds a '-h' or '–help' among the options, it writes a help message to sys.stdout and raises SystemExit.

parse_args also offers possibilities for advanced customization, which I do not cover in this book.

Here is a simple, toy-level example of using optparse. Write the following code into a file named *hello.py*:

```
#!/usr/bin/python
import optparse

def main():
    p = optparse.OptionParser()
    p.add_option('--verbose', '-v', action='store_true')
    p.add_option('--name', '-n', default="world")
```

```
        options, arguments = p.parse_args()
        if options.verbose: print "Greetings and
    salutations,",
        else: print "Hello",
        print '%s!' % options.name

if __name__ == '__main__':
    main()
```

The shebang line at the start of the script (as covered in "Running Python Programs" on page 28) helps mostly on Unix-like systems (although it does no harm in Windows), where it must indicate the complete path to your installation of the *python* interpreter. As also covered in "Running Python Programs" on page 28, you'll probably also want to **chmod +x hello.py** (again, on Unix-like systems) to make the script directly executable (and, on Windows, you can obtain the same effect if the Python distribution you installed associated the extension *.py* with the Python interpreter in the Windows Registry, as most distributions do). Now you can run this script at any command-line prompt, and optparse takes care of reading the command-line options you pass, and reacting appropriately to them. For example, a short command-line session on a Unix-like system, with *hello.py* in the current directory, could go somewhat like the following:

```
$ ./hello.py
Hello world!
$ ./hello.py --help .
usage: hello.py [options]

options:
  -h, --help            show this help message and exit
  -v, --verbose
  -nNAME, --name=NAME
$ ./hello.py -v --name=Alex
Greetings and salutations, Alex!
$ python hello.py -n
usage: hello.py [options]

hello.py: error: -n option requires an argument
$ python hello.py -nthere
Hello there!
```

The last two examples show that (assuming, of course, that the Python interpreter is in your PATH) you also can run the script by passing it to Python explicitly, with options and arguments for the script placed after the script's filename.

The itertools Module

The itertools module offers many powerful, high-performance building blocks to build or manipulate iterator objects. Manipulating iterators is often better than manipulating lists thanks to iterators' intrinsic "lazy evaluation" approach: items of an iterator are produced one at a time, as needed, while all the items of a list (or other sequence) must exist in memory at the same time (this "lazy" approach even makes it feasible to build and manipulate unbounded iterators, while all lists must always have finite numbers of items).

This section documents the most frequently used attributes of module itertools; each of them is an iterator type, which you can call to get an instance of the type in question.

chain	chain(*iterables)

Builds and returns an iterator whose items are all those from the first iterable passed, followed by all those from the second iterable passed, and so on until the end of the last iterable passed, just like the generator expression:

```
(item for iterable in iterables for item in iterable)
```

count	count(firstval=0)

Builds and returns an unbounded iterator whose items are consecutive integers starting from firstval, just like the generator:

```
def count(firstval=0):
    while True:
        yield firstval
        firstval += 1
```

cycle	count(iterable)

Builds and returns an unbounded iterator whose items are the items of iterable, endlessly repeating the items from the beginning each time the cycle reaches the end, just like the generator:

```
def cycle(iterable):
    buffer = []
    for item in iterable:
        yield item
        buffer.append(item)
    while True:
        for item in buffer: yield item
```

ifilter	ifilter(func,iterable)

Builds and returns an iterator whose items are those items of iterable for which func is true, just like the generator expression:

```
(item for item in iterable if func(item))
```

func can be any callable object that accepts a single argument, or None. When *func* is None, ifilter tests for true items, just like the generator expression:

```
(item for item in iterable if item)
```

imap

imap(*func*,**iterables*)

Builds and returns an iterator whose items are the results of *func*, called with one corresponding argument from each of the *iterables*; stops when the shortest of the *iterables* is exhausted. Just like the generator.

```
def imap(func,*iterables):
    next_items = [iter(x).next for x in iterables]
    while True: yield func(*(next() for next in
next_items))
```

islice

islice(*iterable*[,*start*],*stop*[,*step*])

Builds and returns an iterator whose items are items of *iterable*, skipping the first *start* ones (default is 0) until the *stop*th one excluded, and advancing by steps of *step* (default is 1) at a time. All arguments must be nonnegative integers, and *step* must be >0. Apart from checks and optionality of the arguments, just like the generator.

```
def islice(iterable,start,stop,step=1):
    en = enumerate(iterable)
    for n, item in en:
        if n>=start: break
    while n<stop:
        yield item
        for x in range(step): n, item = en.next()
```

izip

izip(**iterables*)

Builds and returns an iterator whose items are tuples with one corresponding item from each of the *iterables*; stops when the shortest of the *iterables* is exhausted. Just like imap(tuple,**iterables*).

repeat

repeat(*item*[,*times*])

Builds and returns an iterator whose *times* items are all the object *item*, just like the generator expression:

```
(item for x in xrange(times))
```

When *times* is absent, the iterator is unbound, with a potentially infinite number of items, which are all the object *item*. Just like the generator.

```
def repeat_unbounded(item):
    while True: yield item
```

tee

tee(*iterable*,*n=2*)

Builds and returns a tuple of *n* independent iterators, each of whom has items that are the same as the items of *iterable*. While the returned iterators are independent from each other, they are *not* independent from *iterable*; therefore, you must avoid altering object *iterable* in any way, as long as you're still using any of the returned iterators (this caveat is roughly the same as for the result of iter(*iterable*)). New in 2.4.

Python's online documentation has abundant examples and explanations about each of these types of module itertools, as well as about other types of itertools that I do not cover in this book. One surprising fact is the sheer speed of itertools types. To take a trivial example, consider repeating some action 10 times. On my laptop:

```
for x in itertools.repeat(0, 10): pass
```

turns out to be about 10 percent faster than the second-fastest alternative:

```
for x in xrange(10): pass
```

and almost twice as fast as using range instead of xrange in this case.

9

Strings and Regular Expressions

Python supports plain and Unicode strings extensively, with statements, operators, built-in functions, methods, and dedicated modules. This chapter covers the methods of string objects, in "Methods of String Objects" on page 186; string formatting, in "String Formatting" on page 193; modules string (in "The string Module" on page 191), pprint (in "The pprint Module" on page 197), and repr (in "The repr Module" on page 198); and issues related to Unicode strings, in "Unicode" on page 198.

Regular expressions let you specify pattern strings and allow searches and substitutions. Regular expressions are not easy to master, but they can be a powerful tool for processing text. Python offers rich regular expression functionality through the built-in re module, documented in "Regular Expressions and the re Module" on page 201.

Methods of String Objects

Plain and Unicode strings are immutable sequences, as covered in "Strings" on page 55. All immutable-sequence operations (repetition, concatenation, indexing, slicing) apply to strings. A string object *s* also supplies several nonmutating methods, as documented in this section. Unless otherwise noted, each method returns a plain string when *s* is a plain string, or a Unicode string when *s* is a Unicode string. Terms such as "letters," "whitespace," and so on, refer to the corresponding attributes of the string module, covered in "The string Module" on page 191. See also "Locale Sensitivity" on page 192.

---

capitalize   `s.capitalize()`

Returns a copy of *s* where the first character, if a letter, is uppercase, and all other letters, if any, are lowercase.

center	`s.center(n, fillchar=' ')`
	Returns a string of length max(len(s),n), with a copy of s in the central part, surrounded by equal numbers of copies of character *fillchar* on both sides (e.g., `'ciao'.center(2)` is `'ciao'` and `'x'.center(4,'_')` is `'_x__'`).
count	`s.count(sub,start=0,end=sys.maxint)`
	Returns the number of nonoverlapping occurrences of substring *sub* in s[*start*:*end*].
encode	`s.encode(codec=None,errors='strict')`
	Returns a plain string obtained from s with the given codec and error handling. See "Unicode" on page 198 for more details.
endswith	`s.endswith(suffix,start=0,end=sys.maxint)`
	Returns True when s[*start*:*end*] ends with *suffix*; otherwise, False.
expandtabs	`s.expandtabs(tabsize=8)`
	Returns a copy of s where each tab character is changed into one or more spaces, with tab stops every *tabsize* characters.
find	`s.find(sub,start=0,end=sys.maxint)`
	Returns the lowest index in s where substring *sub* is found, such that *sub* is entirely contained in s[*start*:*end*]. For example, `'banana'.find('na')` is 2, as is `'banana'.find('na',1)`, while `'banana'.find('na',3)` is 4, as is `'banana'.find('na',-2)`. find returns -1 if *sub* is not found.
index	`s.index(sub,start=0,end=sys.maxint)`
	Like find, but raises ValueError when *sub* is not found.
isalnum	`s.isalnum()`
	Returns True when len(s) is greater than 0 and all characters in s are letters or decimal digits. When s is empty, or when at least one character of s is neither a letter nor a decimal digit, isalnum returns False.

isalpha   `s.isalpha( )`

Returns True when `len(s)` is greater than 0 and all characters in *s* are letters. When *s* is empty, or when at least one character of *s* is not a letter, `isalpha` returns False.

isdigit   `s.isdigit( )`

Returns True when `len(s)` is greater than 0 and all characters in *s* are digits. When *s* is empty, or when at least one character of *s* is not a digit, `isdigit` returns False.

islower   `s.islower( )`

Returns True when all letters in *s* are lowercase. When *s* contains no letters, or when at least one letter of *s* is uppercase, `islower` returns False.

isspace   `s.isspace( )`

Returns True when `len(s)` is greater than 0 and all characters in *s* are whitespace. When *s* is empty, or when at least one character of *s* is not whitespace, `isspace` returns False.

istitle   `s.istitle( )`

Returns True when letters in *s* are *titlecase*: a capital letter at the start of each contiguous sequence of letters, all other letters lower-case (e.g., `'King Lear'.istitle( )` is True). When *s* contains no letters, or when at least one letter of *s* violates the titlecase condition, `istitle` returns False (e.g., `'1900'.istitle( )` and `'Troilus and Cressida'.istitle( )` are False).

isupper   `s.isupper( )`

Returns True when all letters in *s* are uppercase. When *s* contains no letters, or when at least one letter of *s* is lowercase, `isupper` returns False.

join   `s.join(seq)`

Returns the string obtained by concatenating the items of *seq*, which must be a sequence or other iterable whose items are strings, and interposing a copy of *s* between each pair of items (e.g., `''.join(str(x) for x in range(7))` is `'0123456'` and `'x'.join('aeiou')` is `'axexixoxu'`).

ljust	`s.ljust(n,fillchar=' ')`
	Returns a string of length max(len(s),n), with a copy of s at the start, followed by zero or more trailing copies of character *fillchar*.
lower	`s.lower( )`
	Returns a copy of s with all letters, if any, converted to lowercase.
lstrip	`s.lstrip(x=string.whitespace)`
	Returns a copy of s, removing leading characters that are found in string *x*.
replace	`s.replace(old,new,maxsplit=sys.maxint)`
	Returns a copy of s with the first *maxsplit* (or fewer, if there are fewer) nonoverlapping occurrences of substring *old* replaced by string *new* (e.g., 'banana'.replace('a','e',2) is 'benena').
rfind	`s.rfind(sub,start=0,end=sys.maxint)`
	Returns the highest index in s where substring *sub* is found, such that *sub* is entirely contained in s[*start:end*]. rfind returns -1 if *sub* is not found.
rindex	`s.rindex(sub,start=0,end=sys.maxint)`
	Like rfind, but raises ValueError if *sub* is not found.
rjust	`s.rjust(n,fillchar=' ')`
	Returns a string of length max(len(s),n), with a copy of s at the end, preceded by zero or more leading copies of character *fillchar*.
rstrip	`s.rstrip(x=string.whitespace)`
	Returns a copy of s, removing leading characters that are found in string *x*.
split	`s.split(sep=None,maxsplit=sys.maxint)`
	Returns a list *L* of up to *maxsplit*+1 strings. Each item of *L* is a "word" from s, where string *sep* separates words. When s has more than *maxsplit* words, the last item of *L* is the substring of s that follows the first *maxsplit* words. When *sep* is None, any string

of whitespace separates words (e.g., 'four score and seven years ago'.split(None,3) is ['four','score','and','seven years ago']).

Note the difference between splitting on None (any string of whitespace is a separator) and splitting on ' ' (each single space character, *not* other whitespace such as tabs and newlines, and *not* strings, is a separator). For example:

```
>>> x = 'a  b'  # two spaces between a and b
>>> x.split( )
['a', 'b']
>>> x.split(' ')
['a', '', 'b']
```

In the first case, the two-spaces string in the middle is a single separator; in the second case, each single space is a separator so that there is an empty string between the spaces.

---

splitlines   s.splitlines(*keepends*=False)

Like s.split('\n'). When *keepends* is true, however, the trailing '\n' is included in each item of the resulting list.

---

startswith   s.startswith(*prefix,start*=0,*end*=sys.maxint)

Returns True when s[*start:end*] starts with *prefix*; otherwise, False.

---

strip   s.strip(*x*=string.whitespace)

Returns a copy of s, removing both leading and trailing characters that are found in string *x*.

---

swapcase   s.swapcase( )

Returns a copy of s with all uppercase letters converted to lowercase and vice versa.

---

title   s.title( )

Returns a copy of s transformed to titlecase: a capital letter at the start of each contiguous sequence of letters, with all other letters, if any, lowercase.

---

translate   s.translate(*table, deletechars*='') when s is a plain string
s.translate(*table*) when s is a unicode string

When s is a plain string, returns a copy of s where all characters occurring in string *deletechars* are removed, and the remaining characters are mapped through translation-table *table*. *table* must

---

be a plain string of length 256, and is most often built using function `string.maketrans`, covered in `maketrans` on page 192.

When *s* is a Unicode string, returns a copy of *s* where characters found in *table* are translated or deleted. *table* is a dict whose keys are Unicode ordinals; values are Unicode ordinals, Unicode strings, or None (to delete)—for example:

```
u'banna'.translate({ord('a'):None,ord('n'):u'ze'}) is
u'bzeze'
```

upper   `s.upper()`

Returns a copy of *s* with all letters, if any, converted to uppercase.

The string Module

The `string` module supplies functions that duplicate each method of string objects, as covered in "Methods of String Objects" on page 186. Each function takes the (plain or Unicode) string object as its first argument. Module `string` also supplies several useful plain-string attributes:

ascii_letters
> The string `ascii_lowercase+ascii_uppercase`

ascii_lowercase
> The string `'abcdefghijklmnopqrstuvwxyz'`

ascii_uppercase
> The string `'ABCDEFGHIJKLMNOPQRSTUVWXYZ'`

digits
> The string `'0123456789'`

hexdigits
> The string `'0123456789abcdefABCDEF'`

letters
> The string `lowercase+uppercase`

lowercase
> A string containing all characters that are deemed lowercase letters: at least `'abcdefghijklmnopqrstuvwxyz'`, but more letters (e.g., accented ones) may be present, depending on the active locale

octdigits
> The string `'01234567'`

punctuation
> The string `'!"#$%&\'()*+,-./:;<=>?@[\\]^_'{|}~'` (i.e., all ASCII characters that are deemed punctuation characters in the `'C'` locale; does not depend on which locale is active)

Strings

printable

> The string of those characters that are deemed printable (i.e., digits, letters, punctuation, and whitespace)

uppercase

> A string containing all characters that are deemed uppercase letters: at least `'ABCDEFGHIJKLMNOPQRSTUVWXYZ'`, but more letters (e.g., accented ones) may be present, depending on the active locale

whitespace

> A string containing all characters that are deemed whitespace: at least space, tab, linefeed, and carriage return, but more characters (e.g., certain control characters) may be present, depending on the active locale

You should not rebind these attributes, since other parts of the Python library may rely on them and the effects of rebinding them are undefined.

Module `string` also supplies class `Template`, covered in "Template Strings" on page 196.

Locale Sensitivity

The `locale` module is covered in "The locale Module" on page 269. Locale setting affects some attributes of module `string` (`letters`, `lowercase`, `uppercase`, `whitespace`). Through these attributes, locale setting also affects functions of module `string` and methods of plain-string objects that deal with classification of characters as letters, and conversion between upper- and lowercase, such as `capitalize`, `isalnum`, and `isalpha`. The corresponding methods of Unicode strings are not affected by locale setting.

The maketrans Function

The method `translate` of plain strings, covered in `translate` on page 190, takes as its first argument a plain string of length 256 to use as a translation table. The easiest way to build translation tables is to use the `maketrans` function supplied by module `string`.

---

maketrans   maketrans(*from,onto*)

> Returns a translation table—that is, a plain string of length 256 that provides a mapping from characters in ascending ASCII order to another set of characters. *from* and *onto* must be plain strings, with len(*from*) equal to len(*onto*). Each character in *from* is mapped to the character at the corresponding position in *onto*. Each character not listed in *from* is mapped to itself. To get an "identity" table, call maketrans('',''').
>
> With the `translate` string method, you can delete characters as well as translate them. When you use `translate` just to delete characters, the first argument you pass to `translate` should be the

---

identity table. Here's an example of using the maketrans function and the string method translate to delete vowels:

```
import string
identity = string.maketrans('','')
print 'some string'.translate(identity,'aeiou')
# prints: sm strng
```

The Unicode equivalent of this would be:

```
no_vowels = dict.fromkeys(ord(x) for x in 'aeiou')
print u'some string'.translate(no_vowels)    # prints: sm
strng
```

Here are examples of turning all other vowels into a's and also deleting s's:

```
intoas = string.maketrans('eiou','aaaa')
print 'some string'.translate(intoas)                    #
prints: sama strang
print 'some string'.translate(intoas,'s')                #
prints: ama trang
```

The Unicode equivalent of this would be:

```
intoas = dict.fromkeys((ord(x) for x in 'eiou'), 'a')
print u'some string'.translate(intoas)                   #
prints: sama strang
intoas_nos = dict(intoas, s='None')
print u'some string'.translate(intoas_nos)               #
prints: ama trang
```

String Formatting

In Python, a string-formatting expression has the syntax:

format % values

where *format* is a plain or Unicode string containing format specifiers and *values* is any single object or a collection of objects in a tuple or dictionary. Python's string-formatting operator has roughly the same set of features as the C language's printf and operates in a similar way. Each format specifier is a substring of *format* that starts with a percent sign (%) and ends with one of the conversion characters shown in Table 9-1.

Table 9-1. String-formatting conversion characters

Character	Output format	Notes
d, i	Signed decimal integer	Value must be number.
u	Unsigned decimal integer	Value must be number.
o	Unsigned octal integer	Value must be number.
x	Unsigned hexadecimal integer (lowercase letters)	Value must be number.
X	Unsigned hexadecimal integer (uppercase letters)	Value must be number.

Table 9-1. String-formatting conversion characters (continued)

Character	Output format	Notes
e	Floating-point value in exponential form (lowercase e for exponent)	Value must be number.
E	Floating-point value in exponential form (uppercase E for exponent)	Value must be number.
f, F	Floating-point value in decimal form	Value must be number.
g, G	Like e or E when *exp* is >=4 or < precision; otherwise, like f or F	*exp* is the exponent of the number being converted.
c	Single character	Value can be integer or single-character string.
r	String	Converts any value with repr.
s	String	Converts any value with str.
%	Literal % character	Consumes no value.

Between the % and the conversion character, you can specify a number of optional modifiers, as we'll discuss shortly.

The result of a formatting expression is a string that is a copy of *format* where each format specifier is replaced by the corresponding item of *values* converted to a string according to the specifier. Here are some simple examples:

```
x = 42
y = 3.14
z = "george"
print 'result = %d' % x                 # prints: result = 42
print 'answers are: %d %f' % (x,y)       # prints: answers are: 42 3.14
print 'hello %s' % z                     # prints: hello george
```

Format Specifier Syntax

A format specifier can include many modifiers to control how the corresponding item in *values* is converted to a string. The components of a format specifier, in order, are:

- The mandatory leading % character that marks the start of the specifier
- An optional item name in parentheses (e.g., (*name*))
- Zero or more optional conversion flags:

  #

      The conversion uses an alternate form (if any exists for its type).

  0

      The conversion is zero-padded.

  -

      The conversion is left-justified.

  A space

      A space is placed before a positive number.

  +

      The numeric sign (+ or -) is placed before any numeric conversion.

- An optional minimum width of the conversion: one or more digits, or an asterisk (*), meaning that the width is taken from the next item in *values*
- An optional precision for the conversion: a dot (.) followed by zero or more digits, or by a *, meaning that the precision is taken from the next item in *values*
- A mandatory conversion type from Table 9-1

Item names must be given either in all format specifiers in *format* or in none of them. When item names are given, *values* must be a mapping (often the dictionary of a namespace, e.g., *vars*( )), and each item name is a key in *values*. In other words, each format specifier corresponds to the item in *values* keyed by the specifier's item name. When item names are given, you cannot use * in any format specifier.

When item names are absent, *values* must be a tuple; when there is just one item, *values* may be the item itself (of any type *except* tuple) instead of a singleton tuple. Each format specifier corresponds to an item in *values* by position, and *values* must have exactly as many items as *format* has specifiers (plus one extra for each width or precision given by *). When the width or precision component of a specifier is given by *, the * consumes one item in *values*, which must be an integer and is taken as the number of characters to use as width or precision of the conversion.

Common String-Formatting Idioms

It is quite common for *format* to contain several occurrences of %s and for *values* to be a tuple with exactly as many items as *format* has occurrences of %s. The result is a copy of *format* where each %s is replaced with str applied to the corresponding item of *values*. For example:

```
'%s+%s is %s'%(23,45,23+45)          # results in: '23+45 is 68'
```

You can think of %s as a fast and concise way to put together a few values, converted to string form, into a larger string. For example:

```
oneway = 'x' + str(j) + 'y' + str(j) + 'z'
another = 'x%sy%sz' % (j, j)
```

After this code is executed, variables oneway and another will always be equal, but the computation of another, done via string formatting, is measurably faster. Which way is clearer and simpler is a matter of habit. I urge you to get used to the string-formatting idiom, and soon it will come to look simpler and clearer to you.

Besides %s, other reasonably common format specifiers are those used to format floating-point values: %f for decimal formatting, %e for exponential formatting, and %g for either decimal or exponential formatting, depending on the number's magnitude. When formatting floating-point values, you normally specify width and/or precision modifiers. A width modifier is a number right after the % that gives the minimum width for the resulting conversion; you generally use a width modifier if you're formatting a table for display in a fixed-width font. A precision modifier is a number following a dot (.) just before the conversion type letter; you generally use a precision modifier in order to fix the number of decimal digits displayed for a number to avoid giving a misleading impression of excessive precision and wasting display space. For example:

```
'%.2f'%(1/3.0)                          # results in: '0.33'
'%s'%(1/3.0)                            # results in: '0.333333333333'
```

With %s, you cannot specify how many digits to display after the decimal point. It is important to avoid giving a mistaken impression of high precision when your numeric results are accurate only to a few digits. Showing many digits may mislead people examining the results into believing the results are more accurate than is the case.

Template Strings

Python 2.4 introduced the class string.Template, which in some simple cases affords handier formatting facilities than strings' % operator.

Template	class Template(*template*) Builds and returns a new instance *t* of Template, with read-only attribute *t*.template set to the string argument *template*. An instance *t* of Template supplies the following two methods.
safe_substitute	*t*.safe_substitute(*mapping*,**k*) Returns a string that is a copy of *t*.template with: • Each occurrence of $$ changed into a single $ • Each occurrence of $*identifier* or ${*identifier* } (where *identifier* is any valid Python identifier that is a key into *mapping* and/or is one of the argument names in *k*) changed into *mapping*.update(**k*)[*identifier*] Occurrences of $*identifier* or ${*identifier* } (where *identifier* is not a valid Python identifier, or not a key into *mapping* nor one of the argument names in *k*) are just copied from *t*.template into the string result of safe_substitute.
substitute	*t*.substitute(*mapping*,**k*) Like safe_substitute, except that if there are any occurrences of $*identifier* or ${*identifier* } (where *identifier* is not a valid Python identifier, or not a key into *mapping* nor one of the argument names in *k*), substitute raises a KeyError exception. For more advanced (and rarely needed) uses of string.Template, see all the details at *http://docs.python.org/lib/module-string.html*.

Text Wrapping and Filling

The textwrap module supplies a class and a few functions to format a string by breaking it into lines of a given maximum length. To fine-tune the filling and wrapping, you can instantiate the TextWrapper class supplied by module textwrap and apply detailed control. Most of the time, however, one of the two main functions exposed by module textwrap suffices.

wrap

wrap(*s*,*width* =70)

Returns a list of strings (without terminating newlines), each of which is no longer than *width* characters, and which (put back together with whitespaces) equal *s*. wrap also supports other named arguments (equivalent to attributes of instances of class TextWrapper); for such advanced uses, see *http://docs.python.org/lib/module-textwrap.html*.

fill

fill(*s*,*width* =70)

Returns a single multiline string that is exactly equal to '\n'. join(fill(*s*,*width*)).

The pprint Module

The pprint module pretty-prints complicated data structures, with formatting that may be more readable than that supplied by built-in function repr (covered in repr on page 166). To fine-tune the formatting, you can instantiate the PrettyPrinter class supplied by module pprint and apply detailed control, helped by auxiliary functions also supplied by module pprint. Most of the time, however, one of the two main functions exposed by module pprint suffices.

pformat

pformat(*obj*)

Returns a string representing the pretty-printing of *obj*.

pprint

pprint(*obj*,*stream*=sys.stdout)

Outputs the pretty-printing of *obj* to file object *stream*, with a terminating newline.

The following statements are the same:

```
print pprint.pformat(x)
pprint.pprint(x)
```

Either of these constructs will be roughly the same as print *x* in many cases, such as when the string representation of *x* fits within one line. However, with something like *x*=range(30), print *x* displays *x* in two lines, breaking at an arbitrary point, while using module pprint displays *x* over 30 lines, one line per item. You can use module pprint when you prefer the module's specific display effects to the ones of normal string representation.

The repr Module

The repr module supplies an alternative to the built-in function repr (covered in repr on page 198), with limits on length for the representation string. To fine-tune the length limits, you can instantiate or subclass the Repr class supplied by module repr and apply detailed control. Most of the time, however, the main function exposed by module repr suffices.

repr	repr(*obj*)
	Returns a string representing *obj*, with sensible limits on length.

Unicode

Plain strings are converted into Unicode strings either explicitly, with the unicode built-in, or implicitly, when you pass a plain string to a function that expects Unicode. In either case, the conversion is done by an auxiliary object known as a *codec* (for *co*der-*dec*oder). A codec can also convert Unicode strings to plain strings, either explicitly, with the encode method of Unicode strings, or implicitly.

To identify a codec, pass the codec name to unicode or encode. When you pass no codec name, and for implicit conversion, Python uses a default encoding, normally 'ascii'. You can change the default encoding in the startup phase of a Python program, as covered in "The site and sitecustomize Modules" on page 338; see also setdefaultencoding on page 170. However, such a change is not a good idea for most "serious" Python code: it might too easily interfere with code in the standard Python libraries or third-party modules, written to expect the normal 'ascii'.

Every conversion has a parameter *errors*, a string specifying how conversion errors are to be handled. The default is 'strict', meaning any error raises an exception. When *errors* is 'replace', the conversion replaces each character that causes an error with '?' in a plain-string result and with u'\ufffd' in a Unicode result. When *errors* is 'ignore', the conversion silently skips characters that cause errors. When *errors* is 'xmlcharrefreplace', the conversion replaces each character that causes an error with the XML character reference representation of that character in the result. You may also code your own function to implement a conversion-error-handling strategy and register it under an appropriate name by calling codecs.register_error.

The codecs Module

The mapping of codec names to codec objects is handled by the codecs module. This module also lets you develop your own codec objects and register them so that they can be looked up by name, just like built-in codecs. Module codecs also lets you look up any codec explicitly, obtaining the functions the codec uses for encoding and decoding, as well as factory functions to wrap file-like objects. Such advanced facilities of module codecs are rarely used, and are not covered further in this book.

The codecs module, together with the encodings package of the standard Python library, supplies built-in codecs useful to Python developers dealing with internationalization issues. Python comes with over 100 codecs; a list of these codecs, with a brief explanation of each, is at *http://docs.python.org/lib/standard-encodings.html*. Any supplied codec can be installed as the site-wide default by module sitecustomize, but the preferred usage is to always specify the codec by name whenever you are converting explicitly between plain and Unicode strings. The codec installed by default is 'ascii', which accepts only characters with codes between 0 and 127, the 7-bit range of the American Standard Code for Information Interchange (ASCII) that is common to almost all encodings. A popular codec is 'latin-1', a fast, built-in implementation of the ISO 8859-1 encoding that offers a one-byte-per-character encoding of all special characters needed for Western European languages.

The codecs module also supplies codecs implemented in Python for most ISO 8859 encodings, with codec names from 'iso8859-1' to 'iso8859-15'. On Windows systems only, the codec named 'mbcs' wraps the platform's multibyte character set conversion procedures. Many codecs specifically support Asian languages. Module codecs also supplies several standard code pages (codec names from 'cp037' to 'cp1258'), Mac-specific encodings (codec names from 'mac-cyrillic' to 'mac-turkish'), and Unicode standard encodings 'utf-8' and 'utf-16' (the latter also has specific big-endian and little-endian variants: 'utf-16-be' and 'utf-16-le'). For use with UTF-16, module codecs also supplies attributes BOM_BE and BOM_LE, byte-order marks for big-endian and little-endian machines, respectively, and BOM, the byte-order mark for the current platform.

Module codecs also supplies a function to let you register your own conversion-error-handling functions.

---

register_error   register_error(*name*,*func*)

> *name* must be a string. *func* must be callable with one argument *e* that's an instance of exception UnicodeDecodeError and must return a tuple with two items: the Unicode string to insert in the converted-string result and the index from which to continue the conversion (the latter is normally *e*.end). The function's body can use *e*.encoding, the name of the codec of this conversion, and *e*.object[*e*.start:*e*.end], the substring that caused the conversion error.

Module codecs also supplies two functions to ease dealing with files of encoded text.

EncodedFile   EncodedFile(*file*,*datacodec*,*filecodec*=None,*errors*='strict')

Wraps the file-like object *file*, returning a file-like object *ef* that implicitly and transparently applies the given encodings to all data read from or written to the file. When you write a string *s* to *ef*, *ef* first decodes *s* with the codec named by *datacodec*, then encodes the result with the codec named by *filecodec* and writes it to *file*. When you read a string, *ef* applies *filecodec* first, then *datacodec*. When *filecodec* is None, *ef* uses *datacodec* for both steps in either direction.

For example, if you want to write strings that are encoded in latin-1 to sys.stdout and have the strings come out in utf-8, use the following:

```
import sys, codecs
sys.stdout = codecs.EncodedFile(sys.stdout,'latin-1','utf-8')
```

open   open(*filename*,*mode*='rb',*encoding*=None,*errors*='strict', *buffering*=1)

Uses the built-in function open (covered in "Creating a File Object with open" on page 216) to supply a file-like object that accepts and/or provides Unicode strings to/from Python client code, while the underlying file can either be in Unicode (when *encoding* is None) or use the codec named by *encoding*. For example, if you want to write Unicode strings to file *uni.txt* and have the strings implicitly encoded as latin-1 in the file, replacing with '?' any character that cannot be encoded in Latin-1, use the following:

```
import codecs
flout = codecs.open('uni.txt','w','latin-1','replace')

# now you can write Unicode strings directly to flout
flout.write(u'élève')
flout.close( )
```

The unicodedata Module

The unicodedata module supplies easy access to the Unicode Character Database. Given any Unicode character, you can use functions supplied by module unicodedata to obtain the character's Unicode category, official name (if any), and other, more exotic information. You can also look up the Unicode character (if any) that corresponds to a given official name. Such advanced facilities are rarely needed, and are not covered further in this book.

Regular Expressions and the re Module

A *regular expression* (RE) is a string that represents a pattern. With RE function-ality, you can check any string with the pattern and see if any part of the string matches the pattern.

The re module supplies Python's RE functionality. The compile function builds a RE object from a pattern string and optional flags. The methods of a RE object look for matches of the RE in a string or perform substitutions. Module re also exposes functions equivalent to a RE's methods, but with the RE's pattern string as the first argument.

REs can be difficult to master, and this book does not purport to teach them; I cover only the ways in which you can use REs in Python. For general coverage of REs, I recommend the book *Mastering Regular Expressions*, by Jeffrey Friedl (O'Reilly). Friedl's book offers thorough coverage of REs at both tutorial and advanced levels. Many tutorials and references on REs can also be found online.

Pattern-String Syntax

The pattern string representing a regular expression follows a specific syntax:

- Alphabetic and numeric characters stand for themselves. A RE whose pattern is a string of letters and digits matches the same string.
- Many alphanumeric characters acquire special meaning in a pattern when they are preceded by a backslash (\).
- Punctuation works the other way around: self-matching when escaped, spe-cial meaning when unescaped.
- The backslash character is matched by a repeated backslash (i.e., the pattern \\).

Since RE patterns often contain backslashes, you often specify them using raw-string syntax (covered in "Strings" on page 40). Pattern elements (e.g., r'\t', equivalent to the non-raw string literal '\\t') do match the corresponding special characters (e.g., the tab character '\t'). Therefore, you can use raw-string syntax even when you do need a literal match for some such special character.

Table 9-2 lists the special elements in RE pattern syntax. The exact meanings of some pattern elements change when you use optional flags, together with the pattern string, to build the RE object. The optional flags are covered in "Optional Flags" on page 205.

Table 9-2. RE pattern syntax

Element	Meaning
.	Matches any character except \n (if DOTALL, also matches \n)
^	Matches start of string (if MULTILINE, also matches after \n)
$	Matches end of string (if MULTILINE, also matches before \n)
*	Matches zero or more cases of the previous RE; greedy (match as many as possible)
+	Matches one or more cases of the previous RE; greedy (match as many as possible)
?	Matches zero or one case of the previous RE; greedy (match one if possible)

Table 9-2. RE pattern syntax (continued)

Element	Meaning
*?, +?, ??	Nongreedy versions of *, +, and ? (match as few as possible)
{m,n}	Matches m to n cases of the previous RE (greedy)
{m,n}?	Matches m to n cases of the previous RE (nongreedy)
[...]	Matches any one of a set of characters contained within the brackets
|	Matches either preceding expression or following expression
(...)	Matches the RE within the parentheses and indicates a group
(?iLmsux)	Alternate way to set optional flags; no effect on match
(?:...)	Like (...), but does not indicate a group
(?P<id>...)	Like (...), but the group also gets the name *id*
(?P=id)	Matches whatever was previously matched by group named *id*
(?#...)	Content of parentheses is just a comment; no effect on match
(?=...)	*Lookahead assertion*: matches if RE ... matches what comes next, but does not consume any part of the string
(?!...)	*Negative lookahead assertion*: matches if RE ... does not match what comes next, and does not consume any part of the string
(?<=...)	*Lookbehind assertion*: matches if there is a match ending at the current position for RE ... (... must match a fixed length)
(?<!...)	*Negative lookbehind assertion*: matches if there is no match ending at the current position for RE ... (... must match a fixed length)
\number	Matches whatever was previously matched by group numbered *number* (groups are automatically numbered from 1 to 99)
\A	Matches an empty string, but only at the start of the whole string
\b	Matches an empty string, but only at the start or end of a word (a maximal sequence of alphanumeric characters; see also \w)
\B	Matches an empty string, but not at the start or end of a word
\d	Matches one digit, like the set [0-9]
\D	Matches one nondigit, like the set [^0-9]
\s	Matches a whitespace character, like the set [\t\n\r\f\v]
\S	Matches a nonwhite space character, like the set [^\t\n\r\f\v]
\w	Matches one alphanumeric character; unless LOCALE or UNICODE is set, \w is like [a-zA-Z0-9_]
\W	Matches one nonalphanumeric character, the reverse of \w
\Z	Matches an empty string, but only at the end of the whole string
\\	Matches one backslash character

Common Regular Expression Idioms

'.*' as a substring of a regular expression's pattern string means "any number of repetitions (zero or more) of any character." In other words, '.*' matches any substring of a target string, including the empty substring. '.+' is similar, but matches only a nonempty substring. For example:

```
'pre.*post'
```

matches a string containing a substring `'pre'` followed by a later substring `'post'`, even if the latter is adjacent to the former (e.g., it matches both `'prepost'` and `'pre23post'`). On the other hand:

```
'pre.+post'
```

matches only if `'pre'` and `'post'` are not adjacent (e.g., it matches `'pre23post'` but does not match `'prepost'`). Both patterns also match strings that continue after the `'post'`. To constrain a pattern to match only strings that *end* with `'post'`, end the pattern with \Z. For example:

```
r'pre.*post\Z'
```

matches `'prepost'`, but not `'preposterous'`. Note that you need to express the pattern with raw-string syntax (or escape the backslash \ by doubling it into \\), as it contains a backslash. Use raw-string syntax for all rE pattern literals, which ensures you'll never forget to escape a backslash.

Another frequently used element in RE patterns is \b, which matches a word boundary. If you want to match the word `'his'` only as a whole word, and not its occurrences as a substring in such words as `'this'` and `'history'`, the RE pattern is:

```
r'\bhis\b'
```

with word boundaries both before and after. To match the beginning of any word starting with `'her'`, such as `'her'` itself but also `'hermetic'`, but not words that just contain `'her'` elsewhere, such as `'ether'` or `'there'`, use:

```
r'\bher'
```

with a word boundary before, but not after, the relevant string. To match the end of any word ending with `'its'`, such as `'its'` itself but also `'fits'`, but not words that contain `'its'` elsewhere, such as `'itsy'` or `'jujitsu'`, use:

```
r'its\b'
```

with a word boundary after, but not before, the relevant string. To match whole words thus constrained, rather than just their beginning or end, add a pattern element \w* to match zero or more word characters. To match any full word starting with `'her'`, use:

```
r'\bher\w*'
```

To match any full word ending with `'its'`, use:

```
r'\w*its\b'
```

Sets of Characters

You denote sets of characters in a pattern by listing the characters within brackets ([ ]). In addition to listing characters, you can denote a range by giving first and last characters of the range separated by a hyphen (-). The last character of the range is included in the set, differently from other Python ranges. Within a set, special characters stand for themselves, except \,], and -, which you must escape (by preceding them with a backslash) when their position is such that unescaped, they would form part of the set's syntax. You can denote a class of characters within a set by escaped-letter notation, such as \d or \S. \b in a set means a backspace character, not a word boundary. If the first character in the set's pattern, right after the [, is a caret (^), the set is *complemented*: such a set matches any character *except* those that follow ^ in the set pattern notation.

A frequent use of character sets is to match a word using a definition of which characters can make up a word that differs from \w's default (letters and digits). To match a word of one or more characters, each of which can be a letter, an apostrophe, or a hyphen, but not a digit (e.g., 'Finnegan-O'Hara'), use:

```
r"[a-zA-Z'\-]+"
```

It's not strictly necessary to escape the hyphen with a backslash in this case, since its position makes it syntactically unambiguous. However, the backslash is advisable because it makes the pattern somewhat more readable by visually distinguishing the hyphen that you want to have as a character in the set from those used to denote ranges.

Alternatives

A vertical bar (|) in a regular expression pattern, used to specify alternatives, has low syntactic precedence. Unless parentheses change the grouping, | applies to the whole pattern on either side, up to the start or end of the string, or to another |. A pattern can be made up of any number of subpatterns joined by |. To match such a RE, the first subpattern is tried first, and if it matches, the others are skipped. If the first subpattern does not match, the second subpattern is tried, and so on. | is neither greedy nor nongreedy: it just doesn't take the length of the match into consideration.

Given a list *L* of words, a RE pattern that matches any of the words is:

```
'|'.join([r'\b%s\b' % word for word in L])
```

If the items of *L* can be more general strings, not just words, you need to escape each of them with function re.escape (covered in escape on page 212), and you probably don't want the \b word boundary markers on either side. In this case, use the following RE pattern:

```
'|'.join(map(re.escape,L))
```

Groups

A regular expression can contain any number of groups, from 0 to 99 (any number is allowed, but only the first 99 groups are fully supported). Parentheses in a pattern string indicate a group. Element (?P<*id*>...) also indicates a group, and gives the group a name, *id*, that can be any Python identifier. All groups, named and unnamed, are numbered from left to right, 1 to 99; group 0 means the whole RE.

For any match of the RE with a string, each group matches a substring (possibly an empty one). When the RE uses |, some groups may not match any substring, although the RE as a whole does match the string. When a group doesn't match any substring, we say that the group does not *participate* in the match. An empty string ('') is used as the matching substring for any group that does not participate in a match, except where otherwise indicated later in this chapter.

For example:

```
r'(.+)\1+\Z'
```

matches a string made up of two or more repetitions of any nonempty substring. The (.+) part of the pattern matches any nonempty substring (any character, one or more times) and defines a group, thanks to the parentheses. The \1+ part of the pattern matches one or more repetitions of the group, and \Z anchors the match to end-of-string.

Optional Flags

A regular expression pattern element with one or more of the letters iLmsux between (? and) lets you set RE options within the pattern, rather than by the *flags* argument to function compile of module re. Options apply to the whole RE, no matter where the options element occurs in the pattern. For clarity, always place options at the start of the pattern. Placement at the start is mandatory if x is among the options, since x changes the way Python parses the pattern.

Using the explicit *flags* argument is more readable than placing an options element within the pattern. The *flags* argument to function compile is a coded integer built by bitwise ORing (with Python's bitwise OR operator, |) one or more of the following attributes of module re. Each attribute has both a short name (one uppercase letter), for convenience, and a long name (an uppercase multi-letter identifier), which is more readable and thus normally preferable:

I *or* IGNORECASE
: Makes matching case-insensitive

L *or* LOCALE
: Causes \w, \W, \b, and \B matches to depend on what the current locale deems alphanumeric

M *or* MULTILINE
: Makes the special characters ^ and $ match at the start and end of each line (i.e., right after/before a newline), as well as at the start and end of the whole string

S *or* DOTALL
: Causes the special character . to match any character, including a newline

U *or* UNICODE
: Makes \w, \W, \b, and \B matches depend on what Unicode deems alphanumeric

X *or* VERBOSE
: Causes whitespace in the pattern to be ignored, except when escaped or in a character set, and makes a # character in the pattern begin a comment that lasts until the end of the line

For example, here are three ways to define equivalent REs with function compile, covered in compile on page 212. Each of these REs matches the word "hello" in any mix of upper- and lowercase letters:

```
import re
r1 = re.compile(r'(?i)hello')
```

```
r2 = re.compile(r'hello', re.I)
r3 = re.compile(r'hello', re.IGNORECASE)
```

The third approach is clearly the most readable, and thus the most maintainable, even though it is slightly more verbose. The raw-string form is not necessary here, since the patterns do not include backslashes; however, using raw strings is innocuous, and is the recommended style for clarity.

Option re.VERBOSE (or re.X) lets you make patterns more readable and understandable by appropriate use of whitespace and comments. Complicated and verbose RE patterns are generally best represented by strings that take up more than one line, and therefore you normally want to use the triple-quoted raw-string format for such pattern strings. For example:

```
repat_num1 = r'(0[0-7]*|0x[\da-fA-F]+|[1-9]\d*)L?\Z'
repat_num2 = r'''(?x)                  # pattern matching integer numbers
                (0 [0-7]*       |  # octal: leading 0, then 0+ octal digits
                 0x [\da-fA-F]+ |  # hex: 0x, then 1+ hex digits
                 [1-9] \d*      )  # decimal: leading non-0, then 0+ digits
                 L?\Z              # optional trailing L, then end of string
                 '''
```

The two patterns defined in this example are equivalent, but the second one is made somewhat more readable by the comments and the free use of whitespace to group portions of the pattern in logical ways.

Match Versus Search

So far, we've been using regular expressions to match strings. For example, the RE with pattern r'box' matches strings such as 'box' and 'boxes', but not 'inbox'. In other words, a RE match is implicitly anchored at the start of the target string, as if the RE's pattern started with \A.

Often, you're interested in locating possible matches for a RE anywhere in the string, without anchoring (e.g., find the r'box' match inside such strings as 'inbox', as well as in 'box' and 'boxes'). In this case, the Python term for the operation is a *search*, as opposed to a match. For such searches, use the search method of a RE object: the match method deals with matching only from the start. For example:

```
import re
r1 = re.compile(r'box')
if r1.match('inbox'): print 'match succeeds'
else print 'match fails'                                  # prints: match fails
if r1. search('inbox'): print 'search succeeds'  # prints: search succeeds
else print 'search fails'
```

Anchoring at String Start and End

The pattern elements ensuring that a regular expression search (or match) is anchored at string start and string end are \A and \Z, respectively. More traditionally, elements ^ for start and $ for end are also used in similar roles. ^ is the same as \A, and $ is the same as \Z, for RE objects that are not multiline (i.e., that do not contain pattern element (?m) and are not compiled with the flag re.M or re.MULTILINE). For a multiline RE, however, ^ anchors at the start of any line (i.e., either at the start of the whole string or at any position right after a newline character \n). Similarly, with a multiline RE, $ anchors at the end of any line (i.e., either at the end of the whole string or at any position right before \n). On the other hand, \A and \Z anchor at the start and end of the string whether the RE object is multiline or not. For example, here's how to check if a file has any lines that end with digits:

```
import re
digatend = re.compile(r'\d$', re.MULTILINE)
if digatend.search(open('afile.txt').read()): print "some lines end with
digits"
else: print "no lines end with digits"
```

A pattern of r'\d\n' is almost equivalent, but in that case the search fails if the very last character of the file is a digit not followed by an end-of-line character. With the example above, the search succeeds if a digit is at the very end of the file's contents, as well as in the more usual case where a digit is followed by an end-of-line character.

Regular Expression Objects

A regular expression object *r* has the following read-only attributes that detail how *r* was built (by function compile of module re, covered in compile on page 212):

flags
> The *flags* argument passed to compile, or 0 when *flags* is omitted

groupindex
> A dictionary whose keys are group names as defined by elements (?P<*id*>); the corresponding values are the named groups' numbers

pattern
> The pattern string from which *r* is compiled

These attributes make it easy to get back from a compiled RE object to its pattern string and flags, so you never have to store those separately.

A RE object *r* also supplies methods to locate matches for *r* within a string, as well as to perform substitutions on such matches. Matches are generally represented by special objects, covered in "Match Objects" on page 210.

findall	*r*.findall(*s*)

> When *r* has no groups, findall returns a list of strings, each a substring of *s* that is a nonoverlapping match with *r*. For example, to print out all words in a file, one per line:
>
> ```
> import re
> reword = re.compile(r'\w+')
> for aword in reword.findall(open('afile.txt').read()):
>     print aword
> ```
>
> When *r* has one group, findall also returns a list of strings, but each is the substring of *s* that matches *r*'s group. For example, to

print only words that are followed by whitespace (not punctuation), you need to change only one statement in the example:

```
reword = re.compile('(\w+)\s')
```

When r has n groups (with n>1), findall returns a list of tuples, one per nonoverlapping match with r. Each tuple has n items, one per group of r, the substring of s matching the group. For example, to print the first and last word of each line that has at least two words:

```
import re
first_last = re.compile(r'^\W*(\w+)\b.*\b(\w+)\W*$',re.
MULTILINE)
for first, last in \
first_last.findall(open('afile.txt').read()):
    print first, last
```

finditer

`r.finditer(s)`

finditer is like findall except that instead of a list of strings (or tuples), it returns an iterator whose items are match objects. In most cases, finditer is therefore more flexible and performs better than findall.

match

`r.match(s,start=0,end=sys.maxint)`

Returns an appropriate match object when a substring of s, starting at index *start* and not reaching as far as index *end*, matches r. Otherwise, match returns None. Note that match is implicitly anchored at the starting position *start* in s. To search for a match with r at any point in s from *start* onward, call r.search, not r.match. For example, here's how to print all lines in a file that start with digits:

```
import re
digs = re.compile(r'\d+')
for line in open('afile.txt'):
    if digs.match(line): print line,
```

search

`r.search(s,start=0,end=sys.maxint)`

Returns an appropriate match object for the leftmost substring of s, starting not before index *start* and not reaching as far as index *end*, that matches r. When no such substring exists, search returns None. For example, to print all lines containing digits, one simple approach is as follows:

```
import re
digs = re.compile(r'\d+')
for line in open('afile.txt'):
    if digs.search(line): print line,
```

split

`r.split(`*`s,maxsplit=0`*`)`

Returns a list *L* of the *splits* of *s* by *r* (i.e., the substrings of *s* separated by nonoverlapping, nonempty matches with *r*). For example, to eliminate all occurrences of substring `'hello'` (in any mix of lowercase and uppercase) from a string, one way is:

```
import re
rehello = re.compile(r'hello', re.IGNORECASE)
astring = ''.join(rehello.split(astring))
```

When *r* has *n* groups, *n* more items are interleaved in *L* between each pair of splits. Each of the *n* extra items is the substring of *s* that matches *r*'s corresponding group in that match, or None if that group did not participate in the match. For example, here's one way to remove whitespace only when it occurs between a colon and a digit:

```
import re
re_col_ws_dig = re.compile(r'(:)\s+(\d)')
astring = ''.join(re_col_ws_dig.split(astring))
```

If *maxsplit* is greater than 0, at most *maxsplit* splits are in *L*, each followed by *n* items as above, while the trailing substring of *s* after *maxsplit* matches of *r*, if any, is *L*'s last item. For example, to remove only the first occurrence of substring `'hello'` rather than all of them, change the last statement in the first example above to:

```
astring = ''.join(rehello.split(astring, 1))
```

sub

`r.sub(`*`repl,s,count=0`*`)`

Returns a copy of *s* where nonoverlapping matches with *r* are replaced by *repl*, which can be either a string or a callable object, such as a function. An empty match is replaced only when not adjacent to the previous match. When *count* is greater than 0, only the first *count* matches of *r* within *s* are replaced. When *count* equals 0, all matches of *r* within *s* are replaced. For example, here's another way to remove only the first occurrence of substring `'hello'` in any mix of cases:

```
import re
rehello = re.compile(r'hello', re.IGNORECASE)
astring = rehello.sub('', astring, 1)
```

Without the final 1 argument to sub, the example removes all occurrences of `'hello'`.

When *repl* is a callable object, *repl* must accept one argument (a match object) and return a string (or None, which is equivalent to returning the empty string `''`) to use as the replacement for the match. In this case, sub calls *repl*, with a suitable match-object argument, for each match with *r* that sub is replacing. For example, to uppercase all occurrences of words starting with 'h' and ending with 'o' in any mix of cases:

```
import re
h_word = re.compile(r'\bh\w+o\b', re.IGNORECASE)
def up(mo): return mo.group(0).upper( )
astring = h_word.sub(up, astring)
```

When *repl* is a string, sub uses *repl* itself as the replacement, except that it expands back references. A *back reference* is a substring of *repl* of the form \g<*id*>, where *id* is the name of a group in *r* (established by syntax (?P<*id*>) in *r*'s pattern string) or *dd*, where *dd* is one or two digits taken as a group number. Each back reference, named or numbered, is replaced with the substring of *s* that matches the group of *r* that the back reference indicates. For example, here's a way to enclose every word in braces:

```
import re
grouped_word = re.compile('(\w+)')
astring = grouped_word.sub(r'{\1}', astring)
```

---

subn   *r*.subn(*repl*,*s*,*count*=0)

subn is the same as sub, except that subn returns a pair (*new_string*, *n*), where *n* is the number of substitutions that subn has performed. For example, one way to count the number of occurrences of substring 'hello' in any mix of cases is:

```
import re
rehello = re.compile(r'hello', re.IGNORECASE)
junk, count = rehello.subn('', astring)
print 'Found', count, 'occurrences of "hello"'
```

Match Objects

Match objects are created and returned by methods match and search of a regular expression object, and are the items of the iterator returned by method finditer. They are also implicitly created by methods sub and subn when argument *repl* is callable, since in that case a suitable match object is passed as the argument on each call to *repl*. A match object *m* supplies the following read-only attributes that detail how *m* was created:

pos
    The *start* argument that was passed to search or match (i.e., the index into *s* where the search for a match began)

endpos
    The *end* argument that was passed to search or match (i.e., the index into *s* before which the matching substring of *s* had to end)

lastgroup

    The name of the last-matched group (None if the last-matched group has no name, or if no group participated in the match)

lastindex

    The integer index (1 and up) of the last-matched group (None if no group participated in the match)

re

    The RE object *r* whose method created *m*

string

    The string *s* passed to match, search, sub, or subn

A match object *m* also supplies several methods.

---

end, span, start   *m*.end(*groupid*=0) *m*.span(*groupid*=0) *m*.start(*groupid*=0)

    These methods return the limit indices, within *m*.string, of the substring that matches the group identified by *groupid* (a group number or name). When the matching substring is *m*.string[*i:j*], *m*.start returns *i*, *m*.end returns *j*, and *m*.span returns (*i, j*). If the group did not participate in the match, *i* and *j* are -1.

---

expand   *m*.expand(*s*)

    Returns a copy of *s* where escape sequences and back references are replaced in the same way as for method *r*.sub, covered in sub on page 209.

---

group   *m*.group(*groupid*=0,**groupids*)

    When called with a single argument *groupid* (a group number or name), group returns the substring that matches the group identified by *groupid*, or None if that group did not participate in the match. The idiom *m*.group( ), also spelled *m*.group(0), returns the whole matched substring, since group number 0 means the whole RE.

    When group is called with multiple arguments, each argument must be a group number or name. group then returns a tuple with one item per argument, the substring matching the corresponding group, or None if that group did not participate in the match.

---

groups   *m*.groups(*default*=None)

    Returns a tuple with one item per group in *r*. Each item is the substring that matches the corresponding group, or *default* if that group did not participate in the match.

groupdict `m.groupdict(`*default*`=None)`

Returns a dictionary whose keys are the names of all named groups in *r*. The value for each name is the substring that matches the corresponding group, or *default* if that group did not participate in the match.

Functions of Module re

The re module supplies the attributes listed in "Optional Flags" on page 205. It also provides one function for each method of a regular expression object (findall, finditer, match, search, split, sub, and subn), each with an additional first argument, a pattern string that the function implicitly compiles into a RE object. It's generally preferable to compile pattern strings into RE objects explicitly and call the RE object's methods, but sometimes, for a one-off use of a RE pattern, calling functions of module re can be slightly handier. For example, to count the number of occurrences of substring 'hello' in any mix of cases, one function-based way is:

```
import re
junk, count = re.subn(r'(?i)hello', '', astring)
print 'Found', count, 'occurrences of "hello"'
```

In such cases, RE options (here, for example, case insensitivity) must be encoded as RE pattern elements (here, (?i)), since the functions of module re do not accept a *flags* argument. Module re internally caches the RE objects it creates from the patterns passed to its functions; to purge that cache and reclaim some memory, call re.purge( ).

Module re also supplies error, the class of exceptions raised upon errors (generally, errors in the syntax of a pattern string), and two more functions.

compile `compile(`*pattern*`,`*flags*`=0)`

Creates and returns a RE object, parsing string *pattern* as per the syntax covered in "Pattern-String Syntax" on page 201, and using integer *flags*, as in "Optional Flags" on page 205.

escape `escape(`*s*`)`

Returns a copy of string *s* with each nonalphanumeric character escaped (i.e., preceded by a backslash \); useful to match string *s* literally as part of a RE pattern string.

Python Library and Extension Modules

10

File and Text Operations

This chapter covers most of the issues related to dealing with files and the filesystem in Python. A *file* is a stream of bytes that a program can read and/or write; a *filesystem* is a hierarchical repository of files on a computer system.

Other Chapters That Also Deal with Files

Because files are such a crucial concept in programming, even though this chapter is the largest one in the book, several other chapters also contain material that is relevant when you're handling specific kinds of files. In particular, Chapter 11 deals with many kinds of files related to persistence and database functionality (marshal files in "The marshal Module" on page 278, pickle files in "The pickle and cPickle Modules" on page 279, shelve files in "The shelve Module" on page 284, DBM and DBM-like files in "DBM Modules" on page 285, Berkeley database files in "Berkeley DB Interfacing" on page 288), Chapter 23 deals with files in HTML format, and Chapter 24 deals with files in XML format.

Organization of This Chapter

First of all, this chapter, in "File Objects" on page 216, discusses the most typical way in which Python programs read and write data, which is via built-in `file` objects. Immediately after that, the chapter covers the polymorphic concept of file-like objects (objects that are not files but behave to some extent like files) in "File-Like Objects and Polymorphism" on page 222.

The chapter next covers modules that deal with temporary files and file-like objects (`tempfile` in "The tempfile Module" on page 223, `StringIO` and `cStringIO` in "The StringIO and cStringIO Modules" on page 229).

Next comes the coverage of modules that help you access the contents of text and binary files (`fileinput` in "The fileinput Module" on page 224, `linecache` in "The linecache Module" on page 226, struct in "The struct Module" on page 227) and support compressed files and other data archives (gzip in "The gzip Module" on page 230, bz2 in "The bz2 Module" on page 232, tarfile in "The tarfile Module" on page 233, zipfile in "The zipfile Module" on page 235, zlib in "The zlib Module" on page 239).

In Python, the os module supplies many of the functions that operate on the file-system, so this chapter continues by introducing the os module in "The os Module" on page 240. The chapter then covers, in "Filesystem Operations" on page 241, operations on the filesystem (comparing, copying, and deleting directo-ries and files, working with file paths, and accessing low-level file descriptors) offered by os (in "File and Directory Functions of the os Module" on page 242), os.path (in "The os.path Module" on page 246), and other modules (dircache in "listdir", stat in "The stat Module" on page 249, filecmp in "The filecmp Module" on page 250, and shutil in "The shutil Module" on page 252).

Many modern programs rely on a graphical user interface (GUI) (as covered in Chapter 17), but text-based, nongraphical user interfaces are still useful, since they're simple, fast to program, and lightweight. This chapter concludes with material about text input and output in Python in "Text Input and Output" on page 256, richer text I/O in "Richer-Text I/O" on page 258, interactive command-line sessions in "Interactive Command Sessions" on page 265, and, finally, infor-mation about presenting text that is understandable to different users, no matter where they are or what language they speak, in "Internationalization" on page 269. This subject is generally known as *internationalization* (often abbrevi-ated *i18n*).

File Objects

As mentioned in "Organization of This Chapter" on page 215, file is a built-in type in Python and the single most common way for your Python programs to read or write data. With a file object, you can read and/or write data to a file as seen by the underlying operating system. Python reacts to any I/O error related to a file object by raising an instance of built-in exception class IOError. Errors that cause this exception include open failing to open or create a file, calls to a method on a file object to which that method doesn't apply (e.g., calling write on a read-only file object, or calling seek on a nonseekable file), and I/O errors diagnosed by a file object's methods. This section covers file objects, as well as the important issue of making *temporary* files.

Creating a File Object with open

To create a Python file object, call the built-in open with the following syntax:

```
open(filename, mode='r', bufsize=-1)
```

open opens the file named by plain string *filename*, which denotes any path to a file. open returns a Python file object *f*, which is an instance of the built-in type file. Currently, calling file directly is like calling open, but you should call open, which may become a factory function in some future release of Python. If you explicitly pass a *mode* string, open can also create *filename* if the file does not already exist (depending on the value of *mode*, as we'll discuss in a moment). In other words, despite its name, open is not just for opening existing files: it can also create new ones.

File mode

mode is a string that indicates how the file is to be opened (or created). mode can be:

`'r'`
> The file must already exist, and it is opened in read-only mode.

`'w'`
> The file is opened in write-only mode. The file is truncated and overwritten if it already exists, or created if it does not exist.

`'a'`
> The file is opened in write-only mode. The file is kept intact if it already exists, and the data you write is appended to what's already in the file. The file is created if it does not exist. Calling f.seek on the file is innocuous but has no effect.

`'r+'`
> The file must already exist and is opened for both reading and writing, so all methods of f can be called.

`'w+'`
> The file is opened for both reading and writing, so all methods of f can be called. The file is truncated and overwritten if it already exists, or created if it does not exist.

`'a+'`
> The file is opened for both reading and writing, so all methods of f can be called. The file is kept intact if it already exists, and the data you write is appended to what's already in the file. The file is created if it does not exist. Calling f.seek on the file has no effect if the next I/O operation on f writes data but works normally if the next I/O operation on f reads data.

Binary and text modes

The *mode* string may also have any of the values just explained followed by a b or t. b denotes binary mode, while t denotes text mode. When the *mode* string has neither b nor t, the default is text mode (i.e., `'r'` is like `'rt'`, `'w'` is like `'wt'`, and so on).

On Unix, there is no difference between binary and text modes. On Windows, when a file is open in text mode, `'\n'` is returned each time the string that is the value of os.linesep (the line termination string) is encountered while the file is being read. Conversely, a copy of os.linesep is written each time you write `'\n'` to the file.

This widespread convention, originally developed in the C language, lets you read and write text files on any platform without worrying about the platform's line-separation conventions. However, except on Unix-like platforms, you do have to know (and tell Python, by passing the proper *mode* argument to open) whether a file is binary or text. In this chapter, for simplicity, I use \n to refer to the line-termination string, but remember that the string is in fact os.linesep in files on the filesystem, translated to and from \n in memory only for files opened in text mode.

Python also supports *universal newlines*, which let you open a text file for reading in mode 'U' (or, equivalently, 'rU') when you don't know how line separators are encoded in the file. This is useful, for example, when you share text files across a network between machines with different operating systems. Mode 'U' takes any of '\n', '\r', and '\r\n' as a line separator, and translates any line separator to '\n'.

Buffering

bufsize is an integer that denotes the buffer size you're requesting for the file. When *bufsize* is less than 0, the operating system's default is used. Normally, this default is line buffering for files that correspond to interactive consoles and some reasonably sized buffer, such as 8,192 bytes, for other files. When *bufsize* equals 0, the file is unbuffered; the effect is as if the file's buffer were flushed every time you write anything to the file. When *bufsize* equals 1, the file is line-buffered, which means the file's buffer is flushed every time you write \n to the file. When *bufsize* is greater than 1, the file uses a buffer of about *bufsize* bytes, rounded up to some reasonable amount. On some platforms, you can change the buffering for files that are already open, but there is no cross-platform way to do this.

Sequential and nonsequential access

A file object *f* is inherently sequential (i.e., a stream of bytes). When you read from a file, you get bytes in the sequential order in which they're present in the file. When you write to a file, the bytes you write are put in the file in the order in which you write them.

To allow nonsequential access, each built-in file object keeps track of its current position (the position on the underlying file where the next read or write operation will start transferring data). When you open a file, the initial position is at the start of the file. Any call to *f*.write on a file object *f* opened with a *mode* of 'a' or 'a+' always sets *f*'s position to the end of the file before writing data to *f*. When you read or write *n* bytes on file object *f*, *f*'s position advances by *n*. You can query the current position by calling *f*.tell and change the position by calling *f*.seek, which are both covered in the next section.

Attributes and Methods of File Objects

A file object *f* supplies the attributes and methods documented in this section.

---

close   *f*.close( )

Closes the file. You can call no other method on *f* after *f*.close. Multiple calls to *f*.close are allowed and innocuous.

closed   closed

f.closed is a read-only attribute that is True if f.close() has been
called; otherwise, False.

encoding   encoding

f.encoding is a read-only attribute that is either None, if I/O on f
uses the system default encoding, or a string that names the
encoding in use. (Encodings are covered in "Unicode" on page 198.)
In practice, this attribute is set only on the stdin, stdout, and stderr
attributes of module sys (covered in stdin, stdout, stderr on page
171) when they refer to terminals.

flush   f.flush()

Requests that f's buffer be written out to the operating system so
that the file as seen by the system has the exact contents that
Python's code has written. Depending on the platform and the
nature of f's underlying file, f.flush may not be able to ensure the
desired effect.

isatty   f.isatty()

Returns True if f's underlying file is an interactive terminal; otherwise, False.

fileno   f.fileno()

Returns an integer, which is the file descriptor of f's file at operating system level. File descriptors are covered in "File and
Directory Functions of the os Module" on page 242.

mode   mode

f.mode is a read-only attribute that is the value of the *mode* string
used in the open call that created f.

name   name

f.name is a read-only attribute that is the value of the *filename*
string used in the open call that created f.

newlines   newlines

f.newlines is a read-only attribute useful for text files opened for
"universal-newlines reading." f.newlines may be one of the strings
'\n', '\r', or '\r\n' (when that string is the only kind of line

separator met so far while reading *f*); a tuple, whose items are the different kinds of line separators met so far; or None, when no line separators have been met yet while reading *f*, or when *f* was not opened in mode 'U'.

read

f.read(*size*=-1)

Reads up to *size* bytes from *f*'s file and returns them as a string. read reads and returns less than *size* bytes if the file ends before *size* bytes are read. When *size* is less than 0, read reads and returns all bytes up to the end of the file. read returns an empty string if the file's current position is at the end of the file or if *size* equals 0.

readline

f.readline(*size*=-1)

Reads and returns one line from *f*'s file, up to the end of line (\n), included. If *size* is greater than or equal to 0, readline reads no more than *size* bytes. In this case, the returned string might not end with \n. \n might also be absent if readline reads up to the end of the file without finding \n. readline returns an empty string if the file's current position is at the end of the file or if *size* equals 0.

readlines

f.readlines(*size*=-1)

Reads and returns a list of all lines in *f*'s file, each a string ending in \n. If *size*>0, readlines stops and returns the list after collecting data for a total of about *size* bytes rather than reading all the way to the end of the file.

seek

f.seek(*pos*, *how*=0)

Sets *f*'s current position to the signed integer byte offset *pos* away from a reference point. *how* indicates the reference point. When *how* is 0, the reference is the start of the file; when it is 1, the reference is the current position; and when it is 2, the reference is the end of the file. In Python 2.5, module os has attributes named SEEK_SET, SEEK_CUR, and SEEK_END, with values of 0, 1, and 2, respectively. They are usable instead of the bare integer constants to obtain greater readability when calling this method.

When *f* is opened in text mode, *f*.seek may set the current position in unexpected ways, due to the implied translations between os.linesep and \n. This troublesome effect does not occur on Unix platforms, nor when you opened *f* in binary mode or when you called *f*.seek with a *pos* that is the result of a previous call to *f*.tell, and *how* is 0. When *f* is opened in mode 'a' or 'a+', all data written to *f* is appended to the data that is already in *f*, regardless of any calls to *f*.seek.

softspace   softspace

f.softspace is a read-write bool attribute used internally by the print statement (covered in "The print Statement" on page 256) to keep track of its own state. A file object doesn't alter nor interpret softspace in any way: it just lets the attribute be freely read and written, and print takes care of the rest.

tell   *f*.tell( )

Returns *f*'s current position, an integer offset in bytes from the start of the file.

truncate   *f*.truncate([*size*])

Truncates *f*'s file. When *size* is present, truncates the file to be at most *size* bytes. When *size* is absent, uses *f*.tell( ) as the file's new size.

write   *f*.write(*s*)

Writes the bytes of string *s* to the file.

writelines   *f*.writelines(*lst*)

Like:

    for *line* in *lst*: f.write(*line*)

It does not matter whether the strings in iterable *lst* are lines: despite its name, method writelines just writes each of the strings to the file, one after the other.

Iteration on File Objects

A file object *f*, open for text-mode reading, is also an iterator whose items are the file's lines. Thus, the loop:

    for *line* in *f*:

iterates on each line of the file. Due to buffering issues, interrupting such a loop prematurely (e.g., with break), or calling *f*.next( ) instead of *f*.readline( ), leaves the file's position set to an arbitrary value. If you want to switch from using *f* as an iterator to calling other reading methods on *f*, be sure to set the file's position to a known value by appropriately calling *f*.seek. On the plus side, a loop directly on *f* has very good performance, since these specifications allow the loop to use internal buffering to minimize I/O without taking up excessive amounts of memory even for huge files.

File-Like Objects and Polymorphism

An object *x* is file-like when it behaves *polymorphically* to a file, meaning that a function (or some other part of a program) can use *x* as if *x* were a file. Code using such an object (known as the *client code* of the object) typically receives the object as an argument or gets it by calling a factory function that returns the object as the result. For example, if the only method that client code calls on *x* is *x*.read( ), without arguments, then all *x* needs to supply in order to be file-like for that code is a method read that is callable without arguments and returns a string. Other client code may need *x* to implement a larger subset of file methods. File-like objects and polymorphism are not absolute concepts: they are relative to demands placed on an object by some specific client code.

Polymorphism is a powerful aspect of object-oriented programming, and file-like objects are a good example of polymorphism. A client-code module that writes to or reads from files can automatically be reused for data residing elsewhere, as long as the module does not break polymorphism by the dubious practice of type testing. When we discussed the built-ins type and isinstance in type on page 157 and isinstance on page 163, I mentioned that type testing is often best avoided, since it blocks the normal polymorphism that Python otherwise supplies. Sometimes, you may have no choice. For example, the marshal module (covered in "The marshal Module" on page 278) demands real file objects. Therefore, when your client code needs to use marshal, your code must deal with real file objects, not just file-like ones. However, such situations are rare. Most often, to support polymorphism in your client code, all you have to do is avoid type testing.

You can implement a file-like object by coding your own class (as covered in Chapter 5) and defining the specific methods needed by client code, such as read. A file-like object *f1* need not implement all the attributes and methods of a true file object *f*. If you can determine which methods client code calls on *f1*, you can choose to implement only that subset. For example, when *f1* is only going to be written, *f1* doesn't need "reading" methods, such as read, readline, and readlines.

When you implement a writable file-like object *f1*, make sure that *f1*.softspace can be read and written, and don't alter nor interpret softspace in any way, if you want *f1* to be usable by print (covered in "The print Statement" on page 256). Note that this behavior is the default when you write *f1*'s class in Python. You need to take specific care only when *f1*'s class overrides special method __setattr__, or otherwise controls access to its instances' attributes (e.g., by defining __slots__), as covered in Chapter 5. In particular, if your new-style class defines __slots__, then one of the slots must be named softspace if you want instances of your class to be usable as destinations of print statements.

If the main reason you want a file-like object instead of a real file object is to keep the data in memory, use modules StringIO and cStringIO, covered in "The StringIO and cStringIO Modules" on page 229. These modules supply file-like objects that hold data in memory and behave polymorphically to file objects to a wide extent.

The tempfile Module

The `tempfile` module lets you create temporary files and directories in the most secure manner afforded by your platform. Temporary files are often an excellent solution when you're dealing with an amount of data that might not comfortably fit in memory, or when your program needs to write data that another process will then use.

The order of the parameters for the functions in this module is a bit confusing: to make your code more readable, always call these functions with named-argument syntax. Module `tempfile` exposes the following functions.

mkstemp	mkstemp(*suffix*=None, *prefix*=None, *dir*=None, *text*=False)

Securely creates a new temporary file, readable and writable only by the current user, not executable, not inherited by subprocesses; returns a pair (*fd, path*), where *fd* is the file descriptor of the temporary file (as returned by os.open, covered in open on page 231) and string *path* is the absolute path to the temporary file. You can optionally pass arguments to specify strings to use as the start (*prefix*) and end (*suffix*) of the temporary file's filename, and the path to the directory in which the temporary file is created (*dir*); if you want to use the temporary file as a text file, you should explicitly pass the argument *text*=True. Ensuring that the temporary file is removed when you're done using it is up to you. Here is a typical usage example that creates a temporary text file, closes it, passes its path to another function, and finally ensures the file is removed:

```
import tempfile, os
fd, path = tempfile.mkstemp(suffix='.txt', text=True)
try:
    os.close(fd)
    use_filepath(path)
finally:
    os.unlink(path)
```

mkdtemp	mkdtemp(*suffix*=None, *prefix*=None, *dir*=None)

Securely creates a new temporary directory that is readable, writable, and searchable only by the current user, and returns the absolute path to the temporary directory. The optional arguments *suffix*, *prefix*, and *dir* are like for function mkstemp. Ensuring that the temporary directory is removed when you're done using it is your program's responsibility. Here is a typical usage example that creates a temporary directory, passes its path to another function, and finally ensures the directory is removed together with all of its contents:

```
import tempfile, shutil
path = tempfile.mkdtemp()
```

```
        try:
            use_dirpath(path)
        finally:
            shutil.rmtree(path)
```

TemporaryFile	TemporaryFile(*mode*='w+b', *bufsize*=-1,*suffix*=None, *prefix*=None, *dir*=None)

Creates a temporary file with mkstemp (passing to mkstemp the optional arguments *suffix*, *prefix*, and *dir*), makes a file object from it with os.fdopen as covered in fdopen on page 254 (passing to fdopen the optional arguments *mode* and *bufsize*), and returns the file object (or a file-like wrapper around it). The temporary file is removed as soon as the file object is closed (implicitly or explicitly). For greater security, the temporary file has no name on the filesystem, if your platform allows that (Unix-like platforms do; Windows doesn't).

NamedTempor-aryFile	NamedTemporaryFile(*mode*='w+b', *bufsize*=-1,*suffix*=None, *prefix*=None, *dir*=None)

Like TemporaryFile, except that the temporary file does have a name on the filesystem. Use the name attribute of the file or file-like object to access that name. Some platforms, mainly Windows, do not allow the file to be opened again: therefore, the usefulness of the name is limited if you want to ensure your program works cross-platform. If you need to pass the temporary file's name to another program that opens the file, use function mkstemp, instead of NamedTemporaryFile, to guarantee correct cross-platform behavior. Of course, when you choose to use mkstemp, you do have to take care to ensure the file is removed when you're done with it.

Auxiliary Modules for File I/O

File objects supply all the minimal indispensable functionality needed for file I/O. Some auxiliary Python library modules, however, offer convenient supplementary functionality, making I/O even easier and handier in several important cases.

The fileinput Module

The fileinput module lets you loop over all the lines in a list of text files. Performance is good, comparable to the performance of direct iteration on each file, since fileinput uses buffering to minimize I/O. You can therefore use module fileinput for line-oriented file input whenever you find the module's rich functionality convenient, with no worries about performance. The input function is the key function of module fileinput, and the module also provides a FileInput class whose methods support the same functionality as the module's functions.

close	`close( )`
	Closes the whole sequence so that iteration stops and no file remains open.
FileInput	`class FileInput(`*`files`*`=None, `*`inplace`*`=False, `*`backup`*`='',` *`bufsize`*`=0)`
	Creates and returns an instance *f* of class `FileInput`. Arguments are the same as for `fileinput.input`, and methods of *f* have the same names, arguments, and semantics as functions of module `fileinput`. *f* also supplies a method `readline`, which reads and returns the next line. You can use class `FileInput` explicitly when you want to nest or mix loops that read lines from more than one sequence of files.
filelineno	`filelineno( )`
	Returns the number of lines read so far from the file now being read. For example, returns 1 if the first line has just been read from the current file.
filename	`filename( )`
	Returns the name of the file being read, or `None` if no line has been read yet.
input	`input(`*`files`*`=None, `*`inplace`*`=False, `*`backup`*`='', `*`bufsize`*`=0)`
	Returns the sequence of lines in the files, suitable for use in a `for` loop. *files* is a sequence of filenames to open and read one after the other, in order. Filename `'-'` means standard input (`sys.stdin`). If *files* is a string, it's a single filename to open and read. If *files* is `None`, input uses `sys.argv[1:]` as the list of filenames. If the sequence of filenames is empty, input reads `sys.stdin`.
	The sequence object that input returns is an instance of class `FileInput`; that instance is also the global state of module input, so all other functions of module `fileinput` operate on the same shared state. Each function of module `fileinput` corresponds directly to a method of class `FileInput`.
	When *inplace* is false (the default), input just reads the files. When *inplace* is true, input moves each file being read (except standard input) to a backup file and redirects standard output (`sys.stdout`) to write to a new file with the same path as the original one of the file being read. This way, you can simulate overwriting files in-place. If *backup* is a string that starts with a dot, input uses *backup* as the extension of the backup files and does not remove the backup files. If *backup* is an empty string (the default), input uses *.bak* and deletes each backup file as the input files are closed.

bufsize is the size of the internal buffer that input uses to read lines from the input files. If *bufsize* is 0, input uses a buffer of 8,192 bytes.

---

isfirstline   isfirstline( )

Returns True or False, just like filelineno( )==1.

---

isstdin   isstdin( )

Returns True if the current file being read is sys.stdin; otherwise, False.

---

lineno   lineno( )

Returns the total number of lines read since the call to input.

---

nextfile   nextfile( )

Closes the file being read so that the next line to read is the first one of the next file.

The linecache Module

The linecache module lets you read a given line (specified by number) from a file with a given name, keeping an internal cache so that if you read several lines from a file, it's faster than opening and examining the file each time. Module linecache exposes the following functions.

---

checkcache   checkcache( )

Ensures that the module's cache holds no stale data and reflects what's on the filesystem. Call checkcache when the files you're reading may have changed on the filesystem to ensure that future calls to getline return updated information.

---

clearcache   clearcache( )

Drops the module's cache so that the memory can be reused for other purposes. Call clearcache when you know you don't need to perform anymore reading for a while.

---

getline   getline(*filename, lineno*)

Reads and returns the *lineno* line (the first line is 1, not 0 as is usual in Python) from the text file named *filename*, including the trailing \n. For any error, getline does not raise exceptions but rather returns the empty string ''. If *filename* is not found, getline looks for the file in the directories listed in sys.path.

getlines   getlines(*filename*)

Reads and returns all lines from the text file named *filename*, as a list of strings, each including the trailing \n. For any error, getlines does not raise exceptions but rather returns the empty list []. If *filename* is not found, getlines looks for the file in the directories listed in sys.path.

The struct Module

The struct module lets you pack binary data into a string, and unpack the bytes of such a string back into the data they represent. Such operations are useful for many kinds of low-level programming. Most often, you use module struct to interpret data records from binary files that have some specified format, or to prepare records to write to such binary files. The module's name comes from C's keyword struct, which is usable for related purposes. On any error, functions of module struct raise exceptions that are instances of exception class struct.error, the only class the module supplies.

Module struct relies on *struct format strings*, which are plain strings with a specific syntax. The first character of a format string specifies byte order, size, and alignment of packed data:

@

Native byte order, native data sizes, and native alignment for the current platform; this is the default if the first character is none of the characters listed here (note that format P in Table 10-1 is available only for this kind of struct format string)

=

Native byte order for the current platform, but standard size and alignment

<

Little-endian byte order (like Intel platforms); standard size and alignment

>, !

Big-endian byte order (network standard); standard size and alignment

Table 10-1. Format characters for struct

Character	C type	Python type	Standard size
B	unsigned char	int	1 byte
b	signed char	int	1 byte
c	char	str (length 1)	1 byte
d	double	float	8 bytes
f	float	float	4 bytes
H	unsigned short	int	2 bytes
h	signed short	int	2 bytes
I	unsigned int	long	4 bytes
i	signed int	int	4 bytes
L	unsigned long	long	4 bytes
l	signed long	int	4 bytes
P	void*	int	N/A
p	char[ ]	String	N/A
s	char[ ]	String	N/A
x	padding byte	no value	1 byte

Standard sizes are indicated in Table 10-1. Standard alignment means no forced alignment, with explicit padding bytes used if needed. Native sizes and alignment are whatever the platform's C compiler uses. Native byte order is either little-endian or big-endian, depending on the platform.

After the optional first character, a format string is made up of one or more format characters, each optionally preceded by a count (an integer represented by decimal digits). (The format characters are shown in Table 10-1.) For most format characters, the count means repetition (e.g., '3h' is exactly the same as 'hhh'). When the format character is s or p—i.e., a string—the count is not a repetition, but rather the total number of bytes occupied by the string. Whitespace can be freely and innocuously used between formats, but not between a count and its format character.

Format s means a fixed-length string as long as its count (the Python string is truncated, or padded with copies of the null character '\0', if needed). Format p means a Pascal-like string: the first byte is the number of significant characters, and the characters start from the second byte. The count is the total number of bytes, *including* the length byte.

Module struct supplies the following functions.

---

calcsize   calcsize(*fmt*)

Returns the size in bytes of the structure corresponding to struct format string *fmt*.

pack	pack(*fmt*, **values*)
	Packs the given values according to struct format string *fmt* and returns the resulting string. *values* must match in number and types of the values required by *fmt*.

unpack	unpack(*fmt*, *s*)
	Unpacks binary string *s* according to struct format string *fmt* and returns a tuple of values. len(*s*) must be equal to struct.calcsize(*fmt*).

The StringIO and cStringIO Modules

You can implement file-like objects by writing Python classes that supply the methods you need. If all you want is for data to reside in memory, rather than on a file as seen by the operating system, use modules StringIO or cStringIO. The two modules are almost identical: each supplies a factory that is callable to create in-memory file-like objects. The difference between them is that objects created by module StringIO are instances of class StringIO.StringIO. You may inherit from this class to create your own customized file-like objects, overriding the methods that you need to specialize, and you can perform both input and output on objects of this class. Objects created by module cStringIO, on the other hand, are instances of either of two special-purpose types (one just for input, the other just for output), not of a class. Performance is better when you can use cStringIO, but inheritance is not supported, and neither is doing both input and output on the same object. Furthermore, cStringIO does not support Unicode.

Each module supplies a factory function StringIO that returns a file-like object *fl*.

StringIO	StringIO(*[s]*)
	Creates and returns an in-memory file-like object *fl*, with all the methods and attributes of a built-in file object. The data contents of *fl* are initialized to be a copy of argument *s*, which must be a plain string for the StringIO factory function in cStringIO, though it can be a plain or Unicode string for the function in StringIO. When *s* is present, cStringIO.StringIO produces an object suitable for reading from; when *s* is not present, cStringIO.StringIO produces an object suitable for writing to.
	Besides all methods and attributes of built-in file objects (as covered in "Attributes and Methods of File Objects" on page 218), *fl* supplies one supplementary method, getvalue.

getvalue	*f1*. getvalue( )
	Returns the current data contents of *f1* as a string. You cannot call *f1*.getvalue after you call *f1*.close: close frees the buffer that *f1* internally keeps, and getvalue needs to access the buffer to yield its result.

Compressed Files

Storage space and transmission bandwidth are increasingly cheap and abundant, but in many cases you can save such resources, at the expense of some computational effort, by using compression. Computational power grows cheaper and more abundant even faster than other resources, such as bandwidth, so compression's popularity keeps growing. Python makes it easy for your programs to support compression, since the Python standard library contains several modules dedicated to compression.

Since Python offers so many ways to deal with compression, some guidance may be helpful. Files containing data compressed with the zlib module are not automatically interchangeable with other programs, except for those files built with the zipfile module, which respects the standard format of ZIP file archives. You can write custom programs, with any language able to use InfoZip's free *zlib* compression library, to read files produced by Python programs using the zlib module. However, if you do need to interchange compressed data with programs coded in other languages, but have a choice of compression methods, I suggest you use modules bzip2 (best), gzip, or zipfile instead. Module zlib, however, may be useful when you want to compress some parts of datafiles that are in some proprietary format of your own and need not be interchanged with any other program except those that make up your own application.

The gzip Module

The gzip module lets you read and write files compatible with those handled by the powerful GNU compression programs gzip and gunzip. The GNU programs support many compression formats, but module gzip supports only the highly effective native *gzip* format, normally denoted by appending the extension *.gz* to a filename. Module gzip supplies the GzipFile class and an open factory function.

GzipFile	class GzipFile(*filename*=None, *mode*=None, *compresslevel*=9, *fileobj*=None)
	Creates and returns a file-like object *f* wrapping the file or file-like object *fileobj*. When *fileobj* is None, *filename* must be a string that names a file; GzipFile opens that file with the given *mode* (by default, 'rb'), and *f* wraps the resulting file object. *mode* should be

'ab', 'rb', 'wb', or None. When *mode* is None, *f* uses the mode of
fileobj if it can find out the mode; otherwise, it uses 'rb'. When
filename is None, *f* uses the filename of *fileobj* if it can find out the
name; otherwise, it uses ''. *compresslevel* is an integer between 1
and 9: 1 requests modest compression but fast operation; 9 requests
the best compression at the cost of more computation.

File-like object *f* delegates most methods to the underlying file-like
object *fileobj*, transparently accounting for compression as
needed. However, *f* does not allow nonsequential access, so *f* does
not supply methods seek and tell. Calling *f*.close does *not* close
fileobj if *f* was created with a not-None *fileobj*. This matters when
fileobj is an instance of StringIO.StringIO: you can call *fileobj*.
getvalue after *f*.close to get the compressed data string. However,
it also means that you always have to call *fileobj*.close explicitly
after *f*.close.

open   open(*filename*, *mode*='rb', *compresslevel*=9)

Like GzipFile(*filename*, *mode*, *compresslevel*), but *filename* is
mandatory and there is no provision for passing an already opened
fileobj.

A gzip example

Say that you have some function $f(x)$ that writes data to a text
file object *x* passed in as an argument by calling *x*.write and/or
x.writelines. It's easy to make *f* to write data to a *gzip*-
compressed file instead:

```
import gzip
underlying_file = open('x.txt.gz', 'wb')
compressing_wrapper = gzip.
GzipFile(fileobj=underlying_file, mode='wt')
f(compressing_wrapper)
compressing_wrapper.close()
underlying_file.close()
```

This example opens the underlying binary file *x.txt.gz* and explicitly wraps it with gzip.GzipFile, and thus, at the end, we need to
close each object separately. This is necessary because we want to
use two different modes: the underlying file must be opened in
binary mode (any translation of line endings would produce an
invalid compressed file), but the compressing wrapper must be
opened in text mode because we want the implicit translation of \n
to os.linesep. Reading back a compressed text file—for example,
to display it on standard output—is similar:

```
import gzip
underlying_file = open('x.txt.gz', 'rb')
uncompressing_wrapper = gzip.GzipFile(fileobj=
underlying_file, mode='rt')
```

```
for line in uncompressing_wrapper:
    print line,
uncompressing_wrapper.close( )
underlying_file.close( )
```

The bz2 Module

The bz2 module lets you read and write files compatible with those handled by the compression programs bzip2 and bunzip2, which often achieve even better compression than gzip and gunzip. Module bz2 supplies the BZ2File class, for transparent file compression and decompression, and functions compress and decompress to compress and decompress data strings in memory. It also provides objects to compress and decompress data incrementally, enabling you to work with data streams that are too large to comfortably fit in memory at once. For such advanced functionality, consult the Python library's online reference.

BZ2File	class BZ2File(*filename*=None, *mode*='r', *buffering*=0, *compresslevel*=9)
	Creates and returns a file-like object *f*, corresponding to the bzip2-compressed file named by *filename*, which must be a string denoting a file's path. *mode* can be 'r', for reading; 'w', for writing; or 'rU', for reading with universal-newlines translation. When *buffering* is 0, the default, the file is unbuffered. When *buffering* is greater than 0, the file uses a buffer of *buffering* bytes, rounded up to a reasonable amount. *compresslevel* is an integer between 1 and 9: 1 requests modest compression but fast operation; 9 requests the best compression at the cost of more computation.
	f supplies all methods of built-in file objects, including seek and tell. Thus, *f* is seekable; however, the seek operation is emulated, and, while guaranteed to be semantically correct, may in some cases be extremely slow.
compress	compress(*s*, *level*=9)
	Compresses string *s* and returns the string of compressed data. *level* is an integer between 1 and 9: 1 requests modest compression but fast operation; 9 requests the best compression at the cost of more computation.
decompress	decompress(*s*)
	Decompresses the compressed data string *s* and returns the string of uncompressed data.

The tarfile Module

The `tarfile` module lets you read and write TAR files (archive files compatible with those handled by popular archiving programs such as `tar`) optionally with either `gzip` or `bzip2` compression. For invalid TAR file errors, functions of module `tarfile` raise exceptions that are instances of exception class `tarfile.TarError`. Module `tarfile` supplies the following classes and functions.

is_tarfile

`is_tarfile(filename)`

Returns `True` if the file named by string *filename* appears to be a valid TAR file (possibly with compression), judging by the first few bytes; otherwise, returns `False`.

TarInfo

`class TarInfo(name='')`

Methods `getmember` and `getmembers` of `TarFile` instances return instances of `TarInfo`, supplying information about members of the archive. You can also build a `TarInfo` instance with a `TarFile` instance's method `gettarinfo`. The most useful attributes supplied by a `TarInfo` instance *t* are:

linkname
A string that is the target file's name if *t*.type is `LNKTYPE` or `SYMTYPE`

mode
Permission and other mode bits of the file identified by *t*

mtime
Time of last modification of the file identified by *t*

name
Name in the archive of the file identified by *t*

size
Size in bytes (uncompressed) of the file identified by *t*

type
File type, one of many constants that are attributes of module `tarfile` (`SYMTYPE` for symbolic links, `REGTYPE` for regular files, `DIRTYPE` for directories, and so on)

To check the type of *t*, rather than testing *t*.type, you can call *t*'s methods. The most frequently used methods of *t* are:

t.isdir( )
Returns `True` if the file is a directory

t.isfile( )
Returns `True` if the file is a regular file

t.issym( )
Returns `True` if the file is a symbolic link

open   open(*filename, mode=*'r', *fileobj*=None, *bufsize*=10240)

Creates and returns a TarFile instance *f* to read or create a TAR file
through file-like object *fileobj*. When *fileobj* is None, *filename*
must be a string naming a file; open opens the file with the given
mode (by default, 'r'), and *f* wraps the resulting file object. Calling
f.close does *not* close *fileobj* if *f* was opened with a *fileobj* that is
not None. This behavior of *f*.close is important when *fileobj* is an
instance of StringIO.StringIO: you can call *fileobj*.getvalue after
f.close to get the archived and possibly compressed data as a
string. This behavior also means that you have to call *fileobj*.close
explicitly after calling *f*.close.

mode can be 'r', to read an existing TAR file, with whatever
compression it has (if any); 'w', to write a new TAR file, or truncate and rewrite an existing one, without compression or 'a', to
append to an existing TAR file, without compression. Appending
to compressed TAR files is not supported. To write a TAR file with
compression, *mode* can be 'w:gz' for gzip compression, or 'w:bz2'
for bzip2 compression. Special mode strings 'r|' or 'w|' can be
used to read or write uncompressed, nonseekable TAR files (using
a buffer of *bufsize* bytes), and 'r|gz', 'r|bz2', 'w|gz', and 'w|bz2'
can be used to read or write such files with compression.

A TarFile instance *f* supplies the following methods.

add   *f*.add(*filepath, arcname*=None, *recursive*=True)

Adds to archive *f* the file named by *filepath* (can be a regular file,
a directory, or a symbolic link). When *arcname* is not None, it's used
as the archive member name in lieu of *filepath*. When *filepath* is
a directory, add recursively adds the whole filesystem subtree
rooted in that directory, unless you pass *recursive* as False.

addfile   *f*.addfile(*tarinfo, fileobj*=None)

Adds to archive *f* a member identified by *tarinfo*, a TarInfo
instance (the data is the first *tarinfo*.size bytes of file-like object
fileobj if *fileobj* is not None).

close   *f*.close( )

Closes archive *f*. You must call close, or else an incomplete, unusable TAR file might be left on disk. Mandatory finalization is best
performed with a try/finally statement, as covered in try/finally
on page 123.

extract

f.extract(*member, path='.'*)

Extracts the archive member identified by *member* (a name or a TarInfo instance) into a corresponding file in the directory named by *path* (the current directory by default).

extractfile

f.extractfile(*member*)

Extracts the archive member identified by *member* (a name or a TarInfo instance) and returns a read-only file-like object with methods read, readline, readlines, seek, and tell.

getmember

f.getmember(*name*)

Returns a TarInfo instance with information about the archive member named by string *name*.

getmembers

f.getmembers( )

Returns a list of TarInfo instances, one for each member in archive *f*, in the same order as the entries in the archive itself.

getnames

f.getnames( )

Returns a list of strings, the names of each member in archive *f*, in the same order as the entries in the archive itself.

gettarinfo

f.gettarinfo(*name=None, arcname=None, fileobj=None*)

Returns a TarInfo instance with information about the open file object *fileobj*, when not None, or else the existing file whose path is string *name*. When *arcname* is not None, it's used as the name attribute of the resulting TarInfo instance.

list

f.list(*verbose=True*)

Outputs a textual directory of the archive *f* to file *sys.stdout*. If optional argument *verbose* is False, outputs only the names of the archive's members.

The zipfile Module

The zipfile module lets you read and write ZIP files (i.e., archive files compatible with those handled by popular compression programs zip and unzip, pkzip and pkunzip, WinZip, and so on). Detailed information on the formats and capabilities

of ZIP files can be found at *http://www.pkware.com/appnote.html* and *http://www.
info-zip.org/pub/infozip/*. You need to study this detailed information in order to
perform advanced ZIP file handling with module zipfile. If you do not specifically need to interoperate with other programs using the ZIP file standard,
modules gzip and bz2 are most often preferable ways to handle compressed-file
needs.

Module zipfile can't handle ZIP files with appended comments, multidisk ZIP
files, or *.zip* archive members using compression types besides the usual ones,
known as *stored* (a file copied to the archive without compression) and *deflated* (a
file compressed using the ZIP format's default algorithm). For errors related to
invalid *.zip* files, functions of module zipfile raise exceptions that are instances of
exception class zipfile.error. Module zipfile supplies the following classes and
functions.

---

is_zipfile   is_zipfile(*filename*)

Returns True if the file named by string *filename* appears to be a
valid ZIP file, judging by the first few and last bytes of the file;
otherwise, returns False.

ZipInfo   class ZipInfo(*filename*='NoName', *date_time*=(1980, 1, 1, 0, 0,
0))

Methods getinfo and infolist of ZipFile instances return
instances of ZipInfo to supply information about members of the
archive. The most useful attributes supplied by a ZipInfo instance *z*
are:

comment
   A string that is a comment on the archive member

compress_size
   Size in bytes of the compressed data for the archive member

compress_type
   An integer code recording the type of compression of the
   archive member

date_time
   A tuple with six integers recording the time of last modification to the file: the items are year, month, day (1 and up),
   hour, minute, second (0 and up)

file_size
   Size in bytes of the uncompressed data for the archive member

filename
   Name of the file in the archive

ZipFile	class ZipFile(*filename*, *mode*='r', *compression*=zipfile.ZIP_STORED)

Opens a ZIP file named by string *filename*. *mode* can be 'r', to read an existing ZIP file; 'w', to write a new ZIP file or truncate and rewrite an existing one; or 'a', to append to an existing file.

When *mode* is 'a', *filename* can name either an existing ZIP file (in which case new members are added to the existing archive) or an existing non-ZIP file. In the latter case, a new ZIP file–like archive is created and appended to the existing file. The main purpose of this latter case is to let you build a self-unpacking *.exe* file (i.e., a Windows executable file that unpacks itself when run). The existing file must then be a pristine copy of an unpacking *.exe* prefix, as supplied by *www.info-zip.org* and by other purveyors of ZIP file compression tools.

compression is an integer code that can be either of two attributes of module zipfile. zipfile.ZIP_STORED requests that the archive use no compression; zipfile.ZIP_DEFLATED requests that the archive use the *deflation* mode of compression (i.e., the most usual and effective compression approach used in *.zip* files).

A ZipFile instance *z* supplies the following methods.

close	z.close( )

Closes archive file *z*. Make sure the close method gets called, or else an incomplete and unusable ZIP file might be left on disk. Such mandatory finalization is generally best performed with a try/finally statement, as covered in "try/finally" on page 123.

getinfo	z.getinfo(*name*)

Returns a ZipInfo instance that supplies information about the archive member named by string *name*.

infolist	z.infolist( )

Returns a list of ZipInfo instances, one for each member in archive *z*, in the same order as the entries in the archive.

namelist	z.namelist( )

Returns a list of strings, the name of each member in archive *z*, in the same order as the entries in the archive.

printdir	z.printdir( )

Outputs a textual directory of the archive *z* to file *sys.stdout*.

read   z.read(*name*)

Returns a string containing the uncompressed bytes of the file named by string *name* in archive *z*. *z* must be opened for 'r' or 'a'. When the archive does not contain a file named *name*, read raises an exception.

---

testzip   z.testzip( )

Reads and checks the files in archive *z*. Returns a string with the name of the first archive member that is damaged, or None if the archive is intact.

---

write   z.write(*filename, arcname*=None, *compress_type*=None)

Writes the file named by string *filename* to archive *z*, with archive member name *arcname*. When *arcname* is None, write uses *filename* as the archive member name. When *compress_type* is None, write uses *z*'s compression type; otherwise, *compress_type* is zipfile.ZIP_STORED or zipfile.ZIP_DEFLATED, and specifies how to compress the file. *z* must be opened for 'w' or 'a'.

---

writestr   z.writestr(*zinfo, bytes*)

zinfo must be a ZipInfo instance specifying at least *filename* and *date_time*. *bytes* is a string of bytes. writestr adds a member to archive *z* using the metadata specified by *zinfo* and the data in *bytes*. *z* must be opened for 'w' or 'a'. When you have data in memory and need to write the data to the ZIP file archive *z*, it's simpler and faster to use z.writestr rather than z.write. The latter requires you to write the data to disk first and later remove the useless disk file. The following example shows both approaches, each encapsulated into a function and polymorphic to each other:

```
import zipfile
def data_to_zip_direct(z, data, name):
    import time
    zinfo = zipfile.ZipInfo(name, time.localtime( )[:6])
    zinfo.compress_type = zipfile.ZIP_DEFLATED
    z.writestr(zinfo, data)
def data_to_zip_indirect(z, data, name):
    import os
    flob = open(name, 'wb')
    flob.write(data)
    flob.close( )
    z.write(name)
    os.unlink(name)
zz = zipfile.ZipFile('z.zip', 'w', zipfile.ZIP_DEFLATED)
data = 'four score\nand seven\nyears ago\n'
data_to_zip_direct(zz, data, 'direct.txt')
data_to_zip_indirect(zz, data, 'indirect.txt')
zz.close( )
```

Besides being faster and more concise, data_to_zip_direct is handier, since it works in memory and doesn't require the current working directory to be writable, as data_to_zip_indirect does. Of course, method write also has its uses when you already have the data in a file on disk and just want to add the file to the archive.

Here's how you can print a list of all files contained in the ZIP file archive created by the previous example, followed by each file's name and contents:

```
import zipfile
zz = zipfile.ZipFile('z.zip')
zz.printdir( )
for name in zz.namelist( ):
    print '%s: %r' % (name, zz.read(name))
zz.close( )
```

The zlib Module

The zlib module lets Python programs use the free InfoZip *zlib* compression library (*http://www.info-zip.org/pub/infozip/zlib/*), version 1.1.3 or later. Module zlib is used by modules gzip and zipfile, but is also available directly for any special compression needs. The most commonly used functions supplied by module zlib are the following:

compress   compress(s, *level*=6)

Compresses string s and returns the string of compressed data. *level* is an integer between 1 and 9; 1 requests modest compression but fast operation, and 9 requests compression as good as feasible, requiring more computation.

decompress   decompress(s)

Decompresses the compressed data string s and returns the string of uncompressed data.

Module zlib also supplies functions to compute Cyclic-Redundancy Check (CRC) checksums to detect damage in compressed data. It also provides objects to compress and decompress data incrementally to work with data streams too large to fit in memory at once. For such advanced functionality, consult the Python library's online reference.

The os Module

The os module is an umbrella module that presents a reasonably uniform cross-platform view of the different capabilities of various operating systems. The module provides ways to create and handle files and directories, and to create, manage, and destroy processes. This section covers the filesystem-related capabilities of the os module; "Running Other Programs with the os Module" on page 354 covers the process-related capabilities.

The os module supplies a name attribute, which is a string that identifies the kind of platform on which Python is being run. Common values for name are 'posix' (all kinds of Unix-like platforms, including Mac OS X), 'nt' (all kinds of 32-bit Windows platforms), 'mac' (old Mac systems), and 'java' (Jython). You can often exploit unique capabilities of a platform, at least in part, through functions supplied by os. However, this book deals with cross-platform programming, not with platform-specific functionality, so I do not cover parts of os that exist only on one kind of platform, nor do I cover platform-specific modules. All functionality covered in this book is available at least on both 'posix' and 'nt' platforms. However, I do cover any differences among the ways in which a given functionality is provided on different platforms.

OSError Exceptions

When a request to the operating system fails, os raises an exception, which is an instance of OSError. os also exposes built-in exception class OSError with the name os.error. Instances of OSError expose three useful attributes:

errno
> The numeric error code of the operating system error

strerror
> A string that summarily describes the error

filename
> The name of the file on which the operation failed (for file-related functions only)

os functions can also raise other standard exceptions, typically TypeError or ValueError, when the cause of the error is that you have called them with invalid argument types or values so that the underlying operating system functionality has not even been attempted.

The errno Module

The errno module supplies symbolic names for error code numbers. To handle possible system errors selectively, based on error codes, use errno to enhance your program's portability and readability. For example, here's how you might handle "file not found" errors, while propagating all other kinds of errors:

```
try: os.some_os_function_or_other( )
except OSError, err:
    import errno
    # check for "file not found" errors, re-raise other cases
```

```
    if err.errno != errno.ENOENT: raise
    # proceed with the specific case you can handle
    print "Warning: file", err.filename, "not found -- continuing"
```

errno also supplies a dictionary named errorcode: the keys are error code numbers, and the corresponding names are the error names, which are strings such as 'ENOENT'. Displaying errno.errorcode[err.errno], as part of your diagnosis of some os.error instance err, can often make the diagnosis clearer and more understandable to readers who specialize in the specific platform.

Filesystem Operations

Using the os module, you can manipulate the filesystem in a variety of ways: creating, copying, and deleting files and directories, comparing files, and examining filesystem information about files and directories. This section documents the attributes and methods of the os module that you use for these purposes, and covers some related modules that operate on the filesystem.

Path-String Attributes of the os Module

A file or directory is identified by a string, known as its *path*, whose syntax depends on the platform. On both Unix-like and Windows platforms, Python accepts Unix syntax for paths, with a slash (/) as the directory separator. On non-Unix-like platforms, Python also accepts platform-specific path syntax. On Windows, in particular, you may use a backslash (\) as the separator. However, you then need to double-up each backslash as \\ in string literals, or use raw-string syntax as covered in "Literals" on page 37; you also needlessly lose portability. Unix path syntax is handier, and usable everywhere, so I strongly recommend that you *always* use it. In the rest of this chapter, for brevity, I assume Unix path syntax in both explanations and examples.

Module os supplies attributes that provide details about path strings on the current platform. You should typically use the higher-level path manipulation operations covered in "The os.path Module" on page 246 rather than lower-level string operations based on these attributes. However, the attributes may be useful at times.

curdir
      The string that denotes the current directory ('.' on Unix and Windows)

defpath
      The default search path for programs, used if the environment lacks a PATH environment variable

linesep
      The string that terminates text lines ('\n' on Unix; '\r\n' on Windows)

extsep
      The string that separates the extension part of a file's name from the rest of the name ('.' on Unix and Windows)

pardir
      The string that denotes the parent directory ('..' on Unix and Windows)

pathsep

The separator between paths in lists of paths, such as those used for the environment variable PATH (':' on Unix; ';' on Windows)

sep

The separator of path components ('/' on Unix; '\\' on Windows)

Permissions

Unix-like platforms associate nine bits with each file or directory: three each for the file's owner, its group, and anybody else, indicating whether the file or directory can be read, written, and executed by the given subject. These nine bits are known as the file's *permission bits*, and are part of the file's *mode* (a bit string that includes other bits that describe the file). These bits are often displayed in octal notation, with three bits in each digit. For example, mode 0664 indicates a file that can be read and written by its owner and group, and read, but not written, by anybody else. When any process on a Unix-like system creates a file or directory, the operating system applies to the specified mode a bit mask known as the process's *umask*, which can remove some of the permission bits.

Non-Unix-like platforms handle file and directory permissions in very different ways. However, the functions in Python's standard library that deal with file permissions accept a *mode* argument according to the Unix-like approach described in the previous paragraph. The implementation on each platform maps the nine permission bits in a way appropriate for the given platform. For example, on versions of Windows that distinguish only between read-only and read/write files and do not distinguish file ownership, a file's permission bits show up as either 0666 (read/write) or 0444 (read-only). On such a platform, when creating a file, the implementation looks only at bit 0200, making the file read/write if that bit is 0 or read-only if that bit is 1.

File and Directory Functions of the os Module

The os module supplies several functions to query and set file and directory status.

---

access   access(*path, mode*)

Returns True if file *path* has all of the permissions encoded in integer *mode*; otherwise, False. *mode* can be os.F_OK to test for file existence, or one or more of the constant integers named os.R_OK, os.W_OK, and os.X_OK (with the bitwise-OR operator | joining them, if more than one) to test permissions to read, write, and execute the file.

access does not use the standard interpretation for its *mode* argument, covered in "Permissions" on page 242. access tests only if this specific process's real user and group identifiers have the requested permissions on the file. If you need to study a file's permission bits in more detail, see function stat on page 244.

---

chdir	chdir(*path*)

Sets the current working directory to *path*.

chmod	chmod(*path*, *mode*)

Changes the permissions of file *path*, as encoded in integer *mode*. *mode* can be zero or more of os.R_OK, os.W_OK, and os.X_OK (with the bitwise-OR operator | joining them, if more than one) to set permission to read, write, and execute. On Unix-like platforms, *mode* can also be a richer bit pattern (as covered in "Permissions" on page 242) to specify different permissions for user, group, and other.

getcwd	getcwd( )

Returns the path of the current working directory.

listdir	listdir(*path*)

Returns a list whose items are the names of all files and subdirectories found in directory *path*. The returned list is in arbitrary order and does *not* include the special directory names '.' (current directory) and '..' (parent directory).

The dircache module also supplies a function named listdir, which works like os.listdir, with two enhancements. First, dircache.listdir returns a sorted list. Further, dircache caches the list it returns so that repeated requests for lists of the same directory are faster if the directory's contents have not changed in the meantime. dircache automatically detects changes: whenever you call dircache.listdir, you get a list that reflects the directory's contents at that time.

makedirs, mkdir	makedirs(*path*, *mode*=0777) mkdir(*path*, *mode*=0777)

makedirs creates all directories that are part of *path* and do not yet exist. mkdir creates only the rightmost directory of *path* and raises OSError if any of the previous directories in *path* do not exist. Both functions use *mode* as permission bits of directories they create. Both functions raise OSError if creation fails, or if a file or directory named *path* already exists.

remove, unlink	remove(*path*) unlink(*path*)

Removes the file named *path* (see rmdir on page 244 to remove a directory). unlink is a synonym of remove.

removedirs   removedirs(*path*)

Loops from right to left over the directories that are part of *path*, removing each one. The loop ends when a removal attempt raises an exception, generally because a directory is not empty. removedirs does not propagate the exception, as long as it has removed at least one directory.

rename   rename(*source, dest*)

Renames the file or directory named *source* to *dest*.

renames   renames(*source, dest*)

Like rename, except that renames tries to create all intermediate directories needed for *dest*. After renaming, renames tries to remove empty directories from path *source* using removedirs. It does not propagate any resulting exception; it's not an error if the starting directory of *source* does not become empty after the renaming.

rmdir   rmdir(*path*)

Removes the empty directory named *path* (raises OSError if the removal fails, and, in particular, if the directory is not empty).

stat   stat(*path*)

Returns a value *x* of type stat_result, which provides 10 items of information about file or subdirectory *path*. Accessing those items by their numeric indices is generally not advisable because the resulting code is not very readable; use the corresponding attribute names instead. Table 10-2 lists the attributes of a stat_result instance and the meaning of corresponding items.

Table 10-2. Items (attributes) of a stat_result instance

Item index	Attribute name	Meaning
0	st_mode	Protection and other mode bits
1	st_ino	Inode number
2	st_dev	Device ID
3	st_nlink	Number of hard links
4	st_uid	User ID of owner
5	st_gid	Group ID of owner
6	st_size	Size in bytes
7	st_atime	Time of last access
8	st_mtime	Time of last modification
9	st_ctime	Time of last status change

For example, to print the size in bytes of file *path*, you can use any of:

```
import os
print os.path.getsize(path)
print os.stat(path)[6]
print os.stat(path).st_size
```

Time values are in seconds since the epoch, as covered in Chapter 12 (int on most platforms; float on very old versions of the Macintosh). Platforms unable to give a meaningful value for an item use a dummy value for that item.

tempnam,
tmpnam

tempnam(*dir*=None, *prefix*=None) tmpnam( )

Returns an absolute path usable as the name of a new temporary file. **Note**: tempnam and tmpnam are weaknesses in your program's security. Avoid these functions and use instead the standard library module tempfile, covered in "The tempfile Module" on page 223.

utime

utime(*path*, *times*=None)

Sets the accessed and modified times of file or directory *path*. If *times* is None, utime uses the current time. Otherwise, *times* must be a pair of numbers (in seconds since the epoch, as covered in Chapter 12) in the order (*accessed, modified*).

walk

walk(*top*, *topdown*=True, *onerror*=None)

A generator yielding an item for each directory in the tree whose root is directory *top*. When *topdown* is True, the default, walk visits directories from the tree's root downward; when *topdown* is False, walk visits directories from the tree's leaves upward. When *onerror* is None, walk catches and ignores any OSError exception raised during the tree-walk. Otherwise, *onerror* must be a function; walk catches any OSError exception raised during the tree-walk and passes it as the only argument in a call to *onerror*, which may process it, ignore it, or raise it to terminate the tree-walk and propagate the exception.

Each item walk yields is a tuple of three subitems: *dirpath*, a string that is the directory's path; *dirnames*, a list of names of subdirectories that are immediate children of the directory (special directories '.' and '..' are *not* included); and *filenames*, a list of names of files that are directly in the directory. If *topdown* is True, you can alter list *dirnames in-place*, removing some items and/or reordering others, to affect the tree-walk of the subtree rooted at *dirpath*; walk iterates only in subdirectories left in *dirnames*, in the order in which they're left. Such alterations have no effect if *topdown* is False (in this case, walk has already visited all subdirectories by the time it visits the current directory and yields its item).

A typical use of os.walk might be to print the paths of all files (not subdirectories) in a tree, skipping those parts of the tree whose root directories' names start with '.':

```
import os
for dirpath, dirnames, filenames in os.
walk(tree_root_dir):
    # alter dirnames *in-place* to skip subdirectories
    named '.something'
    dirnames[:] = [d for d in dirnames if not d.
startswith('.')]
        # print the path of each file
        for name in filenames:
            print os.path.join(dirpath, name)
```

If argument *top* is a relative path, then the body of a loop on the result of os.walk should not change the working directory, which might cause undefined behavior. os.walk itself never changes the working directory. To transform any name *x*, an item in *dirnames* or *filenames*, into a path, use os.path.join(top, dirpath, x).

The os.path Module

The os.path module supplies functions to analyze and transform path strings. To use this module, you can import os.path; however, if you just import os, you can also access module os.path and all of its attributes.

---

abspath   abspath(*path*)

Returns a normalized absolute path string equivalent to *path*, just like:

```
os.path.normpath(os.path.join(os.getcwd(), path))
```

For example, os.path.abspath(os.curdir) is the same as os.getcwd().

---

basename   basename(*path*)

Returns the base name part of *path*, just like os.path.split(*path*)[1]. For example, os.path.basename('b/c/d.e') returns 'd.e'.

---

commonprefix   commonprefix(*list*)

Accepts a list of strings and returns the longest string that is a prefix of all items in the list. Unlike all other functions in os.path, commonprefix works on arbitrary strings, not just on paths. For example, os.path.commonprefix(['foobar', 'foolish']) returns 'foo'.

dirname   dirname(*path*)

Returns the directory part of *path*, just like os.path.split(*path*)[0]. For example, os.path.dirname('b/c/d.e') returns 'b/c'.

exists   exists(*path*)

Returns True when *path* names an existing file or directory; otherwise, False. In other words, os.path.exists(*x*) is the same as os. access(*x*, os.F_OK).

expandvars   expandvars(*path*)

Returns a copy of string *path*, where each substring of the form $*name* or ${*name*} is replaced with the value of environment variable name. For example, if environment variable HOME is set to /u/alex, the following code:

```
import os
print os.path.expandvars('$HOME/foo/')
```

emits /u/alex/foo/.

getatime,   getatime(*path*) getmtime(*path*) getsize(*path*)
getmtime,
getsize   Each of these functions returns an attribute from the result of os. stat(*path*): respectively, st_atime, st_mtime, and st_size. See stat on page 244 for more details about these attributes.

isabs   isabs(*path*)

Returns True when *path* is absolute. A path is absolute when it starts with a slash (/), or, on some non-Unix-like platforms, with a drive designator followed by os.sep. When *path* is not absolute, isabs returns False.

isfile   isfile(*path*)

Returns True when *path* names an existing regular file (in Unix, however, isfile also follows symbolic links); otherwise, False.

isdir   isdir(*path*)

Returns True when *path* names an existing directory (in Unix, however, isdir also follows symbolic links); otherwise, False.

islink   islink(*path*)

Returns True when *path* names a symbolic link; otherwise (always on platforms that don't support symbolic links), islink returns False.

ismount   ismount(*path*)

Returns True when *path* names a mount point; otherwise (always on platforms that don't support mount points), ismount returns False.

join   join(*path*, **paths*)

Returns a string that joins the argument strings with the appropriate path separator for the current platform. For example, on Unix, exactly one slash character / separates adjacent path components. If any argument is an absolute path, join ignores all previous components. For example:

```
print os.path.join('a/b', 'c/d', 'e/f')
# on Unix prints: a/b/c/d/e/f
print os.path.join('a/b', '/c/d', 'e/f')
# on Unix prints: /c/d/e/f
```

The second call to os.path.join ignores its first argument 'a/b', since its second argument '/c/d' is an absolute path.

normcase   normcase(*path*)

Returns a copy of *path* with case normalized for the current platform. On case-sensitive filesystems (as is typical in Unix-like systems), *path* is returned unchanged. On case-insensitive filesystems (as typical in Windows), all letters in the returned string are lowercase. On Windows, normcase also converts each / to a \.

normpath   normpath(*path*)

Returns a normalized pathname equivalent to *path*, removing redundant separators and path-navigation aspects. For example, on Unix, normpath returns 'a/b' when *path* is any of 'a//b', 'a/./b', or 'a/c/../b'. normpath makes path separators appropriate for the current platform. For example, on Windows, separators become \.

split   split(*path*)

Returns a pair of strings (*dir*, *base*) such that join(*dir*, *base*) equals *path*. *base* is the last pathname component and never contains a path separator. If *path* ends in a separator, *base* is ''. *dir* is the leading part of *path*, up to the last path separator, shorn of

trailing separators. For example, os.path.split('a/b/c/d') returns
the pair ('a/b/c', 'd').

---

splitdrive splitdrive(*path*)

Returns a pair of strings (*drv, pth*) such that *drv+pth* equals *path*.
drv is either a drive specification or ''. *drv* is always '' on platforms that do not support drive specifications, such as all Unix-like
systems. For example, on Windows, os.path.splitdrive('c:d/e')
returns the pair ('c:', 'd/e').

---

splitext splitext(*path*)

Returns a pair of strings (*root, ext*) such that *root+ext* equals *path*.
ext is either '' or starts with a '.' and has no other '.' or path
separator. For example, os.path.splitext('a.a/b.c.d') returns the
pair ('a.a/b.c', '.d').

---

walk walk(*path, func, arg*)

Calls *func*(*arg, dirpath, namelist*) for each directory in the tree
whose root is directory *path*, starting with *path* itself. This function
is complicated to use and obsolete; use, instead, generator os.walk,
covered in walk on page 245.

The stat Module

Function os.stat (covered in stat on page 244) returns instances of stat_result,
whose item indices, attribute names, and meaning are covered in Table 10-2. The
stat module supplies attributes with names like those of stat_result's attributes,
turned into uppercase, and corresponding values that are the corresponding item
indices.

More interesting contents of module stat are functions that examine the st_mode
attribute of a stat_result instance to determine the kind of file. os.path also
supplies functions for such tasks, which operate directly on the file's *path*. The
functions supplied by stat are faster when they perform several tests on the same
file: they require only one os.stat call at the start of a series of tests, while the
functions in os.path implicitly ask the operating system for the information at
each test. Each function returns True if *mode* denotes a file of the given kind; otherwise, False.

S_ISDIR(*mode*)
    Is the file a directory?

S_ISCHR(*mode*)
    Is the file a special device-file of the character kind?

S_ISBLK(*mode*)

    Is the file a special device-file of the block kind?

S_ISREG(*mode*)

    Is the file a normal file (not a directory, special device-file, and so on)?

S_ISFIFO(*mode*)

    Is the file a FIFO (i.e., a "named pipe")?

S_ISLNK(*mode*)

    Is the file a symbolic link?

S_ISSOCK(*mode*)

    Is the file a Unix-domain socket?

Except for stat.S_ISDIR and stat.S_ISREG, the other functions are meaningful only on Unix-like systems, since other platforms do not keep special files such as devices and sockets in the same filesystem as regular files, and don't provide symbolic links as directly as Unix-like systems do.

Module stat supplies two more functions that extract relevant parts of a file's *mode* (*x*.st_mode, for some result *x* of function os.stat).

S_IFMT   S_IFMT(*mode*)

        Returns those bits of *mode* that describe the kind of file (i.e., those bits that are examined by functions S_ISDIR, S_ISREG, etc.).

S_IMODE   S_IMODE(*mode*)

        Returns those bits of *mode* that can be set by function os.chmod (i.e., the permission bits and, on Unix-like platforms, other special bits such as the set-user-id flag).

The filecmp Module

The filecmp module supplies functionality to compare files and directories.

---

cmp   cmp(*f1*, *f2*, *shallow*=True)

        Compares the files named by path strings *f1* and *f2*. If the files seem equal, cmp returns True; otherwise, False. If *shallow* is true, files are "equal" if their stat tuples are. If *shallow* is false, cmp reads and compares files whose stat tuples are equal.

---

cmpfiles   cmpfiles(*dir1*, *dir2*, *common*, *shallow*=True)

        Loops on sequence *common*. Each item of *common* is a string that names a file present in both directories *dir1* and *dir2*. cmpfiles

---

returns a tuple whose items are three lists of strings: (*equal*, *diff*, *errs*). *equal* is the list of names of files that are equal in both directories, *diff* is the list of names of files that differ between directories, and *errs* is the list of names of files that could not be compared (because they do not exist in both directories, or there is no permission to read them). Argument *shallow* is the same as for function cmp.

---

dircmp

class dircmp(*dir1*, *dir2*, *ignore*=('RCS', 'CVS', 'tags'), *hide*=('.', '..'))

Creates a new directory-comparison instance object, comparing directories named *dir1* and *dir2*, ignoring names listed in *ignore*, and hiding names listed in *hide*. A dircmp instance *d* exposes three methods:

d.report( )
> Outputs to sys.stdout a comparison between *dir1* and *dir2*

d.report_partial_closure( )
> Outputs to sys.stdout a comparison between *dir1* and *dir2* and their common immediate subdirectories

d.report_full_closure( )
> Outputs to sys.stdout a comparison between *dir1* and *dir2* and all their common subdirectories, recursively

A dircmp instance *d* supplies several attributes, computed just in time (i.e., only if and when needed, thanks to a __getattr__ special method) so that using a dircmp instance suffers no unnecessary overhead. *d*'s attributes are:

d.common
> Files and subdirectories that are in both *dir1* and *dir2*

d.common_dirs
> Subdirectories that are in both *dir1* and *dir2*

d.common_files
> Files that are in both *dir1* and *dir2*

d.common_funny
> Names that are in both *dir1* and *dir2* for which os.stat reports an error or returns different kinds for the versions in the two directories

d.diff_files
> Files that are in both *dir1* and *dir2* but with different contents

d.funny_files
> Files that are in both *dir1* and *dir2* but could not be compared

d.left_list
> Files and subdirectories that are in *dir1*

d.left_only
> Files and subdirectories that are in *dir1* and not in *dir2*

d.right_list
> Files and subdirectories that are in *dir2*

d.right_only
> Files and subdirectories that are in *dir2* and not in *dir1*

d.same_files
> Files that are in both *dir1* and *dir2* with the same contents

d.subdirs
> A dictionary whose keys are the strings in common_dirs; the corresponding values are instances of dircmp for each subdirectory

The shutil Module

The shutil module (an abbreviation for *shell utilities*) supplies functions to copy and move files, and to remove an entire directory tree. In addition to offering functions that are directly useful, the source file *shutil.py* in the standard Python library is an excellent example of how to use many os functions.

copy	copy(*src*, *dst*)
	Copies the contents of file *src*, creating or overwriting file *dst*. If *dst* is a directory, the target is a file with the same base name as *src* in directory *dst*. copy also copies permission bits, except last-access and modification times.
copy2	copy2(*src*, *dst*)
	Like copy, but also copies times of last access and modification.
copyfile	copyfile(*src*, *dst*)
	Copies just the contents (not permission bits, nor last-access and modification times) of file *src*, creating or overwriting file *dst*.
copyfileobj	copyfileobj(*fsrc*, *fdst*, *bufsize*=16384)
	Copies all bytes from file object *fsrc*, which must be open for reading, to file object *fdst*, which must be open for writing. Copies no more than *bufsize* bytes at a time if *bufsize* is greater than 0. File objects are covered in "File Objects" on page 216.
copymode	copymode(*src*, *dst*)
	Copies permission bits of file or directory *src* to file or directory *dst*. Both *src* and *dst* must exist. Does not change *dst*'s contents, nor its file or directory status.

copystat   copystat(*src*, *dst*)

Copies permission bits and times of last access and modification of
file or directory *src* to file or directory *dst*. Both *src* and *dst* must
exist. Does not change *dst*'s contents, nor its file or directory
status.

copytree   copytree(*src*, *dst*, *symlinks*=False)

Copies the directory tree rooted at *src* into the destination directory named by *dst*. *dst* must not already exist: copytree creates it.
copytree copies each file by using function copy2. When *symlinks* is
true, copytree creates symbolic links in the new tree when it finds
symbolic links in the source tree. When *symlinks* is false, copytree
follows each symbolic link it finds and copies the linked-to file with
the link's name. On platforms that do not have the concept of a
symbolic link, such as Windows, copytree ignores argument
symlinks.

move   move(*src*, *dst*)

Moves file or directory *src* to *dst*. First tries os.rename. Then, if that
fails (because *src* and *dst* are on separate filesystems, or because
they're files and *dst* already exists), copies *src* to *dst* (copy2 for a
file, copytree for a directory), then removes *src* (os.unlink for a file,
rmtree for a directory).

rmtree   rmtree(*path*, *ignore_errors*=False, *onerror*=None)

Removes the directory tree rooted at *path*. When *ignore_errors* is
true, rmtree ignores errors. When *ignore_errors* is false and *onerror*
is None, any error raises an exception. When *onerror* is not None, it
must be callable with three parameters: *func*, *path*, and *excp*. *func* is
the function that raises an exception (os.remove or os.rmdir), *path* is
the path passed to *func*, and *excp* is the tuple of information that
sys.exc_info( ) returns. If *onerror* raises any exception *x*, rmtree
terminates, and exception *x* propagates.

File Descriptor Operations

The os module supplies functions to handle *file descriptors*, which are integers
that the operating system uses as opaque handles to refer to open files. Python file
objects (covered in "File Objects" on page 216) are almost invariably better for
input/output (I/O) tasks, but sometimes working at file-descriptor level lets you
perform some operation more rapidly or elegantly. Note that file objects and file
descriptors are not interchangeable in any way.

You can get the file descriptor *n* of a Python file object *f* by calling *n*=*f*.fileno( ). You can wrap a new Python file object *f* around an open file descriptor *fd* by calling *f*=os.fdopen(*fd*). On Unix-like and Windows platforms, some file descriptors are preallocated when a process starts: 0 is the file descriptor for the process's standard input, 1 for the process's standard output, and 2 for the process's standard error.

os provides the following functions for working with file descriptors.

close
close(*fd*)

Closes file descriptor *fd*.

dup
dup(*fd*)

Returns a file descriptor that duplicates file descriptor *fd*.

dup2
dup2(*fd*, *fd2*)

Duplicates file descriptor *fd* to file descriptor *fd2*. If file descriptor *fd2* is already open, dup2 first closes *fd2*.

fdopen
fdopen(*fd*, *mode*='r', *bufsize*=-1)

Returns a Python file object wrapping file descriptor *fd*. *mode* and *bufsize* have the same meaning as for Python's built-in open, covered in "Creating a File Object with open" on page 216.

fstat
fstat(*fd*)

Returns a stat_result instance *x*, with information about the file that is open on file descriptor *fd*. Table 10-2 covers *x*'s contents.

lseek
lseek(*fd*, *pos*, *how*)

Sets the current position of file descriptor *fd* to the signed integer byte offset *pos* and returns the resulting byte offset from the start of the file. *how* indicates the reference (point 0). When *how* is 0, the reference is the start of the file; when 1, the current position; when 2, the end of the file. In particular, lseek(*fd*, 0, 1) returns the current position's byte offset from the start of the file without affecting the current position. Normal disk files support seeking; calling lseek on a file that does not support seeking (e.g., a file open for output to a terminal) raises an exception. In Python 2.5, module os has attributes named SEEK_SET, SEEK_CUR, and SEEK_END, with values of 0, 1, and 2, respectively, to use instead of the bare integer constants for readability.

open

open(*file*, *flags*, *mode*=0777)

Returns a file descriptor, opening or creating a file named by string *file*. If open creates the file, it uses *mode* as the file's permission bits. *flags* is an int, and is normally obtained by bitwise ORing one or more of the following attributes of os:

O_RDONLY
O_WRONLY
O_RDWR

> Opens *file* for read-only, write-only, or read/write, respectively (mutually exclusive: exactly one of these attributes must be in *flags*)

O_NDELAY
O_NONBLOCK

> Opens *file* in nonblocking (no-delay) mode if the platform supports this

O_APPEND

> Appends any new data to *file*'s previous contents

O_DSYNC
O_RSYNC
O_SYNC
O_NOCTTY

> Sets synchronization mode accordingly if the platform supports this

O_CREAT

> Creates *file* if *file* does not already exist

O_EXCL

> Raises an exception if *file* already exists

O_TRUNC

> Throws away previous contents of *file* (incompatible with O_RDONLY)

O_BINARY

> Opens *file* in binary rather than text mode on non-Unix platforms (innocuous and without effect on Unix-like platforms)

pipe

pipe( )

Creates a pipe and returns a pair of file descriptors (*r*, *w*), respectively open for reading and writing.

read

read(*fd*, *n*)

Reads up to *n* bytes from file descriptor *fd* and returns them as a plain string. Reads and returns *m*<*n* bytes when only *m* more bytes are currently available for reading from the file. In particular, returns the empty string when no more bytes are currently available from the file, typically because the file is finished.

write	write(*fd*, *s*)
	Writes all bytes from plain string *s* to file descriptor *fd* and returns the number of bytes written (i.e., len(*s*)).

Text Input and Output

Python presents non-GUI text input and output channels to your programs as file objects, so you can use the methods of file objects (covered in "Attributes and Methods of File Objects" on page 218) to manipulate these channels.

Standard Output and Standard Error

The sys module (covered in "The sys Module" on page 168) has attributes stdout and stderr, which are writeable file objects. Unless you are using shell redirection or pipes, these streams connect to the terminal running your script. Nowadays, actual terminals are rare: a so-called "terminal" is generally a screen window that supports text I/O (e.g., a Command Prompt console on Windows or an xterm window on Unix).

The distinction between sys.stdout and sys.stderr is a matter of convention. sys.stdout, known as your script's standard output, is where your program emits results. sys.stderr, known as your script's standard error, is where error messages go. Separating results from error messages helps you use shell redirection effectively. Python respects this convention, using sys.stderr for errors and warnings.

The print Statement

Programs that output results to standard output often need to write to sys.stdout. Python's print statement (covered in "The print Statement" on page 61) can be a convenient alternative to sys.stdout.write.

print works well for the kind of informal output used during development to help you debug your code. For production output, you often need more control of formatting than print affords. You may need to control spacing, field widths, number of decimals for floating-point values, and so on. In this case, prepare the output as a string with the string-formatting operator % (covered in "String Formatting" on page 193), then output the string, normally with the write method of the appropriate file object. (You can also pass formatted strings to print, but print adds spaces and newlines, while the write method adds nothing at all, making it easier to control exactly what gets emitted.)

When you want to direct the output from several print statements to another file, as an alternative to repeated use of the >>*destination* clause on each print, you can temporarily change the value of sys.stdout. The following example shows a general-purpose redirection function that you can use for such a temporary change:

```
def redirect(func, *args, **kwds):
    """redirect(func, ...) -> (output string result, func's return value)
    func must be a callable and may emit results to standard output.
    redirect captures those results as a string and returns a pair, with
    the results string as the first item and func's return value as the
    second one.
    """
    import sys, cStringIO
    save_out = sys.stdout
    sys.stdout = cStringIO.StringIO( )
    try:
        retval = func(*args, **kwds)
        return sys.stdout.getvalue( ), retval
    finally:
        sys.stdout.close( )
        sys.stdout = save_out
```

To output some text values to a file object *f* that aren't the current value of sys.stdout, avoid such complicated manipulations: for such simple purposes, just calling *f*.write is usually best, and print>>*f*,... is sometimes a handy alternative.

Standard Input

The sys module provides the stdin attribute, which is a readable file object. When you need a line of text from the user, you can call the built-in function raw_input (covered in raw_input on page 165), optionally with a string argument to use as a prompt.

When the input you need is not a string (for example, when you need a number), you could use built-in function input. However, input is unsuitable for most programs. Rather, use raw_input to obtain a string from the user, then other built-ins, such as int or float, to get a number from the string. You can also use eval (normally preceded by compile, for better control of error diagnostics) to let the user input any expression, as long as you totally trust the user. A malicious user can easily exploit eval to breach security and cause damage; there is no completely effective defense, except to avoid eval (and the exec statement) on any input from sources you do not fully trust. However, the following function, using some advanced introspection, may help:

```
def moderately_secure_input(prompt):
    s = raw_input(prompt)
    c = compile(s, '<your input>', 'eval')
    if c.co_names: raise SyntaxError, 'names %r not allowed'%c.co_names
    return eval(c)
```

This function may raise a SyntaxError exception (which you can, if you want, catch with a try/except statement) and doesn't let the user employ any names (thus, no built-ins, and no other functions or variables either), but otherwise accepts a wide variety of expressions and is moderately safe against abuse.

The getpass Module

Occasionally, you want the user to input a line of text in such a way that somebody looking at the screen cannot see what the user is typing. This often occurs when you're asking the user for a password. The getpass module provides the following functions.

getpass	getpass(*prompt*='Password: ')
	Like raw_input, except that the text the user inputs is not echoed to the screen as the user is typing. getpass's default *prompt* is different from raw_input's.

getuser	getuser()
	Returns the current user's username. getuser tries to get the username as the value of one of the environment variables LOGNAME, USER, LNAME, and USERNAME, in order. If none of these variables are in os.environ, getuser asks the operating system.

Richer-Text I/O

The tools we have covered so far support the minimal subset of text I/O functionality that all platforms supply. Most platforms also offer richer-text I/O capabilities, such as responding to single keypresses (not just entire lines of text) and showing text in any spot on the terminal (not just sequentially).

Python extensions and core Python modules let you access platform-specific functionality. Unfortunately, various platforms expose this functionality in different ways. To develop cross-platform Python programs with rich-text I/O functionality, you may need to wrap different modules uniformly, importing platform-specific modules conditionally (usually with the try/except idiom covered in try/except on page 122).

The readline Module

The readline module wraps the GNU Readline Library. GNU Readline lets the user edit text lines during interactive input, and recall previous lines for editing and reentry. Readline is installed on many Unix-like platforms, and it's available at *http://cnswww.cns.cwru.edu/~chet/readline/rltop.html*. A Windows port (*http://starship.python.net/crew/kernr/*) is available, but is not widely deployed. Chris Gonnerman's module, Alternative Readline for Windows, implements a subset of Python's standard readline module (using a small dedicated *.pyd* file instead of Readline) and is found at *http://newcenturycomputers.net/projects/readline.html*. One way to use Readline on Windows is to install Gary Bishop's version of readline (*http://sourceforge.net/projects/uncpythontools*); this version does, however, require two other Python add-ons (`ctypes` and `PyWin32`), and so is not quite trivial to install.

When readline is available, Python uses it for all line-oriented input, such as raw_input. The interactive Python interpreter always tries to load readline to enable line editing and recall for interactive sessions. Some readline functions control advanced functionality, particularly *history*, for recalling lines entered in previous sessions, and *completion*, for context-sensitive completion of the word being entered. (See *http://cnswww.cns.cwru.edu/~chet/readline/rltop.html#Documentation* for GNU Readline documentation, with details on configuration commands.) Alternative Readline also supports history, but the completion-related functions it supplies are dummy: these functions, in Alternative Readline, don't perform any operation and exist only for compatibility with GNU Readline.

add_history	`add_history(s)`
	Adds string *s* as a line at the end of the history buffer.
clear_history	`clear_history(s)`
	Clears the history buffer.
get_completer	`get_completer( )`
	Returns the current completer function (as last set by `set_completer`), or None if no completer function is set.
get_history_ length	`get_history_length( )`
	Returns the number of lines of history that are saved to the history file. When the returned value is less than 0, all lines in the history are saved.
parse_and_ bind	`parse_and_bind(readline_cmd)`
	Gives Readline a configuration command. To let the user hit Tab to request completion, call `parse_and_bind('tab: complete')`. See the Readline documentation for other useful values of string *readline_cmd*.
	A useful completion function is in module rlcompleter. In an interactive interpreter session (or, more practically, in the startup file that the interpreter runs at the start of each interactive session, as covered in "Environment Variables" on page 22), enter:

```
import readline, rlcompleter
readline.parse_and_bind('tab: complete')
```

For the rest of this interactive session, you can hit Tab during line editing and get completion for global names and object attributes.

read_history_ file	`read_history_file(`*`filename`*`='~/.history')` Loads history lines from the text file whose name or path is *filename*.
read_init_file	`read_init_file(`*`filename`*`=None)` Makes Readline load a text file, where each line is a configuration command. When *filename* is None, Readline loads the same file as last time.
set_completer	`set_completer(`*`f`*`=None)` Sets the completion function. When *f* is None, Readline disables completion. Otherwise, when the user types a partial word *start*, then Tab, Readline calls *f(start, i)*, with *i* initially 0. *f* returns the *i*th possible word starting with *start*, or None when there are no more. Readline loops calling *f*, with *i* set to 0, 1, 2, etc., until *f* returns None.
set_history_ length	`set_history_length(`*`x`*`)` Sets the number of lines of history that are saved to the history file. When *x* is less than 0, all lines in the history are saved.
write_history_ file	`write_history_file(`*`filename`*`='~/.history')` Saves history lines to the text file whose name or path is *filename*.

Console I/O

"Terminals" today are usually text windows on a graphical screen. You may also use a true terminal or the console (main screen) of a personal computer in text mode. All kinds of terminals in use today offer advanced text I/O functionality, but you access this functionality in platform-dependent ways. The curses package works only on Unix-like platforms (there are persistent rumors of Windows ports of it, but I've never found a working one). Modules msvcrt, WConio, and Console work only on Windows.

The curses package

The traditional Unix approach to advanced terminal I/O is named *curses*, for obscure historical reasons.[*] The Python package curses affords reasonably simple use, but still lets you exert detailed control if required. I cover a small subset of curses, just enough to let you write programs with rich-text I/O functionality. (See Eric Raymond's tutorial "Curses Programming with Python," available at *http://py-howto.sourceforge.net/curses/curses.html*, for more information.) Whenever I mention the screen in this section, I mean the screen of the terminal (for example, the text window of a terminal-emulator program).

The simplest and most effective way to use curses is through the curses.wrapper module, which supplies a single function.

wrapper	wrapper(*func*, **args*)

Performs curses initialization, calls *func*(stdscr, **args*), performs curses finalization (setting the terminal back to normal behavior), and finally returns *func*'s result. The first argument that wrapper passes to *func* is stdscr, an object of type curses.Window representing the whole terminal screen. wrapper sets the terminal back to normal behavior, whether *func* terminates normally or propagates an exception.

func should be a function that performs all the tasks in your program that may need curses functionality. In other words, *func* normally contains (or more commonly calls, directly or indirectly, functions containing) all of your program's functionality, save perhaps for some noninteractive initialization and/or finalization tasks.

curses models text and background colors of characters as character attributes. Colors available on the terminal are numbered from 0 to curses.COLORS. Function color_content takes a color number *n* as its argument and returns a tuple (*r*, *g*, *b*) of integers between 0 and 1000 giving the amount of each primary color in *n*. Function color_pair takes a color number *n* as its argument and returns an attribute code that you can pass to various methods of a curses.Window object in order to display text in that color.

curses lets you create multiple instances of type curses.Window, each corresponding to a rectangle on the screen. You can also create exotic variants, such as instances of Panel, polymorphic with Window but not tied to a fixed screen rectangle. You do not need such advanced functionality in simple curses programs: just use the Window object stdscr that curses.wrapper gives you. Call w.refresh( ) to ensure that changes made to any Window instance w, including stdscr, show up on screen. curses can buffer the changes until you

[*] "Curses" does describe well the typical utterances of programmers faced with this rich, complicated approach.

call refresh. An instance *w* of Window supplies, among many others, the following frequently used methods.

---

addstr

w.addstr([*y*, *x*,]*s*[, *attr*])

Puts the characters in string *s*, with attribute *attr*, on *w* at the given coordinates (*x*, *y*), overwriting any previous contents. All curses functions and methods accept coordinate arguments in reverse order, with *y* (the row number) before *x* (the column number). If you omit *y* and *x*, addstr uses *w*'s current cursor coordinates. If you omit *attr*, addstr uses *w*'s current default attribute. In any case, addstr, when done adding the string, sets *w*'s current cursor coordinates to the end of the string it has added.

---

clrtobot,
clrtoeol

w.clrtobot( ) *w*.clrtoeol( )

clrtoeol writes blanks from *w*'s current cursor coordinates to the end of the line. clrtobot, in addition, also blanks all lines lower down on the screen.

---

delch

w.delch([*y*, *x*])

Deletes one character from *w* at coordinates (*x*, *y*). If you omit the *y* and *x* arguments, delch uses *w*'s current cursor coordinates. In any case, delch does not change *w*'s current cursor coordinates. All the following characters in line *y*, if any, shift left by one.

---

deleteln

w.deleteln( )

Deletes from *w* the entire line at *w*'s current cursor coordinates, and scrolls up by one line all lines lower down on the screen.

---

erase

w.erase( )

Writes spaces to the entire terminal screen.

---

getch

w.getch( )

Returns an integer *c* corresponding to a user keystroke. A value between 0 and 255 represents an ordinary character, while a value greater than 255 represents a special key. curses supplies names for special keys, so you can test *c* for equality with readable constants such as curses.KEY_HOME (the Home special key), curses.KEY_LEFT (the left-arrow special key), and so on. (The list of all curses special-key names (about 100 of them) is in Python's free documentation, specifically in the *Python Library Reference*, in the subsection

---

named "Constants" of the section named "curses.") If you have set window *w* to no-delay mode by calling *w*.nodelay(True), *w*.getch raises an exception if no keystroke is ready. By default, *w*.getch waits until the user hits a key.

getyx   *w*.getyx( )

Returns *w*'s current cursor coordinates as a tuple (y, x).

insstr   *w*.insstr([*y*, *x*,]*s*[, *attr*])

Inserts the characters in string *s*, with attribute *attr*, on *w* at coordinates (x, y), shifting the rest of line rightward. Any characters shifted beyond line end are lost. If you omit *y* and *x*, insstr uses *w*'s current cursor coordinates. If you omit *attr*, insstr uses *w*'s current default attribute. In any case, when done inserting the string, insstr sets *w*'s current cursor coordinates to the first character of the string it has inserted.

move   *w*.move(*y*, *x*)

Moves *w*'s cursor to the given coordinates (x, y).

nodelay   *w*.nodelay(*flag*)

Sets *w* to no-delay mode when *flag* is true; resets *w* back to normal mode when *flag* is false. No-delay mode affects method *w*.getch.

refresh   *w*.refresh( )

Updates window *w* on screen with all changes the program has effected on *w*.

The curses.textpad module supplies the Textpad class, which lets you support advanced input and text editing.

Textpad   class Textpad(*window*)

Creates and returns an instance *t* of class Textpad that wraps the curses window instance *window*. Instance *t* has one frequently used method:

t.edit( )

Lets the user perform interactive editing on the contents of the window instance that *t* wraps. The editing session supports simple Emacs-like key bindings: normal characters overwrite the window's previous contents, arrow keys move the cursor, and Ctrl-H deletes the character to the cursor's left. When the user hits Ctrl-G, the editing session ends, and edit returns the window's contents as a single string, with newlines as line separators.

The msvcrt Module

The msvcrt module, available only on Windows, supplies functions that let Python programs access a few proprietary extras supplied by the Microsoft Visual C++'s runtime library *msvcrt.dll*. Some msvcrt functions let you read user input character by character rather than reading a full line at a time.

getch, getche   getch( ) getche( )

Reads and returns one character from keyboard input, and waits if no character is yet available for reading. getche also echoes the character to screen (if printable), while getch doesn't. When the user presses a special key (arrows, function keys, etc.), it's seen as two characters: first a chr(0) or chr(224), then a second character that, together with the first one, defines the special key the user pressed. To find out what getch returns for any key, run the following small script on a Windows machine:

```
import msvcrt
print "press z to exit, or any other key to see the key's
code:"
while 1:
    c = msvcrt.getch( )
    if c == 'z': break
    print "%d (%r)" % (c, c)
```

kbhit   kbhit( )

Returns True when a character is available for reading (getch, if called, would return immediately); otherwise, False (getch, if called, would wait).

ungetch   ungetch(c)

"Ungets" character c; the next call to getch or getche returns c. It's an error to call ungetch twice without intervening calls to getch or getche.

The WConio and Console modules

Two Windows-specific extension modules supply single-character keyboard input (like msvcrt) and the ability to emit characters to specified positions on the screen. Chris Gonnerman's Windows Console I/O module is small, simple, and easy to use; you can freely download it from *http://newcenturycomputers.net/projects/wconio.html*. Fredrik Lundh's Console module is very complete and functionally rich; you can freely download it from *http://www.effbot.org/efflib/console/*.

Interactive Command Sessions

The cmd module offers a simple way to handle interactive sessions of commands. Each command is a line of text. The first word of each command is a verb defining the requested action. The rest of the line is passed as an argument to the method that implements the verb's action.

Module cmd supplies class Cmd to use as a base class, and you define your own subclass of cmd.Cmd. Your subclass supplies methods with names starting with do_ and help_, and may optionally override some of Cmd's methods. When the user enters a command line such as *verb and the rest*, as long as your subclass defines a method named do_*verb*, Cmd.onecmd calls:

```
self.do_verb('and the rest')
```

Similarly, as long as your subclass defines a method named help_*verb*, Cmd.do_help calls the method when the command line starts with 'help *verb*' or '?*verb*'. Cmd, by default, shows suitable error messages if the user tries to use, or asks for help about, a verb for which the subclass does not define the needed method.

Initializing a Cmd Instance

Your subclass of cmd.Cmd, if it defines its own __init__ special method, must call the base class's __init__, whose signature is as follows.

__init__   Cmd.__init__(self, *completekey*='Tab', *stdin*=sys.stdin, *stdout*=sys.stdout)

Initializes instance self with specified or default values for *completekey* (name of the key to use for command completion with the readline module; pass None to disable command completion), *stdin* (file object to get input from), and *stdout* (file object to emit output to).

If your subclass does not define __init__, then it inherits the one from base class cmd.Cmd. In this case, to instantiate your subclass, call it, with optional parameters *completekey*, *stdin*, and *stdout*, as documented in the previous paragraph.

Methods of Cmd Instances

An instance *c* of a subclass of class Cmd supplies the following methods (many of these methods are meant to be overridden by the subclass).

---

cmdloop

c.cmdloop(*intro*=None)

Performs an interactive session of line-oriented commands. cmdloop starts by calling *c*.preloop( ), then emits string *intro* (*c*.intro if *intro* is None). Then *c*.cmdloop enters a loop. In each iteration of the loop, cmdloop reads line *s* with *s*=raw_input(*c*.prompt). When standard input reaches end-of-file, cmdloop sets *s*='EOF'. If *s* is not 'EOF', cmdloop preprocesses string *s* with *s*=*c*.precmd(*s*), then calls *flag*=*c*.onecmd(*s*). When onecmd returns a true value, this is a tentative request to terminate the command loop. Whatever the value of *flag*, cmdloop calls *flag*=*c*.postcmd(*flag*, *s*) to check if the loop should terminate. If *flag* is now true, the loop terminates; otherwise, the loop repeats again. When the loop terminates, cmdloop calls *c*.postloop( ), then terminates. This structure of cmdloop that I just described is easiest to understand by looking at equivalent Python code:

```python
def cmdloop(self, intro=None):
    self.preloop( )
    if intro is None: intro = self.intro
    print intro
    finis_flag = False
    while not finis_flag:
        try: s = raw_input(self.prompt)
        except EOFError: s = 'EOF'
        else: s = self.precmd(s)
        finis_flag = self.onecmd(s)
        finis_flag = self.postcmd(finis_flag, s)
    self.postloop( )
```

cmdloop is a good example of the classic Design Pattern known as *Template Method*. Such a method performs little substantial work itself; rather, it structures and organizes calls to other methods. Subclasses may override some or all of the other methods to define the details of class behavior within the overall framework thus established. When you inherit from Cmd, you almost never override method cmdloop, since cmdloop's structure is the main thing you get by subclassing Cmd.

---

default

c.default(*s*)

c.onecmd calls *c*.default(*s*) when there is no method *c*.do_*verb* for the first word *verb* of line *s*. Subclasses often override default. The base-class method Cmd.default prints an error message.

do_help   *c*.do_help(*verb*)

c.onecmd calls *c*.do_help(*verb*) when command-line *s* starts with
'help *verb*' or '?*verb*'. Subclasses rarely override do_help. The
Cmd.do_help method calls method help_*verb* if the subclass
supplies it; otherwise, it displays the docstring of method do_*verb*
if the subclass supplies that method with a nonempty docstring. If
the subclass does not supply either source of help, Cmd.do_help
outputs a message to inform the user that no help is available on
verb.

emptyline   *c*.emptyline( )

c.onecmd calls *c*.emptyline( ) when command-line *s* is empty or
blank. Unless a subclass overrides this method, the base-class
method Cmd.emptyline reexecutes the last nonblank command line
seen, stored in the attribute *c*.lastcmd of *c*.

onecmd   *c*.onecmd(*s*)

c.cmdloop calls *c*.onecmd(*s*) for each command line *s* that the user
inputs. You can also call onecmd directly if you have independently
obtained a line *s* to process as a command. Normally, subclasses
do not override onecmd. Cmd.onecmd sets *c*.lastcmd=*s*. Then onecmd
calls do_*verb* when *s* starts with the word *verb* and the subclass
supplies such a method; otherwise, it calls emptyline or default, as
explained earlier. In any case, Cmd.onecmd returns the result of whatever other method it calls to be interpreted by postcmd as a
termination-request flag.

postcmd   *c*.postcmd(*flag*, *s*)

c.cmdloop calls *c*.postcmd(*flag*, *s*) for each command-line *s* after
c.onecmd(*s*) has returned value *flag*. If *flag* is true, the command
just executed is posing a tentative request to terminate the
command loop. If postcmd returns a true value, cmdloop's loop
terminates. Unless your subclass overrides this method, the base-
class method Cmd.postcmd is called and returns *flag* itself as the
method's result.

postloop   *c*.postloop( )

c.cmdloop calls *c*.postloop( ) when cmdloop's loop terminates.
Unless your subclass overrides this method, the base-class method
Cmd.postloop does nothing.

precmd	`c.precmd(s)`

        `c.cmdloop` calls `s=c.precmd(s)` to preprocess each command-line `s`. The current leg of the loop bases all further processing on the string that precmd returns. Unless your subclass overrides this method, the base-class method `Cmd.precmd` is called and returns `s` itself as the method's result.

preloop	`c.preloop( )`

        `c.cmdloop` calls `c.preloop( )` before cmdloop's loop begins. Unless your subclass overrides this method, the base-class method `Cmd.preloop` does nothing.

Attributes of Cmd Instances

An instance `c` of a subclass of class Cmd supplies the following attributes:

identchars
    A string whose characters are all those that can be part of a verb; by default, `c.identchars` contains letters, digits, and an underscore (_).

intro
    The message that cmdloop outputs first, when called with no argument.

lastcmd
    The last nonblank command line seen by onecmd.

prompt
    The string that cmdloop uses to prompt the user for interactive input. You almost always bind `c.prompt` explicitly, or override prompt as a class attribute of your subclass, because the default `Cmd.prompt` is just `'(Cmd) '`.

use_rawinput
    When false (default is true), cmdloop prompts and inputs via calls to methods of sys.stdout and sys.stdin, rather than via raw_input.

Other attributes of Cmd instances, which I do not cover here, let you exert fine-grained control on many formatting details of help messages.

A Cmd Example

The following example shows how to use cmd.Cmd to supply the verbs print (to output the rest of the line) and stop (to end the loop):

```
import cmd
class X(cmd.Cmd):
    def do_print(self, rest):
        print rest
```

```
        def help_print(self):
            print "print (any string): outputs (any string)"
        def do_stop(self, rest):
            return True
        def help_stop(self):
            print "stop: terminates the command loop"
    if __name__ == '__main__':
        X( ).cmdloop( )
```

A session using this example might proceed as follows:

```
C:\>\python22\python \examples\chapter10\CmdEx.py
(Cmd) help
Documented commands (type help <topic>):
= == == == == == == == == == == == == == == == == == == =
print           stop
Undocumented commands:
= == == == == == == == == == == =
help
(Cmd) help print
print (any string): outputs (any string)
(Cmd) print hi there
hi there
(Cmd) stop
```

Internationalization

Most programs present some information to users as text. Such text should be understandable and acceptable to the user. For example, in some countries and cultures, the date "March 7" can be concisely expressed as "3/7." Elsewhere, "3/7" indicates "July 3," and the string that means "March 7" is "7/3." In Python, such cultural conventions are handled with the help of standard module locale.

Similarly, a greeting can be expressed in one natural language by the string "Benvenuti," while in another language the string to use is "Welcome." In Python, such translations are handled with the help of standard module gettext.

Both kinds of issues are commonly called *internationalization* (often abbreviated *i18n*, as there are 18 letters between *i* and *n* in the full spelling). This is a misnomer, as the same issues also apply to users of different languages or cultures within a single nation.

The locale Module

Python's support for cultural conventions imitates that of C, though it is slightly simplified. In this architecture, a program operates in an environment of cultural conventions known as a *locale*. The locale setting permeates the program and is typically set at program startup. The locale is not thread-specific, and module locale is not thread-safe. In a multithreaded program, set the program's locale before starting secondary threads.

If a program does not call locale.setlocale, the program operates in a neutral locale known as the *C locale*. The C locale is named from this architecture's origins in the C language and is similar, but not identical, to the U.S. English locale. Alternatively, a program can find out and accept the user's default locale. In this case, module locale interacts with the operating system (via the environment or in other system-dependent ways) to establish the user's preferred locale. Finally, a program can set a specific locale, presumably determining which locale to set on the basis of user interaction or via persistent configuration settings such as a program initialization file.

Locale setting is normally performed across the board for all relevant categories of cultural conventions. This wide-spectrum setting is denoted by the constant attribute LC_ALL of module locale. However, the cultural conventions handled by module locale are grouped into categories, and, in some cases, a program can choose to mix and match categories to build up a synthetic composite locale. The categories are identified by the following constant attributes of module locale:

LC_COLLATE
> String sorting; affects functions strcoll and strxfrm in locale

LC_CTYPE
> Character types; affects aspects of module string (and string methods) that have to do with lowercase and uppercase letters

LC_MESSAGES
> Messages; may affect messages displayed by the operating system—for example, function os.strerror and module gettext

LC_MONETARY
> Formatting of currency values; affects function locale.localeconv

LC_NUMERIC
> Formatting of numbers; affects functions atoi, atof, format, localeconv, and str in locale

LC_TIME
> Formatting of times and dates; affects function time.strftime

The settings of some categories (denoted by the constants LC_CTYPE, LC_TIME, and LC_MESSAGES) affect behavior in other modules (string, time, os, and gettext, as indicated). The settings of other categories (denoted by the constants LC_COLLATE, LC_MONETARY, and LC_NUMERIC) affect only some functions of locale itself.

Module locale supplies functions to query, change, and manipulate locales, as well as functions that implement the cultural conventions of locale categories LC_COLLATE, LC_MONETARY, and LC_NUMERIC.

---

atof   atof(s)

> Converts string s to a floating-point number using the current LC_NUMERIC setting.

---

atoi

atoi(*s*)

Converts string *s* to an integer number using the current LC_NUMERIC setting.

format

format(*fmt*, *num*, *grouping*=False)

Returns the string obtained by formatting number *num* according to the format string *fmt* and the LC_NUMERIC setting. Except for cultural convention issues, the result is like *fmt%num*. If *grouping* is true, format also groups digits in the result string according to the LC_NUMERIC setting. For example:

```
>>> locale.setlocale(locale.LC_NUMERIC, 'en')
'English_United States.1252'
>>> locale.format('%s', 1000*1000)
'1000000'
>>> locale.format('%s', 1000*1000, True)
'1,000,000'
```

When the numeric locale is U.S. English and argument *grouping* is true, format supports the convention of grouping digits by threes with commas.

getdefaultlocale

getdefaultlocale(*envvars*=['LANGUAGE', 'LC_ALL', 'LC_TYPE', 'LANG'])

Checks the environment variables whose names are specified by *envvars*, in order. The first one found in the environment determines the default locale. getdefaultlocale returns a pair of strings (*lang*, *encoding*) compliant with RFC 1766 (except for the 'C' locale), such as ['en_US', 'ISO8859-1']. Each item of the pair may be None if gedefaultlocale is unable to discover what value the item should have.

getlocale

getlocale(*category*=LC_CTYPE)

Returns a pair of strings (*lang*, *encoding*) with the current setting for the given *category*. The category cannot be LC_ALL.

localeconv

localeconv( )

Returns a dict *d* with the cultural conventions specified by categories LC_NUMERIC and LC_MONETARY of the current locale. While LC_NUMERIC is best used indirectly, via other functions of module locale, the details of LC_MONETARY are accessible only through *d*. Currency formatting is different for local and international use. The U.S. currency symbol, for example, is '$' for local use only. '$' is ambiguous in international use, since the same symbol is also used for other currencies called "dollars" (Canadian, Australian, Hong Kong, etc.). In international use, therefore, the U.S. currency symbol is the unambiguous string `'USD'`. The keys into *d* to use for currency formatting are the following strings:

`'currency_symbol'`
> Currency symbol to use locally.

`'frac_digits'`
> Number of fractional digits to use locally.

`'int_curr_symbol'`
> Currency symbol to use internationally.

`'int_frac_digits'`
> Number of fractional digits to use internationally.

`'mon_decimal_point'`
> String to use as the "decimal point" for monetary values.

`'mon_grouping'`
> List of digit-grouping numbers for monetary values.

`'mon_thousands_sep'`
> String to use as digit-groups separator for monetary values.

`'negative_sign'`
`'positive_sign'`
> Strings to use as the sign symbol for negative (positive) monetary values.

`'n_cs_precedes'`
`'p_cs_precedes'`
> True if the currency symbol comes before negative (positive) monetary values.

`'n_sep_by_space'`
`'p_sep_by_space'`
> True if a space goes between sign and negative (positive) monetary values.

`'n_sign_posn'`
`'p_sign_posn'`
> Numeric codes to use to format negative (positive) monetary values:
>
> 0   The value and the currency symbol are placed inside parentheses.
>
> 1   The sign is placed before the value and the currency symbol.
>
> 2   The sign is placed after the value and the currency symbol.
>
> 3   The sign is placed immediately before the value.
>
> 4   The sign is placed immediately after the value.

`CHAR_MAX`
> The current locale does not specify any convention for this formatting.

d[`'mon_grouping'`] is a list of numbers of digits to group when formatting a monetary value. When *d*[`'mon_grouping'`][-1] is 0, there is no further grouping beyond the indicated numbers of digits. When *d*[`'mon_grouping'`][-1] is `locale.CHAR_MAX`, grouping continues indefinitely, as if d['mon_grouping'][-2] were endlessly repeated. locale.CHAR_MAX is a constant used as the value for all entries in d for which the current locale does not specify any convention.

normalize

normalize(*localename*)

Returns a string, suitable as an argument to setlocale, that is the normalized equivalent to *localename*. If normalize cannot normalize string *localename*, then normalize returns *localename* unchanged.

resetlocale

resetlocale(*category*=LC_ALL)

Sets the locale for *category* to the default given by getdefaultlocale.

setlocale

setlocale(*category*, *locale*=None)

Sets the locale for *category* to the given *locale*, if not None, and returns the setting (the existing one when *locale* is None; otherwise, the new one). *locale* can be a string or a pair of strings (*lang*, *encoding*). The *lang* string is normally a language code based on ISO 639 two-letter codes ('en' for English, 'nl' for Dutch, and so on). When *locale* is the empty string '', setlocale sets the user's default locale.

str

str(*num*)

Like locale.format('%f', *num*).

strcoll

strcoll(*str1*, *str2*)

Like cmp(*str1*, *str2*), but according to the LC_COLLATE setting.

strxfrm

strxfrm(*s*)

Returns a string *sx* such that the built-in comparison (e.g., by cmp) of strings so transformed is equivalent to calling locale.strcoll on the original strings. strxfrm lets you use the decorate-sort-undecorate (DSU) idiom for sorts that involve locale-conformant string comparisons. However, if all you need is to sort a list of strings in a locale-conformant way, strcoll's simplicity can make it faster. The following example shows two ways of performing such a sort; in this case, the simple variant is often faster than the DSU one, by about 10 percent for a list of a thousand words:

```
import locale
# simpler and often faster
def locale_sort_simple(list_of_strings):
    list_of_strings.sort(locale.strcoll)
```

```
# less simple and often slower
def locale_sort_DSU(list_of_strings):
    auxiliary_list = [(locale.strxfrm(s), s) for s in
list_of_strings]
    auxiliary_list.sort()
    list_of_strings[:] = [s for junk, s in auxiliary_list]
```

In Python 2.4, the key= argument to the sort method offers both simplicity and speed:

```
# simplest and fastest, but 2.4-only:
def locale_sort_2_4(list_of_strings):
    list_of_strings.sort(key=locale.strxfrm)
```

The gettext Module

A key issue in internationalization is the ability to use text in different natural languages, a task also known as *localization*. Python supports localization via module gettext, which was inspired by GNU *gettext*. Module gettext is optionally able to use the latter's infrastructure and APIs, but is simpler and more general. You do not need to install or study GNU *gettext* to use Python's gettext effectively.

Using gettext for localization

gettext does not deal with automatic translation between natural languages. Rather, gettext helps you extract, organize, and access the text messages that your program uses. Pass each string literal subject to translation, also known as a *message*, to a function named _ (underscore) rather than using it directly. gettext normally installs a function named _ in the __builtin__ module. To ensure that your program runs with or without gettext, conditionally define a do-nothing function, named _, that just returns its argument unchanged. Then you can safely use _('*message*') wherever you would normally use a literal '*message*' that should be translated. The following example shows how to start a module for conditional use of gettext:

```
try: _
except NameError:
    def _(s): return s
def greet(): print _('Hello world')
```

If some other module has installed gettext before you run this example code, function greet outputs a properly localized greeting. Otherwise, greet outputs the string 'Hello world' unchanged.

Edit your source, decorating message literals with function _. Then use any of various tools to extract messages into a text file (normally named *messages.pot*) and distribute the file to the people who translate messages into the various natural languages your application must support. Python supplies a script *pygettext.py* (in directory *Tools/i18n* in the Python source distribution) to perform message extraction on your Python sources.

Each translator edits *messages.pot* to produce a text file of translated messages with extension *.po*. Compile the *.po* files into binary files with extension *.mo*, suitable for fast searching, using any of various tools. Python supplies script *Tools/i18n/msgfmt.py* for this purpose. Finally, install each *.mo* file with a suitable name in a suitable directory.

Conventions about which directories and names are suitable differ among platforms and applications. gettext's default is subdirectory *share/locale/<lang>/LC_MESSAGES/* of directory *sys.prefix*, where *<lang>* is the language's code (two letters). Each file is named *<name>.mo*, where *<name>* is the name of your application or package.

Once you have prepared and installed your *.mo* files, you normally execute, at the time your application starts up, some code such as the following:

```
import os, gettext
os.environ.setdefault('LANG', 'en')      # application-default language
gettext.install('your_application_name')
```

This ensures that calls such as _('message') return the appropriate translated strings. You can choose different ways to access gettext functionality in your program—for example, if you also need to localize C-coded extensions, or to switch back and forth between languages during a run. Another important consideration is whether you're localizing a whole application or just a package that is distributed separately.

Essential gettext functions

Module gettext supplies many functions; the most often used ones are the following.

install	install(*domain*, *localedir*=None, *unicode*=False)
	Installs in Python's built-in namespace a function named _ to perform translations given in file *<lang>/LC_MESSAGES/<domain>.mo* in directory *localedir*, with language code *<lang>* as per getdefaultlocale. When *localedir* is None, install uses directory os.path.join(sys.prefix, 'share', 'locale'). When *unicode* is true, function _ accepts and returns Unicode strings, not plain strings.
translation	translation(*domain*, *localedir*=None, *languages*=None)
	Searches for a *.mo* file similarly to function install. When *languages* is None, translation looks in the environment for the *lang* to use, like *install*. It examines, in order, environment variables LANGUAGE, LC_ALL, LC_MESSAGES, LANG; the first nonempty one is split on ':' to give a list of language names (for example, 'de:en' is split into ['de', 'en']). When not None, *languages* must be a list of one or more language names (for example, ['de', 'en']). Translation uses the first language name in the list for which it finds a *.mo* file. Function translation returns an instance object that supplies

methods gettext (to translate a plain string), ugettext (to translate a Unicode string), and install (to install either gettext or ugettext under name _ into Python's built-in namespace).

Function translation offers more detailed control than install, which is like translation(*domain,localedir*).install(*unicode*). With translation, you can localize a single package without affecting the built-in namespace by binding name _ on a per-module basis—for example, with:

```
_ = translation(domain).ugettext
```

translation also lets you switch globally between several languages, since you can pass an explicit *languages* argument, keep the resulting instance, and call the install method of the appropriate language as needed:

```
import gettext
translators = {}
def switch_to_language(lang, domain='my_app',
use_unicode=True):
    if not translators.has_key(lang):
        translators[lang] = gettext.translation(domain,
languages=[lang])
        translators[lang].install(use_unicode)
```

More Internationalization Resources

Internationalization is a very large topic. For general introductions and useful resources, see *http://www.debian.org/doc/manuals/intro-i18n/* and *http://www.i18ngurus.com/*. One of the best packages of code and information for internationalization is ICU (*http://icu.sourceforge.net/*), which also includes the Unicode Consortium's excellent Common Locale Data Repository (CLDR) database of locale conventions and code to access the CLDR. Unfortunately, at the time of this writing, ICU supports only Java, C, and C++, not (directly) Python. You can easily use the Java version of ICU with Jython (see "Importing Java Packages in Jython" on page 656 for more information about using Java classes from Jython code); with more effort, you can wrap the C/C++ version of ICU with tools such as SWIG or SIP (covered in Chapter 25) to access ICU functionality from Classic Python.

11

Persistence and Databases

Python supports a variety of ways of making data persistent. One such way, known as *serialization*, involves viewing the data as a collection of Python objects. These objects can be saved, or *serialized*, to a byte stream, and later loaded and recreated, or *deserialized*, back from the byte stream. Object persistence is layered on top of serialization and adds such features as object naming. This chapter covers the built-in Python modules that support serialization and object persistence.

Another way to make data persistent is to store it in a database. One simple type of database is just a file format that uses keyed access to enable selective reading and updating of relevant parts of the data. This chapter covers Python standard library modules that support several variations of this file format, known as DBM.

A relational database management system (RDBMS), such as MySQL or Oracle, provides a more powerful approach to storing, searching, and retrieving persistent data. Relational databases rely on dialects of Structured Query Language (SQL) to create and alter a database's schema, insert and update data in the database, and query the database according to search criteria. (This chapter does not provide reference material on SQL. For that purpose, I recommend *SQL in a Nutshell*, by Kevin Kline [O'Reilly].) Unfortunately, despite the existence of SQL standards, no two RDBMSes implement exactly the same SQL dialect.

The Python standard library does not come with an RDBMS interface. However, many free third-party modules let your Python programs access a specific RDBMS. Such modules mostly follow the Python Database API 2.0 standard, also known as the DBAPI. This chapter covers the DBAPI standard and mentions some of the third-party modules that implement it.

Serialization

Python supplies a number of modules dealing with I/O operations that serialize (save) entire Python objects to various kinds of byte streams and deserialize (load and recreate) Python objects back from such streams. Serialization is also known as *marshaling*.

The marshal Module

The marshal module supports the specific serialization tasks needed to save and reload compiled Python files (*.pyc* and *.pyo*). marshal handles only fundamental built-in data types: None, numbers (int, long, float, complex), strings (plain and Unicode), code objects, and built-in containers (tuple, list, dict) whose items are instances of elementary types. marshal does not handle sets nor user-defined types and classes. marshal is faster than other serialization modules, and is the one such module that supports code objects. Module marshal supplies the following functions.

---

dump, dumps   dump(*value*,*fileobj*)
dumps(*value*)

dumps returns a string representing object *value*. dump writes the same string to file object *fileobj*, which must be opened for writing in binary mode. dump(*v*,*f*) is just like *f*.write(dumps(*v*)). *fileobj* cannot be any file-like object: it must be specifically an instance of type file.

---

load, loads   load(*fileobj*)
loads(*str*)

loads creates and returns the object *v* previously dumped to string *str* so that, for any object *v* of a supported type, *v*==loads(dumps(*v*)). If *str* is longer than dumps(*v*), loads ignores the extra bytes. load reads the right number of bytes from file object *fileobj*, which must be opened for reading in binary mode, and creates and returns the object *v* represented by those bytes. *fileobj* cannot be any file-like object: it must be specifically an instance of type file.

Functions load and dump are complementary. In other words, a sequence of calls to load(*f*) deserializes the same values previously serialized when *f*'s contents were created by a sequence of calls to dump(*v*,*f*).

A marshaling example

Say you need to read several text files, whose names are given as your program's arguments, recording where each word appears in the files. What you need to record for each word is a list of (*filename, line-number*) pairs. The following example uses marshal to encode lists of (*filename, line-number*) pairs as strings and store them in a DBM-like file (as covered in "DBM Modules" on page 285). Since these lists contain tuples, each containing a string and a number, they are within marshal's abilities to serialize.

```
import fileinput, marshal, anydbm
wordPos = {}
for line in fileinput.input():
    pos = fileinput.filename(), fileinput.filelineno()
    for word in line.split():
        wordPos.setdefault(word,[]).append(pos)
dbmOut = anydbm.open('indexfilem', 'n')
for word in wordPos:
    dbmOut[word] = marshal.dumps(wordPos[word])
dbmOut.close()
```

We also need marshal to read back the data stored in the DBM-like file *indexfilem*, as shown in the following example:

```
import sys, marshal, anydbm, linecache
dbmIn = anydbm.open('indexfilem')
for word in sys.argv[1:]:
    if not dbmIn.has_key(word):
        sys.stderr.write('Word %r not found in index file\n' % word)
        continue
    places = marshal.loads(dbmIn[word])
    for fname, lineno in places:
        print "Word %r occurs in line %s of file %s:" % (word,lineno,fname)
        print linecache.getline(fname, lineno),
```

The pickle and cPickle Modules

The pickle and cPickle modules supply factory functions, named Pickler and Unpickler, to generate objects that wrap file-like objects and supply serialization mechanisms. Serializing and deserializing via these modules is also known as *pickling* and *unpickling*. The difference between the modules is that, in pickle, Pickler and Unpickler are classes, so you can inherit from these classes to create customized serializer objects, overriding methods as needed. In cPickle, on the other hand, Pickler and Unpickler are factory functions that generate instances of non-subclassable types, not classes. Performance is much better with cPickle, but inheritance is not feasible. In the rest of this section, I'll be talking about module pickle, but everything applies to cPickle too.

Note that unpickling from an untrusted data source is a security risk; an attacker could exploit this to execute arbitrary code. Don't unpickle untrusted data!

Serialization shares some of the issues of deep copying, covered in deepcopy on page 172. Module pickle deals with these issues in much the same way as module copy does. Serialization, like deep copying, implies a recursive walk over a directed graph of references. pickle preserves the graph's shape when the same object is encountered more than once: the object is serialized only the first time, and other occurrences of the same object serialize references to a single copy. pickle also correctly serializes graphs with reference cycles. However, this means that if a mutable object *o* is serialized more than once to the same `Pickler` instance *p*, any changes to *o* after the first serialization of *o* to *p* are not saved. For clarity and simplicity, avoid altering objects that are being serialized while serialization to a `Pickler` instance is in progress.

`pickle` can serialize in an ASCII format or in either of two compact binary ones. The ASCII format is the default, for backward compatibility, but you should normally request binary format 2, which saves time and storage space. When you reload objects, `pickle` transparently recognizes and uses any format. I recommend you always specify binary format 2: the size and speed savings can be substantial, and binary format has basically no downside except loss of compatibility with very old versions of Python.

`pickle` serializes classes and functions by name, not by value. `pickle` can therefore deserialize a class or function only by importing it from the same module where the class or function was found when `pickle` serialized it. In particular, `pickle` can serialize and deserialize classes and functions only if they are top-level names for their module (i.e., attributes of their module). For example, consider the following:

```
def adder(augend):
    def inner(addend, augend=augend): return addend+augend
    return inner
plus5 = adder(5)
```

This code binds a closure to name plus5 (as covered in "Nested functions and nested scopes" on page 77)—a nested function inner plus an appropriate nested scope. Therefore, trying to pickle plus5 raises a `pickle.PicklingError` exception: a function can be pickled only when it is top-level, and function inner, whose closure is bound to name plus5 in this code, is not top-level but rather nested inside function adder. Similar issues apply to all pickling of nested functions and nested classes (i.e., classes that are not top-level).

Functions of pickle and cPickle

Modules `pickle` and `cPickle` expose the following functions.

---

dump, dumps dump(*value,fileobj,protocol=None,bin=None*)
         dumps(*value,protocol=None,bin=None*)

         dumps returns a string representing object *value*. dump writes the same string to file-like object *fileobj*, which must be opened for writing. dump(*v*,*f*) is like *f*.write(dumps(*v*)). Do not pass the *bin* parameter, which exists only for compatibility with old versions of Python. The *protocol* parameter can be 0 (the default, for compatibility reasons; ASCII output, slowest and bulkiest), 1 (binary output is compatible with old versions of Python), or 2 (fastest and leanest). I suggest you always pass the value 2. Unless *protocol* is 0 or absent, implying ASCII output, the *fileobj* parameter to dump must be open for *binary* writing.

---

load, loads

load(*fileobj*) loads(*str*)

loads creates and returns the object *v* represented by string *str* so that for any object *v* of a supported type, *v*==loads(dumps(*v*)). If *str* is longer than dumps(*v*), loads ignores the extra bytes. load reads the right number of bytes from file-like object *fileobj* and creates and returns the object *v* represented by those bytes. load and loads transparently support pickles performed in any binary or ASCII mode. If data is pickled in either binary format, the file must be open as binary for both dump and load. load(*f*) is like Unpickler(*f*).load().

Functions load and dump are complementary. In other words, a sequence of calls to load(*f*) deserializes the same values previously serialized when *f*'s contents were created by a sequence of calls to dump(*v*,*f*).

Pickler

Pickler(*fileobj* protocol=None,bin=None)

Creates and returns an object *p* such that calling *p*.dump is equivalent to calling function dump with the *fileobj*, *protocol*, and *bin* arguments passed to Pickler. To serialize many objects to a file, Pickler is more convenient and faster than repeated calls to dump. You can subclass pickle.Pickler to override Pickler methods (particularly method persistent_id) and create a persistence framework. However, this is an advanced issue and is not covered further in this book.

Unpickler

Unpickler(*fileobj*)

Creates and returns an object *u* such that calling *u*.load is equivalent to calling function load with the *fileobj* argument passed to Unpickler. To deserialize many objects from a file, Unpickler is more convenient and faster than repeated calls to function load. You can subclass pickle.Unpickler to override Unpickler methods (particularly the method persistent_load) and create your own persistence framework. However, this is an advanced issue and is not covered further in this book.

A pickling example

The following example handles the same task as the marshal example shown earlier but uses cPickle instead of marshal to encode lists of (*filename, linenumber*) pairs as strings:

```
import fileinput, cPickle, anydbm
wordPos = {  }
for line in fileinput.input():
    pos = fileinput.filename(), fileinput.filelineno()
    for word in line.split():
```

```
            wordPos.setdefault(word,[ ]).append(pos)
    dbmOut = anydbm.open('indexfilep','n')
    for word in wordPos:
        dbmOut[word] = cPickle.dumps(wordPos[word], 1)
    dbmOut.close( )
```

We can use either cPickle or pickle to read back the data stored to the DBM-like file *indexfilep*, as shown in the following example:

```
    import sys, cPickle, anydbm, linecache
    dbmIn = anydbm.open('indexfilep')
    for word in sys.argv[1:]:
        if not dbmIn.has_key(word):
            sys.stderr.write('Word %r not found in index file\n' % word)
            continue
        places = cPickle.loads(dbmIn[word])
        for fname, lineno in places:
            print "Word %r occurs in line %s of file %s:" % (word,lineno,fname)
            print linecache.getline(fname, lineno),
```

Pickling instances

In order for pickle to reload an instance *x*, pickle must be able to import *x*'s class from the same module in which the class was defined when pickle saved the instance. Here is how pickle saves the state of instance object *x* of class *T* and later reloads the saved state into a new instance *y* of *T* (the first step of the reloading is always to make a new empty instance *y* of *T*, except where I explicitly say otherwise in the following):

- When *T* supplies method __getstate__, pickle saves the result *d* of calling *T*.__getstate__(*x*).
  - When *T* supplies method __setstate__, *d* can be of any type, and pickle reloads the saved state by calling *T*.__setstate__(*y*, *d*).
  - Otherwise, *d* must be a dictionary, and pickle just sets *y*.__dict__ = *d*.
- Otherwise, when *T* is new-style and supplies method __getnewargs__, and pickle is pickling with protocol 2, pickle saves the result *t* of calling *T*.__getnewargs__(*x*); *t* must be a tuple.
  - pickle, in this one case, does not start with an empty *y* but rather creates *y* by executing *y* = *T*.__new__(*T*, *t*), which concludes the reloading.
- Otherwise, when *T* is old-style and supplies method __getinitargs__, pickle saves the result *t* of calling *T*.__getinitargs__(*x*) (*t* must be a tuple) and then, as *d*, the dictionary *x*.__dict__.
  - Pickle reloads the saved state by first calling *T*.__init__(*y*, *t*) and then calling *y*.__dict__.update(*d*).
- Otherwise, by default, pickle saves as *d* the dictionary *x*.__dict__.
  - When *T* supplies method __setstate__, pickle reloads the saved state by calling *T*.__setstate__ (*y*, *d*).
  - Otherwise, pickle just sets *y*.__dict__ = *d*.

All the items in the *d* or *t* object that pickle saves and reloads (normally a dictionary or tuple) must in turn be instances of types suitable for pickling and unpickling (i.e., pickleable objects), and the procedure just outlined may be repeated recursively, if necessary, until pickle reaches primitive pickleable built-in types (dictionaries, tuples, lists, sets, numbers, strings, etc.).

As mentioned in "The copy Module" on page 172, special methods __getinitargs__, __getnewargs__, __getstate__, and __setstate__ also control the way instance objects are copied and deep-copied. If a new-style class defines __slots__, and therefore its instances do not have a __dict__, pickle does it best to save and restore a dictionary equivalent to the names and values of the slots. However, such a new-style class should define __getstate__ and __setstate__; otherwise, its instances may not be correctly pickleable and copy-able through such best-effort endeavors.

Pickling customization with the copy_reg module

You can control how pickle serializes and deserializes objects of an arbitrary type (or new-style class) by registering factory and reduction functions with module copy_reg. This is particularly, though not exclusively, useful when you define a type in a C-coded Python extension. Module copy_reg supplies the following functions.

---

constructor constructor(*fcon*)

Adds *fcon* to the table of constructors, which lists all factory functions that pickle may call. *fcon* must be callable and is normally a function.

---

pickle pickle(*type*,*fred*,*fcon*=None)

Registers function *fred* as the reduction function for type *type*, where *type* must be a type object (not an old-style class). To save any object *o* of type *type*, module pickle calls *fred*(*o*) and saves the result. *fred*(*o*) must return a pair (*fcon,t*) or a tuple (*fcon,t,d*), where *fcon* is a constructor and *t* is a tuple. To reload *o*, pickle calls *o*=*fcon*(**t*). Then, if *fred* returned a *d*, pickle uses *d* to restore *o*'s state (*o*.__setstate__(*d*) if *o* supplies __setstate__; otherwise, *o*.__dict__.update(*d*)), as in "Pickling instances" on page 282. If *fcon* is not None, pickle also calls constructor(*fcon*) to register *fcon* as a constructor.

pickle does not support pickling of code objects, but marshal does. Here is how you can customize pickling to support code objects by delegating the work to marshal thanks to copy_reg:

```
>>> import pickle, copy_reg, marshal
>>> def viaMarshal(x): return marshal.loads, (marshal.
dumps(x),)
...
>>> c=compile('2+2','','eval')
>>> copy_reg.pickle(type(c), viaMarshal)
```

```
>>> s=pickle.dumps(c, 2)
>>> cc=pickle.loads(s)
>>> print eval(cc)
4
```

The shelve Module

The shelve module orchestrates modules cPickle (or pickle, when cPickle is not available in the current Python installation), cStringIO (or StringIO, when cStringIO is not available in the current Python installation), and anydbm (and its underlying modules for access to DBM-like archive files, as discussed in "DBM Modules" on page 285) in order to provide a simple, lightweight persistence mechanism.

shelve supplies a function open that is polymorphic to anydbm.open. The mapping object s returned by shelve.open is less limited than the mapping object a returned by anydbm.open. a's keys and values must be strings. s's keys must also be strings, but s's values may be of any pickleable types or classes. pickle customizations (e.g., copy_reg, __getinitargs__, __getstate__, and __setstate__) also apply to shelve, since shelve delegates serialization to pickle.

Beware of a subtle trap when you use shelve and mutable objects. When you operate on a mutable object held in a shelf, the changes don't "take" unless you assign the changed object back to the same index. For example:

```
import shelve
s = shelve.open('data')
s['akey'] = range(4)
print s['akey']                   # prints: [0, 1, 2, 3]
s['akey'].append('moreover')      # trying direct mutation
print s['akey']                   # doesn't take; prints: [0, 1, 2, 3]

x = s['akey']          # fetch the object
x.append('moreover')   # perform mutation
s['akey'] = x          # store the object back
print s['akey']        # now it takes, prints: [0, 1, 2, 3, 'moreover']
```

You can finesse this issue by passing named argument writeback=True when you call shelve.open, but beware: if you do pass that argument, you may seriously impair the performance of your program.

A shelving example

The following example handles the same task as the earlier pickling and marshaling examples, but uses shelve to persist lists of (*filename, line-number*) pairs:

```
import fileinput, shelve
wordPos = { }
for line in fileinput.input():
    pos = fileinput.filename(), fileinput.filelineno()
```

```
        for word in line.split():
            wordPos.setdefault(word,[ ]).append(pos)
    shOut = shelve.open('indexfiles','n')
    for word in wordPos:
        shOut[word] = wordPos[word]
    shOut.close()
```

We must use shelve to read back the data stored to the DBM-like file *indexfiles*, as shown in the following example:

```
import sys, shelve, linecache
shIn = shelve.open('indexfiles')

for word in sys.argv[1:]:
    if not shIn.has_key(word):
        sys.stderr.write('Word %r not found in index file\n' % word)
        continue
    places = shIn[word]
    for fname, lineno in places:
        print "Word %r occurs in line %s of file %s:" % (word,lineno,fname)
        print linecache.getline(fname, lineno),
```

These two examples are the simplest and most direct of the various equivalent pairs of examples shown throughout this section. This reflects the fact that module shelve is higher-level than the modules used in previous examples.

DBM Modules

A DBM-like file is a file that contains pairs of strings (*key,data*), with support for fetching or storing the data given a key, known as *keyed access*. DBM-like files were developed on early Unix systems, with functionality roughly equivalent to that of access methods popular on mainframe and minicomputers of the time, such as ISAM, the Indexed-Sequential Access Method. Today, many libraries, available for many platforms, let programs written in many different languages create, update, and read DBM-like files.

Keyed access, while not as powerful as the data access functionality of relational databases, may often suffice for a program's needs. If DBM-like files are sufficient, you may end up with a program that is smaller and faster than one using an RDBMS.

The classic *dbm* library, whose first version introduced DBM-like files many years ago, has limited functionality but tends to be available on many Unix platforms. The GNU version, *gdbm*, is richer and very widespread. The BSD version, *dbhash*, offers superior functionality. Python supplies modules that interface with each of these libraries if the relevant underlying library is installed on your system. Python also offers a minimal DBM module, dumbdbm (usable anywhere, as it does not rely on other installed libraries), and generic DBM modules, which are able to automatically identify, select, and wrap the appropriate DBM library to deal with an existing or new DBM file. Depending on your platform, your Python distribution, and what *dbm*-like libraries you have installed on your computer, the default Python build may install some subset of these modules. In general, as a minimum, you can rely on having module dbm on all Unix-like platforms, module dbhash on Windows, and dumbdbm on any platform.

The anydbm Module

The anydbm module is a generic interface to any other DBM module. anydbm supplies a single factory function.

open	open(*filename*,*flag*='r',*mode*=0666)
	Opens or creates the DBM file named by *filename* (a string that can be any path to a file, not just a name) and returns a mapping object corresponding to the DBM file. When the DBM file already exists, open uses module whichdb to determine which DBM library can handle the file. When open creates a new DBM file, open chooses the first available DBM module in order of preference: dbhash, gdbm, dbm, or dumbdbm.

flag is a one-character string that tells open how to open the file and whether to create it, as shown in Table 11-1. *mode* is an integer that open uses as the file's permission bits if open creates the file, as covered in "Creating a File Object with open" on page 216. Not all DBM modules use *flags* and *mode*, but for portability's sake you should always supply appropriate values for these arguments when you call anydbm.open.

Table 11-1. flag values for anydbm.open

Flag	Read-only?	If file exists	If file does not exist
'r'	Yes	open opens the file.	open raises error.
'w'	No	open opens the file.	open raises error.
'c'	No	open opens the file.	open creates the file.
'n'	No	open truncates the file.	open creates the file.

anydbm.open returns a mapping object *m* with a subset of the functionality of dictionaries (covered in "Dictionary Operations" on page 59). *m* only accepts strings as keys and values, and the only mapping methods *m* supplies are *m*.has_key and *m*.keys. You can bind, rebind, access, and unbind items in *m* with the same indexing syntax *m*[*key*] that you would use if *m* were a dictionary. If *flag* is 'r', *m* is read-only, so that you can only access *m*'s items, not bind, rebind, or unbind them. One extra method that *m* supplies is *m*.close, with the same semantics as the close method of a file object. Just like for file objects, you should ensure *m*.close( ) is called when you're done using *m*. The try/finally statement (covered in "try/finally" on page 123) is the best way to ensure finalization (in Python 2.5, the with statement, covered in "The with statement" on page 125, is even better than try/finally).

The dumbdbm Module

The dumbdbm module supplies minimal DBM functionality and mediocre performance. dumbdbm's advantage is that you can use it anywhere, since dumbdbm does not rely on any library. You don't normally import dumbdbm; rather, import anydbm, and let anydbm supply your program with the best DBM module available, defaulting to dumbdbm if nothing better is available on the current Python installation. The only case in which you import dumbdbm directly is the rare one in which you need to create a DBM-like file that you can later read from any Python installation. Module dumbdbm supplies an open function and an exception class error polymorphic to anydbm's.

The dbm, gdbm, and dbhash Modules

The dbm module exists only on Unix platforms, where it can wrap any of the *dbm*, *ndbm*, and *gdbm* libraries, since each supplies a *dbm*-compatibility interface. You hardly ever import dbm directly; rather, import anydbm, and let anydbm supply your program with the best DBM module available, including dbm if appropriate. Module dbm supplies an open function and an exception class error polymorphic to anydbm's.

The gdbm module wraps the GNU DBM library, *gdbm*. The gdbm.open function accepts other values for the *flag* argument and returns a mapping object *m* with a few extra methods. You may import gdbm directly to access nonportable functionality. I do not cover gdbm specifics in this book, since I focus on cross-platform Python.

The dbhash module wraps the BSDDB library in a DBM-compatible way. The dbhash.open function accepts other values for the *flag* argument and returns a mapping object *m* with a few extra methods. You may import dbhash directly to access nonportable functionality. For full access to the BSD DB functionality, however, you should instead import bsddb, as covered in "Berkeley DB Interfacing" on page 288.

The whichdb Module

The whichdb module attempts to guess which of the several DBM modules is appropriate to use. whichdb supplies a single function.

---

whichdb   whichdb(*filename*)

Opens the file specified by *filename* to discover which DBM-like package created the file. whichdb returns None if the file does not exist or cannot be opened and read. whichdb returns '' if the file exists and can be opened and read, but it cannot be determined which DBM-like package created the file (typically, this means that the file is not a DBM file). whichdb returns a string that names a module, such as 'dbm', 'dumbdbm', or 'dbhash', if it finds out which module can read the DBM-like file.

Examples of DBM-Like File Use

Keyed access is suitable when your program needs to record persistently the equivalent of a Python dictionary, with strings as both keys and values. For example, suppose you need to analyze several text files, whose names are given as your program's arguments, and record where each word appears in those files. In this case, the keys are words and, therefore, intrinsically strings. The data you need to record for each word is a list of (*filename, line-number*) pairs. However, you can encode the data as a string in several ways—for example, by exploiting the fact that the path separator string os.pathsep (covered in "Path-String Attributes of the os Module" on page 241) does not normally appear in filenames. (Note that more solid, general, and reliable approaches to the general issue of encoding data as strings are covered in "Serialization" on page 278.) With this simplification, the program that records word positions in files might be as follows:

```
import fileinput, os, anydbm
wordPos = {  }
sep = os.pathsep
for line in fileinput.input():
    pos = '%s%s%s'%(fileinput.filename(), sep, fileinput.filelineno())
    for word in line.split():
        wordPos.setdefault(word,[  ]).append(pos)
dbmOut = anydbm.open('indexfile','n')
sep2 = sep * 2
for word in wordPos:
    dbmOut[word] = sep2.join(wordPos[word])
dbmOut.close()
```

We can read back the data stored to the DBM-like file *indexfile* in several ways. The following example accepts words as command-line arguments and prints the lines where the requested words appear:

```
import sys, os, anydbm, linecache
dbmIn = anydbm.open('indexfile')
sep = os.pathsep
sep2 = sep * 2
for word in sys.argv[1:]:
    if not dbmIn.has_key(word):
        sys.stderr.write('Word %r not found in index file\n' % word)
        continue
    places = dbmIn[word].split(sep2)
    for place in places:
        fname, lineno = place.split(sep)
        print "Word %r occurs in line %s of file %s:" % (word,lineno,fname)
        print linecache.getline(fname, int(lineno)),
```

Berkeley DB Interfacing

Python comes with the bsddb package, which wraps the Berkeley Database (also known as BSD DB) library if that library is installed on your system and your Python installation is built to support it. With the BSD DB library, you can create hash,

---

binary-tree, or record-based files that generally behave like persistent dictionaries. On Windows, Python includes a port of the BSD DB library, thus ensuring that module bsddb is always usable. To download BSD DB sources, binaries for other platforms, and detailed documentation on BSD DB itself, see *http://www.sleepycat.com*.

Simplified and Complete BSD DB Python Interfaces

Module bsddb itself provides a simplified, backward-compatible interface to a subset of BSD DB's functionality, as covered by the Python online documentation at *http://www.python.org/doc/2.4/lib/module-bsddb.html*. However, the standard Python library also comes with many modules in package bsddb, starting with bsddb.db. This set of modules closely mimics BSD DB's current rich, complex functionality and interfaces, and is documented at *http://pybsddb.sourceforge.net/ bsddb3.html*. At this URL, you'll see the package documented under the slightly different name bsddb3, which is the name of a package you can separately download and install even on very old versions of Python. However, to use the version of this package that comes as part of the Python standard library, what you need to import are modules named bsddb.db and the like, not bsddb3.db and the like. Apart from this naming detail, the Sourceforge documentation fully applies to the modules in package bsddb in the Python standard library (db, dbshelve, dbtables, dbutil, dbobj, dbrecio).

Entire books can be (and have been) written about the full interface to BSD DB and its functionality, so I do not cover this rich, complete, and complex interface in this book. (If you need to exploit BSD DB's complete functionality, I suggest, in addition to studying the URLs mentioned above, the book *Berkeley DB*, by Sleepycat Software [New Riders].) However, in Python you can also access a small but important subset of BSD DB's functionality in a much simpler way, through the simplified interface provided by module bsddb and covered in the following.

Module bsddb

Module bsddb supplies three factory functions: btopen, hashopen, and rnopen.

btopen, hashopen, rnopen	btopen(*filename*,*flag*='r',**many_other_optional_arguments*) hashopen(*filename*,*flag*='r',**many_other_optional_arguments*) rnopen(*filename*,*flag*='r',**many_other_optional_arguments*)
	btopen opens or creates the binary tree file named by *filename* (a string that is any path to a file, not just a name), and returns a BTree object to access and manipulate the file. Argument *flag* has the same values and meaning as for anydbm.open. Other arguments indicate options that allow fine-grained control, but are rarely used.
	hashopen and rnopen work the same way, but open or create hash format and record format files, respectively, returning objects of type Hash and Record. hashopen is generally the fastest format and makes sense when you are using keys to look up records. However, if you also need to access records in sorted order, use btopen; if you need to access records in the same order in which you originally

wrote them, use rnopen. Using hashopen does not keep records in order in the file.

An object *b* of any of the types BTree, Hash, and Record can be indexed as a mapping, as long as keys and values are strings. Further, *b* also supports sequential access through the concept of a *current record*. *b* supplies the following methods.

close	*b*.close( )
	Closes *b*. Call no other method on *b* after *b*.close( ).

first	*b*.first( )
	Sets *b*'s current record to the first record and returns a pair (*key,value*) for the first record. The order of records is arbitrary, except for BTree objects, which ensure records are sorted in alphabetical order of key. *b*.first( ) raises KeyError if *b* is empty.

has_key	*b*.has_key(*key*)
	Returns True if string *key* is a key in *b*; otherwise, returns False.

keys	*b*.keys( )
	Returns the list of *b*'s key strings. The order is arbitrary, except for BTree objects, which return keys in alphabetical order.

last	*b*.last( )
	Sets *b*'s current record to the last record and returns a pair (*key,value*) for the last record. Type Hash does not supply method last.

next	*b*.next( )
	Sets *b*'s current record to the next record and returns a pair (*key,value*) for the next record. *b*.next( ) raises KeyError if *b* has no next record.

previous	*b*.previous( )
	Sets *b*'s current record to the previous record and returns a pair (*key,value*) for the previous record. Type Hash does not supply method previous.

set_location   *b*.set_location(*key*)

Sets *b*'s current record to the item with string key *key* and returns a pair (*key,value*). If *key* is not a key in *b*, and *b* is of type BTree, *b*.set_location(*key*) sets *b*'s current record to the item whose key is the smallest key larger than *key* and returns that key/value pair. For other object types, set_location raises KeyError if *key* is not a key in *b*.

Examples of Berkeley DB Use

The Berkeley DB is suited to tasks similar to those for which DBM-like files are appropriate. Indeed, anydbm uses dbhash, the DBM-like interface to BSD DB, to create new DBM-like files. In addition, BSD DB allows other file formats when you use module bsddb directly. The binary tree format is not as fast as the hashed format for keyed access, but excellent when you also need to access keys in alphabetical order.

The following example handles the same task as the DBM example shown earlier, but uses bsddb rather than anydbm:

```
import fileinput, os, bsddb
wordPos = {  }
sep = os.pathsep
for line in fileinput.input():
    pos = '%s%s%s'%(fileinput.filename(), sep, fileinput.filelineno())
    for word in line.split():
        wordPos.setdefault(word,[  ]).append(pos)
btOut = bsddb.btopen('btindex','n')
sep2 = sep * 2
for word in wordPos:
    btOut[word] = sep2.join(wordPos[word])
btOut.close()
```

The differences between this example and the DBM one are minimal: writing a new binary tree format file with bsddb is basically the same task as writing a new DBM-like file with anydbm. Reading back the data using bsddb.btopen('btindex') rather than anydbm.open('indexfile') is also similar. To illustrate the extra features of binary trees regarding access to keys in alphabetical order, let's tackle a slightly more general task. The following example treats its command-line arguments as specifying the beginning of words, and prints the lines in which any word with such a beginning appears:

```
import sys, os, bsddb, linecache
btIn = bsddb.btopen('btindex')
sep = os.pathsep
sep2 = sep * 2

for word in sys.argv[1:]:
    key, pos = btIn.set_location(word)
```

```
        if not key.startswith(word):
            sys.stderr.write('Word-start %r not found in index file\n' % word)
        while key.startswith(word):
            places = pos.split(sep2)
            for place in places:
                fname, lineno = place.split(sep)
                print "%r occurs in line %s of file %s:" % (word,lineno,fname)
                print linecache.getline(fname, int(lineno)),
            try: key, pos = btIn.next()
            except IndexError: break
```

This example exploits the fact that btIn.set_location sets btIn's current position to the smallest key larger than *word*, when *word* itself is not a key in btIn. When *word* is the start of a word, and the keys are words, this means that set_location sets the current position to the first word, in alphabetical order, that begins with *word*. The tests with *key*.startswith(*word*) checks that we're still scanning words with that beginning, and terminate the while loop when that is no longer the case. We perform the first such test in an if statement, right before the while, because we want to single out the case where no word at all starts with the desired beginning, and output an error message in that specific case.

The Python Database API (DBAPI) 2.0

As I mentioned earlier, the Python standard library does not come with an RDBMS interface, but there are many free third-party modules that let your Python programs access specific databases. Such modules mostly follow the Python Database API 2.0 standard, also known as the DBAPI. A new version of the DBAPI (possibly to be known as 3.0) is likely to appear in the future, but currently there are no firm plans or schedules for one. Programs written against DBAPI 2.0 should work with minimal or no changes with any future DBAPI 3.0, although 3.0, if and when it comes, will no doubt offer further enhancements that future programs will be able to take advantage of.

If your Python program runs only on Windows, you might prefer to access databases by using Microsoft's ADO package through COM. For more information on using Python on Windows, see *Python Programming on Win32*, by Mark Hammond and Andy Robinson (O'Reilly). Since ADO and COM are platform-specific, and this book focuses on cross-platform use of Python, I do not cover ADO and COM further in this book. However, at *http://adodbapi.sourceforge.net/* you will find a useful Python extension that lets you access ADO indirectly through DBAPI.

After importing a DBAPI-compliant module, call the module's connect function with suitable parameters. connect returns an instance of Connection, which represents a connection to the database. The instance supplies commit and rollback methods to deal with transactions, a close method to call as soon as you're done with the database, and a cursor method to return an instance of Cursor. The cursor supplies the methods and attributes used for database operations. A DBAPI-compliant module also supplies exception classes, descriptive attributes, factory functions, and type-description attributes.

Exception Classes

A DBAPI-compliant module supplies exception classes Warning, Error, and several subclasses of Error. Warning indicates such anomalies as data truncation during insertion. Error's subclasses indicate various kinds of errors that your program can encounter when dealing with the database and the DBAPI-compliant module that interfaces to it. Generally, your code uses a statement of the form:

```
try:
    ...
except module.Error, err:
    ...
```

to trap all database-related errors that you need to handle without terminating.

Thread Safety

When a DBAPI-compliant module has an attribute threadsafety greater than 0, the module is asserting some level of thread safety for database interfacing. Rather than relying on this, it's safer and more portable to ensure that a single thread has exclusive access to any given external resource, such as a database, as outlined in "Threaded Program Architecture" on page 350.

Parameter Style

A DBAPI-compliant module has an attribute paramstyle to identify the style of markers used as placeholders for parameters. Insert such markers in SQL statement strings that you pass to methods of Cursor instances, such as method execute, to use runtime-determined parameter values. Say, for example, that you need to fetch the rows of database table *ATABLE* where field *AFIELD* equals the current value of Python variable *x*. Assuming the cursor instance is named *c*, you could perform this task by using Python's string-formatting operator %, as follows:

```
c.execute('SELECT * FROM ATABLE WHERE AFIELD=%r' % x)
```

However, this is *not* the recommended approach. This approach generates a different statement string for each value of *x*, requiring such statements to be parsed and prepared anew each time. With parameter substitution, you pass to execute a single statement string, with a placeholder instead of the parameter value. This lets execute perform parsing and preparation just once, giving potentially better performance. For example, if a module's paramstyle attribute is 'qmark', you can express the above query as:

```
c.execute('SELECT * FROM ATABLE WHERE AFIELD=?', [x])
```

The read-only string attribute paramstyle tells your program how it should use parameter substitution with that module. The possible values of paramstyle are:

format
    The marker is %s, as in string formatting. A query looks like:

```
c.execute('SELECT * FROM ATABLE WHERE AFIELD=%s', [x])
```

named

> The marker is :*name*, and parameters are named. A query looks like:
>
> ```
> c.execute('SELECT * FROM ATABLE WHERE AFIELD=:x', {'x':x})
> ```

numeric

> The marker is :*n*, giving the parameter's number. A query looks like:
>
> ```
> c.execute('SELECT * FROM ATABLE WHERE AFIELD=:1', [x])
> ```

pyformat

> The marker is %(*name*)s, and parameters are named. A query looks like:
>
> ```
> c.execute('SELECT * FROM ATABLE WHERE AFIELD=%(x)s', {'x':x})
> ```

qmark

> The marker is ?. A query looks like:
>
> ```
> c.execute('SELECT * FROM ATABLE WHERE AFIELD=?', [x])
> ```

When paramstyle is neither 'pyformat' nor 'named', the second argument of method execute is a sequence. When parameters are named (i.e., paramstyle is 'pyformat' or 'named'), the second argument of method execute is a dictionary.

Factory Functions

Parameters passed to the database via placeholders must typically be of the right type: this means Python numbers (integers or floating-point values), strings (plain or Unicode), and None to represent SQL NULL. There is no type universally used to represent dates, times, and binary large objects (BLOBs). A DBAPI-compliant module supplies factory functions to build such objects. The types used for this purpose by most DBAPI-compliant modules are those supplied by modules datetime and mxDateTime (covered in Chapter 12), and strings or buffer types for BLOBs. The factory functions specified by the DBAPI are as follows.

Binary   Binary(*string*)

> Returns an object representing the given *string* of bytes as a BLOB.

Date   Date(*year,month,day*)

> Returns an object representing the specified date.

DateFromTicks   DateFromTicks(*s*)

> Returns an object representing the date *s* seconds after the epoch of module time, covered in Chapter 12. For example, DateFromTicks(time.time( )) is "today."

Time   Time(*hour,minute,second*)

> Returns an object representing the specified time.

TimeFromTicks	`TimeFromTicks(s)`
	Returns an object representing the time *s* seconds after the epoch of module `time`, covered in Chapter 12. For example, `TimeFromTicks(time.time())` is "now."

Timestamp	`Timestamp(year,month,day,hour,minute,second)`
	Returns an object representing the specified date and time.

Timestamp-FromTicks	`TimestampFromTicks(s)`
	Returns an object representing the date and time *s* seconds after the epoch of module `time`, covered in Chapter 12. For example, `TimestampFromTicks(time.time())` is the current date and time.

Type Description Attributes

A `Cursor` instance's attribute `description` describes the types and other characteristics of each column of a query. Each column's type (the second item of the tuple describing the column) equals one of the following attributes of the DBAPI-compliant module:

BINARY
  Describes columns containing BLOBs

DATETIME
  Describes columns containing dates, times, or both

NUMBER
  Describes columns containing numbers of any kind

ROWID
  Describes columns containing a row-identification number

STRING
  Describes columns containing text of any kind

A cursor's description, and in particular each column's type, is mostly useful for introspection about the database your program is working with. Such introspection can help you write general modules and work with tables using different schemas, including schemas that may not be known at the time you are writing your code.

The connect Function

A DBAPI-compliant module's `connect` function accepts arguments that vary depending on the kind of database and the specific module involved. The DBAPI standard recommends, but does not mandate, that `connect` accept named arguments. In particular, connect should at least accept optional arguments with the following names:

database
> Name of the specific database to connect

dsn
> Data-source name to use for the connection

host
> Hostname on which the database is running

password
> Password to use for the connection

user
> Username for the connection

Connection Objects

A DBAPI-compliant module's connect function returns an object x that is an instance of class Connection. x supplies the following methods.

---

close   `x.close( )`

Terminates the database connection and releases all related resources. Call close as soon as you're done with the database. Keeping database connections needlessly open can be a serious resource drain on the system.

---

commit   `x.commit( )`

Commits the current transaction in the database. If the database does not support transactions, x.commit( ) is an innocuous no-op.

---

cursor   `x.cursor( )`

Returns a new instance of class Cursor, covered in "Cursor Objects" on page 297.

---

rollback   `x.rollback( )`

Rolls back the current transaction in the database. If the database does not support transactions, x.rollback( ) raises an exception. The DBAPI recommends, but does not mandate, that for databases that do not support transactions class Connection supplies no rollback method, so that x.rollback( ) raises AttributeError. You can test whether transaction support is present with hasattr(x, 'rollback').

Cursor Objects

A Connection instance provides a cursor method that returns an object *c* that is an instance of class Cursor. A SQL cursor represents the set of results of a query and lets you work with the records in that set, in sequence, one at a time. A cursor as modeled by the DBAPI is a richer concept, since it represents the only way in which your program executes SQL queries in the first place. On the other hand, a DBAPI cursor allows you only to advance in the sequence of results (some relational databases, but not all, also provide richer cursors that are able to go backward as well as forward), and does not support the SQL clause WHERE CURRENT OF CURSOR. These limitations of DBAPI cursors enable DBAPI-compliant modules to provide cursors even on RDBMSes that provide no real SQL cursors at all. An instance of class Cursor *c* supplies many attributes and methods; the most frequently used ones are documented here.

close
    `c.close()`

Closes the cursor and releases all related resources.

description
    A read-only attribute that is a sequence of seven-item tuples, one per column in the last query executed:

```
name, typecode, displaysize, internalsize, precision,
scale, nullable
```

`c.description` is None if the last operation on *c* was not a query or returned no usable description of the columns involved. A cursor's description is mostly useful for introspection about the database your program is working with. Such introspection can help you write general modules that are able to work with tables using different schemas, including schemas that may not be fully known at the time you are writing your code.

execute
    `c.execute(statement,parameters=None)`

Executes a SQL *statement* string on the database with the given *parameters*. *parameters* is a sequence when the module's paramstyle is `'format'`, `'numeric'`, or `'qmark'`, and a dictionary when it's `'named'` or `'pyformat'`.

executemany
    `c.executemany(statement,*parameters)`

Executes a SQL *statement* on the database, once for each item of the given *parameters*. *parameters* is a sequence of sequences when the module's paramstyle is `'format'`, `'numeric'`, or `'qmark'`, and a sequence of dictionaries when it's `'named'` or `'pyformat'`. For example, the statement:

```
c.executemany('UPDATE atable SET x=? WHERE
y=?',(12,23),(23,34))
```

when paramstyle is 'qmark' is equivalent to, but faster than, the two statements:

```
c.execute('UPDATE atable SET x=12 WHERE y=23')
c.execute('UPDATE atable SET x=23 WHERE y=34')
```

fetchall   `c.fetchall()`

Returns all remaining result rows from the last query as a sequence of tuples. Raises an exception if the last operation was not a SELECT query.

fetchmany   `c.fetchmany(n)`

Returns up to *n* remaining result rows from the last query as a sequence of tuples. Raises an exception if the last operation was not a SELECT query.

fetchone   `c.fetchone()`

Returns the next result row from the last query as a tuple. Raises an exception if the last operation was not a SELECT query.

rowcount   A read-only attribute that specifies the number of rows fetched or affected by the last operation, or -1 if the module is unable to determine this value.

DBAPI-Compliant Modules

Whatever relational database you want to use, there's at least one (often more than one) Python DBAPI-compliant module downloadable from the Internet. All modules listed in the following sections, except mxODBC (and SAPDB, which uses GPL) have liberal licenses that are similar to Python's: you can use them freely in either open source or closed source programs. mxODBC can be used freely for noncommercial purposes, but you must purchase a license for commercial use. There are so many relational databases that I can't list them all, but here are some of the most popular ones:

ODBC

Open DataBase Connectivity (ODBC) is a standard way to connect to many different databases, including some not supported by other DBAPI-compliant modules, such as Microsoft Jet (also known as the Access database). The Python Windows distribution contains an odbc module, but the module is unsupported and follows an older version of the DBAPI, not the current version 2.0. On Unix or Windows, use mxODBC (*http://www.lemburg.com/files/Python/mxODBC.html*). mxODBC's paramstyle is 'qmark'. Its connect function accepts three optional arguments: *dsn*, *user*, and *password*.

Oracle

Oracle is a widespread commercial RDBMS. To interface to Oracle, you can use DCOracle2, available at *http://www.zope.org/Members/matt/dco2*. DCOracle2's paramstyle is 'numeric'. Its connect function accepts a single optional, unnamed argument string with syntax:

```
'user/password@service'
```

cx_oracle (*http://www.python.net/crew/atuining/cx_Oracle/index.html*) is an alternative. paramstyle is 'named'; the connect function accepts a string in the same format as DCOracle2's, or many optional parameters named *dsn*, *user*, *passwd*, and more besides.

Microsoft SQL Server

To interface to Microsoft SQL Server, I recommend module mssqldb, available at *http://www.object-craft.com.au/projects/mssql/*. mssqldb's paramstyle is 'qmark'. Its connect function accepts three arguments—named *dsn*, *user*, and *passwd*—as well as an optional *database* argument. pymssql (*http://pymssql.sourceforge.net/*) is an alternative.

DB/2

For IBM DB/2, try module DB2, available at *http://sourceforge.net/projects/pydb2*. DB2's paramstyle is 'format'. Its connect function accepts three optional arguments: named *dsn*, *uid*, and *pwd*.

MySQL

MySQL is a widespread, open source RDBMS. To interface to MySQL, try MySQLdb, available at *http://sourceforge.net/projects/mysql-python*. MySQLdb's paramstyle is 'format'. Its connect function accepts four optional arguments: named *db*, *host*, *user*, and *passwd*.

PostgreSQL

PostgreSQL is an excellent open source RDBMS. To interface to PostgreSQL, I recommend psycopg, available at *http://initd.org/Software/psycopg*. psycopg's paramstyle is 'pyformat'. Its connect function accepts a single mandatory string argument, named *dsn*, with the syntax:

```
'host=host dbname=dbname user=username password=password'
```

SAP DB

SAP DB, once known as Adabas, is a powerful RDBMS that used to be closed source but is now open source. SAP DB comes with sapdbapi (available at *http://www.sapdb.org/sapdbapi.html*) as well as other useful Python modules. sapdbapi's paramstyle is 'pyformat'. Its connect function accepts three mandatory arguments—named *user*, *password*, and *database*—and an optional argument named *host*.

Gadfly

Gadfly (*http://gadfly.sf.net*) is not an interface to some other RDBMS but rather a complete RDBMS engine written in Python. Gadfly supports a large subset of standard SQL. For example, Gadfly lacks NULL, but it does support VIEW. Gadfly can run as a daemon server, to which clients connect with TCP/IP. Alternatively, you can run the Gadfly engine directly in your application's process if you don't need other processes to be able to access the same database concurrently.

The gadfly module has several discrepancies from the DBAPI 2.0 (covered in "The Python Database API (DBAPI) 2.0" on page 292) because Gadfly implements a variant of the older DBAPI 1.0. The concepts are quite close, but several details differ. The main differences are:

- gadfly does not supply custom exception classes, so Gadfly operations that fail raise normal Python exceptions, such as IOError, NameError, etc.

- gadfly does not supply a paramstyle attribute. However, the module behaves as if it supplied a paramstyle of 'qmark'.

- gadfly does not supply a function named connect; use the gadfly.gadfly or gadfly.client.gfclient functions instead.

- gadfly does not supply factory functions for data types.

- Gadfly cursors do not supply the executemany method. Instead, in the specific case in which the SQL statement is an INSERT, the execute method optionally accepts as its second argument a list of tuples and inserts all the data.

- Gadfly cursors do not supply the rowcount method.

The gadfly module supplies the following functions.

gadfly	gadfly.gadfly(*dbname*,*dirpath*)
	Returns a connection object for the database named *dbname*, which must have been previously created in the directory indicated by string *dirpath*. The database engine runs in the same process as your application.

gfclient	gadfly.client.gfclient(*policyname*, *port*, *password*, *host*)
	Returns a connection object for the database served by a gfserve process on the given *host* and *port*. *policyname* identifies the level of access required, and is often 'admin' to specify unlimited access.

SQLite

SQLite (*http://www.sqlite.org*) is similar to Gadfly in that it's not an interface to some other RDBMS but rather a complete, self-contained RDBMS engine. However, SQLite is written in C and may offer better performance, and accessibility from multiple programming languages, compared to Gadfly. The most popular Python interface to SQLite is PySQLite, available at *http://initd.org/tracker/pysqlite*. It's quite compatible with DBAPI 2.0, except that it doesn't support types (all data is actually held by SQLite as strings). PySQLite's paramstyle is 'qmark'. An alternative is APSW, available at *http://www.rogerbinns.com/apsw.html*. APSW does not even try to meet the DBAPI 2.0's specs but rather faithfully implements SQLite's own preferred API.

In Python 2.5, PySQLite is included in the Python Standard Library as package sqlite3.

12

Time Operations

A Python program can handle time in several ways. Time intervals are floating-point numbers in units of seconds (a fraction of a second is the fractional part of the interval). Particular instants in time are expressed in seconds since a reference instant, known as the *epoch*. (Midnight, UTC, of January 1, 1970, is a popular epoch used on both Unix and Windows platforms.) Time instants often also need to be expressed as a mixture of units of measurement (e.g., years, months, days, hours, minutes, and seconds), particularly for I/O purposes. I/O, of course, also requires the ability to format times and dates into human-readable strings, and parse them back from string formats.

This chapter covers the time module, which supplies Python's core time-handling functionality. The time module is somewhat dependent on the underlying system's C library. The chapter also presents the datetime, sched, and calendar modules from the standard Python library, the third-party modules dateutil and pytz, and some essentials of the popular extension mx.DateTime. mx.DateTime has been around for many years, with behavior across platforms more uniform than time's, which helps account for its popularity, particularly for date-time representation in database interfaces.

The time Module

The underlying C library determines the range of dates that the time module can handle. On Unix systems, years 1970 and 2038 are typical cut-off points, a limitation that datetime and mx.DateTime let you avoid. Time instants are normally specified in UTC (Coordinated Universal Time, once known as GMT, or Greenwich Mean Time). Module time also supports local time zones and daylight saving time (DST), but only to the extent that support is supplied by the underlying C system library.

As an alternative to seconds since the epoch, a time instant can be represented by a tuple of nine integers, called a *time-tuple*. (Time-tuples are covered in

Table 12-1.) All items are integers: time-tuples don't keep track of fractions of a second. A time-tuple is an instance of struct_time. You can use it as a tuple, and access the items as read-only attributes x.tm_year, x.tm_mon, and so on, with the attribute names listed in Table 12-1. Wherever a function requires a time-tuple argument, you can pass an instance of struct_time or any other sequence whose items are nine integers in the right ranges.

Table 12-1. Tuple form of time representation

Item	Meaning	Field name	Range	Notes
0	Year	tm_year	1970–2038	Wider on some platforms.
1	Month	tm_mon	1–12	1 is January; 12 is December.
2	Day	tm_mday	1–31	
3	Hour	tm_hour	0–23	0 is midnight; 12 is noon.
4	Minute	tm_min	0–59	
5	Second	tm_sec	0–61	60 and 61 for leap seconds.
6	Weekday	tm_wday	0–6	0 is Monday; 6 is Sunday.
7	Year day	tm_yday	1–366	Day number within the year.
8	DST flag	tm_isdst	−1 to 1	-1 means library determines DST.

To translate a time instant from a "seconds since the epoch" floating-point value into a time-tuple, pass the floating-point value to a function (e.g., localtime) that returns a time-tuple with all nine items valid. When you convert in the other direction, mktime ignores items six (tm_wday) and seven (tm_yday) of the tuple. In this case, you normally set item eight (tm_isdst) to -1 so that mktime itself determines whether to apply DST.

Module time supplies the following functions and attributes.

asctime

asctime([*tupletime*])

Accepts a time-tuple and returns a readable 24-character string such as 'Tue Dec 10 18:07:14 2002'. asctime( ) without arguments is like asctime(localtime(time( ))) (formats the current time instant, in local time).

clock

clock( )

Returns the current CPU time as a floating-point number of seconds. To measure computational costs of different approaches, the value of time.clock is more useful than that of time.time (standard library module timeit, covered in "Module timeit" on page 484, is even better). On Unix-like platforms, the reason is that time.clock, using CPU time rather than elapsed time, is less dependent than time.time on unpredictable factors due to machine load. On Windows, this reason does not apply, as Windows has no concept of CPU time, but there is another reason: time.clock uses the higher-precision performance-counter machine clock. The epoch (the time corresponding to a 0.0 result from time.clock) is arbitrary, but differences between the results of successive calls to time.clock in the same process are accurate.

ctime   ctime([*secs*])

Like asctime(localtime(*secs*)) (accepts an instant expressed in seconds since the epoch and returns a readable 24-character string form of that instant, in local time). ctime( ) without arguments is like asctime( ) (formats the current time instant).

gmtime   gmtime([*secs*])

Accepts an instant expressed in seconds since the epoch and returns a time-tuple *t* with the UTC time (*t*.tm_isdst is always 0). gmtime( ) without arguments is like gmtime(time( )) (returns the time-tuple for the current time instant).

localtime   localtime([*secs*])

Accepts an instant expressed in seconds since the epoch and returns a time-tuple *t* with the local time (*t*.tm_isdst is 0 or 1, depending on whether DST applies to instant *secs* by local rules). localtime( ) without arguments is like localtime(time( )) (returns the time-tuple for the current time instant).

mktime   mktime(*tupletime*)

Accepts an instant expressed as a time-tuple in local time and returns a floating-point value with the instant expressed in seconds since the epoch. DST, the last item in *tupletime*, is meaningful: set it to 0 to get solar time, to 1 to get DST, or to -1 to let mktime compute whether DST is in effect at the given instant.

sleep   sleep(*secs*)

Suspends the calling thread for *secs* seconds (*secs* is a floating-point number and can indicate a fraction of a second). The calling thread may start executing again before *secs* seconds (if it's the main thread and some signal wakes it up) or after a longer suspension (depending on system scheduling of processes and threads).

strftime   strftime(*fmt*[,*tupletime*])

Accepts an instant expressed as a time-tuple in local time and returns a string representing the instant as specified by string *fmt*. If you omit *tupletime*, strftime uses localtime(time( )) (formats the current time instant in the local time zone). The syntax of string *format* is similar to the syntax specified in "String Formatting" on page 193. Conversion characters are different, as shown in Table 12-2. Refer to the time instant specified by *tupletime*; also, you can't specify width and precision in the format.

Table 12-2. Conversion characters for strftime

Type char	Meaning	Special notes
a	Weekday name, abbreviated	Depends on locale
A	Weekday name, full	Depends on locale
b	Month name, abbreviated	Depends on locale
B	Month name, full	Depends on locale
c	Complete date and time representation	Depends on locale
d	Day of the month	Between 1 and 31
H	Hour (24-hour clock)	Between 0 and 23
I	Hour (12-hour clock)	Between 1 and 12
j	Day of the year	Between 1 and 366
m	Month number	Between 1 and 12
M	Minute number	Between 0 and 59
p	A.M. or P.M. equivalent	Depends on locale
S	Second number	Between 0 and 61
U	Week number (Sunday first weekday)	Between 0 and 53
w	Weekday number	0 is Sunday, up to 6
W	Week number (Monday first weekday)	Between 0 and 53
x	Complete date representation	Depends on locale
X	Complete time representation	Depends on locale
y	Year number within century	Between 0 and 99
Y	Year number	1970 to 2038, or wider
Z	Name of time zone	Empty if no time zone exists
%	A literal % character	Encoded as %%

For example, you can obtain dates just as formatted by asctime (e.g., 'Tue Dec 10 18:07:14 2002') with the format string:

```
'%a %b %d %H:%M:%S %Y'
```

You can obtain dates compliant with RFC 822 (e.g., 'Tue, 10 Dec 2002 18:07:14 EST') with the format string:

```
'%a, %d %b %Y %H:%M:%S %Z'
```

strptime   strptime(*str*,*fmt*='%a %b %d %H:%M:%S %Y')

Parses *str* according to format string *fmt* and returns the instant in time-tuple format. The format string is like the one for strftime, covered in strftime on page 304.

time	time( )
	Returns the current time instant, a floating-point number of seconds since the epoch. On some platforms, the precision of time measurements is as low as one second.
timezone	Attribute time.timezone is the offset in seconds of the local time zone (without DST) from UTC (>0 in the Americas; <=0 in most of Europe, Asia, Africa).
tzname	Attribute time.tzname is a pair of locale-dependent strings, which are the names of the local time zone without and with DST, respectively.

The datetime Module

datetime provides classes representing date and time objects, which can be either *aware* of time zones or *naïve* (the default). Class tzinfo is abstract: module datetime supplies no implementation (for all the gory details, see *http://docs.python.org/lib/ datetime-tzinfo.html*). (See module pytz, in "The pytz Module" on page 313, for a good, simple implementation of tzinfo, which lets you easily create aware objects.) All the types in module datetime have immutable instances, so the instances' attributes are all read-only and the instances can be keys in a dict or items in a set.

Class date

Class date instances represent a date (no time of day in particular within that date), are always naïve, and assume the Gregorian calendar was always in effect. date instances have three read-only integer attributes: year, month, and day.

date	date(*year*,*month*,*day*)
	Class date also supplies some class methods usable as alternative constructors.
fromordinal	date.fromordinal(*ordinal*)
	Returns a date object corresponding to the proleptic Gregorian ordinal *ordinal*, where a value of 1 corresponds to the first day of the year 1.

fromtimestamp   `date.fromtimestamp(`*`timestamp`*`)`

Returns a date object corresponding to the instant *timestamp* expressed in seconds since the epoch.

today   `date.today()`

Returns a date object representing today's date.

Instances of class date support some arithmetic: the difference between date instances is a timedelta instance, and you can add or subtract a date instance and a timedelta instance to construct another date instance. You can also compare any two instances of class date (the one that's later in time is considered greater).

An instance *d* of class date also supplies the following methods.

ctime   `d.ctime()`

Returns a string representing date *d* in the same 24-character format as time.ctime.

isocalendar   `d.isocalendar()`

Returns a tuple with three integers (ISO year, ISO week number, and ISO weekday). See *http://www.phys.uu.nl/~vgent/calendar/ isocalendar.htm* for more details about the ISO (International Standards Organization) calendar.

isoformat   `d.isoformat()`

Returns a string representing date *d* in the format `'YYYY-MM-DD'`; same as str(*d*).

isoweekday   `d.isoweekday()`

Returns the day of the week of date *d* as an integer; 1 for Monday through 7 for Sunday.

replace   `d.replace(`*`year`*`=None,`*`month`*`=None,`*`day`*`=None)`

Returns a new date object, like *d* except for those attributes explicitly specified as arguments, which get replaced. For example:

```
date(x,y,z).replace(month=m) == date(x,m,z)
```

strftime   `d.strftime()`

Returns a string representing date *d* as specified by string *fmt*, like:

```
time.strftime(fmt, d.totuple())
```

timetuple	`d.timetuple()`
	Returns a time tuple corresponding to date *d* at time 00:00:00 (midnight).

toordinal	`d.toordinal()`
	Returns the proleptic Gregorian ordinal corresponding to date *d*. For example:
	`date(1,1,1).toordinal() == 1`

weekday	`d.weekday()`
	Returns the day of the week of date *d* as an integer; 0 for Monday through 6 for Sunday.

Class time

Class time instances represent a time of day (of no particular date), may be naïve or aware regarding time zones, and always ignore leap seconds. They have five attributes: four read-only integers (hour, minute, second, and microsecond) and an optional tzinfo (None for naïve instances).

time	`time(`*hour*`=0,`*minute*`=0,`*second*`=0,`*microsecond*`=0,`*tzinfo*`=None)`
	Instances of class time do not support arithmetic. You can compare two instances of class time (the one that's later in time is considered greater), but only if they are either both aware or both naïve.
	An instance *t* of class time also supplies the following methods.

isoformat	`t.isoformat()`
	Returns a string representing time *t* in the format `'HH:MM:SS'`; same as `str(t)`. If *t*.microsecond!=0, the resulting string is longer: `'HH:MM:SS.mmmmmm'`. If *t* is aware, six more characters, `'+HH:MM'`, are added at the end to represent the time zone's offset from UTC. In other words, this formatting operation follows the ISO1601 standard.

replace	`t.replace(`*hour*`=None,`*minute*`=None,`*second*`=None,`*microsecond*`=None[,`*tzinfo*`])`
	Returns a new time object, like *t* except for those attributes explicitly specified as arguments, which get replaced. For example:
	`time(x,y,z).replace(minute=m) == time(x,m,z)`

strftime	`t.strftime()`

Returns a string representing time *t* as specified by string *fmt*.

An instance *t* of class time also supplies methods dst, tzname, and utcoffset, which delegate to *t*.tzinfo, but return None if *t*.tzinfo is None.

Class datetime

Class datetime instances represent an instant (a date, with a specific time of day within that date), may be naïve or aware regarding time zones, and always ignore leap seconds. Class datetime subclasses date and adds time's attributes; its instances have read-only integers year, month, day, hour, minute, second, and microsecond, and an optional tzinfo (None for naïve instances).

Time
Operations

datetime	`datetime(year,month,day,hour=0,minute=0,second=0,` `microsecond=0,tzinfo=None)`

Class datetime also supplies some class methods usable as alternative constructors.

combine	`datetime.combine(date,time)`

Returns a datetime object with the date attributes taken from *date* and the time attributes (including tzinfo) taken from *time*. `datetime.combine(d,t)` is like:

```
datetime(d.year, d.month, d.day,
         t.hour, t.minute, t.second, t.microsecond,
         t.tzinfo)
```

fromordinal	`datetime.fromordinal(ordinal)`

Returns a datetime object corresponding to the date given proleptic Gregorian ordinal *ordinal*, where a value of 1 corresponds to the first day of the year 1, at midnight.

fromtimestamp	`datetime.fromtimestamp(timestamp,tz=None)`

Returns a datetime object corresponding to the instant *timestamp* expressed in seconds since the epoch, in local time. When *tz* is not None, returns an aware datetime object with the given tzinfo instance *tz*.

now   datetime.now(*tz*=None)

Returns a datetime object representing the current local date and time. When *tz* is not None, returns an aware datetime object with the given tzinfo instance *tz*.

today   datetime.today( )

Returns a datetime object representing the current local date and time.

utcfromtime-   datetime.utcfromtimestamp(*timestamp*)
stamp
Returns a naive datetime object corresponding to the instant *timestamp* expressed in seconds since the epoch, in UTC.

utcnow   datetime.utcnow( )

Returns a datetime object representing the current date and time, in UTC.

Instances of class datetime support some arithmetic: the difference between datetime instances is a timedelta instance, and you can add or subtract a datetime instance and a timedelta instance to construct another datetime instance. You can compare two instances of class datetime (the one that's later in time is considered greater), but only if they are either both aware or both naïve. An instance *d* of class datetime also supplies the following methods.

astimezone   *d*.timezone(*tz*)

Returns a new aware datetime object, like *d* (which must also be aware), except that the time zone is converted to the one in tzinfo object *tz*. Note that *d*.astimezone(*tz*) is different from *d*.replace(tzinfo=*tz*): the latter does no conversion but rather just copies all of *d*'s attributes except for *d*.tzinfo.

ctime   *d*.ctime( )

Returns a string representing date *d* in the same 24-character format as time.ctime.

date   *d*.date( )

Returns a date object representing the same date as *d*.

isocalendar   *d*.isocalendar()

Returns a tuple with three integers (ISO year, ISO week number, and ISO weekday) for *d*'s date. See *http://www.phys.uu.nl/~vgent/ calendar/isocalendar.htm* for more details about the ISO (International Standards Organization) calendar.

isoformat   *d*.isoformat(sep='T')

Returns a string representing *d* in the format 'YYYY-MM-DDxHH:MM:SS', where *x* is the value of argument *sep* (must be a string of length 1). If *d*.microsecond!=0, seven characters, '.mmmmmm', are added after the 'SS' part of the string. If *t* is aware, six more characters, '+HH:MM', are added at the end to represent the time zone's offset from UTC. In other words, this formatting operation follows the ISO1601 standard. str(*d*) is the same as *d*.isoformat(' ').

isoweekday   *d*.isoweekday()

Returns the day of the week of *d*'s date as an integer; 1 for Monday through 7 for Sunday.

replace   *d*.replace(*year*=None,*month*=None,*day*=None,*hour*=None,*minute*= None,*second*=None,*microsecond*=None[,*tzinfo*])

Returns a new datetime object, like *d* except for those attributes explicitly specified as arguments, which get replaced. For example:

    datetime(x,y,z).replace(month=m) == datetime(x,m,z)

strftime   *d*.strftime()

Returns a string representing *d* as specified by string *fmt*, such as:

    time.strftime(*fmt*, *d*.totuple())

time   *d*.time()

Returns a naïve time object representing the same time of day as *d*.

timetz   *d*.timetz()

Returns a time object representing the same time of day as *d*, with the same tzinfo.

timetuple   *d*.timetuple()

Returns a time-tuple corresponding to instant *d*.

toordinal   *d*.toordinal( )

Returns the proleptic Gregorian ordinal corresponding to *d*'s date. For example:

```
datetime(1,1,1).toordinal( ) == 1
```

---

utctimetuple   *d*.utctimetuple( )

Returns a time-tuple corresponding to instant *d*; normalized to UTC if *d* is aware.

---

weekday   *d*.weekday( )

Returns the day of the week of *d*'s date as an integer; 0 for Monday through 6 for Sunday.

An instance *d* of class datetime also supplies methods dst, tzname, and utcoffset, which delegate to *d*.tzinfo, but return None if *d*.tzinfo is None.

Class timedelta

Class timedelta instances represent time intervals with three read-only integer attributes: days, seconds, and microseconds.

---

timedelta   timedelta(*days*=0, *seconds*=0, *microseconds*=0, *milliseconds*=0, *minutes*=0, *hours*=0, *weeks*=0)

Converts all units with the obvious factors (a week is 7 days, an hour is 3,600 seconds, and so on) and normalizes everything to the three integer attributes, ensuring that 0<=seconds<3600*24 and 0<=microseconds<1000000. For example:

```
print repr(timedelta(minutes=0.5)) # emits datetime.
timedelta(0, 30)
print repr(timedelta(minutes=0.5)) # emits datetime.
timedelta(-1, 82800)
```

Instances of class timedelta support arithmetic (between themselves, with integers, and with instances of classes date and datetime) and comparisons between themselves. To compute from a timedelta instance *t* the equivalent time interval as a floating-point number of seconds, use:

```
t.days*86400+t.seconds+t.microseconds/1000000.0
```

The pytz Module

The third-party pytz module offers the simplest way to create tzinfo instances, which are used to make time zone–aware instances of classes time and datetime. (pytz is based on the Olson library of time zones, documented at *http://www.twinsun.com/tz/tz-link.htm*. pytz is available at *http://pytz.source-forge.net/*.) The best general way to program around the traps and pitfalls of time zones is to always use the UTC time zone internally, converting to other time zones only for display purposes.

pytz supplies common_timezones, a list of over 400 strings that name the most common time zones you might want to use (mostly of the form *continent/city*, with some alternatives such as 'UTC' and 'US/Pacific'), and all_timezones, a list of over 500 strings that also supply some synonyms for the time zones. For example, to specify the time zone of Lisbon, Portugal, by Olson library standards, you would normally use the string 'Europe/Lisbon', and that is what you find in common_timezones; however, you may also use 'Portugal', which you find only in all_timezones. pytz also supplies utc and UTC, two names for the same object, a tzinfo instance representing Coordinated Universal Time (UTC).

pytz also supplies two functions.

country_ timezones	country_timezones(*code*) Returns a list of time zone names corresponding to the country whose two-letter ISO code is *code*. For example, pytz. country_timezones('US') returns a list of 22 strings, from 'America/New_York' to 'Pacific/Honolulu'.
timezone	timezone(*name*) Returns an instance of tzinfo corresponding to the time zone named *name*. For example, to display the Honolulu equivalent of midnight, December 31, 2005, in New York: ```dt = datetime.datetime(2005,12,31,tzinfo=pytz.
timezone('America/New_York'))
print dt.astimezone(pytz.timezone('Pacific/Honolulu'))
emits 2005-12-30 19:00:00-10:00```

The dateutil Module

The third-party package dateutil (*http://labix.org/python-dateutil*) offers modules to manipulate dates in various ways, including time deltas, recurrence, time zones, and fuzzy parsing. (See the module's web site for complete documentation of its rich functionality.) dateutil's main modules are the following.

easter   easter.easter(*year*)

Returns the datetime.date object for Easter of the given *year*. For
example:

```
from dateutil import easter
print easter.easter(2006)
```

emits **2006-04-16**.

---

parser   parser.parse(*s*)

Returns the datetime.datetime object denoted by string *s*, with
very permissive (a.k.a. "fuzzy") parsing rules. For example:

```
from dateutil import parser
print parser.parse("Saturday, January 28, 2006, at
11:15pm")
```

emits **2006-01-28 23:15:00**.

---

relativedelta   relativedelta.relativedelta(...)

You can call relativedelta with two instances of datetime.datetime:
the resulting relativedelta instance captures the relative difference
between the two arguments. Alternatively, you can call
relativedelta with a keyword argument representing absolute information (*year*, *month*, *day*, *hour*, *minute*, *second*, *microsecond*); relative
information (*years*, *months*, *weeks*, *days*, *hours*, *minutes*, *seconds*,
microseconds), which may have positive or negative values; or the
special keyword *weekday*, which can be a number from 0 (Monday)
to 6 (Sunday), or one of the module attributes MO, TU,..., SU, which
can also be called with a numeric argument *n* to specify the *n*th
weekday. In any case, the resulting relativedelta instance captures
the information in the call. For example, after:

```
from dateutil import relativedelta
r = relativedelta.relativedelta(weekday=relativedelta.
MO(1))
```

r means "next Monday." You can add a relativedelta instance to
a datetime.datetime instance to get a new datetime.datetime
instance at the stated relative delta from the other:

```
print datetime.datetime(2006,1,29)+r
# emits: 2006-01-30
datetime.datetime(2006,1,30)+r
# emits: 2006-01-30
datetime.datetime(2006,1,31)+r
# emits: 2006-02-06
```

Note that "next Monday," by relativedelta's interpretation, is the
very same date, if that day is already a Monday (so, a more detailed
name might be "the first date, on or following the given date,
which falls on a Monday"). dateutil's site has very detailed explanations of the rules defining the behavior of relativedelta
instances.

---

rrule	`rrule.rrule(freq, ...)`

Module rrule implements RFC2445 (also known as the iCalendar RFC), available in all the glory of its 140+ pages at *ftp://ftp.rfc-editor.org/in-notes/rfc2445.txt*. *freq* must be one of the constant attributes of module rrule: `YEARLY`, `MONTHLY`, `WEEKLY`, `DAILY`, `HOURLY`, `MINUTELY`, or `SECONDLY`. After mandatory argument *freq* may optionally come some of many possible named arguments, such as interval=2, to specify that the recurrence is only on alternate occurrences of the specified frequency (for example, rrule.rrule(rrule.YEARLY) repeats every year, while rrule.rrule(rrule.YEARLY, interval=7) repeats only every seven years).

An instance *r* of type rrule.rrule supplies several methods.

after	`r.after(d, inc=False)`

Returns the earliest `datetime.datetime` instance that's an occurrence of recurrence rule *r* and happens after date *d* (when *inc* is true, an occurrence happening on date *d* itself is also acceptable).

before	`r.before(d, inc=False)`

Returns the latest `datetime.datetime` instance that's an occurrence of recurrence rule *r* and happens before date *d* (when *inc* is true, an occurrence happening on date *d* itself is also acceptable).

between	`r.between(start, finish, inc=False)`

Returns all `datetime.datetime` instances that are occurrences of recurrence rule *r* and happen between dates *start* and *finish* (when *inc* is true, occurrences happening on dates *start* and *finish* themselves are also acceptable).

count	`r.count( )`

Returns the number of occurrences of recurrence rule *r*.

For example, to express "once a week throughout January 2006," you could code:

```
start=datetime.datetime(2006,1,1)
r=rrule.rrule(rrule.WEEKLY, dtstart=start)
for d in r.between(start, datetime.datetime(2006,2,1),
True):
    print d.date( ),
```

to emit **2006-01-01 2006-01-08 2006-01-15 2006-01-22 2006-01-29**.

The sched Module

The sched module implements an event-scheduler, letting you easily deal, along a single thread of execution, with events that may be scheduled in either a "real" or a "simulated" time-scale. sched supplies a scheduler class.

scheduler	class scheduler(*timefunc,delayfunc*)
	An instance *s* of scheduler holds two functions to use for all time-related operations. *timefunc* is callable without arguments to get the current time instant (in any unit of measure); for example, you can pass time.time. *delayfunc* is callable with one argument (a time duration, in the same units as *timefunc*) to delay the current thread for that time; for example, you can pass time.sleep. scheduler calls *delayfunc*(0) after each event to give other threads a chance; this is compatible with time.sleep. By taking functions as arguments, scheduler lets you use whatever "simulated time" or "pseudotime" fits your application's needs.
	A scheduler instance *s* supplies the following methods.

cancel	s.cancel(*event_token*)
	Removes an event from *s*'s queue. *event_token* must be the result of a previous call to *s*.enter or *s*.enterabs, and the event must not yet have happened; otherwise, cancel raises RuntimeError.

empty	s.empty( )
	Returns True if *s*'s queue is empty; otherwise, False.

enterabs	s.enterabs(*when,priority,func,args*)
	Schedules a future event (a callback to *func*(**args*)) at time *when*. *when* is in the units used by the time functions of *s*. If several events are scheduled for the same time, *s* executes them in increasing order of *priority*. enterabs returns an event token *t*, which you may pass to *s*.cancel to cancel this event.

enter	s.enter(*delay,priority,func,args*)
	Like enterabs, except that *delay* is a relative time (different from the current instant), while enterabs's argument *when* is an absolute time (a future instant).

run	s.run( )
	Runs all scheduled events. *s*.run loops until *s*.empty( ), using the *delayfunc* passed on *s*'s initialization to wait for each scheduled

event. If a callback *func* raises an exception, s propagates it, but s keeps its own state, removing the event from the schedule. If a callback *func* runs longer than the time available before the next scheduled event, s falls behind but keeps executing scheduled events in order, never dropping any. Call s.cancel to drop an event explicitly if that event is no longer of interest.

The calendar Module

The calendar module supplies calendar-related functions, including functions to print a text calendar for a given month or year. By default, calendar takes Monday as the first day of the week and Sunday as the last one. To change this, call calendar.setfirstweekday. calendar handles years in module time's range, typically 1970 to 2038. Module calendar supplies the following functions.

calendar	calendar(*year*,w=2,*l*=1,c=6)
	Returns a multiline string with a calendar for year *year* formatted into three columns separated by c spaces. w is the width in characters of each date; each line has length 21*w+18+2*c. *l* is the number of lines for each week.
firstweekday	firstweekday( )
	Returns the current setting for the weekday that starts each week. By default, when calendar is first imported, this is 0, meaning Monday.
isleap	isleap(*year*)
	Returns True if *year* is a leap year; otherwise, False.
leapdays	leapdays(*y1*,*y2*)
	Returns the total number of leap days in the years within range(*y1*,*y2*).
month	month(*year*,*month*,w=2,*l*=1)
	Returns a multiline string with a calendar for month *month* of year *year*, one line per week plus two header lines. w is the width in characters of each date; each line has length 7*w+6. *l* is the number of lines for each week.

monthcalendar   monthcalendar(*year*,*month*)

Returns a list of lists of ints. Each sublist denotes a week. Days outside month *month* of year *year* are set to 0; days within the month are set to their day-of-month, 1 and up.

monthrange   monthrange(*year*,*month*)

Returns two integers. The first one is the code of the weekday for the first day of the month *month* in year *year*; the second one is the number of days in the month. Weekday codes are 0 (Monday) to 6 (Sunday); month numbers are 1 to 12.

prcal   prcal(*year*,w=2,l=1,c=6)

Like print calendar.calendar(*year*,w,l,c).

prmonth   prmonth(*year*,*month*,w=2,l=1)

Like print calendar.month(*year*,*month*,w,l).

setfirstweekday   setfirstweekday(*weekday*)

Sets the first day of each week to weekday code *weekday*. Weekday codes are 0 (Monday) to 6 (Sunday). Module calendar supplies attributes MONDAY, TUESDAY, WEDNESDAY, THURSDAY, FRIDAY, SATURDAY, and SUNDAY, whose values are the integers 0 to 6. Use these attributes when you mean weekday codes (e.g., calendar.FRIDAY instead of 4) to make your code clearer and more readable.

timegm   timegm(*tupletime*)

The inverse of time.gmtime: accepts a time instant in time-tuple form and returns the same instant as a floating-point number of seconds since the epoch.

weekday   weekday(*year*,*month*,*day*)

Returns the weekday code for the given date. Weekday codes are 0 (Monday) to 6 (Sunday); month numbers are 1 (January) to 12 (December).

The mx.DateTime Module

DateTime is one of the modules in the mx package made available by eGenix GmbH. mx is mostly open source, and, at the time of this writing, mx.DateTime has liberal license conditions similar to those of Python itself. mx.DateTime's popularity stems from its functional richness and cross-platform portability. I present only an essential subset of mx.DateTime's rich functionality here; the module comes with detailed documentation about its advanced time- and date-handling features.

Date and Time Types

Package DateTime supplies several date and time types whose instances are immutable (thus, suitable as dictionary keys). Type DateTime represents a time instant and includes an absolute date, the number of days since an epoch of January 1, year 1 CE, according to the Gregorian calendar (0001-01-01 is day 1), and an absolute time, a floating-point number of seconds since midnight. Type DateTimeDelta represents an interval of time, which is a floating-point number of seconds. Class RelativeDateTime lets you specify dates in relative terms, such as "next Monday" or "first day of next month." DateTime and DateTimeDelta are covered in detail (respectively in "The DateTime Type" on page 319 and "The DateTimeDelta Type" on page 324), but RelativeDateTime is not.

Date and time types supply customized string conversion, invoked via the built-in str or automatically during implicit conversion (e.g., in a print statement). The resulting strings are in standard ISO8601 formats, such as:

```
YYYY-MM-DD HH:MM:SS.ss
```

For finer-grained control of string formatting, use method strftime. Function DateTimeFrom constructs DateTime instances from strings. Various modules of package mx.DateTime also supply other formatting and parsing functions.

The DateTime Type

Module DateTime supplies factory functions to build instances of type DateTime, which in turn supply methods, attributes, and arithmetic operators.

Factory functions for DateTime

Module DateTime supplies many factory functions that produce DateTime instances. Several of these factory functions can also be invoked through synonyms. The most commonly used factory functions are the following.

DateTime, Date, Timestamp	DateTime(*year*,*month*=1,*day*=1,*hour*=0,*minute*=0,*second*=0.0) Creates and returns a DateTime instance representing the given absolute time. Date and Timestamp are synonyms of DateTime. *day* can be less than 0 to denote days counted from the end of the

month: -1 is the last day of the month, -2 is the next-to-last day, and so on. For example:

```
print mx.DateTime.DateTime(2002,12,-1)
# prints: 2002-12-31 00:00:00.00
```

second is a floating-point value and can include an arbitrary fraction of a second.

DateTimeFrom,   DateTimeFrom(*args,**kwds)
TimestampFrom

Creates and returns a DateTime instance built from the given arguments. TimestampFrom is a synonym of DateTimeFrom. DateTimeFrom can parse strings that represent a date and/or time. DateTimeFrom also accepts named arguments, with the same names as those of the arguments of function DateTime.

DateTime-   DateTimeFromAbsDays(*days*)
FromAbsDays

Creates and returns a DateTime instance representing an instant *days* days after the epoch. *days* is a floating-point number and can include an arbitrary fraction of a day.

DateTime-   DateTimeFromCOMDate(*comdate*)
FromCOMDate

Creates and returns a DateTime instance representing the COM-format date *comdate*. *comdate* is a floating-point number and can include an arbitrary fraction of a day. The COM date epoch is midnight of January 1, 1900.

DateFromTicks   DateFromTicks(*secs*)

Creates and returns a DateTime instance representing midnight, local time, of the day of instant *secs*. *secs* is an instant as represented by the time module (i.e., seconds since time's epoch).

---

gmt, utc   gmt( )

Creates and returns a DateTime instance representing the current GMT time. utc is a synonym of gmt.

---

gmtime,   gmtime(*secs*=None)
utctime

Creates and returns a DateTime instance representing the GMT time of instant *secs*. *secs* is an instant as represented by the time module (i.e., seconds since time's epoch). When *secs* is None, gmtime uses the current instant as returned by function time.time. utctime is a synonym of gmtime.

---

localtime	`localtime(secs=None)`
	Creates and returns a DateTime instance representing the local time of instant *secs*. *secs* is an instant as represented by the time module (i.e., seconds since time's epoch). When *secs* is None, localtime uses the current instant as returned by function time.time.
mktime	`mktime(timetuple)`
	Creates and returns a DateTime instance representing the instant indicated by nine-item tuple *timetuple*, which is in the format used by module time.
now	`now( )`
	Creates and returns a DateTime instance representing the current local time.
Timestamp-FromTicks	`TimestampFromTicks(secs)`
	Creates and returns a DateTime instance representing the local time of instant *secs*. *secs* is an instant as represented by the time module (seconds since time's epoch).
today	`today(hour=0,minute=0,second=0.0)`
	Creates and returns a DateTime instance representing the local time for the given time (the default is midnight) of today's date.

Methods of DateTime instances

The most commonly used methods of a DateTime instance *d* are the following.

absvalues	`d.absvalues( )`
	Returns a pair (*ad*,*at*) where *ad* is an integer representing *d*'s absolute date and *at* is a floating-point number representing *d*'s absolute time.
COMDate	`d.COMDate( )`
	Returns *d*'s instant in COM format (a floating-point number that is the number of days and fraction of a day since midnight of January 1, 1900).

gmticks　　　　*d*.gmticks()

Returns a floating-point value representing *d*'s instant as seconds (and fraction) since module time's epoch, assuming *d* is represented in GMT.

gmtime　　　　*d*.gmtime()

Returns a DateTime instance *d1* representing *d*'s instant in GMT, assuming *d* is represented in local time.

gmtoffset　　　*d*.gmtoffset()

Returns a DateTimeDelta instance representing the time zone of *d*, assuming *d* is represented in local time. gmtoffset returns negative values in the Americas, and positive ones in most of Europe, Asia, and Africa.

localtime　　　*d*.localtime()

Returns a DateTime instance *d1* representing *d*'s instant in local time, assuming *d* is represented in GMT.

strftime, Format　*d*.strftime(*fmt*="%c")

Returns a string representing *d* as specified by string *fmt*. The syntax of *fmt* is the same as in time.strftime, covered in "strftime". Format is a synonym of strftime.

ticks　　　　　*d*.ticks()

Returns a floating-point number representing *d*'s instant as seconds (and a fraction) since module time's epoch, assuming *d* is represented in local time.

tuple　　　　　*d*.tuple()

Returns *d*'s instant as a nine-item tuple in the format used by module time.

Attributes of DateTime instances

The most commonly used attributes of a DateTime instance *d* are the following (all are read-only):

absdate
> *d*'s absolute date; like *d*.absvalues( )[0]

absdays
> A floating-point number representing days (and fraction of a day) since the epoch

abstime
> *d*'s absolute time; like *d*.absvalues( )[1]

date
> A string in format 'YYYY-MM-DD'; the standard ISO format for the date of *d*

day
> An integer between 1 and 31; the day of the month of *d*

day_of_week
> An integer between 0 and 6; the day of the week of *d* (Monday is 0)

day_of_year
> An integer between 1 and 366; the day of the year of *d* (January 1 is 1)

dst
> An integer between -1 and 1, indicating whether DST is in effect on date *d*, assuming *d* is represented in local time (-1 is unknown, 0 is no, and 1 is yes)

hour
> An integer between 0 and 23; the hour of the day of *d*

iso_week
> A three-item tuple (*year, week, day*) with the ISO week notation for *d* (*week* is week-of-year; *day* is between 1, Monday, and 7, Sunday)

minute
> An integer between 0 and 59; the minute of the hour of *d*

month
> An integer between 1 and 12; the month of the year of *d*

second
> A floating-point number between 0.0 and 60.0; the seconds-within-minute of *d* (DateTime instances do not support leap seconds)

year
> An integer; the year of *d* (1 is 1 CE and 0 is 1 BCE)

Arithmetic on DateTime instances

You can use binary operator - (minus) between two DateTime instances *d1* and *d2*. In this case, *d1-d2* is a DateTimeDelta instance representing the elapsed time between *d1* and *d2*, which is greater than 0 if *d1* is later than *d2*. You can use binary operators + and - between a DateTime instance *d* and a number *n*. *d+n*, *d-n*, and *n+d* are all DateTime instances that differ from *d* by *n* (or *-n*) days (and fraction of a day if *n* is a floating-point number), and *n-d* is arbitrarily defined to be equal to *d-n*.

The DateTimeDelta Type

Instances of type DateTimeDelta represent differences between time instants. Internally, a DateTimeDelta instance stores a floating-point number that represents a number of seconds (and a fraction of a second).

Factory functions for DateTimeDelta

Module DateTime supplies many factory functions that produce DateTimeDelta instances. Some of these factory functions can be invoked through one or more synonyms. The most commonly used are the following.

DateTimeDelta   DateTimeDelta(*days*,*hours*=0.0,*minutes*=0.0,*seconds*=0.0)

Creates and returns a DateTimeDelta instance by the formula:

$$seconds+60.0*(minutes+60.0*(hours+24.0*days))$$

DateTimeDelta-From   DateTimeDeltaFrom(**args*,***kwds*)

Creates and returns a DateTimeDelta instance from the given arguments. See also "DateTimeFrom, TimestampFrom" on page 320.

DateTimeDelta-FromSeconds   DateTimeDeltaFromSeconds(*seconds*)

Like DateTimeDelta(0,0,0,*seconds*).

TimeDelta, Time   TimeDelta(*hours*=0.0,*minutes*=0.0,*seconds*=0.0)

Like DateTimeDelta(0,*hours*,*minutes*,*seconds*). Function TimeDelta is guaranteed to accept named arguments. Time is a synonym for TimeDelta.

TimeDeltaFrom, TimeFrom	`TimeDeltaFrom(*args,**kwds)`
	Like `DateTimeDeltaFrom`, except that positional arguments, if any, indicate hours, not days as for `DateTimeDeltaFrom`. `TimeFrom` is the same as `TimeDeltaFrom`.

TimeFromTicks	`TimeFromTicks(secs)`
	Creates and returns a `DateTimeDelta` instance for the amount of time between instant *secs* (in seconds since the epoch) and midnight of the same day as that of instant *secs*.

Methods of DateTimeDelta instances

The most commonly used methods of a `DateTimeDelta` instance *d* are the following.

absvalues	`d.absvalues()`
	Returns a pair (*ad*,*at*) where *ad* is an integer (*d*'s number of days), *at* is a floating-point number (*d*'s number of seconds modulo 86400), and both have the same sign.

strftime, Format	`d.strftime(fmt="%c")`
	Returns a string representing *d* as specified by string *fmt*. The syntax of *fmt* is the same as in `time.strftime`, covered in strftime on page 304, but not all specifiers are meaningful. The result of `d.strftime` does not reflect the sign of the time interval that *d* represents; to display the sign, affix it to the string by string manipulation. For example:

```
if d.seconds >= 0.0: return d.strftime(fmt)
else: return '-' + d.strftime(fmt)
```

Format is a synonym of `strftime`.

tuple	`d.tuple()`
	Returns a tuple (*day*,*hour*,*minute*,*second*); each item is a signed number in the respective range. *second* is a floating-point number, and the other items are integers.

Attributes of DateTimeDelta instances

A `DateTimeDelta` instance *d* supplies the following attributes (all are read-only):

```
day
hour
minute
second
```
> Like the four items of the tuple returned by *d*.`tuple( )`

```
days
hours
minutes
seconds
```
> Each a floating-point value giving *d*'s value in the given unit of measure so that:

$$d.\text{seconds} == 60.0*d.\text{minutes} == 3600.0*d.\text{hours} == 86400.0*d.\text{days}$$

Arithmetic on DateTimeDelta instances

You can add or subtract two `DateTimeDelta` instances *d1* and *d2* to add or subtract the signed time intervals they represent. You can use binary operators + and - between a `DateTimeDelta` instance *d* and a number *n*; *n* is taken as a number of seconds (and fraction of a second if *n* is a floating-point value). You can multiply or divide *d* by *n* to scale the time interval *d* represents. Each operation returns a `DateTimeDelta` instance. You can also add or subtract a `DateTimeDelta` instance *dd* to or from a `DateTime` instance *d* to get another `DateTime` instance *d1* that differs from *d* by the signed time interval indicated by *dd*.

Other Attributes

Module `mx.DateTime` also supplies many constant attributes. The attributes used most often are:

```
oneWeek
oneDay
oneHour
oneMinute
oneSecond
```
> Instances of `DateTimeDelta` that represent the indicated durations

```
Monday
Tuesday
Wednesday
Thursday
Friday
Saturday
Sunday
```
> Integers that represent the weekdays: Monday is 0, Tuesday is 1, and so on

Weekday

A dictionary that maps integer weekday numbers to their string names and vice versa: 0 maps to 'Monday', 'Monday' maps to 0, and so on

January
February
March
April
May
June
July
August
September
October
November
December

Integers that represent the months: January is 1, February is 2, and so on

Month

A dictionary that maps integer month numbers to their string names and vice versa: 1 maps to 'January', 'January' maps to 1, and so on

Module mx.DateTime supplies one other useful function.

cmp	cmp(*obj1*,*obj2*,*accuracy*=0.0)
	Compares two DateTime or DateTimeDelta instances *obj1* and *obj2*, and returns -1, 0, or 1, like built-in function cmp. It returns 0 (meaning that *obj1* and *obj2* are "equal") if the two instants or durations differ by less than *accuracy* seconds.

Submodules

Package mx.DateTime also supplies several submodules for specialized purposes. Module mx.DateTime.ISO supplies functions to parse and generate date and time strings in ISO8601 format. Module mx.DateTime.ARPA supplies functions to parse and generate date and time strings in ARPA format, as widely used on the Internet:

```
[Day, ]DD Mon YYYY HH:MM[:SS] [ZONE]
```

Module mx.DateTime.Feasts supplies functions to compute the date of Easter Sunday, and other moveable feast days that depend on it, for any given year. If your machine is connected to the Internet, you can use module mx.DateTime.NIST to access the accurate world standard time provided by NIST atomic clocks. Thanks to NIST's atomic clocks, the module is able to compute the current date and time very accurately. The module calibrates your computer's approximate clock with reference to NIST's clocks and compensates for any network delays incurred while accessing NIST.

13

Controlling Execution

Python documents (in other words, directly exposes and supports) many of the internal mechanisms it uses. This support may help you understand Python at an advanced level, and lets you hook your own code into such documented Python mechanisms and control them to some extent. For example, "Python built-ins" on page 141 covers the way Python arranges for built-ins to be made implicitly visible. This chapter covers other advanced Python control techniques, while Chapter 18 covers techniques that apply specifically to testing, debugging, and profiling.

Dynamic Execution and the exec Statement

Python's exec statement can execute code that you read, generate, or otherwise obtain during a program's run. exec dynamically executes a statement or a suite of statements. exec is a simple keyword statement with the following syntax:

```
exec code[ in globals[,locals]]
```

code can be a string, an open file-like object, or a code object. *globals* and *locals* are dictionaries (in Python 2.4, *locals* can be any mapping, but *globals* must be specifically a dict; in Python 2.5, either or both can be any mapping). If both are present, they are the global and local namespaces in which *code* executes. If only *globals* is present, exec uses *globals* in the role of both namespaces. If neither *globals* nor *locals* is present, *code* executes in the current scope. Running exec in the current scope is a bad idea, since it can bind, rebind, or unbind any name. To keep things under control, use exec only with specific, explicit dictionaries.

Avoiding exec

Use exec only when it's really indispensable. Most often, it's best to avoid exec and choose more specific, well-controlled mechanisms instead: exec pries loose your control on your code's namespace, damages your program's performance, and exposes you to numerous, hard-to-find bugs.

For example, a frequently asked question about Python is "How do I set a variable whose name I just read or built?" Strictly speaking, exec lets you do this. For example, if the name of the variable you want to set is in *varname*, you might use:

```
exec varname+'=23'
```

Don't do this. An exec statement like this in current scope makes you lose control of your namespace, leading to bugs that are extremely hard to track, and more generally making your program unfathomably difficult to understand. An improvement is to keep the "variables" that you need to set not as variables, but as entries in a dictionary, say *mydict*. You can then use the following variation:

```
exec varname+'=23' in mydict
```

While this use is not as terrible as the previous example, it is still a bad idea. Keeping such "variables" as dictionary entries is simple and effective, but it also means that you don't need to use exec at all to set them. Just code:

```
mydict[varname] = 23
```

With this approach, your program is clearer, direct, elegant, and faster. While there are valid uses of exec, they are extremely rare and should always use explicit dictionaries.

Expressions

exec can execute an expression because any expression is also a valid statement (called an expression statement). However, Python ignores the value returned by an expression statement in this case. To evaluate an expression and obtain the expression's value, see built-in function eval, covered in eval on page 161.

Compile and Code Objects

To obtain a code object to use with exec, you normally call built-in function compile with the last argument set to 'exec' (as covered in "compile"). A code object *c* exposes many interesting read-only attributes whose names all start with 'co_', such as:

co_argcount
> The number of parameters of the function of which *c* is the code (0 when *c* is not the code object of a function but rather is built directly by compile on a string)

co_code
> A byte-string with *c*'s bytecode

co_consts
> The tuple of constants used in *c*

co_filename
> The name of the file *c* was compiled from (the string that is the second argument to compile when *c* was built that way)

`co_firstlinenumber`
>   The initial line number (within the file named by `co_filename`) of the source code that was compiled to produce *c* if *c* was built by compilation from a file

`co_name`
>   The name of the function of which *c* is the code ('`<module>`' when *c* is not the code object of a function but rather is built directly by `compile` on a string)

`co_names`
>   The tuple of all identifiers used within *c*

`co_varnames`
>   The tuple of local variables' identifiers within *c*, starting with parameter names

Most of these attributes are useful only for debugging purposes, but some may help advanced introspection, as exemplified further on in this section.

If you start with a string that holds some statements, I recommend using `compile` on the string, then calling `exec` on the resulting code object rather than giving `exec` the string to compile and execute. This separation lets you check for syntax errors separately from evaluation-time errors. You can often arrange things so that the string is compiled once and the code object is executed repeatedly, which speeds things up. `eval` can also benefit from such separation. Moreover, the `compile` step is intrinsically safe (while both `exec` and `eval` are enormously risky if you execute them on code that you don't trust), and you may be able to perform some checks on the code object to lessen the risk.

A code object has a read-only attribute `co_names`, which is the tuple of the names used in the code. For example, say that you want the user to enter an expression that contains only literal constants and operators—no function calls nor other names. Before evaluating the expression, you can check that the string the user entered satisfies these constraints:

```
def safe_eval(s):
    code = compile(s, '<user-entered string>', 'eval')
    if code.co_names:
        raise ValueError, ('No names (%r) allowed in expression (%r)' %
                           (code.co_names, s))
    return eval(code)
```

This function `safe_eval` evaluates the expression passed in as argument *s* only if the string is a syntactically valid expression (otherwise, `compile` raises `SyntaxError`) and contains no names at all (otherwise, `safe_eval` explicitly raises `ValueError`).

Knowing what names the code is about to access may sometimes help you optimize the preparation of the dictionary that you need to pass to `exec` or `eval` as the namespace. Since you need to provide values only for those names, you may save work by not preparing other entries. For example, say that your application dynamically accepts code from the user with the convention that variable names starting with `data_` refer to files residing in subdirectory *data* that user-written code doesn't need to read explicitly. User-written code may in turn compute and leave results in global variables with names starting with `result_`, which your application writes back as files in subdirectory *data*. Thanks to this convention, you may later move the data elsewhere (e.g., to BLOBs in a database instead of to files in a subdirectory), and user-written code won't be affected. Here's how you might implement these conventions efficiently:

```
def exec_with_data(user_code_string):
    user_code = compile(user_code_string, '<user code>', 'exec')
    datadict = {  }
    for name in user_code.co_names:
        if name.startswith('data_'):
            datafile = open('data/%s' % name[5:], 'rb')
            datadict[name] = datafile.read( )
            datafile.close( )
    exec user_code in datadict
    for name in datadict:
        if name.startswith('result_'):
            datafile = open('data/%s' % name[7:], 'wb')
            datafile.write(datadict[name])
            datafile.close( )
```

Never exec nor eval Untrusted Code

Note that function exec_with_data is not at all safe against untrusted code: if you pass it as argument *user_code_string*, which is some string obtained in a way that you cannot *entirely* trust, there is essentially no limit to the amount of damage it might do. This is unfortunately true of just about any use of both exec and eval, except for those rare cases in which you can set very strict and checkable limits on the code you're about to execute or evaluate, as was the case for function safe_eval.

Old versions of Python tried to supply tools to ameliorate this situation, under the heading of "restricted execution," but those tools were never entirely proof against the ingenuity of able hackers, and current versions of Python have therefore dropped them. If you need to ward against such attacks, take advantage of your operating system's protection mechanisms: run untrusted code in a separate process, with privileges as restricted as you can possibly make them (study the mechanisms that your OS supplies for the purpose, such as chroot, setuid, and jail). To ward against "denial of service" attacks, have the main process monitor the separate one and terminate it if and when resource consumption becomes excessive. Processes are covered in "Running Other Programs" on page 354.

Internal Types

Some of the internal Python objects that I mention in this section are hard to use. Using such objects correctly and to the best effect requires some study of Python's own C (or Java, or C#) sources. Such black magic is rarely needed, except to build general-purpose development frameworks and similar wizardly tasks. Once you do understand things in depth, Python empowers you to exert control if and when you need to. Since Python exposes many kinds of internal objects to your Python code, you can exert that control by coding in Python, even when a nodding acquaintance with C (or Java, or C#) is needed to read Python's sources in order to understand what is going on.

Type Objects

The built-in type named type acts as a factory object, returning objects that are types. Type objects don't have to support any special operations except equality comparison and representation as strings. However, most type objects are callable and return new instances of the type when called. In particular, built-in types such as int, float, list, str, tuple, set, and dict all work this way. The attributes of the types module are the built-in types, each with one or more names. For example, types.DictType and types.DictionaryType both refer to type({}), also known as dict. Besides being callable to generate instances, many type objects are useful because you can subclass them, as covered in "Classes and Instances" on page 82.

The Code Object Type

As well as by using built-in function compile, you can get a code object via the func_code attribute of a function or method object. (For the attributes of code objects, see "Compile and Code Objects" on page 329.) Code objects are not callable, but you can rebind the func_code attribute of a function object with the correct number of parameters in order to wrap a code object into callable form. For example:

```
def g(x): print 'g', x
code_object = g.func_code
def f(x): pass
f.func_code = code_object
f(23)          # emits g 23
```

Code objects that have no parameters can also be used with statement exec or built-in function eval. Module new supplies a function to create code objects, as well as other functions to create old-style instances and classes, functions, methods, and modules. You can also create a new object by calling the type object you want to instantiate instead of calling a factory function from module new.

The frame Type

Function _getframe in module sys returns a frame object from Python's call stack. A frame object has attributes that supply information about the code executing in the frame and the execution state. Modules traceback and inspect help you access and display information, particularly when an exception is being handled. Chapter 18 provides more information about frames and tracebacks, and covers module inspect, which is generally the best way to perform such introspection.

Garbage Collection

Python's garbage collection normally proceeds transparently and automatically, but you can choose to exert some direct control. The general principle is that Python collects each object x at some time after x becomes unreachable—that is, when no chain of references can reach x by starting from a local variable of a function instance that is executing, nor from a global variable of a loaded module.

Normally, an object *x* becomes unreachable when there are no references at all to *x*. In addition, a group of objects can be unreachable when they reference each other but no global nor local variables reference any of them, even indirectly (such a situation is known as a *mutual reference loop*).

Classic Python keeps with each object *x* a count, known as a *reference count*, of how many references to *x* are outstanding. When *x*'s reference count drops to 0, CPython immediately collects *x*. Function getrefcount of module sys accepts any object and returns its reference count (at least 1, since getrefcount itself has a reference to the object it's examining). Other versions of Python, such as Jython or IronPython, rely on other garbage-collection mechanisms supplied by the platform they run on (e.g., the JVM or the MSCLR). Modules gc and weakref therefore apply only to CPython.

When Python garbage-collects *x* and there are no references at all to *x*, Python then finalizes *x* (i.e., calls *x*.__del__( )) and makes the memory that *x* occupied available for other uses. If *x* held any references to other objects, Python removes the references, which in turn may make other objects collectable by leaving them unreachable.

The gc Module

The gc module exposes the functionality of Python's garbage collector. gc deals only with objects that are unreachable in a subtle way, being part of mutual reference loops. In such a loop, each object in the loop refers to others, keeping the reference counts of all objects positive. However, no outside references to any one of the set of mutually referencing objects exist any longer. Therefore, the whole group, also known as cyclic garbage, is unreachable, and therefore garbage-collectable. Looking for such cyclic garbage loops takes some time, which is why module gc exists. This functionality of "cyclic garbage collection," by default, is enabled with some reasonable default parameters: however, by importing the gc module and calling its functions, you may choose to disable the functionality, change its parameters, or find out exactly what's going on in this respect.

gc exposes functions you can use to help you keep cyclic garbage-collection times under control. These functions can sometimes help you track down a memory leak—objects that are not getting collected even though there *should* be no more references to them—by letting you discover what other objects are in fact holding on to references to them.

---

collect   collect( )

Forces a full cyclic collection run to happen immediately.

---

disable   disable( )

Suspends automatic cyclic garbage collection.

---

enable	enable( ) Reenables automatic cyclic garbage collection previously suspended with disable.
garbage	A read-only attribute that lists the unreachable but uncollectable objects. This happens if any object in a cyclic garbage loop has a __del__ special method, as there may be no demonstrably safe order for Python to finalize such objects.
get_debug	get_debug( ) Returns an int bit string, the garbage-collection debug flags set with set_debug.
get_objects	get_objects( ) Returns a list of all objects currently tracked by the cyclic garbage collector.
get_referrers	get_referrers(*objs) Returns a list of all container objects, currently tracked by the cyclic garbage collector, that refer to any one or more of the arguments.
get_threshold	get_threshold( ) Returns a three-item tuple (*thresh0, thresh1, thresh2*), the garbage-collection thresholds set with set_threshold.
isenabled	isenabled( ) Returns True if cyclic garbage collection is currently enabled. When collection is currently disabled, isenabled returns False.
set_debug	set_debug(*flags*) Sets debugging flags for garbage collection. *flags* is an int bit string built by ORing (with the bitwise-OR operator |) with zero or more constants supplied by module gc: DEBUG_COLLECTABLE 　Prints information on collectable objects found during collection DEBUG_INSTANCES 　If DEBUG_COLLECTABLE or DEBUG_UNCOLLECTABLE are also set, prints information on objects found during collection that are instances of old-style classes

DEBUG_LEAK

> The set of debugging flags that make the garbage collector print all information that can help you diagnose memory leaks; same as the bitwise-OR of all other constants (except DEBUG_STATS, which serves a different purpose)

DEBUG_OBJECTS

> If DEBUG_COLLECTABLE or DEBUG_UNCOLLECTABLE are also set, prints information on objects found during collection that are not instances of old-style classes

DEBUG_SAVEALL

> Saves all collectable objects to list gc.garbage (where uncollectable ones are also always saved) to help you diagnose leaks

DEBUG_STATS

> Prints statistics during collection to help you tune the thresholds

DEBUG_UNCOLLECTABLE

> Prints information on uncollectable objects found during collection

---

set_threshold   set_threshold(*thresh0*[,*thresh1*[,*thresh2*]])

> Sets thresholds that control how often cyclic garbage-collection cycles run. A *thresh0* of 0 disables garbage collection. Garbage collection is an advanced topic, and the details of the generational garbage-collection approach used in Python, and consequently the detailed meanings of its thresholds, are beyond the scope of this book.

When you know you have no cyclic garbage loops in your program, or when you can't afford the delay of cyclic garbage collection at some crucial time, suspend automatic garbage collection by calling gc.disable( ). You can enable collection again later by calling gc.enable( ). You can test if automatic collection is currently enabled by calling gc.isenabled( ), which returns True or False. To control when the time needed for collection is spent, you can call gc.collect( ) to force a full cyclic collection run to happen immediately. An idiom for wrapping time-critical code is:

```
import gc
gc_was_enabled = gc.isenabled( )
if gc_was_enabled:
    gc.collect( )
    gc.disable( )
# insert some time-critical code here
if gc_was_enabled:
    gc.enable( )
```

Other functionality in module gc is more advanced and rarely used, and can be grouped into two areas. Functions get_threshold and set_threshold and debug flag DEBUG_STATS help you fine-tune garbage collection to optimize your program's performance. The rest of gc's functionality can help you diagnose memory leaks in your program. While gc itself can automatically fix many leaks (as long as you avoid defining __del__ in your classes, since the existence of __del__ can block cyclic garbage collection), your program runs faster if it avoids creating cyclic garbage in the first place.

The weakref Module

Careful design can often avoid reference loops. However, at times you need two objects to know about each other, and avoiding mutual references would distort and complicate your design. For example, a container has references to its items, yet it can often be useful for an object to know about a container holding it. The result is a reference loop: due to the mutual references, the container and items keep each other alive, even when all other objects forget about them. Weak references solve this problem by letting you have objects that mutually reference each other but do not keep each other alive.

A *weak reference* is a special object w that refers to some other object x without incrementing x's reference count. When x's reference count goes down to 0, Python finalizes and collects x, then informs w of x's demise. The weak reference w can now either disappear or get marked as invalid in a controlled way. At any time, a given weak reference w refers to either the same target object x as when w was created, or to nothing at all; a weak reference is never retargeted. Not all types of objects support being the target x of a weak reference w, but class instances and functions do.

Module weakref exposes functions and types to create and manage weak references.

getweakrefcount	getweakrefcount(x)
	Returns len(getweakrefs(x)).

getweakrefs	getweakrefs(x)
	Returns a list of all weak references and proxies whose target is x.

proxy	proxy(x[,f])
	Returns a weak proxy p of type ProxyType (CallableProxyType if x is callable) with object x as the target. In most contexts, using p is just like using x, except that if you use p after x has been deleted, Python raises ReferenceError. p is not hashable (therefore, you cannot use p as a dictionary key), even when x is. If f is present, it must be callable with one argument and is the finalization callback for p (i.e., right before finalizing x, Python calls f(p)). When f is called, x is no longer reachable from p.

ref	ref(x[,f])
	Returns a weak reference w of type ReferenceType with object x as the target. w is callable: calling w( ) returns x if x is still alive; otherwise, w( ) returns None. w is hashable if x is hashable. You can compare weak references for equality (==, !=), but not for order (<, >, <=, >=). Two weak references x and y are equal if their targets are alive and equal, or if x is y. If f is present, it must be callable with one argument and is the finalization callback for w (i.e., right before finalizing x, Python calls f(w)). When f is called, x is no longer reachable from w.
WeakKeyDictionary	class WeakKeyDictionary(adict={ })
	A WeakKeyDictionary d is a mapping that references its keys weakly. When the reference count of a key k in d goes to 0, item d[k] disappears. adict is used to initialize the mapping.
WeakValueDictionary	class WeakValueDictionary(adict={ })
	A WeakValueDictionary d is a mapping that references its values weakly. When the reference count of a value v in d goes to 0, all items of d such that d[k] is v disappear. adict is used to initialize the mapping.

WeakKeyDictionary lets you noninvasively associate additional data with some hashable objects without changing the objects. WeakValueDictionary lets you noninvasively record transient associations between objects and build caches. In each case, it's better to use a weak mapping than a normal dict to ensure that an object that is otherwise garbage-collectable is not kept alive just by being used in a mapping.

A typical example of use could be a class that keeps track of its instances, but does not keep them alive just in order to keep track of them:

```
import weakref
class Tracking(object):
    _instances_dict = weakref.WeakValueDictionary( )
    def __init__(self):
        Tracking._instances_dict[id(self)] = self
    def instances( ): return _instances_dict.values( )
    instances = staticmethod(instances)
```

Termination Functions

The atexit module lets you register termination functions (i.e., functions to be called at program termination: "last in, first out"). Termination functions are similar to clean-up handlers established by try/finally. However, termination functions are globally registered and get called at the end of the whole program, while clean-up handlers are established lexically and get called at the end of a specific try clause. Both termination functions and clean-up handlers are called whether the program terminates normally or abnormally, but not when the program ends specifically by calling os._exit. Module atexit supplies a single function called register.

register	register(*func*,**args*,***kwds*)
	Ensures that func(*args,**kwds) is called at program termination time.

Site and User Customization

Python provides a specific "hook" to let each site customize some aspects of Python's behavior at the start of each run. Customization by each single user is not enabled by default, but Python specifies how programs that want to run user-provided code at startup can explicitly request such customization.

The site and sitecustomize Modules

Python loads standard module site just before the main script. If Python is run with option -S, Python does not load site. -S allows faster startup but saddles the main script with initialization chores. site's tasks are:

- Putting sys.path in standard form (absolute paths, no duplicates).
- Interpreting each *.pth* file found in the Python home directory, adding entries to sys.path, and/or importing modules, as each *.pth* file indicates.
- Adding built-ins used to display information in interactive sessions (quit, exit, copyright, credits, and license).
- Setting the default Unicode encoding to 'ascii'. site's source code includes two blocks, each guarded by if 0:, one to set the default encoding to be locale-dependent, and the other to completely disable any default encoding between Unicode and plain strings. You may optionally edit *site.py* to select either block.
- Trying to import sitecustomize (should import sitecustomize raise an ImportError exception, site catches and ignores it). sitecustomize is the module that each site's installation can optionally use for further site-specific customization beyond site's tasks. It is generally best not to edit *site.py*, since any Python upgrade or reinstallation might overwrite such customizations. sitecustomize's main task can be to set the correct default encoding for the site. A Western European site, for example, may choose to call from sitecustomize sys.setdefaultencoding('iso-8859-1').
- After sitecustomize is done, removing from module sys the attribute sys.setdefaultencoding.

Thus, Python's default Unicode encoding can be set only at the start of a run, not changed in midstream during the run. In an emergency, if a specific main script desperately needs to break this guideline and set a different default encoding from that used by all other scripts, you may place the following snippet at the start of the main script:

```
import sys                              # get the sys module object
reload(sys)                            # restore module sys from disk
sys.setdefaultencoding('iso-8859-15')  # or whatever codec you need
del sys.setdefaultencoding             # ensure against later accidents
```

However, this is not good style. You should refactor your script, so that it can accept whatever default encoding the site has chosen, and pass the encoding name explicitly in all of the spots where a specific codec is necessary.

User Customization

Each interactive Python interpreter session runs the script indicated by environment variable PYTHONSTARTUP. Outside of interactive interpreter sessions, there is no automatic per-user customization. To request per-user customization, a Python main script can explicitly import user. Standard library module user, when loaded, first determines the user's home directory, as indicated by environment variable HOME (or, failing that, HOMEPATH, possibly preceded by HOMEDRIVE on Windows systems only). If the environment does not indicate a home directory, user uses the current directory. If module user finds a file named *.pythonrc.py* in the indicated directory, user executes that file, with built-in function execfile, in module user's own global namespace.

Scripts that don't import user do not load *.pythonrc.py*. Of course, any given script is free to arrange other specific ways to load whatever startup or plug-in user-supplied files it requires. Such application-specific arrangements are more common than importing user. A generic *.pythonrc.py*, as loaded via import user, needs to be usable with any application that loads it. Specialized, application-specific startup and plug-in, user-supplied files only need to follow whatever convention a specific application documents.

For example, your application *MyApp.py* could document that it looks for a file named *.myapprc.py* in the user's home directory, as indicated by environment variable HOME, and loads it in the application's main script's global namespace. You could then have the following code in your main script:

```
import os
homedir = os.environ.get('HOME')
if homedir is not None:
    userscript = os.path.join(homedir, '.myapprc.py')
    if os.path.isfile(userscript):
        execfile(userscript)
```

In this case, the *.myapprc.py* user customization script, if present, has to deal only with MyApp-specific user customization tasks.

14

Threads and Processes

A *thread* is a flow of control that shares global state with other threads; all threads appear to execute simultaneously. Threads are not easy to master, but once you do master them, they may let you tackle some problems with a simpler architecture, and sometimes better performance, in comparison to traditional "single-thread" programming. This chapter covers the facilities that Python provides for dealing with threads, including the thread, threading, and Queue modules.

A *process* is an instance of a running program. Sometimes, particularly on Unix-like operating systems or on multiprocessor computers, you can get better results with multiple processes than with threads. The operating system protects processes from one another. Processes that want to communicate must explicitly arrange to do so via local inter-process communication (IPC). Processes may communicate via files (covered in Chapter 10) or via databases (covered in Chapter 11). In both cases, the general way in which processes communicate using such data storage mechanisms is that one process can write data, and another process can later read that data back. This chapter covers Python standard library module process; the process-related parts of module os, including simple IPC by means of pipes; and a cross-platform IPC mechanism known as memory-mapped files, which is supplied to Python programs by module mmap.

Network mechanisms are well suited for IPC, as they work between processes that run on different nodes of a network as well as those that run on the same node. (Chapter 20 covers low-level network mechanisms that provide a flexible basis for IPC.) Other, higher-level mechanisms, known as distributed computing, such as CORBA, DCOM/COM+, EJB, SOAP, XML-RPC, and .NET, make IPC easier, whether locally or remotely. However, distributed computing is not covered in this book.

Threads in Python

Python offers multithreading on platforms that support threads, such as Win32, Linux, and most other variants of Unix. The Classic Python interpreter does not freely switch threads. In the current implementation, Python uses a global interpreter lock (GIL) to ensure that switching between threads happens only between bytecode instructions or when C code deliberately releases the GIL (Python's own C code releases the GIL around blocking I/O and sleep operations). An action is said to be *atomic* if it's guaranteed that no thread switching within Python's process occurs between the start and the end of the action. In practice, in the current implementation, operations that *look* atomic (such as simple assignments and accesses) actually *are* atomic when executed on objects of built-in types (augmented and multiple assignments, however, are not atomic). In general, though, it is not a good idea to rely on atomicity. For example, you never know when you might be dealing with a derived class rather than an object of a built-in type, meaning there might be callbacks to Python code, and any assumptions of atomicity would then prove unwarranted. Moreover, relying on implementation-depended atomicity would lock your code into a specific implementation and might preclude future upgrades. A much better strategy is to use the synchronization facilities covered in the rest of this chapter.

Python offers multithreading in two different flavors. An older and lower-level module, thread, offers a bare minimum of functionality and is not recommended for direct use by your code. The higher-level module threading, built on top of thread, was loosely inspired by Java's threads and is the recommended tool. The key design issue in multithreading systems is most often how best to coordinate multiple threads. threading therefore supplies several synchronization objects. Module Queue is very useful for thread synchronization as it supplies a synchronized FIFO queue type, which is extremely handy for communication and coordination between threads.

The thread Module

The only part of the thread module that your code should use directly is the lock objects that module thread supplies. Locks are simple thread-synchronization primitives. Technically, thread's locks are non-reentrant and unowned: they do not keep track of which thread last locked them, so there is no specific owner thread for a lock. A lock is in one of two states, locked or unlocked.

To get a new lock object (in the unlocked state), call the factory function named allocate_lock without arguments. This function is supplied by both modules thread and threading. A lock object L supplies three methods.

acquire	L.acquire(*wait*=True)
	When *wait* is True, acquire locks L. If L is already locked, the calling thread suspends and waits until L is unlocked, then locks L. Even if the calling thread was the one that last locked L, it still suspends and waits until another thread releases L. When *wait* is

False and *L* is unlocked, acquire locks *L* and returns True. When *wait* is False and *L* is locked, acquire does not affect *L* and returns False.

---

locked   `L.locked()`

Returns True if *L* is locked; otherwise, False.

---

release   `L.release()`

Unlocks *L*, which must be locked. When *L* is locked, any thread may call `L.release`, not just the thread that last locked *L*. When more than one thread is waiting on *L* (i.e., has called `L.acquire`, finding *L* locked, and is now waiting for *L* to be unlocked), release wakes up an arbitrary waiting thread. The thread that calls release is not suspended: it remains ready and continues to execute.

The Queue Module

The Queue module supplies first-in, first-out (FIFO) queues that support multi-thread access, with one main class and two exception classes.

Queue   `class Queue(maxsize=0)`

Queue is the main class for module Queue and is covered in "Methods of Queue Instances" on page 343. When *maxsize* is greater than 0, the new Queue instance *q* is deemed full when *q* has *maxsize* items. A thread inserting an item with the *block* option, when *q* is full, suspends until another thread extracts an item. When *maxsize* is less than or equal to 0, *q* is never considered full and is limited in size only by available memory, like normal Python containers.

Empty   Empty is the class of the exception that `q.get(False)` raises when *q* is empty.

Full   Full is the class of the exception that `q.put(x,False)` raises when *q* is full.

Methods of Queue Instances

An instance *q* of class Queue supplies the following methods.

---

empty　　　　　*q*.empty( )

Returns True if *q* is empty; otherwise, False.

---

full　　　　　　*q*.full( )

Returns True if *q* is full; otherwise, False.

---

get, get_nowait　*q*.get(*block*=True, *timeout*=None)

When *block* is False, get removes and returns an item from *q* if one is available; otherwise, get raises Empty. When *block* is True and *timeout* is None, get removes and returns an item from *q*, suspending the calling thread, if need be, until an item is available. When *block* is True and *timeout* is not None, *timeout* must be a number >=0 (which may include a fractional part to specify a fraction of a second), and get waits for no longer than *timeout* seconds (if no item is yet available by then, get raises Empty). *q*.get_nowait( ) is like *q*.get(False), which is also like *q*.get(timeout=0.0). get removes and returns items in the same order as put inserted them (FIFO).

---

put,　　　　　　*q*.put(*item*, *block*=True, *timeout*=None)
put_nowait

When *block* is False, put adds *item* to *q* if *q* is not full; otherwise, put raises Full. When *block* is True and *timeout* is None, put adds *item* to *q*, suspending the calling thread, if need be, until *q* is not full. When *block* is True and *timeout* is not None, *timeout* must be a number >=0 (which may include a fractional part to specify a fraction of a second), and put waits for no longer than *timeout* seconds (if *q* is still full by then, put raises Full). *q*.put_nowait(*item*) is like *q*.put(*item*, False), which is also like *q*.put(*item*, timeout=0.0).

---

qsize　　　　　　*q*.qsize( )

Returns the number of items that are currently in *q*.

Queue offers a good example of the idiom "It's easier to ask forgiveness than permission" (EAFP), covered in "Error-Checking Strategies" on page 134. Due to multithreading, each nonmutating method of *q* can only be advisory. When some other thread executes and mutates *q*, things can change between the instant a thread gets the information and the very next moment, when the thread acts on the information. Relying on the "look before you leap" (LBYL) idiom is futile, and fiddling with locks to try and fix things is a substantial waste of effort. Just avoid LBYL code such as:

```
if q.empty( ): print "no work to perform"
else: x=q.get_nowait( )
```

and instead use the simpler and more robust EAFP approach:

```
try: x=q.get_nowait( )
except Queue.Empty: print "no work to perform"
```

Customizing Class Queue by Subclassing

If you require the intrinsically thread-safe behavior of class Queue.Queue but do not want a FIFO queuing discipline, you may customize Queue.Queue by subclassing, and you need to override some or all of the *hook methods* that Queue.Queue provides for the purpose: _qsize, _empty, _full, _put, and _get. Each has semantics that correspond to the public method with the corresponding name, but they're simpler, with no worries about threading, timeouts, or error checking. The only one of them that takes an argument (besides the usual self) is _put (which takes as its argument the item to put on the queue).

Queue.Queue ensures that hook methods will get called only in a state already made properly thread-safe (i.e., Queue.Queue's own methods ensure all the needed locking) and that hook methods need not worry about error-checking (for example, _get is called only when the queue is nonempty—i.e., when _empty has just returned a false result). For example, all it takes to make a thread-safe queue class with a LIFO queuing discipline is:

```
import Queue
class LIFOQueue(Queue.Queue):
    def _get(self): return self.queue.pop( )
```

which exploits the self.queue attribute, which Queue.Queue instances already have (an instance of type collections.deque, covered in "The collections Module" on page 173).

The threading Module

The threading module is built on top of module thread and supplies multithreading functionality in a more usable, higher-level form. The general approach of threading is similar to that of Java, but locks and conditions are modeled as separate objects (in Java, such functionality is part of every object), and threads cannot be directly controlled from the outside (which means there are no priorities, groups, destruction, or stopping). All methods of objects supplied by threading are atomic.

threading provides numerous classes for dealing with threads, including Thread, Condition, Event, RLock, and Semaphore. Besides factory functions for the classes detailed in the following sections, threading supplies the currentThread factory function.

currentThread	`currentThread( )`

Returns a `Thread` object for the calling thread. If the calling thread was not created by module `threading`, `currentThread` creates and returns a semi-dummy `Thread` object with limited functionality.

Thread Objects

A `Thread` object *t* models a thread. You can pass *t*'s main function as an argument when you create *t*, or you can subclass `Thread` and override the `run` method (you may also override `__init__` but should not override other methods). *t* is not ready to run when you create it; to make *t* ready (active), call *t*.`start( )`. Once *t* is active, it terminates when its main function ends, either normally or by propagating an exception. A `Thread` *t* can be a daemon, meaning that Python can terminate even if *t* is still active, while a normal (nondaemon) thread keeps Python alive until the thread terminates. Class `Thread` exposes the following constructor and methods.

Thread	`class Thread(`*name=None,target=None,args=( ),kwargs={ }*`)`

Always call `Thread` with named arguments. The number and order of formal arguments may change in the future, but the names of existing arguments are guaranteed to stay. When you instantiate class `Thread` itself, you should specify that *target*: *t*.`run` calls *target(*args,**kwargs)*. When you subclass `Thread` and override `run`, you normally don't specify *target*. In either case, execution doesn't begin until you call *t*.`start( )`. *name* is *t*'s name. If *name* is None, `Thread` generates a unique name for *t*. If a subclass T of `Thread` overrides `__init__`, T.`__init__` must call `Thread.__init__` on `self` before any other `Thread` method.

getName, setName	*t*.`getName( )` *t*.`setName(`*name*`)`

`getName` returns *t*'s name, and `setName` rebinds *t*'s name. The *name* string is arbitrary, and a thread's name need not be unique among threads.

isAlive	*t*.`isAlive( )`

Returns True if *t* is active (i.e., if *t*.`start` has executed and *t*.`run` has not yet terminated). Otherwise, `isAlive` returns False.

isDaemon, setDaemon	*t*.`isDaemon( )` *t*.`setDaemon(`*daemonic*`)`

`isDaemon` returns True if *t* is a daemon (i.e., Python can terminate the whole process even if *t* is still active; such a termination also

terminates *t*); otherwise, isDaemon returns False. Initially, *t* is a
daemon if and only if the thread that creates *t* is a daemon. You
can call *t*.setDaemon only before *t*.start; it sets *t* to be a daemon if
daemonic is true.

join	`t.join(`*timeout*`=None)`

The calling thread (which must not be *t*) suspends until *t* terminates. *timeout* is covered in "Timeout parameters" on page 346.
You can call *t*.join only after *t*.start.

run	`t.run( )`

run is the method that executes *t*'s main function. Subclasses of
Thread often override run. Unless overridden, run calls the target callable passed on *t*'s creation. Do *not* call *t*.run directly; calling *t*.run
appropriately is the job of *t*.start!

start	`t.start( )`

start makes *t* active and arranges for *t*.run to execute in a separate thread. You must call *t*.start only once for any given thread
object *t*.

Thread Synchronization Objects

The threading module supplies several synchronization primitives, which are
objects that let threads communicate and coordinate. Each primitive has specialized uses. However, as long as you avoid global variables that several threads
access, Queue can often provide all the coordination you need. "Threaded Program
Architecture" on page 350 shows how to use Queue objects to give your multithreaded programs simple and effective architectures, often without needing any
synchronization primitives.

Timeout parameters

Synchronization primitives Condition and Event supply wait methods that accept
an optional *timeout* argument. A Thread object's join method also accepts an
optional *timeout* argument. A *timeout* argument can be None (the default) to obtain
normal blocking behavior (the calling thread suspends and waits until the desired
condition is met). If it is not None, a *timeout* argument is a floating-point value that
indicates an interval of time in seconds (*timeout* can have a fractional part, so it can
indicate any time interval, even a very short one). If *timeout* seconds elapse, the
calling thread becomes ready again, even if the desired condition has not been met.
timeout lets you design systems that are able to overcome occasional anomalies in

one or a few threads, and thus are more robust. However, using *timeout* may also make your program slower.

Lock and RLock objects

The Lock objects exposed by module threading are the same as those supplied by module thread and covered in "The thread Module" on page 341. RLock objects supply the same methods as Lock objects. The semantics of an RLock object *r* are, however, often more convenient. An RLock is a "re-entrant" lock, meaning that when *r* is locked, it keeps track of the owning thread (i.e., the thread that locked it). The owning thread can call *r*.acquire again without blocking; *r* just increments an internal count. In a similar situation involving a Lock object, the thread would block forever (until the lock is released by some other thread).

An RLock object *r* is unlocked only when release has been called as many times as acquire. Only the thread owning *r* should call *r*.release. An RLock is useful to ensure exclusive access to an object when the object's methods call each other; each method can acquire at the start, and release at the end, the same RLock instance. try/finally (covered in "try/finally" on page 123) is a good way to ensure the lock is indeed released (in Python 2.5, the new with statement, covered in "The with statement" on page 125, is generally at least as good).

Condition objects

A Condition object *c* wraps a Lock or RLock object *L*. Class Condition exposes the following constructor and methods.

Condition	class Condition(*lock*=None)
	Condition creates and returns a new Condition object *c* with the lock *L* set to *lock*. If *lock* is None, *L* is set to a newly created RLock object.
acquire, release	*c*.acquire(*wait*=1) *c*.release( )
	These methods call *L*'s corresponding methods. A thread must never call any other method on *c* unless the thread holds lock *L*.
notify, notifyAll	*c*.notify( ) *c*.notifyAll( )
	notify wakes up one of the threads waiting on *c*. The calling thread must hold *L* before it calls *c*.notify( ), and notify does not release *L*. The woken-up thread does not become ready until it can acquire *L* again. Therefore, the calling thread normally calls release after calling notify. notifyAll is like notify, but wakes up all waiting threads, not just one.

wait	`c.wait(`*timeout*`=None)`

wait releases *L*, then suspends the calling thread until some other thread calls notify or notifyAll on *c*. The calling thread must hold *L* before it calls `c.wait()`. *timeout* is covered in "Timeout parameters" on page 346. After a thread wakes up, either by notification or timeout, the thread becomes ready when it acquires *L* again. When wait returns, the calling thread always holds *L* again.

In typical use, a Condition object *c* regulates access to some global state *s* that is shared between threads. When a thread needs to wait for *s* to change, the thread loops as follows:

```
c.acquire()
while not is_ok_state(s):
    c.wait()
do_some_work_using_state(s)
c.release()
```

Meanwhile, each thread that modifies *s* calls notify (or notifyAll if it needs to wake up all waiting threads, not just one) each time *s* changes:

```
c.acquire()
do_something_that_modifies_state(s)
c.notify()    # or, c.notifyAll()
c.release()
```

As you can see, you always need to acquire and release *c* around each use of *c*'s methods, which makes using Condition somewhat error-prone.

Event objects

Event objects let any number of threads suspend and wait. All threads waiting on Event object *e* become ready when any other thread calls `e.set()`. *e* has a flag that records whether the event happened; it is initially False when *e* is created. Event is thus a bit like a simplified Condition. Event objects are useful to signal one-shot changes, but brittle for more general use; in particular, relying on calls to `e.clear()` is error-prone. Class Event exposes the following methods.

Event	`class Event()`

Event creates and returns a new Event object *e*, with *e*'s flag set to False.

clear	`e.clear()`

Sets *e*'s flag to False.

isSet	`e.isSet( )`

Returns the value of *e*'s flag, `True` or `False`.

set	`e.set( )`

Sets *e*'s flag to `True`. All threads waiting on *e*, if any, become ready to run.

wait	`e.wait(`*timeout*`=None)`

If *e*'s flag is `True`, `wait` returns immediately. Otherwise, `wait` suspends the calling thread until some other thread calls `set`. *timeout* is covered in "Timeout parameters" on page 346.

Semaphore objects

Semaphores (also known as *counting semaphores*) are a generalization of locks. The state of a `Lock` can be seen as `True` or `False`; the state of a `Semaphore` *s* is a number between 0 and some *n* set when *s* is created. Semaphores can be useful to manage a fixed pool of resources (e.g., 4 printers or 20 sockets), although it's often more robust to use `Queues` for such purposes.

Semaphore	`class Semaphore(`*n*`=1)`

`Semaphore` creates and returns a semaphore object *s* with the state set to *n*. A semaphore object *s* exposes the following methods.

acquire	`s.acquire(`*wait*`=True)`

When *s*'s state is greater than 0, `acquire` decrements the state by 1 and returns `True`. When *s*'s state is 0 and *wait* is `True`, `acquire` suspends the calling thread and waits until some other thread calls `s.release`. When *s*'s state is 0 and *wait* is `False`, `acquire` immediately returns `False`.

release	`s.release( )`

When *s*'s state is > 0 or when the state is 0 but no thread is waiting on *s*, `release` increments the state by 1. When *s*'s state is 0 and some thread is waiting on *s*, `release` leaves *s*'s state at 0 and wakes up an arbitrary waiting thread. The thread that calls `release` is not suspended; it remains ready and continues to execute normally.

Thread Local Storage

In Python 2.4, module threading supplies a class local, which threads can use to obtain *thread-local storage* (TLS), also known as *per-thread data*. An instance L of local has arbitrary named attributes that you can set and get, and stores them in a dictionary L.__dict__ that you can also access. L is fully thread-safe, meaning there is no problem if multiple threads simultaneously set and get attributes on L. Most important, each thread that accesses L sees a completely disjoint set of attributes, and any changes made in one thread have no effect in other threads. For example:

```
import threading
L = threading.local()
print 'in main thread, setting zop to 42'
L.zop = 42
def targ():
    print 'in subthread, setting zop to 23'
    L.zop = 23
    print 'in subthread, zop is now', L.zop
t = threading.Thread(target=targ)
t.start()
t.join()
print 'in main thread, zop is now', L.zop
# emits:
# in main thread, setting zop to 42
# in subthread, setting zop to 23
# in subthread, zop is now 23
# in main thread, zop is now 42
```

TLS makes it easier for you to write code meant to run in multiple threads, since you can use the same namespace (an instance of threading.local) in multiple threads without the separate threads interfering with each other.

Threaded Program Architecture

A threaded program should always arrange for a *single* thread to deal with any given object or subsystem that is external to the program (such as a file, a database, a GUI, or a network connection). Having multiple threads that deal with the same external object can often cause unpredictable problems.

Whenever your threaded program must deal with some external object, devote a thread to such dealings using a Queue object from which the external-interfacing thread gets work requests that other threads post. The external-interfacing thread can return results by putting them on one or more other Queue objects. The following example shows how to package this architecture into a general, reusable class, assuming that each unit of work on the external subsystem can be represented by a callable object:

```
import threading, Queue
class ExternalInterfacing(Threading.Thread):
    def __init__(self, externalCallable, **kwds):
        Threading.Thread.__init__(self, **kwds)
        self.setDaemon(1)
```

```
        self.externalCallable = externalCallable
        self.workRequestQueue = Queue.Queue( )
        self.resultQueue = Queue.Queue( )
        self.start( )
    def request(self, *args, **kwds):
        "called by other threads as externalCallable would be"
        self.workRequestQueue.put((args,kwds))
        return self.resultQueue.get( )
    def run(self):
        while 1:
            args, kwds = self.workRequestQueue.get( )
            self.resultQueue.put(self.externalCallable(*args, **kwds))
```

Once some ExternalInterfacing object *ei* is instantiated, all other threads may call *ei*.request just as they would call *someExternalCallable* without such a mechanism (with or without arguments as appropriate). The advantage of the ExternalInterfacing mechanism is that all calls upon *someExternalCallable* are now serialized. This means they are performed by just one thread (the thread object bound to *ei*) in some defined sequential order, without overlap, race conditions (hard-to-debug errors that depend on which thread happens to get there first), or other anomalies that might otherwise result.

If several callables need to be serialized together, you can pass the callable as part of the work request, rather than passing it at the initialization of class ExternalInterfacing, for greater generality. The following example shows this more general approach:

```
import threading, Queue
class Serializer(Threading.Thread):
    def __init__(self, **kwds):
        Threading.Thread.__init__(self, **kwds)
        self.setDaemon(1)
        self.workRequestQueue = Queue.Queue( )
        self.resultQueue = Queue.Queue( )
        self.start( )
    def apply(self, callable, *args, **kwds):
        "called by other threads as callable would be"
        self.workRequestQueue.put((callable, args,kwds))
        return self.resultQueue.get( )
    def run(self):
        while 1:
            callable, args, kwds = self.workRequestQueue.get( )
            self.resultQueue.put(callable(*args, **kwds))
```

Once a Serializer object *ser* has been instantiated, other threads may call *ser*. apply(*someExternalCallable*) just as they would call *someExternalCallable* without such a mechanism (with or without further arguments as appropriate). The Serializer mechanism has the same advantages as ExternalInterfacing, except that all calls to the same or different callables wrapped by a single *ser* instance are now serialized.

The user interface of the whole program is an external subsystem and thus should be dealt with by a single thread, specifically the main thread of the program (this is mandatory for some user interface toolkits and advisable even when not mandatory). A Serializer thread is therefore inappropriate. Rather, the program's main thread should deal only with user interface issues, and farm out actual work to worker threads that accept work requests on a Queue object and return results on another. A set of worker threads is also known as a *thread pool*. As shown in the following example, all worker threads should share a single queue of requests and a single queue of results, since the main thread will be the only one to post work requests and harvest results:

```
import threading
class Worker(Threading.Thread):
    requestID = 0
    def __init__(self, requestsQueue, resultsQueue, **kwds):
        Threading.Thread.__init__(self, **kwds)
        self.setDaemon(1)
        self.workRequestQueue = requestsQueue
        self.resultQueue = resultsQueue
        self.start()
    def performWork(self, callable, *args, **kwds):
        "called by the main thread as callable would be, but w/o return"
        Worker.requestID += 1
        self.workRequestQueue.put((Worker.requestID, callable, args, kwds))
        return Worker.requestID
    def run(self):
        while 1:
            requestID, callable, args, kwds = self.workRequestQueue.get()
            self.resultQueue.put((requestID, callable(*args, **kwds)))
```

The main thread creates the two queues, then instantiates worker threads as follows:

```
import Queue
requestsQueue = Queue.Queue()
resultsQueue = Queue.Queue()
for i in range(numberOfWorkers):
    worker = Worker(requestsQueue, resultsQueue)
```

Now whenever the main thread needs to farm out work (execute some callable object that may take substantial time to produce results), the main thread calls `worker.performWork(callable)` much as it would call `callable` without such a mechanism (with or without further arguments as appropriate). However, performWork does not return the result of the call. Instead of the results, the main thread gets an *id* that identifies the work request. If the main thread needs the results, it can keep track of that *id*, since the request's results will be tagged with that *id* when they appear. The advantage of the mechanism is that the main thread does not block waiting for the callable's lengthy execution to complete, but rather becomes ready again at once and can immediately return to its main business of dealing with the user interface.

The main thread must arrange to check the resultsQueue, since the result of each work request eventually appears there, tagged with the request's *id*, when the worker thread that took that request from the queue finishes computing the result. How the main thread arranges to check for both user interface events and the results coming back from worker threads onto the results queue depends on what user interface toolkit is used or, if the user interface is text-based, on the platform on which the program runs.

A widely applicable general strategy is for the main thread to *poll* (i.e., check the state of the results queue periodically). On most Unix-like platforms, function alarm of module signal allows polling. The Tkinter GUI toolkit supplies method after, which is usable for polling. Some toolkits and platforms afford more effective strategies, letting a worker thread alert the main thread when it places some result on the results queue, but there is no generally available, cross-platform, cross-toolkit way to arrange for this. Therefore, the following artificial example ignores user interface events, and just simulates work by evaluating random expressions, with random delays, on several worker threads, thus completing the previous example:

```
import random, time
def makeWork( ):
    return "%d %s %d"%(random.randrange(2,10),
        random.choice(('+', '-', '*', '/', '%', '**')),
        random.randrange(2,10))
def slowEvaluate(expressionString):
    time.sleep(random.randrange(1,5))
    return eval(expressionString)
workRequests = {  }
def showResults( ):
    while 1:
        try: id, results = resultsQueue.get_nowait( )
        except Queue.Empty: return
        print 'Result %d: %s -> %s' % (id, workRequests[id], results)
        del workRequests[id]
for i in range(10):
    expressionString = makeWork( )
    id = worker.performWork(slowEvaluate, expressionString)
    workRequests[id] = expressionString
    print 'Submitted request %d: %s' % (id, expressionString)
    time.sleep(1)
    showResults( )
while workRequests:
    time.sleep(1)
    showResults( )
```

Process Environment

The operating system supplies each process *P* with an *environment*, which is a set of environment variables whose names are identifiers (most often, by convention, uppercase identifiers) and whose contents are strings. In "Environment Variables" on page 22, I covered environment variables that affect Python's operations. Operating system shells offer ways to examine and modify the environment via shell commands and other means mentioned in "Environment Variables" on page 22.

The environment of any process *P* is determined when *P* starts. After startup, only *P* itself can change *P*'s environment. Nothing that *P* does affects the environment of *P*'s parent process (the process that started *P*), nor of those of child processes previously started from *P* and now running, nor of processes unrelated to *P*. Changes to *P*'s environment affect only *P* itself: the environment is *not* a means of IPC. Child processes of *P* normally get a copy of *P*'s environment as their starting environment. In this sense, changes to *P*'s environment do affect child processes that *P* starts after such changes.

Module os supplies attribute environ, which is a mapping that represents the current process's environment. os.environ is initialized from the process environment when Python starts. Changes to os.environ update the current process's environment if the platform supports such updates. Keys and values in os.environ must be strings. On Windows, but not on Unix-like platforms, keys into os.environ are implicitly uppercased. For example, here's how to try to determine which shell or command processor you're running under:

```
import os
shell = os.environ.get('COMSPEC')
if shell is None: shell = os.environ.get('SHELL')
if shell is None: shell = 'an unknown command processor'
print 'Running under', shell
```

When a Python program changes its environment (e.g., via os.environ['X']='Y'), this does not affect the environment of the shell or command processor that started the program. As already explained, and for all programming languages including Python, changes to a process's environment affect only the process itself, not others.

Running Other Programs

You can run other programs via functions in the os module or, in Python 2.4, by using the new subprocess module.

Running Other Programs with the os Module

In Python 2.4, the best way for your program to run other processes is with the new subprocess module, covered in "The Subprocess Module" on page 358. However, the os module also offers several ways to do this, which in some cases may be simpler or allow your code to remain backward-compatible to older versions of Python.

The simplest way to run another program is through function os.system, although this offers no way to control the external program. The os module also provides a number of functions whose names start with exec. These functions offer fine-grained control. A program run by one of the exec functions replaces the current program (i.e., the Python interpreter) in the same process. In practice, therefore, you use the exec functions mostly on platforms that let a process duplicate itself by fork (i.e., Unix-like platforms). os functions whose names start with spawn and popen offer intermediate simplicity and power: they are cross-platform and not quite as simple as system, but simple and usable enough for most purposes.

The exec and spawn functions run a specified executable file, given the executable file's path, arguments to pass to it, and optionally an environment mapping. The system and popen functions execute a command, which is a string passed to a new instance of the platform's default shell (typically */bin/sh* on Unix; *command.com* or *cmd.exe* on Windows). A command is a more general concept than an executable file, as it can include shell functionality (pipes, redirection, built-in shell commands) using the normal shell syntax specific to the current platform.

execl, execle, execlp, execv, execve, execvp, execvpe	execl(*path*,**args*) execle(*path*,**args*) execlp(*path*,**args*) execv(*path*,*args*) execve(*path*,*args*,*env*) execvp(*path*,*args*) execvpe(*path*,*args*,*env*)

These functions run the executable file (program) indicated by string *path*, replacing the current program (i.e., the Python interpreter) in the current process. The distinctions encoded in the function names (after the prefix exec) control three aspects of how the new program is found and run:

- Does *path* have to be a complete path to the program's executable file, or can the function accept a name as the *path* argument and search for the executable in several directories, as operating system shells do? execlp, execvp, and execvpe can accept a *path* argument that is just a filename rather than a complete path. In this case, the functions search for an executable file of that name along the directories listed in os.environ['PATH']. The other functions require *path* to be a complete path to the executable file for the new program.

- Are arguments for the new program accepted as a single sequence argument *args* to the function or as separate arguments to the function? Functions whose names start with execv take a single argument *args* that is the sequence of the arguments to use for the new program. Functions whose names start with execl take the new program's arguments as separate arguments (execle, in particular, uses its last argument as the environment for the new program).

- Is the new program's environment accepted as an explicit mapping argument *env* to the function, or is os.environ implicitly used? execle, execve, and execvpe take an argument *env* that is a mapping to be used as the new program's environment (keys and values must be strings), while the other functions use os.environ for this purpose.

Each exec function uses the first item in *args* as the name under which the new program is told it's running (for example, argv[0] in a C program's main); only *args*[1:] is passed as arguments proper to the new program. |
| **popen** | popen(*cmd*,*mode*='r',*bufsize*=-1)

Runs the string command *cmd* in a new process *P* and returns a file-like object *f* that wraps a pipe to *P*'s standard input or from *P*'s standard output (depending on *mode*). *mode* and *bufsize* have the same meaning as for Python's built-in open function, covered in "Creating a File Object with open" on page 216. When *mode* is 'r' |

(or 'rb', for binary-mode reading), *f* is read-only and wraps *P*'s
standard output. When mode is 'w' (or 'wb', for binary-mode
writing), *f* is write-only and wraps *P*'s standard input.

The key difference of *f* with respect to other file-like objects is the
behavior of method *f*.close. *f*.close waits for *P* to terminate and
returns None, as close methods of file-like objects normally do,
when *P*'s termination is successful. However, if the operating
system associates an integer error code *c* with *P*'s termination, indicating that *P*'s termination was unsuccessful, *f*.close also returns *c*.
Not all operating systems support this mechanism: on some platforms, *f*.close therefore always returns None. On Unix-like
platforms, if *P* terminates with the system call exit(*n*) (e.g., if *P* is a
Python program and terminates by calling sys.exit(*n*)), *f*.close
receives from the operating system, and returns to *f*.close's caller,
the code 256**n.

popen2,	popen2(*cmd*,*mode*='t',*bufsize*=-1) popen3(*cmd*,*mode*='t',*bufsize*=-1)
popen3, popen4	popen4(*cmd*,*mode*='t',*bufsize*=-1)

Each of these functions runs the string command *cmd* in a new
process *P*, and returns a tuple of file-like objects that wrap pipes to
P's standard input and from *P*'s standard output and standard
error. *mode* must be 't' to get file-like objects in text mode or 'b' to
get them in binary mode. On Windows, *bufsize* must be -1. On
Unix, *bufsize* has the same meaning as for Python's built-in open
function, covered in "Creating a File Object with open" on
page 216.

popen2 returns a pair (*fi*,*fo*), where *fi* wraps *P*'s standard input
(so the calling process can write to *fi*) and *fo* wraps *P*'s standard
output (so the calling process can read from *fo*). popen3 returns a
tuple with three items (*fi*,*fo*,*fe*), where *fe* wraps *P*'s standard
error (so the calling process can read from *fe*). popen4 returns a pair
(*fi*,*foe*), where *foe* wraps both *P*'s standard output and error (so
the calling process can read from *foe*). While popen3 is in a sense
the most general of the three functions, it can be difficult to coordinate your reading from *fo* and *fe*. popen2 is simpler to use than
popen3 when it's okay for *cmd*'s standard error to go to the same
destination as your own process's standard error, and popen4 is
simpler when it's okay for *cmd*'s standard error and output to be
somewhat arbitrarily mixed with each other.

File objects *fi*, *fo*, *fe*, and *foe* are all normal ones, without the
special semantics of the close method as covered for function
popen. In other words, there is no way in which the caller of popen2,
popen3, or popen4 can learn about *P*'s termination code.

Depending on the buffering strategy of command *cmd* (which is
normally out of your control, unless you're the author of *cmd*), there
may be nothing to read on files *fo*, *fe*, and/or *foe* until your process

has closed file *fi*. Therefore, the normal pattern of usage is something like:

```
import os
def pipethrough(cmd, list_of_lines):
    fi, fo = os.popen2(cmd, 't')
    fi.writelines(list_of_lines)
    fi.close()
    result_lines = fo.readlines()
    fo.close()
    return result_lines
```

Functions in the popen group are generally not suitable for driving another process interactively (i.e., writing something, then reading *cmd*'s response to that, then writing something else, and so on). The first time your program tries to read the response, if *cmd* is following a typical buffering strategy, everything blocks. In other words, your process is waiting for *cmd*'s output but *cmd* has already placed its pending output in a memory buffer, which your process can't get at, and is now waiting for more input. This is a typical case of deadlock.

If you have some control over *cmd*, you can try to work around this issue by ensuring that *cmd* runs without buffering. For example, if *cmd.py* is a Python program, you can run *cmd* without buffering as follows:

```
C:/> python -u cmd.py
```

Other possible approaches include module telnetlib (covered in "Telnet" on page 515) if your platform supports *telnet*, and third-party, Unix-like-only extensions such as *expectpy.sf.net* and packages such as *pexpect.sf.net*. There is no general solution applicable to all platforms and all *cmd*s of interest.

---

spawnv,
spawnve

spawnv(*mode*,*path*,*args*) spawnve(*mode*,*path*,*args*,*env*)

These functions run the program indicated by *path* in a new process *P*, with the arguments passed as sequence *args*. spawnve uses mapping *env* as *P*'s environment (both keys and values must be strings), while spawnv uses os.environ for this purpose. On Unix-like platforms only, there are other variations of os.spawn, corresponding to variations of os.exec, but spawnv and spawnve are the only two that exist on Windows.

mode must be one of two attributes supplied by the os module: os.P_WAIT indicates that the calling process waits until the new process terminates, while os.P_NOWAIT indicates that the calling process continues executing simultaneously with the new process. When *mode* is os.P_WAIT, the function returns the termination code *c* of *P*: 0 indicates successful termination, *c* less than 0 indicates *P* was killed by a *signal*, and *c* greater than 0 indicates normal but unsuccessful termination. When *mode* is os.P_NOWAIT, the function returns *P*'s process ID (on Windows, *P*'s process handle). There is no cross-platform way to use *P*'s ID or handle;

platform-specific ways (not covered further in this book) include function os.waitpid on Unix-like platforms and the win32all extensions (*starship.python.net/crew/mhammond*) on Windows.

For example, your interactive program can give the user a chance to edit a text file that your program is about to read and use. You must have previously determined the full path to the user's favorite text editor, such as *c:\\windows\\notepad.exe* on Windows or */bin/ vim* on a Unix-like platform. Say that this path string is bound to variable *editor* and the path of the text file you want to let the user edit is bound to *textfile*:

```
import os
os.spawnv(os.P_WAIT, editor, [editor, textfile])
```

The first item of the argument *args* is passed to the program being spawned as "the name under which the program is being invoked." Most programs don't look at this, so you can place any string here. Just in case the editor program does look at this special first argument, passing the same string *editor* that is used as the second argument to os.spawnv is the simplest and most effective approach.

---

system   system(*cmd*)

Runs the string command *cmd* in a new process and returns 0 if the new process terminates successfully (or if Python is unable to ascertain the success status of the new process's termination, as happens on Windows 95 and 98). If the new process terminates unsuccessfully (and Python is able to ascertain this unsuccessful termination), system returns an integer error code not equal to 0.

The Subprocess Module

The subprocess module, available only since Python 2.4, supplies one rich class Popen, which supports many diverse ways for your program to run another program.

Popen   class Semaphore(*n*=1)

class Popen(*args*, *bufsize*=0, *executable*=None, *stdin*=None, *stdout*=None, *stderr*=None, *preexec_fn*=None, *close_fds*=False, *shell*=False, *cwd*=None, *env*=None, *universal_newlines*=False, *startupinfo*=None, *creationflags*=0)

Popen starts a subprocess to run a distinct program, and creates and returns an object *p*, which represents that subprocess. The *args* mandatory argument and the many optional (named) arguments control all details of how the subprocess is to be run.

If any exception occurs, during the subprocess creation and before the distinct program starts, the call to Popen re-raises that exception in the calling process with the addition of an attribute named child_traceback, which is the Python traceback object for the subprocess. Such an exception would normally be an instance of OSError (or possibly TypeError or ValueError to indicate that you've passed to Popen an argument that's invalid in type or value).

What to run, and how: args, executable, shell

args is a sequence (normally a list) of strings: the first item is the path to the program to execute, and the following items, if any, are arguments to pass to the program (*args* can also be just a string, when you don't need to pass arguments). *executable*, when not None, overrides *args* in determining which program to execute. When *shell* is true, *executable* specifies which shell to use to run the subprocess; when *shell* is true and *executable* is None, the shell used is */bin/sh* on Unix-like systems (on Windows, it's os.environ['COMSPEC']).

Subprocess files: stdin, stdout, stderr, bufsize, universal_newlines, close_fds

stdin, *stdout*, and *stderr* specify the subprocess's standard input, output, and error files, respectively. Each may be PIPE, which creates a new pipe to/from the subprocess; None, meaning that the subprocess is to use the same file as this ("parent") process; or a file object (or file descriptor) that's already suitably open (for reading, for the standard input; for writing, for the standard output and standard error). *stderr* may also be STDOUT, meaning that the subprocess's standard error is to occur on the same file as its standard output. *bufsize* controls the buffering of these files (unless they're already open), with the same semantics as the same argument to the open function covered in "Creating a File Object with open" on page 216 (the default, 0, means "unbuffered"). When *universal_newlines* is true, *stdout* and *stderr* (unless they're already open) are opened in "universal newlines" ('rU') mode, covered in "File mode" on page 217. When *close_fds* is true, all other files (apart from standard input, output, and error) are closed in the subprocess before the subprocess's program or shell is executed.

Other arguments: preexec_fn, cwd, env, startupinfo, creationflags

When *preexec_fn* is not None, it must be a function, or other callable object, and gets called in the subprocess before the subprocess's program or shell is executed.

When *cwd* is not None, it must be a string that gives the path to an existing directory; the current directory gets changed to *cwd* in the subprocess before the subprocess's program or shell is executed.

When *env* is not None, it must be a mapping (normally a dictionary) with strings as both keys and values, and fully defines the environment for the new process.

startupinfo and *creationflags* are Windows-only arguments to pass to the CreateProcess Win32 API call used to create the subprocess, for Windows-specific purposes (they are not covered further in this book, which focuses on cross-platform uses of Python).

Attributes of subprocess.Popen instances

An instance *p* of class Popen supplies the following attributes:

pid
> The process ID of the subprocess.

returncode
> None to indicate that the subprocess has not yet exited; otherwise, an integer: 0 for successful termination, >0 for termination with an error code, or <0 if the subprocess was killed by a signal.

stderr, stdin, stdout
> When the corresponding argument to Popen was subprocess.PIPE, each of these attributes is a file object wrapping the corresponding pipe; otherwise, each of these attributes is None.

Methods of subprocess.Popen instances

An instance *p* of class Popen supplies the following methods.

communicate	*p*.communicate(*input*=None)
	Sends the string *input* as the subprocess's standard input (when *input* is not None), then reads the subprocess's standard output and error files into in-memory strings *so* and *se* until both files are finished and finally waits for the subprocess to terminate and returns a pair (two-item tuple) (*so, se*).
poll	*p*.poll( )
	Checks if the subprocess has terminated, then returns *p*.returncode.
wait	*p*.wait( )
	Waits for the subprocess to terminate, then returns *p*.returncode.

The mmap Module

The mmap module supplies memory-mapped file objects. An mmap object behaves similarly to a plain (not Unicode) string, so you can often pass an mmap object where a plain string is expected. However, there are differences:

- An mmap object does not supply the methods of a string object.
- An mmap object is mutable, while string objects are immutable.
- An mmap object also corresponds to an open file and behaves polymorphically to a Python file object (as covered in "File-Like Objects and Polymorphism" on page 222).

An mmap object *m* can be indexed or sliced, yielding plain strings. Since *m* is mutable, you can also assign to an indexing or slicing of *m*. However, when you assign to a slice of *m*, the righthand side of the assignment statement must be a string of exactly the same length as the slice you're assigning to. Therefore, many of the useful tricks available with list slice assignment (covered in "Modifying a list" on page 56) do not apply to mmap slice assignment.

Module mmap supplies a factory function that is slightly different on Unix-like systems and Windows.

mmap	`mmap(`*filedesc,length,tagname*`='') # Windows`
	`mmap(`*filedesc,length,flags*`=MAP_SHARED,`
	prot`=PROT_READ|PROT_WRITE) # Unix`

Creates and returns an mmap object *m* that maps into memory the first *length* bytes of the file indicated by file descriptor *filedesc*. *filedesc* must normally be a file descriptor opened for both reading and writing (except, on Unix-like platforms, when argument *prot* requests only reading or only writing). (File descriptors are covered in "File Descriptor Operations" on page 253.) To get an mmap object *m* that refers to a Python file object *f*, use *m*=mmap.mmap(*f*.fileno( ),*length*).

On Windows, all memory mappings are readable and writable and shared between processes so that all processes with a memory mapping on a file can see changes made by each such process. On Windows only, you can pass a string *tagname* to give an explicit tag name for the memory mapping. This tag name lets you have several memory mappings on the same file, but this functionality is rarely necessary. Calling mmap with only two arguments has the advantage of keeping your code portable between Windows and Unix-like platforms.

On Unix-like platforms only, you can pass mmap.MAP_PRIVATE as the *flags* argument to get a mapping that is private to your process and copy-on-write. mmap.MAP_SHARED, the default, gets a mapping that is shared with other processes so that all processes mapping the file can see changes made by one process (same as on Windows). You can pass mmap.PROT_READ as the *prot* argument to get a mapping that you can only read, not write. Passing mmap.PROT_WRITE gets a mapping that you can only write, not read. The bitwise-OR mmap.PROT_READ|mmap.PROT_WRITE, the default, gets a mapping that you can both read and write (same as on Windows).

Methods of mmap Objects

An mmap object *m* supplies the following methods.

close   m.close()

Closes the file of *m*.

---

find   m.find(*str,start*=0)

Returns the lowest index *i* greater than or equal to *start* such that *str* = =*m*[*i*:*i*+len(*str*)]. If no such *i* exists, m.find returns -1. This is the same functionality as for the find method of string objects, covered in find on page 187.

---

flush   m.flush([*offset,n*])

Ensures that all changes made to *m* also exist on *m*'s file. Until you call m.flush, it's uncertain whether the file reflects the current state of *m*. You can pass a starting byte offset *offset* and a byte count *n* to limit the flushing effect's guarantee to a slice of *m*. Pass both arguments, or neither: it is an error to call m.flush with one argument.

---

move   m.move(*dstoff,srcoff,n*)

Like the slicing *m*[*dstoff*:*dstoff*+*n*]=*m*[*srcoff*:*srcoff*+*n*], but potentially faster. The source and destination slices can overlap. Apart from such potential overlap, move does not affect the source slice (i.e., the move method *copies* bytes but does not *move* them, despite the method's name).

---

read   m.read(*n*)

Reads and returns a string *s* containing up to *n* bytes starting from *m*'s file pointer, then advances *m*'s file pointer by len(*s*). If there are less than *n* bytes between *m*'s file pointer and *m*'s length, returns the bytes available. In particular, if *m*'s file pointer is at the end of *m*, returns the empty string ''.

---

read_byte   m.read_byte()

Returns a string of length 1 containing the character at *m*'s file pointer, then advances *m*'s file pointer by 1. m.read_byte() is similar to m.read(1). However, if *m*'s file pointer is at the end of *m*, m.read(1) returns the empty string '', while m.read_byte() raises a ValueError exception.

readline   m.readline( )

Reads and returns one line from the file of m, from m's current file pointer up to the next '\n', included (or up to the end of m if there is no '\n'), then advances m's file pointer to point just past the bytes just read. If m's file pointer is at the end of m, readline returns the empty string ''.

resize   m.resize(n)

Changes the length of m so that len(m) becomes n. Does not affect the size of m's file. m's length and the file's size are independent. To set m's length to be equal to the file's size, call m.resize(m.size( )). If m's length is larger than the file's size, m is padded with null bytes (\x00).

seek   m.seek(pos,how=0)

Sets the file pointer of m to the integer byte offset pos. how indicates the reference point (point 0): when how is 0, the reference point is the start of the file; when 1, m's current file pointer; when 2, the end of m. A seek that tries to set m's file pointer to a negative byte offset, or to a positive offset beyond m's length, raises a ValueError exception.

size   m.size( )

Returns the length (number of bytes) of the file of m, not the length of m itself. To get the length of m, use len(m).

tell   m.tell( )

Returns the current position of the file pointer of m as a byte offset from the start of m's file.

write   m.write(str)

Writes the bytes in str into m at the current position of m's file pointer, overwriting the bytes that were there, and then advances m's file pointer by len(str). If there aren't at least len(str) bytes between m's file pointer and the length of m, write raises a ValueError exception.

write_byte   *m*.write_byte(*byte*)

Writes *byte*, which must be a single-character string, into mapping *m* at the current position of *m*'s file pointer, overwriting the byte that was there, and then advances *m*'s file pointer by 1. When *x* is a single-character string, *m*.write_byte(*x*) is similar to *m*.write(*x*). However, if *m*'s file pointer is at the end of *m*, *m*.write_byte(*x*) silently does nothing, while *m*.write(*x*) raises a ValueError exception. Note that this is the reverse of the relationship between read and read_byte at end-of-file: write and read_byte raise ValueError, while read and write_byte don't.

Using mmap Objects for IPC

The way in which processes communicate using mmap is similar to how IPC uses files: one process can write data, and another process can later read the same data back. Since an mmap object rests on an underlying file, you can also have some processes doing I/O directly on the file (as covered in "File Objects" on page 216), while others use mmap to access the same file. You can choose between mmap and I/O on file objects on the basis of convenience: the functionality is the same, and performance is roughly equivalent. For example, here is a simple program that uses file I/O to make the contents of a file equal to the last line interactively typed by the user:

```
fileob = open('xxx','w')
while True:
    data = raw_input('Enter some text:')
    fileob.seek(0)
    fileob.write(data)
    fileob.truncate()
    fileob.flush()
```

And here is another simple program that, when run in the same directory as the former, uses mmap (and the time.sleep function, covered in sleep on page 304) to check every second for changes to the file and print out the file's new contents:

```
import mmap, os, time
mx = mmap.mmap(os.open('xxx',os.O_RDWR), 1)
last = None
while True:
    mx.resize(mx.size())
    data = mx[:]
    if data != last:
        print data
        last = data
    time.sleep(1)
```

Numeric Processing

You can perform some numeric computations with operators (covered in "Numeric Operations" on page 52) and built-in functions (covered in "Built-in Functions" on page 158). Python also provides modules that support additional numeric computation functionality, as documented in this chapter: math, cmath in "The math and cmath Modules" on page 365, operator in "The operator Module" on page 368, random in "The random module" on page 370, and decimal in "The decimal Module" on page 372. "The gmpy Module" on page 373 also covers third-party module gmpy, which further extends Python's numeric computation abilities. Numeric processing often requires, more specifically, the processing of *arrays* of numbers, covered in Chapter 16.

The math and cmath Modules

The math module supplies mathematical functions on floating-point numbers, while the cmath module supplies equivalent functions on complex numbers. For example, math.sqrt(-1) raises an exception, but cmath.sqrt(-1) returns 1j.

Each module exposes two attributes of type float bound to the values of fundamental mathematical constants, pi and e, and the following functions.

---

acos   acos(*x*)   math and cmath

Returns the arccosine of *x* in radians.

---

acosh   acosh(*x*)   cmath only

Returns the arc hyperbolic cosine of *x* in radians.

---

asin	`asin(x)`	math and cmath

Returns the arcsine of *x* in radians.

asinh	`asinh(x)`	cmath only

Returns the arc hyperbolic sine of *x* in radians.

atan	`atan(x)`	math and cmath

Returns the arctangent of *x* in radians.

atanh	`atanh(x)`	cmath only

Returns the arc hyperbolic tangent of *x* in radians.

atan2	`atan2(y,x)`	math only

Like `atan(y/x)`, except that `atan2` properly takes into account the signs of both arguments. For example:

```
>>> import math
>>> math.atan(-1./-1.)
0.78539816339744828
>>> math.atan2(-1., -1.)
-2.3561944901923448
```

Also, when *x* equals 0, `atan2` returns `pi/2`, while dividing by *x* would raise `ZeroDivisionError`.

ceil	`ceil(x)`	math only

Returns `float(i)`, where *i* is the lowest integer such that *i* >= *x*.

cos	`cos(x)`	math and cmath

Returns the cosine of *x* in radians.

cosh	`cosh(x)`	math and cmath

Returns the hyperbolic cosine of *x* in radians.

e	The mathematical constant *e*.	math and cmath

exp	`exp(x)`	math and cmath

Returns e**x.

fabs   fabs(*x*)   math only

Returns the absolute value of *x*.

---

floor   floor(*x*)   math only

Returns float(*i*), where *i* is the highest integer such that *i* <= *x*.

---

fmod   fmod(*x,y*)   math only

Returns the float *r*, with the same sign as *x*, such that *r==x-n*y* for
some integer *n*, and abs(*r*)<abs(*y*). Like *x%y*, except that, when *x* and
y differ in sign, *x%y* has the same sign as *y*, not the same sign as *x*.

---

frexp   frexp(*x*)   math only

Returns a pair (*m,e*) with the so-called "mantissa" (in fact, the
significand) and exponent of *x*. *m* is a floating-point number, and *e*
is an integer such that *x==m*(2**e)* and 0.5<=abs(*m*)<1, except that
frexp(0) returns (0.0,0).

---

hypot   hypot(*x,y*)   math only

Returns sqrt(*x*x+y*y*).

---

ldexp   ldexp(*x,i*)   math only

Returns *x*(2**i)* (*i* should be an int; if *i* is a float, *i* gets truncated, but that situation also produces a warning).

---

log   log(*x*)   math and cmath

Returns the natural logarithm of *x*.

---

log10   log10(*x*)   math and cmath

Returns the base-10 logarithm of *x*.

---

modf   modf(*x*)   math only

Returns a pair (*f,i*) with fractional and integer parts of *x*, meaning
two floats with the same sign as *x* such that *i==int(i)* and *x==f+i*.

---

pi   The mathematical constant π.   math and cmath

---

pow   pow(*x,y*)   math only

Returns *x**y*.

---

sin	sin(*x*)	math and cmath
	Returns the sine of *x* in radians.	

sinh	sinh(*x*)	math and cmath
	Returns the hyperbolic sine of *x* in radians.	

sqrt	sqrt(*x*)	math and cmath
	Returns the square root of *x*.	

tan	tan(*x*)	math and cmath
	Returns the tangent of *x* in radians.	

tanh	tanh(*x*)	math and cmath
	Returns the hyperbolic tangent of *x* in radians.	

The operator Module

The operator module supplies functions that are equivalent to Python's operators. These functions are handy in cases where callables must be stored, passed as arguments, or returned as function results. The functions in operator have the same names as the corresponding special methods (covered in "Special Methods" on page 104). Each function is available with two names, with and without leading and trailing double underscores (e.g., both operator.add(*a*,*b*) and operator.__add__(*a*,*b*) return *a*+*b*). Table 15-1 lists the functions supplied by the operator module.

Table 15-1. Functions supplied by the operator module

Method	Signature	Behaves like
abs	abs(*a*)	abs(*a*)
add	add(*a*,*b*)	*a*+*b*
and_	and_(*a*,*b*)	*a*&*b*
concat	concat(*a*,*b*)	*a*+*b*
contains	contains(*a*,*b*)	*b* in *a*
countOf	countOf(*a*,*b*)	*a*.count(*b*)
delitem	delitem(*a*,*b*)	del *a*[*b*]
delslice	delslice(*a*,*b*,*c*)	del *a*[*b*:*c*]
div	div(*a*,*b*)	*a*/*b*
eq	eq(*a*,*b*)	*a*==*b*

Table 15-1. Functions supplied by the operator module (continued)

Method	Signature	Behaves like
floordiv	floordiv(*a*,*b*)	*a//b*
ge	ge(*a*,*b*)	*a>=b*
getitem	getitem(*a*,*b*)	*a[b]*
getslice	getslice(*a*,*b*,*c*)	*a[b:c]*
gt	gt(*a*,*b*)	*a>b*
indexOf	indexOf(*a*,*b*)	*a*.index(*b*)
invert, inv	**invert(*a*)**, inv(*a*)	~*a*
is	**is(*a*,*b*)**	*a* is *b*
is_not	**is_not(*a*,*b*)**	*a* is not *b*
le	**le(*a*,*b*)**	*a<=b*
lshift	lshift(*a*,*b*)	*a<<b*
lt	lt(*a*,*b*)	*a<b*
mod	mod(*a*,*b*)	*a%b*
mul	mul(*a*,*b*)	*a*b*
ne	ne(*a*,*b*)	*a!=b*
neg	neg(*a*)	-*a*
not_	not_(*a*)	not *a*
or_	or_(*a*,*b*)	*a|b*
pos	pos(*a*)	+*a*
repeat	repeat(*a*,*b*)	*a*b*
rshift	rshift(*a*,*b*)	*a>>b*
setitem	setitem(*a*,*b*,*c*)	*a[b]=c*
setslice	setslice(*a*,*b*,*c*,*d*)	*a[b:c]=d*
sub	sub(*a*,*b*)	*a-b*
truediv	truediv(*a*,*b*)	*a/b* # "true" div -> no truncation
truth	truth(*a*)	not not *a*, bool(*a*)
xor_	xor(*a*,*b*)	*a^b*

Module operator also supplies two higher-order functions whose results are functions suitable for passing as named argument *key=* to the sort method of lists, the sorted built-in function, and (in Python 2.5) other built-in functions such as min and max.

attrgetter   attrgetter(*attr*)

Returns a callable *f* such that *f(o)* is the same as getattr(*o,attr*).

itemgetter   itemgetter(*key*)

Returns a callable *f* such that *f(o)* is the same as getitem(*o,key*).

For example, say that L is a list of lists, with each sublist at least three items long, and you want to sort L, in-place, based on the third item of each sublist. The simplest way is:

```
import operator
L.sort(key=operator.itemgetter(2))
```

Random and Pseudorandom Numbers

The random module of the standard Python library generates pseudorandom numbers with various distributions. The underlying uniform pseudorandom generator uses the Mersenne Twister algorithm, with a period of length 2**19937-1. (Older versions of Python used the Whichmann-Hill algorithm, with a period of length 6,953,607,871,644.)

Physically random and cryptographically strong random numbers

Pseudorandom numbers provided by module random, while very good, are not of cryptographic quality. If you want higher-quality random numbers (ideally, physically generated random numbers rather than algorithmically generated pseudorandom numbers), in Python 2.4, you can call os.urandom (from module os, *not* random).

---

urandom   urandom(*n*)

Returns *n* random bytes, read from physical sources of random bits such as */dev/urandom* on recent Linux releases or from crypto-graphical-strength sources such as the CryptGenRandom API on Windows. If no suitable source exists on the current system, urandom raises NotImplementedError.

For an alternative source of physically random numbers, see *http://www.four-milab.ch/hotbits*.

The random module

All functions of module random are methods of one hidden global instance of class random.Random. You can instantiate Random explicitly to get multiple generators that do not share state. Explicit instantiation is advisable if you require random numbers in multiple threads (threads are covered in Chapter 14). This section documents the most frequently used functions exposed by module random.

---

choice   choice(*seq*)

Returns a random item from nonempty sequence *seq*.

---

getrandbits   getrandbits(*k*)

Returns a nonnegative long integer with *k* random bits, like choice(xrange(2**k)) (but much faster and with no problems for large *k*).

getstate   getstate( )

Returns a hashable, pickleable, and marshalable object *S* representing current state of the generator. You can later pass *S* to function setstate to restore the generator's state.

jumpahead   jumpahead(*n*)

Advances the generator state as if *n* random numbers had been generated. Computing the new state is faster than generating *n* random numbers would be.

random   random( )

Returns a random float *r* from a uniform distribution such that 0<=*r*<1.

randrange   randrange([*start*,]*stop*[,*step*])

Like choice(xrange(*start*,*stop*,*step*)), but much faster.

sample   sample(*seq*,*k*)

Returns a new list whose *k* items are unique items randomly drawn from *seq*. The list is in random order so that any slice is an equally valid random sample. *seq* may contain duplicate items. In this case, each occurrence of an item is a candidate for selection in the sample, and the sample may also contain duplicates.

seed   seed(*x*=None)

Initializes the generator state. *x* can be any hashable object. When *x* is None, and automatically when module random is first loaded, seed uses the current system time (or some platform-specific source of randomness, if any) to get a seed. *x* is normally a long integer up to 27814431486575L. Larger *x* values are accepted, but may produce the same generator states as smaller ones.

setstate   setstate(*S*)

Restores the generator state. *S* must be the result of a previous call to getstate (such a call may have occurred in another program, or in a previous run of this program, as long as object *S* has correctly been transmitted, or saved and restored).

shuffle	shuffle(*alist*) Shuffles, in place, mutable sequence *alist*.
uniform	uniform(*a*,*b*) Returns a random floating-point number *r* from a uniform distribution such that *a*<=*r*<*b*.

Module random also supplies functions that generate pseudorandom floating-point numbers from other probability distributions (Beta, Gamma, exponential, Gauss, Pareto, etc.) by internally calling random.random as their source of randomness.

The decimal Module

A Python float is a binary floating-point number, normally in accordance with the standard known as IEEE 754 and implemented in hardware in modern computers. A concise, practical introduction to floating-point arithmetic and its issues can be found in David Goldberg's essay "What Every Computer Scientist Should Know about Floating-Point Arithmetic," at *http://docs.sun.com/source/806-3568/ncg_goldberg.html*. Often, particularly for money-related computations, you may prefer to use *decimal* floating-point numbers; Python 2.4 supplies an implementation of the standard known as IEEE 854, for base 10, in standard library module decimal. At *http://docs.python.org/lib/module-decimal.html*, you can find complete reference documentation, pointers to the applicable standards, a tutorial, and an advocacy for decimal. Here, I cover only a small subset of decimal's functionality that corresponds to the most frequently used parts of the module.

Module decimal supplies a class Decimal whose immutable instances are decimal numbers, exception classes, and classes and functions to deal with the *arithmetic context*, which specifies such things as precision, rounding, and which computational anomalies (such as division by zero, overflow, underflow, and so on) will raise exceptions if they occur. In the default context, precision is 28 decimal digits, rounding is "half-even" (round results to the closest representable decimal number: when a result is exactly halfway between two such numbers, round to the one whose last digit is even), and anomalies that raise exceptions are invalid operation, division by zero, and overflow.

To build a decimal number, call decimal.Decimal with one argument: an integer or a string. If you start with a float, you must pass to Decimal a string form of that float to control all the digits involved. For example, decimal.Decimal(0.1) is an error; use decimal.Decimal('0.1') (try decimal.Decimal(repr(0.1)) to help you understand why, and see *http://python.org/doc/2.4.2/tut/node16.html* for a detailed explanation of the issues). If you wish, you can easily write a factory function for ease of experimentation, particularly interactive experimentation, with `decimal`:

```
import decimal
def d(x):
    return decimal.Decimal(str(x))
```

Now $d(0.1)$ is just the same thing as `decimal.Decimal('0.1')`, but far more concise and thus handier to write.

Once you have instances of `decimal`, you can perform arithmetic among them (and with integers, but not with `float`s), pickle and unpickle them, use them as keys in dictionaries and members of sets, and format them (with a string's % operator, covered in "String Formatting" on page 193) with the same formatting choices that are available for `float`s; however, in the latter cases (just as if you pass them as arguments to functions in module math, say) the instances of `decimal` get converted into `float`s, which implies a loss of precision. See *http://docs.python.org/lib/decimal-recipes.html* for some useful recipes for more precise formatting and trigonometric computations.

The gmpy Module

The `gmpy` module (*http://gmpy.sourceforge.net*) wraps the GMP library (*http://www.swox.com/gmp/*) to extend and accelerate Python's abilities for multiple-precision arithmetic, or arithmetic in which the precision of the numbers involved is bounded only by the amount of memory available. Python "out of the box" supplies multiple-precision arithmetic for integers through the built-in type `long`, covered in Chapter 4; `gmpy` supplies another integer-number type, named `mpz`, which affords even faster operations than Python's built-in `long`, and other functions and methods for a vast variety of fast number-theoretical computations (Fibonacci numbers, factorials, binomial coefficients, probabilistic determination of primality, etc.) and bit string operations. `gmpy` also supplies a rational-number type (named `mpq`), a floating-point-number type with arbitrary precision (named `mpf`), and fast random-number generators.

`gmpy`'s reference documentation is part of the `gmpy-sources` tarball, which you can download from *http://sourceforge.net/projects/gmpy/*; on the same page, you will find precompiled, ready-to-install downloads for Windows and Mac OS X 10.4 versions of Python (2.3 and 2.4 at the time of this writing). You need to download and unpack the sources package anyway, even if you're installing a precompiled version, because the sources package is the only one that includes the documentation (which you'll find in subdirectory *doc* once you have unpacked the tarball). Further, in subdirectory *test* there are over 1,000 unit tests to verify the complete correctness of your installation (run **python test/gmpy_test.py**, at a command prompt in the directory into which you've unpacked the tarball, to run all tests; it will take only a few seconds) and a few timing examples to show you the performance, on your specific machine, of `gmpy` types compared to Python's built-in ones. For example, on my laptop, by running **python test/timing2.py** I see that computing the 100,000th Fibonacci number (which starts with 259741 and has a total of 20,898 digits) takes about 1.5 seconds working on Python's built-in `long`s,

0.5 seconds working on `gmpy.mpz` instances, and less than 0.01 seconds by calling the `gmpy.fib` predefined function.

`gmpy` strives to provide heuristically useful conversions from both `decimal.Decimal` instances and floats, using a Stern-Brocot tree to build "sensible" rationals:

```
>>> import gmpy
>>> print gmpy.mpq(0.1)
1/10
```

In this example, `gmpy` manages to compensate for the float's "representation error" and emit the exact fraction that you presumably meant rather than the mathematically exact one, which tends to be less useful:

```
>>> print gmpy.mpq(int(0.1*2**55),2**55)
3602879701896397/36028797018963968
```

16

Array Processing

You can represent arrays with lists (covered in "Lists" on page 43), as well as with the array standard library module (covered in "The array Module" on page 375). You can manipulate arrays with loops; list comprehensions; iterators; generators; genexps (all covered in Chapter 4); built-ins such as map, reduce, and filter (all covered in "Built-in Functions" on page 158); and standard library modules such as itertools (covered in "The itertools Module" on page 183). However, to process large arrays of numbers, such functions may be slower and less convenient than extensions such as Numeric, numarray, and numpy (covered in "Extensions for Numeric Array Computation" on page 377).

The array Module

The array module supplies a type, also called array, whose instances are mutable sequences, like lists. An array *a* is a one-dimensional sequence whose items can be only characters, or only numbers of one specific numeric type, fixed when you create *a*.

array.array's main advantage is that, compared to a list, it can save memory to hold objects all of the same (numeric or character) type. An array object *a* has a one-character, read-only attribute *a*.typecode, which is set on creation and gives the type of *a*'s items. Table 16-1 shows the possible typecodes for array.

Table 16-1. Typecodes for the array module

Typecode	C type	Python type	Minimum size
'c'	char	str (length 1)	1 byte
'b'	char	int	1 byte
'B'	unsigned char	int	1 byte
'U'	unicode char	unicode (lenth 1)	2 bytes
'h'	short	int	2 bytes

Table 16-1. *Typecodes for the array module (continued)*

Typecode	C type	Python type	Minimum size
'H'	unsigned short	int	2 bytes
'i'	int	int	2 bytes
'I'	unsigned	long	2 bytes
'l'	long	int	4 bytes
'L'	unsigned long	long	4 bytes
'f'	float	float	4 bytes
'd'	double	float	8 bytes

The size in bytes of each item may be larger than the minimum, depending on the machine's architecture, and is available as the read-only attribute *a*.itemsize. Module array supplies just the type object called array.

array   array(*typecode,init=''*)

Creates and returns an array object *a* with the given *typecode*. *init* can be a plain string whose length is a multiple of itemsize; the string's bytes, interpreted as machine values, directly initialize *a*'s items. Alternatively, *init* can be any iterable (of characters when *typecode* is 'c', otherwise of numbers): each item of the iterable initializes one item of *a*.

Array objects expose all the methods and operations of mutable sequences (as covered in "Sequence Operations" on page 53), except method sort. Concatenation with + or +=, and assignment to slices, require both operands to be arrays with the same typecode; in contrast, the argument to *a*.extend can be any iterable with items acceptable to *a*. In addition to the methods of mutable sequences, an array object *a* exposes the following methods.

byteswap   *a*.byteswap( )

Swaps the byte order of each item of *a*.

fromfile   *a*.fromfile(*f,n*)

Reads *n* items, taken as machine values, from file object *f* and appends the items to *a*. Note that *f* should be open for reading in binary mode—for example, with mode 'rb'. When less than *n* items are available in *f*, fromfile raises EOFError after appending the items that are available.

fromlist   *a*.fromlist(*L*)

Appends to *a* all items of list *L*.

fromstring   *a*.fromstring(*s*)

Appends to *a* the bytes, interpreted as machine values, of string *s*.
len(*s*) must be an exact multiple of *a*.itemsize.

tofile   *a*.tofile(*f*)

Writes all items of *a*, taken as machine values, to file object *f*. Note
that *f* should be open for writing in binary mode—for example,
with mode 'wb'.

tolist   *a*.tolist( )

Creates and returns a list object with the same items as *a*, like
list(*a*).

tostring   *a*.tostring( )

Returns the string with the bytes from all items of *a*, taken as
machine values. For any *a*, len(*a*.tostring( ))== len(*a*)*a.itemsize.
f.write(*a*.tostring( )) is the same as *a*.tofile(*f*).

Extensions for Numeric Array Computation

From *http://sourceforge.net/project/showfiles.php?group_id=1369*, you can freely
download any of three extension packages that are compatible with each other:
Numeric, Numarray, and NumPy. Each is available either as source code (easy to build
and install on many platforms) or as a pre-built self-installing *.exe* file for
Windows; some are also available in other pre-built forms, such as *.rpm* files for
Linux or *.dmg* files for Apple Mac OS X. From the same URL, you can also download an extensive tutorial on Numeric and find links to other resources, such as bug
trackers, mailing lists, and the Python Scientific Computing home page (*http://
numeric.scipy.org/*).

Each of these extensions focuses on processing large arrays of numbers, which are
often multidimensional (such as matrices). High-performance support for
advanced computations such as linear algebra, Fast Fourier Transforms, and
image processing, is supplied by many auxiliary modules, some of which come
with the extension itself, while others can be downloaded separately from other
sites. Each of the extensions is a large, rich package. For a fuller understanding,
study the tutorial, work through the examples, and experiment interactively. This
chapter presents a reference to an essential subset of Numeric on the assumption
that you already have some grasp of array manipulation and numeric computing
issues. If you are unfamiliar with this subject, the Numeric tutorial can help.

Numeric is not under active development anymore; it is widely considered "stable" by its users and "old" by its detractors. numarray is newer and richer, still under active development, and well documented and supported at its home site, *http://www.stsci.edu/resources/software_hardware/numarray*, where you will also find pointers to abundant, excellent documentation. NumPy is newest, richest, and under very active development (not quite up to a stable 1.0 release at the time of this writing); in the future, as it matures, you can confidently expect that NumPy will supersede both other extensions and become the dominant Python extension for numeric array computation. At the time of this writing, NumPy's documentation, to which *http://numeric.scipy.org/* links, costs a fee, and the proceeds support NumPy's development, present and future. Eventually (when at least 5,000 copies have been sold, or no later than the year 2010 in any case), the documentation is expected to become free.

In this book, I choose to cover Numeric, which is stable, well-performing, and very useful for many applications. Learning about Numeric is also useful to grasp the other alternative packages, given the high degree of mutual compatibility. For a wide range of packages that support numeric and scientific computation in Python, see *http://scipy.org*. The Enthought distribution of Python, mentioned in "Installing Python from Binaries" on page 18, comes with a wide selection of such packages.

The Numeric Package

The main module in the Numeric package is the Numeric module, which supplies the array type, functions that act on array instances, and so-called "universal functions" that operate on arrays and other sequences. Numeric is one of the few Python packages that is often used with the idiom from Numeric import *, even though that idiom does give occasional problems even in this case. A popular alternative, probably the best compromise between conciseness and clarity, is to import Numeric with a short name (e.g., import Numeric as N) and qualify each name by preceding it with N.

Array Objects

Numeric supplies a type array that represents a grid of items. An array object *a* has a given number of dimensions, known as its *rank*, up to some arbitrarily high limit (normally 30, when Numeric is built with default options). A scalar (i.e., a single number) has rank 0, a vector has rank 1, a matrix has rank 2, and so forth.

Typecodes

The values in the grid cells of an array object, known as the *elements* of the array, are homogeneous, meaning they are all of the same type, and all element values are stored within one memory area. This contrasts with a list, where items may be of different types, each stored as a separate Python object. This means a Numeric array occupies far less memory than a Python list with the same number of items. The type of *a*'s elements is encoded as *a*'s typecode, a one-character string, as shown in Table 16-2. Factory functions that build array instances (covered in

"Factory Functions" on page 384) take a *typecode* argument that is one of the values in Table 16-2.

Table 16-2. Typecodes for Numeric arrays

Typecode	C type	Python type	Synonym
'c'	char	str (length 1)	Character
'b'	unsigned char	int	UnsignedInt8
'1'	signed char	int	Int8
's'	short	int	Int16
'w'	unsigned short	int	UnsignedInt16
'i'	int	int	Int32
'u'	unsigned	int	UnsignedInt32
'l'	long	int	Int
'f'	float	float	Float32
'F'	Two floats	complex	Complex32
'd'	double	float	Float
'D'	Two doubles	complex	Complex
'O'	PyObject*	any	PyObject

Numeric supplies readable attribute names for each typecode, as shown in the last column of Table 16-2. Numeric also supplies, on all platforms, the names Int0, Float0, Float8, Float16, Float64, Complex0, Complex8, Complex16, and Complex64. In each case, the name refers to the smallest type of the requested kind with at least that many bits. For example, Float8 is the smallest floating-point type of at least 8 bits (generally the same as Float0 and Float32, but some platforms might, in theory, supply very small floating-point types), while Complex0 is the smallest complex type. On some platforms, Numeric also supplies names Int64, Int128, Float128, and Complex128, with similar meanings. These names are not supplied on all platforms because not all platforms provide numbers with that many bits. A typecode of 'O' means that elements are references to Python objects. In this case, elements can be of different types. This lets you use Numeric array objects as Python containers for array-processing tasks that may have nothing to do with numeric processing.

When you build an array *a* with one of Numeric's factory functions, you can either specify *a*'s typecode explicitly or accept a default data-dependent typecode. To get the typecode of an array *a*, call *a*.typecode(). *a*'s typecode determines how many bytes each element of *a* takes up in memory. Call *a*.itemsize() to get this information. When the typecode is 'O', the item size is small (e.g., 4 bytes on a 32-bit platform), but this size accounts only for the reference held in each of *a*'s cells. The objects indicated by the references are stored elsewhere as separate Python objects; each such object, depending on its type, may occupy an arbitrary amount of extra memory, not accounted for in the item size of an array with typecode 'O'.

Shape and Indexing

Each `array` object *a* has an attribute *a*.`shape`, which is a tuple of `int`s. `len`(*a*.`shape`) is *a*'s rank; for example, a one-dimensional array of numbers (also known as a *vector*) has rank 1, and *a*.`shape` has just one item. More generally, each item of *a*.`shape` is the length of the corresponding dimension of *a*. *a*'s number of elements, known as its *size*, is the product of all items of *a*.`shape`. Each dimension of *a* is also known as an *axis*. Axis indices are from 0 and up, as is usual in Python. Negative axis indices are allowed and count from the right, so -1 is the last (rightmost) axis.

Each array *a* is a Python sequence. Each item *a*[*i*] of *a* is a subarray of *a*, meaning it is an array with a rank one less than *a*'s: *a*[*i*].`shape`==*a*.`shape`[1:]. For example, if *a* is a two-dimensional matrix (*a* is of rank 2), *a*[*i*], for any valid index *i*, is a one-dimensional subarray of *a* that corresponds to a row of the matrix. When *a*'s rank is 1 or 0, *a*'s items are *a*'s elements (just one element, for rank-0 arrays). Since *a* is a sequence, you can index *a* with normal indexing syntax to access or change *a*'s items. Note that *a*'s items are *a*'s subarrays; only for an array of rank 1 or 0 are the array's *items* the same thing as the array's *elements*.

You can also loop on *a* in a `for`, just as you can with any other sequence. For example:

```
for x in a:
    process(x)
```

means the same thing as:

```
for i in range(len(a)):
    x = a[i]
    process(x)
```

In these examples, each item *x* of *a* in the `for` loop is a subarray of *a*. For example, if *a* is a two-dimensional matrix, each *x* in either of these loops is a one-dimensional subarray of *a* that corresponds to a row of the matrix.

You can also index *a* by a tuple. For example, if *a*'s rank is at least 2, you can write *a*[*i*][*j*] as *a*[*i*,*j*], for any valid *i* and *j*, for rebinding as well as for access. Tuple indexing is faster and more convenient. Do not put parentheses inside the brackets to indicate that you are indexing *a* by a tuple: just write the indices one after the other, separated by commas. *a*[*i*,*j*] means the same thing as *a*[(*i*,*j*)], but the form without parentheses is more natural and readable.

If the result of indexing is a single number, Numeric sometimes leaves the result as a rank-0 array, and sometimes as a scalar quantity of the appropriate Python type. In other words, as a result of such an indexing you sometimes get an array with just one number in it, and sometimes the number it contains. For example, consider the snippet:

```
>>> for t in 'blswiufFdDO': print t, type(Numeric.array([0],t)[0])
```

The somewhat surprising output is:

```
b <type 'array'>
l <type 'int'>
s <type 'array'>
w <type 'array'>
```

```
i <type 'int'>
u <type 'array'>
f <type 'array'>
F <type 'array'>
d <type 'float'>
D <type 'complex'>
O <type 'int'>
```

which shows that, for single-result indexing, array types that correspond exactly to a Python number type produce Python numbers, while other array types produce rank-0 arrays.

Storage

An array object *a* is usually stored in a contiguous area of memory, with elements one after the other in what is traditionally called *row-major order*. For example, when *a*'s rank is 2, the elements of *a*'s first row a[0] come first, immediately followed by those of *a*'s second row a[1], and so on.

An array can be noncontiguous when it shares some of the storage of a larger array, as covered in "Slicing" on page 381. For example, when *a*'s rank is 2, the slice b=a[:,0] is the first column of *a*, and is stored noncontiguously because it occupies some of the same storage as *a*. b[0] occupies the same storage as a[0,0], while b[1] occupies the same storage as a[1,0], which cannot be adjacent to the memory occupied by a[0,0] when *a* has more than one column.

Numeric handles contiguous and noncontiguous arrays transparently in most cases so that you can use the most natural approach without wasting memory nor requiring avoidable copies. In the rest of this chapter, I point out the rare exceptions where a contiguous array is needed. When you want to copy a noncontiguous array *b* into a new contiguous array *c*, use method copy, covered in copy on page 387.

Slicing

Arrays may share some or all of their data with other arrays. Numeric shares data between arrays whenever feasible. If you want Numeric to copy data, explicitly ask for a copy. Data sharing, for Numeric, also applies to slices. For built-in Python lists and standard library array objects, slices are (shallow) copies, but for Numeric.array objects, slices share data with the array they're sliced from:

```
from Numeric import *
alist=range(10)
list_slice=alist[3:7]
list_slice[2]=22
print list_slice, alist          # prints: [3,4,22,6] [0,1,2,3,4,5,6,7,8,9]
anarray=array(alist)
arr_slice=anarray[3:7]
arr_slice[2]=33
print arr_slice, anarray          # prints: [3 4 33 6] [0 1 2 3 4 33 6 7 8 9]
```

Rebinding an item of list_slice does not affect the list alist from which list_slice is sliced, since, for built-in lists, slicing performs a copy. However, because, for Numeric arrays, slicing shares data, assigning to an item of arr_slice does affect the array object anarray from which arr_slice is sliced. This behavior may be unexpected for a beginner, but was chosen to enable high performance.

Slicing examples

You can use a tuple to slice an array, just as you can use the tuple to index the array: for arrays, slicing and indexing blend into each other. Each item in a slicing tuple can be an integer, and for each such item, the slice has one fewer axis than the array being sliced: slicing removes the axis for which you give a number by selecting the indicated plane of the array.

A slicing tuple's item can also be a slice expression; the general syntax is *start:stop:step*, and you can omit one or more of the three parts (see "Sequence Operations" on page 53 and slice on page 156, for details on slice semantics and defaults). Here are some example slicings:

```
# a is [[ 0, 1, 2, 3, 4, 5],
#        [10,11,12,13,14,15],
#        [20,21,22,23,24,25],
#        [30,31,32,33,34,35],
#        [40,41,42,43,44,45],
#        [50,51,52,53,54,55]]
a[0,2:4]                  # array([2,3])
a[3:,3:]                  # array([[33,34,35],
#                                  [43,44,45],
#                                  [53,54,55]])
a[:,4]                    # array([4,14,24,34,44,54])
a[2::2,::2]               # array([[20,22,24],
#                                  [40,42,44]])
```

A slicing-tuple item can also use an ellipsis (...) to indicate that the following items in the slicing tuple apply to the last (rightmost) axes of the array you're slicing. For example, consider slicing an array b of rank 3:

```
b.shape                   # (4,2,3)
b[1].shape                # (2,3)
b[...,1].shape            # (4,2)
```

When we slice with b[1] (equivalent to indexing), we give an integer index for axis 0, and therefore we select a specific plane along b's axis 0. By selecting a specific plane, we remove that axis from the result's shape. Therefore, the result's shape is b.shape[1:]. When we slice with b[...,1], we select a specific plane along b's axis -1 (the rightmost axis of b). Again, by selecting a specific plane, we remove that axis from the result's shape. Therefore, the result's shape is b.shape[:-1].

A slicing-tuple item can also be the pseudoindex NewAxis, which is a constant supplied by module Numeric. The resulting slice has an additional axis at the point at which you use NewAxis, with a value of 1 in the corresponding item of the shape tuple. Continuing the previous example:

```
b[Numeric.NewAxis,...,Numeric.NewAxis].shape     # (1,4,2,3,1)
```

Here, rather than selecting and thus removing some of b's axes, we have added two new axes, one at the start of the shape and one at the end, thanks to the ellipsis.

Axis removal and addition can both occur in the same slicing. For example:

```
b[Numeric.NewAxis,:,0,:,Numeric.NewAxis].shape      # (1,4,3,1)
```

Here, we both add new axes at the start and end of the shape, and select a specific index from the middle axis (axis 1) of b by giving an index for that axis. Therefore, axis 1 of b is removed from the result's shape. The colons (:) used as the second and fourth items in the slicing tuple in this example are slice expressions with both *start* and *stop* omitted, meaning that all of the corresponding axis is included in the slice. In all these examples, all slices share some or all of b's data. Slicing affects only the shape of the resulting array. No data is copied, and no operations are performed on the data.

Assigning to array slices

Assignment to array slices is less flexible than assignment to list slices. Normally, the only thing you can assign to an array slice is another array of the same shape as the slice. However, if the righthand side (RHS) of the assignment is not an array, Numeric creates a temporary array from it. Each element of the RHS is coerced to the lefthand side (LHS) type. If the RHS array is not the same shape as the LHS slice, *broadcasting* applies, as covered in "Operations on Arrays" on page 389. For example, you can assign a scalar (meaning a single number) to any slice of a numeric array: the RHS number is coerced, then broadcast (replicated) as needed to make the assignment succeed.

When you assign to an array slice (or indexing) a RHS of a type different from that of the LHS, Numeric coerces the values to the LHS type—for example, by truncating floating-point numbers to integers. This does not apply if the RHS values are complex. Full coercion does not apply to in-place operators, which can only cast the RHS values upward (for example, an integer RHS is okay for in-place operations with a floating-point LHS, but not vice versa), as covered in "In-place operations" on page 391.

Truth Values and Comparisons of Arrays

Although an array object *a* is a Python sequence, *a* does not follow Python's normal rule for the truth value of sequences (a sequence is false when empty; otherwise, it is true). Rather, *a* is false when *a* has no elements *or* when all of *a*'s elements are 0. Since comparisons between arrays produce arrays (whose items are 0 or 1), Numeric's rule is necessary to let you test for element-wise equality of arrays in the natural way:

```
if a==b:
```

Without this proviso, such an if condition would be satisfied by any nonempty comparable arrays *a* and *b*. Despite this rule, array comparison is still tricky, since the comparison of two arrays is true if any *one* of the corresponding elements is equal:

```
print bool(Numeric.array([1,2])==Numeric.array([1,9])) # prints True (!)
```

A better way to express such comparisons is offered by Numeric's functions alltrue and sometrue, covered in Table 16-4; I suggest you *never* rely on the confusing behavior of if a==b but rather make your intentions clear and explicit by coding either if Numeric.alltrue(a==b) or if Numeric.sometrue(a==b).

Do remember, at any rate, that you have to be explicit when you want to test whether *a* has any items or whether *a* has any elements, which are different conditions:

```
a = Numeric.array( [ [ ], [ ], [ ] ] )
if a: print 'a is true'
else: print 'a is false'                        # prints: a is false
print bool(Numeric.alltrue(a))                  # prints: False
print bool(Numeric.sometrue(a))                 # prints: False
if len(a): print 'a has some items'
else: print 'a has no items'                     # prints: a has some items
if Numeric.size(a): print 'a has some elements'
else: print 'a has no elements'                  # prints: a has no elements
```

In most cases, however, the best way to compare arrays of numbers is for *approximate* equality, using Numeric's function allclose, covered in allclose on page 391.

Factory Functions

Numeric supplies several factory functions that create array objects.

---

array, asarray

array(*data*,*typecode*=None,*copy*=True,*savespace*=False)
asarray(*data*,*typecode*=None,*savespace*=False)

Returns a new array object *a*. *a*'s shape depends on *data*. When *data* is a number, *a* has rank 0 and *a*.shape is the empty tuple ( ). When *data* is a sequence of numbers, *a* has rank 1 and *a*.shape is the singleton tuple (len(*data*),). When *data* is a sequence of sequences of numbers, all of *data*'s items (subsequences) must have the same length, *a* has rank 2, and *a*.shape is the pair (len(*data*),len(*data*[0])). This idea generalizes to any nesting level of *data* as a sequence of sequences, up to the arbitrarily high limit on rank mentioned earlier in this chapter. If data is nested over that limit, array raises TypeError. (The limit is unlikely to be a problem in practice: an array of rank 30, with each axis of length 2, would have over a billion elements.)

typecode can be any of the values shown in Table 16-2 or None. When *typecode* is None, array chooses a typecode depending on the types of the elements of *data*. When any one or more elements in *data* are long or are neither numbers nor plain strings (e.g., None or Unicode strings), the typecode is '0', a.k.a. PyObject. When all elements are plain strings, the typecode is Character. When any

---

one or more elements (but not all) are plain strings, all others are numbers (none of them long), and *typecode* is None, array raises TypeError. You must explicitly pass '0' or PyObject as argument *typecode* if you want array to build an array from some plain strings and some ints or floats. When all elements are numbers (none of them long), the typecode depends on the "widest" numeric type among the elements. When any of the elements is a complex, the typecode is Complex. When no elements are complex but some or all are float, the typecode is Float. When all elements are int, the typecode is Int.

Function array, by default, returns an array object *a* that doesn't share data with any other object. If *data* is an array object, and you explicitly pass a false value for argument *copy*, array returns an array object *a* that shares data with *data*, if feasible. Function asarray is just like function array with argument *copy* passed as False.

By default, a numeric array is implicitly cast up when operated with numbers of wider numeric types. When you do not want this implicit casting, you can save some memory by explicitly passing a true value for argument *savespace* to the array factory function to set the resulting array object *a* into space-saving mode. For example:

```
array(range(4),typecode='b')+2.0                    #
array([2.,3.,4.,5.])
array(range(4),typecode='b',savespace=True)+2.0    #
array([2,3,4,5])
array(range(4),typecode='b',savespace=True)+258.7 #
array([2,3,4,5])
```

The first statement creates an array of floating-point values; *savespace* is not specified, so each element is implicitly cast up to a float when added to 2.0. The second and third statements create arrays of 8-bit integers; *savespace* is specified, so, instead of implicit casting up of the array's element, we get implicit casting down of the float added to each element. 258.7 is cast down to 2; the fractional part .7 is lost because of the cast to an integer, and the resulting 258 becomes 2 because, since the cast is to 8-bit integers, only the lowest 8 bits are kept. The *savespace* mode can be useful for large arrays, but be careful lest you suffer unexpected loss of precision when using it.

arrayrange,   arrayrange([*start,*]*stop*[,*step*=1],*typecode*=None)
arange

Like array(range(*start,stop,step*),*typecode*), but faster. (See built-in function range, covered in "range", for details about *start*, *stop*, and *step*.) arrayrange allows floats for these arguments, not just ints. Be careful when exploiting this feature, since floating-point arithmetic may lead to a result with one more or fewer items than you might expect. arange is a synonym of arrayrange.

fromstring   fromstring(*data*,*count*=None,*typecode*=Int)

Returns a one-dimensional array *a* of shape (*count*,) with data copied from the bytes of string *data*. When *count* is None, len(*data*) must be a multiple of *typecode*'s item size, and *a*'s shape is (len(*data*)/*a*.itemsize( ),). When *count* is not None, len(*data*) must be greater than or equal to *count**a.itemsize( ), and fromstring ignores *data*'s trailing bytes, if any.

Together with methods *a*.tostring and *a*.byteswapped (covered in "Attributes and Methods" on page 387), fromstring allows binary I/O of array objects. When you need to save arrays and later reload them, and don't need to use the saved form in non-Python programs, it's simpler and faster to use module cPickle, covered in "The pickle and cPickle Modules" on page 279. Many experienced users prefer to use portable, self-describing file formats such as netCDF (see *http://met-www.cit.cornell.edu/noon/ncmodule.html*).

---

identity   identity(*n*,*typecode*=Int)

Returns a two-dimensional array *a* of shape (*n*,*n*) (a square matrix). *a*'s elements are 0, except those on the main diagonal (*a*[*j*,*j*] for *j* in range(*n*)), which are 1.

---

empty   empty(*shapetuple*,*typecode*=Int,*savespace*=False)

Returns an array *a* with *a*.shape==*shapetuple*. *a*'s elements are *not* initialized, so their values are totally arbitrary (as in other languages that allow "uninitialized variables" and are different than any other situation in Python).

---

ones   ones(*shapetuple*,*typecode*=Int,*savespace*=False)

Returns an array *a* with *a*.shape==*shapetuple*. All of *a*'s elements are 1.

---

zeros   zeros(*shapetuple*,*typecode*=Int,*savespace*=False)

Returns an array *a* with *a*.shape==*shapetuple*. All of *a*'s elements are 0.

By default, identity, ones, and zeros all return arrays whose type is Int. If you want a different typecode, such as Float, pass it explicitly. A common mistake is:

```
a = zeros(3)
a[0] = 0.3                         # a is array([0,0,0])
```

Since a is Int in this snippet, the 0.3 we assign to one of its items gets truncated to the integer 0. Instead, you typically want something closer to the following:

```
a = zeros(3, Float)
a[0] = 0.3                        # a is array([0.3,0.,0.])
```

Here, we have explicitly specified Float as the typecode for a, and therefore no truncation occurs when we assign 0.3 to one of a's items.

Attributes and Methods

For most array manipulations, Numeric supplies functions you can call with array arguments, covered in "Functions" on page 391. Arguments can also be Python lists; this polymorphism offers more flexibility than functionality packaged up as array attributes and methods. Each array object *a* also supplies some methods and attributes for direct (and slightly faster) access to functionality that may not need polymorphism.

astype   *a*.astype(*typecode*)

Returns a new array *b* with the same shape as *a*. *b*'s elements are *a*'s elements coerced to the type indicated by *typecode*. *b* does not share *a*'s data, even if *typecode* equals *a*.typecode( ).

byteswapped   *a*.byteswapped( )

Returns a new array object *b* with the same typecode and shape as *a*. Each element of *b* is copied from the corresponding element of *a*, inverting the order of the bytes in the value. This swapping transforms each value from little-endian to big-endian or vice versa. Together with function fromstring and method *a*.tostring, the swapping helps when you have binary data from one kind of machine and need them for the other kind. For example, all Apple Mac computers sold through 2005 had PowerPC CPUs, which are big-endian, but new Mac computers use Intel CPUs, which are little-endian; byteswapped can help you read, on a new Mac, a binary file written on an older Mac, or vice versa.

copy   *a*.copy( )

Returns a new contiguous array object *b* that is identical to *a* but does not sharing *a*'s data.

flat   *a*.flat is an attribute that is an array of rank 1, with the same size as *a*, and shares *a*'s data. Indexing or slicing *a*.flat lets you access or change *a*'s elements through this alternate view of *a*. Trying to access *a*.flat raises a TypeError exception when *a* is noncontiguous. When *a* is contiguous, *a*.flat is in row-major order. For example, when *a*'s shape is (7,4) (i.e., *a* is a two-dimensional matrix with seven rows and four columns), *a*.flat[*i*] is the same as *a*[divmod(*i*,4)] for all *i* in range(28).

imag, **imaginary, real**	Trying to access *a*.imag raises a ValueError exception unless *a*'s typecode is complex; in this case, *a*.real is an array with the same shape and typecode as *a*, and shares data with *a*. When *a*'s typecode is complex, *a*.real and *a*.imag are noncontiguous arrays with the same shape as *a* and a float typecode, and shares data with *a*. Accessing or modifying *a*.real or *a*.imag accesses or modifies the real or imaginary parts of *a*'s complex elements. imaginary is a synonym of imag.
iscontiguous	*a*.iscontiguous( ) Returns True if *a*'s data occupies contiguous storage; otherwise, False. This matters particularly when interfacing to C-coded extensions. *a*.copy( ) makes a contiguous copy of *a*. Noncontiguous arrays arise when slicing or transposing arrays, as well as for attributes *a*.real and *a*.imag of an array *a* with a complex typecode.
itemsize	*a*.itemsize( ) Returns the number of bytes of memory used by each of *a*'s elements (despite the name; not by each of *a*'s *items*, which in the general case are subarrays of *a*).
savespace	*a*.savespace(*flag*=True) Sets or resets the space-saving mode of array *a*, depending on *flag*. When *flag* is true, *a*.savespace(*flag*) sets *a*'s space-saving mode, so that *a*'s elements are *not* implicitly cast up when operated with wider numeric types. (For more details on this, see the discussion of the *savespace* argument of function array in array on page 376.) When *flag* is false, *a*.savespace(*flag*) resets *a*'s space-saving mode so that *a*'s elements *are* implicitly cast up when needed.
shape	*a*.shape is a tuple with one item per axis of *a*, giving the length of that axis. You can assign a sequence of ints to *a*.shape to change the shape of *a*, but *a*'s size (total number of elements) must remain the same. When you assign to *a*.shape a sequence *s*, one of *s*'s items can be -1, meaning that the length along that axis is whatever is needed to keep *a*'s size unchanged. The product of the other items of *s* must evenly divide *a*'s size, or else the reshaping raises an

exception. When you need to change the total number of elements in *a*, call function `resize` (covered in resize on page 397).

---

spacesaver *a*.spacesaver( )

Returns `True` if space-saving mode is on for array *a*; otherwise, `False`. See the discussion of the `savespace` method earlier in this section.

---

tolist *a*.tolist( )

Returns a list *L* equivalent to *a*. For example, if *a*.shape is (2,3) and *a*'s typecode is 'd', *L* is a list of two lists of three `float` values each such that, for each valid *i* and *j*, *L*[*i*][*j*]==*a*[*i*,*j*]. list(*a*) converts only the top-level (axis 0) of array *a* into a list, and thus is not equivalent to *a*.tolist( ) if *a*'s rank is 2 or more. For example:

```
a=array([[1,2,3],[4,5,6]],typecode='d')
print a.shape          # prints: (2,3)
print a                # prints: [[1. 2. 3.]
                       #          [4. 5. 6.]]
print list(a)
# prints: [array([1.,2.,3.]), array([4.,5.,6.])]
print a.tolist( )
# prints: [[1.0,2.0,3.0],[4.0,5.0,6.0]]
```

---

toscalar *a*.toscalar( )

Returns the first element of *a* as a Python scalar (normally a number) of the appropriate type, depending on *a*'s typecode.

---

tostring *a*.tostring( )

Returns a binary string *s* whose bytes are a copy of the bytes of *a*'s elements.

---

typecode *a*.typecode( )

Returns the typecode of *a* as a one-character string.

Operations on Arrays

Arithmetic operators +, -, *, /, //, %, and **; comparison operators >, >=, <, <=, ==, and !=; and bitwise operators &, |, ^, and ~ (all covered in "Numeric Operations" on page 52) also apply to arrays. If both operands *a* and *b* are arrays with equal shapes and typecodes, the result is a new array *c* with the same shape (and the same typecode, except for comparison operators). Each element of *c* is the result of the operator on corresponding elements of *a* and *b* (element-wise operation). Order comparisons are not allowed between arrays whose typecode is complex, just as they are not allowed between complex numbers; in all other cases, comparison operators between arrays return arrays with integer typecode.

Arrays do not follow sequence semantics for * (replication) and + (concatenation): * and + perform element-wise arithmetic. Similarly, * does not mean matrix multiplication, but element-wise multiplication. Numeric supplies functions to perform replication, concatenation, and matrix multiplication; all operators on arrays work element-wise.

When the typecodes of *a* and *b* differ, the narrower numeric type is converted to the wider one, like for other Python numeric operations. Operations between numeric and nonnumeric values are disallowed. In the case of arrays, you can inhibit casting by setting an array into space-saving mode with method savespace. Use space-saving with care, since it can result in a silent loss of significant data. For more details on this, see the discussion of the *savespace* argument of function array in array on page 376.

Broadcasting

Element-wise operations between arrays of different shapes are generally not possible: attempting such operations raises an exception. Numeric allows some such operations by broadcasting (replicating) a smaller array up to the shape of the larger one when feasible. To make broadcasting efficient, the replication is only conceptual: Numeric does not physically copy the data (i.e., you need not worry that performance will be degraded because an operation involves broadcasting).

The simplest and most common case of broadcasting is when one operand, *a*, is a scalar (or an array of rank 0), while *b*, the other operand, is any array. In this case, Numeric conceptually builds a temporary array *t*, with shape *b*.shape, where each element of *t* equals *a*. Numeric then performs the requested operation between *t* and *b*. In practice, therefore, when you operate an array *b* with a scalar *a*, as in *a+b* or *b-a*, the resulting array has the same shape as *b*, and each element is the result of applying the operator to the corresponding element of *b* and the single number *a*.

More generally, broadcasting can also apply when both operands *a* and *b* are arrays. Conceptually, broadcasting works according to rather complicated general rules:

- When *a* and *b* differ in rank, the one whose shape tuple is shorter is padded up to the other's rank by adding leading axes, each with a length of 1.
- *a*.shape and *b*.shape, padded to the same length as per the first rule, are compared starting from the right (i.e., from the length of the last axis).
- When the axis length along the axis being examined is the same for *a* and *b*, that axis is okay, and examination moves leftward to the previous axis.
- When the lengths of the axes differ and both are >1, Numeric raises an exception.
- When one axis length is 1, Numeric broadcasts the corresponding array by replication along that plane to the axis length of the other array.

The rules of broadcasting are complicated because of their generality, but most typical applications of broadcasting are simple. For example, say we compute *a+b*, and *a*.shape is (5,3) (a matrix of five rows and three columns). Typical values for *b*.shape include ( ) (a scalar), (3,) (a one-dimensional vector with three elements), and (5,1) (a matrix with five rows and one column). In each of these cases, *b* is conceptually broadcast up to a temporary array *t* with shape (5,3) by replicating *b*'s elements along the needed axis (both axes when *b* is a scalar), and Numeric computes *a+t*. The simplest and most frequent case, of course, is when *b*.shape is (5,3), the same shape as *a*'s. In this case, no broadcasting is needed.

In-place operations

Arrays support in-place operations through augmented assignment operators +=, -=, and so on. The LHS array or slice cannot be broadcast, but the RHS can be. Similarly, the LHS cannot be cast up, but the RHS can be. In other words, in-place operations treat the LHS as rigid in both shape and type, but the RHS is subject to the normal, more lenient rules.

Functions

Numeric defines several functions that operate on arrays, or polymorphically on Python sequences, conceptually forming temporary arrays from nonarray operands.

allclose	allclose(*x*,*y*,*rtol*=1.e-5,*atol*=1.e-8)
	Returns a single number: 0 when every element of *x* is *close* to the corresponding element of *y*; otherwise, 1. Two elements *ex* and *ey* are defined to be close if:
	abs(*ex-ey*) < *atol* + *rtol**abs(*ey*)
	In other words, *ex* and *ey* are close if both are tiny (less than *atol*) or if the relative difference is small (less than *rtol*). allclose is generally a better way to check array equality than ==, since floating-point arithmetic requires some comparison tolerance. However, allclose is not applicable to complex arrays, only to floating-point and integer arrays. To compare two complex arrays *x* and *y* for approximate equality, use:
	allclose(x.real, y.real) and allclose(x.imag, y.imag)
argmax, argmin	argmax(*a*,*axis*=-1) argmin(*a*,*axis*=-1)
	argmax returns a new integer array *m* whose shape tuple is *a*.shape minus the indicated *axis*. Each element of *m* is the index of a maximal element of *a* along *axis*. argmin is similar, but indicates minimal elements rather than maximal ones.

argsort   argsort(*a*,*axis*=-1)

Returns a new integer array *m* with the same shape as *a*. Each vector
of *m* along *axis* is the index sequence needed to sort the corresponding axis of *a*. In particular, if *a* has rank 1, the most common
case, take(*a*,argsort(*a*))==sort(*a*). For example:

```
x = [52, 115, 99, 111, 114, 101, 97, 110, 100, 55]
print Numeric.argsort(x)   # prints: [0 9 6 2 8 5 7 3 4 1]
print Numeric.sort(x)
# prints: [52 55 97 99 100 101 110 111 114 115]
print Numeric.take(x, Numeric.argsort(x))
# prints: [52 55 97 99 100 101 110 111 114 115]
```

Here, the result of Numeric.argsort(*x*) tells us that *x*'s smallest
element is *x*[0], the second smallest is *x*[9], the third smallest is
x[6], and so on. The call to Numeric.take in the last print statement takes *x*'s items in this order, producing the same sorted array
as the call to Numeric.sort in the second print statement.

around   around(*a*,*decimals*=0)

Returns a new float array *m* with the same shape as *a*. Each element
of *m* is like the result of calling Python's built-in function round on
the corresponding element of *a*.

array2string   array2string(*a*,*max_line_width*=77,*precision*=8,
                    suppress_small=False,*separator*=' ', *array_output*=False)

Returns a string representation *s* of array *a*, with elements in
brackets, separated by string *separator*. The last dimension is horizontal, the penultimate one vertical, and further dimensions are
shown by bracket nesting. When *array_output* is true, *s* starts with
'array(' and ends with ')', or ",'X')" when X, which is *a*'s typecode, is not Float, Complex, or Int (so you can later use eval(*s*) if
separator is ',').

Lines longer than *max_line_width* get split. *precision* determines
how many digits each element shows. If *suppress_small* is true, very
small numbers are shown as 0. To change defaults, set attributes of
module sys named output_line_width, float_output_precision, and
float_output_suppress_small. For example:

```
>>> Numeric.array2string(Numeric.array([1e-20]*3))
'[  1.00000000e-20   1.00000000e-20   1.00000000e-20]'
>>> import sys
>>> sys.float_output_suppress_small = True
>>> Numeric.array2string(Numeric.array([1e-20]*3))
'[ 0.  0.  0.]'
```

str(*a*) is like array2string(*a*). repr(*a*) is like array2string(*a*,
separator=',', array_output=True). You can also access these
formatting functions by the names array_repr and array_str in
module Numeric.

average average(*a*,*axis*=0,*weights*=None,*returned*=False)

Returns *a*'s average along *axis*. When *axis* is None, returns the average of all of *a*'s elements. When *weights* is not None, *weights* must be an array with *a*'s shape, or a one-dimensional array with the length of *a*'s given *axis*, and average computes a weighted average. When *returned* is true, returns a pair: the first item is the average; the second item is the sum of weights (the count of values when *weights* is None).

choose choose(*a*,*values*)

Returns an array *c* with the same shape as *a*. *values* is any Python sequence. *a*'s elements are integers between 0, included, and len(*values*), excluded. Each element of *c* is the item of *values* whose index is the corresponding element of *a*. For example:

```
print Numeric.choose(Numeric.identity(3),'ox')
# prints: [[x o o]
#          [o x o]
#          [o o x]]
```

clip clip(*a*,*min*,*max*)

Returns an array *c* with the same typecode and shape as *a*. Each element *ec* of *c* is the corresponding element *ea* of *a*, where *min*<=*ea*<=*max*. Where *ea*<*min*, *ec* is *min*; where *ea*>*max*, *ec* is *max*. For example:

```
print Numeric.clip(Numeric.arange(10),2,7)
# prints: [2 2 2 3 4 5 6 7 7 7]
```

compress compress(*condition*,*a*,*axis*=0)

Returns an array *c* with the same typecode and rank as *a*. *c* includes only the elements of *a* for which the item of *condition*, corresponding along the given *axis*, is true. For example, compress((1,0,1),*a*) == take(*a*,(0,2),0) since (1,0,1) has true values only at indices 0 and 2. Here's how to get only the even numbers from an array:

```
a = Numeric.arange(10)
print Numeric.compress(a%2==0, a)   # prints: [0 2 4 6 8]
```

concatenate concatenate(*arrays*, *axis*=0)

arrays is a sequence of arrays, all with the same shape except possibly along the given *axis*. concatenate returns an array concatenating the *arrays* along the given *axis*. concatenate((s,)*n) has the same sequence replication semantics that *s*n* would have if *s* were a generic Python sequence rather than an array. For example:

```
print Numeric.concatenate([Numeric.arange(5), Numeric.
arange(3)])
# prints: [0 1 2 3 4 0 1 2]
```

convolve

convolve(*a,b,mode=2*)

Returns an array *c* with rank 1, the linear convolution of rank 1 arrays *a* and *b*. Linear convolution is defined over unbounded sequences. convolve conceptually extends *a* and *b* to infinite length by padding with 0, then clips the infinite-length result to its central part, yielding *c*. When *mode* is 2, the default, convolve clips only the padding, so *c*'s shape is (len(*a*)+len(*b*)-1,). Otherwise, convolve clips more. Say len(*a*) is greater than or equal to len(*b*). When *mode* is 0, len(*c*) is len(*a*)-len(*b*)+1; when *mode* is 1, len(*c*) is len(*a*). When len(*a*) is less than len(*b*), the effect is symmetrical. For example:

```
a = Numeric.arange(6)
b = Numeric.arange(4)
print Numeric.convolve(a, b)        # prints: [0 0 1 4
10 16 22 22 15]
print Numeric.convolve(a, b, 1)     # prints: [0 1 4 10
16 22]
print Numeric.convolve(a, b, 0)     # prints: [4 10 16]
```

cross_correlate

cross_correlate(*a,b,mode=0*)

Like convolve(*a,b*[::-1],*mode*).

diagonal

diagonal(*a,k=0,axis1=0,axis2=1*)

Returns the elements of *a* whose indices along *axis1* and *axis2* differ by *k*. When *a* has rank 2, that's the main diagonal when *k* == 0, subdiagonals above the main one when *k* > 0, and subdiagonals below the main one when *k* < 0. For example:

```
# a is [[ 0  1  2  3]
#       [ 4  5  6  7]
#       [ 8  9 10 11]
#       [12 13 14 15]]
print Numeric.diagonal(a)        # prints: [0 5 10 15]
print Numeric.diagonal(a,1)      # prints: [1 6 11]
print Numeric.diagonal(a,-1)     # prints: [4 9 14]
```

As shown, diagonal(*a*) is the main diagonal, diagonal(*a*,1) is the subdiagonal just above the main one, and diagonal(*a*,-1) is the subdiagonal just below the main one.

dot

dot(*a*,*b*)

Returns an array *m* with *a* times *b* in the matrix-multiplication sense, rather than element-wise multiplication. *a*.shape[-1] must equal *b*.shape[-2], and *m*.shape is the tuple *a*.shape[:-1]+*b*.shape[:-2]+*b*.shape[-1:].

indices

indices(*shapetuple*,*typecode*=None)

Returns an integer array *x* of shape (len(*shapetuple*),)+*shapetuple*. Each element of subarray *x*[*i*] is equal to the element's *i* index in the subarray. For example:

```
print Numeric.indices((2,4))    # prints: [[[0 0 0 0]
                                #           [1 1 1 1]]
                                #          [[0 1 2 3]
                                #           [0 1 2 3]]]
```

innerproduct

innerproduct(*a*,*b*)

Returns an array *m* with the result of the inner product of *a* and *b*, like matrixmultiply(*a*,transpose(*b*)). *a*.shape[-1] must equal *b*.shape[-1], and *m*.shape is the tuple *a*.shape[:-1]+*b*.shape[0:-1:-1].

matrixmultiply

matrixmultiply(*a*,*b*)

Returns an array *m* with *a* times *b* in the matrix-multiplication sense, rather than element-wise multiplication. *a*.shape[-1] must equal *b*.shape[0], and *m*.shape is the tuple *a*.shape[:-1]+*b*.shape[1:].

nonzero

nonzero(*a*)

Returns the indices of those elements of *a* that are not equal to 0, like the expression:

```
array([i for i in range(len(a)) if a[i] != 0])
```

a must be a sequence or vector (meaning a one-dimensional array).

outerproduct

outerproduct(*a*,*b*)

Returns an array *m*, which is the outer products of vectors *a* and *b* (in other words, for every valid pair of indices *i* and *j*, *m*[*i*,*j*] equals *a*[*i*]**b[*j*]).

put

put(*a*,*indices*,*values*)

a must be a contiguous array. *indices* is a sequence of integers, taken as indices into *a*.flat. *values* is a sequence of values that can be converted to *a*'s typecode (if shorter than *indices*, *values* is repeated as needed). Each element of *a* indicated by an item in *indices* is replaced by the corresponding item in *values*. put is therefore similar to (but much faster than) the loop:

```
for i,v in zip(indices,list(values)*len(indices)):
    a.flat[i]=v
```

---

putmask

putmask(*a*,*mask*,*values*)

a must be a contiguous array. *mask* is a sequence with the same length as *a*.flat. *values* is a sequence of values that can be converted to *a*'s typecode (if shorter than *mask*, *values* is repeated as needed). Each element of *a* corresponding to a true item in *mask* is replaced by the corresponding item in *values*. putmask is therefore similar to (but faster than) the loop:

```
for i,v in zip(xrange(len(mask)),list(values)*len(mask)):
    if mask[i]: a.flat[i]=v
```

---

rank

rank(*a*)

Returns the rank of *a*, just like len(array(*a*,copy=False).shape).

---

ravel

ravel(*a*)

Returns the flat form of *a*, just like array(*a*, copy=not a.iscontiguous())).flat.

---

repeat

repeat(*a*,*repeat*,*axis*=0)

Returns an array with the same typecode and rank as *a*, where each of *a*'s elements is repeated along *axis* as many times as the value of the corresponding item of *repeat*. *repeat* is an int or an int sequence of length *a*.shape[*axis*]. For example:

```
>>> print N.repeat(range(4),range(4))  # emits  [1 2 2 3 3
3]
```

---

reshape

reshape(*a*,*shapetuple*)

Returns an array *r* with shape *shapetuple*, and shares *a*'s data. *r*=reshape(*a*,*shapetuple*) is like *r*=*a*;*r*.shape=*shapetuple*. The product of *shapetuple*'s items must equal the product of *a*.shape's; one of *shapetuple*'s items may be -1 to ask for adaptation of that axis's length. For example:

```
print Numeric.reshape(range(12),(3,-1))
# prints: [[0 1 2 3]
#          [4 5 6 7]
#          [8 9 10 11]]
```

---

resize   resize(*a*,*shapetuple*)

Returns an array *r* with shape *shapetuple* and data copied from *a*. If *r*'s size is smaller than *a*'s size, *r*.flat is copied from the start of ravel(*a*); if *r*'s size is larger, the data in ravel(*a*) is replicated as many times as needed. In particular, resize(*s*,(*n**len(*s*),)) has the sequence replication semantics that *s**n would have if *s* were a generic Python sequence rather than an array. For example:

```
print Numeric.resize(range(5),(3,4))
# prints: [[0 1 2 3]
#          [4 0 1 2]
#          [3 4 0 1]]
```

searchsorted   searchsorted(*a*,*values*)

a must be a sorted rank 1 array. searchsorted returns an array of integers *s* with the same shape as *values*. Each element of *s* is the index in *a* where the corresponding element of *values* would fit in the sorted order of *a*. For example:

```
print Numeric.searchsorted([0,1], [0.2,-0.3,0.5,1.3,1.0,0.
0,0.3])
# prints: [1 0 1 2 1 0 1]
```

This specific idiom returns an array with: 0 in correspondence to each element *x* of *values* when *x* is less than or equal to 0;, 1 when *x* is greater than 0 and less than or equal to 1, and 2 when *x* is greater than 1. With slight generalization, and with appropriate thresholds as the elements of sorted array *a*, this idiom allows very fast classification of the subrange each element *x* of *values* falls into.

shape   shape(*a*)

Returns the shape of *a*, just like array(*a*,copy=False).shape.

size   size(*a*,*axis*=None)

When *axis* is None, returns the total number of elements in *a*. Otherwise, returns the number of elements of *a* along *axis*, like array(*a*,copy=False).shape[*axis*].

sort   sort(*a*,*axis*=-1)

Returns an array *s* with the same typecode and shape as *a*, with elements along each plane of *axis* reordered so that the plane is sorted in increasing order. For example:

```
# x is [[0 1 2 3]
#       [4 0 1 2]
#       [3 4 0 1]]
print Numeric.sort(x)        # prints: [[0 1 2 3]
```

```
#              [0 1 2 4]
#              [0 1 3 4]]
print Numeric.sort(x,0)    # prints: [[0 0 0 1]
#              [3 1 1 2]
#              [4 4 2 3]]
```

Here, sort(x) sorts each row, while sort(x,0) sorts each column.

---

swapaxes

swapaxes(a,axis1,axis2)

Returns an array s with the same typecode, rank, and size as a, and shares a's data. s's shape is the same as a, but with the lengths of axes *axis1* and *axis2* swapped. In other words, s=swapaxes(a,axis1,axis2) is like:

```
swapped_shape=range(length(a.shape))
swapped_shape[axis1]=axis2
swapped_shape[axis2]=axis1
s=transpose(a,swapped_shape)
```

---

take

take(a,indices,axis=0)

Returns an array t with the same typecode and rank as a, and contains the subset of a's elements that would be in a slice along *axis* comprising the given *indices*. For example, after t=take(a,(1,3)), t.shape==(2,)+a.shape[1:], and t's items are copies of the second and fourth rows of a.

---

trace

trace(a,k=0)

Returns the sum of a's elements along the k diagonal, like sum(diagonal(a,k)).

---

transpose

transpose(a,axes=None)

Returns an array t, with the same typecode, rank, and size as a, and shares a's data. t's axes are permuted with respect to a's by the axis indices in sequence *axes*. When *axes* is None, t's axes invert the order of a's, as if *axes* were reversed(a.shape).

---

vdot

vdot(a,b)

Returns a scalar that is the dot products of vectors a and b. If a is complex, this operation uses the complex conjugate of a.

---

where

where(condition,x,y)

Returns an array w with the same shape as *condition*. Where an element of *condition* is true, the corresponding element of w is

---

the corresponding element of *x*; otherwise, it is the corresponding element of *y*. For example, clip(*a*,*min*,*max*) is the same as where(greater(*a*,*max*),*max*,where(greater(*a*,*min*),*a*,*min*)).

Universal Functions (ufuncs)

Numeric supplies named functions with the same semantics as Python's arithmetic, comparison, and bitwise operators, and mathematical functions like those supplied by built-in modules math and cmath (covered in "The math and cmath Modules" on page 365), such as sin, cos, log, and exp.

These functions are objects of type ufunc (which stands for "universal function") and share several traits in addition to those they have in common with array operators (element-wise operation, broadcasting, coercion). Every ufunc instance *u* is callable, is applicable to sequences as well as to arrays, and accepts an optional *output* argument. If *u* is binary (i.e., if *u* accepts two operand arguments), *u* also has four callable attributes, named *u*.accumulate, *u*.outer, *u*.reduce, and *u*.reduceat. The ufunc objects supplied by Numeric apply only to arrays with numeric typecodes (i.e., not to arrays with typecode '0' or 'c') and Python sequences of numbers.

When you start with a list *L*, it's faster to call *u* directly on *L* rather than to convert *L* to an array. *u*'s return value is an array *a*; you can perform further computation, if any, on *a*; if you need a list result, convert the resulting array to a list at the end by calling method tolist. For example, say you must compute the logarithm of each item of a list and return another list. On my laptop, with N set to 2222, a list comprehension such as:

```
def logsupto(N):
    return [math.log(x) for x in range(2,N)]
```

takes about 5.2 milliseconds. Using Python's built-in map:

```
def logsupto(N):
    return map(math.log, range(2,N))
```

is faster, about 3.7 milliseconds. Using Numeric's ufunc named log:

```
def logsupto(N):
    return Numeric.log(Numeric.arange(2,N)).tolist()
```

reduces the time to about 2.1 milliseconds. Taking some care to exploit the *output* argument to the log ufunc:

```
def logsupto(N):
    temp = Numeric.arange(2, N, typecode=Numeric.Float)
    Numeric.log(temp, output=temp)
    return temp.tolist()
```

further reduces the time, down to just 2 milliseconds. The ability to accelerate such simple but massive computations (here by almost three times) with so little effort is a good part of the attraction of Numeric, and particularly of Numeric's ufunc objects. Do take care *not* to carelessly code something like:

```
def logsupto(N):
    return Numeric.log(range(2,N)).tolist()
```

which, on my laptop, takes about 18 milliseconds; clearly, the conversions from list to array and from integer to float may dominate actual computations in a case like this one.

The Optional output Argument

Any ufunc *u* accepts an optional last argument *output* that specifies an output array. If supplied, *output* must be an array or array slice of the right shape and type for *u*'s results (no coercion, no broadcasting). *u* stores results in *output* and does not create a new array. *output* can be the same as an input array argument *a* of *u*. Indeed, *output* is normally specified in order to substitute common idioms such as *a=u(a,b)* with faster equivalents such as *u(a,b,a)*. However, *output* cannot share data with *a* without being *a* (i.e., *output* can't be a different view of some or all of *a*'s data). If you pass such a disallowed *output* argument, Numeric is normally unable to diagnose your error and raise an exception, so instead you may get wrong results.

Whether you pass the optional *output* argument or not, a ufunc *u* returns its results as the function's return value. When you do not pass *output*, *u* stores the results it returns in a new array object, so you normally bind *u*'s return value to some reference in order to be able to access *u*'s results later. When you pass the *output* argument, *u* stores the results in *output*, so you need not bind *u*'s return value. You can later access *u*'s results as the new contents of the array object passed as *output*.

Callable Attributes

Every binary ufunc *u* supplies four attributes that are also callable objects.

---

accumulate   `u.accumulate(a,axis=0)`

Returns an array *r* with the same shape and typecode as *a*. Each element of *r* is the accumulation of elements of *a* along the given *axis* with the function or operator underlying *u*. For example:

```
print add.accumulate(range(10))
# prints: [0 1 3 6 10 15 21 28 36 45]
```

Since add's underlying operator is +, and *a* is the sequence 0,1,2,...,9, *r* is 0,0+1,0+1+2,...,0+1+...+8+9. In other words, *r*[0] is *a*[0], *r*[1] is *r*[0] + *a*[1], *r*[2] is *r*[1] + *a*[2], and so on (*r*[*i*] is *r*[*i*-1] + *a*[*i*] for each *i*>0).

---

outer

u.outer(a,b)

Returns an array r whose shape tuple is a.shape+b.shape. For each tuple ta indexing a and tb indexing b, $a[ta]$, operated (with the function or operator underlying u) with $b[tb]$, is put in $r[ta+tb]$ (the + here indicates tuple concatenation). The overall operation is known in mathematics as the outer product when u is multiply. For example:

```
a = Numeric.arange(3, 5)
b = Numeric.arange(1, 6)
c = Numeric.multiply.outer(a, b)
print a.shape, b.shape, c.shape # prints: (2,) (5,) (2,5)
print c                         # prints: [[3 6 9 12 15]
                                #          [4 8 12 16 20]]
```

c.shape is (2,5), which is the concatenation of the shape tuples of operands a and b. Each ith row of c is the whole of b multiplied by the corresponding ith element of a.

reduce

u.reduce(a,$axis$=0)

Returns an array r with the same typecode as a and a rank one less than a's rank. Each element of r is the reduction of the elements of a, along the given $axis$, with the function or operator underlying u. The functionality of u.reduce is therefore close to that of Python's built-in reduce function, covered in "reduce". For example, since 0+1+2+...+9 is 45, add.reduce(range(10)) is 45. With built-in reduce and import operator, reduce(operator.add,range(10)) is also 45, just like the simpler and faster expression sum(range(10)).

reduceat

u.reduceat(a,$indices$)

Returns an array r with the same typecode as a and the same shape as $indices$. Each element of r is the reduction, with the function or operator underlying u, of elements of a starting from the corresponding item of $indices$ up to the next one excluded (up to the end, for the last one). For example:

```
print Numeric.add.reduceat(range(10),(2,6,8)) # emits: [14
13 17]
```

Here, r's elements are the partial sums 2+3+4+5, 6+7, and 8+9.

Array
Processing

ufunc Objects Supplied by Numeric

Numeric supplies several ufunc objects, as listed in Table 16-3.

Table 16-3. ufunc objects supplied by Numeric

ufunc	Behavior
absolute	Like the abs built-in function
add	Like the + operator
arccos	Like the acos function in math and cmath
arccosh	Like the acosh function in cmath
arcsin	Like the asin function in math and cmath
arcsinh	Like the asinh function in cmath
arctan	Like the atan function in math and cmath
arctanh	Like the atanh function in cmath
bitwise_and	Like the & operator
bitwise_not	Like the ~ operator
bitwise_or	Like the | operator
bitwise_xor	Like the ^ operator
ceil	Like the ceil function in math
conjugate	Complex conjugate of each element (unary)
cos	Like the cos function in math and cmath
cosh	Like the cosh function in cmath
divide	Like the / operator (but with result inf for division by zero)
divide_safe	Like the / operator (raises an exception for division by zero)
equal	Like the == operator
exp	Like the exp function in math and cmath
fabs	Like the fabs function in math
floor	Like the floor function in math
fmod	Like the fmod function in math
greater	Like the > operator
greater_equal	Like the >= operator
less	Like the < operator
less_equal	Like the <= operator
log	Like the log function in math and cmath
log10	Like the log10 function in math and cmath
logical_and	Like the & operator; returns array of 0s and 1s
logical_not	Like the ~ operator; returns array of 0s and 1s
logical_or	Like the | operator; returns array of 0s and 1s
logical_xor	Like the ^ operator; returns array of 0s and 1s
maximum	Element-wise, the larger of the two elements being operated on
minimum	Element-wise, the smaller of the two elements being operated on
multiply	Like the * operator
not_equal	Like the != operator
power	Like the ** operator
remainder	Like the % operator
sin	Like the sin function in math and cmath
sinh	Like the sinh function in cmath

Table 16-3. ufunc objects supplied by Numeric (continued)

ufunc	Behavior
sqrt	Like the sqrt function in math and cmath
subtract	Like the - operator
tan	Like the tan function in math and cmath
tanh	Like the tanh function in cmath

Here's how you can use ufunc to get a "ramp" of numbers, decreasing then increasing:

```
print Numeric.maximum(range(1,20),range(20,1,-1))
# prints: [20 19 18 17 16 15 14 13 12 11 11 12 13 14 15 16 17 18 19]
```

Shorthand for Commonly Used ufunc Methods

Numeric defines function synonyms for some commonly used methods of ufunc objects, as listed in Table 16-4.

Table 16-4. Synonyms for ufunc methods

Synonym	Stands for
alltrue	logical_and.reduce
cumproduct	multiply.accumulate
cumsum	add.accumulate
product	multiply.reduce
sometrue	logical_or.reduce
sum	add.reduce

Auxiliary Numeric Modules

Many other modules are built on top of Numeric or cooperate with it. Some of these extra modules are included in the Numeric package, and their documentation is also part of Numeric's documentation. A rich collection of scientific and engineering computing tools that work with Numeric is available at *http://www.scipy.org*; have a look at it if you are using Python for any kind of scientific or engineering computing.

Here are the key auxiliary modules that come with Numeric:

MLab

> MLab supplies many Python functions, written on top of Numeric, but is similar in name and operation to functions supplied by the product Matlab.

FFT

> FFT supplies Python-callable Fast Fourier Transforms (FFTs) of data held in Numeric arrays. FFT can wrap either the well-known *FFTPACK* Fortran-coded library or the compatible C-coded *fftpack* library, which comes with FFT.

LinearAlgebra

> LinearAlgebra supplies Python-callable functions, operating on data held in Numeric arrays, wrapping either the *LAPACK* Fortran-coded library or the compatible C-coded *lapack_lite* library. LinearAlgebra lets you invert matrices, solve linear systems, compute eigenvalues and eigenvectors, perform singular value decomposition, and least-squares-solve overdetermined linear systems.

RandomArray

> RandomArray supplies fast, high-quality pseudorandom number generators to build Numeric arrays with various random distributions.

MA

> MA supports *masked* arrays (i.e., arrays that can have missing or invalid values). MA supplies a large subset of Numeric's functionality, albeit sometimes at reduced speed. MA also lets you associate to each array an optional mask, which is an auxiliary array of Booleans, where True indicates array elements that are missing, unknown, or invalid. Computations propagate masks; you can turn masked arrays into plain Numeric ones by supplying a fill-in value for invalid elements. MA is widely applicable because experimental data often has missing or inapplicable elements. Should you need to extend or specialize some aspect of Numeric's behavior for your application's purposes, it may be simplest and most effective to start with MA's sources rather than with Numeric's. The latter are often quite hard to understand and modify due to the degree of optimization applied to them over the years.

These modules' performance is generally quite good. For example:

```
import RandomArray
x = RandomArray.random((13,23))
```

On my laptop, this takes 109 microseconds. The pure-Python equivalent:

```
from random import random
x = [[random( ) for i in xrange(13)] for j in xrange(23)]
```

takes 230 microseconds, over twice as long.

17

Tkinter GUIs

Most professional client-side applications interact with the user through a graphical user interface (GUI). A GUI is programmed through a *toolkit*, which is a library that supplies *controls* (also known as *widgets*), visible objects such as buttons, labels, text entry fields, and menus. A GUI toolkit lets you compose controls into a coherent whole, display them on-screen, and interact with the user, receiving input via keyboard and mouse.

Python gives you a choice among many GUI toolkits. Some are platform-specific, but most are cross-platform, supporting at least Windows and Unix-like platforms and often the Mac as well. *http://wiki.python.org/moin/GuiProgramming* lists dozens of GUI toolkits for Python. The most popular Python GUI toolkit today is probably wxPython (*http://www.wxpython.org/*), but the one distributed with Python itself is Tkinter.

Tkinter is an object-oriented Python wrapper around the cross-platform toolkit Tk, which is also used with other scripting languages such as Tcl (for which it was originally developed), Ruby, and Perl. Tkinter, like the underlying Tcl/Tk, runs on Windows, Macintosh, and Unix-like platforms. On Windows, the standard Python distribution also includes, as well as Tkinter itself, the Tcl/Tk library needed to run Tkinter. On other platforms, you may have to obtain and install Tcl/Tk separately (you may also have to install or reinstall Python after Tcl/Tk, depending on the Python distribution's details).

This chapter covers an essential subset of Tkinter that is sufficient to build simple graphical frontends for Python applications. (More complete documentation is available at *http://docs.python.org/lib/tkinter.html*.) All the scripts in this chapter are meant to be run standalone (i.e., from a command line, or in a platform-dependent way, such as by double-clicking on a script's icon). Running a GUI script from inside another program that has its own GUI, such as a Python integrated development environment (e.g., IDLE or PythonWin), can often cause anomalies. This can be a particular problem when the GUI script attempts to terminate (and thus close down the GUI), since the script's GUI and the development environment's GUI may interfere with each other.

Tkinter Fundamentals

Tkinter makes it easy to build simple GUI applications. You import Tkinter, create, configure, and position the widgets you want, then enter the Tkinter main loop. Your application becomes *event-driven*: the user interacts with the widgets, causing events, and your application responds via the functions you installed as handlers for these events.

The following example shows a simple application that exhibits this general structure:

```
import sys, Tkinter
Tkinter.Label(text="Welcome!").pack( )
Tkinter.Button(text="Exit", command=sys.exit).pack( )
Tkinter.mainloop( )
```

The calls to Label and Button create the respective widgets and return them as results. Since we specify no parent windows, Tkinter puts the widgets directly in the application's main window. The named arguments specify each widget's configuration. In this simple case, we don't need to bind variables to the widgets. We just call the pack method on each widget, handing control of the widget's layout to a layout manager object known as the packer. A *layout manager* is an invisible component whose job is to position widgets within other widgets (known as *container* or *parent* widgets), handling geometrical layout issues. The previous example passes no arguments to control the packer's operation, which lets the packer operate in a default way.

When the user clicks on the button, the command callable of the Button widget executes without arguments. The example passes function sys.exit as the argument named command when it creates the Button. Therefore, when the user clicks on the button, sys.exit( ) executes and terminates the application (as covered in exit on page 169).

After creating and packing the widgets, the example calls Tkinter's mainloop function, and thus enters the Tkinter main loop and becomes event-driven. Since the only event for which the example installs a handler is a click on the button, nothing happens from the application's viewpoint until the user clicks the button. Meanwhile, however, the Tkinter toolkit responds in the expected way to other user actions, such as moving the Tkinter window, covering and uncovering the window, and so on. When the user resizes the window, the packer layout manager works to update the widgets' layout. In this example, the widgets remain centered, close to the upper edge of the window, with the label above the button.

All strings going to or coming from Tkinter are Unicode strings, so be sure to review "Unicode" on page 198 if you need to show, or accept as input, characters outside of the ASCII encoding (you will then need to use the appropriate codec).

This chapter uses many all-uppercase, multiletter identifiers (e.g., LEFT, RAISED, and ACTIVE). All these identifiers are constant attributes of module Tkinter and are used for a wide variety of purposes. If your code uses from Tkinter import *, you can use the identifiers directly. If your code uses import Tkinter instead, you need to qualify these identifiers, just like all others you import from Tkinter, by preceding them with 'Tkinter.'. Tkinter is one of the rare Python modules designed to support from Tkinter import *, but using import Tkinter is still advisable, sacrificing some convenience in favor of greater clarity. A good compromise between convenience and clarity is to import Tkinter with a shorter name (e.g., import Tkinter as Tk).

Dialogs

Tkinter comes with several auxiliary modules to define *dialogs*, which are modal boxes that, when you activate them, return control to your application only when the user is done with them, either providing an answer you requested, or declining to answer by some button such as Cancel. These useful modules are not well documented and lack functionality your application may well need, such as internationalization (covered in "Internationalization" on page 269). For detailed understanding, as well as for adding such functionality, I suggest you examine the Python sources of these modules in Python's standard library: these sources are also good examples of how to use various aspects of Tkinter's functionality. In this section, I present only a general overview of the modules and some highlights of their most important functionality.

The tkMessageBox module

tkMessageBox supplies classes, functions, and constants that use Tk's "message boxes." You can specify the set of buttons to show, which one of the buttons you want to be the default, which icon to display, and title and message strings. Normally, you just call one of the following functions, with optional parameters *title* and *message*:

askokcancel
> Asks if an operation should proceed; returns True if the user clicks OK

askquestion
> Asks a yes/no question; returns 'yes' or 'no'

askretrycancel
> Asks if an operation should be tried again; returns True if the user clicks RETRY

askyesno
> Asks a yes/no question; returns True if the user clicks YES

showerror
> Shows an error message

showinfo
> Shows an informational message

showwarning
> Shows a warning message

The tkSimpleDialog module

tkSimpleDialog supplies a Dialog class, which is a base class that you subclass to create your own custom dialogs, and three convenience functions, each with optional parameters *title* and *prompt*, and each returning a user response (when the user clicks OK) or None (when the user clicks Cancel):

askfloat
> Asks the user to enter a floating-point number; returns a float

askinteger
> Asks the user to enter an integer number; returns an int

askstring
> Asks the user to enter a string; returns a plain str (when the user has entered only ASCII characters) or a unicode string (in all other cases)

The tkFileDialog module

tkFileDialog supplies classes and functions to let the user select a file or directory for loading (reading) or saving (writing). These classes and functions support many options, such as *defaultextension* to specify a default extension for files, *filetypes* to specify which extensions are accepted, and *initialdir* to specify where to start looking. The most commonly used utility functions in the module are:

askdirectory
> Returns the path of a directory

askopenfilename
> Returns the path of an existing file to open

askopenfilenames
> Returns the paths of one or more existing files to open

asksaveasfilename
> Returns the path of a file to save to (with confirmation, if already existing)

The tkColorChooser module

tkColorChooser supplies a function askcolor, which you call without arguments, and returns a color chosen by the user, which is a tuple with four items: red, green, and blue components, followed by the Tkinter color string.

Widget Fundamentals

Tkinter supplies many kinds of widgets, and most of them have several things in common. All widgets are instances of classes that inherit from class Widget. Class Widget itself is *abstract*; that is, you never instantiate Widget itself. You only instantiate concrete subclasses corresponding to specific kinds of widgets. Class Widget's functionality is common to all the widgets you instantiate.

To instantiate any kind of widget, call the widget's class. The first argument is the parent window of the widget, also known as the widget's *master*. If you omit this

---

positional argument, the widget's master is the application's main window. All other arguments are in named form: *option=value*. To set or change options on an existing widget *w*, call *w*.config(*option=value*). To get an option of *w* call *w*.cget('*option*'), which returns the option's value. Each widget *w* is a mapping, so you can also get an option as *w*['*option*'], and set or change it with *w*['*option*']=*value*.

Common Widget Options

Many widgets accept some common options. Some options affect a widget's colors, while others affect lengths (normally in pixels), and there are various other kinds. This section details the most commonly used options.

Color options

Tkinter represents colors with strings. The string can be a color name, such as 'red' or 'orange', or it may be of the form '#*RRGGBB*', where each *R*, *G*, and *B* are hexadecimal digits that represent a color by the values of red, green, and blue components on a scale of 0 to 255. Don't worry if your screen can't display millions of different colors, as implied by this scheme: Tkinter maps any requested color to the closest color that your screen can display. The common color options are:

activebackground
:   Background color for the widget when the widget is *active*, meaning that the mouse is over the widget and clicking on it makes something happen

activeforeground
:   Foreground color for the widget when the widget is active

background *(also* bg)
:   Background color for the widget

disabledforeground
:   Foreground color for the widget when the widget is *disabled*, meaning that clicking on the widget is ignored

foreground *(also* fg)
:   Foreground color for the widget

highlightbackground
:   Background color of the highlight region when the widget has focus

highlightcolor
:   Foreground color of the highlight region when the widget has focus

selectbackground
:   Background color for the selected items of the widget; for widgets that have selectable items, such as Listbox

selectforeground
:   Foreground color for the selected items of the widget

Length options

Tkinter normally expresses a length as an integer number of pixels; other units of measure are possible, but rarely used. The common length options are:

borderwidth
> Width of the border (if any), giving a three-dimensional look to the widget

highlightthickness
> Width of the highlight rectangle when the widget has focus (when 0, the widget does not draw a highlight rectangle)

padx
pady
> Extra space the widget requests from its layout manager beyond the minimum the widget needs to display its contents in the x and y directions

selectborderwidth
> Width of the three-dimentional border (if any) around selected items of the widget

wraplength
> Maximum line length for widgets that perform word wrapping (when less than or equal to 0, there is no wrapping: the widget breaks lines of text only at '\n')

Options expressing numbers of characters

Some options indicate a widget's requested layout not in pixels but rather as a number of characters, using average width or height of the widget's fonts:

height
> Desired height of the widget; must be greater than or equal to 1

underline
> Index of the character to underline in the widget's text (0 is the first character, 1 the second one, and so on); the underlined character is the shortcut key to reach or activate the widget

width
> Desired width of the widget (when less than or equal to 0, the desired width is just enough to hold the widget's current contents)

Other common options

Other options accepted by many kinds of widgets are a mixed bag that deals with both behavior and looks:

anchor
> Where the information in the widget is displayed; must be N, NE, E, SE, S, SW, W, NW, or CENTER (all except CENTER are compass directions).

command
> Callable without arguments; executes when the user clicks on the widget (only for widgets Button, Checkbutton, and Radiobutton).

font
>   Font for the text in this widget (see "Fonts" on page 433).

image
>   An image to display in the widget instead of text; the value must be a Tkinter image object (see "Tkinter Images" on page 414).

justify
>   How lines are justified when a widget shows more than a line of text; must be LEFT, CENTER, or RIGHT.

relief
>   The three-dimensional effect that indicates how the interior of the widget appears relative to the exterior; must be RAISED, SUNKEN, FLAT, RIDGE, SOLID, or GROOVE.

state
>   Widget look and behavior on mouse and keyboard clicks; must be NORMAL, ACTIVE, or DISABLED.

takefocus
>   If true, the widget accepts focus when the user navigates among widgets by pressing the Tab or Shift-Tab keys.

text
>   The text string displayed by the widget.

textvariable
>   The Tkinter variable object associated with the widget (see "Tkinter Variable Objects" on page 413).

Common Widget Methods

A widget *w* supplies many methods. Besides event-related methods (covered in "Event-Related Methods" on page 448), commonly used widget methods are the following.

---

cget
> `w.cget(option)`
>
> Returns the value configured in *w* for *option*.

---

config
> `w.config(**options)`
>
> `w.config()`, called without arguments, returns a dictionary where each possible option of *w* is mapped to a tuple that describes the option's current setting. Called with one or more named arguments, config sets those options in *w*'s configuration.

---

focus_set
> `w.focus_set()`
>
> Sets focus to *w* so that all keyboard events for the application are sent to *w*.

---

grab_set, **grab_release**	`w.grab_set( ) w.grab_release( )`
	grab_set ensures that all of the application's events are sent to `w` until a corresponding call is made to grab_release.
mainloop	`w.mainloop( )`
	Enters a Tkinter event loop. Event loops may be nested; each call to `mainloop` enters one further nested level of the event loop.
quit	`w.quit( )`
	Quits a Tkinter event loop. When event loops are nested, each call to `quit` exits one nested level of the event loop.
update	`w.update( )`
	Handles all pending events. *Never* call this while you're already handling an event!
update_ **idletasks**	`w.update_idletasks( )`
	Handles those pending events that would normally be handled only when the event loop is idle (such as layout-manager updates and widget redrawing), but does not perform any callbacks. You can safely call this method at any time.
wait_variable	`w.wait_variable(v)`
	`v` must be a Tkinter variable object (covered in "Tkinter Variable Objects" on page 413). `wait_variable` returns only when the value of `v` changes. Meanwhile, other parts of the application remain active.
wait_visibility	`w.wait_visibility(w1)`
	`w1` must be a widget. `wait_visibility` returns only when `w1` becomes visible. Meanwhile, other parts of the application remain active.
wait_window	`w.wait_window(w1)`
	`w1` must be a widget. `wait_window` returns only when `w1` is destroyed. Meanwhile, other parts of the application remain active.

winfo_height	*w*.winfo_height( )
	Returns *w*'s height in pixels.

winfo_width	*w*.winfo_width( )
	Returns *w*'s width in pixels.

w supplies many other methods whose names start with winfo_, but the two above are the most often called, typically after calling *w*.update_idletasks. They let you ascertain a widget's dimensions after the user has resized a window, causing the layout manager to rearrange the widgets' layout.

Tkinter Variable Objects

The Tkinter module supplies classes whose instances represent *variables*. Each class deals with a specific data type: DoubleVar for float, IntVar for int, StringVar for str. Instantiate any of these classes without arguments to obtain an instance *x*, also known in Tkinter as a *variable object*, set to 0 or ''. *x*.set(*datum*) sets *x*'s value to the given value; *x*.get( ) returns *x*'s current value.

You can pass *x* as the textvariable or variable configuration option for a widget. Once you do this, the widget's text changes to track any change to *x*'s value, and, for some kinds of widgets, *x*'s value tracks changes to the widget. A Tkinter variable can control more than one widget. Tkinter variables let you control widgets more transparently, and sometimes more conveniently, than explicitly querying and setting widget properties. The following example shows how to use a StringVar to connect an Entry widget and a Label widget automatically:

```
import Tkinter

root = Tkinter.Tk( )
tv = Tkinter.StringVar( )
Tkinter.Label(textvariable=tv).pack( )
Tkinter.Entry(textvariable=tv).pack( )
tv.set('Welcome!')
Tkinter.Button(text="Exit", command=root.quit).pack( )

Tkinter.mainloop( )
print 'Final value is', tv.get( )
```

As you edit the Entry, you'll see the Label change automatically. This example instantiates the Tkinter main window explicitly, binds it to name *root*, and then sets as the Button's command the bound method *root*.quit, which quits Tkinter's main loop but does not terminate the Python application. Thus, the example ends with a print statement to show on standard output the final value of variable object *tv*.

Tkinter

Tkinter Images

The Tkinter class PhotoImage handles Graphical Interchange Format (GIF) and Portable PixMap (PPM) images. Call PhotoImage with a named argument file=*path* to load image data from the file at the given *path* and get an instance *x*.

You can set *x* as the image configuration option for one or more widgets. The widgets display the image rather than text. For image-processing functionality on many image formats (including JPEG, PNG, and TIFF), use PIL, the Python Imaging Library (*http://www.pythonware.com/products/pil/*), which is designed to work with Tkinter. I do not cover PIL further in this book.

Tkinter also supplies class BitmapImage, whose instances are usable wherever instances of PhotoImage are. BitmapImage supports some file formats known as "bitmaps." I do not cover BitmapImage further in this book.

Being set as the image configuration option of a widget is not enough to keep instances of PhotoImage and BitmapImage alive. Hold such instances in a Python container object, such as a list or dictionary, so that the instances are not garbage-collected. The following example shows how to display some GIF images:

```
import os
import Tkinter

root = Tkinter.Tk()
L = Tkinter.Listbox(selectmode=Tkinter.SINGLE)
gifsdict = {}

dirpath = 'imgs'
for gifname in os.listdir(dirpath):
    if not gifname[0].isdigit(): continue
    gifpath = os.path.join(dirpath, gifname)
    gif = Tkinter.PhotoImage(file=gifpath)
    gifsdict[gifname] = gif
    L.insert(Tkinter.END, gifname)

L.pack()
img = Tkinter.Label()
img.pack()
def list_entry_clicked(*ignore):
    imgname = L.get(L.curselection()[0])
    img.config(image=gifsdict[imgname])
L.bind('<ButtonRelease-1>', list_entry_clicked)
root.mainloop()
```

Assuming you have in some directory ('imgs' in the example) several GIF files whose filenames start with digits, the example loads the images into memory, shows the names in a Listbox instance, and shows in a Label instance the GIF whose file you click on. For simplicity, the example does not give the Listbox widget a Scrollbar (we'll see how to equip a Listbox with a Scrollbar in "Scrollbar" on page 419).

Commonly Used Simple Widgets

The Tkinter module provides a number of simple widgets that cover most of the needs of simple GUI applications. This section documents the Button, Checkbutton, Entry, Label, Listbox, Radiobutton, Scale, and Scrollbar widgets.

Button

Class Button implements a *pushbutton*, which the user clicks to execute an action. Instantiate Button with option text=*somestring* to let the button show text, or image=*imageobject* to let the button show an image. You normally also use command=*callable* to have *callable* execute without arguments when the user clicks the button. *callable* can be a function, a bound method of an object, an instance of a class with a __call__ method, or a lambda.

Besides methods common to all widgets, an instance *b* of class Button supplies two button-specific methods.

flash   *b*.flash( )

Draws the user's attention to button *b* by redrawing *b* a few times, alternatively in normal and active states.

invoke   *b*.invoke( )

Calls without arguments the callable object that is *b*'s command option, just like *b*.cget('command')( ). This can be handy when, within some other action, you want the program to act just as if the button had been clicked.

Checkbutton

Class Checkbutton implements a *checkbox*, which is a little box, optionally displaying a checkmark, that the user clicks to toggle on or off. Instantiate Checkbutton with exactly one of the two options text=*somestring* to label the box with text, or image=*imageobject* to label the box with an image. Optionally, use command=*callable* to have *callable* execute without arguments when the user clicks the box. *callable* can be a function, a bound method of an object, an instance of a class with a __call__ method, or a lambda.

An instance *c* of Checkbutton must be associated with a Tkinter variable object *v*, using configuration option variable=*v* of *c*. Normally, *v* is an instance of IntVar, and *v*'s value is 0 when the box is unchecked, and 1 when the box is checked. The value of *v* changes when the box gets checked or unchecked (either by the user clicking on it or by your code calling *c*'s methods deselect, select, and toggle). Vice versa, when the value of *v* changes, *c* shows or hides the checkmark as appropriate.

Besides methods common to all widgets, an instance *c* of class `Checkbutton` supplies five checkbox-specific methods.

deselect	`c.deselect()`
	Removes *c*'s checkmark, like `c.cget('variable').set(0)`.

flash	`c.flash()`
	Draws the user's attention to checkbox *c* by redrawing *c* a few times, alternately in normal and active states.

invoke	`c.invoke()`
	Calls without arguments the callable object that is *c*'s `command` option, just like `c.cget('command')()`.

select	`c.select()`
	Shows *c*'s checkmark, like `c.cget('variable').set(1)`.

toggle	`c.toggle()`
	Toggles the state of *c*'s checkmark, as if the user had clicked on *c*.

Entry

Class Entry implements a *text entry field* (a widget in which the user can input and edit a line of text). An instance *e* of Entry supplies several methods and configuration options that allow fine-grained control of widget operation and contents, but, in most GUI programs, you can get by with just three Entry-specific idioms:

```
e.delete(0, END)             # clear the widget's contents
e.insert(END, somestring)    # append somestring to the widget's contents
somestring = e.get()         # get the widget's contents
```

An Entry instance with `state=DISABLED` displays a line of text and lets the user copy it to the clipboard. To display more than one line of text, use class Text, covered in "The Text Widget" on page 426. DISABLED stops your program, as well as the user, from altering *e*'s contents. To perform any alteration, temporarily set `state=NORMAL`:

```
e.config(state=NORMAL)       # allow alteration of e's contents
# call e.delete and/or e.insert as needed
e.config(state=DISABLED)     # make e's contents inalterable again
```

Label

Class Label implements a widget that just displays text or an image without interacting with user input. Instantiate Label either with option text=*somestring* to let the widget display text, or image=*imageobject* to let the widget display an image.

An instance L of class Label does *not* let the user copy text from L to the clipboard. L is therefore not the right widget to use when you show text that the user may want to copy and paste into an email or other document. Use an instance e of class Entry, with option state=DISABLED to avoid changes to e, as discussed in the previous section.

Listbox

Class Listbox displays textual items and lets the user select one or more items. To set the text items for an instance L of class Listbox, in most GUI programs you can get by with just two Listbox-specific idioms:

```
L.delete(0, END)            # clear the listbox's items
L.insert(END, somestring)   # add somestring to the listbox's items
```

To get the text item at index *idx*, call L.get(*idx*). To get a list of all text items between indices *idx1* and *idx2*, call L.get(*idx1*,*idx2*). To get the list of all text items, call L.get(0,END).

Option selectmode defines the *selection mode* of a Listbox instance L. The selection mode indicates how many items the user can select at once: one in modes SINGLE and BROWSE; more in modes MULTIPLE and EXTENDED. selectmode also defines which user actions cause items to be selected or unselected. BROWSE is the default; it differs from SINGLE in that the user may change the one selected item by moving up and down while holding down the left mouse button. In MULTIPLE mode, each click on a list item selects or deselects the item without affecting the selection state of other items. In EXTENDED mode, a click on a list item selects that item and deselects all other items; however, clicking while holding down a Ctrl key selects an item without deselecting others, and clicking while holding down a Shift key selects a range of items.

An instance L of class Listbox supplies three selection-related methods.

---

curselection   L.curselection()

> Returns a sequence of zero or more indices, from 0 upward, of selected items. Depending on the underlying release of Tk, curselection may return string representations of the int indices rather than ints. To remove this uncertainty, use:
>
> > *indices* = [int(x) for x in L.curselection()]
>
> [L.get(x) for x in L.curselection()] is always the list of the zero or more text items selected, no matter what form of indices curselection returns. So, if you care about selected text items rather than selected indices, the uncertainty is not an issue.

Tkinter

select_clear	`L.select_clear(i,j=None)`
	Deselects item *i* (all items from *i* to *j*, included, if *j* is not None).

select_set	`L.select_set(i,j=None)`
	Selects item *i* (all items from *i* to *j* if *j* is not None). select_set does not automatically deselect other items, even if *L*'s selection mode is SINGLE or BROWSE.

Radiobutton

Class Radiobutton implements a little box that is optionally checked. The user clicks the radiobutton to toggle it on or off. Radiobuttons come in groups; checking a radiobutton automatically unchecks all other radiobuttons of the same group. Call Radiobutton with text=*somestring* to label the button with text, or image=*imageobject* to label the button with an image. Optionally, use command=*callable* to have *callable* execute without arguments when the user clicks the radiobutton. *callable* can be a function, a bound method of an object, an instance of a class with a __call__ method, or a lambda.

An instance *r* of Radiobutton must be associated with a Tkinter variable object *v*, using configuration option variable=*v* of *r*, and with a designated value *X*, using option value=*X* of *r*. Most often, *v* is an instance of IntVar. The value of *v* changes to *X* when *r* is checked, either by the user clicking on *r* or by your code calling *r*.select( ). Vice versa, when the value of *v* changes, *r* is checked if, and only if, *v*.get( )==*X*. Several instances of Radiobutton form a group if, and only if, they have the same variable and different values; selecting an instance changes the variable's value, which automatically unchecks whichever other instance was previously checked. There is no special container to use to make Radiobutton instances into a group, nor is it even necessary for the Radiobutton instances to be children of the same widget. However, it would be confusing to the user if you spread a group of Radiobutton instances in disparate locations.

Besides methods common to all widgets, an instance *r* of class Radiobutton supplies four radiobutton-specific methods.

deselect	`r.deselect( )`
	Unchecks *r* and sets the associated variable object to an empty string, like *r*.cget('variable').set('').

flash	`c.flash( )`
	Draws the user's attention to *r* by redrawing *r* a few times, alternately in normal and active states.

invoke	c.invoke( )
	Calls without arguments the callable object that is *r*'s command option, just like r.cget('command')( ).

select	r.select( )
	Checks *r* and sets the associated variable object to *r*'s value, like r.cget('variable').set(r.cget('value')).

Scale

Class Scale implements a widget that lets the user input a value by sliding a cursor along a line. Scale sports configuration options to control the widget's looks and the value's range, but, in most GUI programs, the only option you specify is orient=HORIZONTAL when you want the line to be horizontal (by default, the line is vertical).

Besides methods common to all widgets, an instance *s* of class Scale supplies two scale-specific methods.

get	s.get( )
	Returns the current position of *s*'s cursor, normally on a scale of 0 to 100.

set	s.set(*p*)
	Sets the current position of *s*'s cursor, normally on a scale of 0 to 100.

Scrollbar

Class Scrollbar implements a widget similar to class Scale, which is used to scroll another widget (most often a Listbox, covered in "Listbox" on page 417; a Text, covered in "The Text Widget" on page 426 [see also "The ScrolledText Module" on page 426]; or a Canvas, covered in "The Canvas Widget" on page 436) rather than to let the user input a value.

A Scrollbar instance *s* is connected to the widget that *s* controls (e.g., a Listbox instance *L*) through a configuration option on each of *s* and *L*. For this purpose, widgets often associated with a scrollbar supply a method named yview and a configuration option named yscrollcommand for vertical scrolling. (For horizontal scrolling, widgets such as Text, Canvas, and Entry supply a method named xview and a configuration option named xscrollcommand.) For vertical scrolling, use *s*'s option command=*L*.yview so that user actions on *s* call *L*'s bound method yview to control *L*'s scrolling, and use *L*'s option yscrollcommand=*s*.set so that changes to *L*'s scrolling, in turn, adjust the way *s* displays by calling *s*'s bound method set. The following example uses a Scrollbar to control vertical scrolling of a Listbox:

```
import Tkinter
s = Tkinter.Scrollbar( )
L = Tkinter.Listbox( )
s.pack(side=Tkinter.RIGHT, fill=Tkinter.Y)
L.pack(side=Tkinter.LEFT, fill=Tkinter.Y)
s.config(command=L.yview)
L.config(yscrollcommand=s.set)
for i in range(30): L.insert(Tkinter.END, str(i)*3)
Tkinter.mainloop( )
```

Since *s* and *L* refer to each other, we cannot set their respective options on construction in both cases; for uniformity, we call their config methods to set the options later. In this example, we need to bind names to the widgets to be able to call pack and config methods of the widgets, use the widgets' bound methods, and populate the Listbox. *L*=Tkinter.Listbox( ).pack( ) would not bind *L* to the Listbox but rather to the result of pack (i.e., None). Code this in two statements (as in the previous example):

```
L = Tkinter.Listbox( )
L.pack( )
```

Container Widgets

The Tkinter module supplies widgets whose purpose is to contain other widgets. A Frame instance does nothing else but act as a container. A Toplevel instance (including Tkinter's *root window*, also known as the application's main window) is a top-level window, so your window manager interacts with it (typically by supplying suitable decoration and handling requests). To ensure that a widget *parent*, which must be a Frame or Toplevel instance, is the parent (a.k.a. the master) of another widget *child*, pass *parent* as the first parameter when you instantiate *child*.

Frame

Class Frame is a rectangular area of the screen contained in other frames or top-level windows. Frame's only purpose is to contain other widgets. Option borderwidth defaults to 0, so an instance of Frame normally displays no border. You can configure the option with borderwidth=1 if you want the frame border's outline to be visible.

Toplevel

Class Toplevel represents a rectangular area of the screen that is a top-level window and therefore receives decoration from whichever window manager handles your screen. Each instance of Toplevel interacts with the window manager and contains other widgets. Every Tkinter program has at least one top-level window, known as the root window. Instantiate Tkinter's root window with *root*=Tkinter.Tk( ); otherwise, Tkinter instantiates its root window implicitly as and when it is first needed. If you want more than one top-level window, instantiate the main one with *root*=Tkinter.Tk( ). Later, instantiate other top-level windows as needed, with calls such as *another_toplevel*=Tkinter.Toplevel( ).

An instance *T* of class Toplevel supplies many methods that enable interaction with the window manager. Many are platform-specific, relevant only with some window managers for the X Window System (used mostly on Unix-like systems). The cross-platform methods used most often are as follows.

deiconify   *T*.deiconify( )

Makes *T* display normally, even if previously *T* was iconic or invisible.

geometry   *T*.geometry([*geometry_string*])

T.geometry( ), without arguments, returns a string that encodes *T*'s size and position: *widthxheight+x_offset+y_offset*, with *width*, *height*, *x_offset*, and *y_offset* being decimal forms of the numbers of pixels. *T*.geometry(*S*), with one argument *S* (a string of the same form), sets *T*'s size and position according to *S*.

iconify   *T*.iconify( )

Makes *T* display as an icon (in Windows, as a button in the taskbar).

maxsize   *T*.maxsize([*width,height*])

T.maxsize( ), without arguments, returns a pair of integers whose two items are *T*'s maximum width and height in pixels. *T*.maxsize(*w,h*), with two integer arguments *w* and *h*, sets *T*'s maximum width and height in pixels to *w* and *h*, respectively.

minsize   *T*.minsize([*width,height*])

T.minsize( ), without arguments, returns a pair of integers whose two items are *T*'s minimum width and height in pixels. *T*.minsize(*w,h*), with two integer arguments *w* and *h*, sets *T*'s maximum width and height in pixels to *w* and *h*, respectively.

Tkinter

overrideredirect   *T*.overrideredirect([*avoid_decoration*])

T.overrideredirect( ), without arguments, returns False for a normal window, and True for a window that has asked the window manager to avoid decorating it. *T*.overrideredirect(*x*), with one argument *x*, asks the window manager to avoid decorating *T* if, and only if, *x* is true. A top-level window *T* without decoration has no title, and the user cannot act via the window manager to close, move, or resize *T*.

protocol   *T*.protocol(*protocol_name*,*callable*)

By calling protocol with a first argument of 'WM_DELETE_WINDOW' (the only valid value on most platforms), you install *callable* as the handler for attempts by the user to close *T* through the window manager (e.g., by clicking on the X in the upper-right corner on Windows and KDE). Python calls *callable* without arguments when the user makes such an attempt. *callable* itself must call *T*.destroy( ) to close *T*; otherwise, *T* stays open. By default, if *T*.protocol has not been called, such attempts implicitly call *T*.destroy( ) and thus unconditionally close *T*.

resizable   *T*.resizable([*width*,*height*])

T.resizable( ), without arguments, returns a pair of integers (each 0 or 1) that indicate if user action via the window manager can change *T*'s width and height, respectively. *T*.resizable(*w*,*h*), with two integer arguments *w* and *h* (each 0 or 1), sets the user's ability to change *T*'s width and height accordingly. With some releases of Tk, resizable, when called without arguments, returns a string such as '1 1' rather than a pair of integers such as (1,1). To remove this uncertainty, use:

```
resizable_wh = T.resizable( )
if len(resizable_wh) != 2: resizable_wh = map(int,
resizable_wh.split( ))
resizable_w, resizable_h = resizable_wh
```

state   *T*.state( )

Returns 'normal' if *T* is showing normally, 'withdrawn' if *T* is invisible, or 'icon' or 'iconic' (depending on the window manager) if *T* is showing as an icon (e.g., in Windows, only as a button in the taskbar).

title	T.title([title_string])

T.title( ), without arguments, returns a string that is *T*'s window title. T.title(*title_string*), with one argument *title_string*, sets *T*'s window title to string *title_string*.

withdraw	T.withdraw( )

Makes *T* invisible.

The following example shows a root window with an Entry widget that lets the user edit the window's title, and buttons to perform various root window operations:

```
import Tkinter
root = Tkinter.Tk( )
var = Tkinter.StringVar( )
entry = Tkinter.Entry(root, textvariable=var)
entry.focus_set( )
entry.pack( )
var.set(root.title( ))
def changeTitle( ): root.title(var.get( ))
Tkinter.Button(root, text="Change Title", command=changeTitle).pack( )
Tkinter.Button(root, text="Iconify", command=root.iconify).pack( )
Tkinter.Button(root, text="Close", command=root.destroy).pack( )
Tkinter.mainloop( )
```

Menus

Class Menu implements all kinds of menus: menu bars of top-level windows, submenus, and pop-up menus. To use a Menu instance *m* as the menu bar for a top-level window *w*, set *w*'s configuration option menu=*m*. To use *m* as a submenu of a Menu instance *x*, call *x*.add_cascade with menu=*m*. To use *m* as a pop-up menu, call *m*.post.

Besides configuration options covered in "Common Widget Options" on page 409, a Menu instance *m* supports option postcommand=*callable*. Tkinter calls *callable* without arguments each time it is about to display *m* (because of a call to *m*.post or because of user actions). Use this option to update a dynamic menu just in time when necessary.

By default, a Tkinter menu shows a tear-off entry (a dashed line before other entries), which lets the user get a copy of the menu in a separate Toplevel window. Since such tear-offs are not part of user interface standards on popular platforms, you may want to disable tear-off functionality by using configuration option tearoff=0 for the menu.

Tkinter

Menu-Specific Methods

Besides methods common to all widgets, an instance *m* of class Menu supplies several menu-specific methods.

add, **add_cascade,** **add_** **checkbutton,** **add_command,** **add_** **radiobutton,** **add_separator**	`m.add(entry_kind, **entry_options)` Adds after *m*'s existing entries a new entry whose kind is the string *entry_kind*, one of `'cascade'`, `'checkbutton'`, `'command'`, `'radiobutton'`, or `'separator'`. "Menu Entries" on page 425 covers entry kinds and options. Methods whose names start with add_ work like method add, but accept no positional argument; the kind of entry each method adds is implied by the method's name.
delete	`m.delete(i[,j])` `m.delete(i)` removes *m*'s *i* entry. `m.delete(i,j)` removes *m*'s entries from *i* to *j*, included. The first entry has index 0.
entryconfigure, **entryconfig**	`m.entryconfigure(i, **entry_options)` Changes entry options for *m*'s *i* entry. entryconfig is an exact synonym.
insert, **insert_cascade,** **insert_** **checkbutton,** **insert_** **command,** **insert_** **radiobutton,** **insert_** **separator**	`m.insert(i,entry_kind, **entry_options)` Adds before *m*'s entry *i* a new entry whose kind is the string *entry_kind*, one of `'cascade'`, `'checkbutton'`, `'command'`, `'radiobutton'`, or `'separator'`. "Menu Entries" on page 425 covers entry kinds and options. Methods whose names start with insert_ work just like method insert, without a second argument; the kind of entry each inserts is implied by the method's name.
invoke	`m.invoke(i)` Invokes *m*'s *i* entry, just as if the user clicked on it.
post	`m.post(x,y)` Displays *m* as a pop-up menu, with *m*'s upper-left corner at coordinates *x*, *y* (offsets in pixels from the upper-left corner of Tkinter's root window).

| **unpost** | `m.unpost( )` |
| | Closes *m* if *m* was displaying as a pop-up menu; otherwise, does nothing. |

Menu Entries

When a menu *m* displays, it shows a vertical (horizontal for a menu bar) list of entries. Each entry can be one of the following kinds:

cascade
> A submenu; option menu=*x* must give as *x* another Menu instance

checkbutton
> Similar to a Checkbutton widget; typical options are variable (to indicate a Tkinter variable object), onvalue, offvalue, and, optionally, command, like for a Checkbutton instance

command
> Similar to a Button widget; a typical option is command=*callable*

radiobutton
> Similar to a Radiobutton widget; typical options are variable (to indicate a Tkinter variable object), value, and, optionally, command, like for a Radiobutton instance

separator
> A line segment that separates groups of other entries

Other options often used with menu entries are:

image
> Option image=*x* uses *x*, a Tkinter image object, to label the entry with an image rather than text.

label
> Option label=*somestring* labels the entry with a text string.

underline
> Option underline=*x* gives *x* as the index of the character to underline within the entry's label (0 is the first character, 1 the second one, and so on).

Menu Example

The following example shows how to add a menu bar with typical File and Edit menus:

```
import Tkinter

root = Tkinter.Tk( )
bar = Tkinter.Menu( )
```

```
    def show(menu, entry): print menu, entry

    fil = Tkinter.Menu( )
    for x in 'New', 'Open', 'Close', 'Save':
        fil.add_command(label=x,command=lambda x=x:show('File',x))
    bar.add_cascade(label='File',menu=fil)

    edi = Tkinter.Menu( )
    for x in 'Cut', 'Copy', 'Paste', 'Clear':
        edi.add_command(label=x,command=lambda x=x:show('Edit',x))
    bar.add_cascade(label='Edit',menu=edi)
    root.config(menu=bar)
    Tkinter.mainloop( )
```

In this example, each menu command just outputs information to standard output for demonstration purposes. (Note the *x=x* idiom to snapshot the value of *x* at the time we create each lambda.) Otherwise, the current value of *x* at the time a lambda executes, 'Clear', would show up at each menu selection. A better alternative to the lambda expressions with the *x=x* idiom is a closure. Instead of def show, use:

```
    def mkshow(menu, entry):
        def emit( ): print menu, entry
        return emit
```

and use command=mkshow('File', x) and command=mkshow('Edit', x), respectively, in the calls to the add_command methods of *fil* and *edi*.

The Text Widget

Class Text implements a powerful multiline text editor, which can display images and embedded widgets as well as text in one or more fonts and colors. An instance *t* of Text supports many ways to refer to specific points in *t*'s contents. *t* supplies methods and configuration options, which allows fine-grained control of operations, content, and rendering. This section covers a large, frequently used subset of this vast functionality. In some very simple cases, you can get by with just three Text-specific idioms:

```
    t.delete('1.0', END)              # clear the widget's contents
    t.insert(END, astring)            # append astring to the widget's contents
    somestring = t.get('1.0', END)    # get the widget's contents as a string
```

END is an index on any Text instance *t*, indicating the end of *t*'s text. '1.0' is also an index, indicating the start of *t*'s text (first line, first column). For more about indices, see "Indices" on page 432.

The ScrolledText Module

The ScrolledText module of Python's standard library supplies a class named ScrolledText. To construct a ScrolledText instance, call ScrolledText.ScrolledText in exactly the same way you would call Tkinter.Text. A ScrolledText instance *s* is exactly the same as a Text instance, except that *s* automatically provides a scrollbar for the Text instance it wraps.

Text Widget Methods

An instance *t* of Text supplies many methods. (Methods dealing with marks and tags are covered in "Marks" on page 428 and "Tags" on page 429.) Many methods accept one or two indices into *t*'s contents. The most frequently used methods are the following.

delete	*t*.delete(*i*[,*j*])
	t.delete(*i*) removes *t*'s character at index *i*. *t*.delete(*i*,*j*) removes all characters from index *i* to index *j*, included.

get	*t*.get(*i*[,*j*])
	t.get(*i*) returns *t*'s character at index *i*. *t*.get(*i*,*j*) returns a string that joins all characters from index *i* to index *j*, included.

image_create	*t*.image_create(*i*,**window_options*)
	Inserts an embedded image in *t*'s contents at index *i*. Call image_create with option image=*e*, where *e* is a Tkinter image object, as covered in "Tkinter Images" on page 414.

insert	*t*.insert(*i*,*s*[,*tags*])
	Inserts string *s* in *t*'s contents at index *i*. *tags*, if supplied, is a sequence of strings to attach as tags to the new text, as covered in "Tags" on page 429.

search	*t*.search(*pattern*,*i*,**search_options*)
	Finds the first occurrence of string *pattern* in *t*'s contents not earlier than index *i* and returns a string that is the index of the occurrence, or an empty string '' if it is not found. Option nocase=True makes the search case-insensitive; by default, or with an explicit option nocase=False, the search is case-sensitive. Option stop=*j* makes the search stop at index *j*; by default, the search wraps around to the start of *t*'s contents. When you need to avoid wrapping, use stop=END.

see	*t*.see(*i*)
	Scrolls *t*, if needed, to make sure the contents at index *i* are visible. If the contents at index *i* are already visible, see does nothing.

window_create   *t*.window_create(*i*,***window_options*)

Inserts an embedded widget in *t*'s contents at index *i*. *t* must be the parent of the widget *w* that you are inserting. Call window_create either with option window=*w* to insert an already existing widget *w*, or with option create=*callable*. If you use option create, Tkinter calls *callable* without arguments the first time the embedded widget needs to be displayed, and *callable* must create and return a widget *w* whose parent is *t*. Option create lets you arrange the creation of embedded widgets just in time, which is a useful optimization when you have many embedded widgets in a very long text.

xview, yview   *t*.xview([...]) *t*.yview([...])

xview and yview handle scrolling in horizontal and vertical directions, respectively, and accept several different patterns of arguments. *t*.xview( ), without arguments, returns a tuple of two floats between 0.0 and 1.0, indicating the fraction of *t*'s contents corresponding to the first (leftmost) and last (rightmost) currently visible columns. *t*.xview(MOVETO,*frac*) scrolls *t* left or right so that the first (leftmost) visible column becomes the one that corresponds to fraction *frac* of *t*'s contents, between 0.0 and 1.0. yview supports the same patterns of arguments, but uses lines rather than columns, and scrolls up and down rather than left and right. yview supports one more pattern of arguments: *t*.yview(*i*), for any index *i*, scrolls *t* up or down so that the first (topmost) visible line becomes the one of index *i*.

Marks

A *mark* on a Text instance *t* is a name that indicates a point within the contents of *t*. INSERT and CURRENT are predefined marks on any Text instance *t*, with predefined meanings. INSERT names the point where the *insertion cursor* (also known as the text caret) is located in *t*. By default, when the user enters text at the keyboard with the focus on *t*, *t* inserts the text at index INSERT. CURRENT names the point in *t* that was closest to the mouse cursor when the user last moved the mouse within *t*. By default, when the user clicks the mouse on *t*, *t* gets focus and sets INSERT to CURRENT.

To set other marks on *t*, call method *t*.mark_set. Each mark is an arbitrary string without whitespace. To avoid confusion with other forms of index, use no punctuation in a mark. A mark is an index, as covered in "Indices" on page 432; you can pass a string that is a mark on *t* wherever a method of *t* accepts an index argument.

When you insert or delete text before a mark *m*, *m* moves accordingly. Deleting a portion of text that surrounds *m* does not remove *m*. To remove a mark on *t*, call method *t*.mark_unset. What happens when you insert text at a mark *m* depends on *m*'s gravity setting, which can be RIGHT (the default) or LEFT. When *m* has gravity RIGHT, *m* moves to remain at the end (i.e., to the right) of text inserted at *m*. When *m* has gravity LEFT, *m* does not move when you insert text at *m*: text inserted at *m* goes after *m*, and *m* itself remains at the start (i.e., to the left) of such inserted text.

A Text instance *t* supplies the following methods related to marks on *t*.

---

mark_gravity   *t*.mark_gravity(*mark*[,*gravity*])

> *mark* is a mark on *t*. *t*.mark_gravity(*mark*) returns *mark*'s gravity setting, RIGHT or LEFT. *t*.mark_gravity(*mark*,*gravity*) sets *mark*'s gravity to *gravity*, which must be RIGHT or LEFT.

---

mark_set   *t*.mark_set(*mark*,*i*)

> If *mark* was not yet a mark on *t*, mark_set creates *mark* at index *i*. If *mark* was already a mark on *t*, mark_set moves *mark* to index *i*.

---

mark_unset   *t*.mark_unset(*mark*)

> *mark* is a user-defined mark on *t* (not one of the predefined marks INSERT or CURRENT). mark_unset removes *mark* from among the marks on *t*.

Tags

A *tag* on a Text instance *t* is a symbolic name that indicates zero or more regions (ranges) in the contents of a Text instance *t*. SEL is a predefined tag on any Text instance *t* and names a single range of *t* that is selected, normally by the user dragging over it with the mouse. Tkinter typically displays the SEL range with distinctive background and foreground colors. To create other tags on *t*, call the *t*.tag_add or *t*.tag_config method, or use optional parameter *tags* of method *t*.insert. The ranges of various tags on *t* may overlap. *t* renders text that has several tags by using options from the uppermost tag, according to calls to methods *t*.tag_raise or *t*.tag_lower. By default, a tag created more recently is above one created earlier.

Each tag is an arbitrary string that contains no whitespace. Each tag has two indices: first (start of the tag's first range) and last (end of the tag's last range). You can pass a tag's index wherever a method of *t* accepts an index argument. SEL_FIRST and SEL_LAST indicate the first and last indices of predefined tag SEL.

A Text instance *t* supplies the following methods related to tags on *t*.

tag_add t.tag_add(*tag*,*i*[,*j*])

   t.tag_add(*tag*,*i*) adds tag *tag* to the single character at index *i* in
   t. t.tag_add(*tag*,*i*,*j*) adds tag *tag* to characters from index *i* to
   index *j*.

---

tag_bind t.tag_bind(*tag*,*event_name*,*callable*[,'+'])

   t.tag_bind(*tag*,*event_name*,*callable*) sets *callable* as the callback
   for *event_name* on *tag*. t.tag_bind(*tag*,*event_name*,*callable*,'+')
   adds *callable* to the previous bindings. Events, callbacks, and
   bindings are covered in "Tkinter Events" on page 446.

---

tag_cget t.tag_cget(*tag*,*tag_option*)

   Returns the value currently associated with option *tag_option* for
   tag *tag*. For example, t.tag_cget(SEL,'background') returns the
   color that t is using as the background of t's selected range.

---

tag_config t.tag_config(*tag*,**tag_options*)

   Sets or changes tag options associated with tag *tag*, which determines the way t renders text in *tag*'s region. The most frequently
   used tag options are:

   background
   foreground
       Background and foreground colors

   bgstipple
   fgstipple
       Background and foreground stipples, typically 'gray12',
       'gray25', 'gray50', or 'gray75'; solid colors by default (no
       stippling)

   borderwidth
       Width in pixels of the text border; default is 0 (no border)

   font
       Font used for text in the tag's ranges (see "Fonts" on page 433)

   justify
       Text justification: LEFT (default), CENTER, or RIGHT

   lmargin1
   lmargin2
   rmargin
       Left margin (first line, other lines) and right margin (all lines),
       in pixels; default is 0 (no margin)

offset
> Offset from baseline in pixels (greater than 0 for superscript, less than 0 for subscript); default is 0 (no offset—i.e., the text is aligned with the baseline)

overstrike
> If true, draws a line right over the text

relief
> Text relief: FLAT (default), SUNKEN, RAISED, GROOVE, or RIDGE

spacing1, spacing2, spacing3
> Extra spacing in pixels (before first line, between lines, or after last line); default is 0 (no extra spacing)

underline
> If true, draws a line under the text

wrap
> Wrapping mode: WORD (default), CHAR, or NONE

For example:

```
t.tag_config(SEL,background='black',foreground='yellow')
```

tells *t* to display *t*'s selected range with yellow text on a black background.

---

tag_delete `t.tag_delete(`*tag*`)`

Forgets all information associated with tag *tag* on *t*.

---

tag_lower `t.tag_lower(`*tag*`)`

Gives *tag*'s options minimum priority for ranges overlapping with other tags.

---

tag_names `t.tag_names([`*i*`])`

Returns a list of strings whose items are all the tags that include index *i*. Called without arguments, returns a list of strings whose items are all the tags that currently exist on *t*.

---

tag_raise `t.tag_raise(`*tag*`)`

Gives *tag*'s options maximum priority for ranges overlapping with other tags.

---

tag_ranges `t.tag_ranges(`*tag*`)`

Returns a list with an even number of strings (zero if *tag* is not a tag on *t* or has no ranges), alternating start and stop indices of *tag*'s ranges.

tag_remove	*t*.tag_remove(*tag*,*i*[,*j*])
	t.tag_remove(*tag*,*i*) removes tag *tag* from the single character at index *i* in *t*. *t*.tag_remove(*tag*,*i*,*j*) removes tag *tag* from characters from index *i* to index *j*. Removing a tag from characters that do not have that tag is an innocuous no-operation.
tag_unbind	*t*.tag_unbind(*tag*,*event*)
	t.tag_unbind(*tag*,*event*) removes any binding for *event* on *tag*'s ranges. Events and bindings are covered in "Tkinter Events" on page 446.

Indices

All ways to indicate a spot in the contents of a Text instance *t* are known as *indices* on *t*. The basic form of an index is a string of the form '%d.%d'%(*L*,*C*), which indicates the spot in the text that is at line *L* (the first line is 1), column *C* (the first column is 0). For example, '1.0' is a basic-form index that indicates the start of text for any *t*. *t*.index(*i*) returns the basic-form equivalent to an index *i* of any form.

END is an index that indicates the end of text for any *t*. '%d.end'%*L*, for any line number *L*, is an index that indicates the end (the '\n' end-of-line marker) of line *L*. For example, '1.end' indicates the end of the first line. To get the number of characters in line number *L* of a Text instance *t*, you can use:

```
def line_length(t, L):
    return int(t.index('%d.end'%L).split('.')[-1])
```

'@%d,%d'%(*x*,*y*) is also an index on *t*, where *x* and *y* are coordinates in pixels within *t*'s window.

Any tag on *t* is associated with two indices: strings '%s.first'%*tag* (start of *tag*'s first range) and '%s.last'%*tag* (end of *tag*'s last range). For example, right after *t*.tag_add('mytag',*i*,*j*), 'mytag.first' indicates the same spot in *t* as index *i*, and 'mytag.last' indicates the same spot in *t* as index *j*. Using index 'x.first' or 'x.last' when *t* has no tag 'x' raises an exception.

SEL_FIRST and SEL_LAST are indices (start and end of the selection, SEL tag). Using SEL_FIRST or SEL_LAST when there is no selected range on *t* raises an exception.

Marks (covered in "Marks" on page 428), including predefined marks INSERT and CURRENT, are also indices. Any image or widget embedded in *t* is also an index on *t* (methods image_create and window_create are covered in image_create on page 427 and window_create on page 428).

Another form of index, *index expressions*, concatenates to the string form of any index one or more of the following modifier string literals:

`'+n chars'`
`'-n chars'`
> *n* characters toward the end or start of the text (including newlines)

`'+n lines'`
`'-n lines'`
> *n* lines toward the end or start of the text

`'linestart'`
`'lineend'`
> Column 0 in the index's line or the `'\n'` in the index's line

`'wordstart'`
`'wordend'`
> Start or end of the word that comprises the index (in this context, a *word* means a sequence of letters, digits, and underscores)

You can optionally omit spaces and abbreviate keywords down to one character. For example, `'%s-4c'%END` means "four characters before the end of *t*'s text contents," and `'%s+1line linestart'%SEL_LAST` means "the start of the line immediately after the line where *t*'s selection ends."

A Text instance *t* supplies two methods related to indices on *t*.

---

compare t.compare(i,op,j)

Returns True or False, reflecting the comparison of indices i and j, where a lower number means earlier, and *op* is one of `'<'`,`'>'`,`'<='`,`'>='`,`'=='`, or `'!='`. For example, t.compare(`'1.0+90c'`,`'<'`,END) returns True if *t* contains more than 90 characters, counting each line end as a character.

---

index t.index(i)

Returns the basic form `'L.C'` of index i, where L and C are decimal string forms of the line and column of i (lines start from 1; columns start from 0).

Fonts

You can change the font on any Tkinter widget with option font=*font*. In most cases, it makes no sense to change widgets' fonts. However, in Text instances, and for specific tags on them, changing fonts can be quite useful.

Module tkFont supplies class Font; attributes BOLD, ITALIC, and NORMAL to define font characteristics; and functions families (returns a sequence of strings that name all families of available fonts) and names (returns a sequence of strings that name all user-defined fonts). Frequently used font options are:

family
> Font family (e.g., 'courier' or 'helvetica')

size
> Font size (in points if positive, in pixels if negative)

slant
> NORMAL (default) or ITALIC

weight
> NORMAL (default) or BOLD

An instance F of Font supplies the following frequently used methods.

actual	F.actual([*font_option*])
	F.actual(), without arguments, returns a dictionary with all options actually used in F (best available approximations to those requested). F.actual(*font_option*) returns the value actually used in F for option *font_option*.
cget	F.cget(*font_option*)
	Returns the value configured (i.e., requested) in F for *font_option*.
config	F.config(**font_options*)
	F.config(), called without arguments, returns a dictionary with all options configured (i.e., requested) in F. Called with one or more named arguments, config sets font options in F's configuration.
copy	F.copy()
	Returns a font G that is a copy of F. You can then modify either or both of F and G separately, and any modifications on one do not affect the other.

Text Example

To exemplify some of the many features of class Text, the following example shows one way to highlight all occurrences of a string in the text:

```
from Tkinter import *
```

```
root = Tk()

# at top of root, left to right, put a Label, an Entry, and a Button
fram = Frame(root)
Label(fram,text='Text to find:').pack(side=LEFT)
edit = Entry(fram)
edit.pack(side=LEFT, fill=BOTH, expand=1)
edit.focus_set()
butt = Button(fram, text='Find')
butt.pack(side=RIGHT)
fram.pack(side=TOP)

# fill rest of root with a Text and put some text there
text = Text(root)
text.insert('1.0',
'''Nel mezzo del cammin di nostra vita
mi ritrovai per una selva oscura
che la diritta via era smarrita
''')
text.pack(side=BOTTOM)

# action-function for the Button: highlight all occurrences of string
def find():
    # remove previous uses of tag `found', if any
    text.tag_remove('found', '1.0', END)
    # get string to look for (if empty, no searching)
    s = edit.get()
    if s:
        # start from the beginning (and when we come to the end, stop)
        idx = '1.0'
        while 1:
            # find next occurrence, exit loop if no more
            idx = text.search(s, idx, nocase=1, stopindex=END)
            if not idx: break
            # index right after the end of the occurrence
            lastidx = '%s+%dc' % (idx, len(s))
            # tag the whole occurrence (start included, stop excluded)
            text.tag_add('found', idx, lastidx)
            # prepare to search for next occurrence
            idx = lastidx
        # use a red foreground for all the tagged occurrences
        text.tag_config('found', foreground='red')
    # give focus back to the Entry field
    edit.focus_set()

# install action-function to execute when user clicks Button
butt.config(command=find)

# start the whole show (go event-driven)
root.mainloop()
```

This example also shows how to use a Frame to perform a simple widget layout task (put three widgets side by side with the Text below them all). Figure 17-1 shows this example in action.

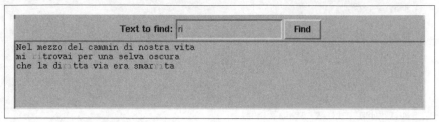

Figure 17-1. Highlighting in a Text instance

The Canvas Widget

Class Canvas is a powerful, flexible widget used for many purposes, including plotting and, in particular, building custom widgets. Building custom widgets is an advanced topic, and I do not cover it further in this book. This section covers only a subset of Canvas functionality used for the simplest kind of plotting.

Coordinates within a Canvas instance *c* are in pixels, with origin at the upper-left corner of *c*, and positive coordinates growing rightward and down. Some advanced methods let you change *c*'s coordinate system, but I do not cover them in this book.

What you draw on a Canvas instance *c* are *canvas items*: lines, polygons, Tkinter images, arcs, ovals, texts, and others. Each item has an *item handle* by which you can refer to the item. You can also assign symbolic names called *tags* to sets of canvas items (the sets of items with different tags can overlap). ALL is a predefined tag that applies to all items; CURRENT is a predefined tag that applies to the item under the mouse pointer.

Tags on a Canvas are different from tags on a Text. Canvas tags are nothing more than sets of items, with no independent existence. When you perform any operation with a Canvas tag as the item identifier, the operation occurs on the items that are in the tag's current set. It makes no difference if items are later removed from or added to that tag.

To create a canvas item, call on *c* a method with a name of the form create_*kindofitem*, which returns the new item's handle. Methods itemcget and itemconfig of *c* let you get and change items' options.

Canvas Methods on Items

A Canvas instance *c* supplies methods that you can call on items. The *item* argument can be an item's handle—as returned, for example, by c.create_line—or a tag, meaning all items in that tag's set (no items at all if the tag's set is currently empty), unless otherwise indicated in the method's description.

bbox   `c.bbox(`*item*`)`

Returns an approximate bounding box for *item*, which is a tuple of
four integers: the pixel coordinates of minimum x, minimum y,
maximum x, and maximum y, in that order. For example, `c.`
`bbox(ALL)` returns the minimum and maximum x and y coordinates
of all items on *c*. When *c* has no items at all, `c.bbox(ALL)` returns
`None`.

coords   `c.coords(`*item,*coordinates*`)`

Changes the coordinates for *item*. Operates on just one item. If
item is a tag, coords operates on an arbitrary item currently in the
tag's set. If *item* is a tag with an empty set, coords is an innocuous
no-operation.

delete   `c.delete(`*item*`)`

Deletes *item*. For example, `c.delete(ALL)` deletes all items on *c*.

gettags   `c.gettags(`*item*`)`

Returns the sequence of all tags whose sets include *item* (but not
tag `ALL`, which includes all items, nor `CURRENT`, whether or not it
includes *item*).

itemcget   `c.itemcget(`*item,option*`)`

Returns the value of *option* for *item*. Operates on just one item. If
item is a tag, itemcget returns the value of *option* for an arbitrary
item currently in the tag's set. If *item* is a tag with an empty set,
itemcget returns the empty string `''`.

itemconfig   `c.itemconfig(`*item,*options*`)`

Sets or changes the value of *options* for *item*. For example, `c.`
`itemconfig(ALL, fill='red')` sets all items on *c* to fill-color red.

tag_bind   `c.tag_bind(`*tag,event_name,callable*`[,'+'])`

`c.tag_bind(`*tag,event_name,callable*`)` sets *callable* as the callback
for *event_name* on the items currently in *tag*'s set. `c.`
`tag_bind(`*tag,event_name,callable*`,'+')` adds *callable* to the
previous bindings. Events, callbacks, and bindings are covered in
"Tkinter Events" on page 446.

tag_unbind   `c.tag_unbind(`*`tag`*`,`*`event`*`)`

                `c.tag_unbind(`*`tag`*`,`*`event`*`)` removes bindings for *event* on the items currently in *tag*'s set. Events and bindings are covered in "Tkinter Events" on page 446.

The Line Canvas Item

A Canvas instance *c* supplies one method to create a line item.

create_line   `c.create_line(*`*`coordinates`*`, **`*`line_options`*`)`

                Creates a line item with vertices at given *coordinates* and returns the item's handle. *coordinates* must be an even number of positional parameters, alternately x and y for each vertex of the line. Coordinates are in pixels, with origin (0,0) in the upper-left corner, x growing rightward, and y growing downward. You may set different coordinate systems on *c*, but I do not cover this option in this book. *line_options* may include:

                `arrow`
                      Which ends of the line have arrow heads: `NONE` (default), `FIRST`, `LAST`, or `BOTH`

                `fill`
                      The line's color (default is `black`)

                `smooth`
                      If true, the line is drawn as a smooth curve (a B-spline); otherwise (default), the line is drawn as a polygonal (a sequence of line segments)

                `tags`
                      A string to set one tag on the item or a tuple of strings to set multiple tags on the item

                `width`
                      Width of the line in pixels (default is 1)

                For example:

```
x=c.create_line(0,150, 50,100, 0,50, 50,0 smooth=1)
```

                draws an S-like curve on *c*, binding the curve's handle to name *x*. You can then change the curve's color to blue with:

```
c.itemconfig(x,fill='blue')
```

The Polygon Canvas Item

A Canvas instance *c* supplies one method to create a polygon item.

create_polygon   `c.create_polygon(*coordinates, **poly_options)`

Creates a polygon item with vertices at the given *coordinates* and returns the item's handle. *coordinates* must be an even number of positional parameters, alternately x and y for each vertex of the polygon, and there must be at least six positional parameters (at least three vertices). *poly_options* may include:

fill
>The polygon's interior color (default is black)

outline
>The polygon's perimeter color (default is black)

smooth
>If true, the polygon is drawn as a smooth curve (a B-spline); otherwise (default), the line is drawn as a normal polygon (a sequence of sides)

tags
>A string to set one tag on the item or a tuple of strings to set multiple tags on the item

width
>Width of the perimeter line in pixels (default 1)

For example:

```
x=c.create_polygon(0,150, 50,100, 0,50, 50,0, fill='',
outline='red')
```

draws two empty red triangles on *c* as a single polygon and binds the polygon's handle to name *x*. You can then fill the triangles with blue using:

```
c.itemconfig(x,fill='blue')
```

The Rectangle Canvas Item

A Canvas instance *c* supplies one method to create a rectangle item.

create_ rectangle   `c.create_rectangle(x0,y0,x1,y1,**rect_options)`

Creates a rectangle item with vertices at the given coordinates and returns the item's handle. *rect_options* may include:

fill
>The rectangle's interior color (default is empty)

outline
>The rectangle's perimeter color (default is black)

tags
>   A string to set one tag on the item or a tuple of strings to set
>   multiple tags on the item

width
>   Width of the perimeter line in pixels (default is 1)

The Text Canvas Item

A Canvas instance *c* supplies one method to create a text item.

create_text	`c.create_text(x,y,**text_options)`

Creates a text item at the given *x* and *y* coordinates and returns the item's handle. *text_options* may include:

anchor
>   The exact spot of the text's bounding box that *x* and *y* refer to;
>   may be N, E, S, W, NE, NW, SE, or SW—which are compass direc-
>   tions that indicate the corners and sides of the bounding
>   box—or CENTER (the default)

fill
>   The text's color (default is black)

font
>   Font to use for this text

tags
>   A string to set one tag on the item or a tuple of strings to set
>   multiple tags on the item

text
>   The text to display

A Simple Plotting Example

The following example shows how to use a Canvas to perform an elementary plot-ting task, graphing a user-specified function:

```
from Tkinter import *
import math

root = Tk()

# first, a row for function entry and action button
fram = Frame(root)
Label(fram,text='f(x):').pack(side=LEFT)
func = Entry(fram)
func.pack(side=LEFT, fill=BOTH, expand=1)
```

```
butt = Button(fram, text='Plot')
butt.pack(side=RIGHT)
fram.pack(side=TOP)

# then a row to enter bounds in
fram = Frame(root)
bounds = [  ]
for label in 'minX', 'maxX', 'minY', 'maxY':
    Label(fram,text=label+':').pack(side=LEFT)
    edit = Entry(fram, width=6)
    edit.pack(side=LEFT)
    bounds.append(edit)
fram.pack(side=TOP)

# and finally the canvas
c = Canvas(root)
c.pack(side=TOP, fill=BOTH, expand=1)

def minimax(values=[0.0, 1.0, 0.0, 1.0]):
    "Adjust and display X and Y bounds"
    for i in range(4):
        edit = bounds[i]
        try: values[i] = float(edit.get())
        except: pass
        edit.delete(0, END)
        edit.insert(END, '%.2f'%values[i])
    return values

def plot():
    "Plot given function with given bounds"
    minx, maxx, miny, maxy = minimax()

    # get and compile the function
    f = func.get()
    f = compile(f, f, 'eval')

    # get Canvas X and Y dimensions
    CX = c.winfo_width()
    CY = c.winfo_height()

    # compute coordinates for line
    coords = [  ]
    for i in range(0,CX,5):
        coords.append(i)
        x = minx + ((maxx-minx)*i)/CX
        y = eval(f, vars(math), {'x':x})
        j = CY - CY*(y-miny)/(maxy-miny)
        coords.append(j)

    # draw line
    c.delete(ALL)
    c.create_line(*coords)
```

```
butt.config(command=plot)

# give an initial sample in lieu of docs
f = 'sin(x) + cos(x)'
func.insert(END, f)
minimax([0.0, 10.0, -2.0, 2.0])

root.mainloop( )
```

Figure 17-2 shows the output that results from this example.

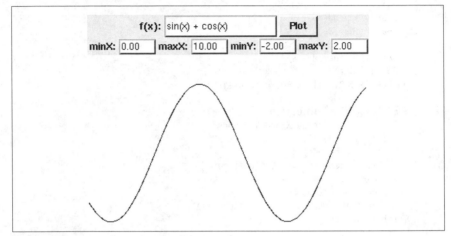

Figure 17-2. A sample canvas

Layout Management

In all examples so far, we have made widgets visible via method pack. This is typical of real-life Tkinter usage. However, two other layout managers are sometimes useful. This section covers all three layout managers provided by Tkinter: the packer, gridder, and placer. Never mix layout managers for the same container widget: all children of a given container widget must be handled by the same layout manager, or very strange effects (including Tkinter going into infinite loops) may result.

The Packer

Calling method pack on a widget delegates widget layout management to a simple, flexible layout manager known as the Packer. The Packer sizes and positions widgets within a container (parent) widget according to each widget's space needs (including padx and pady). Each widget w supplies the following Packer-related methods.

pack	w.pack(**pack_options)

Delegates layout management to the packer. *pack_options* may include:

expand
> When true, *w* expands to fill any space not otherwise used in *w*'s parent.

fill
> Determines whether *w* fills any extra space allocated to it by the packer or keeps its own minimal dimensions: NONE (default), X (fill only horizontally), Y (fill only vertically), or BOTH (fill both horizontally and vertically).

side
> Determines which side of the parent *w* packs against: TOP (default), BOTTOM, LEFT, or RIGHT. To avoid confusion, don't mix different values for option side= in widgets that are children of the same container. When more than one child requests the same side (for example, TOP), the rule is first come, first served: the first child packs at the top, the second child packs second from the top, and so on.

pack_forget	w.pack_forget( )

The packer forgets about *w*. *w* remains alive but becomes invisible; you may show *w* again later by calling w.pack again (or, perhaps, w.grid or w.place).

pack_info	w.pack_info( )

Returns a dictionary with the current *pack_options* of *w*.

The Gridder

Calling method grid on a widget delegates widget layout management to a specialized layout manager called the Gridder. The Gridder sizes and positions each widget into cells of a table (grid) within a container (parent) widget. Each widget *w* supplies the following Gridder-related methods.

Tkinter

grid

w.grid(**grid_options*)

Delegates layout management to the gridder. *grid_options* may include:

column
> The column to put *w* in; the default is 0 (leftmost column).

columnspan
> How many columns *w* occupies; the default is 1.

ipadx, ipady
> How many pixels to pad *w*, horizontally and vertically, inside *w*'s borders.

padx, pady
> How many pixels to pad *w*, horizontally and vertically, outside *w*'s borders.

row
> The row to put *w* in; the default is the first row that is still empty.

rowspan
> How many rows *w* occupies; the default is 1.

sticky
> What to do if the cell is larger than *w*. By default, with sticky='', *w* is centered in its cell. sticky may be the string concatenation of zero or more of N, E, S, W, NE, NW, SE, and SW, which are compass directions that indicate the sides and corners of the cell to which *w* sticks. For example, sticky=N means that *w* sticks to the cell's top and is centered horizontally, while sticky=N+S means that *w* expands vertically to fill the cell and is centered horizontally.

For example:

```
import Tkinter
root = Tkinter.Tk( )
for r in range(3):
    for c in range(4):
        Tkinter.Label(root, text='R%s/C%s'%(r,c),
            borderwidth=1 ).grid(row=r,column=c)
root.mainloop( )
```

displays 12 labels arrayed in a 3 × 4 grid.

---

grid_forget

w.grid_forget( )

The gridder forgets about *w*. *w* remains alive but becomes invisible; you may show *w* again later by calling *w*.grid again (or, perhaps, *w*.pack or *w*.place).

grid_info   `w.grid_info()`

Returns a dictionary with the current *grid_options* of *w*.

The Placer

Calling method place on a widget explicitly handles widget layout management
thanks to a simple layout manager called the Placer. The Placer sizes and positions each widget *w* within a container (parent) widget exactly as *w* explicitly
requires. Other layout managers are usually preferable, but the Placer can help
you implement custom layout managers. Each widget *w* supplies the following
Placer-related methods.

place   `w.place(**place_options)`

Delegates layout management to the placer. *place_options* may
include:

anchor
> The exact spot of *w* other options refer to: N, E, S, W, NE, NW, SE,
> or SW, which are compass directions that indicate the corners
> and sides of *w*; the default is NW (upper-left corner of *w*)

bordermode
> INSIDE (the default) to indicate that other options refer to the
> parent's inside (ignoring the parent's border); OUTSIDE otherwise

height
width
> Height and width in pixels

relheight
relwidth
> Height and width as a float between 0.0 and 1.0, and as a frac-
> tion of the height and width of the parent widget

relx
rely
> Horizontal and vertical offset as a float between 0.0 and 1.0,
> and as a fraction of the height and width of the parent widget

x, y
> Horizontal and vertical offset in pixels

place_forget   `w.place_forget()`

The placer forgets about *w*. *w* remains alive but becomes invisible;
you may show *w* again later by calling *w*.place again (or, perhaps,
w.pack or *w*.grid).

place_info	w.place_info()

Returns a dictionary with the current *place_options* of w.

Tkinter Events

So far, we've seen only one kind of event handling: callbacks performed on callables set with the command= option of buttons and menu entries. Tkinter also lets you set callables to handle a variety of events. Tkinter does not let you create custom events: you are limited to working with events predefined by Tkinter itself.

The Event Object

General event callbacks must accept one argument *event* that is a Tkinter event object. Such an event object has several attributes that describe the event:

char
: A single-character string that is the key's code (only for keyboard events)

keysym
: A string that is the key's symbolic name (only for keyboard events)

num
: Button number (only for mouse-button events); 1 and up

x, y
: Mouse position, in pixels, relative to the upper-left corner of the widget

x_root
y_root
: Mouse position, in pixels, relative to the upper-left corner of the screen

widget
: The widget in which the event has occurred

Binding Callbacks to Events

To bind a callback to an event in a widget w, call w.bind and describe the event with a string, usually enclosed in angle brackets ('<...>'). The following example prints 'Hello World' each time the user presses the Enter key:

```
from Tkinter import *

root = Tk()
def greet(*ignore): print 'Hello World'
root.bind('<Return>', greet)
root.mainloop()
```

Method tag_bind of classes Canvas and Text (covered in tag_bind on page 430 and tag_bind on page 437) binds event callbacks to sets of items of a Canvas instance, or ranges within a Text instance.

Event Names

Common event names, almost all of which are enclosed in angle brackets, fall into a few categories.

Keyboard events

Key

> The user clicked any key. The event object's attribute char tells you which key, for normal keys only. Attribute keysym is equal to char for letters and digits, the character's name for punctuation, and the key's name for special keys.

Special keys

> Special keys have event names: F1, F2, and up are function keys; Left, Right, Up, and Down are arrows; Prior and Next are page-up and page-down; BackSpace, Delete, End, Home, Insert, Print, and Tab are the keys so labeled; Escape is the key labeled Esc; Return is the key labeled Enter; Caps_Lock, Num_Lock, and Scroll_Lock are lock-request keys; and Alt_L, Control_L, Shift_L are the modifier keys Alt, Ctrl, Shift (without distinction among multiple instances of such modifier keys in a keyboard). All of these event names are placed within angle brackets, like almost all event names.

Normal keys

> Normal keys have event names *without* surrounding angle brackets—the only event names that lack brackets. The event name of each normal key is the key's character, such as 'w', '1', or '+'. Exceptions are the Space key, with event name '<space>', and the key of the less-than character, with event name '<less>'.
>
> Key names can be modified by the prefixes 'Alt-', 'Shift-', and 'Control-'. In this case, the event name is always surrounded with '<...>'; for example, '<Control-Q>' and '<Alt-Up>'.

Mouse events

Button-1
Button-2
Button-3

> The user pressed the left, middle, or right mouse-button. A two-button mouse produces only events Button-1 and Button-3, since it has no middle button.

B1-Motion
B2-Motion
B3-Motion

> The user moved the mouse while pressing the left, middle, or right mouse button (mouse motion without pressing a button can produce only Enter and Leave).

```
ButtonRelease-1
ButtonRelease-2
ButtonRelease-3
```
The user released the left, middle, or right mouse button.

```
Double-Button-1
Double-Button-2
Double-Button-3
```
The user double-clicked the left, middle, or right mouse button (such an action also generates Button-1, Button-2, or Button-3 before the double-click event).

`Enter`
The user moved the mouse so that the mouse entered the widget.

`Leave`
The user moved the mouse so that the mouse exited the widget.

Event-Related Methods

Each widget *w* supplies the following event-related methods.

bind	w.bind(*event_name*,*callable*[,'+'])
	w.bind(*event_name*,*callable*) sets *callable* as the callback for *event_name* on w. w.bind(*event_name*,*callable*,'+') adds *callable* to the previous bindings for *event_name* on w.
bind_all	w.bind_all(*event_name*,*callable*[,'+'])
	w.bind_all(*event_name*,*callable*) sets *callable* as the callback for *event_name* on all widgets. w.bind_all(*event_name*,*callable*,'+') adds *callable* to the previous bindings for *event_name* on all widgets.
unbind	w.unbind(*event_name*)
	Removes all callbacks for *event_name* on w.
unbind_all	w.unbind_all(*event_name*)
	Removes all callbacks for *event_name* on any widget, as set by bind_all.

An Events Example

The following example detects key and mouse events with bind_all:

```
import Tkinter
from Tkinter import *

root = Tk()
prompt='Click any button, or press a key'
L = Label(root, text=prompt, width=len(prompt))
L.pack()

def key(event):
    if event.char==event.keysym:
        msg ='Normal Key %r' % event.char
    elif len(event.char)==1:
        msg ='Punctuation Key %r (%r)' % (event.keysym, event.char)
    else:
        msg ='Special Key %r' % event.keysym
    L.config(text=msg)
L.bind_all('<Key>', key)

def do_mouse(eventname):
    def mouse_binding(event):
        L.config(text='Mouse event %s' % eventname)
    L.bind_all('<%s>'%eventname, mouse_binding)
for i in range(1,4):
    do_mouse('Button-%s'%i)
    do_mouse('ButtonRelease-%s'%i)
    do_mouse('Double-Button-%s'%i)

root.mainloop()
```

Other Callback-Related Methods

Each widget *w* supplies the following other callback-related methods.

---

after   w.after(*ms,callable,*args*)

Starts a timer to call *callable(*args)* *ms* milliseconds from now. Returns an ID that you can pass to after_cancel to cancel the timer. The timer is one-shot: to call a function periodically, the function itself must call after to install itself again.

---

after_cancel   w.after_cancel(*id*)

Cancels the timer identified by *id*.

Tkinter

after_idle   `w.after_idle(callable,*args)`

Registers a callback to *callable(*args)* to be performed when the event loop is idle (i.e., when all pending events have been processed).

The following example uses `after` to implement a simple digital clock:

```
import Tkinter
import time

curtime = ''
clock = Tkinter.Label()
clock.pack()

def tick():
    global curtime
    newtime = time.strftime('%H:%M:%S')
    if newtime != curtime:
        curtime = newtime
        clock.config(text=curtime)
    clock.after(200, tick)
tick()
clock.mainloop()
```

Method `after` is crucially important. Many widgets have no callbacks to let you know about user actions on them; to track such actions, polling is the only option. For example, here's how to poll with `after` to track a `Listbox` selection in real time:

```
import Tkinter

F1 = Tkinter.Frame()
s = Tkinter.Scrollbar(F1)
L = Tkinter.Listbox(F1)
s.pack(side=Tkinter.RIGHT, fill=Tkinter.Y)
L.pack(side=Tkinter.LEFT, fill=Tkinter.Y, yscrollcommand=s.set)
s['command'] = L.yview
for i in range(30): L.insert(Tkinter.END, str(i))
F1.pack(side=Tkinter.TOP)

F2 = Tkinter.Frame()
lab = Tkinter.Label(F2)
def poll():
    lab.after(200, poll)
    sel = L.curselection()
    lab.config(text=str(sel))
lab.pack()
F2.pack(side=Tkinter.TOP)

poll()
Tkinter.mainloop()
```

Testing, Debugging, and Optimizing

You're not finished with a programming task when you're done writing the code; you're finished when the code runs correctly and with acceptable performance. *Testing* (covered in "Testing" on page 452) means verifying that code runs correctly by exercising the code under known conditions and checking that results are as expected. *Debugging* (covered in "Debugging" on page 461) means discovering causes of incorrect behavior and repairing them (repair is often easy, once you figure out the causes).

Optimizing (covered in "Optimization" on page 474) is often used as an umbrella term for activities meant to ensure acceptable performance. Optimizing breaks down into *benchmarking* (measuring performance for given tasks to check that it's within acceptable bounds), *profiling* (instrumenting the program to identify performance bottlenecks), and optimizing proper (removing bottlenecks to make overall program performance acceptable). Clearly, you can't remove performance bottlenecks until you've found out where they are (using profiling), which in turn requires knowing that there *are* performance problems (using benchmarking).

This chapter covers the three subjects in the natural order in which they occur in development: testing first and foremost, debugging next, and optimizing last. However, most programmers' enthusiasm focuses on optimization: testing and debugging are often (wrongly, in my opinion) perceived as being chores, while optimization is perceived as being fun. As a consequence, if you were to read only one section of the chapter, I would suggest that section be "Developing a Fast-Enough Python Application" on page 474, which summarizes the Pythonic approach to optimization—close to Jackson's classic "Rules of Optimization: Rule 1: Don't do it. Rule 2 (for experts only): Don't do it yet."

All of these tasks are large and important, and each could fill at least a book by itself. This chapter does not even come close to exploring every related technique and implication; it focuses on Python-specific techniques, approaches, and tools.

Testing

In this chapter, I distinguish between two rather different kinds of testing: unit testing and system testing. Testing is a rich and important field, and many more distinctions could be drawn, but I focus on the issues of most immediate importance to software developers. Many developers are reluctant to spend time on testing, seeing it as time subtracted from "real" development, but this attitude is short-sighted: defects are easier to fix the earlier you find out about them, so each hour spent developing tests can amply pay back for itself by finding defects ASAP, thus saving many hours of debugging that would otherwise have been needed in later phases of the software development cycle.

Unit Testing and System Testing

Unit testing means writing and running tests to exercise a single module or an even smaller unit, such as a class or function. *System testing* (also known as *functional* or *integration* testing) involves running an entire program with known inputs. Some classic books on testing also draw the distinction between *white-box testing*, done with knowledge of a program's internals, and *black-box testing*, done without such knowledge. This classic viewpoint parallels, but does not exactly duplicate, the modern one of unit versus system testing.

Unit and system testing serve different goals. Unit testing proceeds apace with development; you can and should test each unit as you're developing it. One modern approach is known as *test-driven development* (TDD): for each feature that your program must have, you first write unit tests and only then do you proceed to write code that implements the feature. TDD may seem upside-down, but it has several advantages. For example, it ensures that you won't omit unit tests for some feature. Further, developing test-first is helpful because it urges you to focus first on the tasks a certain function, class, or method should accomplish, and to deal only afterward with how to implement that function, class, or method. A recent important innovation along the lines of TDD is *behavior-driven development*; see *http://behavior-driven.org/* for all details about this new and promising development methodology.

In order to test a unit, which may depend on other units not yet fully developed, you often have to write *stubs*, which are fake implementations of various units' interfaces that give known and correct responses in cases needed to test other units. The Mock module (*http://python-mock.sourceforge.net/*) can be very helpful in the implementation of many such stubs (a good tutorial, with links to other useful documents about Mock Objects, is at *http://xper.org/wiki/seminar/ PythonMockObjectTutorial*).

System testing comes afterward, since it requires the system to exist, with some subset of system functionality believed to be in working condition. System testing provides a sanity check: given that each module in the program works properly (passes unit tests), does the whole program work? If each unit is okay but the system as a whole is not, there is a problem in the integration between units, meaning the way the units cooperate. For this reason, system testing is also known as integration testing.

System testing is similar to running the system in production use, except that you fix the inputs in advance so that any problems you may find are easy to reproduce. The cost of failures in system testing is lower than in production use, since outputs from system testing are not used to make decisions, serve customers, control external systems, and so on. Rather, outputs from system testing are systematically compared with the outputs that the system should produce given the known inputs. The purpose is to find, in a cheap and reproducible way, any discrepancy between what the program should do and what the program actually does.

Failures discovered by system testing, just like system failures in production use, may reveal some defects in unit tests, as well as defects in the code. Unit testing may have been insufficient: a module's unit tests may have failed to exercise all needed functionality of that module. In this case, the unit tests clearly need to be beefed up. Do that *before* you change your code to fix the problem, then run the newly strengthened unit tests to confirm that they do now show the existence of the problem. Then fix the problem and run unit tests again to confirm they show no problem anymore. Finally, rerun the system tests to confirm that the problem has indeed gone away.

Most often, failures in system testing reveal communication problems within the development team: a module correctly implements a certain functionality, but another module expects different functionality. This kind of problem (an integration problem in the strict sense) is hard to pinpoint in unit testing. In good development practice, unit tests must run often, so it is crucial that they run fast. It's therefore essential that each unit can assume other units are working correctly and as expected.

Unit tests that are run in reasonably late stages of development can reveal integration problems if the system architecture is hierarchical, a common and reasonable organization. In such an architecture, lower-level modules depend on no others (except perhaps library modules, which you can assume to be correct), and thus the unit tests of such lower-level modules, if complete, suffice to assure correctness. Higher-level modules depend on lower-level ones, and therefore also depend on correct understanding about what functionality each module expects and supplies. Running complete unit tests on higher-level modules, using the true lower-level modules rather than stubs, exercises the interface between modules, as well as the higher-level modules' own code.

Unit tests for higher-level modules are thus run in two ways. You run the tests with stubs for the lower levels during the early stages of development when the lower-level modules are not yet ready or, later, when you need to check only the correctness of the higher levels. During later stages of development, you also regularly run the higher-level modules' unit tests using the true lower-level modules. In this way, you check the correctness of the whole subsystem, from the higher levels downward. Nevertheless, even in this favorable case, you *still* need to write and run system tests to make sure the whole system's functionality is exercised and checked, and that no interface between modules is neglected.

System testing is similar to running the program in normal ways. You need special support only to ensure that known inputs are supplied and that outputs are captured for comparison with expected outputs. This is easy for programs that perform I/O on files, but terribly hard for programs whose I/O relies on a GUI, network, or other communication with independent external entities. To simulate such external entities and make them predictable and entirely observable, you generally need platform-dependent infrastructure. Another useful piece of supporting infrastructure for system testing is a *testing framework* that automates the running of system tests, including logging of successes and failures. Such a framework can also help testers prepare sets of known inputs and corresponding expected outputs.

Both free and commercial programs for these purposes exist, but they are not dependent on which programming languages are used in the system under test. System testing is a close kin to what was classically known as black-box testing, or testing that is independent from the implementation of the system under test (and therefore, in particular, independent from the programming languages used for implementation). Instead, testing frameworks usually depend on the operating system platform on which they run, since the tasks they perform are platform-dependent: running programs with given inputs, capturing their outputs, and particularly simulating and capturing GUI, network, and other interprocess communication I/O. Since frameworks for system testing depend on the platform and not on programming languages, I do not cover them further in this book.

The doctest Module

The doctest module has the primary purpose of letting you create good usage examples in your code's docstrings by checking that the examples do in fact produce the results that your docstrings show for them. doctest recognizes such examples by looking within the docstring for the interactive Python prompt '>>> ', followed on the same line by a Python statement, and the statement's expected output on the next line.

As you're developing a module, keep the docstrings up to date and gradually enrich them with examples. Each time part of the module (e.g., a function) is ready, or even partially ready, make it a habit to add examples to the docstrings. Import the module into an interactive session, and interactively use the parts you just developed in order to provide examples with a mix of typical cases, limit cases, and failing cases. For this specific purpose only, use from *module* import * so that your examples don't prefix *module*. to each name the module supplies. Copy and paste the text of the interactive session into the docstring in an editor, adjust any mistakes, and you're almost done.

Your documentation is now enriched with examples, and readers will have an easier time following it, assuming you choose a good mix of examples and season it wisely with nonexample text. Make sure you have docstrings, with examples, for your module as a whole, and for each function, class, and method that the module exports. You may choose to skip functions, classes, and methods whose names start with _, since, as their names indicate, they're meant to be private implementation details; doctest by default ignores them, and so should most readers of your module.

Examples that don't match the way your code works are worse than useless. Documentation and comments are useful only if they match reality. Docstrings and comments often get out of date as code changes, and then they become misinformation, hampering rather than helping any reader of the source. Better to have no comments and docstrings at all than to have ones that lie. doctest can help you through the examples in your docstrings. A failing doctest run should prompt you to review the docstring that contains the failing examples, reminding you to keep the docstring's text updated, too.

At the end of your module's source, insert the following small snippet:

```
if __name__ == '__main__':
    import doctest
    doctest.testmod( )
```

This code calls function testmod of module doctest when you run your module as the main program. testmod examines all relevant docstrings (the module docstring, and docstrings of all public functions, public classes, and public methods of public classes). In each docstring, testmod finds all examples (by looking for occurrences of the interpreter prompt '>>> ', possibly preceded by whitespace) and runs each example. testmod checks that each example's results are equal to the output given in the docstring right after the example. In the case of exceptions, testmod ignores the traceback, and just checks that the expected and observed error messages are equal.

When everything goes right, testmod terminates silently. Otherwise, it outputs detailed messages about examples that failed, showing expected and actual output. Example 18-1 shows a typical example of doctest at work on a module *mod.py*.

Example 18-1. Using doctest

```
"""
This module supplies a single function reverseWords that reverses
a string by words.

>>> reverseWords('four score and seven years')
'years seven and score four'
>>> reverseWords('justoneword')
'justoneword'
>>> reverseWords('')
''

You must call reverseWords with one argument, and it must be a string:

>>> reverseWords( )
Traceback (most recent call last):
   ...
TypeError: reverseWords( ) takes exactly 1 argument (0 given)
>>> reverseWords('one', 'another')
Traceback (most recent call last):
   ...
TypeError: reverseWords( ) takes exactly 1 argument (2 given)
>>> reverseWords(1)
```

Example 18-1. Using doctest (continued)

```
Traceback (most recent call last):
  ...
AttributeError: 'int' object has no attribute 'split'
>>> reverseWords(u'however, unicode is all right too')
u'too right all is unicode however,'
```

As a side effect, reverseWords eliminates any redundant spacing:

```
>>> reverseWords('with   redundant   spacing')
'spacing redundant with'

"""
def reverseWords(astring):
    words = astring.split( )
    words.reverse( )
    return ' '.join(words)

if __name__=='__main__':
    import doctest, sys
    doctest.testmod(sys.modules[__name__])
```

In this module's docstring, I have snipped the tracebacks from the docstring and replaced them with an ellipsis: this is good common practice, since doctest ignores tracebacks and they add nothing to the explanatory value of each failing case. Apart from this snipping, the docstring is the copy and paste of an interactive session, with the addition of some explanatory text and empty lines for readability. Save this source as *mod.py*, and then run it with *python mod.py*. It produces no output, meaning that all examples work right. Try *python mod.py -v* to get an account of all tests tried and a verbose summary at the end. Finally, alter the example results in the module docstring, making them incorrect, to see the messages doctest provides for errant examples.

While doctest is not primarily meant for general-purpose unit testing, it can nevertheless be a very convenient tool for the purpose. The recommended way to do unit testing in Python is with module unittest, covered in "The unittest Module" on page 457. However, unit testing with doctest can be easier and faster to set up, since it requires little more than copy and paste from an interactive session. If you need to maintain a module that lacks unit tests, retrofitting such tests into the module with doctest is a reasonable compromise. It's certainly better to have doctest-based unit tests than not to have any unit tests at all, as might otherwise happen should you decide that setting up tests "properly" with unittest would take you too long.

If you do decide to use doctest for unit testing, don't cram extra tests into your module's docstrings. This would damage the docstrings by making them too long and hard to read. Keep in the docstrings the right amount and kind of examples, strictly for explanatory purposes, just as if unit testing was not in the picture. Instead, put the extra tests into a global variable of your module, a dictionary named __test__. The keys in __test__ are strings used as arbitrary test names, and the corresponding values are strings that doctest picks up and uses in just the same way as it uses docstrings. The values in __test__ may also be function and class objects, in which case doctest examines their docstrings for tests to run. This latter feature is a convenient way to run doctest on objects with private names, which doctest skips by default.

In Python 2.4, the doctest module also supplies two functions that return instances of the unittest.TestSuite class based on doctests so that you can integrate such tests into testing frameworks based on unittest. The documentation for this advanced functionality is at *http://docs.python.org/lib/doctest-unittest-api.html*.

The unittest Module

The unittest module is the Python version of a unit-testing framework originally developed by Kent Beck for Smalltalk. Similar, widespread versions of the framework also exist for many other programming languages (e.g., the JUnit package for Java) and are often collectively referred to as xUnit.

To use unittest, you don't put your testing code in the same source file as the tested module, but instead write a separate test module for each module you're testing. A popular convention is to name the test module the same as the module being tested, with a prefix such as 'test_', and put it in a subdirectory named *test* of the directory where you keep your sources. For example, the test module for *mod.py* can be *test/test_mod.py*. You need a simple and consistent naming convention to make it easy for you to write and maintain auxiliary scripts that find and run all unit tests for a package.

Separation between a module's source code and its unit-testing code lets you refactor the module more easily, including possibly recoding its functionality in C, without perturbing the unit-testing code. Knowing that *test_mod.py* stays intact, whatever changes you make to *mod.py*, enhances your confidence that passing the tests in *test_mod.py* indicates that *mod.py* still works correctly after the changes.

A unit-testing module defines one or more subclasses of unittest's TestCase class. Each subclass specifies one or more test cases by defining *test-case methods*, which are methods that are callable without arguments and whose names start with test. The subclass may also override method setUp, which the framework calls to prepare a new instance just before calling each test-case method, and tearDown, which the framework calls to clean things up just after calling each test-case method. Each test-case method calls methods of class TestCase whose names start with assert in order to express the conditions that the test must meet. unittest runs the test-case methods within a TestCase subclass in arbitrary order, each on a new instance of the subclass, running setUp just before each test case and tearDown just after each test case.

unittest provides other facilities, such as grouping test cases into test suites, and other more advanced functionality. You do not need such extras unless you're defining a custom unit-testing framework or, at the very least, structuring complicated testing procedures for equally complicated packages. In almost all cases, the concepts and details covered in this section are sufficient to perform effective and systematic unit testing. Example 18-2 shows how to use unittest to provide unit tests for the module *mod.py* of Example 18-1. For illustration purposes, this example uses unittest to perform exactly the same tests that Example 18-1 uses as examples in docstrings using doctest.

Example 18-2. Using unittest

```
""" This module tests function reverseWords provided by module mod.py. """
import unittest
import mod

class ModTest(unittest.TestCase):

    def testNormalCase(self):
        self.assertEqual(mod.reverseWords('four score and seven years'),
            'years seven and score four')

    def testSingleWord(self):
        self.assertEqual(mod.reverseWords('justoneword'), 'justoneword')

    def testEmpty(self):
        self.assertEqual(mod.reverseWords(''), '')

    def testRedundantSpacing(self):
        self.assertEqual(mod.reverseWords('with    redundant    spacing'),
            'spacing redundant with')

    def testUnicode(self):
        self.assertEqual(mod.reverseWords(u'unicode is all right too'),
            u'too right all is unicode')

    def testExactlyOneArgument(self):
        self.assertRaises(TypeError, mod.reverseWords)
        self.assertRaises(TypeError, mod.reverseWords, 'one', 'another')

    def testMustBeString(self):
        self.assertRaises((AttributeError,TypeError), mod.reverseWords, 1)

if __name__ = ='__main__':
    unittest.main()
```

Running this script with *python test_mod.py* is a bit more verbose than using *python mod.py* to run doctest, as in Example 18-1. *test_mod.py* outputs a . (dot) for each test-case method it runs, then a separator line of dashes, and finally a summary line, such as "Ran 7 tests in 0.110s," and a final line of "OK" if every test passed.

Each test-case method makes one or more calls to methods whose names start with assert (or their synonyms whose names start with fail). Here, method testExactly1Argument is the only one with two such calls. In more complicated cases, multiple calls to assert methods from a single test-case method are quite common.

Even in a case as simple as this, one minor aspect shows that, for unit testing, unittest is more powerful and flexible than doctest. In method testMustBeString, we pass as the first argument to assertRaises a pair of exception classes, meaning we accept either kind of exception. *test_mod.py* therefore accepts as valid multiple implementations of *mod.py*. It accepts the implementation in Example 18-1, which tries calling method split on its argument, and therefore raises AttributeError when called with an argument that is not a string. However, it also accepts a different hypothetical implementation, one that raises TypeError instead when called with an argument of the wrong type. It would be possible to code this testing functionality with doctest, but it would be awkward and nonobvious, while unittest makes it simple and natural.

This kind of flexibility is crucial for real-life unit tests, which to some extent are executable specifications for their modules. You could, pessimistically, view the need for flexibility as indicating that the interface of the code you're testing is not well defined. However, it's best to view the interface as being defined with a useful amount of flexibility for the implementer: under circumstance *X* (argument of invalid type passed to function reverseWords, in this example), either of two things (raising AttributeError or TypeError) is allowed to happen.

Thus, implementations with either of the two behaviors are correct, and the implementer can choose between them on the basis of such considerations as performance and clarity. By viewing unit tests as executable specifications for their modules (the modern view, and the basis of test-first development) rather than as white-box tests strictly constrained to a specific implementation (as in some traditional taxonomies of testing), the tests become a more vital component of the software development process.

The TestCase class

With unittest, you write test cases by subclassing class TestCase and adding methods, callable without arguments, whose names start with test. Such test-case methods, in turn, call methods that your subclass inherits from TestCase, whose names start with assert (or their synonyms, whose names start with fail), to indicate conditions that must hold for the test to succeed.

Class TestCase also defines two methods that your subclass can optionally override in order to group actions to perform right before and right after each test-case method runs. This doesn't exhaust TestCase's functionality, but you won't need the rest unless you're developing testing frameworks or performing some similarly advanced task. The frequently called methods in a TestCase instance *t* are the following.

assert_, **failUnless**	*t*.assert_(*condition*,*msg*=None)
	Fails and outputs *msg* if *condition* is false; otherwise, does nothing. The underscore in the name is needed because assert is a Python keyword. failUnless is a synonym. Do not use these methods when you can use more specific ones, such as assertEqual.

assertAlmost-Equal, failUnlessAlmostEqual	`t.assertAlmostEqual(`*first,second,places*`=7,`*msg*`=None)` Fails and outputs *msg* if *first*`!=`*second* to within *places* decimal digits; otherwise, does nothing. `failUnlessAlmostEqual` is a synonym. Almost always, these methods are preferable to `assertEqual` when what you are comparing are floats.
assertEqual, failUnlessEqual	`t.assertEqual(`*first,second,msg*`=None)` Fails and outputs *msg* if *first*`!=`*second*; otherwise, does nothing. `failUnlessEqual` is a synonym.
assertNotAlmostEqual, failIfAlmostEqual	`t.assertNotAlmostEqual(`*first,second,places*`=7,`*msg*`=None)` Fails and outputs *msg* if *first*`==`*second* to within *places* decimal digits; otherwise, does nothing. `failIfAlmostEqual` is a synonym.
assertNotEqual, failIfEqual	`t.assertNotEqual(`*first,second,msg*`=None)` Fails and outputs *msg* if *first*`==`*second*; otherwise, does nothing. `failIfEqual` is a synonym.
assertRaises, failUnlessRaises	`t.assertRaises(`*exceptionSpec,callable,*`*`*args,*`**`*kwargs*`)` Calls *callable*(`*`*args,*`**`*kwargs*). Fails if the call doesn't raise any exception. If the call raises an exception that does not meet *exceptionSpec*, `assertRaises` propagates the exception. If the call raises an exception that meets *exceptionSpec*, `assertRaises` does nothing. *exceptionSpec* can be an exception class or a tuple of classes, just like the first argument of the except clause in a try/except statement. `failUnlessRaises` is a synonym.
fail	`t.fail(`*msg*`=None)` Fails unconditionally and outputs *msg*.
failIf	`t.failIf(`*condition, msg*`=None)` Fails and outputs *msg* if *condition* is true; otherwise, does nothing.
setUp	`t.setUp( )` The framework calls `t.setUp( )` just before calling a test-case method. The implementation in `TestCase` does nothing. This method is provided in order to let your subclass override it if it needs to perform some preparation for each test.

tearDown	`t.tearDown( )`
	The framework calls `t.tearDown( )` just after calling a test-case method. The implementation in `TestCase` does nothing. This method is provided in order to let your subclass override it if it needs to perform some cleanup after each test.

Unit tests dealing with large amounts of data

Unit tests must be fast, since they are run frequently during development. Therefore, it's best to unit-test each aspect of your modules' functionality on small amounts of data when possible. This makes each unit test faster and lets you conveniently embed all needed data in the test's source code. When you test a function that reads from or writes to a file object, in particular, you normally use an instance of class `cStringIO` (covered in "The StringIO and cStringIO Modules" on page 229) to simulate a file object while holding the data in memory; this approach is faster than writing to disk and saves you the bother of having to remove disk files after your tests have run.

However, in some rare cases, it may be impossible to fully exercise a module's functionality without supplying and/or comparing data in quantities larger than can be reasonably embedded in a test's source code. In such cases, your unit test will have to rely on auxiliary, external datafiles to hold the data it needs to supply to the module it tests and/or the data it needs to compare to the tested module's output. Even then, you're generally better off reading the data into instances of `cStringIO` rather than directing the tested module to perform actual disk I/O. Even more important, I strongly suggest that you generally use stubs to test modules meant to interact with other external entities, such as a database, a GUI, or some other program over a network. It's easier for you to control all aspects of the test when using stubs rather than real external entities. Also, to reiterate, the speed at which you can run unit tests is important, and it's invariably faster to perform simulated operations in stubs, rather than real operations.

Debugging

Since Python's development cycle is so fast, the most effective way to debug is often to edit your code so that it outputs relevant information at key points. Python has many ways to let your code explore its own state in order to extract information that may be relevant for debugging. The `inspect` and `traceback` modules specifically support such exploration, which is also known as reflection or introspection.

Once you have obtained debugging-relevant information, the `print` statement is often the simplest way to display it. You can also log debugging information to files. Logging is particularly useful for programs that run unattended for a long time, such as server programs. Displaying debugging information is just like displaying other kinds of information, as covered in Chapters 10 and 17. Logging such information is mostly like writing to files (as covered in Chapter 10) or otherwise persisting information, as covered in Chapter 11; however, to help with the specific task of logging, Python's standard library also supplies a logging module, covered in "The logging module" on page 136. As covered in excepthook on page 168, rebinding attribute excepthook of module sys lets your program log detailed error information just before your program is terminated by a propagating exception.

Python also offers hooks that enable interactive debugging. Module pdb supplies a simple text-mode interactive debugger. Other interactive debuggers for Python are part of integrated development environments (IDEs), such as IDLE and various commercial offerings. However, I do not cover IDEs in this book.

Before You Debug

Before you embark on possibly lengthy debugging explorations, make sure you have thoroughly checked your Python sources with the tools mentioned in Chapter 3. Such tools can catch only a subset of the bugs in your code, but they're much faster than interactive debugging, and so their use amply repays itself.

Moreover, again before starting a debugging session, make sure that all the code involved is well covered by unit tests, as seen at "Unit Testing and System Testing" on page 452. Once you have found a bug, *before* you fix it, add to your suite of unit tests (or, if needed, to the suite of system tests) a test or two that would have found the bug if they had been present from the start, and run the tests again to confirm that they now do reveal and isolate the bug; only once that is done should you proceed to fix the bug. By regularly following this procedure, you will soon have a much better suite of tests, learn to write better tests, and gain much sounder assurance about the overall correctness of your code.

Remember, even with all the facilities offered by Python, its standard library, and whatever IDEs you fancy, debugging is still *hard*. Take this fact into account even before you start designing and coding: write and run plenty of unit tests and keep your design and code *simple*, so as to reduce to the absolute minimum the amount of debugging you will need! The classic advice in this regard was phrased by Brian Kernighan as follows: "Debugging is twice as hard as writing the code in the first place. Therefore, if you write the code as cleverly as possible, you are, by definition, not smart enough to debug it."

The inspect Module

The inspect module supplies functions to get information from all kinds of objects, including the Python call stack (which records all function calls currently executing) and source files. The most frequently used functions of module inspect are as follows.

getargspec, formatargspec	getargspec(*f*)
	f is a function object. getargspec returns a tuple with four items: (*arg_names, extra_args, extra_kwds, arg_defaults*). *arg_names* is the sequence of names of *f*'s parameters. *extra_args* is the name of

the special parameter of the form *args*, or None if *f* has no such parameter. *extra_kwds* is the name of the special parameter of the form **kwds*, or None if *f* has no such parameter. *arg_defaults* is the tuple of default values for *f*'s arguments. You can deduce other details of *f*'s signature from getargspec's results: *f* has len(*arg_names*)-len(*arg_defaults*) mandatory parameters, and the names of *f*'s optional parameters are the strings that are the items of the list slice *arg_names*[-len(*arg_defaults*):].

formatargspec accepts one to four arguments that are the same as the items of the tuple that getargspec returns, and returns a string with this information. Thus, formatargspec(*getargspec(*f*)) returns a string with *f*'s parameters (i.e., *f*'s *signature*) in parentheses, as used in the def statement that created *f*. For example:

```
import inspect
def f(a,b=23,**c): pass
print inspect.formatargspec(*inspect.getargspec(f))
# emits: (a, b=23, **c)
```

| **getargvalues,**
formatarg-
values | getargvalues(*f*) |

f is a frame object—for example, the result of a call to the function _getframe in module sys (covered in "_getframe") or to function currentframe in module inspect. getargvalues returns a tuple with four items: (*arg_names*, *extra_args*, *extra_kwds*, *locals*). *arg_names* is the sequence of names of *f*'s function's parameters. *extra_args* is the name of the special parameter of form *args*, or None if *f*'s function has no such parameter. *extra_kwds* is the name of the special parameter of form **kwds*, or None if *f*'s function has no such parameter. *locals* is the dictionary of local variables for *f*. Since arguments, in particular, are local variables, the value of each argument can be obtained from *locals* by indexing the *locals* dictionary with the argument's corresponding parameter name.

formatargvalues accepts one to four arguments that are the same as the items of the tuple that getargvalues returns, and returns a string with this information. formatargvalues(*getargvalues(*f*)) returns a string with *f*'s arguments in parentheses, in named form, as used in the call statement that created *f*. For example:

```
def f(x=23): return inspect.currentframe()
print inspect.formatargvalues(inspect.getargvalues(f()))
# emits: (x=23)
```

| **currentframe** | currentframe() |

Returns the frame object for the current function (caller of currentframe). formatargvalues(getargvalues(currentframe())), for example, returns a string with the arguments of the calling function.

getdoc	getdoc(*obj*)
	Returns the docstring for *obj*, with tabs expanded to spaces and redundant whitespace stripped from each line.
getfile, **getsourcefile**	getfile(*obj*)
	Returns the name of the file that defined *obj* and raises TypeError when unable to determine the file. For example, getfile raises TypeError if *obj* is built-in. getfile returns the name of a binary or source file. getsourcefile returns the name of a source file and raises TypeError when all it can find is a binary file, not the corresponding source file.
getmembers	getmembers(*obj*, *filter*=None)
	Returns all attributes (members), both data and methods (including special methods), of *obj*, a sorted list of (*name*,*value*) pairs. When *filter* is not None, returns only attributes for which callable *filter* is true when called on the attribute's *value*, like:

```
sorted((n, v) for n, v in getmembers(obj) if filter(v))
```

getmodule	getmodule(*obj*)
	Returns the module object that defined *obj*, or None if it is unable to determine it.
getmro	getmro(*c*)
	Returns a tuple of bases and ancestors of class *c* in method resolution order. *c* is the first item in the tuple. Each class appears only once in the tuple. For example:

```
class oldA: pass
class oldB(oldA): pass
class oldC(oldA): pass
class oldD(oldB,oldC): pass
for c in inspect.getmro(oldD): print c.__name__,
# emits: oldD oldB oldA oldC
class newA(object): pass
class newB(newA): pass
class newC(newA): pass
class newD(newB,newC): pass
for c in inspect.getmro(newD): print c.__name__,
# emits: newD newB newC newA object
```

getsource, **getsourcelines**	getsource(*obj*)
	Returns one multiline string that is the source code for *obj*, and raises IOError if it is unable to determine or fetch it. getsourcelines

returns a pair: the first item is the source code for *obj* (a list of lines), and the second item is the line number of first line.

isbuiltin, isclass, iscode, isframe, isfunction, ismethod, ismodule, isroutine	`isbuiltin(obj)` Each of these functions accepts a single argument *obj* and returns True if *obj* belongs to the type indicated in the function name. Accepted objects are, respectively: built-in (C-coded) functions, class objects, code objects, frame objects, Python-coded functions (including `lambda` expressions), methods, modules, and, for isroutine, all methods or functions, either C-coded or Python-coded. These functions are often used as the *filter* argument to getmembers.
stack	`stack(context=1)` Returns a list of six-item tuples. The first tuple is about stack's caller, the second tuple is about the caller's caller, and so on. Each tuple's items, in order, are: frame object, filename, line number, function name, list of *context* source code lines around the current line, and index of current line within the list.

An example of using inspect

Suppose that somewhere in your program you execute a statement such as:

```
x.f()
```

and unexpectedly receive an AttributeError informing you that object *x* has no attribute named *f*. This means that object *x* is not as you expected, so you want to determine more about *x* as a preliminary to ascertaining why *x* is that way and what you should do about it. Change the statement to:

```
try: x.f()
except AttributeError:
    import sys, inspect
    print>>sys.stderr, 'x is type %s, (%r)' % (type(x), x)
    print>>sys.stderr, "x's methods are:",
    for n, v in inspect.getmembers(x, callable):
        print>>sys.stderr, n,
    print>>sys.stderr
    raise
```

This example uses sys.stderr (covered in stdin, stdout, stderr on page 171), since it displays information related to an error, not program results. Function getmembers of module inspect obtains the name of all the methods available on *x* in order to display them. If you need this kind of diagnostic functionality often, package it up into a separate function, such as:

```
import sys, inspect
def show_obj_methods(obj, name, show=sys.stderr.write):
```

```
    show('%s is type %s(%r)\n'%(name,obj,type(obj)))
    show("%s's methods are: "%name)
    for n, v in inspect.getmembers(obj, callable):
        show('%s '%n)
    show('\n')
```

And then the example becomes just:

```
try: x.f( )
except AttributeError:
    show_obj_methods(x, 'x')
    raise
```

Good program structure and organization are just as necessary in code intended for diagnostic and debugging purposes as they are in code that implements your program's functionality. See also "The _ _debug_ _ built-in variable" on page 138 for a good technique to use when defining diagnostic and debugging functions.

The traceback Module

The traceback module lets you extract, format, and output information about tracebacks as normally produced by uncaught exceptions. By default, module traceback reproduces the formatting Python uses for tracebacks. However, module traceback also lets you exert fine-grained control. The module supplies many functions, but in typical use you need only one of them.

---

print_exc   print_exc(*limit*=None, *file*=sys.stderr)

Call print_exc from an exception handler or a function directly or indirectly called by an exception handler. print_exc outputs to file-like object *file* the traceback information that Python outputs to stderr for uncaught exceptions. When *limit* is not None, print_exc outputs only *limit* traceback nesting levels. For example, when, in an exception handler, you want to cause a diagnostic message just as if the exception propagated, but actually stop the exception from propagating any further (so that your program keeps running and no further handlers are involved), call traceback.print_exc( ).

The pdb Module

The pdb module exploits the Python interpreter's debugging and tracing hooks to implement a simple command-line-oriented interactive debugger. pdb lets you set breakpoints, single-step on sources, examine stack frames, and so on.

To run some code under pdb's control, import pdb and then call pdb.run, passing as the single argument a string of code to execute. To use pdb for post-mortem debugging (meaning debugging of code that just terminated by propagating an exception at an interactive prompt), call pdb.pm( ) without arguments. When pdb starts, it first reads text files named *.pdbrc* in your home directory and in the current directory. Such files can contain any pdb commands, but most often they use the alias command in order to define useful synonyms and abbreviations for other commands.

When pdb is in control, it prompts you with the string '(Pdb) ', and you can enter pdb commands. Command help (which you can also enter in the abbreviated form h) lists all available commands. Call help with an argument (separated by a space) to get help about any specific command. You can abbreviate most commands to the first one or two letters, but you must always enter commands in lowercase: pdb, like Python itself, is case-sensitive. Entering an empty line repeats the previous command. The most frequently used pdb commands are the following.

!	! *statement*
	Executes Python statement *statement* in the currently debugged context.
alias, unalias	alias [*name* [*command*]]
	alias without arguments lists currently defined aliases. alias *name* outputs the current definition of the alias *name*. In the full form, *command* is any pdb command, with arguments, and may contain %1, %2, and so on to refer to specific arguments passed to the new alias *name* being defined, or %* to refer to all such arguments together. Command unalias *name* removes an alias.
args, a	args
	Lists all actual arguments passed to the function you are currently debugging.
break, b	break [*location* [,*condition*]]
	break without arguments lists currently defined breakpoints and the number of times each breakpoint has triggered. With an argument, break sets a breakpoint at the given *location*. *location* can be a line number or a function name, optionally preceded by *filename*: to set a breakpoint in a file that is not the current one or at the start of a function whose name is ambiguous (i.e., a function that exists in more than one file). When *condition* is present, it is an expression to evaluate (in the debugged context) each time the given line or function is about to execute; execution breaks only when the expression returns a true value. When setting a new breakpoint, break returns a breakpoint number, which you can then use to refer to the new breakpoint in any other breakpoint-related pdb command.

clear, cl   clear [*breakpoint-numbers*]

Clears (removes) one or more breakpoints. clear without arguments removes all breakpoints after asking for confirmation. To deactivate a breakpoint without removing it, see disable on page 468.

condition   condition *breakpoint-number* [*expression*]

condition *n expression* sets or changes the condition on breakpoint *n*. condition *n*, without *expression*, makes breakpoint *n* unconditional.

continue, c, cont continue

Continues execution of the code being debugged, up to a breakpoint, if any.

disable   disable [*breakpoint-numbers*]

Disables one or more breakpoints. disable without arguments disables all breakpoints (after asking for confirmation). This differs from clear in that the debugger remembers the breakpoint, and you can reactivate it via enable.

down, d   down

Moves down one frame in the stack (i.e., toward the most recent function call). Normally, the current position in the stack is at the bottom (i.e., at the function that was called most recently and is now being debugged). Therefore, command down can't go further down. However, command down is useful if you have previously executed command up, which moves the current position upward.

enable   enable [*breakpoint-numbers*]

Enables one or more breakpoints. enable without arguments enables all breakpoints after asking for confirmation.

ignore   ignore *breakpoint-number* [*count*]

Sets the breakpoint's ignore count (to 0 if *count* is omitted). Triggering a breakpoint whose ignore count is greater than 0 just decrements the count. Execution stops, presenting you with an interactive pdb prompt, when you trigger a breakpoint whose ignore count is 0. For example, say that module *fob.py* contains the following code:

```
def f( ):
    for i in range(1000):
        g(i)
def g(i):
    pass
```

Now consider the following interactive pdb session (in Python 2.4; minor details may change depending on the Python version you're running):

```
>>> import pdb
>>> import fob
>>> pdb.run('fob.f( )')
> <string>(1)?( )
(Pdb) break fob.g
Breakpoint 1 at C:\mydir\fob.py:5
(Pdb) ignore 1 500
Will ignore next 500 crossings of breakpoint 1.
(Pdb) continue
> C:\mydir\fob.py(5)g( )
-> pass
(Pdb) print i
500
```

The ignore command, as pdb says, asks pdb to ignore the next 500 hits on breakpoint 1, which we set at *fob.g* in the previous break statement. Therefore, when execution finally stops, function g has already been called 500 times, as we show by printing its argument i, which indeed is now 500. The ignore count of breakpoint 1 is now 0; if we give another continue and print i, i will show as 501. In other words, once the ignore count decrements to 0, execution stops every time the breakpoint is hit. If we want to skip some more hits, we must give pdb another ignore command, setting the ignore count of breakpoint 1 at some value greater than 0 yet again.

---

list, l

list [*first* [, *last*]]

list without arguments lists 11 lines centered on the current one, or the next 11 lines if the previous command was also a list. Arguments to the list command can optionally specify the first and last lines to list within the current file. The list command lists physical lines, including comments and empty lines, not logical lines.

---

next, n

next

Executes the current line, without stepping into any function called from the current line. However, hitting breakpoints in functions called directly or indirectly from the current line does stop execution.

print, p	p *expression*
	Evaluates *expression* in the current context and displays the result.

quit, q	quit
	Immediately terminates both pdb and the program being debugged.

return, r	return
	Executes the rest of the current function, stopping only at breakpoints if any.

step, s	step
	Executes the current line, stepping into any function called from the current line.

tbreak	tbreak [*location* [,*condition*]]
	Like break, but the breakpoint is temporary (i.e., pdb automatically removes the breakpoint as soon as the breakpoint is triggered).

up, u	up
	Moves up one frame in the stack (i.e., away from the most recent function call and toward the calling function).

where, w	where
	Shows the stack of frames and indicates the current one (i.e., in which frame's context command ! executes statements, command args shows arguments, command *print* evaluates expressions, etc.).

Debugging in IDLE

IDLE, the Interactive DeveLopment Environment that comes with Python, offers debugging functionality similar to that of pdb, although not quite as powerful. Thanks to IDLE's GUI, the functionality is easier to access. For example, instead of having to ask for source lists and stack lists explicitly with such pdb commands as list and where, you just activate one or more of four checkboxes in the Debug Control window to see source, stack, locals, and globals always displayed in the same window at each step.

To start IDLE's interactive debugger, use Debug → Debugger in IDLE's *Python Shell* window. IDLE opens the Debug Control window, outputs [DEBUG ON] in the shell window, and gives you another >>> prompt in the shell window. Keep using the shell window as you normally would; any command you give at the shell window's prompt now runs under the debugger. To deactivate the debugger, use Debug → Debugger again; IDLE then toggles the debug state, closes the Debug Control window, and outputs [DEBUG OFF] in the shell window. To control the debugger when the debugger is active, use the GUI controls in the Debug Control window. You can toggle the debugger away only when it is not busy actively tracking code; otherwise, IDLE disables the Quit button in the Debug Control window.

The warnings Module

Warnings are messages about errors or anomalies that may not be serious enough to be worth disrupting the program's control flow (as would happen by raising a normal exception). The warnings module affords fine-grained control over which warnings are output and what happens to them. You can conditionally output a warning by calling function warn in module warnings. Other functions in the module let you control how warnings are formatted, set their destinations, and conditionally suppress some warnings (or transform some warnings into exceptions).

Classes

Module warnings supplies several exception classes that represent warnings. Class Warning subclasses Exception and is the base class for all warnings. You may define your own warning classes; they must subclass Warning, either directly or via one of its other existing subclasses, which are:

DeprecationWarning
 Uses deprecated features supplied only for backward compatibility

RuntimeWarning
 Uses features whose semantics are error-prone

SyntaxWarning
 Uses features whose syntax is error-prone

UserWarning
 Other user-defined warnings that don't fit any of the above cases

Objects

Python supplies no concrete warning objects. A warning is composed of a *message* (a text string), a *category* (a subclass of Warning), and two pieces of information that identify where the warning was raised from: *module* (name of the module that raised the warning) and *lineno* (line number of the source code line that raised the warning). Conceptually, you may think of these as attributes of a warning object *w*, and I use attribute notation later for clarity, but no specific warning object *w* actually exists.

Filters

At any time, module warnings keeps a list of active filters for warnings. When you import warnings for the first time in a run, the module examines sys.warnoptions to determine the initial set of filters. You can run Python with option -W to set sys.warnoptions for a given run. Do not rely on the initial set of filters being held specifically in sys.warnoptions, as this is an implementation aspect that may change in future releases of Python.

As each warning _w_ occurs, warnings tests _w_ against each filter until a filter matches. The first matching filter determines what happens to _w_. Each filter is a tuple of five items. The first item, _action_, is a string that defines what happens on a match. The other four items, _message_, _category_, _module_, and _lineno_, control what it means for _w_ to match the filter, and all conditions must be satisfied for a match. Here are the meanings of these items (using attribute notation to indicate conceptual attributes of _w_):

message
> A regular expression object; the match condition is _message_.match(w.message) (the match is case-insensitive).

category
> Warning or a subclass of Warning; the match condition is issubclass(w. category,_category_).

module
> A regular expression object; the match condition is _module_.match(w.module) (the match is case-sensitive).

lineno
> An int; the match condition is _lineno_ in (0,w.lineno). _lineno_ is 0, meaning w.lineno does not matter, or w.lineno must exactly equal _lineno_.

Upon a match, the first field of the filter, the _action_, determines what happens:

'always'
> w.message is output whether or not _w_ has already occurred.

'default'
> w.message is output if, and only if, this is the first time _w_ occurs from this specific location (i.e., this specific w.module, w.location pair).

'error'
> w.category(w.message) is raised as an exception.

'ignore'
> _w_ is ignored.

'module'
> w.message is output if, and only if, this is the first time _w_ occurs from w.module.

'once'
> w.message is output if, and only if, this is the first time _w_ occurs from any location.

Functions

Module warnings supplies the following functions.

filterwarnings   `filterwarnings(`*`action,message`*`='.*',`*`category`*`=Warning,`
                                      `*`module`*`='.*',`*`lineno`*`=0, `*`append`*`=False)`

Adds a filter to the list of active filters. When *append* is true, `filterwarnings` adds the filter after all other existing filters (i.e., appends the filter to the list of existing filters); otherwise, `filterwarnings` inserts the filter before any other existing filter. All components, save *action*, have default values that mean "match everything." As detailed above, *message* and *module* are pattern strings for regular expressions, *category* is some subclass of Warning, *lineno* is an integer, and *action* is a string that determines what happens when a message matches this filter.

formatwarning   `formatwarning(`*`message,category,filename,lineno`*`)`

Returns a string that represents the given warning with standard formatting.

resetwarnings   `resetwarnings( )`

Removes all filters from the list of filters. `resetwarnings` also discards any filters originally added with the -*W* command-line option.

showwarning   `showwarning(`*`message,category,filename,lineno,file`*`=sys.stderr)`

Outputs the given warning to the given file object. Filter actions that output warnings call `showwarning`, letting argument *file* default to `sys.stderr`. To change what happens when filter actions output warnings, code your own function with this signature and bind it to `warnings.showwarning`, thus overriding the default implementation.

warn   `warn(`*`message,category`*`=UserWarning,*`stacklevel`*=1)`

Sends a warning so that the filters examine and possibly output it. The location of the warning is the current function (caller of `warn`) if *stacklevel* is 1, or the caller of the current function if *stacklevel* is 2. Thus, passing 2 as the value of *stacklevel* lets you write functions that send warnings on their caller's behalf, such as:

```
def toUnicode(astr):
    try:
        return unicode(astr)
    except UnicodeError:
        warnings.warn("Invalid characters in (%s)"%astr,
                      stacklevel=2)
        return unicode(astr, errors='ignore')
```

Debugging

Thanks to parameter *stacklevel=2*, the warning appears to come from the caller of toUnicode, rather than from toUnicode itself. This is very important when the *action* of the filter that matches this warning is *default* or *module*, since these actions output a warning only the first time the warning occurs from a given location or module.

Optimization

"First make it work. Then make it right. Then make it fast." This quotation, often with slight variations, is widely known as "the golden rule of programming." As far as I've been able to ascertain, the quotation is by Kent Beck, who credits his father with it. Being widely known makes the principle no less important, particularly because it's more honored in the breach than in the observance. A negative form, slightly exaggerated for emphasis, is in a quotation by Don Knuth (who credits Hoare with it): "Premature optimization is the root of all evil in programming."

Optimization is premature if your code is not working yet, or if you're not sure about what, exactly, your code should be doing (since then you cannot be sure if it's working). First make it work. Optimization is also premature if your code is working but you are not satisfied with the overall architecture and design. Remedy structural flaws before worrying about optimization: first make it work, then make it right. These first two steps are not optional; working, well-architected code is *always* a must.

In contrast, you don't always need to make it fast. Benchmarks may show that your code's performance is already acceptable after the first two steps. When performance is not acceptable, profiling often shows that all performance issues are in a small part of the code, perhaps 10 to 20 percent of the code where your program spends 80 or 90 percent of the time. Such performance-crucial regions of your code are known as its *bottlenecks*, or *hot spots*. It's a waste of effort to optimize large portions of code that account for, say, 10 percent of your program's running time. Even if you made that part run 10 times as fast (a rare feat), your program's overall runtime would only decrease by 9 percent, a speedup no user would even notice. If optimization is needed, focus your efforts where they'll matter—on bottlenecks. You can optimize bottlenecks while keeping your code 100 percent pure Python, thus not preventing future porting to other Python implementations. In some cases, you can resort to recoding some computational bottlenecks as Python extensions (as covered in Chapter 25), potentially gaining even better performance (possibly at the expense of some potential future portability).

Developing a Fast-Enough Python Application

Start by designing, coding, and testing your application in Python, using available extension modules if they save you work. This takes much less time than it would with a classic compiled language. Then benchmark the application to find out if the resulting code is fast enough. Often it is, and you're done—congratulations! Ship it!

Since much of Python itself is coded in highly optimized C, as are many of its standard and extension modules, your application may even turn out to be already faster than typical C code. However, if the application is too slow, you need to reexamine your algorithms and data structures. Check for bottlenecks due to application architecture, network traffic, database access, and operating system interactions. For typical applications, each of these factors is more likely than language choice to cause slowdowns. Tinkering with large-scale architectural aspects can often speed up an application dramatically, and Python is an excellent medium for such experimentation.

If your program is still too slow, profile it to find out where the time is going. Applications often exhibit computational bottlenecks: small areas of the source code, often between 10 and 20 percent, which account for 80 percent or more of the running time. Then optimize the bottlenecks, applying the techniques suggested in the rest of this chapter.

If normal Python-level optimizations still leave some outstanding computational bottlenecks, you can recode them as Python extension modules, as covered in Chapter 25. In the end, your application will run at roughly the same speed as if you had coded it all in C, C++, or Fortran—or faster, when large-scale experimentation has let you find a better architecture. Your overall programming productivity with this process is not much less than if you coded everything in Python. Future changes and maintenance are easy, since you use Python to express the overall structure of the program and lower-level, harder-to-maintain languages for only a few specific computational bottlenecks.

As you build applications in a given area according to this process, you accumulate a library of reusable Python extension modules. You therefore become more and more productive at developing other fast-running Python applications in the same field.

Even if external constraints eventually force you to recode the whole application in a lower-level language, you're still better off for having started in Python. Rapid prototyping has long been acknowledged as the best way to get software architecture just right. A working prototype lets you check that you have identified the right problems and taken a good path to their solution. A prototype also affords the kind of large-scale architectural experiments that can make a real difference to performance. Starting your prototype with Python allows a gradual migration to other languages by way of extension modules. The application remains fully functional and testable at each stage. This ensures against the risk of compromising a design's architectural integrity in the coding stage. The resulting software is faster and more robust than if all of the coding had been lower-level from the start, and your productivity, while not quite as good as with a pure Python application, is still better than if you had been coding at a lower level throughout.

Benchmarking

Benchmarking (also known as *load testing*) is similar to system testing: both activities are much like running the program for production purposes. In both cases, you need to have at least some subset of the program's intended functionality working, and you need to use known, reproducible inputs. For benchmarking, you don't need to capture and check your program's output: since you make it work and make it right before you make it fast, you are already fully confident about your program's correctness by the time you load-test it. You do need inputs that are representative of typical system operations, ideally ones that may be most challenging for your program's performance. If your program performs several kinds of operations, make sure you run some benchmarks for each different kind of operation.

Elapsed time as measured by your wristwatch is probably precise enough to benchmark most programs. Programs with hard real-time constraints are obviously another matter, but they have needs very different from those of normal programs in most respects. A 5 or 10 percent difference in performance, except for programs with very peculiar constraints, makes no practical difference to a program's real-life usability.

When you benchmark "toy" programs or snippets in order to help you choose an algorithm or data structure, you may need more precision: the timeit module of Python's standard library (mentioned in "Module timeit" on page 484) is quite suitable for such tasks. The benchmarking discussed in this section is of a different kind: it is an approximation of real-life program operation for the sole purpose of checking whether the program's performance at each task is acceptable, before embarking on profiling and other optimization activities. For such system benchmarking, a situation that approximates the program's normal operating conditions is best, and high accuracy in timing is not particularly important.

Large-Scale Optimization

The aspects of your program that are most important for performance are large-scale ones: choice of algorithms, overall architecture, choice of data structures.

The performance issues that you must often take into account are those connected with the traditional big-O notation of computer science. Informally, if you call N the input size of an algorithm, big-O notation expresses algorithm performance, for large values of N, as proportional to some function of N (in precise computer science lingo, this should be called big-Theta, but in real life, most programmers call this big-O, perhaps because a Greek uppercase Theta looks like an O with a dot in the center!).

An O(1) algorithm (also known as a "constant time" algorithm) is one that takes a time that does not grow with N. An O(N) algorithm (also known as a "linear time" algorithm) is one where, for large enough N, handling twice as much data takes about twice as much time, three times as much data three times as much time, and so on, growing proportionally to N. An O(N^2) algorithm (also known as a "quadratic time" algorithm) is one where, for large enough N, handling twice as much data takes about four times as much time, three times as much data nine times as much time, and so on, growing proportionally to N squared. Identical concepts and notation are used to describe a program's consumption of memory ("space") rather than of time.

You will find more information on big-O notation, and about algorithms and their complexity, in any good book about algorithms and data structures. Unfortunately, at the time of this writing, there aren't yet any such books that use Python. However, if you are familiar with C, I recommend *Mastering Algorithms with C*, by Kyle Loudon (O'Reilly).

To understand the practical importance of big-O considerations in your programs, consider two different ways to accept all items from an input iterable and accumulate them into a list in reverse order:

```
def slow(it):
    result = []
    for item in it: result.insert(0, item)
    return result

def fast(it):
    result = []
    for item in it: result.append(item)
    result.reverse()
    return result
```

We could express each of these functions more concisely, but the key difference is best appreciated by presenting the functions in elementary terms. Function slow builds the result list by inserting each input item before all previously received ones. Function fast appends each input item after all previously received ones, then reverses the result list at the end. Intuitively, one might think that the final reversing represents extra work, and therefore slow should be faster than fast. But that's not the way things work out.

Each call to result.append takes roughly the same amount of time, independent of how many items are already in list result, since there is always a free slot for an extra item at the end of the list (in pedantic terms, append is *amortized* O(1), but I don't cover amortization in this book). The for loop in function fast executes N times to receive N items. Since each iteration of the loop takes a constant time, overall loop time is O(N). result.reverse also takes time O(N), as it is directly proportional to the total number of items. Thus, the total running time of fast is O(N). (If you don't understand why a sum of two quantities, each O(N), is also O(N), consider that the sum of any two linear functions of N is also a linear function of N—and "being O(N)" has exactly the same meaning as "consuming an amount of time that is a linear function of N.")

In contrast, each call to result.insert must make space at slot 0 for the new item to insert by moving all items that are already in list result forward one slot. This takes a time proportional to the number of items that are already in the list. The overall amount of time to receive N items is therefore proportional to 1+2+3+...N-1, a sum whose value is O(N²). Therefore, the total running time of slow is O(N²).

It's almost always worth replacing an O(N²) solution with an O(N) one, unless you can somehow assign rigorous small limits to the input size N. If N can grow without very strict bounds, the O(N²) solution will inevitably turn out to be disastrously slower than the O(N) one for large enough values of N, no matter what the proportionality constants in each case may be (and no matter what profiling tells you). Unless you have other O(N²) or even worse bottlenecks elsewhere that you

Debugging

cannot eliminate, a part of the program that is O(N²) will inevitably turn into the program's bottleneck and dominate runtime for large enough values of N. Do yourself a favor and watch out for the big O: all other performance issues, in comparison, are almost always insignificant.

Incidentally, function fast can be made even faster by expressing it in more idiomatic Python. Just replace the first two lines with the single statement:

```
result = list(it)
```

This change does not affect fast's big-O character (fast is still O(N) after the change), but does speed things up by a large constant factor. Often, in Python, the simplest, clearest, most idiomatic way to express something is also the fastest.

Choosing algorithms with good big-O characteristics is roughly the same task in Python as in any other language. You just need a few indications about the big-O performance of Python's elementary building blocks, and I provide them in the following sections.

List operations

Python lists are internally implemented as vectors (also known as *dynamic arrays*), not as "linked lists." This fundamental implementation choice determines just about all performance characteristics of Python lists, in big-O terms.

Chaining two lists L1 and L2, of length N1 and N2 (i.e., L1+L2) is O(N1+N2). Multiplying a list L of length N by the integer M (i.e., L*M) is O(N*M). Accessing or rebinding any list item is O(1). len( ) on a list is also O(1). Accessing any slice of length M is O(M). Rebinding a slice of length M with one of identical length is also O(M). Rebinding a slice of length M1 with one of different length M2 is O(M1+M2+N1), where N1 is the number of items *after* the slice in the target list (in other words, such length-changing slice rebindings are very cheap when they occur at the *end* of a list, and costly when they occur at the *beginning* or around the middle of a long list). If you need first-in, first-out (FIFO) operations, a list is probably not the fastest data structure for the purpose: instead, try type collections.deque, covered in "deque" on page 173.

Most list methods, as shown back in Table 4-3, are equivalent to slice rebindings and have the same big-O performance. Methods count, index, remove, and reverse, and operator in, are O(N). Method sort is generally O(N*log(N)), but is highly optimized to be O(N) in some important special cases, like when the list is already sorted, reverse-sorted, or sorted except for a few items. range(a,b,c) is O((b-a)/c). xrange(a,b,c) is O(1), but looping on xrange's result is O((b-a)/c).

String operations

Most methods on a string of length N (be it plain or Unicode) are O(N). len(astring) is O(1). The fastest way to produce a copy of a string with transliterations and/or removal of specified characters is the string's method translate. The single most practically important big-O consideration involving strings is covered in "Building up a string from pieces" on page 484.

Dictionary operations

Python dictionaries are internally implemented with hash tables. This fundamental implementation choice determines just about all performance characteristics of Python dictionaries, in big-O terms.

Accessing, rebinding, adding, or removing a dictionary item is generally O(1), as are methods has_key, get, setdefault, and popitem, and operator in. d1.update(d2) is O(len(d2)). len(adict) is O(1). Methods keys, items, and values are O(N). Methods iterkeys, iteritems, and itervalues are O(1), but looping on the iterators that those methods return is O(N) (the methods with names that start with iter do save memory compared to their counterparts that return lists, which in turn may make them faster), and looping directly on a dict has the same big-O performance as iterkeys. *Never* test with if x in d.keys(). That would be O(N), while the equivalent test if x in d: is O(1) (if d.has_key(x): is also O(1), but is slower than if x in d: and has no compensating advantage).

When the keys in a dictionary are instances of classes that define __hash__ and equality comparison methods, dictionary performance is of course affected by those methods. The performance indications presented in this paragraph hold only when hashing and equality comparison are O(1).

Set operations

Python sets, like dictionaries, are internally implemented with hash tables. All performance characteristics of sets are, in big-O terms, the same as those of dictionaries.

Adding or removing a set item is generally O(1), as is operator in. len(aset) is O(1). Looping on a set is O(N). When the items in a set are instances of classes that define __hash__ and equality comparison methods, set performance is of course affected by those methods. The performance indications presented in this paragraph hold only when hashing and equality comparison are O(1).

Summary of big-O times for operations on Python built-in types

Let L be any list, T any string (plain or Unicode); D any dict; S any set, with (say) numbers as items (with O(1) hashing and comparison) and x any number:

O(1)

   len(L), len(T), len(D), len(S), L[i], T[i], D[i], del D[i], if x in D, if x in S, S.add(x), S.remove(x), additions or removals to/from the right end of L

O(N)

   Loops on L, T, D, S, general additions or removals to/from L (not at the right end), all methods on T, if x in L, if x in T, most methods on L, all shallow copies

O(N log N)

   L.sort in general (but O(N) if L is already nearly sorted or reverse-sorted)

Profiling

Most programs have hot spots (i.e., regions of source code that account for most of the time elapsed during a program run). Don't try to guess where your program's hot spots are: a programmer's intuition is notoriously unreliable in this field. Use module profile to collect profile data over one or more runs of your program, with known inputs. Then use module pstats to collate, interpret, and display that profile data. To gain accuracy, you can calibrate the Python profiler for your machine (i.e., determine what overhead profiling incurs on your machine). Module profile can then subtract this overhead from the times it measures so that the profile data you collect is closer to reality. Python 2.5 introduces a new standard library module cProfile with similar functionality to profile; cProfile is preferable, since it's faster, which imposes less overhead. Yet another profiling module in Python's standard library is hotshot (covered at *http://docs.python.org/lib/module-hotshot.html* and present since Python 2.2); unfortunately, hotshot is not compatible with threads.

The profile module

The profile module supplies one function you will often use.

run	run(*code*,*filename*=None)
	code is a string that is usable with statement exec, normally a call to the main function of the program you're profiling. *filename* is the path of a file that run creates or rewrites with profile data. Usually, you call run a few times, specifying different filenames, and different arguments to your program's main function, in order to exercise various program parts in proportion to what you expect will be their use "in real life." Then you use module pstats to display collated results.
	You may call run without a *filename* to get a summary report, similar to the one module pstats could give you, on standard output. However, this approach gives no control over output format, nor any way to consolidate several runs into one report. In practice, you should rarely use this feature: it's better to collect profile data into files.
	Module profile also supplies class Profile (mentioned in the next section). By instantiating Profile directly, you can access advanced functionality, such as the ability to run a command in specified local and global dictionaries. I do not cover such advanced functionality of class profile.Profile further in this book.

Calibration

To calibrate profile for your machine, you need to use class Profile, which module profile supplies and internally uses in function run. An instance *p* of Profile supplies one method you use for calibration.

calibrate   `p.calibrate(N)`

Loops *N* times, then returns a number that is the profiling overhead per call on your machine. *N* must be large if your machine is fast. Call `p.calibrate(10000)` a few times and check that the various numbers it returns are close to each other, then pick the smallest one of them. If the numbers vary a lot, try again with larger values of *N*.

The calibration procedure can be time-consuming. However, you need to perform it only once, repeating it only when you make changes that could alter your machine's characteristics, such as applying patches to your operating system, adding memory, or changing Python version. Once you know your machine's overhead, you can tell `profile` about it each time you import it, right before using `profile.run`. The simplest way to do this is as follows:

```
import profile
profile.Profile.bias = ...the overhead you measured...
profile.run('main( )', 'somefile')
```

The pstats module

The pstats module supplies a single class, Stats, to analyze, consolidate, and report on the profile data contained in one or more files written by function `profile.run`.

Stats   `class Stats(filename,*filenames)`

Instantiates Stats with one or more filenames of files of profile data written by function `profile.run`.

An instance *s* of class Stats provides methods to add profile data and sort and output results. Each method returns *s*, so you can chain several calls in the same expression. *s*'s main methods are as follows.

add   `s.add(filename)`

Adds another file of profile data to the set that *s* is holding for analysis.

print_callees,   `s.print_callees(*restrictions)`
print_callers

Outputs the list of functions in *s*'s profile data, sorted according to the latest call to `s.sort_stats` and subject to given restrictions, if any. You can call each printing method with zero or more *restrictions*, to be applied one after the other, in order, to reduce the number of output lines. A restriction that is an int *n* limits the output to the first *n* lines. A restriction that is a float *f* between 0.0 and 1.0 limits the output to a fraction *f* of the lines. A restriction that is a string is compiled as a regular expression (covered in "Regular Expressions and the re Module" on page 201); only lines that satisfy a search method call on the regular expressions are output. Restrictions are cumulative. For example, `s.print_calls(10,0.5)` outputs the first 5 lines (half of 10). Restrictions apply only after the summary and header lines: the summary and header are output unconditionally.

Each function *f* that is output is accompanied by the list of *f*'s callers (the functions that called *f*) or *f*'s callees (the functions that *f* called) according to the name of the method.

print_stats	`s.print_stats(*restrictions)`

Outputs statistics about *s*'s profile data, sorted according to the latest call to `s.sort_stats` and subject to given restrictions, if any, as covered in `print_callees`, `print_callers` on page 481. After a few summary lines (date and time on which profile data was collected, number of function calls, and sort criteria used), the output, absent restrictions, is one line per function, with six fields per line, labeled in a header line. For each function *f*, `print_stats` outputs six fields:

- Total number of calls to *f*
- Total time spent in *f*, exclusive of other functions that *f* called
- Total time per call to *f* (i.e., field 2 divided by field 1)
- Cumulative time spent in *f*, and all functions directly or indirectly called from *f*
- Cumulative time per call to *f* (i.e., field 4 divided by field 1)
- The name of function *f*

sort_stats	`s.sort_stats(key, *keys)`

Gives one or more keys on which to sort future output, in priority order. Each key is a string. The sort is descending for keys that indicate times or numbers, and alphabetical for key `'nfl'`. The most frequently used keys when calling `sort_stats` are:

`'calls'`
  Number of calls to the function (like field 1 covered in "print_stats")

`'cumulative'`
  Cumulative time spent in the function and all functions it called (like field 4 covered in `print_stats` on page 482)

'nfl'
> Name of the function, its module, and the line number of the function in its file (like field 6 covered in print_stats on page 482)

'time'
> Total time spent in the function itself, exclusive of functions it called (like field 2 covered in print_stats on page 482)

---

strip_dirs
    `s.strip_dirs()`

Alters *s* by stripping directory names from all module names to make future output more compact. *s* is unsorted after *s.* `strip_dirs()`, and therefore you normally call `s.sort_stats` right after calling `s.strip_dirs`.

Small-Scale Optimization

Fine-tuning of program operations is rarely important. Tuning may make a small but meaningful difference in some particularly hot spot, but hardly ever is it a decisive factor. And yet, fine-tuning, in the pursuit of mostly irrelevant micro-efficiencies, is where a programmer's instincts are likely to lead. It is in good part because of this that most optimization is premature and best avoided. The most that can be said in favor of fine-tuning is that, if one idiom is always speedier than another when the difference is measurable, it's worth getting into the habit of always using the former and not the latter.

Most often, in Python, if you do what comes naturally and choose simplicity and elegance, you end up with code that has good performance as well as clarity and maintainability. In a few cases, an approach that may not be intuitively preferable still does offer performance advantages, as discussed in the rest of this section.

The simplest possible optimization is to run your Python programs using *python -O* or *-OO*. *-OO* makes little direct difference to performance compared to *-O*, but *-OO* may save memory, since it removes docstrings from the bytecode, and memory availability is sometimes (indirectly) a performance bottleneck. The optimizer is not very powerful in current releases of Python, but it may still gain you performance advantages on the order of 5 percent, sometimes as large as 10 percent (potentially larger if you make use of assert statements and if __debug__: guards, as suggested in "The assert Statement" on page 138). The best aspect of *-O* is that it costs nothing—as long as your optimization isn't premature, of course (don't bother using *-O* on a program you're still developing).

Module timeit

Standard library module `timeit` is very handy for measuring the precise performance of specific snippets of code. You can have module `timeit` use `timeit`'s functionality in your programs, but the simplest and most normal use is from the command line:

```
python -mtimeit -s'setup statement(s)' 'statement(s) to be timed'
```

For example, say you're wondering about the performance of x=x+1 versus x+=1. At some command prompt, you can easily try:

```
$ python -mtimeit -s'x=0' 'x=x+1'
1000000 loops, best of 3: 0.25 usec per loop
$ python -mtimeit -s'x=0' 'x+=1'
1000000 loops, best of 3: 0.258 usec per loop
```

and find out that performance is for all intents and purposes identical in both cases.

Building up a string from pieces

The single Python "anti-idiom" that's likeliest to kill your program's performance, to the point that you should *never* use it, is to build up a large string from pieces by looping on string concatenation statements such as *big_string+=piece*. Python strings are immutable, so each such concatenation means that Python must free the M bytes previously allocated for *big_string*, and allocate and fill M+K bytes for the new version. Doing this repeatedly in a loop, you end up with roughly $O(N^2)$ performance, where N is the total number of characters. More often than not, $O(N^2)$ performance where $O(N)$ is available is a performance disaster. On some platforms, things may be even bleaker due to memory fragmentation effects caused by freeing many memory areas of progressively larger sizes.

To achieve $O(N)$ performance, accumulate intermediate pieces in a list rather than build up the string piece by piece. Lists, unlike strings, are mutable, so appending to a list has $O(1)$ performance (amortized). Change each occurrence of *big_string+=piece* into *temp_list*.append(*piece*). Then, when you're done accumulating, use the following to build your desired string result in $O(N)$ time:

```
big_string = ''.join(temp_list)
```

Using a list comprehension, generator expression, or other direct means (such as a call to map, or use of standard library module `itertools`) to build *temp_list* may often offer further optimization over repeated calls to *temp_list*.append. Other $O(N)$ ways to build up big strings, which some Python programmers find more readable, are to concatenate the pieces to an instance of array.array('c') with the array's extend method, or to write the pieces to an instance of cStringIO.StringIO.

In the special case where you want to output the resulting string, you may gain a further small slice of performance by using `writelines` on *temp_list* (never building *big_string* in memory). When feasible (i.e., when you have the output file object open and available in the loop), it's just as effective to perform a `write` call for each *piece*, without any accumulation.

Although not nearly as crucial as += on a big string in a loop, another case where removing string concatenation may give a slight performance improvement is when you're concatenating several values in an expression:

```
oneway = str(x)+' eggs and '+str(y)+' slices of '+k+' ham'
another = '%s eggs and %s slices of %s ham' % (x, y, k)
```

Using operator % for string formatting is often a good performance choice.

Searching and sorting

Operator in, the most natural tool for searching, is O(1) when the righthand side operand is a set or dictionary, but O(N) when the righthand side operand is a string, list, or tuple. If you need to perform many searches on a container, you're generally much better off using a set or dictionary, rather than a list or tuple, as the container. Python sets and dictionaries are highly optimized for searching and fetching items by key.

Method sort of Python lists is also a highly optimized and sophisticated tool. You can rely on sort's performance. Performance dramatically degrades, however, if you pass sort a custom callable to perform comparisons in order to sort a list based on anything but built-in comparisons. To satisfy such needs, consider using the decorate-sort-undecorate (DSU) idiom instead. In spelled-out form, this idiom has the following steps:

Decorate
> Build an auxiliary list A where each item is a tuple made up of the sort keys, ending with the item of the original list L or with the item's index.

Sort
> Call A.sort( ) without arguments.

Undecorate
> Extract the items in order from the now-sorted A.

The decorate and undecorate steps are often handily performed with list comprehensions. If you need the sort to be in-place, assign the final sorted list to L[:]. Otherwise, DSU provides a sorted copy, without disturbing the original list L.

For example, say we have in L a large list of strings, each of at least two words, and we want to sort L in-place by the second word of each string:

```
A = [ (s.split( )[1], s) for s in L ]
A.sort( )
L[:] = [ t[1] for t in A ]
```

This is much faster than passing to L.sort a function that compares two strings by their second words, as in:

```
def cmp2ndword(a, b): return cmp(a.split( )[1], b.split( )[1])
L.sort(cmp2ndword)
```

On a series of benchmarks with Python 2.4 on lists of 10,000 strings, I measured the DSU version as about five times faster than the non-DSU one.

A particularly fast and effective way to use DSU is to specify a named argument key= to sort, a possibility that was introduced in Python 2.4. Module operator

Debugging

supplies functions `attrgetter` and `itemgetter` that are particularly suitable for this use. The fastest way to perform the task mentioned above is:

```
import operator
L.sort(key=operator.itemgetter(1))
```

On the same benchmarks, this is another five times faster than the plain DSU version.

Occasionally, you may avoid the need for sorting by using heaps, covered in "The heapq Module" on page 177.

Avoiding exec and from...import *

Code in a function runs faster than code at the top level in a module because access to a function's local variables is optimized to be very fast. If a function contains an exec statement without explicit dictionaries, however, the whole function slows down. The presence of such an exec statement forces the Python compiler to avoid the modest but important optimizations it normally performs regarding access to local variables, since the exec might cause any alteration at all to the function's namespace. A from statement of the form:

```
from MyModule import *
```

wastes performance, too, since it also can alter a function's namespace unpredictably.

exec itself is also quite slow, and even more so if you apply it to a string of source code rather than to a code object. By far the best approach—for performance, for correctness, and for clarity—is to avoid exec altogether. It's most often possible to find better (faster, more robust, and clearer) solutions. If you must use exec, always use it with explicit dictionaries. If you need to exec a dynamically obtained string more than once, compile the string just once and then repeatedly exec the resulting code object.

eval works on expressions, not on statements; therefore, while still slow, it avoids some of the worst performance impacts of exec. With eval, too, you're best advised to use explicit dictionaries. If you need several evaluations of the same dynamically obtained string, compile the string once and then repeatedly eval the resulting code object.

See "Dynamic Execution and the exec Statement" on page 328 for more details and advice about exec, eval, and compile.

Optimizing loops

Most of your program's bottlenecks will be in loops, particularly nested loops, because loop bodies tend to execute repeatedly. Python does not implicitly perform any code hoisting: if you have any code inside a loop that might be executed just once by hoisting it out of the loop, and the loop is a performance bottleneck, hoist the code out yourself. Sometimes the presence of code to hoist may not be immediately obvious:

```
def slower(anobject, ahugenumber):
    for i in xrange(ahugenumber): anobject.amethod(i)
```

```
def faster(anobject, ahugenumber):
    themethod = anobject.amethod
    for i in xrange(ahugenumber): themethod(i)
```

In this case, the code that `faster` hoists out of the loop is the attribute lookup `anobject.amethod`. `slower` repeats the lookup every time, while `faster` performs it just once. The two functions are not 100 percent equivalent: it is (barely) conceivable that executing `amethod` might cause such changes on `anobject` that the next lookup for the same named attribute fetches a different method object. This is part of why Python doesn't perform such optimizations itself. In practice, such subtle, obscure, and tricky cases happen quite seldom; you're quite safe performing such optimizations yourself, to squeeze the last drop of performance out of some crucial bottleneck.

Python is faster with local variables than with global ones. If a loop repeatedly accesses a global whose value does not change between iterations, cache the value in a local variable and have the loop access the local instead. This also applies to built-ins:

```
def slightly_slower(asequence, adict):
    for x in asequence: adict[x] = hex(x)
def slightly_faster(asequence, adict):
    myhex = hex
    for x in asequence: adict[x] = myhex(x)
```

Here, the speedup is very modest, on the order of five percent or so.

Do not cache `None`. `None` is a keyword, so no further optimization is needed.

List comprehensions can be faster than loops, and so can `map` and `filter`. For optimization purposes, try changing loops into list comprehensions or `map` and `filter` calls where feasible. The performance advantage of `map` and `filter` is nullified if you have to use a `lambda` or an extra level of function call. Only when you pass to `map` or `filter` a built-in function, or a function you'd have to call anyway even from an explicit loop, do you stand to gain.

The loops that you can replace most naturally with list comprehensions, or `map` and `filter` calls, are ones that build up a list by repeatedly calling `append` on the list. The following example shows this optimization in a micro-performance benchmark script:

```
import time, operator

def slow(asequence):
    result = []
    for x in asequence: result.append(-x)
    return result

def middling(asequence):
    return map(operator.neg, asequence)

def fast(asequence):
    return [-x for x in asequence]

biggie = xrange(500*1000)
tentimes = [None]*10
```

```
def timit(afunc):
    lobi = biggie
    start = time.clock()
    for x in tentimes: afunc(lobi)
    stend = time.clock()
    return "%-10s: %.2f" % (afunc.__name__, stend-start)

for afunc in slow, middling, fast, fast, middling, slow:
    print timit(afunc)
```

Running this example with Python 2.4 on my laptop shows that fast takes 3.62 seconds, middling 4.71 seconds, and slow 6.91 seconds. In other words, on this machine, slow (the loop of append method calls) is about 47 percent slower than middling (the single map call), and middling, in turn, is about 30 percent slower than fast (the list comprehension). The list comprehension is the most direct way to express the task being micro-benchmarked in this example, so, not surprisingly, it's also fastest—almost two times faster than the loop of append method calls.

Optimizing I/O

If your program does substantial amounts of I/O, it's likely that performance bottlenecks are due to I/O, not to computation. Such programs are said to be I/O-bound, rather than CPU-bound. Your operating system tries to optimize I/O performance, but you can help it in a couple of ways. One such way is to perform your I/O in chunks of a size that is optimal for performance, rather than simply being convenient for your program's operations. Another way is to use threading.

From the point of view of a program's convenience and simplicity, the ideal amount of data to read or write at a time is often small (one character or one line) or very large (an entire file at a time). That's often okay: Python and your operating system work behind the scenes to let your program use convenient logical chunks for I/O, while arranging physical I/O operations with chunk sizes more attuned to performance. Reading and writing a whole file at a time is quite likely to be okay for performance as long as the file is not very large. Specifically, file-at-a-time I/O is fine as long as the file's data fits comfortably in physical memory, leaving ample memory available for your program and operating system to perform whatever other tasks they're performing at the same time. The hard problems of I/O-bound performance tend to come with huge files.

If performance is an issue, don't use a file's readline method, which is limited in the amount of chunking and buffering it can perform. (Using writeline, on the other hand, gives no performance problem when that method is convenient for your program.) When reading a text file, loop directly on the file object to get one line at a time with best performance. If the file isn't too huge, and so can conveniently fit in memory, time two versions of your program—one looping directly on the file object, the other calling readlines to read the whole file into memory. Either may prove faster.

For binary files, particularly large binary files whose contents you need just a part of on each run of your program, module mmap (covered in "The mmap Module" on page 360) can often give you both good performance and program simplicity.

Making an I/O-bound program multithreaded may sometimes afford substantial performance gains if you can arrange your program's architecture accordingly. Start a few worker threads devoted exclusively to I/O, have the computational threads request I/O operations from the I/O threads via Queue instances, and post the request for each input operation as soon as you know you'll eventually need that data. Performance will increase only if there are other tasks your computational threads can perform while I/O threads are blocked waiting for data. Basically, you get better performance this way if you can manage to overlap computation and waiting for data by having different threads do the computing and the waiting. (See "Threads in Python" on page 341 for detailed coverage of Python threading and a suggested architecture.) On the other hand, if a substantial fraction of your I/O is on the Net, an even faster and definitely more scalable approach is to eschew threads in favor of asynchronous (event-driven) architectures, as covered in "Event-Driven Socket Programs" on page 533.

IV

Network and Web Programming

19

Client-Side Network Protocol Modules

A program can work on the Internet as a *client* (a program that accesses resources) or as a *server* (a program that makes services available). Both kinds of programs deal with protocol issues, such as how to access and communicate data, and with data-formatting issues. For order and clarity, the Python library deals with these issues in several different modules. This book covers these topics in several chapters. This chapter deals with the modules in the Python library that support protocol issues of client programs. Chapter 20 deals with lower-level modules such as socket, used in both client and server programs, and modules that support protocol issues in server programs. Data-format issues are covered in Chapters 22, 23, and 24. Chapter 21 deals specifically with server-side programs that produce web pages, either standalone or in cooperation with existing web servers such as Apache or IIS.

Data access can often be achieved most simply through Uniform Resource Locators (URLs). Python supports URLs with modules urlparse, urllib, and urllib2. For rarer cases, such as when you need fine-grained control of data access protocols normally accessed via URLs, Python supplies modules httplib and ftplib. Protocols for which URLs are often insufficient include mail (modules poplib and smtplib), Network News (module nntplib), and Telnet (module telnetlib). Python also supports the XML-RPC protocol for distributed computing with module xmlrpclib.

URL Access

A URL identifies a resource on the Internet. A URL is a string composed of several optional parts, called components, known as scheme, location, path, query, and fragment. A URL with all its parts looks something like:

```
scheme://lo.ca.ti.on/pa/th?query#fragment
```

For example, in *http://www.python.org:80/faq.cgi?src=fie*, the scheme is *http*, the location is *www.python.org:80*, the path is */faq.cgi*, the query is *src=fie*, and there is no fragment. Some of the punctuation characters form a part of one of the components they separate, while others are just separators and are part of no component. Omitting punctuation implies missing components. For example, in *mailto:me@you.com*, the scheme is *mailto*, the path is *me@you.com*, and there is no location, query, or fragment. The missing *//* means the URL has no location part, the missing *?* means it has no query part, and the missing *#* means it has no fragment part.

The urlparse Module

The urlparse module supplies functions to analyze and synthesize URL strings. The most frequently used functions of module urlparse are urljoin, urlsplit, and urlunsplit.

urljoin	urljoin(*base_url_string*,*relative_url_string*)

Returns a URL string *u*, obtained by joining *relative_url_string*, which may be relative, with *base_url_string*. The joining procedure that urljoin performs to obtain its result *u* may be summarized as follows:

- When either of the argument strings is empty, *u* is the other argument.

- When *relative_url_string* explicitly specifies a scheme that is different from that of *base_url_string*, *u* is *relative_url_string*. Otherwise, *u*'s scheme is that of *base_url_string*.

- When the scheme does not allow relative URLs (e.g., *mailto*), or *relative_url_string* explicitly specifies a location (even when it is the same as the location of *base_url_string*), all other components of *u* are those of *relative_url_string*. Otherwise, *u*'s location is that of *base_url_string*.

- *u*'s path is obtained by joining the paths of *base_url_string* and *relative_url_string* according to standard syntax for absolute and relative URL paths. For example:

```
import urlparse
urlparse.urljoin('http://somehost.com/some/path/
here','../other/path')
# Result is: 'http://somehost.com/some/other/path'
```

urlsplit	urlsplit(*url_string*,*default_scheme*='',*allow_fragments*=True)

Analyzes *url_string* and returns a tuple with five string items: scheme, location, path, query, and fragment. *default_scheme* is the first item when the *url_string* lacks a scheme. When *allow_fragments* is False, the tuple's last item is always '', whether or not *url_string* has a fragment. Items corresponding to missing parts are always ''. For example:

```
urlparse.urlsplit('http://www.python.org:80/faq.
cgi?src=fie')
# Result is: ('http','www.python.org:80','/faq.
cgi','src=fie','')
```

urlunsplit urlunsplit(*url_tuple*)

url_tuple is any iterable with exactly five items, all strings. For example, any return value from a urlsplit call is an acceptable argument for urlunsplit. urlunsplit returns a URL string with the given components and the needed separators, but with no redundant separators (e.g., there is no # in the result when the fragment, *url_tuple*'s last item, is ''). For example:

```
urlparse.urlunsplit(('http','www.python.org:80','/faq.
cgi','src=fie',''))
# Result is: 'http://www.python.org:80/faq.cgi?src=fie'
```

urlunsplit(urlsplit(*x*)) returns a normalized form of URL string *x*, which is not necessarily equal to *x* because *x* need not be normalized. For example:

```
urlparse.urlunsplit(urlparse.urlsplit('http://a.com/path/
a?'))
# Result is: 'http://a.com/path/a'
```

In this case, the normalization ensures that redundant separators, such as the trailing *?* in the argument to urlsplit, are not present in the result.

The urllib Module

The urllib module supplies simple functions to read data from URLs. urllib supports the following protocols (schemes): *http*, *https*, *ftp*, *gopher*, and *file*. *file* indicates a local file. urllib uses *file* as the default scheme for URLs that lack an explicit scheme. You can find simple, typical examples of urllib use in Chapter 23, where urllib.urlopen is used to fetch HTML and XML pages that all the various examples parse and analyze.

Functions

Module urllib supplies a number of functions, with urlopen being the most frequently used.

quote quote(*str*,*safe*='/')

Returns a copy of *str* where special characters are changed into Internet-standard quoted form %*xx*. Does not quote alphanumeric characters, spaces, any of the characters _,.-, nor any of the characters in string *safe*. For example:

```
print urllib.quote('zip&zap')
# emits: zip%26zap
```

---

quote_plus   quote_plus(*str*, *safe*='/')

Like quote, but also changes spaces into plus signs.

---

unquote   unquote(*str*)

Returns a copy of *str* where each quoted form *%xx* is changed into the corresponding character. For example:

```
print urllib.unquote('zip%26zap')
# emits: zip&zap
```

---

unquote_plus   unquote_plus(*str*)

Like unquote, but also changes plus signs into spaces.

---

urlcleanup   urlcleanup( )

Clears the cache of function urlretrieve, covered in "urlretrieve".

---

urlencode   urlencode(*query*,*doseq*=False)

Returns a string with the URL-encoded form of *query*. *query* can be either a sequence of (*name, value*) pairs, or a mapping, in which case the resulting string encodes the mapping's (*key, value*) pairs. For example:

```
urllib.urlencode([('ans',42),('key','val')])
# 'ans=42&key=val'
urllib.urlencode({'ans':42, 'key':'val'})
# 'key=val&ans=42'
```

The order of items in a dictionary is arbitrary: if you need the URL-encoded form to have key/value pairs in a specific order, use a sequence as the *query* argument, as in the first call in this snippet.

When *doseq* is true, any *value* in *query* that is a sequence and is not a string is encoded as separate parameters, one per item in *value*. For example:

```
urllib.urlencode([('K',('x','y','z'))],True)
# 'K=x&K=y&K=z'
```

When *doseq* is false (the default), each value is encoded as the quote_plus of its string form given by built-in str, whether the value is a sequence or not:

```
urllib.urlencode([('K',('x','y','z'))],False)
# 'K=%28%27x%27%2C+%27y%27%2C+%27z%27%29'
```

---

urlopen   urlopen(*urlstring*,*data*=None,*proxies*=None)

Accesses the given URL and returns a read-only file-like object *f*. *f* supplies file-like methods read, readline, readlines, and close, as well as two others:

f.geturl( )

> Returns the URL of *f*. This may differ from *urlstring* by normalization (as mentioned for function urlunsplit earlier) and because of HTTP redirects (i.e., indications that the requested data is located elsewhere). urllib supports redirects transparently, and method geturl lets you check for them if you want.

f.info( )

> Returns an instance *m* of class Message of module mimetools, covered in "The Message Classes of the rfc822 and mimetools Modules" on page 573. *m*'s headers provide metadata about *f*. For example, *m*['Content-Type'] is the MIME type of the data in *f*, and *m*'s methods *m*.gettype( ), *m*.getmaintype( ), and *m*.getsubtype( ) provide the same information.

When *data* is None and *urlstring*'s scheme is *http*, urlopen sends a GET request. When *data* is not None, *urlstring*'s scheme must be *http*, and urlopen sends a POST request. *data* must then be in URL-encoded form, and you normally prepare it with function urlencode, covered in urlencode on page 496.

urlopen can use proxies that do not require authentication. Set environment variables http_proxy, ftp_proxy, and gopher_proxy to the proxies' URLs to exploit this. You normally perform such settings in your system's environment, in platform-dependent ways, before you start Python. On the Macintosh only, urlopen transparently and implicitly retrieves proxy URLs from your Internet configuration settings. Alternatively, you can pass as argument *proxies* a mapping whose keys are scheme names, with the corresponding values being proxy URLs. For example:

```
f=urllib.urlopen('http://python.org',
proxies={'http':'http://prox:999'})
```

urlopen does not support proxies that require authentication; for such advanced needs, use the richer library module urllib2, covered in "The urllib2 Module" on page 498.

urlretrieve   urlretrieve(*urlstring*,*filename*=None,*reporthook*=None,*data*=None)

Similar to urlopen(*urlstring*,*data*), but instead returns a pair (*f*,*m*). *f* is a string that specifies the path to a file on the local file-system. *m* is an instance of class Message of module mimetools, like the result of method info called on the result value of urlopen, covered in "urlopen".

When *filename* is None, urlretrieve copies retrieved data to a temporary local file, and *f* is the path to the temporary local file.

When *filename* is not None, urlretrieve copies retrieved data to the file named *filename*, and *f* is *filename*. When *reporthook* is not None, it must be a callable with three arguments, as in the function:

```
def reporthook(block_count, block_size, file_size):
    print block_count
```

urlretrieve calls *reporthook* zero or more times while retrieving data. At each call, it passes *block_count*, the number of blocks of data retrieved so far; *block_size*, the size in bytes of each block; and *file_size*, the total size of the file in bytes. urlretrieve passes *file_size* as -1 when it cannot determine file size, which depends on the protocol involved and on how completely the server implements that protocol. The purpose of *reporthook* is to allow your program to give graphical or textual feedback to the user about the progress of the file-retrieval operation that urlretrieve performs.

The FancyURLopener class

You normally use module urllib through the functions it supplies (most often urlopen). To customize urllib's functionality, however, you can subclass urllib's FancyURLopener class and bind an instance of your subclass to attribute _urlopener of module urllib. The customizable aspects of an instance *f* of a subclass of FancyURLopener are the following.

prompt_user_ passwd

f.prompt_user_passwd(*host*,*realm*)

Returns a pair (*user*,*password*) to use to authenticate access to *host* in the security *realm*. The default implementation in class FancyURLopener prompts the user for this data in interactive text mode. Your subclass can override this method in order to interact with the user via a GUI or to fetch authentication data from persistent storage.

version

f.version

The string that *f* uses to identify itself to the server—for example, via the User-Agent header in the HTTP protocol. You can override this attribute by subclassing or rebind it directly on an instance of FancyURLopener.

The urllib2 Module

The urllib2 module is a rich, highly customizable superset of module urllib. urllib2 lets you work directly with advanced aspects of protocols such as HTTP.

For example, you can send requests with customized headers as well as URL-encoded POST bodies, and handle authentication in various realms, in both Basic and Digest forms, directly or via HTTP proxies.

In the rest of this section, I cover only the ways in which urllib2 lets your program customize these advanced aspects of URL retrieval. I do not try to impart the advanced knowledge of HTTP and other network protocols, independent of Python, that you need to make full use of urllib2's rich functionality. As an HTTP tutorial, I recommend *Python Web Programming*, by Steve Holden (New Riders): it offers good coverage of HTTP basics with examples coded in Python and a good bibliography if you need further details about network protocols.

Functions

urllib2 supplies a function urlopen that is basically identical to urllib's urlopen. To customize urllib2, install, before calling urlopen, any number of handlers grouped into an *opener*, using the build_opener and install_opener functions.

You can also optionally pass to urlopen an instance of class Request instead of a URL string. Such an instance may include both a URL string and supplementary information on how to access it, as covered in "The Request class" on page 500.

build_opener	build_opener(*handlers*)

Creates and returns an instance of class OpenerDirector (covered in "The OpenerDirector class" on page 502) with the given *handlers*. Each handler can be a subclass of class BaseHandler, instantiable without arguments, or an instance of such a subclass, however instantiated. build_opener adds instances of various handler classes provided by module urllib2 in front of the handlers you specify to handle proxies; unknown schemes; the *http*, *file*, and *https* schemes; HTTP errors; and HTTP redirects. However, if you have instances or subclasses of said classes in *handlers*, this indicates that you want to override these defaults.

install_opener	install_opener(*opener*)

Installs *opener* as the opener for further calls to urlopen. *opener* can be an instance of class OpenerDirector, such as the result of a call to function build_opener, or any signature-compatible object.

urlopen	urlopen(*url*,*data*=None)

Almost identical to the urlopen function in module urllib. However, you customize behavior via the opener and handler classes of urllib2 (covered in "The OpenerDirector class" on page 502 and "Handler classes" on page 502) rather than via class FancyURLopener as in module urllib. Argument *url* can be a URL string, like for the urlopen function in module urllib. Alternatively, *url* can be an instance of class Request, covered in the next section.

The Request class

You can optionally pass to function urlopen an instance of class Request instead of a URL string. Such an instance can embody both a URL and, optionally, other information on how to access the target URL.

Request   class Request(*urlstring*,*data*=None,*headers*={})

urlstring is the URL that this instance of class Request embodies. For example, if there are no *data* and *headers*, calling:

    urllib2.urlopen(urllib2.Request(*urlstring*))

is just like calling:

    urllib2.urlopen(*urlstring*)

When *data* is not None, the Request constructor implicitly calls on the new instance *r* its method *r*.add_data(*data*). *headers* must be a mapping of header names to header values. The Request constructor executes the equivalent of the loop:

    for *k*,*v* in *headers*.items( ): *r*.add_header(*k*,*v*)

The Request constructor also accepts optional parameters allowing fine-grained control of HTTP Cookie behavior, but such advanced functionality is rarely necessary: the class's default handling of cookies is generally sufficient. For fine-grained, client-side control of cookies, see also *http://docs.python.org/lib/module-cookielib.html*; I do not cover the cookielib module of the standard library in this book.

An instance *r* of class Request supplies the following methods.

add_data   *r*.add_data(*data*)

Sets *data* as *r*'s data. Calling urlopen(*r*) then becomes like calling urlopen(*r*,*data*)—i.e., it requires *r*'s scheme to be *http* and uses a POST request with a body of *data*, which must be a URL-encoded string.

Despite its name, method add_data does not necessarily *add* the *data*. If *r* already had data, set in *r*'s constructor or by previous calls to *r*.add_data, the latest call to *r*.add_data *replaces* the previous value of *r*'s data with the new given one. In particular, *r*.add_data(None) removes *r*'s previous data, if any.

add_header	`r.add_header(`*key*`,`*value*`)`
	Adds a header with the given *key* and *value* to *r*'s headers. If *r*'s scheme is *http*, *r*'s headers are sent as part of the request. When you add more than one header with the same *key*, later additions overwrite previous ones, so out of all headers with one given *key*, only the one given last matters.
add_unredirec-ted_header	`r.add_unredirected_header(`*key*`,`*value*`)`
	Like add_header, except that the header is added only for the first request, and is not used if the requesting procedure meets and follows any further HTTP redirection.
get_data	`r.get_data( )`
	Returns the data of *r*, either None or a URL-encoded string.
get_full_url	`r.get_full_url( )`
	Returns the URL of *r*, as given in the constructor for *r*.
get_host	`r.get_host( )`
	Returns the host component of *r*'s URL.
get_method	`r.get_method( )`
	Returns the HTTP method of *r*, either of the strings `'GET'` or `'POST'`.
get_selector	`r.get_selector( )`
	Returns the selector components of *r*'s URL (path and all following components).
get_type	`r.get_type( )`
	Returns the scheme component of *r*'s URL (i.e., the protocol).
has_data	`r.has_data( )`
	Like *r*.get_data( ) is not None.

has_header	r.has_header(*key*)
	Returns True if *r* has a header with the given *key*; otherwise, returns False.

set_proxy	r.set_proxy(*host*,*scheme*)
	Sets *r* to use a proxy at the given *host* and *scheme* for accessing *r*'s URL.

The OpenerDirector class

An instance *d* of class OpenerDirector collects instances of handler classes and orchestrates their use to open URLs of various schemes and to handle errors. Normally, you create *d* by calling function build_opener and then install it by calling function install_opener. For advanced uses, you may also access various attributes and methods of *d*, but this is a rare need and I do not cover it further in this book.

Handler classes

Module urllib2 supplies a class BaseHandler to use as the superclass of any custom handler classes you write. urllib2 also supplies many concrete subclasses of BaseHandler that handle schemes *gopher*, *ftp*, *http*, *https*, and *file*, as well as authentication, proxies, redirects, and errors. Writing custom handlers is an advanced topic, and I do not cover it further in this book.

Handling authentication

urllib2's default opener does no authentication. To get authentication, call build_opener to build an opener with instances of HTTPBasicAuthHandler, ProxyBasicAuthHandler, HTTPDigestAuthHandler, and/or ProxyDigestAuthHandler, depending on whether you want authentication to be directly in HTTP or to a proxy, and on whether you need Basic or Digest authentication.

To instantiate each of these authentication handlers, use an instance *x* of class HTTPPasswordMgrWithDefaultRealm as the only argument to the authentication handler's constructor. You normally use the same *x* to instantiate all the authentication handlers you need. To record users and passwords for given authentication realms and URLs, call *x*.add_password one or more times.

add_password	x.add_password(*realm*,*URLs*,*user*,*password*)
	Records in *x* the pair (*user*,*password*) as the credentials in the given *realm* for URLs given by *URLs*. *realm* is a string that names an authentication realm, or None, to supply default credentials for any

realm not specifically recorded. *URLs* is a URL string or a sequence of URL strings. A URL *u* is deemed applicable for these credentials if there is an item *u1* of *URLs* such that the location components of *u* and *u1* are equal, and the path component of *u1* is a prefix of that of *u*. Other components (scheme, query, fragment) don't affect applicability for authentication purposes.

The following example shows how to use urllib2 with basic HTTP authentication:

```
import urllib2

x = urllib2.HTTPPasswordMgrWithDefaultRealm( )
x.add_password(None, 'http://myhost.com/', 'auser',
'apassword')
auth = urlib2.HTTPBasicAuthHandler(x)
opener = urllib2.build_opener(auth)
urllib2.install_opener(opener)

flob = urllib2.urlopen('http://myhost.com/index.html')
for line in flob.readlines( ): print line,
```

Email Protocols

Most email today is sent via servers that implement the Simple Mail Transport Protocol (SMTP) and received via servers that implement the Post Office Protocol version 3 (POP3). These protocols are supported by the Python standard library modules smtplib and poplib. Some servers, instead of or in addition to POP3, implement the richer and more advanced Internet Message Access Protocol version 4 (IMAP4), supported by the Python standard library module imaplib, which I do not cover in this book.

The poplib Module

The poplib module supplies a class POP3 to access a POP mailbox. The specifications of the POP protocol are at *http://www.ietf.org/rfc/rfc1939.txt*.

POP3   class POP3(*host*,*port*=110)

Returns an instance *p* of class POP3 connected to the given *host* and *port*.

Instance *p* supplies many methods, of which the most frequently used are the following.

dele   `p.dele(msgnum)`

Marks message *msgnum* for deletion. The server will perform deletions when this connection terminates by calling *p*.quit. dele returns the server response string.

list   `p.list(msgnum=None)`

Returns a pair (*response,messages*), where *response* is the server response string and *messages* is a list of strings, each of two words '*msgnum bytes*', giving the message number and the length in bytes of each message in the mailbox. When *msgnum* is not None, *messages* has only one item: a '*msgnum bytes*' for the given *msgnum*.

pass_   `p.pass_(password)`

Sends the password. Must be called after *p*.user. The trailing underscore in the name is needed because pass is a Python keyword. Returns the server response string.

quit   `p.quit( )`

Ends the session and tells the server to perform the deletions that were requested by calls to *p*.dele. Returns the server response string.

retr   `p.retr(msgnum)`

Returns a three-item tuple (*response,lines,bytes*), where *response* is the server response string, *lines* is the list of all lines in message *msgnum*, and *bytes* is the total number of bytes in the message.

set_debuglevel   `p.set_debuglevel(debug_level)`

Sets the debug level to integer *debug_level*: 0, the default, for no debugging; 1 to get a modest amount of debugging output; and 2 or more to get a complete output trace of all control information exchanged with the server.

stat   `p.stat( )`

Returns a pair (*num_messages,bytes*), where *num_messages* is the number of messages in the mailbox and *bytes* is the total number of bytes.

top	`p.top(msgnum,maxlines)`

Like retr, but returns no more than *maxlines* lines of text from the message after the headers. Can be useful to view the start of long messages.

user	`p.user(username)`

Sends the username. Must be followed by a call to `p.pass_`.

The smtplib Module

The smtplib module supplies a class SMTP to send mail to any SMTP server. The specifications of the SMTP protocol are at *http://www.ietf.org/rfc/rfc2821.txt*.

SMTP	`class SMTP([host,port=25])`

Returns an instance *s* of class SMTP. When *host* (and optionally *port*) is given, implicitly calls *s*.connect(*host,port*).

Instance *s* supplies many methods, of which the most frequently used are the following.

connect	`s.connect(host=127.0.0.1,port=25)`

Connects to an SMTP server on the given *host* (by default, the local host) and *port* (port 25 is the default port for the SMTP service).

login	`s.login(user,password)`

Logs in to the server with the given *user* and *password*. Needed only if the SMTP server requires authentication.

quit	`s.quit( )`

Terminates the SMTP session.

sendmail	`s.sendmail(from_addr,to_addrs,msg_string)`

Sends mail message *msg_string* from the sender whose address is in string *from_addr* to each of the recipients whose addresses are the items of list *to_addrs*. *msg_string* must be a complete RFC 822 message in a single multiline string: the headers, an empty line for separation, then the body. *from_addr* and *to_addrs* only direct the mail transport, and do not add or change headers in *msg_string*. To prepare RFC 822–compliant messages, use package email, covered in "MIME and Email Format Handling" on page 564.

The HTTP and FTP Protocols

Modules urllib and urllib2 are often the handiest ways to access servers for *http*, *https*, and *ftp* protocols. The Python standard library also supplies specific modules for these protocols. The protocols' specifications are at *http://www.ietf.org/rfc/rfc2616.txt*, *http://www.ietf.org/rfc/rfc2818.txt*, and *http://www.ietf.org/rfc/rfc959.txt*.

The httplib Module

Module httplib supplies a class HTTPConnection to connect to an HTTP server.

HTTPConnection	class HTTPConnection(*host*,*port*=80)
	Returns an instance *h* of class HTTPConnection, ready for connection (but not yet connected) to the given *host* and *port*.
	Instance *h* supplies several methods, of which the most frequently used are the following.
close	*h*.close( )
	Closes the connection to the HTTP server.
getresponse	*h*.getresponse( )
	Returns an instance *r* of class HTTPResponse, which represents the response received from the HTTP server. Call after method request has returned. Instance *r* supplies the following attributes and methods:
	r.getheadeeypr(*name*,*default*=None)
	Returns the contents of header *name*, or *default* if no such header exists.
	r.msg
	An instance of class Message of module mimetools, covered in "The Message Classes of the rfc822 and mimetools Modules" on page 573. You can use *r*.msg to access the response's headers and body.
	r.read( )
	Returns a string that is the body of the server's response.

r.reason

> The string that the server gave as the reason for errors or anomalies, if any. If the request was successful, *r*.reason is normally the string 'OK'.

r.status

> An int, which is the status code that the server returned. If the request was successful, *r*.status should be between 200 and 299 according to the HTTP standard. Values between 400 and 599 are HTTP error codes: for example, 404 is the error code that a server sends when the page you request cannot be found.

r.version

> 10 if the server supports only HTTP 1.0, 11 if the server supports HTTP 1.1.

---

request   *h*.request(*command*,*URL*,*data*=None,*headers*={})

Sends a request to the HTTP server. *command* is an HTTP command string, such as 'GET' or 'POST'. *URL* is an HTTP selector (i.e., a URL string without the scheme and location components—just the path, possibly followed by a query and/or fragment). *data*, if not None, is a string sent as the body of the request, and is normally meaningful only for commands 'POST' and 'PUT'. request computes and sends the Content-Length header giving the length of *data*. To send other headers, pass them in dict argument *headers*, with the header name as the key and the contents as the corresponding value.

Module httplib also supplies class HTTPSConnection, which is used in exactly the same way as class HTTPConnection for connections with protocol *https* rather than *http*.

The ftplib Module

The ftplib module supplies a class FTP to connect to an FTP server.

FTP   class FTP([*host*[,*user*,*passwd*='']])

Returns an instance *f* of class FTP. When *host* is given, implicitly calls *f*.connect(*host*). When *user* (and optionally *passwd*) are also given, implicitly calls *f*.login(*user*,*passwd*) after *f*.connect.

Instance *f* supplies many methods, of which the most frequently used are the following.

abort   *f*.abort( )

Tries to interrupt an ongoing file transfer by immediately sending the FTP 'ABOR' command as "out-of-band" data.

---

connect   *f*.connect(*host*,*port*=21)

Connects to an FTP server on the given *host* and *port*. Call once per instance *f*, as *f*'s first method call. Don't call if *host* was given on creation.

---

cwd   *f*.cwd(*pathname*)

Sets the current directory on the FTP server to *pathname*.

---

delete   *f*.delete(*filename*)

Tells the FTP server to delete a file and returns a string, which is the server's response.

---

getwelcome   *f*.getwelcome( )

Returns the string that's the server's "Welcome" response, as saved at the time you called *f*.connect.

---

login   *f*.login(*user*='anonymous',*passwd*='')

Logs in to the FTP server. When *user* is 'anonymous' and *passwd* is '', login determines the real user and host and sends *user@host* as the password, as normal anonymous FTP conventions require. Call once per instance of *f*, as the first method call on *f* after connecting.

---

mkd   *f*.mkd(*pathname*)

Makes a new directory, named *pathname*, on the FTP server.

---

pwd   *f*.pwd( )

Returns the current directory on the FTP server.

---

quit   *f*.quit( )

Closes the connection to the FTP server. Call as the last method call on *f*.

rename

f.rename(*oldname*,*newname*)

Tells the FTP server to rename a file from *oldname* to *newname*.

retrbinary

f.retrbinary(*command*,*callback*,*blocksize*=8192,*rest*=None)

Retrieves data in binary mode. *command* is a string with an appropriate FTP command, typically 'RETR *filename*'. *callback* is a callable that retrbinary calls for each block of data returned, passing the block of data, a string, as the only argument. *blocksize* is the maximum size of each block of data. When *rest* is not None, it's the offset in bytes from the start of the file at which you want to start the retrieval, if the FTP server supports the 'REST' command. When *rest* is not None and the FTP server does not support the 'REST' command, retrbinary raises an exception.

retrlines

f.retrlines(*command*,*callback*=None)

Retrieves data in text mode. *command* is a string with an appropriate FTP command, typically 'RETR *filename*' or 'LIST'. *callback* is a callable that retrlines calls for each line of text returned, passing the line of text, a string, as the only argument (without the end-of-line marker). When *callback* is None, retrlines writes the lines of text to sys.stdout.

rmd

f.rmd(*pathname*)

Removes directory *pathname* on the FTP server.

sendcmd

f.sendcmd(*command*)

Sends string *command* as a command to the server and returns the server's response string. Suitable only for commands that don't open data connections.

set_pasv

f.set_pasv(*pasv*)

Sets passive mode on if *pasv* is true, off if false. Passive mode defaults to on.

size

f.size(*filename*)

Returns the size in bytes of the named file on the FTP server, or None if unable to determine the file's size.

storbinary   *f*.storbinary(*command*,*file*,*blocksize*=8192)

Stores data in binary mode. *command* is a string with an appropriate FTP command, typically 'STOR *filename*'. *file* is a file open in binary mode, which storbinary reads, repeatedly calling *file*.read(*blocksize*), to obtain the data to transfer to the FTP server.

storlines   *f*.storlines(*command*,*file*)

Stores data in text mode. *command* is a string with an appropriate FTP command, typically 'STOR *filename*'. *file* is a file open in text mode, which storlines reads, repeatedly calling *file*.readline, to get the data to transfer to the FTP server.

Here is a typical, simple example of ftplib use in an interactive interpreter session:

```
>>> import ftplib
>>> f = ftplib.FTP('ftp.python.org')
>>> f.login( )
'230 Anonymous access granted, restrictions apply.'
>>> f.retrlines('LIST')
drwxrwxr-x   4 webmaster webmaster       512 Oct 12  2001 pub
'226 Transfer complete.'
>>> f.cwd('pub')
'250 CWD command successful.'
>>> f.retrlines('LIST')
drwxrwsr-x   2 barry     webmaster       512 Oct 12  2001 jython
lrwx------   1 root      ftp            25 Aug  3  2001 python -> www.python.
org/ftp/python
drwxrwxr-x  43 webmaster webmaster      2560 Sep  3 17:22 www.python.org
'226 Transfer complete.'
>>> f.cwd('python')
'250 CWD command successful.'
>>> f.retrlines('LIST')
drwxrwxr-x   2 webmaster webmaster       512 Aug 23  2001 2.0
  [ many result lines snipped ]
drwxrwxr-x   2 webmaster webmaster       512 Aug  2  2001 wpy
'226 Transfer complete.'
>>> f.retrlines('RETR README')
Python Distribution
====================

Most subdirectories have a README or INDEX files explaining the
contents.
  [ many result lines snipped ]
gzipped version of this file, and 'get misc.tar.gz' will fetch a
gzipped tar archive of the misc subdir.
'226 Transfer complete.'
```

```
>>> f.close()
>>>
```

In this case, the following far simpler code is equivalent:

```
print urllib.urlopen('ftp://ftp.python.org/pub/python/README').read()
```

However, ftplib affords much more detailed control of FTP operations than urllib does. Thus, in some cases, ftplib may be useful in your programs.

Network News

Network News, also known as Usenet, is mostly transmitted with the Network News Transport Protocol (NNTP). The specifications of the POP protocol are at *http://www.ietf.org/rfc/rfc977.txt* and *http://www.ietf.org/rfc/rfc2980.txt*. The Python standard library supports this protocol in module nntplib. The nntplib module supplies a class NNTP to connect to an NNTP server.

NNTP

class NNTP(*host, port*=119, *user*=None, *password*=None, *readermode*=False, *usenetrc*=True)

Returns an instance *n* of class NNTP connected to the *host* and *port*, and optionally authenticated with the given *user* and *password* if *user* is not None. When *readermode* is True, also sends a 'mode reader' command; you may need this, depending on the NNTP server and on the NNTP commands you send to that server. When *usenetrc* is True, tries getting user and password for authentication from a file named *.netrc* in the current user's home directory, if not explicitly specified.

Response Strings

An instance *n* of NNTP supplies many methods. Each of *n*'s methods returns a tuple whose first item is a string (known as *response* in the following), which is the response from the NNTP server to the NNTP command that corresponds to the method (method post just returns the *response* string, not a tuple). Each method returns the *response* string just as the NNTP server supplies it. The string starts with an integer in decimal form (the integer is known as the return code), followed by a space, followed by explanatory text.

For some commands, the extra text after the return code is just a comment or explanation supplied by the NNTP server. For other commands, the NNTP standard specifies the format of the text that follows the return code on the response line. In those cases, the relevant method also parses the text in question, yielding other items in the method's resulting tuple, so your code need not perform such parsing itself; rather, you just access further items in the method's result tuple, as specified in the following sections.

Return codes of the form 2*xx*, for any two digits *xx*, are success codes (i.e., they indicate that the corresponding NNTP command succeeded). Return codes of other forms, such as 4*xx* and 5*xx*, indicate failures in some NNTP command. In these cases, the method does not return a result. Rather, the method raises an instance of exception class nntplib.NNTPError, or some subclass of it, such as NNTPTemporaryError for errors that may (or may not) be automatically resolved if you try again, or NNTPPermanentError for errors that are sure to occur again if you retry. When a method of an NNTP instance raises an NNTPError instance *e*, the server's response string, starting with a return code such as 4*xx*, is str(*e*).

Methods

The most frequently used methods of an NNTP instance *n* are as follows.

---

article | *n*.article(*id*)

id is a string, either an article ID enclosed in angle brackets (<>) or an article number in the current group. Returns a tuple with three strings and a list (*response,number,id,lines*), where *number* is the article number in the current group, *id* is the article ID enclosed in angle brackets, and *lines* is a list of strings that are the lines in the article (headers, then body, with an empty-line separator, and without end-of-line characters).

---

body | *n*.body(*id,file*)

id is a string, either an article ID enclosed in angle brackets (<>) or an article number in the current group. Returns a tuple with three strings and a list (*response,number,id,lines*), where *number* is the article number in the current group, *id* is the article ID enclosed in angle brackets, and *lines* is a list of strings that are the lines in the article's body, without end-of-line characters. When *file* is not None, it can be either a string that names a file that body then opens for writing, or a file object already open for writing. In either case, body writes the article's body to the file, and, in these cases, *lines* in the tuple body returns is an empty list.

---

group | *n*.group(*group_name*)

Makes *group_name* the current group and returns a tuple of five strings (*response,count,first,last,group_name*), where *count* is the total number of articles in the group, *last* is the number of the most recent article, *first* is the number of the oldest article, and *group_name* is the group's name. *group_name* is usually the same one you requested (i.e., the argument to *n*.group). However, an NNTP server can set up aliases, or synonyms; therefore, you may want to check the last item of the returned tuple to ascertain which newsgroup has been set as current.

| **head** | `n.head(id)`

Returns an article's headers. *id* is a string, either an article ID enclosed in angle brackets (<>) or an article number in the current group. head returns a tuple of three strings and a list (*response,number,id,lines*), where *number* is the article number in the current group, *id* is the article ID enclosed in angle brackets, and *lines* is a list of strings that are the lines in the article's headers, without end-of-line characters.

| **last** | `n.last()`

Returns a tuple of three strings (*response,number,id*), where *number* is the latest (highest) article number in the current group and *id* is the article ID, enclosed in angle brackets, for the last article in the current group.

| **list** | `n.list()`

Returns a pair (*response,group_stats*), where *group_stats* is a list of tuples with information about each group on the server. Each item of *group_stats* is a tuple of four strings (*group_name,last,first,group_flag*), where *group_name* is the group's name, *last* is the number of the most recent article, *first* is the number of the oldest article, and *group_flag* is `'y'` when you're allowed to post, `'n'` when you're not allowed to post, and `'m'` when the group is moderated.

| **newgroups** | `n.newgroups(date,time)`

date is a string that indicates a date, of the form `'yymmdd'`. *time* is a string that indicates a time, of the form `'hhmmss'`. newgroups returns a pair (*response,group_names*), where *group_names* is the list of the names of groups created since the given date and time.

| **newnews** | `n.newnews(group,date,time)`

group is a string that is either a group name, meaning you only want data about articles in that group, or `'*'`, meaning you want data about articles in any newsgroup on the server. *date* is a string that indicates a date, of the form `'yymmdd'`. *time* is a string that indicates a time, of the form `'hhmmss'`. newnews returns a pair (*response,article_ids*), where *article_ids* is the list of the identifiers of articles received since the given date and time.

| **next** | `n.next()`

Returns a tuple of three strings (*response,number,id*), where *number* is the next article number in the current group and *id* is the article ID, enclosed in angle brackets, for the next article in the current group. The current group is set by calling *n*.group. Each time you call *n*.next, you receive information about another article (i.e., *n* implicitly maintains a pointer to a current article within the group and advances the pointer on each call to *n*.next). When there is no next article (i.e., the current article is the last one in the current group), *n*.next raises NNTPTemporaryError (the error is deemed to be "temporary" because, presumably, there will be more articles in the future).

post	*n*.post(*file*)

Posts an article to the current group, reading it from *file*. *file* is a file-like object open for reading; post reads the article's headers and body from the file by repeatedly calling *file*.readline. *file* contains all headers, then an empty-line separator, then the body. post returns a string, which is the *response* from the server to the posting request.

quit	*n*.quit( )

Closes the connection to the NNTP server. Call as the last method call on *n*.

stat	*n*.stat(*id*)

id is a string, either an article ID in angle brackets or an article number in the current group. Returns a tuple of three strings (*response*,*number*,*id*), where *number* is the article number in the current group and *id* is the article ID in angle brackets.

Example

Here is a typical, simple example of nntplib use in an interactive interpreter session, using the free public NNTP server at news.gmane.org:

```
>>> import nntplib
>>> n = nntplib.NNTP('news.gmane.org')
>>> response, groups = n.list( )
>>> print response
215 Newsgroups in form "group high low flags".
>>> print 'gmane.org carries', len(groups), 'newsgroups'
gmane.org carries 8094 newsgroups
>>> pg_groups = [g for g in groups if 'postgresql' in g[0]]
>>> print 'gmane.org carries', len(pg_groups), 'groups about postgresql'
gmane.org carries 1162 groups about postgresql
>>> n.group('gmane.comp.db.postgresql.announce')
 ('211 699 1 699 gmane.comp.db.postgresql.announce', '699', '1', '699',
'gmane.comp.db.postgresql.announce')
```

```
>>> response, artnum, artid, headers = n.head('699')
>>> len(headers)
71
>>> [h for h in headers if h.startswith('Subject:')]
['Subject: EMS SQL Manager 2005 for PostgreSQL ver. 3.4 released']
>>> n.quit()
'205 .'
```

Telnet

Telnet is an old protocol, specified by RFC 854 (see *http://www.ietf.org/rfc/rfc854.txt*), and is normally used for interactive user sessions. The Python standard library supports this protocol in its module `telnetlib`. Module `telnetlib` supplies a class Telnet to connect to a Telnet server.

Telnet

`class Telnet(host=None,port=23)`

Returns an instance *t* of class Telnet. When *host* (and optionally *port*) is given, implicitly calls *t*.open(*host*,*port*).

Instance *t* supplies many methods, of which the most frequently used are as follows.

close

`t.close()`

Closes the connection.

expect

`t.expect(res,timeout=None)`

Reads data from the connection until it matches any of the regular expressions that are the items of list *res*, or until *timeout* seconds elapse when *timeout* is not None. (Regular expressions and match objects are covered in "Regular Expressions and the re Module" on page 201.) Returns a tuple of three items (*i*,*mo*,*txt*), where *i* is the index in *res* of the regular expression that matched, *mo* is the match object, and *txt* is all the text read until the match, included. Raises EOFError when the connection is closed and no data is available; otherwise, when it gets no match, returns (-1,None,*txt*), where *txt* is all the text read, or possibly '' if nothing was read before a timeout. Results are nondeterministic if more than one item in *res* can match, or if any of the items in *res* include greedy parts (such as '.*').

interact

`t.interact()`

Enters interactive mode, connecting standard input and output to the two channels of the connection, like a dumb Telnet client.

open	`t.open(host,port=23)`
	Connects to a Telnet server on the given *host* and *port*. Call once per instance *t*, as *t*'s first method call. Don't call if *host* was given on creation.
read_all	`t.read_all()`
	Reads data from the connection until the connection is closed, then returns all available data. Blocks until the connection is closed.
read_eager	`t.read_eager()`
	Reads and returns all that can be read from the connection without blocking; may be the empty string `''`. Raises `EOFError` if the connection is closed and no data is available.
read_some	`t.read_some()`
	Reads and returns at least one byte of data from the connection, unless the connection is closed, in which case it returns `''`. Blocks until at least one byte of data is available.
read_until	`t.read_until(expected,timeout=None)`
	Reads data from the connection until it finds string *expected*, or *timeout* seconds elapse when *timeout* is not None. Returns the data available at that time, possibly the empty string `''`. Raises `EOFError` if the connection is closed and no data is available.
write	`t.write(astring)`
	Writes string *astring* to the connection.

Distributed Computing

There are many standards for distributed computing, from simple Remote Procedure Call (RPC) ones to rich object-oriented ones such as CORBA. You can find many third-party Python modules that support these standards on the Internet.

The Python standard library supports both server and client use of a simple yet powerful standard known as XML-RPC. For in-depth coverage of XML-RPC, I recommend the book *Programming Web Services with XML-RPC*, by Simon St. Laurent and Joe Johnson (O'Reilly). XML-RPC uses HTTP or HTTPS as the underlying transport and encodes requests and replies in XML. For server-side support, see "The Message Classes of the rfc822 and mimetools Modules" on page 573. Client-side support is supplied by module xmlrpclib.

The xmlrpclib module supplies a class ServerProxy, which you instantiate to connect to an XML-RPC server. An instance *s* of ServerProxy is a proxy for the server it connects to: you call arbitrary methods on *s*, and *s* packages the method name and argument values as an XML-RPC request, sends the request to the XML-RPC server, receives the server's response, and unpacks the response as the method's result. The arguments to such method calls can be of any type supported by XML-RPC:

Boolean
    The built-in bool constants True and False

Integers, floating-point numbers, strings, arrays
    Passed and returned as Python int, float, Unicode, and list values

Structures
    Passed and returned as Python dict values whose keys must be strings

Dates
    Passed as instances of class xmlrpclib.DateTime; value is represented in seconds since the epoch, as in module time (see Chapter 12).

Binary data
    Passed as instances of class xmlrpclib.Binary; value is an arbitrary byte string

Module xmlrpclib supplies several classes.

Binary   class Binary(*x*)

                    x is a Python string of arbitrary bytes. *b* wraps the bytes as an XML-RPC binary object.

DateTime   class DateTime(*x*)

                    x is the number of seconds since the epoch, as in module time, covered in "The time Module" on page 302.

ServerProxy   class ServerProxy(*uri*, *transport*=None, *encoding*='utf-8', *verbose*=False, *allow_none*=False)

                    The *uri* string is normally the server's URL and may be of the form '*protocol://user:pass@host/*...' to include a username and password for basic authentication; *protocol* is http or https, and you normally do not pass optional argument *transport*, allowing the module to pick the right transport for the given protocol. You may optionally pass optional argument *encoding* as the name of the 8-bit encoding to use, *verbose* as True to get verbose debugging information during the following XML-RPC operations, and *allow_none* as True to add None to the set of data types supported (this requires a server that sports a popular but not universal extension to the basic XML-RPC protocol).

If the server at the given *uri* supports introspection, *s* supplies an attribute *s*.system that in turn supplies three methods:

s.system.listMethods( )
> Returns a list of strings, one per each method supported by the server.

s.system.methodSignature(*name*)
> Returns a list of strings, each a signature of method *name* on the server. A signature string is composed of type names separated by commas: first the type of the return value, then the type of each argument. When method *name* has no defined signature, *s*.server.methodSignature(*name*) returns some object that is not a list.

s.system.methodHelp(*name*)
> Returns a string with help about method *name*. The string can be either plain text or HTML. When the method *name* has no defined help, *s*.server.methodHelp(*name*) returns an empty string ' '.

The following example uses xmlrpclib to access O'Reilly's Meerkat open wire service (see *http://www.oreillynet.com/meerkat/* for more information about Meerkat) and displays a few recent news items about Python:

```
import xmlrpclib

proxy = xmlrpclib.ServerProxy(
    'http://www.oreillynet.com/meerkat/xml-rpc/server.php')
results = proxy.meerkat.getItems({'search':'Python', 'num_items':7})

want_keys = 'title link description'.split( )
n = 0
for result in results:
    n = n + 1
    for key in want_keys:
        print '%d. %s: %s' % (n, key.title( ), result.get(key))
    print
```

Other Protocols

While the standard Python library is quite rich, the set of protocols used on the Net is even richer. You can find support for these protocols in many third-party extensions. For the RSS protocol (described at *http://blogs.law.harvard.edu/tech/rss*), for example, you can check *http://wiki.python.org/moin/RssLibraries*, where you will find a fair summary of many available modules. For SSH (see *http://www.snailbook.com/protocols.html*), a very secure protocol that does not require third-party involvement of a Certification Authority, your best choice is probably paramiko, found at *http://www.lag.net/paramiko/*. SSH is often the most secure, handiest alternative to Telnet, FTP, and similar old protocols, and paramiko is an excellent implementation of SSH for Python.

20

Sockets and Server-Side Network Protocol Modules

To communicate with the Internet, programs use objects known as *sockets*. The Python library supports sockets through module socket, as well as wrapping them into higher-level client-side modules, as covered in Chapter 19. To help you write server programs, the Python library also supplies higher-level modules to use as frameworks for socket servers. Standard and third-party Python modules and extensions also support asynchronous socket operations. This chapter covers socket, in "The socket Module" on page 521; server-side framework modules, in "The SocketServer Module" on page 528; asynchronous operation with standard Python library modules, in "Event-Driven Socket Programs" on page 533; and the bare essentials of the rich and powerful Twisted third-party package, in "The Twisted Framework" on page 539.

The modules covered in this chapter offer many conveniences compared to C-level socket programming. However, in the end, the modules rely on native socket functionality supplied by the underlying operating system. While it is often possible to write effective network clients by using just the modules covered in Chapter 19 without really needing to understand sockets, writing effective network servers most often does require some understanding of sockets. Thus, the lower-level module socket is covered in this chapter and not in Chapter 19, even though both clients and servers use sockets.

However, I cover only the ways in which module socket lets your program access sockets; I do not try to impart a detailed understanding of sockets, TCP/IP, and other aspects of network behavior independent of Python that you may need to make use of socket's functionality. To understand socket behavior in detail on any kind of platform, I recommend W. Richard Stevens's *Unix Network Programming, Volume 1* (Prentice Hall). Higher-level modules are simpler and more powerful, but a detailed understanding of the underlying technology is always useful, and sometimes it can prove indispensable.

The socket Module

The socket module supplies a factory function, also named socket, that you call to generate a socket object s. To perform network operations, call methods on s. In a client program, connect to a server by calling s.connect. In a server program, wait for clients to connect by calling s.bind and s.listen. When a client requests a connection, accept the request by calling s.accept, which returns another socket object s1 connected to the client. Once you have a connected socket object, transmit data by calling its method send and receive data by calling its method recv.

Python supports both current Internet Protocol (IP) standards. IPv4 is more widespread; IPv6 is newer. In IPv4, a network address is a pair (*host,port*). *host* is a Domain Name System (DNS) hostname such as 'www.python.org' or a dotted-quad IP address such as '194.109.137.226'. *port* is an integer that indicates a socket's port number. In IPv6, a network address is a tuple (*host,port,flowinfo,scopeid*). IPv6 infrastructure is not yet widely deployed; I do not cover IPv6 further in this book. When *host* is a DNS hostname, Python looks up the name on your platform's DNS infrastructure, using the IP address that corresponds to the name.

Module socket supplies an exception class error. Functions and methods of socket raise error to diagnose socket-specific errors. Module socket also supplies many functions. Many of these functions translate data, such as integers, between your host's native format and network standard format. The higher-level protocol that your program and its counterpart are using on a socket determines what conversions you must perform.

socket Functions

The most frequently used functions of module socket are as follows.

getdefault-timeout	getdefaulttimeout( )
	Returns a float that is the timeout (in seconds, possibly with a fractional part) currently set by default on newly created socket objects, or None if newly created socket objects currently have no timeout behavior.
getfqdn	getfqdn(*host=''*)
	Returns the fully qualified domain name string for the given *host* (a string that is most often a domain name that is not fully qualified). When *host* is '', returns the fully qualified domain name string for the local host.
gethostbyaddr	gethostbyaddr(*ipaddr*)
	Returns a tuple with three items (*hostname,alias_list,ipaddr_list*). *hostname* is a string, the primary name of the host whose IP address you pass as string *ipaddr*. *alias_list* is a list of zero or more alias

names for the host. *ipaddr_list* is a list of one or more dotted-quad addresses for the host.

gethostby-name_ex	gethostbyname_ex(*hostname*)
	Returns the same results as gethostbyaddr, but takes as an argument a *hostname* string that can be either an IP dotted-quad address or a DNS name.
htonl	htonl(*i32*)
	Converts the 32-bit integer *i32* from this host's format into network format.
htons	htons(*i16*)
	Converts the 16-bit integer *i16* from this host's format into network format.
inet_aton	inet_aton(*ipaddr_string*)
	Converts the IP address *ipaddr_string* to 32-bit network format; returns a 4-byte string.
inet_ntoa	inet_ntoa(*packed_string*)
	Converts the 4-byte network-format string *packed_string*; returns IP dotted-quad string.
ntohl	ntohl(*i32*)
	Converts the 32-bit integer *i32* from network format into this host's format; returns int.
ntohs	ntohs(*i16*)
	Converts the 16-bit integer *i16* from network format into this host's format; returns int.
setdefault-timeout	setdefaulttimeout(*t*)
	Sets float *t* as the timeout (in seconds, possibly with a fractional part) set by default on newly created socket objects. If *t* is None, sets newly created socket objects to have no timeout behavior.

socket	socket(*family,type*)
	Creates and returns a socket object with the given family and type. *family* is usually attribute AF_INET of module socket, indicating you want an Internet (TCP/IP) kind of socket. Depending on your platform, *family* may also be another attribute of module socket. AF_UNIX, on Unix-like platforms only, indicates that you want a Unix-like socket. (This book does not cover non-Internet sockets, since it focuses on cross-platform Python.) *type* is one of a few attributes of module socket—usually SOCK_STREAM for a TCP (connection) socket, or SOCK_DGRAM for a UDP (datagram) socket.

The socket Class

A socket object *s* supplies many methods. The commonly used ones are as follows.

accept	s.accept()
	Accepts a connection request and returns a pair (*s1*,(*ipaddr*,*port*)). *s1* is a new connected socket; *ipaddr* and *port* are the IP address and port number of the counterpart. *s* must be SOCK_STREAM; you must have previously called s.bind and s.listen. If no client is trying to connect, accept blocks until some client tries to connect.
bind	s.bind((*host,port*))
	Binds socket *s* to accept connections from host *host* on port number *port*. *host* can be the empty string ' ' to accept connections from any host. It's an error to call s.bind twice on any socket object *s*.
close	s.close()
	Closes the socket, terminating any listening or connection on it. It's an error to call any other method on *s* after s.close.
connect	s.connect((*host,port*))
	Connects socket *s* to the server on the given *host* and *port*. Blocks until the server accepts or rejects the connection attempt, and raises an exception in case of errors.

getpeername   `s.getpeername( )`

Returns a pair (*ipaddr,port*) with the IP address and port number of the counterpart. *s* must be connected, either because you called `s.connect` or because *s* was generated by another socket object's accept method.

getsockname   `s.getpeername( )`

Returns a pair (*ipaddr,port*) with the IP address and port number of this socket on the local machine.

getsockopt   `s.getsockopt(`*level,optname*`[,`*bufsize*`])`

Returns the current value of an option on *s*. *level* can be any of four constants supplied for the purpose by module socket: SOL_SOCKET, for options related to the socket itself, or SOL_IP, SOL_TCP, or SOL_UDP, for options related to protocols IP, TCP, and UDP, respectively. *optname* can be any of many constants supplied by module socket to identify each socket option, with names starting with SO_. *bufsize* is normally absent, and then getsockopt returns the int value of the option. However, some options have values that are structures, not integers. In these cases, pass as *bufsize* the size of the appropriate structure, in bytes—getsockopt returns a binary string of bytes suitable for unpacking with module struct, covered in "The struct Module" on page 227.

For example, here is how to find out if by default sockets are allowed to reuse addresses:

```
import socket
s = socket.socket( )
print s.getsockopt(s.SOL_SOCKET, s.SO_REUSEADDR)
# emits 0, meaning that by default sockets do not reuse
addresses
```

gettimeout   `s.gettimeout( )`

Returns a float, which is the timeout (in seconds, possibly with a fractional part) currently set on *s*, or None if *s* currently has no timeout behavior.

listen   `s.listen(`*maxpending*`)`

Listens for connection attempts to the socket, allowing up to *maxpending* queued attempts at any time. *maxpending* must be greater than 0 and less than or equal to a system-dependent value, which on all contemporary systems is at least 5.

makefile	`s.makefile(mode='r')`

Creates and returns a file object *f* (as covered in "File Objects" on page 216) that reads from and/or writes to the socket. You can close *f* and *s* independently; Python closes the underlying socket only when both *f* and *s* are closed.

recv	`s.recv(bufsize)`

Receives up to *bufsize* bytes from the socket and returns a string with the data received. Returns an empty string when the socket is disconnected. If there is currently no data, blocks until the socket is disconnected or some data arrives.

recvfrom	`s.recvfrom(bufsize)`

Receives up to *bufsize* bytes from the socket and returns a tuple (*data*,(*ipaddr*,*port*)). *data* is a string of the data received, and *ipaddr* and *port* are the IP address and port number of the sender. Useful with datagram sockets, which can receive data from many senders. If there is no data in the socket, blocks until data arrives.

send	`s.send(string)`

Sends the bytes of *string* on the socket. Returns the number *n* of bytes sent. *n* may be lower than len(*string*); you must check for this, and resend substring *string*[*n*:] if needed. If there is no space in the socket's buffer, blocks until space appears.

sendall	`s.sendall(string)`

Sends the bytes of *string* on the socket, blocking until all the bytes are sent.

sendto	`s.sendto(string,(host,port))`

Sends the bytes of *string* on the socket to destination *host* and *port*, and returns the number *n* of bytes sent. Useful with datagram sockets, which can send data to many destinations. You must not have called method s.bind. *n* may be lower than len(*string*); you must check for this, and resend *string*[*n*:] if it is nonempty.

Echo Server and Client Using TCP Sockets

Example 20-1 shows a TCP server that listens for connections on port 8881. When connected, the server loops, echoes all data back to the client, and goes back to accept another connection when the client is done. To terminate the server, hit the interrupt key with focus on the server's terminal window (console). The interrupt key, depending on your platform and settings, may be Ctrl-Break (typical on Windows) or Ctrl-C.

Example 20-1. TCP echo server

```
import socket
sock = socket.socket(socket.AF_INET, socket.SOCK_STREAM)
sock.bind(('', 8881))
sock.listen(5)

# loop waiting for connections
# terminate with Ctrl-Break on Win32, Ctrl-C on Unix
try:
    while True:
        newSocket, address = sock.accept()
        print "Connected from", address
        while True:
            receivedData = newSocket.recv(8192)
            if not receivedData: break
            newSocket.sendall(receivedData)
        newSocket.close()
        print "Disconnected from", address
finally:
    sock.close()
```

The argument passed to the newSocket.recv call, here 8192, is the maximum number of bytes to receive at a time. Receiving up to a few thousand bytes at a time is a good compromise between performance and memory consumption, and it's usual to specify a power of 2 (e.g., 8192==2**13) since memory allocation tends to round up to such powers anyway. It's important to close sock (to ensure we free its well-known port 8881 as soon as possible), so we use a try/finally statement to ensure we call sock.close. Closing newSocket, system-allocated on any suitable free port, is not as crucial, so we do not use a try/finally for it, although it would be fine to do so.

Example 20-2 shows a simple TCP client that connects to port 8881 on the local host, sends lines of data, and prints what it receives back from the server.

Example 20-2. TCP echo client

```
import socket
sock = socket.socket(socket.AF_INET, socket.SOCK_STREAM)
sock.connect(('localhost', 8881))
print "Connected to server"
data = """A few lines of data
to test the operation
of both server and client."""
for line in data.splitlines():
    sock.sendall(line)
    print "Sent:", line
    response = sock.recv(8192)
```

Example 20-2. TCP echo client (continued)

```
    print "Received:", response
sock.close( )
```

Run the Example 20-1 server in a terminal window and try a few runs of Example 20-2.

Echo Server and Client Using UDP Sockets

Examples 20-3 and 20-4 implement an echo server and client with UDP (i.e., using datagram rather than stream sockets).

Example 20-3. UDP echo server

```
import socket
sock = socket.socket(socket.AF_INET, socket.SOCK_DGRAM)
sock.bind(('', 8881))

# loop waiting for datagrams
(terminate with Ctrl-Break on Win32, Ctrl-C on Unix)
try:
    while True:
        data, address = sock.recvfrom(8192)
        print "Datagram from", address
        sock.sendto(data, address)
finally:
    sock.close( )
```

Example 20-4. UDP echo client

```
import socket
sock = socket.socket(socket.AF_INET, socket.SOCK_DGRAM)
data = """A few lines of data
to test the operation
of both server and client."""
for line in data.splitlines( ):
    sock.sendto(line, ('localhost', 8881))
    print "Sent:", line
    response = sock.recv(8192)
    print "Received:", response
sock.close( )
```

Run the server of Example 20-3 on a terminal window and try a few runs of Example 20-4. Examples 20-3 and 20-4, as well as Examples 20-1 and 20-2, can run independently at the same time. There is no interference or interaction, even though all are using port number 8881 on the local host, because TCP and UDP ports are separate. If you run Example 20-4 when the server of Example 20-3 is not running, you don't receive an error message: the client of Example 20-4 hangs forever, waiting for a response that will never arrive. Datagrams are not as robust and reliable as connections.

Socket Timeout Behavior

Standard C-level sockets, on most platforms, have no concept of timing out. By default, each socket operation blocks until it either succeeds or fails. There are advanced ways to ask for nonblocking sockets and to ensure that you perform socket operations only when they can't block (such as relying on module select, covered in "The select Module" on page 533). However, explicitly arranging for such behavior, particularly in a cross-platform way, can sometimes be complicated and difficult.

It's often simpler to deal with socket objects enriched by a timeout behavior. Each operation on such an object fails, with an exception indicating a timeout condition, if the operation has neither succeeded nor failed after the timeout period has elapsed. Such objects are internally implemented by using nonblocking sockets and selects, but your program is shielded from the complexities and deals only with objects that present a simple and intuitive interface. Functions getdefaulttimeout and setdefaulttimeout in the socket module, and methods gettimeout and settimeout on socket objects, let you set sockets' timeout behavior: the timeout value of each socket can be a floating-point number of seconds (thus you can also use a fraction of a second) or None to have a "normal" socket that doesn't time out.

With "normal" sockets (ones whose timeout value t is None), many methods, such as connect, accept, recv, and send, may block and wait "forever." When you call such methods on a socket s whose timeout value t is not None, if t seconds elapse since the call and the wait is still going on, then s stops waiting and raises socket.error.

The SocketServer Module

The Python library supplies a framework module, SocketServer, to help you implement simple Internet servers. SocketServer supplies server classes TCPServer, for connection-oriented servers using TCP, and UDPServer, for datagram-oriented servers using UDP, with the same interface.

An instance s of either TCPServer or UDPServer supplies many attributes and methods, and you can subclass either class and override some methods to architect your own specialized server framework. However, I do not cover such advanced and rarely used possibilities in this book.

Classes TCPServer and UDPServer implement synchronous servers that can serve one request at a time. Classes ThreadingTCPServer and ThreadingUDPServer implement threaded servers, spawning a new thread per request. You are responsible for synchronizing the resulting threads as needed. Threading is covered in "Threads in Python" on page 341.

The BaseRequestHandler Class

For normal use of SocketServer, subclass the BaseRequestHandler class provided by SocketServer and override the handle method. Then instantiate a server class, passing the address pair on which to serve and your subclass of BaseRequestHandler. Finally, call serve_forever on the server instance.

An instance *h* of `BaseRequestHandler` supplies the following methods and attributes.

client_address	The *h*.client_address attribute is the pair (*host*,*port*) of the client, set by the base class at connection.
handle	*h*.handle( ) Your subclass overrides this method, and the server calls the method on a new instance of your subclass for each incoming request. For a TCP server, your implementation of handle conducts a conversation with the client on socket *h*.request to service the request. For a UDP server, your implementation of handle examines the datagram in *h*.request[0] and sends a reply string with *h*.request[1].sendto.
request	For a TCP server, the *h*.request attribute is the socket connected to the client. For a UDP server, the *h*.request attribute is a pair (*data*,*sock*), where *data* is the string of data the client sent as a request (up to 8,192 bytes) and *sock* is the the server socket. Your handle method can call method sendto on *sock* to send a reply to the client.
server	The *h*.server attribute is the server instance that instantiated this handler object.

Example 20-5 uses module SocketServer to reimplement the server of Example 20-1 with the added ability to serve multiple clients simultaneously by threading.

Example 20-5. Threaded TCP echo server using SocketServer

```
import SocketServer
class EchoHandler(SocketServer.BaseRequestHandler):
    def handle(self):
        print "Connected from", self.client_address
        while True:
            receivedData = self.request.recv(8192)
            if not receivedData: break
            self.request.sendall(receivedData)
        self.request.close( )
        print "Disconnected from", self.client_address
srv = SocketServer.ThreadingTCPServer(('',8881),EchoHandler)
srv.serve_forever( )
```

Run the server of Example 20-5 on a terminal window and try a few runs of Example 20-2. Try also *telnet localhost 8881* on other terminal windows (or other

---

platform-dependent Telnet-like programs) to verify the behavior of longer-lived connections.

HTTP Servers

The BaseHTTPServer, SimpleHTTPServer, CGIHTTPServer, and SimpleXMLRPCServer modules implement HTTP servers of different completeness and sophistication on top of module SocketServer.

The BaseHTTPServer module

The BaseHTTPServer module supplies a server class HTTPServer that subclasses SocketServer.TCPServer and is used in the same way. It also provides a request handler class BaseHTTPRequestHandler, which subclasses SocketServer.BaseRequestHandler and adds attributes and methods useful for HTTP servers, of which the most commonly used are as follows.

command	The *h*.command attribute is the HTTP verb of the client's request, such as 'get', 'head', or 'post'.
handle	*h*.handle( ) Overrides the superclass's method handle and delegates request handling to methods whose names start with 'do_', such as do_get, do_head, and do_post. Class BaseHTTPRequestHandler supplies no do_ methods: subclass it and supply the methods you want to implement.
end_headers	*h*.end_headers( ) Terminates the response's MIME headers by sending a blank line.
path	The *h*.path attribute is the HTTP path of the client's request, such as '/index.html'.
rfile	The *h*.rfile attribute is a file-like object open for reading, from which you can read data sent as the body of the client's request (e.g., URL-encoded form data for a POST).
send_header	*h*.send_header(*keyword*,*value*) Adds to the response a MIME header with given *keyword* and *value*. At each call to send_header, another header is added to the response. When you call send_header repeatedly with the same *keyword*, multiple headers with that *keyword* get added, one per call to send_header, in the same order as the calls to send_header.

send_error	h.send_error(*code*,*message*=None)
	Sends a complete error reply with HTTP code *code*, and text from string *message*, when *message* is not None.

send_response	h.send_response(*code*,*message*=None)
	Sends a response header with HTTP code *code*, and text from string *message*, when message is not None. Headers Server and Date are always sent automatically.

wfile	The *h*.wfile attribute is a file-like object open for writing, to which you can write the response body after you call send_response, send_header, and end_headers.

As an example, here's a trivial HTTP server that answers every request with the 404 error code and the corresponding message 'File not found':

```
import BaseHTTPServer

class TrivialHTTPRequestHandler(BaseHTTPServer.BaseHTTPRequestHandler):
    """Trivial HTTP request handler, answers not found to every request"""
    server_version = "TrivialHTTP/1.0"
    def do_GET(self):
        """Serve a GET request."""
        self.send_error(404, "File not found")
    do_HEAD = do_POST = do_GET

server = BaseHTTPServer.HTTPServer(('',80), TrivialHTTPRequestHandler)
server.serve_forever()
```

The SimpleHTTPServer module

The SimpleHTTPServer module builds on top of BaseHTTPServer, supplying what's needed to serve HTTP GET requests for files in a directory. It is most useful as an example of how to use BaseHTTPServer for a simple real-world HTTP serving task.

The CGIHTTPServer module

The CGIHTTPServer module builds on top of SimpleHTTPServer, supplying the ability to serve HTTP GET and POST requests via CGI scripts, covered in Chapter 19. You can use it, for example, to debug CGI scripts on your local machine.

The SimpleXMLRPCServer module

XML-RPC is a higher-level protocol that runs on top of HTTP. Python supports XML-RPC clients with module xmlrpclib, covered in "Distributed Computing" on page 516. The SimpleXMLRPCServer module supplies class SimpleXMLRPCServer to instantiate with the address pair on which to serve.

An instance *x* of class SimpleXMLRPCServer supplies two methods to call before *x*.serve_forever( ).

register_ **function**	*x*.register_function(*callable*,*name*=None) Registers *callable*, callable with a single argument, to respond to XML-RPC requests for string *name*. *name* is an identifier or a sequence of identifiers joined by dots. When *name* is None, uses name *callable*.__name__. The argument to *callable* is the result of xmlrpclib.loads(*payload*), where *payload* is the request's payload.
register_ **instance**	*x*.register_instance(*inst*) Registers *inst* to respond to XML-RPC requests with names not registered via register_function. When *inst* supplies a method _dispatch, *inst*._dispatch is called with the request name and parameters as arguments. When *inst* does not supply _dispatch, the request name is used as an attribute name to search in *inst*. When the request name contains dots, the search repeats for each component. The attribute found by this search is called with the request parameters as arguments. Only one instance at a time can be registered with register_instance: if you call *x*.register_instance again, the instance passed in the previous call to *x*.register_instance is replaced by the one passed in the later call.

Simple examples of all typical usage patterns for SimpleXMLRPCServer are given in the docstring of module SimpleXMLRPCServer.py, which you can find in the *Lib* directory of your Python installation. Here is a toy example of using the _dispatch method. In one terminal window, run the following tiny script:

```
import SimpleXMLRPCServer
class with_dispatch:
    def _dispatch(self, *args):
        print '_dispatch', args
        return args
server = SimpleXMLRPCServer.SimpleXMLRPCServer(('localhost',8888))
server.register_instance(with_dispatch())
server.serve_forever()
```

From a Python interactive session on another terminal window of the same machine (or an IDLE interactive session on the same machine), you can now run:

```
>>> import xmlrpclib
>>> proxy = xmlrpclib.ServerProxy('http://localhost:8888')
>>> print proxy.whatever.method('any', 'args')
['whatever.method', ['any', 'args']]
```

Event-Driven Socket Programs

Socket programs, particularly servers, must often perform many tasks at once. Example 20-1 accepts a connection request, then serves a single client until that client has finished—other requests must wait. This is not acceptable for servers in production use. Clients cannot wait too long: the server must be able to service multiple clients at once.

One way to let your program perform several tasks at once is threading, covered in "Threads in Python" on page 341. Module SocketServer optionally supports threading, as covered in "The SocketServer Module" on page 528. An alternative to threading that can offer better performance and scalability is *event-driven* (also known as *asynchronous*) programming.

An event-driven program sits in an event loop and waits for events. In networking, typical events are "a client requests connection," "data arrived on a socket," and "a socket is available for writing." The program responds to each event by executing a small slice of work to service that event, then goes back to the event loop to wait for the next event. The Python library provides minimal support for event-driven network programming with the low-level select module and the higher-level asyncore and asynchat modules. Much richer support for event-driven programming is in the Twisted package (available at *http://www.twistedmatrix.com*), particularly in subpackage twisted.internet.

The select Module

The select module exposes a cross-platform, low-level function to implement asynchronous network servers and clients. Module select has additional functionality on Unix-like platforms, but I cover only cross-platform functionality in this book.

select	select(*inputs*,*outputs*,*excepts*,*timeout*=None)

<blockquote>

inputs, *outputs*, and *excepts* are lists of socket objects that wait for input events, output events, and exceptional conditions, respectively. *timeout* is a float, which is the maximum time to wait in seconds. When *timeout* is None, there is no maximum wait: select waits until some objects receive events. When *timeout* is 0, select returns at once, without waiting, whether some objects have already received events or not.

select returns a tuple with three items (*i*,*o*,*e*). *i* is a list of zero or more of the items of *inputs*, those that received input events. *o* is a list of zero or more of the items of *outputs*, those that received output events. *e* is a list of zero or more of the items of *excepts*, those that received exceptional conditions (i.e., out-of-band data). Any or all of *i*, *o*, and *e* can be empty, but at least one of them is nonempty if *timeout* is None.

In addition to sockets, you can have in lists *inputs*, *outputs*, and *excepts* other objects that supply a method fileno, callable without arguments, returning a socket's file descriptor. For example, the

</blockquote>

server classes of module SocketServer, covered in "The Socket-
Server Module" on page 528, follow this protocol. Therefore, you
can have instances of these classes in the lists. On Unix-like platforms, select.select has wider applicability, since it also accepts
file descriptors that do not refer to sockets. On Windows, however,
select.select accepts only file descriptors that do refer to sockets.

Example 20-6 uses module select to reimplement the server of Example 20-1
with the added ability to serve any number of clients simultaneously.

Example 20-6. Asynchronous TCP echo server using select

```
import socket
import select
sock = socket.socket(socket.AF_INET, socket.SOCK_STREAM)
sock.bind(('', 8881))
sock.listen(5)

# lists of sockets to watch for input and output events
ins = [sock]
ous = []
# mapping socket -> data to send on that socket when feasible
data = {}
# mapping socket -> (host, port) on which the client is running
adrs = {}

try:
    while True:
        i, o, e = select.select(ins, ous, [])  # no excepts nor timeout
        for x in i:
            if x is sock:
                # input event on sock means a client is trying to connect
                newSocket, address = sock.accept()
                print "Connected from", address
                ins.append(newSocket)
                adrs[newSocket] = address
            else:
                # other input events mean data arrived, or disconnections
                newdata = x.recv(8192)
                if newdata:
                    # data arrived, prepare and queue the response to it
                    print "%d bytes from %s" % (len(newdata), adrs[x])
                    data[x] = data.get(x, '') + newdata
                    if x not in ous: ous.append(x)
                else:
                    # a disconnect, give a message and clean up
                    print "disconnected from", adrs[x]
                    del adrs[x]
                    try: ous.remove(x)
                    except ValueError: pass
                    x.close()
                    ins.remove(x)
```

Example 20-6. Asynchronous TCP echo server using select (continued)

```
        for x in o:
            # output events always mean we can send some data
            tosend = data.get(x)
            if tosend:
                nsent = x.send(tosend)
                print "%d bytes to %s" % (nsent, adrs[x])
                # remember data still to be sent, if any
                tosend = tosend[nsent:]
            if tosend:
                print "%d bytes remain for %s" % (len(tosend), adrs[x])
                data[x] = tosend
            else:
                try: del data[x]
                except KeyError: pass
                ous.remove(x)
                print "No data currently remain for", adrs[x]
finally:
    sock.close( )
```

Programming at such a low level incurs substantial complications, as shown by the complexity of Example 20-6 and its data structures. Run the server of Example 20-6 on a terminal window and try a few runs of Example 20-2. Try also *telnet localhost 8881* on other terminal windows (or other platform-dependent, Telnet-like programs) to verify the behavior of longer-lived connections.

The asyncore and asynchat Modules

The asyncore and asynchat modules help you implement asynchronous network servers and clients at a higher, more productive level than module select affords.

The asyncore module

Module asyncore supplies one function.

---

loop   loop( )

Implements the asynchronous event loop, dispatching all network events to previously instantiated dispatcher objects. loop terminates when all dispatcher objects (i.e., all communication channels) are closed.

Module asyncore also supplies class dispatcher, which supplies all methods of socket objects, plus specific methods for event-driven programming, with names starting with 'handle_'. Subclass dispatcher and override the handle_ methods for all events you need to handle. To initialize an instance *d* of dispatcher, you can pass an argument *s*, which is an already connected socket object. Otherwise, first call:

d.create_socket(socket.AF_INET,socket.SOCK_STREAM)

and then call on *d* either connect, to connect to a server, or bind and listen, to have *d* itself be a server. The most frequently used methods of an instance *d* of a subclass *X* of dispatcher are the following.

create_socket   *d*.create_socket(*family*,*type*)

Creates *d*'s socket with the given family and type. *family* is generally socket.AF_INET. *type* is generally socket.SOCK_STREAM, since class dispatcher normally uses a TCP (i.e., connection-based) socket.

handle_accept   *d*.handle_accept( )

Called when a new client has connected. Your class *X* normally responds by calling self.accept, then instantiating another subclass *Y* of dispatcher with the resulting new socket, in order to handle the new client connection.

Your implementation of handle_accept need not return the new instance of *Y*: all instances of subclasses of dispatcher register themselves with the asyncore framework in dispatcher.__init__ so that asyncore later calls back to them.

handle_close   *d*.handle_close( )

Called when the connection is closing.

handle_connect   *d*.handle_connect( )

Called when the connection is starting.

handle_read   *d*.handle_read( )

Called when the socket has new data that you can read without blocking.

handle_write   *d*.handle_write( )

Called when the socket has some free buffer space, so you can write without blocking.

Module asyncore also supplies class dispatcher_with_send, a subclass of dispatcher that overrides one method.

send   *d*.send(*data*)

In class dispatcher_with_send, method *d*.send is equivalent to a socket object's method send_all in that it sends all the data.

However, *d*.send does not send all the data at once, and does not block; rather, *d* sends the data in small packets of 512 bytes each in response to handle_write events (callbacks). This strategy ensures good performance in simple cases.

Example 20-7 uses module asyncore to reimplement the server of Example 20-1, with the added ability to serve any number of clients simultaneously.

Example 20-7. Asynchronous TCP echo server using asyncore

```python
import asyncore
import socket

class MainServerSocket(asyncore.dispatcher):
    def __init__(self, port):
        asyncore.dispatcher.__init__(self)
        self.create_socket(socket.AF_INET, socket.SOCK_STREAM)
        self.bind(('',port))
        self.listen(5)
    def handle_accept(self):
        newSocket, address = self.accept( )
        print "Connected from", address
        SecondaryServerSocket(newSocket)

class SecondaryServerSocket(asyncore.dispatcher_with_send):
    def handle_read(self):
        receivedData = self.recv(8192)
        if receivedData: self.send(receivedData)
        else: self.close( )
    def handle_close(self):
        print "Disconnected from", self.getpeername( )

MainServerSocket(8881)
asyncore.loop( )
```

The complexity of Example 20-7 is modest when compared to Example 20-1. The additional functionality of serving multiple clients, with the high performance and scalability of asynchronous, event-driven programming, comes cheap, thanks to asyncore's power.

Note that method handle_read of SecondaryServerSocket can freely use self.send without precautions: SecondaryServerSocket subclasses dispatcher_with_send, which overrides method send appropriately. We could not do this if we had instead chosen to subclass asyncore.dispatcher directly.

The asynchat module

The asynchat module supplies class async_chat, which subclasses asyncore. dispatcher and adds methods to support buffering and line-oriented protocols. Subclass async_chat and override some methods. The most frequently used additional methods of an instance *x* of a subclass of async_chat are the following.

collect_ incoming_data	`x.collect_incoming_data(data)` Called whenever a byte string *data* of data arrives. Normally, *x* adds *data* to some buffer that *x* keeps; generally, the buffer is a list, and *x* adds data by calling the list's append method.
found_ terminator	`x.found_terminator( )` Called whenever the terminator, set by method set_terminator, is found. Normally, *x* processes the buffer it keeps, then clears the buffer.
push	`x.push(data)` Your class normally doesn't override this method. The implementation in base class async_chat adds string *data* to an output buffer that it sends as appropriate. Method push is therefore quite similar to method send of class asyncore.dispatcher_with_send, but method push has a more sophisticated implementation to ensure good performance in more cases.
set_terminator	`x.set_terminator(terminator)` Your class normally doesn't override this method. *terminator* is normally '\r\n', the line terminator specified by most Internet protocols. *terminator* can also be None, to disable calls to found_terminator.

Example 20-8 uses module asynchat to reimplement the server of Example 20-7, using asynchat.async_chat instead of asyncore.dispatcher_with_send. To highlight async_chat's typical use, Example 20-8 responds (by echoing the received data back to the client, like all other server examples in this chapter) only when it has received a complete line (i.e., one ending with \n).

Example 20-8. Asynchronous TCP echo server using asynchat

```
import asyncore, asynchat, socket

class MainServerSocket(asyncore.dispatcher):
    def __init__(self, port):
        print 'initing MSS'
        asyncore.dispatcher.__init__(self)
        self.create_socket(socket.AF_INET, socket.SOCK_STREAM)
        self.bind(('',port))
        self.listen(5)
    def handle_accept(self):
        newSocket, address = self.accept( )
        print "Connected from", address
        SecondaryServerSocket(newSocket)
```

Example 20-8. Asynchronous TCP echo server using asynchat (continued)

```
class SecondaryServerSocket(asynchat.async_chat):
    def __init__(self, *args):
        print 'initing SSS'
        asynchat.async_chat.__init__(self, *args)
        self.set_terminator('\n')
        self.data = []
    def collect_incoming_data(self, data):
        self.data.append(data)
    def found_terminator(self):
        self.push(''.join(self.data))
        self.data = []
    def handle_close(self):
        print "Disconnected from", self.getpeername()
        self.close()

MainServerSocket(8881)
asyncore.loop()
```

To try out Example 20-8, we cannot use Example 20-2 as it stands because that code does not ensure that it sends only entire lines terminated with \n. It doesn't take much to fix this, however. The following client program, for example, is quite suitable for testing Example 20-8, as well as any of the other server examples in this chapter:

```
import socket
sock = socket.socket(socket.AF_INET, socket.SOCK_STREAM)
sock.connect(('localhost', 8881))
print "Connected to server"
data = """A few lines of data
to test the operation
of both server and client."""
for line in data.splitlines():
    sock.sendall(line+'\n')
    print "Sent:", line
    response = sock.recv(8192)
    print "Received:", response
sock.close()
```

The only difference in this code with respect to Example 20-2 is the change to the argument in the call to sock.sendall, in the first line of the loop body. This code simply adds a line terminator '\n' to ensure it interoperates with Example 20-8.

The Twisted Framework

The Twisted package (available at *http://www.twistedmatrix.com*) is a freely available framework for network clients and servers. Twisted includes powerful, high-level components such as web servers, user authentication systems, mail servers and clients, instant messaging, SSH clients and servers, a DNS server and client, and so on, as well as the lower-level infrastructure on which all these high-level components are built. Each component is highly scalable and easily customizable, and all are integrated to interoperate smoothly. It's a tribute to the power of

Python and to the ingenuity of Twisted's developers that so much can be accomplished within two megabytes' worth of download.

The twisted.internet and twisted.protocols packages

"Twisted Core" is the low-level part of Twisted that supports event-driven clients and servers, centered on modules twisted.internet and twisted.protocols. twisted.protocols supplies protocol handlers and factories. twisted.internet supplies object reactor, embodying the concept of an event loop. To make optimal use of Twisted Core, you need a good understanding of the design patterns used in distributed computing. Douglas Schmidt, of the Center for Distributed Object Computing of Washington University, documents such design patterns at *http://www.cs.wustl.edu/~schmidt/patterns-ace.html*.

twisted.protocols supplies many protocols using twisted.internet's infrastructure, including FTP, HTTP, Finger, GPS-NMEA, IRC, Jabber, NNTP, POP3, IMAP4, SMTP, SIP, SocksV4, and Telnet.

Reactors

A reactor object lets you establish protocol factories as listeners (servers) on given TCP/IP ports (or other transports, such as SSL) and connect protocol handlers as clients. You can choose different reactor implementations, depending on which module you import (the reactor is instantiated at the time you import a reactor module for the first time in your program's run: no need to call any factory). The default reactor uses the select module covered in "The select Module" on page 533. Other specialized reactors integrate with many GUI toolkits' event loops, or use platform-specific techniques such as the Windows event loop, the poll system call support available in the select module on some Unix-like systems, and even more specialized system calls such as FreeBSD's kqueue. The default reactor is often sufficient, but the extra flexibility of being able to use other implementations can help you integrate GUIs or other platform-specific capabilities, or achieve even higher performance and scalability.

A reactor object r implements many interfaces, each of which supplies many methods. The reactor methods most frequently used for programs that implement TCP/IP clients and servers with twisted.internet are the following.

callLater	r.callLater(*delay,callable,*args,**kwds*)
	Schedules a call to *callable(*args,**kwds*) to happen *delay* seconds from now. *delay* is a float, so it can also express fractions of a second.

callInThread	r.callInThread(*callable,*args,**kwds*)
	Calls *callable(*args,**kwds*) in a worker thread separate from the reactor's.

callFromThread	*r*.callFromThread(*callable*,**args*,***kwds*)
	Calls *callable*(**args*,***kwds*) in the reactor's thread. *r*.callFrom-Thread must be called only from a separate thread and, per se, does no synchronization.
callWhenRun-ning	*r*.callWhenRunning(*callable*,**args*,***kwds*)
	Schedules a call to *callable*(**args*,***kwds*) to happen when *r* is running.
connectTCP	*r*.listenTCP(*host*,*port*,*factory*,*timeout*=30,*bindAddress*=None)
	Establishes *factory*, which must be an instance of class ClientFactory (or any subclass of ClientFactory), as the protocol handler factory for a TCP client that connects to the given *host* and *port*. If no connection takes place within *timeout* seconds, the connection attempt is deemed to have failed. When *bindAddress* is not None, it is a tuple with two items, (*clienthost*,*clientport*); the client locally binds to that local host and port.
listenTCP	*r*.listenTCP(*port*,*factory*,*backlog*=50,*interface*='')
	Establishes *factory*, which must be an instance of class ServerFactory (or any subclass of ServerFactory), as the protocol handler factory for a TCP server that listens on the given *port*. No more than *backlog* clients can be kept queued waiting for connection at any given time. When *interface* is not '', binds to hostname *interface*.
run	*r*.run( )
	Runs the reactor's event loop until *r*.stop( ) is called.
stop	*r*.stop( )
	Stops the reactor's event loop that was started by calling *r*.run( ).

Transports

A transport object embodies a network connection. Each protocol object calls methods on self.transport to write data to its counterpart and to disconnect. A transport object *t* supplies the following methods.

getHost	`t.getHost( )`
	Returns an object *a* that identifies this side of the connection. *a*'s attributes are type (a string such as `'TCP'` or `'UDP'`), host (a string with a dotted-quad IP address), and port (an integer that identifies the port number).

getPeer	`t.getPeer( )`
	Returns an object that identifies the other side of the connection (easily confused by proxies, masquerading, NATting, firewalls, and so on), and is of the same type as getHost's result.

loseConnection	`t.loseConnection( )`
	Tells *t* to disconnect as soon as *t* has finished writing all pending data.

write	`t.write(data)`
	Transmits string *data* to the counterpart or queues it for transmission. *t* tries its best to ensure that all data you pass to write is eventually sent.

writeSequence	`t.writeSequence(seq)`
	Transmits each string item data of iterable *seq* to the counterpart or queues it for eventual transmission. *t* tries its best to ensure that all data you pass to writeSequence is eventually sent.
	Specific transports add some methods to this small set; for example, a TCP transport also has methods to let you set and get attributes `SO_KEEPALIVE` and `TCP_NODELAY`, and an SSL transport, in addition to those, also supplies a further method to let you get the certificate information for the peer (the other side of the connection).

Protocol handlers and factories

The reactor instantiates protocol handlers using a factory and calls methods on protocol handler instances when events occur. A protocol handler subclasses class Protocol and overrides some methods. A protocol handler may use its factory, available as self.factory, as a repository for state that needs to be shared among handlers or persist across multiple instantiations. A protocol factory may subclass class Factory, but this subclassing is often not necessary since in most cases the stock Factory supplies all you need. Just set the protocol attribute of a Factory instance *f* to a class object that is an appropriate subclass of Protocol, then pass *f* to the reactor.

An instance *p* of a subclass of Protocol supplies the following methods.

connectionLost	*p*.connectionLost(*reason*)
	Called when the connection to the counterpart has been closed. Argument *reason* is an object that explains why the connection has been closed. *reason* is not an instance of a Python exception, but has an attribute *reason*.value that often is such an instance. You can use str(*reason*) to get an explanation string, including a brief traceback, or str(*reason*.value) to get just the explanation string without any traceback.
connection-Made	*p*.connectionMade( )
	Called when the connection to the counterpart has just succeeded.
dataReceived	*p*.dataReceived(*data*)
	Called when string *data* has just been received from the counterpart.
makeConnec-tion	*p*.makeConnection(*transport*)
	Initiates a connection with the given *transport*, and calls *p*.connectionMade when the connection attempt succeeds or *p*.connectionLost when the attempt fails.

Echo server using Twisted

Example 20-9 uses twisted.internet to implement an echo server with the ability to serve any number of clients simultaneously.

Example 20-9. Asynchronous TCP echo server using twisted

```
from twisted.internet import protocol, reactor

class EchoProtocol(protocol.Protocol):
    def connectionMade(self):
        p = self.transport.getPeer( )
        self.peer = '%s:%s' % (p.host, p.port)
        print "Connected from", self.peer
    def dataReceived(self, data):
        self.transport.write(data)
    def connectionLost(self, reason):
        print "Disconnected from %s: %s" % (self.peer, reason.value)

factory = protocol.Factory( )
factory.protocol = EchoProtocol
```

Example 20-9. Asynchronous TCP echo server using twisted (continued)

```
reactor.listenTCP(8881, factory)
def hello( ): print 'Listening on port', 8881
reactor.callWhenRunning(hello)
reactor.run( )
```

Example 20-9 exhibits scalability at least as good as Example 20-7, yet it's easily the simplest of the echo server examples in this chapter—a good indication of Twisted's power and simplicity, even when used for such low-level tasks. Note the statement:

```
factory.protocol = EchoProtocol
```

This binds the class object EchoProtocol as the attribute protocol of object factory. The righthand side of the assignment must not be EchoProtocol( ), with parentheses after the class name. Such a righthand side would call, and therefore instantiate, class EchoProtocol, and therefore the statement would bind to factory.protocol a protocol instance object rather than a protocol class object. Such a mistake would make the server fail pretty quickly.

For a task-oriented book that shows how to implement a variety of tasks with Twisted at both low and high levels, check out *Twisted Network Programming Essentials*, by Abe Fettig (O'Reilly).

21

CGI Scripting and Alternatives

When a web browser (or any other web client) requests a page from a web server, the server may return either static or dynamic content. Serving dynamic content involves server-side web programs to generate and deliver content on the fly, often based on information stored in a database. The long-standing web-wide standard for server-side programming is known as CGI, which stands for Common Gateway Interface:

1. A web client (typically a browser) sends a structured request to a web server.

2. The server executes another program, passing the content of the request.

3. The server captures the standard output of the other program.

4. The server sends that output to the client as the response to the original request.

In other words, the server's role is that of a gateway between the client and the other program. The other program is called a CGI program, or CGI script.

CGI enjoys the typical advantages of standards. When you program to the CGI standard, your program can be deployed on all web servers, and work despite the differences. This chapter focuses on CGI scripting in Python. It also mentions the downsides of CGI (basically, issues of scalability under high load) and, in "Other Server-Side Approaches" on page 557, some of the many alternative, nonstandard server-side architectures that you can use instead of CGI. Nowadays, the nonstandard alternatives are often superior because they do not constrain your deployment much, and they can support higher-level abstractions to enhance productivity. (For example, use cookies implicitly and transparently to provide a "session" abstraction (while in CGI you must deal with cookies directly if you want any session continuity) with the Cookie module covered in "The Cookie Module" on page 553). However, at least for low-level CGI alternatives (such as FastCGI, mentioned in "FastCGI" on page 557), most of what you learn about CGI programming still comes in handy.

This chapter assumes familiarity with HTML and HTTP. For reference material on these standards, see *Webmaster in a Nutshell*, by Stephen Spainhour and Robert Eckstein (O'Reilly). For detailed coverage of HTML, I recommend *HTML & XHTML: The Definitive Guide*, by Chuck Musciano and Bill Kennedy (O'Reilly). For additional coverage of HTTP, see the *HTTP Pocket Reference*, by Clinton Wong (O'Reilly).

CGI in Python

The CGI standard lets you use any language to code CGI scripts. Python is a very high-level, high-productivity language, and thus quite suitable for CGI coding. The Python standard library supplies modules to handle typical CGI-related tasks.

Form Submission Methods

CGI scripts often handle submitted HTML forms. In this case, the action attribute of the form tag specifies the URL for a CGI script to handle the form, and the method attribute is GET or POST, indicating how the form data is sent to the script. According to the CGI standard, the GET method should be used only for forms without side effects, such as asking the server to query a database and display results, while the POST method is meant for forms with side effects, such as asking the server to update a database. In practice, however, GET is also often used to create side effects. The distinction between GET and POST in practical use is that GET encodes the form's contents as a query string joined to the action URL to form a longer URL, while POST transmits the form's contents as an encoded stream of data, which a CGI script sees as standard input.

GET is slightly faster. You can use a fixed GET-form URL wherever you can use a hyperlink. However, GET cannot send large amounts of data to the server, since many clients and servers limit URL lengths (you're safe up to about 200 bytes). The POST method has no size limits. You must use POST when the form contains input tags with type=file—the form tag must then have enctype=multipart/form-data.

The CGI standard does not specify whether a single script can access both the query string (used for GET) and the script's standard input (used for POST). Many clients and servers let you get away with it, but relying on this nonstandard practice may negate the portability advantages that you would otherwise get from the fact that CGI is a standard. Python's standard module cgi (covered in the next section) recovers form data only from the query string, when any query string is present; otherwise, when no query string is present, cgi recovers form data from standard input.

The cgi Module

The cgi module supplies one function and one class that your CGI scripts use often.

escape

escape(*str*,*quote*=False)

Returns a copy of string *str*, replacing characters &, <, and > with appropriate HTML entities (&, <, >). When *quote* is true, escape also replaces double-quote characters (") with ". escape lets a script prepare text strings for output within an HTML document, whether or not the strings contain HTML special characters.

FieldStorage

class FieldStorage(*keep_blank_values*=0)

When your script instantiates a FieldStorage instance *f*, module cgi parses the query string, and/or standard input, as appropriate. cgi hides the distinction between POST and GET. Your script must instantiate FieldStorage only once, since the instantiation may consume standard input.

f is a mapping: *f*'s keys are the name attributes of the form's controls. When *keep_blank_values* is true, *f* also includes controls whose values are blank strings. By default, *f* ignores such controls. *f* supplies a subset of dict's functionality: you can iterate on *f* to obtain each key *n* (for *n* in *f*), check if key *n* is present (if *n* in *f*), and index *f* to get the value for a key *n* (*f*[*n*]). The value you obtain can be either:

- A list of *k* FieldStorage instances if name *n* occurs more than once in the form (*k* is the number of occurrences of *n*)
- A single FieldStorage instance if name *n* occurs exactly once in the form

name occurrence counts follow HTML form rules. Groups of radio or checkbox controls share a name, but the whole group is just *one* occurrence of the name.

Values in a FieldStorage instance are in turn FieldStorage instances to handle nested forms. In practice, you don't need such complications. For each nested instance, just access the value (and occasionally other attributes), ignoring potential nested-mapping aspects. Avoid type tests: module cgi can optimize, using instances of MiniFieldStorage, a lightweight signature-compatible class instead of FieldStorage instances. You may know in advance which names are repeated in the form, and therefore which items of *f* can be lists. When you don't know, find out with try/except, not with type tests (see "Error-Checking Strategies" on page 134 for details on this idiom). Even better, use one of the following two methods of *f*.

getfirst

f.getfirst(*key*,*default*=None)

When *key* in *f*, and *f*[*key*].value is a single value, not a list, getfirst returns *f*[*key*].value. When *key* in *f*, and *f*[*key*].value is a list, getfirst returns *f*[*key*].value[0]. When *key* not in *f*, getfirst returns *default*.

Use getfirst when you know that there should be at most one input field named *key* in the form from which your script's input comes.

getlist   *f*.getlist(*key*)

When *key* in *f*, and *f*[*key*].value is a single value, not a list, getlist returns [*f*[*key*].value], i.e., a list whose only item is *f*[*key*].value. When *key* in *f*, and *f*[*key*].value is a list, getlist returns *f*[*key*].value. When *key* not in *f*, getlist returns the empty list [].

Use getlist when you know that there could be more than one input field named *key* in the form from which your script's input comes.

An instance *f* of class FieldStorage supplies the following attributes:

disposition
> The Content-Disposition header, or None if no such header is present

disposition_options
> A mapping built with all the options in the Content-Disposition header, if any

headers
> A mapping of all the headers: header names as keys and header values as values

file
> A file-like object from which you can read the control's value, if applicable; None if the value is held in memory as a string, as is the case for most controls

filename
> The filename as specified by the client, for file controls; otherwise, None

name
> The name attribute of the control, or None if no such attribute is present

type
> The Content-Type header, or None if no such header is present

type_options
> A mapping built with all the options in the Content-Type header, if any

value
> The control's value as a string; if *f* is keeping the control's value in a file, then *f* implicitly reads the file into memory when you access *f*.value

In most cases, attribute value is all you need. Other attributes are useful for file controls, which may have metadata such as Content-Type and Content-Disposition headers. The values of checkbox controls that share a name, and multiple-choice select controls, are strings that represent comma-separated lists of options. The idiom:

```
values=f.getfirst(n,'').split(',')
```

breaks apart such composite value strings into a list of their individual component strings.

CGI Output and Errors

When the server runs a CGI script to meet a request, the response to the request is the standard output of the script. The script must output HTTP headers, then an empty line, then the response's body. In particular, the script must always output a Content-Type header. Most often, the script outputs the Content-Type header as:

```
Content-Type: text/html
```

In this case, the response body must be HTML. However, the script may also choose to output a content type of text/plain (i.e., the response body must be plain text), or any other MIME type followed by a response body that conforms to that MIME type. The MIME type must be compatible with the Accept header that the client sent, if any.

Here is the simplest possible Python CGI script in the tradition of "Hello World," ignoring its input and outputting just one line of plain text output:

```
print "Content-Type: text/plain"
print
print "Hello, CGI World!"
```

Most often, you want to output HTML, and this is similarly easy:

```
print "Content-Type: text/html"
print
print "<html><head><title>Hello, HTML</title></head>"
print "<body><p>Hello, CGI and HTML together!</p></body></html>"
```

Browsers are quite forgiving in parsing HTML: you could get by without the HTML structure tags that this code outputs. However, being fully correct costs little. For some other ways to generate HTML output, see "Generating HTML" on page 586.

The web server collects all output from a CGI script, then sends it to the client browser in one gulp. Therefore, you cannot send to the client progress information, just final results.

If you need to output binary data (on a platform where binary and text files differ, i.e., Windows), you must ensure *python* is called with the *-u* switch, covered in "Command-Line Syntax and Options" on page 23. A more robust approach is to text-encode your output, using the encoding modules covered in "Encoding Binary Data as Text" on page 561 (typically with Base-64 encoding) and a suitable Content-Transfer-Encoding header. A standard-compliant browser then decodes your output according to the Content-Transfer-Encoding header and recovers the binary data you encoded. Encoding enlarges output by about 30 percent, which sometimes gives performance problems. In such cases, it's better to ensure that your script's standard output stream is a binary file. To ensure binary output on Windows, here is an alternative to the *-u* switch:

```
try: import msvcrt, os
except ImportError: pass
else: msvcrt.setmode(1, os.OS_BINARY)
```

Error messages

If exceptions propagate from your script, Python outputs traceback diagnostics to standard error. With most web servers, error information ends up in error logs. The client browser receives a concise generic error message. This may be okay, if you can access the server's error logs. Seeing detailed error information in the client browser, however, makes your life easier when you debug a CGI script. When you think that a script may have bugs, and you need an error trace for debugging, you can use a content type of text/plain and redirect standard error to standard output, as shown here:

```
print "Content-Type: text/plain"
print
import sys
sys.stderr = sys.stdout
def witherror():
    return 1/0
print "Hello, CGI with an error!"
print "Trying to divide by 0 produces:",witherror()
print "The script does not reach this part..."
```

If your script fails only occasionally and you want to see HTML-formatted output up to the point of failure, you could also use a more sophisticated approach based on the traceback module covered in "The traceback Module" on page 466, as shown here:

```
import sys
sys.stderr = sys.stdout
import traceback
print "Content-Type: text/html"
print
try:
    def witherror():
        return 1/0
    print "<html><head><title>Hello, traceback</title></head><body>"
    print "<p>Hello, CGI with an error traceback!"
    print "<p>Trying to divide by 0 produces:",witherror()
    print "<p>The script does not reach this part..."
except ZeroDivisionError:
    print "<br><strong>ERROR detected:</strong><br><pre>"
    traceback.print_exc()
    sys.stderr = sys.__stderr__
    traceback.print_exc()
```

After imports, redirection, and content-type output, this example runs the script's substantial part in the try clause of a try/except statement. In the except clause, the script outputs a <br> tag, terminating any current line, and then a <pre> tag to ensure that further line breaks are honored. Function print_exc of module traceback outputs all error information. Lastly, the script restores standard error and outputs error information again. Thus, the information is also in the error logs for later study, not just transiently displayed in the client browser: not very useful in this specific example, since the error is repeatable, but necessary to track down real-life errors.

The cgitb module

The simplest way to provide good error reporting in CGI scripts, although not quite as flexible as the approach just outlined in the previous section, is to use module cgitb. Module cgitb supplies two functions.

handle	handle(*exception*=None)
	Reports an exception's traceback to the browser. *exception* is a tuple with three items (*type,value,tb*), just like the result of calling sys.exc_info( ), covered in exc_info on page 168. When *exception* is None, the default, handle calls exc_info to get the information about the exception to display.
enable	enable(*display*=True,*logdir*=None,*context*=5)
	Installs an exception hook, via sys.excepthook, to diagnose propagated exceptions. The hook displays the exception traceback on the browser if *display* is true. The hook logs the exception traceback to a file in directory *logdir* if *logdir* is not None. In the traceback, the hook shows *context* lines of source code per frame.
	In practice, you can start all of your CGI scripts with:

```
import cgitb
cgitb.enable( )
```

and be assured of good error reporting to the browser with minimal effort on your part. When you don't want users of your page to see Python tracebacks from your scripts on their browsers, you can call cgitb.enable(False,'/my/log/dir') and get the error reports, with tracebacks, as files in directory */my/log/dir* instead.

Installing Python CGI Scripts

Installation of CGI scripts depends on the web browser and host platform. A script coded in Python is no different in this respect from scripts coded in other languages. Of course, you must ensure that the Python interpreter and standard library are installed and accessible. On Unix-like platforms, you must set the x permission bits for the script and use a so-called shebang line as the script's first line—for example:

```
#!/usr/local/bin/python
```

depending on the details of your platform and Python installation. If you copy or share files between Unix and Windows platforms, make sure the shebang line does not end with a carriage return (\r), which might confuse the shell or web server that parses the shebang line to find out which interpreter to use for your script.

Python CGI scripts on Microsoft web servers

If your web server is Microsoft IIS or Microsoft PWS (Personal Web Server), assign file extensions to CGI scripts via entries in registry path *HKLM\System\CurrentControlSet\Services\W3Svc\Parameters\Script_Map*. Each value in this path is named by a file extension, such as *.pyg* (value names start with a period). The value is the interpreter command (e.g., C:\Python24\Python.Exe -u %s %s). You may use file extensions such as *.cgi* or *.py* for this purpose, but I recommend a unique one such as *.pyg* instead. Assigning Python as the interpreter for all scripts named *.cgi* might interfere with your ability to use other interpreters for CGI purposes. Having all modules with a *.py* extension interpreted as CGI scripts is more accident-prone than dedicating a unique extension such as *.pyg* to this purpose and may interfere with your ability to have your Python-coded CGI scripts import modules from the same directories.

With IIS 5 and later, you can use the Administrative Tools → Computer Management applet to associate a file extension with an interpreter command line. This is performed via Services and Applications → Internet Information Services. Right-click either on [IISAdmin], for all sites, or on a specific web site, and choose Properties → Configuration → Add Mappings → Add. Enter the extension, such as *.pyg*, in the Extension field, and the interpreter command line, such as C:\Python22\Python.Exe -u %s %s, in the Executable field.

Python CGI scripts on Apache

The popular free web server Apache is configured via directives in a text file (by default, *httpd.conf*). When the configuration has ScriptAlias entries, such as:

```
ScriptAlias /cgi-bin/ /usr/local/apache/cgi-bin/
```

any executable script in the aliased directory can run as a CGI script. You may enable CGI execution in a specific directory by using for the Apache directive for that directory:

```
Options +ExecCGI
```

In this case, to let scripts with a certain extension run as CGI scripts, you may also add a global AddHandler directive, such as:

```
AddHandler cgi-script pyg
```

to enable scripts with extension *.pyg* to run as CGI scripts. Apache determines the interpreter to use for a script by the shebang line at the script's start. Another way to enable CGI scripts in a directory (if global directive AllowOverride Options is set) is to use Options +ExecCGI in a file named *.htaccess* in that directory.

Python CGI scripts on Xitami

The free, lightweight, simple web server Xitami (*http://www.xitami.org*) makes it easy to install CGI scripts. When any component of a URL is named *cgi-bin*, Xitami takes the URL as a request for CGI execution. Xitami determines the interpreter to use for a script by the shebang line at the script's start, even on Windows platforms.

Cookies

HTTP, per se, is a stateless protocol, meaning that it retains no session state between transactions. Cookies, as specified by the HTTP 1.1 standard, let web clients and servers cooperate to build a stateful session from a sequence of HTTP transactions.

Each time a server sends a response to a client's request, the server may initiate or continue a session by sending one or more Set-Cookie headers, whose contents are small data items called *cookies*. When a client sends another request to the server, the client may continue a session by sending Cookie headers with cookies previously received from that server or other servers in the same domain. Each cookie is a pair of strings, the name and value of the cookie, plus optional attributes. Attribute max-age is the maximum number of seconds the cookie should be kept. The client should discard saved cookies after their maximum age. If max-age is missing, then the client should discard the cookie when the user's interactive session ends.

Cookies provide no intrinsic privacy or authentication. Cookies travel in the clear on the Internet and are vulnerable to sniffing. A malicious client might return cookies different from cookies previously received. To use cookies for authentication or identification, or to hold sensitive information, the server must encrypt and encode cookies sent to clients, and decode, decrypt, and verify cookies received back from clients.

Encryption, encoding, decoding, decryption, and verification may all be slow when applied to large amounts of data. Decryption and verification require the server to keep some amount of server-side state. Sending substantial amounts of data back and forth on the network is also slow. The server should therefore persist most state data locally in files or databases. In most cases, a server should use cookies only as small, encrypted, verifiable keys that confirm the identity of a user or session, using DBM files or a relational database (both covered in Chapter 11) for session state. HTTP sets a limit of 2 KB on cookie size, but I suggest you normally use even smaller cookies.

The Cookie Module

The Cookie module supplies several classes, mostly for backward compatibility. CGI scripts normally use the following classes from module Cookie.

Morsel
A script does not directly instantiate class `Morsel`. However, instances of cookie classes hold instances of `Morsel`. An instance *m* of class `Morsel` represents a single cookie element: a key string, a value string, and optional attributes. *m* is a mapping. The only valid keys in *m* are cookie attribute names: `'comment'`, `'domain'`, `'expires'`, `'max-age'`, `'path'`, `'secure'`, and `'version'`. Keys into *m* are case-insensitive. Values in *m* are strings, each holding the value of the corresponding cookie attribute.

SimpleCookie
class `SimpleCookie(`*input*`=None)`

A `SimpleCookie` instance *c* is a mapping. *c*'s keys are strings. *c*'s values are `Morsel` instances that wrap strings. *c*[*k*]=*v* implicitly expands to:

```
c[k]=Morsel( ); c[k].set(k,str(v),str(v))
```

If *input* is not None, instantiating *c* implicitly calls *c*.load(*input*).

SmartCookie
class `SmartCookie(`*input*`=None)`

A `SmartCookie` instance *c* is a mapping. *c*'s keys are strings. *c*'s values are `Morsel` instances that wrap arbitrary values serialized with pickle. *c*[*k*]=*v* has the semantics:

```
c[k]=Morsel( ); c[k].set(k,str(v),pickle.dumps(v))
```

(Module `pickle` is covered in "The pickle and cPickle Modules" on page 279.) Since you have no control over the code that executes during deserialization via `pickle.loads`, class `SmartCookie` offers no security whatsoever. Unless your script is exposed only on a trusted intranet, avoid `SmartCookie`; use `SimpleCookie` instead. You can use any cryptographic approach to build, and take apart again, the strings wrapped by `Morsel` instance values in `SimpleCookie` instances. Modules covered in "Encoding Binary Data as Text" on page 561 make it easy to encode arbitrary byte strings as text strings, quite apart from any cryptographic measures.

`SmartCookie` is more convenient than `SimpleCookie` plus cryptography, encoding, and decoding. Convenience and security, however, are often in conflict. The choice is yours. Do not labor under the misapprehension that your system is secure because "after all, nobody knows what I'm doing"—to quote a famous principle of secure design, "Security through obscurity isn't." Good cryptography is a necessary (but not sufficient) condition for strong security. To use cryptography with Python, see the Python Cryptography Toolkit at *http://www.amk.ca/python/code/crypto*.

Cookie methods

An instance *c* of SimpleCookie or SmartCookie supplies the following methods.

js_output   *c*.js_output(*attrs*=None)

Returns a string *s*, which is a JavaScript snippet that sets document.cookie to the cookies held in *c*. You can embed *s* in an HTML response to simulate cookies without sending an HTTP Set-Cookie header if the client browser supports JavaScript. If *attrs* is not None, *s*'s JavaScript sets only cookie attributes whose names are in *attrs*.

load   *c*.load(*data*)

When *data* is a string, load parses it and adds to *c* each parsed cookie. When *data* is a mapping, load adds to *c* a new Morsel instance for each item in *data*. Normally, *data* is string os.environ.get('HTTP_COOKIE','') to recover the cookies the client sent.

output   *c*.output(*attrs*=None,*header*='Set-Cookie',*sep*='\n')

Returns a string *s* formatted as HTTP headers. You can print *c*.output( ) among your response's HTTP headers to send to the client the cookies held in *c*. Each header's name is string *header*, and headers are separated by string *sep*. If *attrs* is not None, *s*'s headers contain only cookie attributes whose names are in *attrs*.

Morsel attributes and methods

An instance *m* of class Morsel supplies three read/write attributes:

coded_value
    The cookie's value, encoded as a string; *m*'s output methods use *m*.coded_value

key
    The cookie's name

value
    The cookie's value, which is an arbitrary Python object

Instance *m* also supplies the following methods.

js_output   *m*.js_output(*attrs*=None)

Returns a string *s*, which is a JavaScript snippet that sets document.cookie to the cookie held in *m*. See also the js_output method of cookie instances.

output	`m.output(attrs=None,header='Set-Cookie')`

Returns a string *s* formatted as an HTTP header that sets the cookie held in *m*. See also the output method of cookie instances.

OutputString	`m.OutputString(attrs=['path','comment','domain','max-age','secure','version','expires'])`

Returns a string *s* that represents the cookie held in *m*, without decorations. *attrs* can be any container suitable as the righthand operand of in, such as a list, dict, or set; *s* contains only attributes whose names are in *attrs*.

set	`m.set(key,value,coded_value)`

Sets *m*'s attributes. *key* and *coded_value* must be strings.

Using module Cookie

Module Cookie supports cookie handling in both client-side and server-side scripts. Typical usage is server-side, often in a CGI script (where you have no alternatives, to maintain session state, to the direct manipulation of cookies). The following example shows a simple CGI script using cookies:

```
import Cookie, time, os, sys, traceback

sys.stderr = sys.stdout

try:
    # first, the script emits HTTP headers
    c = Cookie.SimpleCookie()
    c["lastvisit"]=str(time.time())
    print c.output()
    print "Content-Type: text/html"
    print
    # then, the script emits the response's body
    print "<html><head><title>Hello, visitor!</title></head><body>"
    # for the rest of the response, the scripts gets and decodes the cookie
    c = Cookie.SimpleCookie(os.environ.get("HTTP_COOKIE"))
    when = c.get("lastvisit")
    if when is None:
        print "<p>Welcome to this site on your first visit!</p>"
        print "<p>Please click the 'Refresh' button to proceed</p>"
    else:
        try: lastvisit = float(when.value)
        except:
            print "<p>Sorry, cannot decode cookie (%s)</p>"%when.value
            print "</br><pre>"
            traceback.print_exc()
```

```
    else:
        formwhen = time.asctime(time.localtime(lastvisit))
        print "<p>Welcome back to this site!</p>"
        print "<p>You last visited on %s</p>"%formwhen
    print "</body></html>"
except:
    print "Content-Type: text/html"
    print
    print "</br><pre>"
    traceback.print_exc( )
```

Each time a client visits the script, the script sets a cookie encoding the current time. On successive visits, if the client browser supports cookies, the script greets the visitor appropriately. Module time is covered in "The time Module" on page 302. This example uses no cryptography or server-side persistence, since session state is small and not confidential.

Other Server-Side Approaches

A CGI script runs as a new process each time a client requests it. Process startup time, interpreter initialization, connection to databases, and script initialization add up to measurable overhead. On fast, modern server platforms, the overhead is bearable for light to moderate loads. On a busy server, CGI may not scale up well. Web servers support many server-specific ways to reduce overhead, running scripts in processes that can serve for several hits rather than starting up a new CGI process per hit.

Microsoft's ASP (Active Server Pages) is a server extension that leverages a lower-level library, ISAPI, and Microsoft's COM technology. Most ASP pages are coded in the VBScript language, but ASP is language-independent. As the reptilian connection suggests, Python and ASP go very well together, as long as Python is installed with the platform-specific win32all extensions, specifically ActiveScripting. Many other server extensions are cross-platform, not tied to specific operating systems.

The popular application server Zope (*http://www.zope.org*) is a Python application. If you need advanced management features, Zope (and the higher-level content-management system Plone, *http://plone.org/*, built on top of Zope) should be among the solutions you consider. Zope and Plone are large, powerful systems and need full books of their own to do them justice. I do not cover Zope and Plone further in this book.

FastCGI

FastCGI lets you write scripts similar to CGI scripts, in a variety of languages, using each process to handle multiple hits, either sequentially or simultaneously in separate threads. See *http://www.fastcgi.com* for FastCGI overviews and details, including pointers about FastCGI support on all kinds of servers as well as Python support for FastCGI. A streamlined variant of FastCGI is SCGI (*http://www.mems-exchange.org/software/scgi/*).

WSGI

The Python Web Server Gateway Interface (WSGI) is the emerging standard "middleware" approach that interfaces higher-level Python web development frameworks to underlying web servers, and is documented at *http://www.python.org/peps/pep-0333.html*. Although not mainly intended for direct use by your application programs (rather, you code your programs using any of several higher-abstraction frameworks, which, in turn, use WSGI to talk to the web server), it's not impossible to use WSGI directly. To ease this task, *http://www.owlfish.com/software/wsgiutils/* and *http://pythonpaste.org/* offer several modules you may want to explore. Mike Orr has published in the *Linux Gazette* an excellent article (*http://linuxgazette.net/115/orr.html*) that explore the state of WSGI. For much interesting information and discussion on how best to integrate WSGI with the fast, lightweight *lighttpd* server (*http://www.lighttpd.org/*), see the blog post and comments at *http://www.cleverdevil.org/computing/24/python-fastcgi-wsgi-and-lighttpd*.

A reference implementation of WSGI, known as wsgiref, may be included in the standard library of Python 2.5 (this was still not fully decided at the time of this writing). In any case, the reference implementation is available at *http://svn.eby-sarna.com/wsgiref/* and should work with any release of Python from 2.3 upward.

mod_python

Apache's architecture is highly modular. Beyond CGI and FastCGI, mod_python (*http://www.modpython.org*) affords full Python/Apache integration, with Python access to all needed Apache internals, including the ability to write authentication scripts.

Custom Pure Python Servers

In "HTTP Servers" on page 530, we saw that the standard Python library includes modules that implement web servers. You can subclass BaseHTTPServer and implement special-purpose web servers with little effort. Such special-purpose servers are useful in low-volume applications, but may not scale up well to handle moderate to high server loads.

Modules asyncore and asynchat (covered in "The asyncore and asynchat Modules" on page 535) exhibit very different performance characteristics. The event-driven architecture of asynchat-based applications affords high scalability and performance, beating applications that use lower-level languages and traditional architectures (multiprocess or multithreading).

The Twisted framework (covered in "The Twisted Framework" on page 539) has performance advantages even over asyncore, and supplies much richer functionality. With Twisted, you can program a web site at high levels of abstraction and still obtain superb scalability and performance. In particular, Twisted Web2 (*http://twistedmatrix.com/projects/web2/*) offers a higher-abstraction web-programming framework that can also be used with a different web server (i.e., without Twisted proper underneath); vice versa, you can also choose to use Twisted as the web server, and a different higher-abstraction framework, since WSGI acts as middleware, letting the low-level server layer and the high-level application layer interface transparently to each other. Nevow (*http://divmod.org/trac/wiki/DivmodNevow*) is another powerful web framework, optimized for Twisted but also usable with WSGI, which, among many notable features, provides excellent, transparent integration with client-side JavaScript in "AJAX" style.

Other Higher-Level-of-Abstraction Frameworks

It has been said that "Python is the language with more web app frameworks than keywords"; the language's power and simplicity conspire to tempt many developers to write their own, unique frameworks. Fortunately, these days, WSGI affords some interoperability. It may be worth your while to examine some of these frameworks, just in case one of them is a perfect match for your needs and desires (it's certainly a better use of your time than developing *yet another* such framework!). Coverage and discussion of many, *many* frameworks (including many no longer being actively developed), with URLs to find out more about them and download them, can be found in the essay at *http://www.python.org/pycon/papers/framework/web.html* and at the Wiki page *http://wiki.python.org/moin/WebProgramming*.

In my personal opinion, among the most promising frameworks, all under current active development and already rich and stable enough for mission-critical use, are CherryPy (*http://www.cherrypy.org/*), Django (*http://www.djangoproject.com/*), Pylons (*http://pylonshq.com/*), and TurboGears (*http://www.turbogears.org/*). They adopt very different approaches and philosophies: some integrate and even emphasize templating, or database access, while others focus on the web part and let you access databases or perform templating via separate modules; some require (and exploit) good understanding of HTTP issues, and/or SQL, while others shield you from those layers. Given such differences, each may prove optimal for different programmers and teams. In the rest of this chapter, I single out three frameworks (two mature and still actively developed ones, and one that is "the new kid on the block" and, in my personal opinion, is especially promising and interesting).

Webware

Webware for Python (*http://www.webwareforpython.org/*) is a modular collection of software components for Python server-side web scripting. You can code Python scripts according to different programming models, such as CGI scripts with added-value wrappers, servlets, or Python Server Pages (PSP), and run them all on Webware. Webware, in turn, interfaces to your web server in many ways, including CGI, FastCGI, mod_python, the specialized Apache module mod_webkit, and Python Paste (*http://pythonpaste.org/*) for WSGI interfacing. Webware offers you a lot of flexibility in architecting, coding, and deploying your server-side Python web scripts.

Among the many ways that Webware offers for you to generate web pages, one that will often be of interest is templating (i.e., automatic insertion of Python-computed values and some control logic in nearly formed HTML scripts). Webware supports templating via PSP, but also, with more power and sharper separation between logic and presentation parts, via the Cheetah package, covered in "The Cheetah Package" on page 586.

Quixote

Quixote (*http://www.mems-exchange.org/software/quixote/*) is another framework for Python web applications that can interface to your web server via the usual huge variety of ways, including CGI, FastCGI, WSGI, and mod_python. Quixote defines a new language, the Python Template Language (PTL), and an import hook that lets your Python application directly import PTL-coded modules.

Quixote's PTL is nearly the same as Python, but has a few extras that may be handy in web applications. For example, PTL keyword `template` defines functions that return string results, automatically called to respond to web requests; within such functions, all expression statements are taken as appending strings to the function's return value. For example, the PTL code:

```
template hw( ):
    'hello'
    'world'
```

is roughly the same as the following Python code:

```
def hw( ):
    _result = []
    _result.append('hello')
    _result.append('world')
    return ''.join(_result)
```

web.py

Based on my own skills, needs, and tastes, my current favorite web framework is web.py (*http://webpy.org*). It's small (*web.py* itself is currently a single Python module of less than 2,500 lines, including comments), simple, works smoothly with other open source components (such as Cheetah for templating and PostgreSQL or MySQL as a database), and supports WSGI without *requiring* any such component (your script may also run with CGI, FastCGI, or as a standalone web server, which is particularly useful for ease of testing during development). Canonical "Hello world" example is:

```
import web
urls = '/', 'greet'
class greet(object):
    def GET(self):
        print 'Hello, web.py world!'
if __name__ == '__main__':
    web.run(urls)
```

The *urls* list maps regular expressions (matching HTTP paths) to class names, and classes implement methods GET and POST (and possibly others) to serve HTTP requests. Visit *http://webpy.org* for more information and to download web.py.

MIME and Network Encodings

What travels on a network are streams of bytes or text. However, what you want to send over the network often has more structure. The Multipurpose Internet Mail Extensions (MIME) and other encoding standards bridge the gap by specifying how to represent structured data as bytes or text. Python supports such encodings through many library modules, such as base64, quopri, and uu (covered in "Encoding Binary Data as Text" on page 561), and the modules of the email package (covered in "MIME and Email Format Handling" on page 564).

Encoding Binary Data as Text

Several kinds of media (e.g., email messages) contain only text. When you want to transmit arbitrary binary data via such media, you need to encode the data as text strings. The Python standard library supplies modules that support the standard encodings known as Base 64, Quoted Printable, and UU.

The base64 Module

The base64 module supports the encoding specified in RFC 1521 as Base 64. The Base 64 encoding is a compact way to represent arbitrary binary data as text, without any attempt to produce human-readable results. Module base64 supplies four functions.

decode	decode(*infile*,*outfile*)
	Reads text-file-like object *infile* by calling *infile*.readline until end of file (i.e., until a call to *infile*.readline returns an empty string), decodes the Base 64–encoded text thus read, and writes the decoded data to binary-file-like object *outfile*.

decodestring   decodestring(*s*)

Decodes text string *s*, which contains one or more complete lines of Base 64–encoded text, and returns the byte string with the corresponding decoded data.

encode   encode(*infile,outfile*)

Reads binary-file-like object *infile* by calling *infile*.read (for 57 bytes at a time, which is the amount of data that Base 64 encodes into 76 characters in each output line) until end of file (i.e., until a call to *infile*.read returns an empty string). It encodes the data thus read in Base 64, and writes the encoded text, one line at a time, to text-file-like object *outfile*, appending \n to each line of text it emits, including the last one.

encodestring   encodestring(*s*)

Encodes binary string *s*, which contains arbitrary bytes, and returns a text string with one or more complete lines of Base 64–encoded data joined by newline characters (\n). encodestring always returns a text string that ends with \n.

The quopri Module

The quopri module supports the encoding specified in RFC 1521 as Quoted Printable (QP). QP can represent any binary data as text, but it's mainly intended for data that is textual, with a modest amount of characters with the high bit set (i.e., characters outside the ASCII range). For such data, QP produces results that are both compact and human-readable. Module quopri supplies four functions.

decode   decode(*infile,outfile,header*=False)

Reads file-like object *infile* by calling *infile*.readline until end of file (i.e., until a call to *infile*.readline returns an empty string), decodes the QP-encoded ASCII text thus read, and writes the decoded data to file-like object *outfile*. When *header* is true, decode also decodes _ (underscores) into spaces.

decodestring   decodestring(*s,header*=False)

Decodes string *s*, which contains QP-encoded ASCII text, and returns the byte string with the decoded data. When *header* is true, decodestring also decodes _ (underscores) into spaces.

encode	encode(*infile*,*outfile*,*quotetabs*,*header*=False)
	Reads file-like object *infile* by calling *infile*.readline until end of file (i.e., until a call to *infile*.readline returns an empty string), encodes the data thus read in QP, and writes the encoded ASCII text to file-like object *outfile*. When *quotetabs* is true, encode also encodes spaces and tabs. When *header* is true, encode encodes spaces as _ (underscores).
encodestring	encodestring(*s*,*quotetabs* =False,*header*=False)
	Encodes string *s*, which contains arbitrary bytes, and returns a string with QP-encoded ASCII text. When *quotetabs* is true, encodestring also encodes spaces and tabs. When *header* is true, encodestring encodes spaces as _ (underscores).

The uu Module

The uu module supports the traditional Unix-to-Unix (UU) encoding, as implemented by Unix programs *uuencode* and *uudecode*. UU begins encoded data with a begin line, which also gives the filename and permissions of the file being encoded, and ends it with an end line. Therefore, UU encoding lets you embed encoded data in otherwise unstructured text, while Base 64 encoding relies on the existence of other indications of where the encoded data starts and finishes. Module uu supplies two functions.

decode	decode(*infile*,*outfile*=None,*mode*=None)
	Reads file-like object *infile* by calling *infile*.readline until end of file (i.e., until a call to *infile*.readline returns an empty string) or until a terminator line (the string 'end' surrounded by any amount of whitespace). decode decodes the UU-encoded text thus read and writes the decoded data to file-like object *outfile*. When *outfile* is None, decode creates the file specified in the UU-format begin line, with the permission bits given by *mode* (the permission bits specified in the begin line when *mode* is None). In this case, decode raises an exception if the file already exists.
encode	encode(*infile*,*outfile*,*name*='-',*mode*=0666)
	Reads file-like object *infile* by calling *infile*.read (for 45 bytes at a time, which is the amount of data that UU encodes into 60 characters in each output line) until end of file (i.e, until a call to *infile*.read returns an empty string). It encodes the data thus read

in UU and writes the encoded text to file-like object *outfile*. encode also writes a UU begin line before the encoded text and a UU end line after the encoded text. In the begin line, encode specifies the filename as *name* and the mode as *mode*.

MIME and Email Format Handling

Python supplies the email package to handle parsing, generation, and manipulation of MIME files such as email messages, network news posts, and so on. The Python standard library also contains other modules that handle some parts of these jobs. However, the email package offers a complete and systematic approach to these important tasks. I suggest you use package email, not the older modules that partially overlap with parts of email's functionality. Package email has nothing to do with receiving or sending email; for such tasks, see modules poplib and smtplib, covered in "Email Protocols" on page 503. email deals with handling messages after you receive them or before you send them.

Functions in Package email

Package email supplies two factory functions that return an instance *m* of class email.Message.Message. These functions rely on class email.Parser.Parser, but the factory functions are handier and simpler. Therefore, I do not cover module Parser further in this book.

message_ from_string	message_from_string(*s*) Builds *m* by parsing string *s*.
message_ from_file	message_from_file(*f*) Builds *m* by parsing the contents of file-like object *f*, which must be open for reading.

The email.Message Module

The email.Message module supplies class Message. All parts of package email make, modify, or use instances of class Message. An instance *m* of Message models a MIME message, including headers and a payload (data content). To create an initially empty *m*, call class Message with no arguments. More often, you create *m* by parsing via functions message_from_string and message_from_file of module email, or by other indirect means such as the classes covered in "Creating Messages" on page 568. *m*'s payload can be a string, a single other instance of Message, or a list of other Message instances for a multipart message.

You can set arbitrary headers on email messages you're building. Several Internet RFCs specify headers for a wide variety of purposes. The main applicable RFC is RFC 2822 (see *http://www.faqs.org/rfcs/rfc2822.html*). An instance *m* of class Message holds headers as well as a payload. *m* is a mapping, with header names as keys and header value strings as values. To make *m* more convenient, the semantics of *m* as a mapping are different from those of a dictionary. *m*'s keys are case-insensitive. *m* keeps headers in the order in which you add them, and methods keys, values, and items return headers in that order. *m* can have more than one header named *key*: *m*[*key*] returns an arbitrary header, and del *m*[*key*] deletes all of them. len(*m*) returns the total number of headers, counting duplicates, not just the number of distinct header names. If there is no header named *key*, *m*[*key*] returns None and does not raise KeyError (i.e., behaves like *m*.get(*key*)), and del *m*[*key*] is a no-operation in this case. You cannot loop directly on *m*; loop on *m*.keys( ) instead.

An instance *m* of Message supplies the following attributes and methods that deal with *m*'s headers and payload.

MIME

add_header	*m*.add_header(*_name, _value,**_params*)
	Like *m*[*_name*]=*_value*, but you can also supply header parameters as named arguments. For each named argument *pname=pvalue*, add_header changes underscores to dashes, then appends to the header's value a parameter of the form:
	; *pname*="*pvalue*"
	If *pvalue* is None, add_header appends only a parameter '; *pname*'.
as_string	*m*.as_string(*unixfrom*=False)
	Returns the entire message as a string (the message's payload must be a string). When *unixfrom* is true, also includes a first line, normally starting with 'From ', known as the *envelope header* of the message.
attach	*m*.attach(*payload*)
	Adds the *payload* to *m*'s payload. If *m*'s payload was None, *m*'s payload is now the single-item list [*payload*]. If *m*'s payload was a list, appends *payload* to the list. Otherwise, *m*.attach(*payload*) raises MultipartConversionError.
epilogue	Attribute *m*.epilogue can be None or a string that becomes part of the message's string-form after the last boundary line. Mail programs normally don't display this text. epilogue is a normal attribute of *m*: your program can access it when you're handling an *m* built by whatever means, and bind it when you're building or modifying *m*.

get_all

m.get_all(*name*,*default*=None)

Returns a list with all values of headers named *name* in the order in which the headers were added to *m*. When *m* has no header named *name*, get_all returns *default*.

get_boundary

m.get_boundary(*default*=None)

Returns the string value of the boundary parameter of *m*'s Content-Type header. When *m* has no Content-Type header, or the header has no boundary parameter, get_boundary returns *default*.

get_charsets

m.get_charsets(*default*=None)

Returns the list *L* of string values of parameter charset of *m*'s Content-Type headers. When *m* is multipart, *L* has one item per part; otherwise, *L* has length 1. For parts that have no Content-Type, no charset parameter, or a main type different from 'text', the corresponding item in *L* is *default*.

get_content_ maintype

m.get_content_maintype(*default*=None)

Returns *m*'s main content type: a lowercased string '*maintype*' taken from header Content-Type. When *m* has no header Content-Type, get_content_maintype returns *default*.

get_content_ subtype

m.get_content_subtype(*default*=None)

Returns *m*'s content subtype: a lowercased string '*subtype*' taken from header Content-Type. When *m* has no header Content-Type, get_content_subtype returns *default*.

get_content_ type

m.get_content_type(*default*=None)

Returns *m*'s content type: a lowercased string '*maintype/subtype*' taken from header Content-Type. When *m* has no header Content-Type, get_content_type returns *default*.

get_filename

m.get_filename(*default*=None)

Returns the string value of the filename parameter of *m*'s Content-Disposition header. When *m* has no Content-Disposition, or the header has no filename parameter, get_filename returns *default*.

get_param

m.get_param(*param*,*default*=None,*header*='Content-Type')

Returns the string value of parameter *param* of *m*'s header *header*. Returns the empty string for a parameter specified just by name.

When *m* has no header *header*, or the header has no parameter named *param*, get_param returns *default*.

get_params	*m*.get_params(*default*=None,*header*='Content-Type')

Returns the parameters of *m*'s header *header*, a list of pairs of strings that give each parameter's name and value. Uses the empty string as the value for parameters specified just by name. When *m* has no header *header*, get_params returns *default*.

get_payload	*m*.get_payload(*i*=None,*decode*=False)

Returns *m*'s payload. When *m*.is_multipart( ) is False, *i* must be None, and *m*.get_payload( ) returns *m*'s entire payload, a string or Message instance. If *decode* is true, and the value of header Content-Transfer-Encoding is either 'quoted-printable' or 'base64', *m*.get_payload also decodes the payload. If *decode* is false, or header Content-Transfer-Encoding is missing or has other values, *m*.get_payload returns the payload unchanged.

When *m*.is_multipart( ) is True, *decode* must be false. When *i* is None, *m*.get_payload( ) returns *m*'s payload as a list. Otherwise, *m*.get_payload( ) returns the *i*th item of the payload, or raises TypeError if *i*<0 or *i* is too large.

get_unixfrom	*m*.get_unixfrom( )

Returns the envelope header string for *m*, or None if *m* has no envelope header.

is_multipart	*m*.is_multipart( )

Returns True when *m*'s payload is a list; otherwise, False.

preamble	Attribute *m*.preamble can be None or a string that becomes part of the message's string form before the first boundary line. A mail program shows this text only if it doesn't support multipart messages, so you can use this attribute to alert the user that your message is multipart and a different mail program is needed to view it. preamble is a normal attribute of *m*: your program can access it when you're handling an *m* that is built by whatever means and bind it when you're building or modifying *m*.

set_boundary	*m*.set_boundary(*boundary*)

Sets the boundary parameter of *m*'s Content-Type header to *boundary*. When *m* has no Content-Type header, raises HeaderParseError.

set_payload	`m.set_payload(payload)`
	Sets *m*'s payload to *payload*, which must be a string or list, as appropriate.
set_unixfrom	`m.set_unixfrom(unixfrom)`
	Sets the envelope header string for *m*. *unixfrom* is the entire envelope header line, including the leading `'From '` but *not* including the trailing `'\n'`.
walk	`m.walk( )`
	Returns an iterator on all parts and subparts of *m* to walk the tree of parts depth-first.

The email.Generator Module

The `email.Generator` module supplies class `Generator`, which you can use to generate the textual form of a message *m*. *m.as_string* and `str(m)` may be sufficient, but class `Generator` gives you more flexibility. You instantiate `Generator` with a mandatory argument and two optional arguments.

Generator	`class Generator(outfp,mangle_from_=False,maxheaderlen=78)`
	outfp is a file or file-like object that supplies method `write`. When *mangle_from_* is true, *g* prepends `'>'` to any line in the payload that starts with `'From '` to make the message's textual form easier to parse. *g* wraps each header line at semicolons into physical lines of no more than *maxheaderlen* characters. To use *g*, call *g*.`flatten`:
	`g.flatten(m, unixfrom=False)`
	This emits *m* as text to *outfp*, like *outfp*.`write(m.as_string(unixfrom))`.

Creating Messages

Package `email` supplies modules with names that start with `'MIME'`, each module supplying a subclass of `Message` named like the module. These classes make it easier to create `Message` instances of various MIME types. The MIME classes are as follows.

MIMEAudio   class MIMEAudio(_audiodata, _subtype=None, _encoder=None, **_params)

audiodata is a byte string of audio data to pack in a message of MIME type 'audio/_subtype'. When _subtype_ is None, _audiodata_ must be parseable by standard Python module sndhdr to determine the subtype; otherwise, MIMEAudio raises a TypeError. When _encoder_ is None, MIMEAudio encodes data as Base 64, which is generally optimal. Otherwise, _encoder_ must be callable with one parameter _m_, which is the message being constructed; _encoder_ must then call _m_.get_payload() to get the payload, encode the payload, put the encoded form back by calling _m_.set_payload, and set _m_['Content-Transfer-Encoding'] appropriately. MIMEAudio passes the _params_ dictionary of named-argument names and values to _m_.add_header to construct _m_'s Content-Type.

MIMEBase   class MIMEBase(_maintype, _subtype, **_params)

The base class of all MIME classes; directly subclasses Message. Instantiating:

    m = MIMEBase(main, sub, **parms)

is equivalent to the longer and less convenient idiom:

    m = Message()
    m.add_header('Content-Type','%s/%s'%(main, sub), **parms)
    m.add_header('Mime-Version','1.0')

MIMEImage   class MIMEImage(_imagedata, _subtype=None, _encoder=None, **_params)

Like MIMEAudio, but with main type 'image'; uses standard Python module imghdr to determine the subtype, if needed.

MIMEMessage   class MIMEMessage(msg, _subtype='rfc822')

Packs _msg_, which must be an instance of Message (or a subclass), as the payload of a message of MIME type 'message/_subtype'.

MIMEText   class MIMEText(_text, _subtype='plain', _charset='us-ascii', _encoder=None)

Packs text string _text_ as the payload of a message of MIME type 'text/_subtype' with the given charset. When _encoder_ is None, MIMEText does not encode the text, which is generally optimal. Otherwise, _encoder_ must be callable with one parameter _m_, which is the message being constructed; _encoder_ must then call *m*.get_payload( ) to get the payload, encode the payload, put the encoded form back by calling *m*.set_payload, and set *m*['Content-Transfer-Encoding'] appropriately.

The email.Encoders Module

The email.Encoders module supplies functions that take a message *m* as their only argument, encode *m*'s payload, and set *m*'s headers appropriately.

encode_base64   encode_base64(*m*)

Uses Base 64 encoding, optimal for arbitrary binary data.

encode_noop   encode_noop(*m*)

Does nothing to *m*'s payload and headers.

encode_quopri   encode_quopri(*m*)

Uses Quoted Printable encoding, optimal for text that is almost but not fully ASCII.

encode_7or8bit   encode_7or8bit(*m*)

Does nothing to *m*'s payload, and sets header Content-Transfer-Encoding to '8bit' if any byte of *m*'s payload has the high bit set; otherwise, to '7bit'.

The email.Utils Module

The email.Utils module supplies several functions useful for email processing.

formataddr   formataddr(*pair*)

pair is a pair of strings (*realname,email_address*). formataddr returns a string *s* with the address to insert in header fields such as To and Cc. When *name* is false (e.g., ''), dump_address_pair returns *email_address*.

formatdate formatdate(*timeval*=None,*localtime*=False)

timeval is a number of seconds since the epoch. When *timeval* is None, formatdate uses the current time. When *localtime* is true, formatdate uses the local time zone; otherwise, it uses UTC. formatdate returns a string with the given time instant formatted in the way specified by RFC 2822.

---

getaddresses getaddresses(*L*)

Parses each item of *L*, a list of address strings as used in header fields such as To and Cc, and returns a list of pairs of strings (*name,email_address*). When getaddresses cannot parse an item of *L* as an address, getaddresses uses (None,None) as the corresponding item in the list it returns.

---

mktime_tz mktime_tz(*t*)

t is a tuple with 10 items. The first nine items of *t* are in the same format used in module time, covered in "The time Module" on page 302. *t*[-1] is a time zone as an offset in seconds from UTC (with the opposite sign from time.timezone, as specified by RFC 2822). When *t*[-1] is None, mktime_tz uses the local time zone. mktime_tz returns a float with the number of seconds since the epoch, in UTC, corresponding to the instant that *t* denotes.

---

parseaddr parseaddr(*s*)

Parses string *s*, which contains an address as typically specified in header fields such as To and Cc, and returns a pair of strings (*realname,email_address*). When parseaddr cannot parse *s* as an address, parseaddr returns ('','').

---

parsedate parsedate(*s*)

Parses string *s* as per the rules in RFC 2822 and returns a tuple *t* with nine items, as used in module time, covered in "The time Module" on page 302 (the items *t*[-3:] are not meaningful). parsedate also attempts to parse some erroneous variations on RFC 2822 that widespread mailers use. When parsedate cannot parse *s*, parsedate returns None.

---

parsedate_tz parsedate_tz(*s*)

Like parsedate, but returns a tuple *t* with 10 items, where *t*[-1] is *s*'s time zone as an offset in seconds from UTC (with the opposite sign from time.timezone, as specified by RFC 2822), like in the argument that mktime_tz accepts. Items *t*[-4:-1] are not meaningful. When *s* has no time zone, *t*[-1] is None.

quote	quote(s)
	Returns a copy of string *s*, where each double quote (") becomes '\"' and each existing backslash is repeated.

unquote	unquote(s)
	Returns a copy of string *s* where leading and trailing double-quote characters (") and angle brackets (<>) are removed if they surround the rest of *s*.

Example Uses of the email Package

The email package helps you both in reading and composing email and email-like messages (the email package, on the other hand, has absolutely nothing to do with receiving and transmitting such messages: these tasks belong to the completely different and separate modules covered in Chapters 19 and 20). Here is an example of how to use the email package to read a possibly multipart message and unpack each part into a file in a given directory:

```
import os, email
def unpack_mail(mail_file, dest_dir):
    ''' Given file object mail_file, open for reading, and dest_dir, a
        string that is a path to an existing, writable directory, unpack
        each part of the mail message from mail_file to a file within
        dest_dir.
    '''
    try: msg = email.message_from_file(mail_file)
    finally: mail_file.close()
    for part_number, part in enumerate(msg.walk()):
        if part.get_content_maintype( ) == "multipart":
            continue
        dest = part.get_filename()
        if dest is None: dest = part.get_param("name")
        if dest is None: dest = "part-%i" % partCounter
        # In real life, make sure that dest is a reasonable filename
        # for your OS; otherwise, mangle that name until it is!
        f = open(os.path.join(dest_dir, dest), "wb")
        try: f.write(part.get_payload(decode=True))
        finally: f.close()
```

And here is an example that performs roughly the reverse task, packaging all files that are directly under a given source directory into a file suitable for mailing:

```
def pack_mail(source_dir, **headers):
    ''' Given source_dir, a string that is a path to an existing, readable
        directory, and arbitrary header name/value pairs passed in as named
```

```
        arguments, packs all the files directly under source_dir (assumed to
        be plain text files) into a mail message returned as a string.
    '''
    msg = email.Message.Message( )
    for name, value in headers.iteritems( ):
        msg[name] = value
    msg['Content-type'] = 'multipart/mixed'
    filenames = os.walk(source_dir).next( )[-1]
    for filename in filenames:
        m = email.Message.Message( )
        m.add_header("Content-type", 'text/plain', name=filename)
        f = open(os.path.join(source_dir, filename), "r")
        m.set_payload(f.read( ))
        f.close( )
        msg.attach(m)
    return msg.as_string( )
```

The Message Classes of the rfc822 and mimetools Modules

The best way to handle email-like messages is with package email. However, some
other modules covered in Chapters 19 and 21 use instances of class rfc822.Message
or its subclass, mimetools.Message. This section covers the subset of these classes'
functionality that you need to make effective use of the modules covered in Chapters 19 and 21.

An instance *m* of class Message is a mapping, with the headers' names as keys and
the corresponding header value strings as values. Keys and values are strings, and
keys are case-insensitive. *m* supports all mapping methods except clear, copy,
popitem, and update. get and setdefault default to '' instead of None. Instance *m*
also supplies convenience methods (e.g., to combine getting a header's value and
parsing it as a date or an address). I suggest you use for such purposes the functions of module email.Utils (covered in "The email.Utils Module" on page 570)
and use *m* just as a mapping.

When *m* is an instance of mimetools.Message, *m* supplies additional methods.

---

getmaintype   *m*.getmaintype( )

Returns *m*'s main content type, taken from header Content-Type
converted to lowercase. When *m* has no header Content-Type,
getmaintype returns 'text'.

---

getparam   *m*.getparam(*param*)

Returns the string value of the parameter named *param* of *m*'s header
Content-Type.

getsubtype   *m*.getsubtype( )

Returns *m*'s content subtype, taken from header Content-Type converted to lowercase. When *m* has no Content-Type, getsubtype returns 'plain'.

gettype   *m*.gettype( )

Returns *m*'s content type, taken from header Content-Type converted to lowercase. When *m* has no Content-Type, gettype returns 'text/plain'.

Structured Text: HTML

Most documents on the Web use HTML, the HyperText Markup Language. *Markup* is the insertion of special tokens, known as *tags*, in a text document to give structure to the text. HTML is, in theory, an application of the large, general standard known as SGML, the Standard General Markup Language. In practice, many of the Web's documents use HTML in sloppy or incorrect ways. Browsers have evolved many practical heuristics over the years to try and compensate for this, but even so, it still sometimes happens that a browser displays an incorrect web page in some weird way (don't blame the browser: 9 times out of 10, all the blame and then some is deserved by the web page's author!).

HTML is not suitable for much more than presenting documents on a screen. Complete and precise extraction of the information in the document, working backward from the document's presentation, is often unfeasible. To tighten things up, HTML has evolved into a more rigorous standard called XHTML. XHTML is very similar to traditional HTML, but it is defined in terms of XML and more precisely than HTML. You can handle XHTML with the tools covered in Chapter 24.

Despite the difficulties, it's often possible to extract at least some useful information from HTML documents (a task often known as *screen-scraping*, or just *scraping*). Python supplies the sgmllib, htmllib, and HTMLParser modules for the task of parsing HTML documents, whether this parsing is for the purpose of presenting the documents, or, more typically, as part of an attempt to extract (scrape) information. When you're dealing with broken web pages, third-party module BeautifulSoup offers your best, last hope. Generating HTML and embedding Python in HTML are also frequent tasks. No standard Python library module supports HTML generation or embedding directly, but you can use normal Python string manipulation, and third-party modules can also help.

The sgmllib Module

The name of the sgmllib module is misleading: sgmllib parses only a tiny subset of SGML, but it is still a good way to get information from HTML files. sgmllib supplies one class, SGMLParser, which you subclass, overriding methods. The most frequently used methods of an instance *s* of your subclass *X* of SGMLParser are as follows.

close	s.close( )
	Tells the parser that there is no more input data. When *X* overrides close, s.close must call SGMLParser.close to ensure that buffered data is processed.
do_tag	s.do_tag(*attributes*)
	X supplies a method with such a name for each *tag*, with no corresponding end tag, that *X* wants to process. *tag* must be lowercase in the method name, but can be in any case in the parsed text (the SGML standard, like HTML, is case-insensitive, in contrast to XML and XHTML, which are case-sensitive). SGMLParser's handle_tag method calls do_tag when appropriate. *attributes* is a list of pairs (*name*,*value*), where *name* is an attribute's name, lowercased, and *value* is the value, processed to resolve entity and character references and remove surrounding quotes.
end_tag	s.end_tag( )
	X supplies a method with such a name for each *tag* whose end tag *X* wants to process. *tag* must be lowercase in the method name, but can be in any case in the parsed text. *X* must also supply a method named start_*tag*; otherwise, end_*tag* is ignored. SGMLParser's handle_endtag method calls end_*tag* when appropriate.
feed	s.feed(*data*)
	Passes to the parser some of the text being parsed. The parser may process some prefix of the text, holding the rest in a buffer until the next call to s.feed or s.close.
handle_charref	s.handle_charref(*ref*)
	Called to process a character reference '&#*ref*;'. SGMLParser's implementation of handle_charref handles only decimal numbers in range(0,256), like:

```
def handle_charref(self, ref):
    try:
        c = chr(int(ref[1:]))
```

```
                    except (TypeError, ValueError):
                        self.unknown_charref(ref)
                    else: self.handle_data(c)
```

Your subclass *X* may override handle_charref or unknown_charref in
order to support other forms of character references '&#...;'.

handle_ comment	s.handle_comment(*comment*)

Called to handle comments. *comment* is the string within '<!--...-->',
without the delimiters. SGMLParser's implementation of
handle_comment does nothing.

handle_data	s.handle_data(*data*)

Called to process each arbitrary string *data*. Your subclass *X*
normally overrides handle_data. SGMLParser's implementation of
handle_data does nothing.

handle_endtag	s.handle_endtag(*tag*,*method*)

Called to handle termination tags for which *X* supplies methods
named start_*tag* and end_*tag*. *tag* is the tag string, lowercased.
method is the bound method for end_*tag*. SGMLParser's implementation of handle_endtag just calls *method*( ), and it's rarely necessary
to override it.

handle_ entityref	s.handle_entityref(*ref*)

Called to process an entity reference '&*ref*;'. SGMLParser's implementation of handle_entityref looks *ref* up in s.entitydefs.

Your subclass *X* may override handle_entityref or unknown_entityref
in order to support entity references '&...;' in different ways.
SGMLParser's attribute entitydefs includes keys 'amp', 'apos', 'gt',
'lt', and 'quot'. Suppose your subclass *X* needs to add entities
defined in module htmlentitydefs, covered in "The htmlentitydefs
Module" on page 582. One approach would be:

```
class X(sgmllib.SGMLParser):
    entitydefs = dict(sgmllib.SGMLParser)
    entitydefs.update((k, unichr(v))
        for k, v in htmlentitydefs.name2codepoint.
iteritems( ))
```

Of course, method *X*.handle_data must then also be ready to
process Unicode rather than just plain-string arguments (an
enhancement that is a good idea in any case).

handle_starttag	`s.handle_starttag(`*`tag, method, attributes`*`)`
	Called to handle tags for which *X* supplies a method `start_`*`tag`* or `do_`*`tag`*. *`tag`* is the tag string, lowercased. *`method`* is the bound method for `start_`*`tag`* or `do_`*`tag`*. *`attributes`* is a list of pairs (*`name,value`*), where *`name`* is each attribute's name, lowercased, and *`value`* is the value, processed to resolve entity references and character references and to remove surrounding quotes. When *X* supplies both `start_`*`tag`* and `do_`*`tag`* methods, `start_`*`tag`* has precedence and `do_`*`tag`* is ignored. SGMLParser's implementation of `handle_starttag` just calls *`method`*(*`attributes`*), and it's rarely necessary to override it.
report_ unbalanced	`s.report_unbalanced(`*`tag`*`)`
	Called when tags terminate without being open. *`tag`* is the tag string, lowercased. SGMLParser's implementation of `report_unbalanced` does nothing.
start_tag	`s.start_`*`tag`*`(`*`attributes`*`)`
	X supplies a method thus named for each *`tag`*, with an end tag, that *X* wants to process. *`tag`* must be lowercase in the method name, but can be in any case in the parsed text. SGMLParser's `handle_tag` method calls `start_`*`tag`* when appropriate. *`attributes`* is a list of pairs (*`name,value`*), where *`name`* is each attribute's name, lowercased, and *`value`* is the value, processed to resolve entity references and character references and to remove surrounding quotes.
unknown_ charref	`s.unknown_charref(`*`ref`*`)`
	Called to process invalid or unrecognized character references. SGMLParser's implementation of `unknown_charref` does nothing.
unknown_ endtag	`s.unknown_endtag(`*`tag`*`)`
	Called to process termination tags for which *X* supplies no specific method. SGMLParser's implementation of `unknown_endtag` does nothing.
unknown_ entityref	`s.unknown_entityref(`*`ref`*`)`
	Called to process unknown entity references. SGMLParser's implementation of `unknown_entityref` does nothing.

| **unknown_** | s.unknown_starttag(*tag*, *attributes*) |
| **starttag** | |

Called to process tags for which *X* supplies no specific method. *tag* is the tag string, lowercased. *attributes* is a list of pairs (*name*,*value*), where *name* is each attribute's name, lowercased, and *value* is the value, processed to resolve entity references and character references and to remove surrounding quotes. SGMLParser's implementation of unknown_starttag does nothing.

Parsing HTML with sgmllib

The following example uses sgmllib for a typical HTML-related task that could be at the core of a "web spider": fetch a page from the Web with urllib, parse it, and output the targets of outgoing hyperlinks. The example uses urlparse to check the page's links and outputs only links whose URLs have an explicit scheme of 'http'.

```python
import sgmllib, urllib, urlparse

class LinksParser(sgmllib.SGMLParser):
    def __init__(self):
        sgmllib.SGMLParser.__init__(self)
        self.seen = set()
    def do_a(self, attributes):
        for name, value in attributes:
            if name == 'href' and value not in self.seen:
                self.seen.add(value)
                pieces = urlparse.urlparse(value)
                if pieces[0] != 'http': return
                print urlparse.urlunparse(pieces)
                return

p = LinksParser()
f = urllib.urlopen('http://www.python.org/index.html')
BUFSIZE = 8192
while True:
    data = f.read(BUFSIZE)
    if not data: break
    p.feed(data)
p.close()
```

Class LinksParser only needs to define method do_a. The superclass calls back to this method for all <a> tags, and the method loops on the attributes, looking for one named 'href', then works with the corresponding value (i.e., the relevant URL).

The htmllib Module

The htmllib module supplies a class named HTMLParser that subclasses SGMLParser and defines start_*tag*, do_*tag*, and end_*tag* methods for HTML 2.0 tags. HTMLParser implements and overrides methods to perform calls to methods of a formatter object, covered in "The formatter Module" on page 581. You can subclass HTMLParser and override methods. In addition to start_*tag*, do_*tag*, and end_*tag* methods, an instance *h* of HTMLParser supplies the following attributes and methods.

---

anchor_bgn   *h*.anchor_bgn(*href,name,type*)

Called for each <a> tag. *href*, *name*, and *type* are the string values of the tag's attributes with the same names. HTMLParser's implementation of anchor_bgn maintains a list of outgoing hyperlink targets (i.e., *href* arguments of method *s*.anchor_bgn) in an instance attribute named *s*.anchorlist.

---

anchor_end   *h*.anchor_end( )

Called for each </a> end tag. HTMLParser's implementation of anchor_end emits to the formatter a footnote reference that is an index within *s*.anchorlist. In other words, by default, HTMLParser asks the formatter to format an <a>/</a> tag pair as the text inside the tag, followed by a footnote reference number that points to the URL in the <a> tag. Of course, it's up to the formatter to deal with this formatting request.

---

anchorlist   The *h*.anchor_list attribute contains the list of outgoing hyperlink target URLs, as built by method *h*.anchor_bgn.

---

formatter   The *h*.formatter attribute is the formatter object *f* associated with *h*, which you pass as the only argument when you instantiate HTMLParser(*f*).

---

handle_image   *h*.handle_image(*source,alt,ismap='',align='',width='',height=''*)

Called for each <img> tag. Each argument is the string value of the tag's attribute of the same name. HTMLParser's implementation of handle_image calls *h*.handle_data(*alt*) (in other words, the default implementation ignores the image proper and formats the alternate text instead).

---

nofill	*h*.nofill
	The *h*.nofill attribute is false when the parser is collapsing whitespace, the normal case. It is true when the parser must preserve whitespace, typically within a <pre> tag.
save_bgn	*h*.save_bgn( )
	Diverts data to an internal buffer instead of passing it to the formatter, until the next call to *h*.save_end( ). *h* has only one buffer, so you cannot nest save_bgn calls.
save_end	*h*.save_end( )
	Returns a string with all data in the internal buffer and directs data back to the formatter from now on. If save_bgn state was not on, raises TypeError.

The formatter module defines formatter and writer classes. Instantiate a formatter by passing a writer instance to the class, then pass the formatter instance to class HTMLParser of module htmllib. You can define your own formatters and writers by subclassing formatter's classes and overriding methods appropriately, but I do not cover this advanced and rarely used possibility in this book. An application with special output requirements would typically define an appropriate writer, subclassing AbstractWriter and overriding all methods, and use class AbstractFormatter without needing to subclass it. Module formatter supplies the following classes.

Abstract-Formatter	class AbstractFormatter(*writer*)
	The standard formatter implementation, suitable for most tasks.
AbstractWriter	class AbstractWriter( )
	A writer implementation that prints each of its method names when called, suitable for debugging purposes only.
DumbWriter	class DumbWriter(*file*=sys.stdout,*maxcol*=72)
	A writer implementation that emits text to file object *file*, with word wrapping to ensure that no text line is longer than *maxcol* characters.

NullFormatter	class NullFormatter(*writer*=None)
	A formatter implementation whose methods are do-nothing stubs. When *writer* is None, instantiates NullWriter. Suitable when you subclass HMTLParser to analyze an HTML document but don't want any output to occur.

NullWriter	class NullWriter()
	A writer implementation whose methods are do-nothing stubs.

The htmlentitydefs Module

The htmlentitydefs module supplies three attributes:

codepoint2name
> A mapping from Unicode codepoints to HTML entity names. For example, htmlentitydefs.codepoint2name[229] is 'auml', since Unicode character 229, "lowercase a with umlaut," is encoded in HTML as 'ä'.

entitydefs
> A mapping from HTML entity names to Latin-1 characters or HTML character references. For example, htmlentitydefs.entitydefs['auml'] is '\xe4', and htmlentitydefs.entitydefs['sigma'] is 'σ'.

name2codepoint
> A mapping from HTML entity names to Unicode codepoints. For example, htmlentitydefs.name2codepoint['auml'] is 228.

Module htmllib uses module htmlentitydefs internally.

Parsing HTML with htmllib

The following example uses htmllib to perform the same task as in the previous example for sgmllib, fetching a page from the Web with urllib, parsing it, and outputting the hyperlinks:

```
import htmllib, formatter, urllib, urlparse

p = htmllib.HTMLParser(formatter.NullFormatter())
f = urllib.urlopen('http://www.python.org/index.html')
BUFSIZE = 8192
while True:
    data = f.read(BUFSIZE)
    if not data: break
    p.feed(data)
p.close()

seen = set()
for url in p.anchorlist:
```

```
if url in seen: continue
seen.add(url)
pieces = urlparse.urlparse(url)
if pieces[0] == 'http':
    print urlparse.urlunparse(pieces)
```

The example exploits the anchorlist attribute of class htmllib.HTMLParser, and therefore does not need to perform any subclassing. htmllib.HTMLParser builds the anchorlist attribute as it parses the HTML page, so the code need only loop on the list and work with the list's items, each a relevant URL.

The HTMLParser Module

Module HTMLParser supplies one class, HTMLParser, that you subclass to override methods. HTMLParser.HTMLParser is similar to sgmllib.SGMLParser, but is simpler and able to parse XHTML as well. The main differences between HTMLParser and SGMLParser are the following:

- HMTLParser does not call methods named do_*tag*, start_*tag*, and end_*tag*. To process tags and end tags, your subclass *X* of HTMLParser must override methods handle_starttag and/or handle_endtag and check explicitly for the tags it wants to process.

- HMTLParser does not keep track of, nor check, tag nesting in any way.

- HMTLParser does nothing, by default, to resolve character and entity references. Your subclass *X* of HTMLParser must override methods handle_charref and/or handle_entityref if it needs to perform processing of such references.

Commonly used methods of an instance *h* of subclass *X* of HTMLParser are as follows.

---

close   *h*.close( )

Tells the parser that there is no more input data. When *X* overrides close, *h*.close must also call HTMLParser.close to ensure that all buffered data is processed.

---

feed   *h*.feed(*data*)

Passes to the parser a part of the text being parsed. The parser processes some prefix of the text and holds the rest in a buffer until the next call to *h*.feed or *h*.close.

---

handle_charref   *h*.handle_charref(*ref*)

Called to process a character reference '&#*ref*;'. HTMLParser's implementation of handle_charref does nothing.

handle_ comment	*h*.handle_comment(*comment*)
	Called to handle comments. *comment* is the string within '`<!--...-->`', without the delimiters. HTMLParser's implementation of handle_comment does nothing.
handle_data	*h*.handle_data(*data*)
	Called to process each arbitrary string *data*. Your subclass *X* almost always overrides handle_data. HTMLParser's implementation of handle_data does nothing.
handle_endtag	*h*.handle_endtag(*tag*)
	Called to handle termination tags. *tag* is the tag string, lowercased. HTMLParser's implementation of handle_endtag does nothing.
handle_ entityref	*h*.handle_entityref(*ref*)
	Called to process an entity reference '`&ref;`'. HTMLParser's implementation of handle_entityref does nothing.
handle_starttag	*h*.handle_starttag(*tag, attributes*)
	Called to handle tags. *tag* is the tag string, lowercased. *attributes* is a list of pairs (*name,value*): *name* is each attribute's name, lowercased, and *value* is the value, processed to resolve entity and character references and remove surrounding quotes. HTMLParser's implementation of handle_starttag does nothing.

Parsing HTML with HTMLParser

The following example uses HTMLParser to perform the same task as previous examples: fetching a page from the Web with urllib, parsing it, and emitting hyperlinks:

```
import HTMLParser, urllib, urlparse

class LinksParser(HTMLParser.HTMLParser):
    def __init__(self):
        HTMLParser.HTMLParser.__init__(self)
        self.seen = set()
    def handle_starttag(self, tag, attributes):
        if tag != 'a': return
        for name, value in attributes:
            if name == 'href' and value not in self.seen:
                self.seen.add(value)
```

```
                pieces = urlparse.urlparse(value)
                if pieces[0] != 'http': return
                print urlparse.urlunparse(pieces)
                return

    p = LinksParser( )
    f = urllib.urlopen('http://www.python.org/index.html')
    BUFSIZE = 8192
    while True:
        data = f.read(BUFSIZE)
        if not data: break
        p.feed(data)

    p.close( )
```

Since `HTMLParser.HTMLParser` performs no per-tag dispatching to methods, `LinksParser` overrides method `handle_starttag` and checks if the *tag* is `'a'`.

The BeautifulSoup Extension

BeautifulSoup (*http://www.crummy.com/software/BeautifulSoup/*) lets you parse HTML that may be badly formed and uses simple heuristics to compensate for likely HTML brokenness (it succeeds in this difficult task with surprisingly good frequency). Module `BeautifulSoup` supplies a class, also named `BeautifulSoup`, which you instantiate with either a file-like object (which is read to give the HTML text to parse) or a string (which is the text to parse). The module also supplies other classes (`BeautifulStoneSoup` and `ICantBelieveItsBeautifulSoup`) that are quite similar, but suitable for slightly different XML parsing tasks. An instance *b* of class `BeautifulSoup` supplies many attributes and methods to ease the task of searching for information in the parsed HTML input, returning instances of classes `Tag` and `NavigableText`, which in turn let you keep navigating or dig for more information.

Parsing HTML with BeautifulSoup

The following example uses `BeautifulSoup` to perform the same task as previous examples: fetch a page from the Web with `urllib`, parse it, and output the hyperlinks:

```
    import urllib, urlparse, BeautifulSoup

    f = urllib.urlopen('http://www.python.org/index.html')
    b = BeautifulSoup.BeautifulSoup(f)

    seen = set( )
    for anchor in b.fetch('a'):
        url = anchor.get('href')
        if url is None or url in seen: continue
        seen.add(url)
        pieces = urlparse.urlparse(url)
        if pieces[0]=='http':
            print urlparse.urlunparse(pieces)
```

The example calls the `fetch` method of class `BeautifulSoup.BeautifulSoup` to obtain all instances of a certain tag (here, tag `'<a>'`), then the get method of instances of class `Tag` to obtain the value of an attribute (here, `'href'`), or `None` when that attribute is missing. The logic to analyze and emit the target URLs of outgoing hyperlinks is just the same as in previous examples.

Generating HTML

Python does not come with tools to generate HTML. If you want an advanced framework for structured HTML generation, I recommend Robin Friedrich's HTMLGen 2.2 (available at *http://starship.python.net/crew/friedrich/HTMLgen/ html/main.html*), but I do not cover the package in this book. To generate XHTML, you can use the approaches covered in Chapter 24.

Embedding

If your favorite approach is to embed Python code within HTML in the manner made popular by JSP, ASP, and PHP, one possibility is to use the Python Server Pages (PSP) supplied by Webware (mentioned in "Webware" on page 559). Another package, focused particularly on the embedding approach, is Spyce (available at *http://spyce.sf.net/*). For all but the simplest problems, however, development and maintenance are eased by separating logic and presentation issues through templating, covered in the next section. Both Webware and Spyce optionally support templating in lieu of embedding.

Templating

To generate HTML, the best approach is often templating. With templating, you start with a *template*, which is a text string (often read from a file, database, etc.) that is valid HTML, but includes markers, also known as placeholders, where dynamically generated text must be inserted. Your program generates the needed text and substitutes it into the template. In the simplest case, you can use markers of the form `'%(name)s'`. Set the dynamically generated text as the value for key `'name'` in some dictionary *d*. The Python string formatting operator `%` (covered in "String Formatting" on page 193) now does all you need: if *t* is your template, *t%d* is a copy of the template with all values properly substituted.

The Cheetah Package

For advanced templating tasks, I recommend Cheetah (available at *http://www.chee-tahtemplate.org*). Cheetah interoperates particularly well with Webware and other Python server-side web frameworks, as mentioned in "Webware" on page 559. When you have Webware installed, Cheetah's template objects are Webware servlets, so you can immediately deploy them under Webware. You can also use Cheetah in many other contexts: for example, Spyce and `web.py` (covered in "web.py" on page 560) can optionally use Cheetah for templating, and TurboGears (mentioned in "Other Higher-Level-of-Abstraction Frameworks" on page 559) also relies on Cheetah. Cheetah can process HTML templates for any purpose whatsoever. In fact,

Cheetah is quite suitable for templating with any kind of structured text, HTML or otherwise.

The Cheetah templating language

In a Cheetah template, use $*name* or ${*name*} to request the insertion of the value of a variable named *name*. *name* can contain dots to request lookups of object attributes or dictionary keys. For example, $a.b.c requests insertion of the value of attribute c of attribute b of the variable named a. When b is a dictionary, this translates to the Python expression *a.b['c']*. If an object encountered during $ substitution is callable, Cheetah calls the object, without arguments, during the lookup. This high degree of polymorphism makes authoring and maintaining Cheetah templates easier for nondevelopers, as it saves them the need to learn and understand these distinctions.

A Cheetah template can contain *directives*, which are verbs that start with # that allow comments, file inclusion, flow control (conditionals, loops, exception handling), and more; Cheetah provides a rich templating language on top of Python. The most frequently used verbs in simple Cheetah templates are the following (similar to Python, but with $ in front of names, no trailing :, and no mandatory indents but #end clauses instead):

comment text
> Single-line comments start with two # characters (you can also use multiline comments: start with #* and end with *#); a comment that starts with doc (with no whitespace between the start-of-comment marker and the d) is used as a docstring.

#break
#continue
#from
#import
#pass
> Like the Python statements with the same names.

#echo *expression*
> Computes a Python expression (with $ in front of names) and outputs the result.

#for $*variable* in $*container* ... #end for
> Like the Python for statement.

#include *filename_expression*
> Reads the named file and includes its text, parsing it for Cheetah syntax.

#include raw *filename_expression*
> Reads the named file and includes its text verbatim, without parsing.

#if ... #else if ... #else ... #end if
> Like the Python if statement (#else if and #else are optional).

#if ... then ... else ...
> Single-line if statement (else is mandatory; no else if is allowed).

`#raw`... `#end raw`
> Emits some text verbatim, without checking for `$name` or `#directive` occurrences.

`#repeat $times` ... `#end repeat`
> Repeats some text `$times` times.

`#set $variable = expression`
> Assigns a value to a variable (the variable is local to this template).

`#silent expression`
> Computes a Python expression (with `$` in front of names) and hides the result.

`#slurp`
> Consumes the following newline (i.e., joins the following line onto this one).

`#stop`
> Stops the processing of the current template file.

`#while $condition` ... `#end while`
> Like the Python `while` statement.

Note the differences between `#echo`, `#silent`, and `$` substitution. `#echo $a(2)` inserts in the template's output the result of calling function a with an argument of 2. Without the `#echo`, `$a(2)` inserts the string form of a (calling a( ) without arguments, if a is callable) followed by the three characters `(2)`. `#silent $a(2)` calls a with an argument of 2 and inserts nothing in the template's output.

Cheetah has many other verbs that let you control advanced functionality such as caching, filtering, setting and deleting of variables, and method definitions. A Cheetah template object is a class instance, and may use inheritance, override methods, and so on. However, for simple templates you will most often not need such powerful mechanisms.

The Template class

The `Cheetah.Template` module supplies one class.

Template

`class Template(source=None, searchList=[], file=None)`

Always call `Template` with named arguments (except, optionally, the first one); the number and order of parameters may change in the future, but the names are guaranteed to stay. You must pass either *source* or *file*, but not both. *source* is a template string. *file* is a file-like object open for reading, or the path to a file to open for reading.

searchList is a sequence of objects to use as top-level sources for `$name` insertion. The instance *t* of class `Template` is implicitly appended at the end of *t*'s search list (e.g., `$a` in the template inserts the value of `t.a` if no other object in the search list has an attribute a or an item with a key of `'a'`). *searchList* defaults to the empty list, so, by default, *t*'s template expansion uses only *t*'s attributes as variables for $ substitution.

Class Template also allows other keyword arguments, but these are the most frequently used. The instance *t* supplies many methods, but normally you call only str(*t*), which returns the string form of the expanded template.

A Cheetah example

The following example uses Cheetah.Template to output HTML with dynamic content:

```
import Cheetah.Template
import os, time, socket

tt = Cheetah.Template.Template('''
<html><head><title>Report by $USER</title></head><body>
<h1>Report on host data</h1>
<p>Report written at $asctime:<br/>
#for $hostline in $uname
  $hostline<br/>
#end for
</p></body></html>
''', searchList=[time, os.environ])

try: tt.uname = os.uname
except AttributeError:
    tt.uname = [socket.gethostname()]

print tt
```

This example instantiates and binds to name *tt* a Template instance, whose *source* is an HTML document string with some Cheetah placeholders (*$USER*, *$asctime*, *$uname*) and a Cheetah #for...#end for directive. The placeholder *$hostline* is the loop variable in the #for directive, so the template does not search the search-list objects for name 'hostline' when it expands. The example instantiates *tt* with a *searchList* argument, setting module time and dictionary os.environ as part of the search. For names that cannot be found in objects on the search list, *tt*'s expansion looks in instance *tt* itself. Therefore, the example binds attribute *tt.uname* either to function os.uname (which returns a tuple of host description data, but exists only on certain platforms), if available, or else to a list whose only item is the hostname returned by function gethostname of module socket.

The last statement of the example is print *tt*. The print statement transforms its arguments into strings, as if str were called on each argument. Therefore, print *tt* expands *tt*. Some of the placeholders' expansions use dictionary lookup (*$USER* looks up os.environ['USER']), some perform a function call (*$asctime* calls time.asctime()), and some may behave in different ways (*$uname*, depending on what it finds as *tt.uname*, calls that attribute—if it is callable, as when it's os.uname—or just takes it as is, when it's already a list).

One important note applies to all templating tasks, not just to Cheetah. Templates are almost invariably not the right place for program logic to reside. Don't put in your templates more logic than is strictly needed. Templating engines let you separate the task of computing results (best done in Python, outside of any template) from that of presenting the results as HTML or other kinds of structured text. Templates should deal just with presentation issues and contain as little program logic as feasible.

24

Structured Text: XML

XML, the eXtensible Markup Language, has become very widespread over the last few years. Like SGML (mentioned in "The sgmllib Module" on page 576), XML is a *metalanguage*, a language to describe markup languages. On top of XML 1.0, the XML community (mostly within the World Wide Web Consortium [W3C]) has standardized many other technologies, such as schema languages, Namespaces, XPath, XLink, XPointer, and XSLT.

Industry consortia in many fields have defined industry-specific markup languages on top of XML to facilitate data exchange among applications in those fields. Such industry standards let applications exchange data even when the applications are coded in different languages and deployed on different platforms by different firms. XML, related technologies, and XML-based markup languages are the basis for inter-application, cross-language, cross-platform data interchange in modern applications.

Python has excellent support for XML. The standard Python library supplies the xml package, which lets you use fundamental XML technology quite simply. The third-party package PyXML (*http://pyxml.sf.net*) extends the standard library's xml with validating parsers, richer DOM implementations, and advanced technologies such as XPath and XSLT. Downloading and installing PyXML upgrades Python's own xml packages, so it can be a good idea to do so even if you don't use PyXML-specific features.

On top of PyXML, you can choose to install yet another freely available third-party package, 4Suite (available at *http://4suite.org*). 4Suite provides even more XML parsers for special niches, advanced technologies such as XLink and XPointer, and code supporting standards built on top of XML, such as the Resource Description Framework (RDF).

A highly Pythonic alternative for XML processing is ElementTree (*http://effbot.org/ zone/element-index.htm*), most of whose functionality is also slated for release in Python 2.5 as standard library module xml.etree (for use in Python 2.3 or 2.4, or even 2.5 but with more complete functionality, you can, in any case, download and install the complete ElementTree from the URL at *effbot.org*). ElementTree's elegance, speed, and highly Pythonic architecture make it the package of choice for most Python XML applications, particularly, but not exclusively, if you can restrict your application to run on Python 2.5. However, I do not cover Element-Tree in this book.

In this chapter, I cover only the essentials of the standard library's xml package, taking for granted some elementary knowledge of XML itself.

An Overview of XML Parsing

When your application must parse XML documents, your first, fundamental choice is what kind of parsing to use. You can use *event-driven* parsing, in which the parser reads the document sequentially and calls back to your application each time it parses a significant aspect of the document (such as an element), or you can use *object-based* parsing, in which the parser reads the whole document and builds in-memory data structures, representing the document, that you can then navigate. SAX is the main way to perform event-driven parsing, and DOM is the main way to perform object-based parsing. In each case, there are alternatives, such as direct use of expat for event-driven parsing, or ElementTree for object-based parsing, but I do not cover these alternatives in this book. Another interesting possibility is *pull-based parsing*, supported by pulldom, covered later in this chapter (and also, to some extent, by ElementTree, via the iterparse function of C-coded module cElementTree).

Event-driven parsing requires fewer resources, which makes it particularly suitable to parse very large documents. However, event-driven parsing requires you to structure your application accordingly, performing your processing (and typically building auxiliary data structures) in your methods called by the parser. Object-based parsing gives you more flexibility to structure your application, which may make it more suitable when you need to perform very complicated processing, as long as you can afford the extra resources needed for object-based parsing (typically, this means that you are not dealing with very large documents). Object-based approaches also support programs that need to modify or create XML documents, as covered in "Changing and Generating XML" on page 606.

As a general guideline, when you are still undecided after studying the various trade-offs, I suggest you try event-driven parsing first, whenever you can see a reasonably direct way to perform your program's tasks through this approach. Event-driven parsing is more scalable: if your program can perform its task via event-driven parsing, it will be more applicable to larger documents than it would be otherwise. If event-driven parsing is just too confining, then try pull-based parsing instead, via pulldom (or cElementTree.iterparse). I suggest you consider (non-pull) DOM only when you think DOM is the only way to perform your program's tasks without excessive contortions. In that case (and assuming you cannot use ElementTree, which offers a more Pythonic API that is also faster and less memory-hungry), DOM may be best, as long as you can accept the resulting limitations in terms of the maximum size of documents that your program can support and the costs in time and memory for processing.

Parsing XML with SAX

In most cases, the best way to extract information from an XML document is to parse the document with an event-driven parser compliant with SAX, the Simple API for XML. SAX defines a standard API that can be implemented on top of many different underlying parsers. The SAX approach to parsing has similarities to most of the HTML parsers covered in Chapter 23. As the parser encounters XML elements, text contents, and other significant events in the input stream, the parser calls back to methods of your classes. Such event-driven parsing, based on callbacks to your methods as relevant events occur, also has similarities to the event-driven approach that is almost universal in GUIs and in some of the best, most scalable networking frameworks, such as Twisted, mentioned in Chapter 19. Event-driven approaches in various programming fields may not appear natural to beginners, but enable high performance and particularly high scalability, making them very suitable for high-workload cases.

To use SAX, you define a content handler class, subclassing a library class and overriding some methods. Then you build a parser object *p*, install an instance of your class as *p*'s handler, and feed *p* the input stream to parse. *p* calls methods on your handler to reflect the document's structure and contents. Your handler's methods perform application-specific processing. The xml.sax package supplies a factory function to build *p*, and convenience functions for simpler operation in typical cases. xml.sax also supplies exception classes, raised in cases of invalid input and other errors.

Optionally, you can also register with parser *p* other kinds of handlers besides the content handler. You can supply a custom error handler to use an error diagnosis strategy different from normal exception raising, for example in order to diagnose several errors during a parse. You can supply a custom DTD handler to receive information about notation and unparsed entities from the XML document's Document Type Definition (DTD). You can supply a custom entity resolver to handle external entity references in advanced, customized ways. These advanced possibilities are rarely used, and I do not cover them further in this book.

The xml.sax Package

The xml.sax package supplies exception class SAXException and subclasses of it to support fine-grained exception handling. xml.sax also supplies three functions.

make_parser   make_parser(*parsers_list*=[])

parsers_list is a list of strings, which are the names of modules from which you would like to build your parser. make_parser tries each module in sequence until it finds one that defines a function create_parser. After the modules in *parsers_list*, if any, make_parser continues by trying a list of default modules. make_parser terminates as soon as it can generate a parser *p*, and returns *p*.

parse   parse(*file*,*handler*,*error_handler*=None)

file is either a filename string or a file-like object open for reading, that contains an XML document. *handler* is an instance of your own subclass of class ContentHandler, covered in "ContentHandler" on page 594. *error_handler*, if given, is an instance of your own subclass of class ErrorHandler. You don't necessarily have to subclass ContentHandler and/or ErrorHandler; you just need to provide the same interfaces as the classes do. Subclassing is a convenient means to this end.

Function parse is equivalent to the code:

```
p = make_parser( )
p.setContentHandler(handler)
if error_handler is not None:
    p.setErrorHandler(error_handler)
p.parse(file)
```

This idiom is quite frequent in SAX parsing, so having it in a single function is convenient. When *error_handler* is None, the parser reacts to errors by propagating an exception that is an instance of some subclass of SAXException.

parseString   parseString(*string*,*handler*,*error_handler*=None)

Like parse, except that *string* is the XML document in string form.

xml.sax also supplies a class, which you subclass to define your content handler.

ContentHandler   class ContentHandler( )

A subclass of ContentHandler (whose instance we name *h* in the following) may override several methods, of which the most frequently useful are the following:

h.characters(*data*)
    Called when textual content *data* (a unicode string) is parsed. The parser may split each range of text in the document into any number of separate callbacks to *h*.characters. Therefore,

your implementation of method characters usually buffers *data*, generally by appending it to a list attribute. When your class knows from some other event that all relevant data has arrived, your class calls ''.join on the list and processes the resulting string.

h.endDocument( )
> Called once when the document finishes.

h.endElement(*tag*)
> Called when the element named *tag* finishes.

h.endElementNS(*name,qname*)
> Called when an element finishes and the parser is handling namespaces. *name* and *qname* are the same for startElementNS, covered below.

h.startDocument( )
> Called once when the document begins.

h.startElement(*tag,attrs*)
> Called when the element named *tag* begins. *attrs* is a mapping of attribute names to values, as covered in "Attributes" on page 595.

h.startElementNS(*name,qname,attrs*)
> Called when an element begins and the parser is handling namespaces. *name* is a pair (*uri,localname*), where *uri* is the namespace's URI or None, and *localname* is the name of the tag. *qname* (which stands for qualified name) is either None, if the parser does not supply the namespace prefixes feature, or the string *prefix:name* used in the document's text for this tag. *attrs* is a mapping of attribute names to values, as covered in "Attributes" on page 595.

XML

Attributes

The last argument of methods startElement and startElementNS is an attributes object *attr*, a read-only mapping of attribute names to attribute values. For method startElement, names are identifier strings. For method startElementNS, names are pairs (*uri,localname*), where *uri* is the namespace's URI or None, and *localname* is the name of the tag. In addition to some mapping methods, *attr* also supports methods that let you work with the *qname* (qualified name) of each attribute.

getValueByQ-Name   attr.getValueByQName(*name*)

Returns the attribute value for a qualified name *name*.

getNameByQ- Name	`attr.getNameByQName(`*name*`)`
	Returns the (*namespace, localname*) pair for a qualified name *name*.

getQNameBy- Name	`attr.getQNameByName(`*name*`)`
	Returns the qualified name for *name*, which is a (*namespace, localname*) pair.

getQNames	`attr.getQNames( )`
	Returns the list of qualified names of all attributes.

For `startElement`, each *qname* is the same string as the corresponding name. For `startElementNS`, a *qname* is the corresponding local name for attributes not associated with a namespace (i.e., attributes whose *uri* is None); otherwise, the *qname* is the string *prefix:name* used in the document's text for this attribute.

The parser may reuse in later processing the *attr* object that it passes to methods `startElement` and `startElementNS`. If you need to keep a copy of the attributes of an element, call *attr*`.copy( )` to get the copy.

Incremental parsing

All parsers support a method parse, which you call with the XML document as either a string or a file-like object open for reading. parse does not return until the end of the XML document. Most SAX parsers, though not all, also support incremental parsing, letting you feed the XML document to the parser a little at a time, as the document arrives from a network connection or other source; good incremental parsers perform all possible callbacks to your handler class's methods as soon as possible, so you don't have to wait for the whole document to arrive before you start processing it (the processing can instead proceed as incrementally as the parsing itself does, which is a great idea for asynchronous networking approaches, covered in "Event-Driven Socket Programs" on page 533). A parser *p* that is capable of incremental parsing supplies three more methods.

close	`p.close( )`
	Call when the XML document is finished.

feed	`p.feed(`*data*`)`
	Passes to the parser a part of the document. The parser processes some prefix of the text and holds the rest in a buffer until the next call to *p*`.feed` or *p*`.close`.

reset   `p.reset()`

Call after an XML document is finished or abandoned, before you start feeding another XML document to the parser.

The xml.sax.saxutils module

The `saxutils` module of package `xml.sax` supplies two functions and a class that provide handy ways to generate XML output based on an input XML document.

escape   `escape(data,entities={})`

Returns a copy of string *data* with characters <, >, and & changed into entity references <, >, and &. *entities* is a dictionary with strings as keys and values; each substring *s* of *data* that is a key in *entities* is changed in escape's result string into string *entities*[*s*]. For example, to escape single- and double-quote characters, in addition to angle brackets and ampersands, you can call:

```
xml.sax.saxutils.escape(data, {'"': '&quot;', "'":
'&apos;'})
```

quoteattr   `quoteattr(data,entities={})`

Same as `escape`, but also quotes the result string to make it immediately usable as an attribute value and escapes any quote characters that have to be escaped.

XMLGenerator   `class XMLGenerator(out=sys.stdout, encoding='iso-8859-1')`

Subclasses `xml.sax.ContentHandler` and implements all that is needed to reproduce the input XML document on the given file-like object *out* with the specified *encoding*. When you must generate an XML document that is a small modification of the input one, you can subclass `XMLGenerator`, overriding methods and delegating most of the work to `XMLGenerator`'s implementations of the methods. For example, if all you need to do is rename some tags according to a dictionary, `XMLGenerator` makes it extremely simple, as shown in the following example:

```
import xml.sax, xml.sax.saxutils

def tagrenamer(infile, outfile, renaming_dict):
    base = xml.sax.saxutils.XMLGenerator

    class Renamer(base):
        def rename(self, name):
            return renaming_dict.get(name, name)
```

```
                            def startElement(self, name, attrs):
                                base.startElement(self, self.rename(name),
            attrs)
                            def endElement(self, name):
                                base.endElement(self, self.rename(name))

                        xml.sax.parse(infile, Renamer(outfile))
```

Parsing XHTML with xml.sax

The following example uses xml.sax to perform a typical XHTML-related task
that is very similar to the tasks performed in the examples of Chapter 22. The
example fetches an XHTML page from the Web with urllib, parses it, and
outputs all unique links from the page to other sites. The example uses urlparse
to examine the links for the given site and outputs only the links whose URLs
have an explicit scheme of 'http'.

```
import xml.sax, urllib, urlparse

class LinksHandler(xml.sax.ContentHandler):
    def startDocument(self):
        self.seen = set()
    def startElement(self, tag, attributes):
        if tag != 'a': return
        value = attributes.get('href')
        if value is not None and value not in self.seen:
            self.seen.add(value)
            pieces = urlparse.urlparse(value)
            if pieces[0] != 'http': return
            print urlparse.urlunparse(pieces)

p = xml.sax.make_parser()
p.setContentHandler(LinksHandler())
f = urllib.urlopen('http://www.w3.org/MarkUp/')
BUFSIZE = 8192

while True:
    data = f.read(BUFSIZE)
    if not data: break
    p.feed(data)

p.close()
```

This example is quite similar to the HTMLParser example in Chapter 22. With the
xml.sax module, the parser and the handler are separate objects (while in the
examples of Chapter 22 they coincided). Method names differ (startElement in
this example versus handle_starttag in the HTMLParser example). The *attributes*
argument is a mapping here, so its method get immediately gives us the attribute
value we're interested in, while in the examples of Chapter 22, attributes were
given as a sequence of (*name,value*) pairs, so we had to loop on the sequence until

we found the right name. Despite these differences in detail, the overall structure is very close, and typical of simple event-driven parsing tasks.

Parsing XML with DOM

SAX parsing does not build any structure in memory to represent the XML document. This makes SAX fast and highly scalable, as your application builds exactly as little or as much in-memory structure as needed for its specific tasks. However, for particularly complicated processing tasks involving reasonably small XML documents, you may prefer to let the library build in-memory structures that represent the whole XML document, and then traverse those structures. The XML standards describe the DOM (Document Object Model) for XML. A DOM object represents an XML document as a tree whose root is the *document object*, while other nodes correspond to elements, text contents, element attributes, and so on. The ElementTree module mentioned in the introduction of this chapter provides a different, more Pythonic (and faster) approach to build an in-memory representation of an XML document, while DOM mimics existing W3C standards (mostly developed with other languages, such as Java, in mind).

The Python standard library supplies a minimal implementation of the XML DOM standard: xml.dom.minidom. minidom builds everything up in memory, with the typical pros and cons of the DOM approach to parsing. The Python standard library also supplies a different DOM-like approach in module xml.dom.pulldom. pulldom occupies an interesting middle ground between SAX and DOM, presenting the stream of parsing events as a Python iterator object so that you do not code callbacks, but rather loop over the events and examine each event to see if it's of interest. When you do find an event of interest to your application, you ask pulldom to build the DOM subtree rooted in that event's node by calling method expandNode, and then work with that subtree as you would in minidom. Paul Prescod, pulldom's author and XML and Python expert, describes the net result as "80 percent of the performance of SAX, 80 percent of the convenience of DOM." Other DOM parsers are part of the PyXML and 4Suite extension packages, mentioned at the start of this chapter.

The xml.dom Package

The xml.dom package supplies exception class DOMException and subclasses of it to support fine-grained exception handling. xml.dom also supplies a class Node, typically used as a base class for all nodes by DOM implementations. Class Node itself supplies only constant attributes that give the codes for node types, such as ELEMENT_NODE for elements, ATTRIBUTE_NODE for attributes, and so on. xml.dom also supplies constant module attributes with the URIs of some important namespaces: XML_NAMESPACE, XMLNS_NAMESPACE, XHTML_NAMESPACE, and EMPTY_NAMESPACE.

The xml.dom.minidom Module

The xml.dom.minidom module supplies two functions.

parse	parse(*file*,*parser*=None)
	file is a filename string or a file-like object open for reading, and contains an XML document. *parser*, if given, is an instance of a SAX parser class; otherwise, parse generates a default SAX parser by calling xml.sax.make_parser( ). parse returns a minidom document object instance that represents the given XML document.
parseString	parseString(*string*,*parser*=None)
	Like parse, except that *string* is the XML document in string form.

xml.dom.minidom also supplies many classes as specified by the XML DOM standard. Almost all of these classes subclass Node. Class Node supplies the methods and attributes that all kinds of nodes have in common. A notable class of module xml.dom.minidom that is not a subclass of Node is AttributeList, identified in the DOM standard as NamedNodeMap, which is a mapping that collects the attributes of a single node of class Element.

For methods and attributes related to changing and creating XML documents, see "Changing and Generating XML" on page 606. Here, I present the classes, methods, and attributes that you use most often to traverse a DOM tree, usually after the tree has been built by parsing an XML document. For concreteness and simplicity, I mention Python classes. However, the DOM specifications deal with abstract interfaces, never with concrete classes. Your code must never deal with the class objects directly, only with instances of those classes. Do not type-test nodes (for example, don't use isinstance on them) and do not instantiate node classes directly (rather, use the factory methods covered in "Factory Methods of a Document Object" on page 607). This is good Python practice in general, but it's particularly important here.

Node objects

Each node *n* in the DOM tree is an instance of some subclass of Node; thus, *n* supplies all attributes and methods of Node, with appropriate overriding implementations if needed. The most frequently used methods and attributes are as follows.

attributes	The *n*.attributes attribute is either None or an AttributeList instance with all attributes of *n*.
childNodes	The *n*.childNodes attribute is a list of all nodes that are children of *n*, possibly an empty list.

firstChild	The *n*.firstChild attribute is None when *n*.childNodes is empty; otherwise, *n*.childNodes[0].
hasChildNodes	*n*.hasChildNodes( ) Like len(*n*.childNodes)!=0, but possibly faster.
isSameNode	*n*.isSameNode(*other*) True when *n* and *other* refer to the same DOM node; otherwise, False. Do not use the normal Python idiom *n* is *other*: a DOM implementation is free to generate multiple Node instances that refer to the same DOM node. Therefore, to check the identity of DOM node references, always and exclusively use method isSameNode.
lastChild	The *n*.lastChild attribute is None when *n*.childNodes is empty; otherwise, *n*.childNodes[-1].
localName	The *n*.localName attribute is the local part of *n*'s qualified name (relevant when namespaces are involved).
namespaceURI	The *n*.namespaceURI attribute is None when *n*'s qualified name has no namespace part; otherwise, the namespace's URI.
nextSibling	The *n*.nextSibling attribute is None when *n* is the last child of *n*'s parent; otherwise, the next child of *n*'s parent.
nodeName	The *n*.nodeName attribute is *n*'s name string. The string is a node-specific name when that makes sense for *n*'s node type (e.g., the tag name when *n* is an Element); otherwise, a string starting with '#'.
nodeType	The *n*.nodeType attribute is *n*'s type code, an integer that is one of the constant attributes of class Node.
nodeValue	The *n*.nodeValue attribute is None when *n* has no value (e.g., when *n* is an Element); otherwise, *n*'s value (e.g., the text content when *n* is an instance of Text).

normalize n.normalize( )

Normalizes the entire subtree rooted at n, merging adjacent Text nodes. Parsing may separate ranges of text in the XML document into arbitrary chunks; normalize ensures that text ranges remain separate only when there is markup between them.

ownerDocument   The n.ownerDocument attribute is the Document instance that contains n.

parentNode   The n.parentNode attribute is n's parent node in the DOM tree, or None for attribute nodes and nodes not in the tree.

prefix   The n.prefix attribute is None when n's qualified name has no namespace prefix; otherwise, the namespace prefix. Note that a name may have a namespace even if it has no namespace prefix.

previousSibling   The n.previousSibling attribute is None when n is the first child of n's parent; otherwise, the previous child of n's parent.

Attr objects

The Attr class is a subclass of Node that represents an attribute of an Element. Besides attributes and methods of class Node, an instance a of Attr supplies the following attributes.

ownerElement   The a.ownerElement attribute is the Element instance of which a is an attribute.

specified   The a.specified attribute is true if a was explicitly specified in the document, and false if obtained by default.

Document objects

The Document class is a subclass of Node whose instances are returned by the parse and parseString functions of module xml.dom.minidom. All nodes in the document refer to the same Document node as their ownerDocument attribute. To check this, however, you must exclusively use the isSameNode method, *not* Python identity checking (operator is). Besides the attributes and methods of class Node, d supplies the following attributes and methods.

doctype	The *d*.doctype attribute is the DocumentType instance that corresponds to *d*'s DTD. This attribute comes directly from the !DOCTYPE declaration in *d*'s XML source.
document-Element	The *d*.documentElement attribute is the Element instance that is *d*'s root element.
getElementById	*d*.getElementById(*elementId*) Returns the Element instance within the document that has the given ID (which element attributes are IDs is specified by the DTD), or None if there is no such instance (or the underlying parser does not supply ID information).
getElementsBy-TagName	*d*.getElementsByTagName(*tagName*) Returns the list of Element instances in the document whose tag equals string *tagName*, in the same order as in the XML document. May be the empty list. When *name* is '*', returns the list of all Element instances in the document, with any tag.
getElementsBy-TagNameNS	*d*.getElementsByTagNameNS(*namespaceURI*,*localName*) Returns the list of Element instances in the document with the given *namespaceURI* and *localName*, in the same order in the XML document. May be the empty list. A value of '*' for *namespaceURI*, *localName*, or both matches all values of the field.

Element objects

Element is a subclass of Node that represents tagged elements. Besides attributes and methods of Node, an instance *e* of Element supplies the following methods.

getAttribute	*e*.getAttribute(*name*) Returns the value of *e*'s attribute with the given *name*. Returns the empty string ' ' if *e* has no attribute with the given *name*.
getAttributeNS	*e*.getAttributeNS(*namespaceURI*,*localName*) Returns the value of *e*'s attribute with the given *namespaceURI* and *localName*.

getAttribute- Node	`e.getAttributeNode(`*name*`)`
	Returns the `Attr` instance that is *e*'s attribute with the given *name*, or None if *e* has no attribute with the given *name*.
getAttribute- NodeNS	`e.getAttributeNodeNS(`*namespaceURI*`,`*localName*`)`
	Returns the `Attr` instance that is *e*'s attribute with the given *namespaceURI* and *localName*, or None if *e* has no attribute with the given namespace and name.
getElementsBy- TagName	`e.getElementsByTagName(`*tagName*`)`
	Returns the list of `Element` instances in the subtree rooted at *e* whose tag equals string *tagName*, in the same order as in the XML document. *e* is also included in the list, if *e*'s tag equals *tagName*. getElementsbyTagName returns the empty list when no node in the subtree rooted at *e* has a tag equal to *tagName*. When *tagName* is '*', getElementsbyTagName returns the list of all `Element` instances within the subtree, starting with *e*.
getElementsBy- TagNameNS	`e.getElementsByTagNameNS(`*namespaceURI*`,`*localName*`)`
	Returns the list of `Element` instances within the subtree rooted at *e*, with the given *namespaceURI* and *localname*, in the same order as in the XML document. A value of '*' for *namespaceURI*, *localname*, or both matches all values of the corresponding field. The list may include *e* or may be empty, just as for method getElementsByTagName.
hasAttribute	`e.hasAttribute(`*name*`)`
	True if and only if *e* has an attribute with the given *name*. If the underlying parser extracts the relevant information from the DTD, hasAttribute is also true for attributes of *e* that have a default value, even when they are not explicitly specified.
hasAttributeNS	`e.hasAttributeNS(`*namespaceURI*`,`*localName*`)`
	True if and only if *e* has an attribute with the given *namespaceURI* and *localName*. Same as method hasAttribute for attributes with default values in the DTD.

Parsing XHTML with xml.dom.minidom

The following example uses xml.dom.minidom to perform the same task as in the previous example for xml.sax, fetching a page from the Web with urllib, parsing it, and outputting the hyperlinks:

```
import xml.dom.minidom, urllib, urlparse

f = urllib.urlopen('http://www.w3.org/MarkUp/')
doc = xml.dom.minidom.parse(f)
links = doc.getElementsByTagName('a')
seen = set( )
for a in links:
    value = a.getAttribute('href')
    if value and value not in seen:
        seen.add(value)
        pieces = urlparse.urlparse(value)
        if pieces[0] == 'http' and pieces[1]!='www.w3.org':
            print urlparse.urlunparse(pieces)
```

In this example, we get the list of all elements with tag 'a', and the relevant attribute, if any, for each of them. We then work in the usual way with the attribute's value.

The xml.dom.pulldom Module

The xml.dom.pulldom module supplies two functions.

parse	parse(*file*,*parser*=None)

file is a filename or a file-like object open for reading, and contains an XML document. *parser*, if given, is an instance of a SAX parser class; otherwise, parse generates a default SAX parser by calling xml.sax.make_parser( ). parse returns a pulldom event stream instance that represents the given XML document.

parseString	parseString(*string*,*parser*=None)

Like parse, except that *string* is the XML document in string form.

xml.dom.pulldom also supplies class DOMEventStream, an iterator whose items are pairs (*event*,*node*), where *event* is a string that gives the event type, and *node* is an instance of an appropriate subclass of class Node. The possible values for *event* are constant uppercase strings that are also available as constant attributes of module xml.dom.pulldom with the same names: CHARACTERS, COMMENT, END_DOCUMENT, END_ELEMENT, IGNORABLE_WHITESPACE, PROCESSING_INSTRUCTION, START_DOCUMENT, and START_ELEMENT.

An instance *d* of class DOMEventStream supplies one other important method.

expandNode   *d*.expandNode(*node*)

> *node* must be the latest instance of Node so far returned by iterating
> on *d*, i.e., the instance of Node returned by the latest call to *d*.next( ).
> expandNode processes the part of the XML document stream that
> corresponds to the subtree rooted at *node* so that you can then
> access the subtree with the usual minidom approach. *d* iterates on
> itself for the purpose so that after calling expandNode, the next call to
> *d*.next( ) continues right after the subtree thus expanded.

Parsing XHTML with xml.dom.pulldom

The following example uses xml.dom.pulldom to perform the same task as our
previous examples, fetching a page from the Web with urllib, parsing it, and
outputting the hyperlinks:

```
import xml.dom.pulldom, urllib, urlparse

f = urllib.urlopen('http://www.w3.org/MarkUp/')
doc = xml.dom.pulldom.parse(f)
seen = set( )
for event, node in doc:
    if event=='START_ELEMENT' and node.nodeName=='a':
        doc.expandNode(node)
        value = node.getAttribute('href')
        if value and value not in seen:
            seen.add(value)
            pieces = urlparse.urlparse(value)
            if pieces[0] == 'http' and pieces[1]!='www.w3.org':
                print urlparse.urlunparse(pieces)
```

In this example, we select only elements with tag 'a'. For each of them, we
request full expansion, and then proceed just like in the minidom example (i.e., we
get the relevant attribute, if any, then work in the usual way with the attribute's
value). The expansion is in fact not necessary in this specific case, since we do not
need to work with the subtree rooted in each element with tag 'a', just with the
attributes, and attributes can be accessed *without* calling expandNode. Therefore,
this example works just as well if you remove the call to doc.expandNode.
However, I put the expandNode call in the example to show how this crucial
method of pulldom is normally used in context.

Changing and Generating XML

Just like for HTML and other kinds of structured text, the simplest way to output
an XML document is often to prepare and write it using Python's normal string
and file operations, covered in Chapter 9 and "File Objects" on page 216.

Templating (covered in "Templating" on page 586) is also often the best approach. Subclassing class XMLGenerator (covered in "XMLGenerator" on page 597) is a good way to generate an XML document that is like an input XML document except for a few changes.

The xml.dom.minidom module offers yet another possibility because its classes support methods to generate, insert, remove, and alter nodes in a DOM tree that represents the document. You can create a DOM tree by parsing and then alter it, or you can create an empty DOM tree and populate it from scratch. You can output the resulting XML document with methods toxml, toprettyxml, or writexml of the Document instance. You can also output a subtree by calling these methods on the Node that is the subtree's root. The ElementTree module, mentioned in this chapter's introduction, also offers similar functionality (but with a more Pythonic API and much better performance).

Factory Methods of a Document Object

The Document class supplies factory methods to create instances of Node subclasses. The most frequently used factory methods of a Document instance *d* are as follows.

createComment   *d*.createComment(*data*)

Builds and returns an instance *c* of class Comment for a comment with text *data*.

createElement   *d*.createElement(*tagname*)

Builds and returns an instance *e* of class Element for an element with the given tag.

createTextNode   *d*.createTextNode(*data*)

Builds and returns an instance *t* of class TextNode for a text node with text *data*.

Mutating Methods of an Element Object

An instance *e* of class Element supplies methods to remove and add attributes.

removeAttribute   *e*.removeAttribute(*name*)

Removes *e*'s attribute with the given *name*.

setAttribute   *e*.setAttribute(*name*,*value*)

Changes *e*'s attribute with the given *name* to have the given *value*, or adds to *e* a new attribute with the given *name* and *value* if *e* had no attribute named *name*.

Mutating Methods of a Node Object

An instance *n* of class Node supplies methods to remove, add, and replace children.

appendChild   *n*.appendChild(*child*)

Makes *child* the last child of *n*, whatever *child*'s parent was (including *n* or None).

insertBefore   *n*.insertBefore(*child*,*nextChild*)

Makes *child* the child of *n* immediately before *nextChild*, whatever *child*'s parent was (including *n* or None). *nextChild* must be a child of *n*.

removeChild   *n*.removeChild(*child*)

Makes *child* parentless and returns *child*. *child* must be a child of *n*.

replaceChild   *n*.replaceChild(*child*,*oldChild*)

Makes *child* the child of *n* in *oldChild*'s place, whatever *child*'s parent was (including *n* or None). *oldChild* must be a child of *n*. Returns *oldChild*.

Output Methods of a Node Object

An instance *n* of class Node supplies methods to output the subtree rooted at *n*.

toprettyxml   *n*.toprettyxml(*indent*='\t',*newl*='\n')

Returns a string, plain or Unicode, with the XML source for the subtree rooted at *n*, using *indent* to indent nested tags and *newl* to end lines.

toxml	*n*.toxml( )
	Like *n*.toprettyxml('',''), i.e., inserts no extraneous whitespace.

writexml	*n*.writexml(*file*,*encoding*='None')
	Writes the XML source for the subtree rooted at *n* to file-like object *file*, open for writing, using the specified *encoding*. If *encoding* is not given, then *file*.write must accept a unicode argument.

Changing and Outputting XHTML with xml.dom.minidom

The following example uses xml.dom.minidom to analyze an XHTML page and output it to standard output with each hyperlink's destination URL shown, within triple parentheses, just before the hyperlink:

```
import xml.dom.minidom, urllib, sys

f = urllib.urlopen('http://www.w3.org/MarkUp/')
doc = xml.dom.minidom.parse(f)
as = doc.getElementsByTagName('a')
for a in as:
    value = a.getAttribute('href')
    if value:
        newtext = doc.createTextNode(' (((%s)))'%value)
        a.parentNode.insertBefore(newtext,a)

doc.writexml(sys.stdout, 'utf-8')
```

This example uses encoding 'utf-8' because that is the encoding that the XML standard specifies as the default, but you may want to change this detail, depending on the encoding your terminal window supports.

V

Extending and Embedding

25

Extending and Embedding Classic Python

Classic Python runs on a portable, C-coded virtual machine. Python's built-in objects, such as numbers, sequences, dictionaries, sets, and files, are coded in C, as are several modules in Python's standard library. Modern platforms support dynamic-load libraries, with file extensions such as *.dll* on Windows and *.so* on Linux and Mac, and building Python produces such binary files. You can code your own extension modules for Python in C, using the Python C API covered in this chapter, to produce and deploy dynamic libraries that Python scripts and interactive sessions can later use with the import statement, covered in "The import Statement" on page 140.

Extending Python means building modules that Python code can import to access the features the modules supply. Embedding Python means executing Python code from your application. For such execution to be useful, Python code must in turn be able to access some of your application's functionality. In practice, therefore, embedding implies some extending, as well as a few embedding-specific operations. The three main reasons for wishing to extend Python can be summarized as follows:

- Reimplementing some functionality (originally coded in Python) in a lower-level language, hoping to get better performance
- Letting Python code access some existing functionality supplied by libraries coded in (or, at any rate, callable from) lower-level languages
- Letting Python code access some existing functionality of an application that is in the process of embedding Python as the application's scripting language

Embedding and extending are covered extensively in Python's online documentation; you can find an in-depth tutorial at *http://www.python.org/doc/ext/ext.html* and a reference manual at *http://www.python.org/doc/api/api.html*. Many details are best studied in Python's extensively documented sources. Download Python's source distribution and study the sources of Python's core, C-coded extension modules and the example extensions supplied for study purposes.

This chapter covers the basics of extending and embedding Python with C. It also mentions, but does not cover in depth, other possibilities for extending Python.

Extending Python with Python's C API

A Python extension module named *x* resides in a dynamic library with the same filename (*x.pyd* on Windows; *x.so* on most Unix-like platforms) in an appropriate directory (often the *site-packages* subdirectory of the Python library directory). You generally build the *x* extension module from a C source file *x.c* whose the overall structure is:

```
#include <Python.h>

/* omitted: the body of the x module */

void
initx(void)
{
    /* omitted: the code that initializes the module named x */
}
```

When you have built and installed the extension module, a Python statement import *x* loads the dynamic library, then locates and calls the function named initx, which must do all that is needed to initialize the module object named *x*.

Building and Installing C-Coded Python Extensions

To build and install a C-coded Python extension module, it's simplest and most productive to use the distribution utilities, distutils, covered in "The Distribution Utilities (distutils)" on page 150. In the same directory as *x.c*, place a file named *setup.py* that contains the following statements:

```
from distutils.core import setup, Extension
setup(name='x', ext_modules=[ Extension('x',sources=['x.c']) ])
```

From a shell prompt in this directory, you can now run:

```
C:\> python setup.py install
```

to build the module and install it so that it becomes usable in your Python installation. distutils performs all needed compilation and linking steps, with the right compiler and linker commands and flags, and copies the resulting dynamic library into an appropriate directory, dependent on your Python installation (depending on that installation's details, you may need to have administrator or super-user privileges for the installation; for example, on a Mac or Linux, you may need to run **sudo python setup.py install**). Your Python code can then access the resulting module with the statement import *x*.

The C compiler you need

To compile C-coded extensions to Python, you normally need the same C compiler that was used to build the Python version you want to extend. For most platforms, this usually means the free *gcc* compiler that normally comes with your

---

platform or can be freely downloaded for it. On the Macintosh, *gcc* comes with Apple's free XCode (a.k.a. Developer Tools) Integrated Development Environment (IDE).

For Windows, you normally need the Microsoft product known as Visual Studio 7.1 (a.k.a. Visual Studio 2003). However, it may be possible to compile C-coded extensions on Windows without having to purchase that Microsoft product. At *http://www.vrplumber.com/programming/mstoolkit/*, you will find instructions that show how to perform this task by downloading, installing, and configuring five other Microsoft components, ones that can be downloaded without paying license fees. Unfortunately, at the time of this writing, the freely downloadable Microsoft Visual Studio 2005 is not suitable for compiling extensions for the standard distributions of Python for Windows, which (for both Python 2.4 and 2.5) are compiled with Visual Studio 2003.

Compatibility of C-coded extensions among Python versions

In general, a C-coded extension compiled to run with one version of Python is not guaranteed to run with another. For example, a version compiled for Python 2.4 is only certain to run with 2.4, not with 2.3 nor 2.5. On some platforms, such as Windows, you cannot even try to run an extension with a different version of Python; on others, such as Linux or Mac OS X, a given extension may happen to work right on more than one version of Python, but you will at least get a warning when the module is imported, and the most prudent course is to heed the warning and recompile the extension appropriately.

At a C-source level, on the other hand, compatibility is almost always preserved. One exception is with the new Python 2.5, in which many values that used to be C ints are now of type Py_ssize_t—equivalent to int on 32-bit platforms, but a 64-bit signed integer (specifically, the signed equivalent of size_t) on 64-bit platforms. This C API change lets you address more than two billion items in a Python 2.5 sequence on a 64-bit platform, and makes no difference on 32-bit platforms. If your C-coded extension, originally developed and tested under previous versions of Python, produces errors and warnings from the C compiler when you recompile your sources for Python 2.5, the cause is almost certainly this: you need (with the help of the errors and warnings from the C compiler) to find and change the occurrences of int that must become Py_ssize_t. A simple checking tool to make this process easier can be freely downloaded from *http://svn.effbot.python-hosting.com/stuff/sandbox/python/ssizecheck.py*. To ensure that your extension remains compilable for Python 2.4 and earlier, as well as becoming correct for Python 2.5 on 64-bit machines, insert, early in your source files, the lines:

```
#if PY_VERSION_HEX < 0x02050000
typedef int Py_ssize_t;
#endif
```

Overview of C-Coded Python Extension Modules

Your C function init*x* generally has the following overall structure:

```
void
initx(void)
```

```
{
    PyObject* thismod = Py_InitModule3("x", x_methods, "docstring for x");
    /* optional: calls to PyModule_AddObject(thismod, "somename", someobj)
       and other Python C API calls to finish preparing module object
       thismod and its types (if any) and other objects.
    */
}
```

More details are covered in "Module Initialization" on page 617. *x_methods* is an array of `PyMethodDef` structs. Each `PyMethodDef` struct in the *x_methods* array describes a C function that your module *x* makes available to Python code that imports *x*. Each such C function has the following overall structure:

```
static PyObject*
func_with_named_arguments(PyObject* self, PyObject* args, PyObject* kwds)
{
    /* omitted: body of function, accessing arguments via the Python C
       API function PyArg_ParseTupleAndKeywords, returning a PyObject*
       result, NULL for errors */
}
```

or some slightly simpler variant, such as:

```
static PyObject*
func_with_positional_args_only(PyObject* self, PyObject* args)
{
    /* omitted: body of function, accessing arguments via the Python C
       API function PyArg_ParseTuple, returning a PyObject* result,
       NULL for errors */
}
```

How C-coded functions access arguments passed by Python code is covered in "Accessing Arguments" on page 621. How such functions build Python objects is covered in "Creating Python Values" on page 624, and how they raise or propagate exceptions back to the Python code that called them is covered in "Exceptions" on page 625. When your module defines new Python types (as well as or instead of Python-callable functions), your C code defines one or more instances of struct `PyTypeObject`. This subject is covered in "Defining New Types" on page 638.

A simple example that makes use of all these concepts is shown in "A Simple Extension Example" on page 635. A toy-level "Hello World" example could be as simple as:

```
#include <Python.h>

static PyObject*
helloworld(PyObject* self)
{
    return Py_BuildValue("s", "Hello, C-coded Python extensions world!");
}

static char helloworld_docs[] =
    "helloworld( ): return a popular greeting phrase\n";
```

```
static PyMethodDef helloworld_funcs[] = {
    {"helloworld", (PyCFunction)helloworld, METH_NOARGS, helloworld_docs},
    {NULL}
};

void
inithelloworld(void)
{
    Py_InitModule3("helloworld", helloworld_funcs,
                   "Toy-level extension module");
}
```

Save this as *helloworld.c* and build it through a *setup.py* script with distutils. After you have run *python setup.py install*, you can use the newly installed module—for example, from a Python interactive session—such as:

```
>>> import helloworld
>>> print helloworld.helloworld( )
Hello, C-coded Python extensions world!
>>>
```

Return Values of Python's C API Functions

All functions in the Python C API return either an int or a PyObject*. Most functions returning int return 0 in case of success and -1 to indicate errors. Some functions return results that are true or false: these functions return 0 to indicate false and an integer not equal to 0 to indicate true, and never indicate errors. Functions returning PyObject* return NULL in case of errors. See "Exceptions" on page 625 for more details on how C-coded functions handle and raise errors.

Module Initialization

Function init*x* must contain, at a minimum, a call to one of the module initialization functions supplied by the C API. You can always use the Py_InitModule3 function.

Py_InitModule3   PyObject* Py_InitModule3(char* *name*,PyMethodDef* *methods*,char* *doc*)

name is the C string name of the module you are initializing (e.g., "name"). *methods* is an array of PyMethodDef structures, covered in "The PyMethodDef structure" on page 619. *doc* is the C string that becomes the docstring of the module. Py_InitModule3 returns a PyObject* that is a borrowed reference to the new module object, as covered in "Reference Counting" on page 620. In practice, this means that you can ignore the return value if you need to perform no more initialization operations on this module. Otherwise, assign the return value to a C variable of type PyObject* and continue initialization.

Py_InitModule3 initializes the module object to contain the functions described in table *methods*. Further initialization, if any, may add other module attributes and is generally best performed with calls to the following convenience functions.

PyModule_ AddIntConstant	int PyModule_AddIntConstant(PyObject* *module*,char* *name*,int *value*) Adds to module *module* an attribute named *name* with integer value *value*.
PyModule_ AddObject	int PyModule_AddObject(PyObject* *module*,char* *name*,PyObject* *value*) Adds to module *module* an attribute named *name* with value *value* and steals a reference to value, as covered in "Reference Counting" on page 620.
PyModule_ AddStringCon-stant	int PyModule_AddStringConstant(PyObject* *module*,char* *name*,char* *value*) Adds to module *module* an attribute named *name* with string value *value*. Some module initialization operations may be conveniently performed by executing Python code with PyRun_String (covered in "PyRun_String" on page 649) with the module's dictionary as both the *globals* and *locals* argument. If you find yourself using PyRun_String extensively, rather than just as an occasional convenience, consider the possibility of splitting your extension module in two: a C-coded extension module that offers raw, fast functionality, and a Python module that wraps the C-coded extension to provide further convenience and handy utilities. When you do need to get a module's dictionary, use the PyModule_GetDict function.
PyModule_ GetDict	PyObject* PyModule_GetDict(PyObject* *module*) Returns a borrowed reference to the dictionary of module *module*. You should not use PyModule_GetDict for the specific tasks supported by PyModule_Add functions (as covered in "PyModule_ AddObject" on page 618): use PyModule_GetDict only for such purposes as supporting the use of PyRun_String. If you need to access another module, you can import it by calling the PyImport_Import function.
PyImport_ Import	PyObject* PyImport_Import(PyObject* *name*) Imports the module named in Python string object *name* and returns a new reference to the module object, like Python's

`__import__`(*name*). `PyImport_Import` is the highest-level, simplest, and most often used way to import a module.

Beware, in particular, of using function `PyImport_ImportModule`, which may often look more convenient because it accepts a `char*` argument. `PyImport_ImportModule` operates on a lower level, bypassing any import hooks that may be in force, so extensions that use it will be far harder to incorporate in packages such as those built by tools py2exe and cxFreeze, covered in "py2exe" and "cxFreeze". Always do any needed importing by calling `PyImport_Import`, unless you have very specific needs and know exactly what you're doing.

The PyMethodDef structure

To add functions to a module (or nonspecial methods to new types, as covered in "Defining New Types" on page 638), you must describe the functions or methods in an array of `PyMethodDef` structures and terminate the array with a *sentinel* (i.e., a structure whose fields are all 0 or NULL). `PyMethodDef` is defined as follows:

```
typedef struct {
    char* ml_name;          /* Python name of function or method */
    PyCFunction ml_meth;    /* pointer to C function impl */
    int ml_flags;           /* flag describing how to pass arguments */
    char* ml_doc;           /* docstring for the function or method */
} PyMethodDef
```

You must cast the second field to (PyCFunction) unless the C function's signature is exactly `PyObject*` *function*(`PyObject*` *self*, `PyObject*` *args*), which is the typedef for `PyCFunction`. This signature is correct when `ml_flags` is `METH_O`, which indicates a function that accepts a single argument, or `METH_VARARGS`, which indicates a function that accepts positional arguments. For `METH_O`, *args* is the only argument. For `METH_VARARGS`, *args* is a tuple of all arguments, to be parsed with the C API function `PyArg_ParseTuple`. However, `ml_flags` can also be `METH_NOARGS`, which indicates a function that accepts no arguments, or `METH_KEYWORDS`, which indicates a function that accepts both positional and named arguments. For `METH_NOARGS`, the signature is `PyObject*` *function*(`PyObject*` *self*), without arguments. For `METH_KEYWORDS`, the signature is:

`PyObject*` *function*(`PyObject*` *self*, `PyObject*` *args*, `PyObject*` *kwds*)

args is the tuple of positional arguments, and *kwds* is the dictionary of named arguments; both are parsed with the C API function `PyArg_ParseTupleAndKeywords`. In these cases, you do need to cast the second field to (PyCFunction).

When a C-coded function implements a module's function, the `self` parameter of the C function is always NULL for any value of the `ml_flags` field. When a C-coded function implements a nonspecial method of an extension type, the `self` parameter points to the instance on which the method is being called.

Reference Counting

Python objects live on the heap, and C code sees them as pointers of type PyObject*. Each PyObject counts how many references to itself are outstanding and destroys itself when the number of references goes down to 0. To make this possible, your code must use Python-supplied macros: Py_INCREF to add a reference to a Python object and Py_DECREF to abandon a reference to a Python object. The Py_XINCREF and Py_XDECREF macros are like Py_INCREF and Py_DECREF, but you may also use them innocuously on a null pointer. The test for a non-null pointer is implicitly performed inside the Py_XINCREF and Py_XDECREF macros, which saves you from needing to write out that test explicitly when you don't know whether the pointer might be null.

A PyObject* *p*, which your code receives by calling or being called by other functions, is known as a *new reference* if the code that supplies *p* has already called Py_INCREF on your behalf. Otherwise, it is known as a *borrowed reference*. Your code is said to *own* new references it holds, but not borrowed ones. You can call Py_INCREF on a borrowed reference to make it into a reference that you own; you must do this if you need to use the reference across calls to code that might cause the count of the reference you borrowed to be decremented. You must always call Py_DECREF before abandoning or overwriting references that you own, but never on references you don't own. Therefore, understanding which interactions transfer reference ownership and which rely on reference borrowing is absolutely crucial. For most functions in the C API, and for *all* functions that you write and Python calls, the following general rules apply:

- PyObject* arguments are borrowed references.
- A PyObject* returned as the function's result transfers ownership.

For each of the two rules, there are a few exceptions for some functions in the C API. PyList_SetItem and PyTuple_SetItem *steal* a reference to the item they are setting (but not to the list or tuple object into which they're setting it). So do the faster versions of these two functions that exist as C preprocessor macros, PyList_SET_ITEM and PyTuple_SET_ITEM. So does PyModule_AddObject, covered in "PyModule_ AddObject" on page 618. There are no other exceptions to the first rule. The rationale for these exceptions, which may help you remember them, is that the object you're setting is most often one you created for the purpose, so the reference-stealing semantics save you from having to call Py_DECREF immediately afterward.

The second rule has more exceptions than the first one. There are several cases in which the returned PyObject* is a borrowed reference rather than a new reference. The abstract functions, whose names begin with PyObject_, PySequence_, PyMapping_, and PyNumber_, return new references. This is because you can call them on objects of many types, and there might not be any other reference to the resulting object that they return (i.e., the returned object might have to be created on the fly). The concrete functions, whose names begin with PyList_, PyTuple_, PyDict_, and so on, return a borrowed reference when the semantics of the object they return ensure that there must be some other reference to the returned object somewhere.

In this chapter, I indicate all cases of exceptions to these rules (i.e., the return of borrowed references and the rare cases of reference stealing from arguments) regarding all functions that I cover. When I don't explicitly mention a function as being an exception, it means that the function follows the rules: its PyObject* arguments, if any, are borrowed references, and its PyObject* result, if any, is a new reference.

Accessing Arguments

A function that has ml_flags in its PyMethodDef set to METH_NOARGS is called from Python with no arguments. The corresponding C function has a signature with only one argument, *self*. When ml_flags is METH_O, Python code must call the function with exactly one argument. The C function's second argument is a borrowed reference to the object that the Python caller passes as the argument's value.

When ml_flags is METH_VARARGS, Python code can call the function with any number of positional arguments, which the Python interpreter implicitly collects into a tuple. The C function's second argument is a borrowed reference to the tuple. Your C code can then call the PyArg_ParseTuple function.

PyArg_ ParseTuple	int PyArg_ParseTuple(PyObject* *tuple*,char* *format*,...) Returns 0 for errors, and a value not equal to 0 for success. *tuple* is the PyObject* that was the C function's second argument. *format* is a C string that describes mandatory and optional arguments. The following arguments of PyArg_ParseTuple are addresses of C variables in which to put the values extracted from the tuple. Any PyObject* variables among the C variables are borrowed references. Table 25-1 lists the commonly used code strings, of which zero or more are joined to form string *format*.

Table 25-1. Format codes for PyArg_ParseTuple

Code	C type	Meaning
c	char	A Python string of length 1 becomes a C char.
d	double	A Python float becomes a C double.
D	Py_Complex	A Python complex becomes a C Py_Complex.
f	float	A Python float becomes a C float.
i	int	A Python int becomes a C int.
l	long	A Python int becomes a C long.
L	long long	A Python int becomes a C long long (__int64 on Windows).
O	PyObject*	Gets non-NULL borrowed reference to Python argument.
O!	type+PyObject*	Like code O, plus type checking (see below).
O&	convert+void*	Arbitrary conversion (see below).
s	char*	Python string without embedded nulls to C char*.

Table 25-1. Format codes for PyArg_ParseTuple (continued)

Code	C type	Meaning
s#	char*+int	Any Python string to C address and length.
t#	char*+int	Read-only single-segment buffer to C address and length.
u	Py_UNICODE*	Python Unicode without embedded nulls to C.
u#	Py_UNICODE*+int	Any Python Unicode C address and length.
w#	char*+int	Read/write single-segment buffer to C address and length.
z	char*	Like s, also accepts None (sets C char* to NULL).
z#	char*+int	Like s#, also accepts None (sets C char* to NULL).
(...)	as per ...	A Python sequence is treated as one argument per item.
|		The following arguments are optional.
:		Format end, followed by function name for error messages.
;		Format end, followed by entire error message text.

Code formats d to L accept numeric arguments from Python. Python coerces the corresponding values. For example, a code of i can correspond to a Python float; the fractional part gets truncated, as if built-in function int had been called. Py_Complex is a C struct with two fields named real and imag, both of type double.

O is the most general format code and accepts any argument, which you can later check and/or convert as needed. Variant O! corresponds to two arguments in the variable arguments: first the address of a Python type object, then the address of a PyObject*. O! checks that the corresponding value belongs to the given type (or any subtype of that type) before setting the PyObject* to point to the value; otherwise, it raises TypeError (the whole call fails, and the error is set to an appropriate TypeError instance, as covered in "Exceptions" on page 625). Variant O& also corresponds to two arguments in the variable arguments: first the address of a converter function you coded, then a void* (i.e., any address). The converter function must have signature int *convert*(PyObject*, void*). Python calls your conversion function with the value passed from Python as the first argument and the void* from the variable arguments as the second argument. The conversion function must either return 0 and raise an exception (as covered in "Exceptions" on page 625) to indicate an error, or return 1 and store whatever is appropriate via the void* it gets.

Code format s accepts a string from Python and the address of a char* (i.e., a char**) among the variable arguments. It changes the char* to point at the string's buffer, which your C code must treat as a read-only, null-terminated array of chars (i.e., a typical C string; however, your code must *not* modify it). The Python string must contain no embedded null characters. s# is similar, but corresponds to two arguments among the variable arguments: first the address of a char*, then the address of an int to set to the string's length. The Python string can contain embedded nulls, and therefore so can the buffer to which the char* is set to point. u and u# are similar, but accept a Unicode string, and the C-side pointers must be Py_UNICODE* rather than char*. Py_UNICODE is a macro defined in *Python.h*, and corresponds to the type of a Python Unicode character in the implementation (this is often, but not always, a C wchar_t).

t# and w# are similar to s#, but the corresponding Python argument can be any object of a type respecting the buffer protocol, respectively read-only and read/write. Strings are a typical example of read-only buffers. mmap and array instances are typical examples of read/write buffers, and like all read/write buffers they are also acceptable where a read-only buffer is required (i.e., for a t#).

When one of the arguments is a Python sequence of known fixed length, you can use format codes for each of its items, and corresponding C addresses among the variable arguments, by grouping the format codes in parentheses. For example, code (ii) corresponds to a Python sequence of two numbers and, among the remaining arguments, corresponds to two addresses of ints.

The format string may include a vertical bar (|) to indicate that all following arguments are optional. In this case, you must initialize the C variables, whose addresses you pass among the variable arguments for later arguments, to suitable default values before you call PyArg_ParseTuple. PyArg_ParseTuple does not change the C variables corresponding to optional arguments that were not passed in a given call from Python to your C-coded function.

The format string may optionally end with :*name* to indicate that *name* must be used as the function name if any error messages are needed. Alternatively, the format string may end with ;*text* to indicate that *text* must be used as the entire error message if PyArg_ParseTuple detects errors (this form is rarely used).

A function that has ml_flags in its PyMethodDef set to METH_KEYWORDS accepts positional and keyword arguments. Python code calls the function with any number of positional arguments, which the Python interpreter collects into a tuple, and keyword arguments, which the Python interpreter collects into a dictionary. The C function's second argument is a borrowed reference to the tuple, and the third one is a borrowed reference to the dictionary. Your C code then calls the PyArg_ParseTupleAndKeywords function.

PyArg_ ParseTuple- AndKeywords

int PyArg_ParseTupleAndKeywords(PyObject* *tuple*, PyObject* *dict*, char* *format*, char** *kwlist*,...)

Returns 0 for errors, and a value not equal to 0 for success. *tuple* is the PyObject* that was the C function's second argument. *dict* is the PyObject* that was the C function's third argument. *format* is the same as for PyArg_ParseTuple, except that it cannot include the (...) format code to parse nested sequences. *kwlist* is an array of char* terminated by a NULL sentinel, with the names of the parameters, one after the other. For example, the following C code:

```
static PyObject*
func_c(PyObject* self, PyObject* args, PyObject* kwds)
```

```
        {
            static char* argnames[] = {"x", "y", "z", NULL};
            double x, y=0.0, z=0.0;
            if(!PyArg_ParseTupleAndKeywords(
                args,kwds,"d|dd",argnames,&x,&y,&z))
                return NULL;
            /* rest of function snipped */
```

is roughly equivalent to this Python code:

```
        def func_py(x, y=0.0, z=0.0):
            x, y, z = map(float, (x,y,z))
            # rest of function snipped
```

Creating Python Values

C functions that communicate with Python must often build Python values, both
to return as their PyObject* result and for other purposes, such as setting items
and attributes. The simplest and handiest way to build a Python value is most
often with the Py_BuildValue function.

Py_BuildValue   PyObject* Py_BuildValue(char* *format*,...)

format is a C string that describes the Python object to build. The
following arguments of Py_BuildValue are C values from which the
result is built. The PyObject* result is a new reference. Table 25-2
lists the commonly used code strings, of which zero or more are
joined into string *format*. Py_BuildValue builds and returns a tuple
if *format* contains two or more format codes, or if *format* begins
with (and ends with). Otherwise, the result is not a tuple. When
you pass buffers—as, for example, in the case of format code s#—
Py_BuildValue copies the data. You can therefore modify, abandon,
or free() your original copy of the data after Py_BuildValue
returns. Py_BuildValue always returns a new reference (except for
format code N). Called with an empty *format*, Py_BuildValue("")
returns a new reference to None.

Table 25-2. Format codes for Py_BuildValue

Code	C type	Meaning
c	char	A C char becomes a Python string of length 1.
D	double	A C double becomes a Python float.
d	Py_Complex	A C Py_Complex becomes a Python complex.
i	int	A C int becomes a Python int.
l	long	A C long becomes a Python int.
N	PyObject*	Passes a Python object and steals a reference.
O	PyObject*	Passes a Python object and INCREFs it as normal.
O&	convert+void*	Arbitrary conversion (see below).

Table 25-2. Format codes for Py_BuildValue (continued)

Code	C type	Meaning
s	char*	C 0-terminated char* to Python string, or NULL to None.
s#	char*+int	C char* and length to Python string, or NULL to None.
u	Py_UNICODE*	C-wide, null-terminated string to Python Unicode, or NULL to None.
u#	Py_UNICODE*+int	C-wide string and length to Python Unicode, or NULL to None.
(...)	As per ...	Builds Python tuple from C values.
[...]	As per ...	Builds Python list from C values.
{...}	As per ...	Builds Python dictionary from C values, alternating keys and values (must be an even number of C values).

Code 0& corresponds to two arguments among the variable arguments: first the address of a converter function you code, then a void* (i.e., any address). The converter function must have signature PyObject* *convert*(void*). Python calls the conversion function with the void* from the variable arguments as the only argument. The conversion function must either return NULL and raise an exception (as covered in "Exceptions" on page 625) to indicate an error, or return a new reference PyObject* built from data obtained through the void*.

Code {...} builds dictionaries from an even number of C values, alternately keys and values. For example, Py_BuildValue("{issi}",23,"zig","zag",42) returns a dictionary like Python's {23:'zig','zag':42}.

Note the crucial difference between codes N and 0. N steals a reference from the corresponding PyObject* value among the variable arguments, so it's convenient to build an object including a reference you own that you would otherwise have to Py_DECREF. 0 does no reference stealing, so it's appropriate to build an object including a reference you don't own, or a reference you must also keep elsewhere.

Exceptions

To propagate exceptions raised from other functions you call, return NULL as the PyObject* result from your C function. To raise your own exceptions, set the current-exception indicator and return NULL. Python's built-in exception classes (covered in "Standard Exception Classes" on page 130) are globally available, with names starting with PyExc_, such as PyExc_AttributeError, PyExc_KeyError, and so on. Your extension module can also supply and use its own exception classes. The most commonly used C API functions related to raising exceptions are the following.

PyErr_Format

`PyObject* PyErr_Format(PyObject* type,char* format,...)`

Raises an exception of class *type*, which must be either a built-in such as `PyExc_IndexError` or an exception class created with `PyErr_NewException`. Builds the associated value from format string *format*, which has syntax similar to `printf`'s, and the following C values indicated as variable arguments above. Returns NULL, so your code can just call:

```
return PyErr_Format(PyExc_KeyError,
    "Unknown key name (%s)", thekeystring);
```

PyErr_ NewException

`PyObject* PyErr_NewException(char* name,PyObject* base,PyObject* dict)`

Subclasses exception class *base*, with extra class attributes and methods from dictionary *dict* (normally NULL, meaning no extra class attributes or methods), creating a new exception class named *name* (string *name* must be of the form "*modulename.classname*") and returning a new reference to the new class object. When *base* is NULL, uses `PyExc_Exception` as the base class. You normally call this function during initialization of a module object *module*. For example:

```
PyModule_AddObject(module, "error",
    PyErr_NewException("mymod.error", NULL, NULL));
```

PyErr_ NoMemory

`PyObject* PyErr_NoMemory( )`

Raises an out-of-memory error and returns NULL, so your code can just call:

```
return PyErr_NoMemory( );
```

PyErr_SetObject

`void PyErr_SetObject(PyObject* type,PyObject* value)`

Raises an exception of class *type*, which must be a built-in such as `PyExc_KeyError` or an exception class created with `PyErr_NewException`, with *value* as the associated value (a borrowed reference). `PyErr_SetObject` is a void function (i.e., returns no value).

PyErr_ SetFromErrno

`PyObject* PyErr_SetFromErrno(PyObject* type)`

Raises an exception of class *type*, which must be a built-in such as `PyExc_OSError` or an exception class created with `PyErr_NewException`. Takes all details from global variable errno, which C standard library functions and system calls set for many error cases, and the standard C library function strerror, which translates such error codes into appropriate strings. Returns NULL, so your code can just call:

```
return PyErr_SetFromErrno(PyExc_IOError);
```

PyErr_ SetFromErrno- WithFilename	`PyObject* PyErr_SetFromErrnoWithFilename(PyObject* ` *`type`*`,char* ` *`filename`*`)` Like `PyErr_SetFromErrno`, but also provides string *filename* as part of the exception's value. When *filename* is NULL, works like `PyErr_SetFromErrno`. Your C code may want to deal with an exception and continue, as a try/except statement would let you do in Python code. The most commonly used C API functions related to catching exceptions are the following.
PyErr_Clear	`void PyErr_Clear( )` Clears the error indicator. Innocuous if no error is pending.
PyErr_ Exception- Matches	`int PyErr_ExceptionMatches(PyObject* ` *`type`*`)` Call only when an error is pending, or the whole program might crash. Returns a value not equal to 0 when the pending exception is an instance of the given *type* or any subclass of *type*, or 0 when the pending exception is not such an instance.
PyErr_Occurred	`PyObject* PyErr_Occurred( )` Returns NULL if no error is pending; otherwise, a borrowed reference to the type of the pending exception. (Don't use the returned value; call `PyErr_ExceptionMatches` instead, in order to catch exceptions of subclasses as well, as is normal and expected.)
PyErr_Print	`void PyErr_Print( )` Call only when an error is pending, or the whole program might crash. Outputs a standard traceback to `sys.stderr`, then clears the error indicator. If you need to process errors in highly sophisticated ways, study other error-related functions of the C API, such as `PyErr_Fetch`, `PyErr_Normalize`, `PyErr_GivenExceptionMatches`, and `PyErr_Restore`. However, I do not cover such advanced and rarely needed possibilities in this book.

Abstract Layer Functions

The code for a C extension typically needs to use some Python functionality. For example, your code may need to examine or set attributes and items of Python objects, call Python-coded and built-in functions and methods, and so on. In most cases, the best approach is for your code to call functions from the abstract layer of Python's C API. These are functions that you can call on any Python object (functions whose names start with PyObject_), or on any object within a wide category, such as mappings, numbers, or sequences (with names starting with PyMapping_, PyNumber_, and PySequence_, respectively).

Some of the functions callable on specifically typed objects within these categories duplicate functionality that is also available from PyObject_ functions. In these cases, you should almost invariably use the more general PyObject_ function instead. I don't cover such almost-redundant functions in this book.

Functions in the abstract layer raise Python exceptions if you call them on objects to which they are not applicable. All of these functions accept borrowed references for PyObject* arguments and return a new reference (NULL for an exception) if they return a PyObject* result.

The most frequently used abstract layer functions are the following.

PyCallable_Check	int PyCallable_Check(PyObject* x)
	True if x is callable, like Python's callable(x).
PyEval_CallObject	PyObject* PyEval_CallObject(PyObject* x,PyObject* args)
	Calls callable Python object x with the positional arguments held in tuple args. Returns the call's result, like Python's return x(*args).
PyEval_CallObjectWith-Keywords	PyObject* PyEval_CallObjectWithKeywords(PyObject* x,PyObject* args,PyObject* kwds)
	Calls callable Python object x with the positional arguments held in tuple args and the named arguments held in dictionary kwds. Returns the call's result, like Python's return x(*args,**kwds).
PyIter_Check	int PyIter_Check(PyObject* x)
	True if x supports the iterator protocol (i.e., if x is an iterator).
PyIter_Next	PyObject* PyIter_Next(PyObject* x)
	Returns the next item from iterator x. Returns NULL *without* raising any exception if x's iteration is finished (i.e., when Python's x.next() raises StopIteration).
PyNumber_Check	int PyNumber_Check(PyObject* x)
	True if x supports the number protocol (i.e., if x is a number).

PyObject_ CallFunction	`PyObject* PyObject_CallFunction(PyObject* x,char* `*`format`*`,...)`
	Calls the callable Python object *x* with positional arguments described by format string *format*, using the same format codes as Py_BuildValue, covered in "Py_BuildValue" on page 624. When *format* is NULL, calls *x* with no arguments. Returns the call's result.
PyObject_ CallMethod	`PyObject* PyObject_CallMethod(PyObject* x,char* `*`method`*`,char* `*`format`*`,...)`
	Calls the method named *method* of Python object *x* with positional arguments described by format string *format*, using the same format codes as Py_BuildValue. When *format* is NULL, calls the method with no arguments. Returns the call's result.
PyObject_Cmp	`int PyObject_Cmp(PyObject* x1,PyObject* x2,int* `*`result`*`)`
	Compares objects *x1* and *x2* and places the result (-1, 0, or 1) in **result*, like Python's *result*=cmp(*x1,x2*).
PyObject_ DelAttrString	`int PyObject_DelAttrString(PyObject* x,char* `*`name`*`)`
	Deletes *x*'s attribute named *name*, like Python's del *x.name*.
PyObject_ DelItem	`int PyObject_DelItem(PyObject* x,PyObject* key)`
	Deletes *x*'s item with key (or index) *key*, like Python's del *x*[*key*].
PyObject_ DelItemString	`int PyObject_DelItemString(PyObject* x,char* `*`key`*`)`
	Deletes *x*'s item with key *key*, like Python's del *x*[*key*].
PyObject_ GetAttrString	`PyObject* PyObject_GetAttrString(PyObject* x,char* `*`name`*`)`
	Returns *x*'s attribute *name*, like Python's *x.name*.
PyObject_ GetItem	`PyObject* PyObject_GetItem(PyObject* x,PyObject* key)`
	Returns *x*'s item with key (or index) *key*, like Python's *x*[*key*].
PyObject_ GetItemString	`int PyObject_GetItemString(PyObject* x,char* `*`key`*`)`
	Returns *x*'s item with key *key*, like Python's *x*[*key*].
PyObject_ GetIter	`PyObject* PyObject_GetIter(PyObject* x)`
	Returns an iterator on *x*, like Python's iter(*x*).

PyObject_ HasAttrString	int PyObject_HasAttrString(PyObject* x,char* name) True if x has an attribute name, like Python's hasattr(x,name).
PyObject_IsTrue	int PyObject_IsTrue(PyObject* x) True if x is true for Python, like Python's bool(x).
PyObject_ Length	int PyObject_Length(PyObject* x) Returns x's length, like Python's len(x).
PyObject_ Repr	PyObject* PyObject_Repr(PyObject* x) Returns x's detailed string representation, like Python's repr(x).
PyObject_ RichCompare	PyObject* PyObject_RichCompare(PyObject* x,PyObject* y,int op) Performs the comparison indicated by op between x and y, and returns the result as a Python object. op can be Py_EQ, Py_NE, Py_LT, Py_LE, Py_GT, or Py_GE, corresponding to Python comparisons x==y, x!=y, x<y, x<=y, x>y, or x>=y.
PyObject_ RichCompare- Bool	int PyObject_RichCompareBool(PyObject* x,PyObject* y,int op) Like PyObject_RichCompare, but returns 0 for false and 1 for true.
PyObject_ SetAttrString	int PyObject_SetAttrString(PyObject* x,char* name,PyObject* v) Sets x's attribute named name to v, like Python's x.name=v.
PyObject_ SetItem	int PyObject_SetItem(PyObject* x,PyObject* k,PyObject *v) Sets x's item with key (or index) key to v, like Python's x[key]=v.
PyObject_ SetItemString	int PyObject_SetItemString(PyObject* x,char* key,PyObject *v) Sets x's item with key key to v, like Python's x[key]=v.
PyObject_Str	PyObject* PyObject_Str(PyObject* x) Returns x's readable string form, like Python's str(x).
PyObject_Type	PyObject* PyObject_Type(PyObject* x) Returns x's type object, like Python's type(x).

PyObject_ Unicode	PyObject* PyObject_Unicode(PyObject* x) Returns x's Unicode string form, like Python's unicode(x).
PySequence_ Contains	int PySequence_Contains(PyObject* x,PyObject* v) True if v is an item in x, like Python's v in x.
PySequence_ DelSlice	int PySequence_DelSlice(PyObject* x,int start,int stop) Deletes x's slice from start to stop, like Python's del x[start:stop].
PySequence_ Fast	PyObject* PySequence_Fast(PyObject* x) Returns a new reference to a tuple with the same items as x, unless x is a list, in which case returns a new reference to x. When you need to get many items of an arbitrary sequence x, it's fastest to call t=PySequence_Fast(x) once, then call PySequence_Fast_GET_ITEM(t,i) as many times as needed, and finally call Py_DECREF(t).
PySequence_ Fast_GET_ITEM	PyObject* PySequence_Fast_GET_ITEM(PyObject* x,int i) Returns the i item of x, where x must be the result of PySequence_Fast, x!=NULL, and 0<=i<PySequence_Fast_GET_SIZE(t). Violating these conditions can cause program crashes. This approach is optimized for speed, not for safety.
PySequence_ Fast_GET_SIZE	int PySequence_Fast_GET_SIZE(PyObject* x) Returns the length of x. x must be the result of PySequence_Fast, x!=NULL.
PySequence_ GetSlice	PyObject* PySequence_GetSlice(PyObject* x,int start,int stop) Returns x's slice from start to stop, like Python's x[start:stop].
PySequence_ List	PyObject* PySequence_List(PyObject* x) Returns a new list object with the same items as x, like Python's list(x).
PySequence_ SetSlice	int PySequence_SetSlice(PyObject* x,int start,int stop,PyObject* v) Sets x's slice from start to stop to v, like Python's x[start:stop]=v. Just as in the equivalent Python statement, v must also be a sequence.

PySequence_
Tuple
    PyObject* PySequence_Tuple(PyObject* x)

    Returns a new reference to a tuple with the same items as x, like
    Python's tuple(x).

    Other functions whose names start with PyNumber_ allow you to
    perform numeric operations. Unary PyNumber functions, which take
    one argument PyObject* x and return a PyObject*, are listed in
    Table 25-3 with their Python equivalents.

Table 25-3. Unary PyNumber functions

Function	Python equivalent
PyNumber_Absolute	abs(x)
PyNumber_Float	float(x)
PyNumber_Int	int(x)
PyNumber_Invert	~x
PyNumber_Long	long(x)
PyNumber_Negative	-x
PyNumber_Positive	+x

Binary PyNumber functions, which take two PyObject* arguments x and y and
return a PyObject*, are similarly listed in Table 25-4.

Table 25-4. Binary PyNumber functions

Function	Python equivalent
PyNumber_Add	x + y
PyNumber_And	x & y
PyNumber_Divide	x / y
PyNumber_Divmod	divmod(x, y)
PyNumber_FloorDivide	x // y
PyNumber_Lshift	x << y
PyNumber_Multiply	x * y
PyNumber_Or	x | y
PyNumber_Remainder	x % y
PyNumber_Rshift	x >> y
PyNumber_Subtract	x - y
PyNumber_TrueDivide	x / y (nontruncating)
PyNumber_Xor	x ^ y

All the binary PyNumber functions have in-place equivalents whose names start
with PyNumber_InPlace, such as PyNumber_InPlaceAdd and so on. The in-place
versions try to modify the first argument in place, if possible, and in any case

return a new reference to the result, be it the first argument (modified) or a new object. Python's built-in numbers are immutable; therefore, when the first argument is a number of a built-in type, the in-place versions work just the same as the ordinary versions. Function `PyNumber_Divmod` returns a tuple with two items (the quotient and the remainder) and has no in-place equivalent.

There is one ternary `PyNumber` function, `PyNumber_Power`.

PyNumber_Power	`PyObject* PyNumber_Power(PyObject* x,PyObject* y,PyObject* z)`
	When *z* is `Py_None`, returns *x* raised to the *y* power, like Python's *x**y* or, equivalently, pow(*x*,*y*). Otherwise, returns *x**y%z*, like Python's pow(*x*,*y*,*z*). The in-place version is named `PyNumber_InPlacePower`.

Concrete Layer Functions

Each specific type of Python built-in object supplies concrete functions to operate on instances of that type, with names starting with P*ytype_* (e.g., `PyInt_` for functions related to Python ints). Most such functions duplicate the functionality of abstract-layer functions or auxiliary functions covered earlier in this chapter, such as `Py_BuildValue`, which can generate objects of many types. In this section, I cover some frequently used functions from the concrete layer that provide unique functionality or substantial convenience or speed. For most types, you can check if an object belongs to the type by calling P*ytype_*Check, which also accepts instances of subtypes, or P*ytype_*CheckExact, which accepts only instances of *type*, not of subtypes. Signatures are the same as for function `PyIter_Check`, covered in "PyIter_Check" on page 628.

PyDict_GetItem	`PyObject* PyDict_GetItem(PyObject* x,PyObject* key)`
	Returns a borrowed reference to the item with key *key* of dictionary *x*.

PyDict_GetItemString	`int PyDict_GetItemString(PyObject* x,char* key)`
	Returns a borrowed reference to the item with key *key* of dictionary *x*.

PyDict_Next	`int PyDict_Next(PyObject* x,int* pos,PyObject** k,PyObject** v)`
	Iterates over items in dictionary *x*. You must initialize **pos* to 0 at the start of the iteration: `PyDict_Next` uses and updates **pos* to keep track of its place. For each successful iteration step, returns 1; when there are no more items, returns 0. Updates **k* and **v* to point to the next key and value, respectively (borrowed references), at each step that returns 1. You can pass either *k* or *v* as NULL if you are not

interested in the key or value. During an iteration, you must not
change in any way the set of x's keys, but you can change x's values
as long as the set of keys remains identical.

PyDict_Merge	`int PyDict_Merge(PyObject* x,PyObject* y,int override)` Updates dictionary x by merging the items of dictionary y into x. *override* determines what happens when a key k is present in both x and y: if *override* is 0, then x[k] remains the same; otherwise, x[k] is replaced by the value y[k].
PyDict_ MergeFromSeq2	`int PyDict_MergeFromSeq2(PyObject* x,PyObject* y,int override)` Like PyDict_Merge, except that y is not a dictionary but a sequence of sequences, where each subsequence has length 2 and is used as a (*key,value*) pair.
PyFloat_AS_ DOUBLE	`double PyFloat_AS_DOUBLE(PyObject* x)` Returns the C double value of Python float x, very fast, without any error checking.
PyList_New	`PyObject* PyList_New(int length)` Returns a new, uninitialized list of the given *length*. You must then initialize the list, typically by calling PyList_SET_ITEM *length* times.
PyList_GET_ ITEM	`PyObject* PyList_GET_ITEM(PyObject* x,int pos)` Returns the *pos* item of list x, without any error checking.
PyList_SET_ ITEM	`int PyList_SET_ITEM(PyObject* x,int pos,PyObject* v)` Sets the *pos* item of list x to v, without any error checking. Steals a reference to v. Use only immediately after creating a new list x with PyList_New.
PyString_AS_ STRING	`char* PyString_AS_STRING(PyObject* x)` Returns a pointer to the internal buffer of string x, very fast, without any error checking. You must not modify the buffer in any way, unless you just allocated it by calling PyString_FromStringAndSize(NULL,*size*).

PyString_ AsStringAndSize	int PyString_AsStringAndSize(PyObject* *x*,char** *buffer*,int* *length*)
	Puts a pointer to the internal buffer of string *x* in **buffer*, and *x*'s length in **length*. You must not modify the buffer in any way, unless you just allocated it by calling PyString_FromStringAnd-Size(NULL,*size*).
PyString_ FromFormat	PyObject* PyString_FromFormat(char* *format*,...)
	Returns a Python string built from format string *format*, which has syntax similar to printf's, and the following C values indicated as variable arguments (...) above.
PyString_ FromStringAnd-Size	PyObject* PyString_FromFormat(char* *data*,int *size*)
	Returns a Python string of length *size*, copying *size* bytes from *data*. When *data* is NULL, the Python string is uninitialized, and you must initialize it. You can get the pointer to the string's internal buffer by calling PyString_AS_STRING.
PyTuple_New	PyObject* PyTuple_New(int *length*)
	Returns a new, uninitialized tuple of the given *length*. You must then initialize the tuple, typically by calling PyTuple_SET_ITEM *length* times.
PyTuple_GET_ ITEM	PyObject* PyTuple_GET_ITEM(PyObject* *x*,int *pos*)
	Returns the *pos* item of tuple *x*, without error checking.
PyTuple_SET_ ITEM	int PyTuple_SET_ITEM(PyObject* *x*,int *pos*,PyObject* *v*)
	Sets the *pos* item of tuple *x* to *v*, without error checking. Steals a reference to *v*. Use only immediately after creating a new tuple *x* with PyTuple_New.

A Simple Extension Example

Example 25-1 exposes the functionality of Python C API functions PyDict_Merge and PyDict_MergeFromSeq2 for Python use. The update method of dictionaries works like PyDict_Merge with *override*=1, but Example 25-1 is more general.

Example 25-1. A simple Python extension module merge.c

```c
#include <Python.h>

static PyObject*
merge(PyObject* self, PyObject* args, PyObject* kwds)
{
    static char* argnames[] = {"x","y","override",NULL};
    PyObject *x, *y;
    int override = 0;
    if(!PyArg_ParseTupleAndKeywords(args, kwds, "O!O|i", argnames,
        &PyDict_Type, &x, &y, &override))
            return NULL;
    if(-1 == PyDict_Merge(x, y, override)) {
        if(!PyErr_ExceptionMatches(PyExc_TypeError))
            return NULL;
        PyErr_Clear();
        if(-1 == PyDict_MergeFromSeq2(x, y, override))
            return NULL;
    }
    return Py_BuildValue("");
}

static char merge_docs[] = "\
merge(x,y,override=False): merge into dict x the items of dict y (or the pairs\n\
    that are the items of y, if y is a sequence), with optional override.\n\
    Alters dict x directly, returns None.\n\
";

static PyObject*
mergenew(PyObject* self, PyObject* args, PyObject* kwds)
{
    static char* argnames[] = {"x","y","override",NULL};
    PyObject *x, *y, *result;
    int override = 0;
    if(!PyArg_ParseTupleAndKeywords(args, kwds, "O!O|i", argnames,
        &PyDict_Type, &x, &y, &override))
            return NULL;
    result = PyObject_CallMethod(x, "copy", "");
    if(!result)
        return NULL;
    if(-1 == PyDict_Merge(result, y, override)) {
        if(!PyErr_ExceptionMatches(PyExc_TypeError))
            return NULL;
        PyErr_Clear();
        if(-1 == PyDict_MergeFromSeq2(result, y, override))
            return NULL;
    }
    return result;
}

static char mergenew_docs[] = "\
mergenew(x,y,override=False): merge into dict x the items of dict y (or\n\
    the pairs that are the items of y, if y is a sequence), with optional\n\
```

Example 25-1. A simple Python extension module merge.c (continued)

```
      override.  Does NOT alter x, but rather returns the modified copy as\n\
      the function's result.\n\
";

static PyMethodDef funcs[] = {
    {"merge", (PyCFunction)merge, METH_KEYWORDS, merge_docs},
    {"mergenew", (PyCFunction)mergenew, METH_KEYWORDS, mergenew_docs},
    {NULL}
};

void
initmerge(void)
{
    Py_InitModule3("merge", funcs, "Example extension module");
}
```

This example declares as static every function and global variable in the C source file, except initmerge, which must be visible from the outside so Python can call it. Since the functions and variables are exposed to Python via PyMethodDef structures, Python does not need to see their names directly. Therefore, declaring them static is best: this ensures that names don't accidentally end up in the whole program's global namespace, as might otherwise happen on some platforms, possibly causing conflicts and errors.

The format string "O!O|i" passed to PyArg_ParseTupleAndKeywords indicates that function merge accepts three arguments from Python: an object with a type constraint, a generic object, and an optional integer. At the same time, the format string indicates that the variable part of PyArg_ParseTupleAndKeywords's arguments must contain four addresses in the following order: the address of a Python type object, two addresses of PyObject* variables, and the address of an int variable. The int variable must be previously initialized to its intended default value, since the corresponding Python argument is optional.

And indeed, after the *argnames* argument, the code passes &PyDict_Type (i.e., the address of the dictionary type object). Then it passes the addresses of the two PyObject* variables. Finally, it passes the address of variable *override*, an int that was previously initialized to 0, since the default, when the *override* argument isn't explicitly passed from Python, is "no overriding." If the return value of PyArg_ParseTupleAndKeywords is 0, the code immediately returns NULL to propagate the exception; this automatically diagnoses most cases where Python code passes wrong arguments to our new function merge.

When the arguments appear to be okay, it tries PyDict_Merge, which succeeds if *y* is a dictionary. When PyDict_Merge raises a TypeError, indicating that *y* is not a dictionary, the code clears the error and tries again, this time with PyDict_MergeFromSeq2, which succeeds when *y* is a sequence of pairs. If that also fails, it returns NULL to propagate the exception. Otherwise, it returns None in the simplest way (i.e., with return Py_BuildValue("")) to indicate success.

Function mergenew basically duplicates merge's functionality; however, mergenew does not alter its arguments, but rather builds and returns a new dictionary as the function's result. The C API function PyObject_CallMethod lets mergenew call the copy method of its first Python-passed argument, a dictionary object, and obtain a new dictionary object that it then alters (with exactly the same logic as function merge). It then returns the altered dictionary as the function result (thus, no need to call Py_BuildValue in this case).

The code of Example 25-1 must reside in a source file named *merge.c*. In the same directory, create the following script named *setup.py*:

```
from distutils.core import setup, Extension
setup(name='merge', ext_modules=[ Extension('merge',sources=['merge.c']) ])
```

Now, run *python setup.py install* at a shell prompt in this directory (with a user ID having appropriate privileges to write into your Python installation, or sudo on Unix-like systems if necessary). This command builds the dynamically loaded library for the merge extension module, and copies it to the appropriate directory, depending on your Python installation. Now your Python code can use the module. For example:

```
import merge
x = {'a':1,'b':2 }
merge.merge(x,[['b',3],['c',4]])
print x                              # prints: {'a':1, 'b':2, 'c':4 }
print merge.mergenew(x,{'a':5,'d':6},override=1)
# prints: {'a':5, 'b':2, 'c':4, 'd':6 }
print x                              # prints: {'a':1, 'b':2, 'c':4 }
```

This example shows the difference between merge (which alters its first argument) and mergenew (which returns a new object and does not alter its argument). It also shows that the second argument can be either a dictionary or a sequence of two-item subsequences. Further, it demonstrates default operation (where keys that are already in the first argument are left alone) as well as the override option (where keys coming from the second argument take precedence, as in Python dictionaries' update method).

Defining New Types

In your extension modules, you often want to define new types and make them available to Python. A type's definition is held in a large struct named PyTypeObject. Most of the fields of PyTypeObject are pointers to functions. Some fields point to other structs, which in turn are blocks of pointers to functions. PyTypeObject also includes a few fields that give the type's name, size, and behavior details (option flags). You can leave almost all fields of PyTypeObject set to NULL if you do not supply the related functionality. You can point some fields to functions in the Python C API in order to supply certain aspects of fundamental object functionality in standard ways.

The best way to implement a type is to copy from the Python sources the file *Modules/xxsubtype.c*, which Python supplies exactly for such didactical purposes, and edit it. It's a complete module with two types, subclassing from list and dict, respectively. Another example in the Python sources, *Objects/xxobject.c*, is not a complete module, and the type in this file is minimal and old-fashioned, and does not use modern recommended approaches. See *http://www.python.org/dev/*

---

doc/devel/api/type-structs.html for detailed documentation on `PyTypeObject` and other related structs. File *Include/object.h* in the Python sources contains the declarations of these types, as well as several important comments that you would do well to study.

Per-instance data

To represent each instance of your type, declare a C struct that starts, right after the opening brace, with macro `PyObject_HEAD`. The macro expands into the data fields that your struct must begin with in order to be a Python object. These fields include the reference count and a pointer to the instance's type. Any pointer to your structure can be correctly cast to a `PyObject*`. You can choose to look at this practice as a kind of C-level implementation of a (single) inheritance mechanism.

The `PyTypeObject` struct that defines your type's characteristics and behavior must contain the size of your per-instance struct, as well as pointers to the C functions you write to operate on your structure. Therefore, you normally place the `PyTypeObject` toward the end of your C-coded module's source code, after the definitions of the per-instance struct, and of all the functions that operate on instances of the per-instance struct. Each *x* that points to a structure starting with `PyObject_HEAD`, and in particular each `PyObject* ` *x*, has a field *x*->ob_type that is the address of the `PyTypeObject` structure that is *x*'s Python type object.

The PyTypeObject definition

Given a per-instance struct such as:

```
typedef struct {
    PyObject_HEAD
    /* other data needed by instances of this type, omitted */
} mytype;
```

the corresponding `PyTypeObject` struct almost invariably begins in a way similar to:

```
static PyTypeObject t_mytype = {
/* tp_head */        PyObject_HEAD_INIT(NULL)   /* use NULL, for MSVC++ */
/* tp_internal */    0,                /* must be 0 */
/* tp_name */        "mymodule.mytype", /* type name, including module */
/* tp_basicsize */   sizeof(mytype),
/* tp_itemsize */    0,                /* 0 except variable-size type */
/* tp_dealloc */     (destructor)mytype_dealloc,
/* tp_print */       0,                /* usually 0, use str instead */
/* tp_getattr */     0,                /* usually 0 (see getattro) */
/* tp_setattr */     0,                /* usually 0 (see setattro) */
/* tp_compare*/      0,                /* see also richcompare */
/* tp_repr */        (reprfunc)mytype_str,   /* like Python's __repr__ */
    /* rest of struct omitted */
```

For portability to Microsoft Visual C++, the `PyObject_HEAD_INIT` macro at the start of the `PyTypeObject` must have an argument of `NULL`. During module initialization, you must call `PyType_Ready(&t_mytype)`, which, among other tasks, inserts in t_mytype the address of its type (the type of a type is also known as a *metatype*), normally `&PyType_Type`. Another slot in `PyTypeObject` that points to another type object is tp_base, which comes later in the structure. In the structure definition itself, you must have a tp_base of NULL, again for compatibility with Microsoft Visual C++. However, before you invoke PyType_Ready(&t_mytype), you can optionally set t_mytype.tp_base to the address of another type object. When you do so, your type inherits from the other type, just as a class coded in Python can optionally inherit from a built-in type. For a Python type coded in C, inheriting means that, for most fields in the PyTypeObject, if you set the field to NULL, PyType_Ready copies the corresponding field from the base type. A type must specifically assert in its field tp_flags that it is usable as a base type; otherwise, no other type can inherit from it.

The tp_itemsize field is of interest only for types that, like tuples, have instances of different sizes, and can determine instance size once and forever at creation time. Most types just set tp_itemsize to 0. Fields tp_getattr and tp_setattr are generally set to NULL because they exist only for backward compatibility; modern types use fields tp_getattro and tp_setattro instead. Field tp_repr is typical of most of the following fields, which are omitted here: the field holds the address of a function, which corresponds directly to a Python special method (here, __repr__). You can set the field to NULL, indicating that your type does not supply the special method, or else set the field to point to a function with the needed functionality. If you set the field to NULL, but also point to a base type from the tp_base slot, you inherit the special method, if any, from your base type. You often need to cast your functions to the specific typedef type that a field needs (here, type reprfunc for field tp_repr) because the typedef has a first argument PyObject* self, while your functions, being specific to your type, normally use more specific pointers. For example:

```
static PyObject* mytype_str(mytype* self) { ... /* rest omitted */
```

Alternatively, you can declare mytype_str with a PyObject* self, then use a cast (mytype*)self in the function's body. Either alternative is acceptable style, but it's more common to locate the casts in the PyTypeObject declaration.

Instance initialization and finalization

The task of finalizing your instances is split among two functions. The tp_dealloc slot must never be NULL, except for immortal types (i.e., types whose instances are never deallocated). Python calls x->ob_type->tp_dealloc(x) on each instance x whose reference count decreases to 0, and the function thus called must release any resource held by object x, including x's memory. When an instance of mytype holds no other resources that must be released (in particular, no owned references to other Python objects that you would have to DECREF), mytype's destructor can be extremely simple:

```
static void mytype_dealloc(PyObject *x)
{
    x->ob_type->tp_free((PyObject*)x);
}
```

The function in the tp_free slot has the specific task of freeing x's memory. Often, you can just put in slot tp_free the address of the C API function _PyObject_Del.

The task of initializing your instances is split among three functions. To allocate memory for new instances of your type, put in slot tp_alloc the C API function

PyType_GenericAlloc, which does absolutely minimal initialization, clearing the newly allocated memory bytes to 0 except for the type pointer and reference count. Similarly, you can often set field tp_new to the C API function PyType_GenericNew. In this case, you can perform all per-instance initialization in the function you put in slot tp_init, which has the signature:

```
int init_name(PyObject *self,PyObject *args,PyObject *kwds)
```

The positional and named arguments to the function in slot tp_init are those passed when calling the type to create the new instance, just like, in Python, the positional and named arguments to __init__ are those passed when calling the class object. Again, as for types (classes) defined in Python, the general rule is to do as little initialization as feasible in tp_new and do as much as possible in tp_init. Using PyType_GenericNew for tp_new accomplishes this. However, you can choose to define your own tp_new for special types, such as ones that have immutable instances, where initialization must happen earlier. The signature is:

```
PyObject* new_name(PyObject *subtype,PyObject *args,PyObject *kwds)
```

The function in tp_new must return the newly created instance, normally an instance of *subtype* (which may be a type that inherits from yours). The function in tp_init, on the other hand, must return 0 for success, or -1 to indicate an exception.

If your type is subclassable, it's important that any instance invariants be established before the function in tp_new returns. For example, if it must be guaranteed that a certain field of the instance is never NULL, that field must be set to a non-NULL value by the function in tp_new. Subtypes of your type might fail to call your tp_init function; therefore, such indispensable initializations, needed to establish invariants, should always be in tp_new for subclassable types.

Attribute access

Access to attributes of your instances, including methods (as covered in "Attribute Reference Basics" on page 89), is mediated by the functions you put in slots tp_getattro and tp_setattro of your PyTypeObject struct. Normally, you put there the standard C API functions PyObject_GenericGetAttr and PyObject_GenericSetAttr, which implement standard semantics. Specifically, these API functions access your type's methods via the slot tp_methods, pointing to a sentinel-terminated array of PyMethodDef structs, and your instances' members via the slot tp_members, which is a similar sentinel-terminated array of PyMemberDef structs:

```
typedef struct {
    char* name;      /* Python-visible name of the member */
    int type;        /* code defining the data-type of the member */
    int offset;      /* offset of the member in the per-instance struct */
    int flags;       /* READONLY for a read-only member */
    char* doc;       /* docstring for the member */
} PyMemberDef
```

As an exception to the general rule that including *Python.h* gets you all the declarations you need, you have to include *structmember.h* explicitly in order to have your C source see the declaration of PyMemberDef.

type is generally T_OBJECT for members that are PyObject*, but many other type codes are defined in *Include/structmember.h* for members that your instances hold as C-native data (e.g., T_DOUBLE for double or T_STRING for char*). For example, say that your per-instance struct is something like:

```
typedef struct {
    PyObject_HEAD
    double datum;
    char* name;
} mytype;
```

Expose to Python per-instance attributes *datum* (read/write) and *name* (read-only) by defining the following array and pointing your PyTypeObject's tp_members to it:

```
static PyMemberDef[] mytype_members = {
    {"datum", T_DOUBLE, offsetof(mytype, datum), 0, "The current datum"},
    {"name", T_STRING, offsetof(mytype, name), READONLY, "Datum name"},
    {NULL}
};
```

Using PyObject_GenericGetAttr and PyObject_GenericSetAttr for tp_getattro and tp_setattro also provides further possibilities, which I do not cover in detail in this book. Field tp_getset points to a sentinel-terminated array of PyGetSetDef structs, the equivalent of having property instances in a Python-coded class. If your PyTypeObject's field tp_dictoffset is not equal to 0, the field's value must be the offset, within the per-instance struct, of a PyObject* that points to a Python dictionary. In this case, the generic attribute access API functions use that dictionary to allow Python code to set arbitrary attributes on your type's instances, just like for instances of Python-coded classes.

Another dictionary is per-type, not per-instance; the PyObject* for the per-type dictionary is slot tp_dict of your PyTypeObject struct. You can set slot tp_dict to NULL, and then PyType_Ready initializes the dictionary appropriately. Alternatively, you can set tp_dict to a dictionary of type attributes, and then PyType_Ready adds other entries to that same dictionary, in addition to the type attributes you set. It's generally easier to start with tp_dict set to NULL, call PyType_Ready to create and initialize the per-type dictionary, and then, if need be, add any further entries to the dictionary via explicit C code.

Field tp_flags is a long whose bits determine your type struct's exact layout, mostly for backward compatibility. Normally, set this field to Py_TPFLAGS_DEFAULT to indicate that you are defining a normal, modern type. You should set tp_flags to Py_TPFLAGS_DEFAULT|Py_TPFLAGS_HAVE_GC if your type supports cyclic garbage collection. Your type should support cyclic garbage collection if instances of the type contain PyObject* fields that might point to arbitrary objects and form part of a reference loop. However, to support cyclic garbage collection, it's not enough to add Py_TPFLAGS_HAVE_GC to field tp_flags; you also have to supply appropriate functions, indicated by slots tp_traverse and tp_clear, and register and unregister your instances appropriately with the cyclic garbage collector. Supporting cyclic garbage collection is an advanced subject, and I do not cover it further in this book. Similarly, I do not cover the advanced subject of supporting weak references.

Field tp_doc, a char*, is a null-terminated character string that is your type's docstring. Other fields point to structs (whose fields point to functions); you can set each such field to NULL to indicate that you support none of the functions of that kind. The fields pointing to such blocks of functions are tp_as_number, for special methods typically supplied by numbers; tp_as_sequence, for special methods typically supplied by sequences; tp_as_mapping, for special methods typically supplied by mappings; and tp_as_buffer, for the special methods of the buffer protocol.

For example, objects that are not sequences can still support one or a few of the methods listed in the block to which tp_as_sequence points, and in this case the PyTypeObject must have a non-NULL field tp_as_sequence, even if the block of function pointers it points to is in turn mostly full of NULLs. For example, dictionaries supply a __contains__ special method so that you can check if x in d when d is a dictionary. At the C code level, the method is a function pointed to by field sq_contains, which is part of the PySequenceMethods struct to which field tp_as_sequence points. Therefore, the PyTypeObject struct for the dict type, named PyDict_Type, has a non-NULL value for tp_as_sequence, even though a dictionary supplies no other field in PySequenceMethods except sq_contains, and therefore all other fields in *(PyDict_Type.tp_as_sequence) are NULL.

Type definition example

Example 25-2 is a complete Python extension module that defines the very simple type intpair, each instance of which holds two integers named first and second.

Example 25-2. Defining a new intpair type

```
#include "Python.h"
#include "structmember.h"

/* per-instance data structure */
typedef struct {
    PyObject_HEAD
    int first, second;
} intpair;

static int
intpair_init(PyObject *self, PyObject *args, PyObject *kwds)
{
    static char* nams[] = {"first","second",NULL};
    int first, second;
    if(!PyArg_ParseTupleAndKeywords(args, kwds, "ii", nams, &first, &second))
        return -1;
    ((intpair*)self)->first = first;
    ((intpair*)self)->second = second;
    return 0;
}

static void
intpair_dealloc(PyObject *self)
```

Example 25-2. Defining a new intpair type (continued)

```
{
    self->ob_type->tp_free(self);
}

static PyObject*
intpair_str(PyObject* self)
{
    return PyString_FromFormat("intpair(%d,%d)",
        ((intpair*)self)->first, ((intpair*)self)->second);
}

static PyMemberDef intpair_members[] = {
    {"first", T_INT, offsetof(intpair, first), 0, "first item" },
    {"second", T_INT, offsetof(intpair, second), 0, "second item" },
    {NULL}
};

static PyTypeObject t_intpair = {
    PyObject_HEAD_INIT(0)           /* tp_head */
    0,                              /* tp_internal */
    "intpair.intpair",              /* tp_name */
    sizeof(intpair),                /* tp_basicsize */
    0,                              /* tp_itemsize */
    intpair_dealloc,                /* tp_dealloc */
    0,                              /* tp_print */
    0,                              /* tp_getattr */
    0,                              /* tp_setattr */
    0,                              /* tp_compare */
    intpair_str,                    /* tp_repr */
    0,                              /* tp_as_number */
    0,                              /* tp_as_sequence */
    0,                              /* tp_as_mapping */
    0,                              /* tp_hash */
    0,                              /* tp_call */
    0,                              /* tp_str */
    PyObject_GenericGetAttr,        /* tp_getattro */
    PyObject_GenericSetAttr,        /* tp_setattro */
    0,                              /* tp_as_buffer */
    Py_TPFLAGS_DEFAULT,
    "two ints (first,second)",
    0,                              /* tp_traverse */
    0,                              /* tp_clear */
    0,                              /* tp_richcompare */
    0,                              /* tp_weaklistoffset */
    0,                              /* tp_iter */
    0,                              /* tp_iternext */
    0,                              /* tp_methods */
    intpair_members,                /* tp_members */
    0,                              /* tp_getset */
    0,                              /* tp_base */
    0,                              /* tp_dict */
    0,                              /* tp_descr_get */
```

Example 25-2. Defining a new intpair type (continued)

```
    0,                              /* tp_descr_set */
    0,                              /* tp_dictoffset */
    intpair_init,                   /* tp_init */
    PyType_GenericAlloc,            /* tp_alloc */
    PyType_GenericNew,              /* tp_new */
    _PyObject_Del,                  /* tp_free */
};

void
initintpair(void)
{
    static PyMethodDef no_methods[] = { {NULL} };
    PyObject* this_module = Py_InitModule("intpair", no_methods);
    PyType_Ready(&t_intpair);
    PyObject_SetAttrString(this_module, "intpair", (PyObject*)&t_intpair);
}
```

The intpair type defined in Example 25-2 gives just about no substantial benefits when compared to an equivalent definition in Python, such as:

```
class intpair(object):
    __slots__ = 'first', 'second'
    def __init__(self, first, second):
        self.first = first
        self.second = second
    def __repr__(self):
        return 'intpair(%s,%s)' % (self.first, self.second)
```

The C-coded version does, however, ensure that the two attributes are integers, truncating float or complex number arguments as needed. For example:

```
import intpair
x=intpair.intpair(1.2,3.4)                      # x is: intpair(1,3)
```

Each instance of the C-coded version of intpair occupies somewhat less memory than an instance of the Python version in the above example. However, the purpose of Example 25-2 is purely didactic: to present a C-coded Python extension that defines a simple new type.

Extending Python Without Python's C API

You can code Python extensions in other classic compiled languages besides C. For Fortran, the choice is between Paul Dubois's Pyfort (available at *http://pyfortran.sf.net*) and Pearu Peterson's F2PY (available at *http://cens.ioc.ee/projects/f2py2e/*). Both packages support and require the Numeric package covered in "The Numeric Package" on page 378, since numeric processing is Fortran's typical application area.

For C++, you have many choices. SCXX (available at *http://davidf.sjsoft.com/mirrors/mcmillan-inc/scxx.html*) is a simple, lightweight package that uses no templates and is thus suitable for older C++ compilers. PyCXX (available at *http://cxx.sf.net*) uses a modest amount of templates, essentially ones from the C++ standard library. SIP (available at *http://www.riverbankcomputing.co.uk/sip/index.php*) also supports the C++ extensions needed to use the powerful Qt cross-platform libraries, but, while it fully supports Qt, it does not *require* it. The Boost Python Library (available at *http://www.boost.org/libs/python/doc*) is part of Boost, a vast treasury of powerful, template-rich C++ libraries, of uniformly high quality, that need and support modern C++ compilers that support templates very well.

Of course, you may also choose to use Python's C API from your C++ code, using C++ in this respect as if it were C, and foregoing the extra convenience that C++ affords. However, if you're already using C++ rather than C anyway, then using SCXX, PyCXX, SIP, or Boost can substantially improve your programming productivity when compared to using Python's underlying C API.

If your Python extension is basically a wrapper over an existing C or C++ library (as many are), consider SWIG, the Simplified Wrapper and Interface Generator (available at *http://www.swig.org*). SWIG generates the C source code for your extension based on the library's header files, generally with some help in terms of further annotations in an interface description file. If you specifically need to wrap an existing dynamic library (a *.dll* on Windows, and a *.so* on most Unix-like systems, including Linux and Mac OS X) in order to use the library from your Python code, look into the ctypes extension (*http://starship.python.net/crew/theller/ctypes/*), which offers excellent support for this task. In Python 2.5, ctypes is scheduled to be included in the standard Python library.

Greg Ewing is developing a language called Pyrex, which is specifically for coding Python extensions. Pyrex (found at *http://www.cosc.canterbury.ac.nz/~greg/python/Pyrex/*) is an interesting mix of Python and C concepts, and is already quite usable despite being a relatively new development. Pyrex is suitable both for wrapping existing C libraries and for writing fast extension modules for Python that are compiled to machine language, like C-coded extensions would be. Pyrex works by generating intermediate C code that is then compiled. Pyrex is covered in "Pyrex" on page 650.

The weave package (available at *http://www.scipy.org/site_content/weave*) lets you run inline C/C++ code within Python. The blitz function, in particular, generates and runs C++ code from expressions using the Numeric package, and thus requires Numeric.

If your application runs only on Windows, the most practical way to extend and embed Python may sometimes be through COM. In particular, COM is by far the best way to use Visual Basic modules (packaged as ActiveX classes) from Python. COM is also the best way to make Python-coded functionality (packaged as COM servers) available to Visual Basic programs. The standard Python distribution for Windows (as of Python 2.4) does not directly support COM: you need to use ctypes (which is part of the standard Python library starting only with Python 2.5, but can be downloaded and installed for use with previous versions of Python too), or download and install the platform-specific win32all extension package (available at *http://starship.python.net/crew/mhammond/*). I do not cover Windows-specific functionality, including COM, any further in this book. For excellent coverage of platform-specific Python use on Windows, I recommend *Python Programming on Win32*, by Mark Hammond and Andy Robinson (O'Reilly).

Embedding Python

If you have an application already written in C or C++ (or another classic compiled language), you may want to embed Python as your application's scripting language. To embed Python in languages other than C, the other language must be able to call C functions. In the following, I cover only the C view of things, since other languages vary widely regarding what you have to do in order to call C functions from them.

Installing Resident Extension Modules

In order for Python scripts to communicate with your application, your application must supply extension modules with Python-accessible functions and classes that expose your application's functionality. If these modules are linked with your application, rather than residing in dynamic libraries that Python can load when necessary, register your modules with Python as additional built-in modules by calling the PyImport_AppendInittab C API function.

PyImport_ AppendInittab	int PyImport_AppendInittab(char* *name*,void (*initfunc*)(void))
	name is the module name, which Python scripts use in import statements to access the module. *initfunc* is the module initialization function, taking no argument and returning no result, as covered in "Module Initialization" on page 617 (i.e., *initfunc* is the module's function that would be named init*name* for a normal extension module in a dynamic library). PyImport_AppendInittab must be called before Py_Initialize.

Setting Arguments

You may want to set the program name and arguments, which Python scripts can access as sys.argv, by calling either or both of the following C API functions.

Py_SetPro- gramName	void Py_SetProgramName(char* *name*)
	Sets the program name, which Python scripts can access as sys.argv[0]. Must be called before Py_Initialize.
PySys_SetArgv	void PySys_SetArgv(int *argc*,char** *argv*)
	Sets the program arguments, which Python scripts can access as sys.argv[1:], to the *argc* 0-terminated strings in array *argv*. Must be called after Py_Initialize.

Python Initialization and Finalization

After installing extra built-in modules and optionally setting the program name, your application initializes Python. At the end, when Python is no longer needed, your application finalizes Python. The relevant functions in the C API are as follows.

Py_Finalize	void Py_Finalize(void)
	Frees all memory and other resources that Python is able to free. You should not make any other Python C API call after calling this function.

Py_Initialize	void Py_Initialize(void)
	Initializes the Python environment. Make no other Python C API call before this one, except PyImport_AppendInittab and Py_SetProgramName, covered in "PyImport_ AppendInittab" on page 647 and "Py_SetPro-gramName" on page 647.

Running Python Code

Your application can run Python source code from a character string or from a file. To run or compile Python source code, choose the mode of execution as one of the following three constants defined in *Python.h*:

Py_eval_input
: The code is an expression to evaluate (like passing 'eval' to Python built-in function compile).

Py_file_input
: The code is a block of one or more statements to execute (like 'exec' for compile; just like in that case, a trailing '\n' must close compound statements).

Py_single_input
: The code is a single statement for interactive execution (like 'single' for compile; implicitly outputs the results of expression statements).

Running Python source code directly is similar to passing a source code string to Python statement exec or built-in function eval, or a source code file to built-in function execfile. Two general functions you can use for this task are the following.

PyRun_File	PyObject* PyRun_File(FILE* *fp*,char* *filename*,int *start*, PyObject* *globals*,PyObject* *locals*)
	fp is a file of source code open for reading. *filename* is the name of the file, to use in error messages. *start* is one of the constants

Py_..._input that define execution mode. *globals* and *locals* are dictionaries (may be the same dictionary twice) to use as global and local namespace for the execution. Returns the result of the expression when *start* is Py_eval_input, a new reference to Py_None otherwise, or NULL to indicate that an exception has been raised (often, but not always, due to a syntax error).

PyRun_String

PyObject* PyRun_String(char* *astring*,int *start*, PyObject* *globals*,PyObject* *locals*)

Like PyRun_File, but the source code is in null-terminated string *astring*.

Dictionaries *locals* and *globals* are often new, empty dictionaries (most conveniently built by Py_BuildValue("{}")) or the dictionary of a module. PyImport_Import is a convenient way to obtain an existing module object; PyModule_GetDict obtains a module's dictionary. Sometimes you want to create a new module object on the fly and populate it with PyRun_ calls. To create a new, empty module, you can use the PyModule_New C API function.

PyModule_New

PyObject* PyModule_New(char* *name*)

Returns a new, empty module object for a module named *name*. Before the new object is usable, you must add to the object a string attribute named __file__. For example:

```
PyObject* newmod = PyModule_New("mymodule");
PyModule_AddStringConstant(newmod, "__file__",
"<synthetic>");
```

After this code runs, module object *newmod* is ready; you can obtain the module's dictionary with PyModule_GetDict(*newmod*) and pass the dict to such functions as PyRun_String as the *globals* and possibly the *locals* argument.

To run Python code repeatedly, and to separate the diagnosis of syntax errors from that of runtime exceptions raised by the code when it runs, you can compile the Python source to a code object, then keep the code object and run it repeatedly. This is just as true when using the C API as when dynamically executing in Python, as covered in "Dynamic Execution and the exec Statement" on page 328. Two C API functions you can use for this task are the following.

Py_CompileString

PyObject* Py_CompileString(char* *code*,char* *filename*,int *start*)

code is a null-terminated string of source code. *filename* is the name of the file to use in error messages. *start* is one of the constants that define execution mode. Returns the Python code object that contains the bytecode, or NULL for syntax errors.

PyEval_ EvalCode	`PyObject* PyEval_EvalCode(PyObject* co,PyObject* globals,` `PyObject* locals)`

co is a Python code object, as returned by `Py_CompileString`, for example. *globals* and *locals* are dictionaries (may be the same dictionary twice) to use as global and local namespace for the execution. Returns the result of the expression when *co* was compiled with `Py_eval_input`, a new reference to `Py_None` otherwise, or `NULL` to indicate the execution has raised an exception.

Pyrex

The Pyrex language (*http://www.cosc.canterbury.ac.nz/~greg/python/Pyrex/*) is often the most convenient way to write extensions for Python. Pyrex is a large subset of Python, with the addition of optional C-like types for variables: you can automatically compile Pyrex programs (source files with extension *.pyx*) into machine code (via an intermediate stage of generated C code), producing Python-importable extensions. See the above URL for all the details of Pyrex programming; in this section, I cover only a few essentials to let you get started with Pyrex.

The limitations of the Pyrex language, compared with Python, are the following:

- No nesting of `def` and `class` statements in other statements (except that one level of `def` within one level of `class` is okay, and indeed is the proper and normal way to define a class's methods).
- No `import *`, generators, list comprehensions, decorators, or augmented assignment.
- No `globals` and `locals` built-ins.
- To give a class a `staticmethod` or `classmethod`, you must first `def` the function *outside* the class statement (in Python, it's normally `def`ed *within* the class).

As you can see, while not quite as rich as Python proper, Pyrex is a vast subset indeed. More importantly, Pyrex adds to Python a few statements that allow C-like declarations, enabling easy generation of machine code (via an intermediate C-code generation step). Here is a simple example; code it in source file *hello.pyx* in a new empty directory:

```
def hello(char *name):
    return "Hello, " + name + "!"
```

This is almost exactly like Python—except that parameter *name* is preceded by a char*, declaring that its type must always be a C 0-terminated string (but, as you see from the body, in Pyrex, you can use its value as you would a normal Python string).

When you install Pyrex (by the usual *python setup.py install* route), you also gain a way to build Pyrex source files into Python dynamic-library extensions through the usual `distutils` approach. Code the following in file *setup.py* in the new directory:

```
from distutils.core import setup
from distutils.extension import Extension
from Pyrex.Distutils import build_ext

setup(name='hello',ext_modules=[Extension("hello",["hello.pyx"])],
    cmdclass = {'build_ext': build_ext})
```

Now run **python setup.py install** in the new directory (ignore compilation warnings; they're fully expected and benign). Now you can import and use the new module—for example, from an interactive Python session:

```
>>> import hello
>>> hello.hello("Alex")
'Hello, Alex!'
```

Due to the way we've coded this Pyrex source, we *must* pass a string to `hello.hello`: passing no arguments, more than one argument, or a nonstring raises an exception:

```
>>> hello.hello( )
Traceback (most recent call last):
  File "<stdin>", line 1, in ?
TypeError: function takes exactly 1 argument (0 given)
>>> hello.hello(23)
Traceback (most recent call last):
  File "<stdin>", line 1, in ?
TypeError: argument 1 must be string, not int
```

The cdef Statement and Function Parameters

You can use the keyword `cdef` mostly as you would `def`, but `cdef` defines functions that are internal to the extension module and are not visible on the outside, while `def` functions can also be called by Python code that imports the module. For both types of functions, parameters and return values with unspecified types, or, better, ones explicitly typed as `object`, become `PyObject*` pointers in the generated C code (with implicit and standard handling of reference incrementing and decrementing). `cdef` functions may also have parameters and return values of any other C type; `def` functions, in addition to untyped (or, equivalently, `object`), can only accept `int`, `float`, and `char*` types. For example, here's a `cdef` function to specifically sum two integers:

```
cdef int sum2i(int a, int b):
    return a + b
```

You can also use `cdef` to declare C variables: scalars, arrays, and pointers like in C:

```
cdef int x, y[23], *z
```

and struct, union, and enum with Pythonic syntax (colon on head clause, then indent):

```
cdef struct Ure:
    int x, y
    float z
```

(Afterward, refer to the new type by name only—e.g., *Ure*. Never use the keywords struct, union, and enum anywhere outside of the cdef that declares the type.)

External declarations

To interface with external C code, you can declare variables as cdef extern, with the same effect that extern has in the C language. More commonly, you will have the C declarations regarding some library you want to use available in a *.h* C header file; to ensure that the Pyrex-generated C code includes that header file, use the following form of cdef:

```
cdef external from "someheader.h":
```

and follow with a block of indented cdef-style declarations (*without* repeating the keyword cdef in the block). You need only declare the functions and variables that you want to use in your Pyrex code; Pyrex does not read the C header file, but rather trusts your Pyrex declarations in the block, without generating any C code for them. Do *not* use const in your Pyrex declarations, since const is not a keyword known to Pyrex!

cdef classes

A cdef class statement lets you define a new Python type in Pyrex. It may include cdef declarations of attributes (which apply to every instance, not to the type as a whole), which are normally invisible from Python code; however, you can specifically declare attributes as cdef public to make them normal attributes from Python's viewpoint, or cdef readonly to make them visible but read-only from Python (such Python-visible attributes must be numbers, strings, or objects).

A cdef class supports special methods (with some caveats), properties (with a special syntax), and inheritance (single inheritance only). To declare a property, use the following within the body of the cdef class:

```
property name:
```

then use indented, def statements for methods __get__(self), __set__(self, value), and __del__(self) (you may omit one or more of these methods if the property must not allow setting or deletion).

A cdef class's __new__ is different from that of a normal Python class: the first argument is self, the new instance, already allocated and with its memory filled with 0s. At object destruction time, Pyrex calls a special method __dealloc__(self) to let you undo whatever allocations __new__ may have done (cdef classes have no __del__ special method).

There are no *righthand-side* versions of arithmetic special methods, such as __radd__ to go with __add__, like in Python; rather, if (say) a+b can't find or use type(a).__add__, it next calls type(b).__add__(a, b)—note the order of arguments (*no* swapping!). You may need to attempt some type checking to ensure that you perform the correct operation in all cases.

To make the instances of a cdef class into iterators, define a special method __next__(self), not a method called next as you would do in Python.

Here is a Pyrex equivalent of Example 25-2:

```
cdef class intpair:
    cdef public int first, second
    def __init__(self, first, second):
        self.first = first
        self.second = second
    def __repr__(self):
        return 'intpair(%s,%s)' % (self.first, self.second)
```

Like the C-coded extension in Example 25-2, this Pyrex-coded extension also offers no substantial advantage with respect to a Python-coded equivalent. However, note that the simplicity and conciseness of the Pyrex code is much closer to that of Python than to the verbosity and boilerplate needed in C, and yet the machine code generated from this Pyrex file is very close to what gets generated from the C code in Example 25-2.

The ctypedef Statement

You can use the keyword ctypedef to declare a name (synonym) for a type:

```
ctypedef char* string
```

The for...from Statement

In addition to the usual Python statements, Pyrex allows another form of for statement:

```
for variable from lower_expression<=variable<upper_expression:
```

This is the most common form, but you can use either < or <= on either side of the variable after the from keyword; alternatively, you can use > and/or >= to have a backward loop (but you cannot mix a < or <= on one side and > or >= on the other). This statement is much faster than the usual Python for variable in range(...):, as long as the variable and both loop boundaries are all C-kind ints.

Pyrex Expressions

In addition to Python expression syntax, Pyrex can use some, but not all, of C's additions to it. To take the address of variable *var*, use &*var*, like in C. To dereference a pointer *p*, however, use *p*[0]; the C syntax **p* is not valid Pyrex. Similarly, where in C you would use *p*->*q*, use *p.q* in Pyrex. The null pointer uses the Pyrex keyword NULL. For character constants, use the syntax c'x'. For casts, use angle brackets—such as <int>*somefloat* where in C you would code (int)*somefloat*—also, use only casts on C values and onto C types, *never* with Python values and types (let Pyrex perform type conversion for you automatically when Python values or types occur).

A Pyrex Example: Greatest Common Divisor

Euclid's algorithm for GCD (Greatest Common Divisor) of two numbers is, of course, quite simple to implement in pure Python:

```python
def gcd(dividend, divisor):
    remainder = dividend % divisor
    while remainder:
        dividend = divisor
        divisor = remainder
        remainder = dividend % divisor
    return divisor
```

The Pyrex version is very similar:

```python
def gcd(int dividend, int divisor):
    cdef int remainder
    remainder = dividend % divisor
    while remainder:
        dividend = divisor
        divisor = remainder
        remainder = dividend % divisor
    return divisor
```

On my laptop, gcd(454803,278255) takes about 6 microseconds in the Python version, while the Pyrex version takes 1.75 microseconds. A speed three to four times faster for so little effort can be well worth the bother (assuming, of course, that this function takes up a substantial fraction of your program's execution time!), even though the pure Python version could have several practical advantages (it runs in Jython or IronPython just as well as in Classic Python, it works with longs just as well as with ints, it's perfectly cross-platform, and so on).

26

Extending and Embedding Jython

Jython implements the Python language on a Java Virtual Machine (JVM). Jython's built-in objects, such as numbers, sequences, dictionaries, and files, are coded in Java. To extend Classic Python with C, you code C modules using the Python C API (as covered in "Extending Python with Python's C API" on page 614). To extend Jython with Java, you do not have to code Java modules in special ways: every Java package on the Java CLASSPATH (or on Jython's sys.path) is automatically available to your Jython scripts and Jython interactive sessions for use with the import statement covered in "The import Statement" on page 140. This automatic availability applies to Java's standard libraries, third-party Java libraries you have installed, and Java classes you have coded yourself. You can extend Java with C using the Java Native Interface (JNI), and such extensions will be available to Jython code, just as if they were coded in pure Java rather than in JNI-compliant C.

For details on interoperation between Java and Jython, I recommend *Jython Essentials*, by Samuele Pedroni and Noel Rappin (O'Reilly). In this chapter, I offer a brief overview of the simplest interoperation scenarios, just enough for a large number of practical needs. In most cases, importing, using, extending, and implementing Java classes and interfaces in Jython *just works*. In some cases, however, you need to be aware of issues related to accessibility, type conversions, and overloading, as covered in this chapter. Embedding the Jython interpreter in Java-coded applications is similar to embedding the Python interpreter in C-coded applications (as covered in "Embedding Python" on page 647), but the Jython task is easier. Jython offers yet another possibility for interoperation with Java, using the *jythonc* compiler to turn your Python sources into classic, static JVM bytecode .*class* and .*jar* files. You can then use these bytecode files in Java applications and frameworks, exactly as if their source code had been in Java rather than in Python.

In this book, I do not cover the very similar task of extending and embedding IronPython with C# or other languages running on the CLR (Microsoft .NET, or the Mono open source implementation of CLR). However, most issues you will meet during this task are very similar to those covered in this chapter, considering the similarities between C# and Java, and the fact that the same programmer, Jim Hugunin, was responsible for initiating both Jython and IronPython. See *http://ironpython.com* for all details about IronPython, including ones related to extending and embedding tasks. At the time of this writing, the site *http://ironpython.com* was not being actively maintained, and the most up-to-date site about IronPython was instead *http://workspaces.gotdotnet.com/ironpython*. However, the IronPython team plans to revive *http://ironpython.com*, making it once more the reference site for IronPython, as soon as the team has released IronPython 1.0, which should be out by the time you read this book.

Importing Java Packages in Jython

Unlike Java, Jython does not implicitly and automatically import java.lang. Your Jython code can explicitly import java.lang, or even just import java, and then use classes such as java.lang.System and java.lang.String as if they were Python classes. Specifically, your Jython code can use imported Java classes as if they were Python classes with a __slots__ class attribute (i.e., you cannot create arbitrary new instance attributes). You can subclass a Java class with your own Python class, and instances of your class do let you create new attributes just by binding them, as usual.

You may choose to import a top-level Java package (such as java) rather than specific subpackages (such as java.lang). Your Python code acquires the ability to access all subpackages when you import the top-level package. For example, after import java, your code can use classes java.lang.String, java.util.Vector, and so on.

The Jython runtime wraps every Java class you import in a transparent proxy, which manages communication between Python and Java code behind the scenes. This gives an extra reason to avoid the dubious idiom from *somewhere* import *, in addition to the reasons mentioned in "The from ... import * statement" on page 143. When you perform such a bulk import, the Jython runtime must build proxy wrappers for *all* the Java classes in package *somewhere*, spending substantial amounts of memory and time wrapping many classes your code will probably not use. Avoid from ... import *, except for occasional convenience in interactive exploratory sessions, and stick with the import statement. Alternatively, it's okay to use specific, explicit from statements for classes you know your Python code specifically wants to use (e.g., from java.lang import System).

The Jython Registry

Jython relies on a *registry* of Java properties as a cross-platform equivalent of the kind of settings that would normally use the Windows Registry, or environment variables on Unix-like systems. Jython's registry file is a standard Java properties file named *registry*, located in a directory known as the Jython root directory. The Jython root directory is normally the directory where *jython.jar* is located, but you can override this by setting Java properties python.home or install.root. For special needs, you may tweak the Jython registry settings via an auxiliary Java properties file named *.jython* in your home directory, and/or via command-line options to the *jython* interpreter command. The registry option `python.path` is equivalent to Classic Python's `PYTHONPATH` environment variable. This is the option you may most often be interested in, as it can help you install extra Python packages outside of the Jython installation directories (e.g., sharing pure-Python packages that you have already installed for CPython use).

Accessibility

Normally, your Jython code can access only `public` features (methods, fields, inner classes) of Java classes. You may also choose to make `private` and `protected` features available by setting an option in the Jython registry before you run Jython:

```
python.security.respectJavaAccessibility=false
```

Such bending of normal Java rules is not necessary for normal operation. However, the ability to access private and protected features may be useful in Jython scripts meant to thoroughly test a Java package, which is why Jython gives you this option.

Type Conversions

The Jython runtime transparently converts data between Python and Java. However, when a Java method expects a `boolean` argument, you have to pass an `int` or an instance of `java.lang.Boolean` in order to call that method from Python. In Python, any object can be taken as true or false, but Jython does not perform the conversion to `boolean` implicitly on method calls to avoid confusion and the risk of errors. The new Version 2.2 of Jython, which is only out in alpha-stage at the time of this writing, also supports the more natural choice of Python type `bool` for this purpose.

Calling overloaded Java methods

A Java class can supply *overloaded* methods (i.e., several methods with the same name, distinguished by the number and types of their arguments). Jython resolves calls to overloaded methods at runtime, based on the number and types of arguments that Python code passes in each given call. If Jython's implicit overload resolution is not giving the results you expect, you can help it along by explicitly passing instances of Java's `java.lang` wrapper classes, such as `java.lang.Integer` where the Java method expects an `int` argument, `java.lang.Float` where the Java method expects a `float` argument, and so on. For example, if a Java class `C` supplies a method `M` in two overloaded versions, `M(long x)` and `M(int x)`, consider the following code:

```
import C, java.lang

c = C( )
c.M(23)                     # calls M(long)
c.M(java.lang.Integer(23))  # calls M(int)
```

`c.M(23)` calls the `long` overloaded method due to the rules of Jython overload resolution. `c.M(java.lang.Integer(23))`, however, explicitly calls the `int` overloaded method.

The jarray module

When you pass Python sequences to Java methods that expect array arguments, Jython performs automatic conversion, copying each item of the Python sequence into an element of the Java array. When you call a Java method that accepts and modifies an array argument, the Python sequence that you pass cannot reflect any changes the Java method performs on its array argument. To let you effectively call methods that change their array arguments, Jython offers module `jarray`, which supplies two factory functions that let you build Java arrays directly.

---

array   `array(seq,typecode)`

seq is any Python sequence. *typecode* is either a Java class or a single character (specifying a primitive Java type according to Table 26-1). array creates a Java array *a* with the same length as *seq* and elements of the class or type given by *typecode*. array initializes *a*'s elements from *seq*'s corresponding items.

Table 26-1. Typecodes for the jarray module

Typecode	Java type
'b'	Byte
'c'	Char
'd'	Double
'f'	Float
'h'	Short
'i'	Int
'l'	Long
'z'	Boolean

---

zeros   `zeros(length,typecode)`

Creates a Java array *z* with length *length* and elements of the class or type given by *typecode*, which has the same meaning as in function array. zeros initializes each element of *z* to 0, null, or false, as appropriate for the type or class. Of course, when you access such elements from Jython code, you see them as the equivalent Python 0 values (or None as the Jython equivalent of Java null), but when Java code accesses the elements, it sees them with the appropriate Java types and values.

You can use instances created by functions array and zeros as Python sequences of fixed length. When you pass such an instance to a Java method that accepts an array argument and modifies the argument, the changes are visible in the instance you passed so that your Python code can effectively call such methods.

The java.util collection classes

Jython performs no automatic conversion either way between Python containers and the collection classes of package java.util, such as java.util.Vector, java.util.Dictionary, and so on. However, Jython adds to the wrappers it builds for the Java collection classes a minimal amount of support to let you treat instances of collection classes as Python sequences, iterables, or mappings, as appropriate.

Subclassing a Java Class

A Python class may inherit from a Java class (equivalent to Java construct extends) and/or from Java interfaces (equivalent to Java construct implements), as well as from other Python classes. A Jython class cannot inherit, directly or indirectly, from more than one Java class. There is no limit on inheriting from interfaces. Your Jython code can access protected methods of the Java superclass, but not protected fields. You can override non-final superclass methods. In particular, you should always override the methods of interfaces you inherit from and abstract methods, if any, when your superclass is abstract. If a method is overloaded in the superclass, your overriding method must support all of the signatures of the overloads. To accomplish this, you can define your method to accept a variable number of arguments (by having its last formal argument use special form *args) and check at runtime for the number and types of arguments you receive on each call to know which overloaded variant was called.

JavaBeans

Jython offers special support for the JavaBeans idiom of naming accessor methods get*SomeThing*, is*SomeThing*, set*SomeThing*. When such methods exist in a Java class, Python code can access and set a property named *someThing* on instances of that Java class, using Python syntax for attribute access and binding: the Jython runtime transparently translates that syntax into calls to appropriate accessor methods.

Embedding Jython in Java

Your Java-coded application can embed the Jython interpreter in order to use Jython for scripting. *jython.jar* must be in your Java CLASSPATH. Your Java code must import `org.python.core.*` and `org.python.util.*` in order to access Jython's classes. To initialize Jython's state and instantiate an interpreter, use the Java statements:

```
PySystemState.initialize( );
PythonInterpreter interp = new PythonInterpreter( );
```

Jython also supplies several advanced overloads of this method and constructor in order to let you determine in detail how `PySystemState` is set up, and to control the system state and global scope for each interpreter instance. However, in typical, simple cases, the previous Java code is all your application needs.

The PythonInterpreter Class

Once you have an instance *interp* of class `PythonInterpreter`, you can call method *interp*.eval to have the interpreter evaluate a Python expression held in a Java string. You can also call any of several overloads of *interp*.exec and *interp*.execfile to have the interpreter execute Python statements held in a Java string, a precompiled Jython code object, a file, or a Java `InputStream`.

The Python code you execute can `import` your Java classes in order to access your application's functionality. Your Java code can set attributes in the interpreter namespace by calling overloads of *interp*.set, and get attributes from the interpreter namespace by calling overloads of *interp*.get. The methods' overloads give you a choice. You can work with native Java data and let Jython perform type conversions, or you can work directly with `PyObject`, the base class of all Python objects, covered in "The PyObject Class" on page 661. The most frequently used methods and overloads of a `PythonInterpreter` instance *interp* are the following.

eval	PyObject *interp*.eval(String s)
	Evaluates, in *interp*'s namespace, the Python expression held in Java string s, and returns the PyObject that is the expression's result.
exec	void *interp*.exec(String s) void *interp*.exec(PyObject code)
	Executes, in *interp*'s namespace, the Python statements held in Java string s or in compiled PyObject code (produced by function __builtin__.compile of package org.python.core, covered in "The __builtin__ class" on page 661).
execfile	void *interp*.execfile(String name) void *interp*.execfile(java.io.InputStream s) void *interp*.execfile(java.io.InputStream s,String name)
	Executes, in *interp*'s namespace, the Python statements read from the stream s or from the file name. When you pass both s and name, execfile reads the statements from s and uses name as the filename in error messages.

get	PyObject *interp*.get(String *name*) Object *interp*.get(String *name*,Class *javaclass*)
	Fetches the value of the attribute *name* from *interp*'s namespace. The overload with two arguments also converts the value to the specified *javaclass*, throwing a Java PyException exception that wraps a Python TypeError if the conversion is unfeasible. Either overload raises a NullPointerException if *name* is unbound. Typical use of the two-argument form might be a Java statement such as:
	`String s = (String)interp.get("attname", String.class);`

set	void *interp*.set(String *name*,PyObject *value*) void *interp*.set(String *name*,Object *value*)
	Binds the attribute named *name* in *interp*'s namespace to *value*. The second overload also converts the value to a PyObject.

The _ _builtin_ _ class

The org.python.core package supplies a class _ _builtin_ _ whose static methods let your Java code access the functionality of Python built-in functions. The compile method, in particular, is quite similar to Python built-in function compile, covered in compile on page 160. Your Java code can call compile with three String arguments (a string of source code, a filename to use in error messages, and a *kind* that is normally "exec"), and compile returns a PyObject instance *p* that is a precompiled Python bytecode object. You can repeatedly call *interp*.exec(*p*) to execute the Python statements in *p* without the overhead of compiling the Python source for each execution. The advantages are the same as those covered in "Compile and Code Objects" on page 329.

The PyObject Class

Seen from Java, all Jython objects are instances of classes that extend PyObject. Class PyObject supplies methods named like Python objects' special methods, such as _ _len_ _, _ _str_ _, and so on. Concrete subclasses of PyObject override some special methods to supply meaningful implementations. For example, _ _len_ _ makes sense for Python sequences and mappings, but not for numbers; _ _add_ _ makes sense for numbers and sequences, but not for mappings. When your Java code calls a special method on a PyObject instance that does not in fact supply the method, the call raises a Java PyException exception that wraps a Python AttributeError.

PyObject methods that set, get, and delete attributes exist in two overloads, as the attribute name can be a PyString or a Java String. PyObject methods that set, get, and delete items exist in three overloads, as the key or index can be a PyObject, a Java String, or an int. The Java String instances that you use as attribute names or item keys must be Java interned strings (i.e., either string literals or the result of calling s.intern( ) on any Java String instance s). In addition to the usual Python special methods __getattr__ and __getitem__, class PyObject provides similar methods __findattr__ and __finditem__, the difference being that, when the attribute or item is not found, the __find... methods return a Java null, while the __get... methods raise exceptions.

Every PyObject instance *p* has a method __tojava__ that takes a single argument, a Java Class *c*, and returns an Object that is the value of *p* converted to *c* (or raises an exception if the conversion is unfeasible). Typical use might be a Java statement such as:

```
String s = (String)mypyobj.__tojava__(String.class);
```

Method __call__ of PyObject has several convenience overloads, but the semantics of all the overloads boil down to __call__'s fundamental form:

```
PyObject p.__call__(PyObject args[], String keywords[]);
```

When array *keywords* has length *L*, array *args* must have length *N* >= *L*, and the last *L* items of *args* are taken as named arguments, the names being the corresponding items in *keywords*. When *args* has length *N* > *L*, *args*'s first *N-L* items are taken as positional actual arguments. The equivalent Python code is therefore similar to:

```
def docall(p, args, keywords):
    assert len(args) >= len(keywords)
    deltalen = len(args) - len(keywords)
    return p(*args[:deltalen], ** dict(zip(keywords, args[deltalen:])))
```

Jython supplies concrete subclasses of PyObject that represent all built-in Python types. You can instantiate such a concrete subclass in order to create a PyObject for further use. For example, class PyList extends PyObject, implements a Python list, and has constructors that take an array or a java.util.Vector of PyObject instances, as well as an empty constructor that builds the empty list [].

The Py Class

The Py class supplies several utility class attributes and static methods. Py.None is Python's None. Method Py.java2py takes a Java Object argument and returns the corresponding PyObject. Methods Py.py2*type*, for all values of *type* that name a Java primitive type (boolean, byte, long, short, etc.), take a PyObject argument and return the corresponding value of the given primitive Java type.

Compiling Python into Java

Jython comes with the *jythonc* compiler. You can feed *jythonc* your *.py* source files, and *jythonc* compiles them into normal JVM bytecode and packages them into *.class* and *.jar* files. Since *jythonc* generates traditional static bytecode, it cannot quite cope with the whole range of dynamic possibilities that Python allows. For example, *jythonc* cannot successfully compile Python classes that determine their base classes dynamically at runtime, as the normal Python interpreters allow. However, except for such extreme examples of dynamically changeable class structures, *jythonc* does support compilation of essentially the whole Python language into Java bytecode.

The jythonc Command

jythonc resides in the *Tools/jythonc* directory of your Jython installation. You invoke it from a shell (console) command line with the syntax:

```
jythonc options modules
```

options are zero or more option flags starting with --. *modules* are zero or more names of Python source files to compile, either as Python-style names of modules residing on Python's sys.path, or as relative or absolute paths to Python source files. Include the *.py* extension in each path to a source file, but not in a module name.

More often than not, you will specify the *jythonc* option *--jar jarfile* to build a *.jar* file of compiled bytecode rather than separate *.class* files. Most other options deal with what to put in the *.jar* file. You can choose to make the file self-sufficient (for browsers and other Java runtime environments that do not support the use of multiple *.jar* files) at the expense of making the file larger. Option *--all* ensures all Jython core classes are copied into the *.jar* file, while *--core* tries to be more conservative, copying as few core classes as feasible. Option *--addpackages packages* lets you list (in *packages*, a comma-separated list) those external Java packages whose classes are copied into the *.jar* file if any of the Python classes *jythonc* is compiling depends on them. An important alternative to *--jar* is *--bean jarfile*, which also includes a bean manifest in the *.jar* file as needed for Python-coded JavaBeans components.

Another useful *jythonc* option is *--package package*, which instructs Jython to place all the new Java classes it's creating in the given *package* (and any subpackages of *package* needed to reflect the Python-side package structure).

Adding Java-Visible Methods

The Java classes that *jythonc* creates normally extend existing classes from Java libraries and/or implement existing interfaces. Other Java-coded applications and frameworks instantiate the *jythonc*-created classes via constructor overloads, which have the same signatures as the constructors of their Java superclasses. The Python-side _ _init_ _ executes after the superclass is initialized, and with the same arguments (therefore, don't _ _init_ _ a Java superclass in the _ _init_ _ of a Python class meant to be compiled by *jythonc*). Afterward, Java code can access the functionality of instances of Python-coded classes by calling instance methods defined in known interfaces or superclasses and overridden by Python code.

Python code can never supply Java-visible static methods or attributes, only instance methods. By default, each Python class supplies only the instance methods it inherits from the Java class it extends or the Java interfaces it implements. However, Python code can also supply other Java-visible instance methods via the @sig directive.

To expose a method of your Python class to Java when *jythonc* compiles the class, code the method's docstring as @sig followed by a Java method signature. For example:

```
class APythonClass:
    def __init__ _(self, greeting="Hello, %s!"):
        "@sig public APythonClass(String greeting)"
        self.greeting = greeting
    def hello(self, name):
        "@sig public String hello(String name)"
        return self.greeting % name
```

To expose a constructor, use the @sig signature for the class, as shown in the previous example's __init__ method docstring. All names of classes in @sig signatures must be fully qualified, except for names that come from java.lang and names supplied by the Python-coded module being compiled. When a Python method with a @sig has optional arguments, *jythonc* generates Java-visible overloads of the method with each legal signature and deals with supplying the default argument values where needed. An __init__ constructor with a @sig, for a Python class that extends a Java class, implicitly initializes the superclass using the superclass's empty constructor.

Since a Python class cannot expose data attributes directly to Java, you may need to code accessors with the usual JavaBeans convention and expose them via the @sig mechanism. For example, instances of APythonClass in the above example do not allow Java code to directly access or change the greeting attribute. When such functionality is needed, you can supply it in a subclass as follows:

```
class APythonBean(APythonClass):
    def getGreeting(self):
        "@sig public String getGreeting( )"
        return self.greeting
    def setGreeting(self, greeting):
        "@sig public void setGreeting(String greeting)"
        self.greeting = greeting
```

Python Applets and Servlets

Two simple examples of using Jython within existing Java frameworks are applets and servlets. Applets are typical examples of *jythonc* use (with specific caveats), while servlets are specifically supported by a Jython-supplied utility.

Python applets

A Jython applet class must import java.applet.Applet and extend it, typically overriding method paint and others. You compile the applet into a *.jar* file by calling *jythonc* with options *--jar somejar.jar* and either *--core* or *--all*. Normally, Jython is installed in a modern Java 2 environment, which is okay for most uses. It is fine for applets, as long as the applets run only in browsers that support Java 2, typically with a Sun-supplied browser plug-in. However, if you need to support browsers that are limited to Java 1.1, you must ensure that the JDK you use is Release 1.1, and that you compile your applet with Jython under a JDK 1.1 environment. It's possible to share a single Jython installation between different JDKs, such as 1.1 and 1.4. However, I suggest you perform separate installations of Jython, one under each JDK you need to support, in separate directories, in order to minimize the risk of confusion and accidents.

Python servlets

You can use *jythonc* to build and deploy servlets. However, Jython also supports an alternative that lets you deploy Python-coded servlets as source *.py* files. Use the servlet class org.python.util.PyServlet, supplied with Jython, and a servlet mapping of all **.py* URLs to PyServlet. Each servlet *.py* file must reside in the *web-app* top-level directory, and must expose an object callable without arguments (normally a class) with the same name as the file. PyServlet uses that callable as a factory for instances of the servlet, and calls methods on the instance according to the Java Servlet API. Your servlet instance, in turn, accesses Servlet API objects such as the *request* and *response* objects, passed as method arguments, and these objects' attributes and methods, such as *response*.outputStream and *request*.getSession. PyServlet provides an excellent, fast-turnaround way to experiment with servlets and rapidly deploy them.

27

Distributing Extensions and Programs

Python's distutils allows you to package Python programs and extensions in several ways, and to install programs and extensions to work with your Python installation. As I mentioned in "Building and Installing C-Coded Python Extensions" on page 614, distutils also affords the simplest and most effective way to build C-coded extensions you write yourself, even when you are not interested in distributing such extensions to anybody else. This chapter covers distutils, as well as third-party tools that complement distutils and let you package Python programs for distribution as standalone applications, installable on machines with specific hardware and operating systems without a separate installation of Python. A simpler and more powerful way to package Python programs and extensions is offered by the freely downloadable third-party framework covered in "Python Eggs" on page 151.

Python's distutils

distutils is a rich and flexible set of tools to package Python programs and extensions for distribution to third parties. I cover typical, simple uses of distutils for the most common packaging needs. For an in-depth, highly detailed discussion of distutils, I recommend two manuals that are part of Python's online documentation: *Distributing Python Modules* (available at *http://www.python.org/doc/current/dist/*) and *Installing Python Modules* (available at *http://www.python.org/doc/current/inst/*), both by Greg Ward, the principal author of distutils.

The Distribution and Its Root

A *distribution* is the set of files to package into a single file for distribution purposes. A distribution may include zero, one, or more Python packages and other Python modules (as covered in Chapter 7), as well as, optionally, Python scripts, C-coded (and other) extensions, supporting datafiles, and auxiliary files containing metadata about the distribution itself. A distribution is said to be *pure* if all code it includes is Python, and *nonpure* if it includes non-Python code (most often, C-coded or Pyrex extensions).

You should normally place all the files of a distribution in a directory, known as the *distribution root directory*, and in subdirectories of the distribution root. Mostly, you can arrange the subtree of files and directories rooted at the distribution root to suit your own organizational needs. However, as covered in "Packages" on page 149, a Python package must reside in its own directory, and a package's directory must contain a file named *__init__.py* (and subdirectories with *__init__.py* files, for the package's subpackages, if any) as well as other modules that belong to that package.

The setup.py Script

The distribution root directory must contain a Python script that by convention is named *setup.py*. The *setup.py* script can, in theory, contain arbitrary Python code. However, in practice, *setup.py* always boils down to some variation of:

```
from distutils.core import setup, Extension

setup( many named arguments go here )
```

All the action is in the parameters you supply in the call to setup. You should not import Extension if your *setup.py* deals with a pure distribution. Extension is needed only for nonpure distributions, and you should import it only when you need it. It is fine, of course, to have a few statements before the call to setup in order to arrange setup's arguments in clearer and more readable ways than could be managed by having everything inline as part of the setup call.

The distutils.core.setup function accepts only named arguments, and there are a large number of such arguments that you could potentially supply. A few arguments deal with the internal operations of distutils itself, and you never supply such arguments unless you are extending or debugging distutils, an advanced subject that I do not cover in this book. Other named arguments to setup fall into two groups: metadata about the distribution and information about which files are in the distribution.

Metadata About the Distribution

You should provide metadata about the distribution by supplying some of the following keyword arguments when you call the distutils.core.setup function. The value you associate with each argument name you supply is a string, intended mostly to be human-readable; the specifications about the string's format are mostly advisory. The explanations and recommendations about the metadata fields in the following are also non-normative and correspond only to common, not universal, conventions. Whenever the following explanations refer to "this distribution," the phrase can be taken to refer to the material included in the distribution rather than to the packaging of the distribution:

author
> The name(s) of the author(s) of material included in the distribution. You should always provide this information, since authors deserve credit for their work.

author_email
> Email address(es) of the author(s) named in argument author. You should provide this information only if the author is willing to receive email about this work.

classifiers
> A list of Trove strings to classify your package; each string must be one of those listed at *http://www.python.org/pypi?%3Aaction=list_classifiers*.

contact
> The name of the principal contact person or mailing list for this distribution. You should provide this information if there is somebody who should be contacted in preference to people named in arguments author and maintainer.

contact_email
> Email address of the contact named in argument contact. You should provide this information if and only if you supply the contact argument.

description
> A concise description of this distribution, preferably fitting within one line of 80 characters or less. You should always provide this information.

fullname
> The full name of this distribution. You should provide this information if the name supplied as argument name is in abbreviated or incomplete form (e.g., an acronym).

keywords
> A list of keywords that would likely be searched for by somebody looking for the functionality provided by this distribution. You should provide this information if it might prove useful to somebody indexing this distribution in a search engine.

license
> The licensing terms of this distribution, in a concise form that may refer for details to a file in the distribution or to a URL. You should always provide this information.

maintainer
> The name(s) of the current maintainer(s) of this distribution. You should normally provide this information if the maintainer is different from the author.

`maintainer_email`

> Email address(es) of the maintainer(s) named in argument `maintainer`. You should provide this information only if you supply the `maintainer` argument and if the maintainer is willing to receive email about this work.

`name`

> The name of this distribution as a valid Python identifier (this often requires abbreviations, e.g., as an acronym). You should always provide this information.

`platforms`

> A list of platforms on which this distribution is known to work. You should provide this information if you have reasons to believe this distribution may not work everywhere. This information should be reasonably concise, so this field may refer for details to a file in the distribution or to a URL.

`url`

> A URL at which more information can be found about this distribution. You should always provide this information if any such URL exists.

`version`

> The version of this distribution and/or its contents, normally structured as *major.minor* or even more finely. You should always provide this information.

Distribution Contents

A distribution can contain a mix of Python source files, C-coded extensions, and datafiles. `setup` accepts optional keyword arguments that detail which files to put in the distribution. Whenever you specify file paths, the paths must be relative to the distribution root directory and use / as the path separator. `distutils` adapts location and separator appropriately when it installs the distribution. Note, however, that the keyword arguments `packages` and `py_modules` do not list file paths, but rather Python packages and modules, respectively. Therefore, in the values of these keyword arguments, don't use path separators or file extensions. When you list subpackage names in argument `packages`, use Python syntax instead (e.g., *top_package.sub_package*).

Python source files

By default, `setup` looks for Python modules (which you list in the value of the keyword argument `py_modules`) in the distribution root directory, and for Python packages (which you list in the value of the keyword argument `packages`) as subdirectories of the distribution root directory. You may specify keyword argument `package_dir` to change these defaults. However, things are simpler when you locate files according to `setup`'s defaults, so I do not cover `package_dir` further in this book.

The `setup` keyword arguments you will most frequently use to detail which Python source files are part of the distribution are the following.

packages packages=[*list of package name strings*]

For each package name string *p* in the list, setup expects to find a subdirectory *p* in the distribution root directory and includes in the distribution the file *p/_ _init_ _.py*, which must be present, as well as any other file *p/*.py* (i.e., all the modules of package *p*). setup does not search for subpackages of *p*: you must explicitly list all subpackages, as well as top-level packages, in the value of keyword argument packages.

py_modules py_modules=[*list of module name strings*]

For each module name string *m* in the list, setup expects to find a file *m.py* in the distribution root directory and includes *m.py* in the distribution.

scripts scripts=[*list of script file path strings*]

Scripts are Python source files that are meant to be run as main programs (generally from the command line). The value of the scripts keyword lists the path strings of these files, complete with *.py* extension, relative to the distribution root directory.

Each script file should have as its first line a shebang line, i.e., a line starting with #! and containing the substring python. When distutils installs the scripts included in the distribution, distutils alters each script's first line to point to the Python interpreter. This is quite useful on many platforms, since the shebang line is used by the platform's shells or by other programs that may run your scripts, such as web servers.

Datafiles

To put datafiles of any kind in the distribution, supply the following keyword argument.

data_files data_files=[*list of pairs* (*target_directory*,[*list of files*])]

The value of keyword argument data_files is a list of pairs. Each pair's first item is a string and names a *target directory* (i.e., a directory where distutils places datafiles when installing the distribution); the second item is the list of file path strings for files to put in the target directory. At installation time, distutils places each target directory as a subdirectory of Python's sys.prefix for a pure distribution, or of Python's sys.exec_prefix for a nonpure distribution. distutils places the given files directly in the respective target directory, never in subdirectories of the target. For example, given the following data_files usage:

```
data_files = [('miscdata', ['conf/config.txt', 'misc/
sample.txt'])]
```

distutils includes in the distribution the file *config.txt* from subdirectory *conf* of the distribution root, and the file *sample.txt* from subdirectory *misc* of the distribution root. At installation time, distutils creates a subdirectory named *miscdata* in Python's sys.prefix directory (or in the sys.exec_prefix directory, if the distribution is nonpure), and copies the two files into *miscdata/config.txt* and *miscdata/sample.txt*.

C-coded extensions

To put C-coded extensions in the distribution, supply the following keyword argument.

ext_modules　　ext_modules=[*list of instances of class* Extension]

All the details about each extension are supplied as arguments when instantiating the distutils.core.Extension class.

Extension's constructor accepts two mandatory arguments and many optional keyword arguments, as follows.

Extension　　class Extension(*name, sources, **kwds*)

name is the module name string for the C-coded extension. *name* may include dots to indicate that the extension module resides within a package. *sources* is the list of C source files that the distutils must compile and link in order to build the extension. Each item of *sources* is a string that gives a source file's path relative to the distribution root directory, complete with file extension .*c*. *kwds* lets you pass other, optional arguments to Extension, as covered later in this section.

The Extension class also supports other file extensions besides *.c*, indicating other languages you may use to code Python extensions. On platforms having a C++ compiler, file extension *.cpp* indicates C++ source files. Other file extensions that may be supported, depending on the platform and on various add-ons to the distutils, include *.f* for Fortran, *.i* for SWIG, and *.pyx* for Pyrex files. See "Extending Python Without Python's C API" on page 645 for information about using different languages to extend Python.

In some cases, your extension needs no further information besides mandatory arguments *name* and *sources*. distutils implicitly performs all that is necessary to make the Python headers directory and the Python library available for your extension's compilation and linking, and provides whatever compiler or linker flags or options are needed to build extensions on a given platform.

When additional information is required to compile and link your extension correctly, you can supply such information via the keyword arguments of class Extension. Such arguments may potentially interfere with the cross-platform portability of your distribution. In particular, whenever you specify file or directory paths as the values of such arguments, the paths should be relative to the distribution root directory; using absolute paths seriously impairs your distribution's cross-platform portability.

Portability is not a problem when you just use distutils as a handy way to build your extension, as suggested in "Building and Installing C-Coded Python Extensions" on page 614. However, when you plan to distribute your extensions to other platforms, you should examine whether you really need to provide build information via keyword arguments to Extension. It is sometimes possible to bypass such needs by careful coding at the C level, and the already mentioned *Distributing Python Modules* manual provides important examples.

The keyword arguments that you may pass when calling Extension are the following:

define_macros = [(*macro_name*,*macro_value*) ...]
Each of the items *macro_name* and *macro_value*, in the pairs listed as the value of define_macros, is a string, respectively the name and value for a C preprocessor macro definition, equivalent in effect to the C preprocessor directive:

    #define *macro_name macro_value*

macro_value can also be None, to get the same effect as the C preprocessor directive:

    #define *macro_name*

extra_compile_args = [*list of compile_arg strings*]
Each of the strings *compile_arg* listed as the value of extra_compile_args is placed among the command-line arguments for each invocation of the C compiler.

extra_link_args = [*list of link_arg strings*]
Each of the strings *link_arg* listed as the value of extra_link_args is placed among the command-line arguments for the invocation of the linker.

extra_objects = [*list of object_name strings*]
Each of the strings *object_name* listed as the value of extra_objects names an object file to add to the invocation of the linker. Do not specify the file extension as part of the object name: distutils adds the platform-appropriate file extension (such as *.o* on Unix-like platforms and *.obj* on Windows) to help you keep cross-platform portability.

`include_dirs = [`*`list of directory_path strings`*` ]`
> Each of the strings *directory_path* listed as the value of `include_dirs` identifies a directory to supply to the compiler as one where header files are found.

`libraries = [`*`list of library_name strings`*` ]`
> Each of the strings *library_name* listed as the value of `libraries` names a library to add when invoking of the linker. Do not specify the file extension or any prefix as part of the library name: distutils, in cooperation with the linker, adds the platform-appropriate file extension and prefix (such as *.a*, and a prefix *lib*, on Unix-like platforms, and *.lib* on Windows) to help you keep cross-platform portability.

`library_dirs = [ `*`list of directory_path strings`*` ]`
> Each of the strings *directory_path* listed as the value of `library_dirs` identifies a directory to supply to the linker as one where library files are found.

`runtime_library_dirs = [ `*`list of directory_path strings`*` ]`
> Each of the strings *directory_path* listed as the value of `runtime_library_dirs` identifies a directory where dynamically loaded libraries are found at runtime.

`undef_macros = [ `*`list of macro_name strings`*` ]`
> Each of the strings *macro_name* listed as the value of `undef_macros` is the name for a C preprocessor macro definition, equivalent in effect to the C preprocessor directive:
>
> ```
> #undef macro_name
> ```

The setup.cfg File

distutils lets a user who's installing your distribution specify many options at installation time. Most often the user will simply enter at a command line:

```
C:\> python setup.py install
```

but the already mentioned manual *Installing Python Modules* explains many alternatives. To provide suggested values for installation options, you can put a *setup.cfg* file in your distribution root directory. *setup.cfg* can also provide appropriate defaults for options you can supply to build-time commands. For copious details on the format and contents of file *setup.cfg*, see the already mentioned manual *Distributing Python Modules*.

The MANIFEST.in and MANIFEST Files

When you run:

```
python setup.py sdist
```

to produce a packaged-up source distribution (typically a *.zip* file on Windows or a *.tgz* file, a.k.a. a *tarball*, on Unix), the distutils by default inserts in the distribution:

- All Python and C source files, as well as datafiles, explicitly mentioned or directly implied by your *setup.py* file's options, as covered earlier in this chapter
- Test files, located at *test/test*.py* under the distribution root directory
- Files *README.txt* (if any), *setup.cfg* (if any), and *setup.py*

To add yet more files in the source distribution *.zip* file or tarball, place in the distribution root directory a *manifest template* file named *MANIFEST.in*, whose lines are rules, applied sequentially, about files to add (include) or subtract (prune) from the list of files to place in the distribution. The sdist command of the distutils produces an exact list of the files placed in the source distribution in a text file named *MANIFEST* in the distribution root directory.

Creating Prebuilt Distributions with distutils

The packaged source distributions you create with *python setup.py sdist* are the most useful files you can produce with distutils. However, you can make life even easier for users with specific platforms by also creating prebuilt forms of your distribution with the command *python setup.py bdist*.

For a pure distribution, supplying prebuilt forms is merely a matter of convenience for the users. You can create prebuilt, pure distributions for any platform, including ones different from those on which you work, as long as you have the needed commands (such as *zip*, *gzip*, *bzip2*, and *tar*) available on your path. Such commands are freely available on the Internet for all sorts of platforms, so you can easily stock up on them in order to provide maximum convenience to users who want to install your distribution.

For a nonpure distribution, making prebuilt forms available may be more than just an issue of convenience. A nonpure distribution, by definition, includes code that is not pure Python—generally, C code. Unless you supply a prebuilt form, users need to have the appropriate C compiler installed in order to build and install your distribution. This is not a terrible problem on platforms where the appropriate C compiler is the free and ubiquitous *gcc* (nowadays, this means most Unix-like platforms, including Mac OS X, where *gcc* is part of the free XCode IDE that comes with the operating system). However, on other platforms (mostly Windows), the C compiler needed for normal building of Python extensions is commercial and costly. For example, on Windows, the normal C compiler used by Python and its C-coded extensions is Microsoft Visual Studio (VS 2003, for Python 2.4 and 2.5). It is possible to substitute other compilers, including free ones such as the *mingw32* and *cygwin* versions of *gcc*. However, using such alternative compilers, as documented in the Python online manuals, is rather intricate, particularly for end users who may not be experienced programmers.

Therefore, if you want your nonpure distribution to be widely adopted on such platforms as Windows, it's highly advisable to make your distribution also available in prebuilt form. However, unless you have developed or purchased advanced cross-compilation environments, building a nonpure distribution and packaging it in prebuilt form is feasible only on the target platform. You also need to have the necessary C compiler installed. When all of these conditions are satisfied, however, distutils makes the procedure quite simple. In particular, the command:

```
python setup.py bdist_wininst
```

creates an *.exe* file that is a Windows installer for your distribution. If your distribution is nonpure, the prebuilt distribution is dependent on the specific Python version. The distutils reflect this fact in the name of the *.exe* installer they create for you. Say, for example, that your distribution's name metadata is mydist, your distribution's version metadata is 0.1, and the Python version you use is 2.4. In this case, the distutils build a Windows installer named *mydist-0.1.win32-py2.4.exe*.

py2exe

distutils helps you package your Python extensions and applications. However, an end user can install the resulting packaged form only after installing Python. This is particularly a problem on Windows, where end users want to run a single installer to get an application working on their machine. Installing Python first and then running your application's installer may prove too much of a hassle for such end users.

Thomas Heller has developed a simple solution, a distutils add-on named py2exe, freely available for download from *http://starship.python.net/crew/theller/py2exe/*. This URL also contains detailed documentation of py2exe, and I recommend you study this documentation if you intend to use py2exe in advanced ways. However, the simplest uses, which I cover in the rest of this section, cover most practical needs.

After downloading and installing py2exe (on a Windows machine where Microsoft VS 2003 is also installed), you just need to add the line:

    import py2exe

at the start of your otherwise normal distutils script *setup.py*. Now, in addition to other distutils commands, you have one more option. Running:

    python setup.py py2exe

builds and collects in a subdirectory of your distribution root directory an *.exe* file and one or more *.dll* files. If your distribution's name metadata is, for example, myapp, then the directory into which the *.exe* and *.dll* files are collected is named *dist\myapp*. Any files specified by option data_files in your *setup.py* script are placed in subdirectories of *dist\myapp*. The *.exe* file corresponds to your application's first or only entry in the scripts keyword argument value, and contains the bytecode-compiled form of all Python modules and packages that your *setup.py* specifies or implies. Among the *.dll* files is, at minimum, the Python dynamic load library—for example, *python24.dll* if you use Python 2.4—plus any other *.pyd* or *.dll* files that your application needs, excluding *.dll* files that py2exe knows are system files (i.e., guaranteed to be available on any Windows installation).

py2exe provides no direct means to collect the contents of the *dist\myapp* directory for easy distribution and installation. You have several options, ranging from a *.zip* file (which may be given an *.exe* extension and made self-extracting, in ways that vary depending on the ZIP file–handling tools you choose) all the way to a professional Windows installer construction system, such as those sold by companies such as Wise and InstallShield. One option that is particularly worth considering is Inno Setup, a free, professional-quality installer construction system (see *http://www.jrsoftware.org/isinfo.php*). Since the files to be packaged for end user installation are an *.exe* file, one or more *.dll* files, and perhaps some data files in subdirectories, the issue now becomes totally independent from Python. You may package and redistribute such files just as if they had originally been built from sources written in any other programming language.

py2app

py2app (*http://undefined.org/python/py2app.html*) is a distutils extension that builds standalone Python applications for the Mac. py2app is distributed with PyObjC (*http://pyobjc.sourceforge.net/*), the Python/Objective C bridge that offers an excellent way to create Mac applications with Cocoa interfaces in Python; however, py2app is also fully compatible with all major cross-platform GUI tool-kits for Python, including Tkinter, wxPython, pygame, and PyQt. Moreover, py2app lets you build installer packages (*.mpkg* files) directly. Refer to the URL for all practical usage details.

cx_Freeze

cx_Freeze (*http://starship.python.net/crew/atuining/cx_Freeze/*) is a standalone utility (not a distutils extension) that builds standalone Python applications for Windows and Linux. Refer to the URL for all practical usage details.

PyInstaller

PyInstaller (*http://pyinstaller.hpcf.upr.edu/cgi-bin/trac.cgi*) is another standalone utility that builds standalone Python applications for Windows, Linux, and Irix. Refer to the URL for all practical usage details.

Index

Numbers
4Suite, 591

Symbols
See also
    complete list of operators, Table 4-2,
        50
    regular expression pattern syntax,
        Table 9-2, 201–202
    string-formatting specifier syntax,
        193–194
& (ampersand), set intersection
        operator, 59
<> (angle brackets)
    Tkinter event names, 447
    obsolete form of !=, 50
* (asterisk)
    from statement, 143
    sequence repetition operator, 54
    special form in def parameters, 72
    special form in function call, 75
@ (at-sign), decorators, 37, 115–116
` (backquote), string conversion, 50
\ (backslash)
    in directory paths, 24
    escape sequences in string literals, 42
    joining physical lines into one logical
        line, 34
    in regular expressions, 202

^ (caret), set symmetric difference
        operator, 59
: (colon)
    compound statements, 38
    dictionary literals, 44
, (comma)
    class statement, 82–83
    def statement, 70
    function call, 74
    tuples, 42
{} (curly braces), dictionary literals, 44
$ (dollar sign), in template strings, 196
** (double asterisk)
    exponentiation operator, 53
    special form in def parameters, 72
    special form in function call, 75
== (double equals), equality
        comparison, 53
// (double forward slash), truncating
        division operator, 52–53
" (double quote), string literals, 40–41
__ (double underscore)
    class-private variables, 85
    special methods, 82, 104
… (ellipsis)
    in array slicing, 382–383
    in doctest tracebacks, 456
    prompt in interactive sessions, 25
= (equals)
    assignment, 47
    augmented assignment, 36, 49

We'd like to hear your suggestions for improving our indexes. Send email to *index@oreilly.com*.

= (continued)
    in long-form option strings, 180
    named arguments, 44, 74–75
    optional parameters, 71
! (exclamation point), pdb command,
        467
/ (forward slash)
    in directory paths, 24
    semantics of division, 24, 52–53
- (hyphen)
    command-line options, 23–24, 179
    set difference operator, 59
() (parentheses)
    class statement, 82
    def statement, 70
    function call, 74
    genexps, 79–80
    ternary operator, 51
    tuples, 42
% (percent sign)
    remainder operator, 52
    string formatting, 193
. (period)
    attribute syntax, 46, 84, 87, 89–91
    in docstrings, 73
    in floating-point literals, 39
+ (plus sign)
    to form complex numbers, 40
    sequence concatenation operator, 53
(pound sign)
    comments, 33
    coding directive, 35
    shebang line, 29
; (semicolon)
    not needed at end of line, 34
    separator for multistatement lines,
        24, 37–38
' (single quote), string literals, 40
[] (square brackets)
    indexing, 54, 60, 380
    list comprehensions, 67
    list literals, 43
    slicing, 55, 381–383
""" (triple double quote), string literals,
        40–41
>>> (triple right-angle bracket)
    prompt in interactive sessions, 25
    recognized by doctest, 454–455
''' (triple single quote), string literals,
        40–41

_ (underscore)
    class-private variables, 85
    in gettext (i18n), 274
    in interactive sessions, 25
    module-private variables, 142
| (vertical bar), set union operator, 59

A

Active Server Pages (ASP), 557
ActivePython, 19
ActiveState
    Python Cookbook, 11
    Python IDEs offered by, 27
anydbm module, 286
Apache servers
    installing Python CGI scripts, 552
    Webware/mod_webkit for, 559
Apple Macintosh (see Macintosh)
applets, Jython, 6, 664
applications
    developing, 474
    event-driven, 406, 533
    multithreaded, 350
    Windows, with COM, 676
arguments (when calling functions),
        73–75
arithmetic operators, 52–53, 112–115,
        369–370
ArithmeticError exception, 129
ARPA module, 327
array module, 375
array objects (Numeric module), 378
    attributes and methods, 388–390
    comparisons, 384–385
    factory functions, 385–388
    indexing and slicing, 381–384
    operations, 390–392
    type codes, 379–380
ascii, default encoding in Python,
        199–200
    character to code ordinal (ord), 166
    code ordinal to character (chr), 161
ASP (Active Server Pages), 557
assert statement, 138
AssertionError class (built-in), assert
        statement, 138
assignment statements
    assignment, 47
    augmented assignment, 36, 49
    in long-form option strings, 180

named arguments, 44, 74
  to Numeric.array slices, 383
asynchat module, 537
  performance characteristics, 558
asynchronous programming, 533
asyncore module, 535
  performance characteristics, 558
atexit module, 337
atomic operations, 341, 344
Attr class (minidom module), 602
AttributeError exception, 90
AttributeList class (minidom
        module), 600
attributes
  binding, 84–87
  of class objects, 84
  deleting, 98
  of module objects, 140
  overriding, 95
  unbinding, 84, 87
attributes attribute (Node object), 600
Attributes object (xml.sax
        package), 595
augmented assignment statements, 49
authentication
  SMTP servers, 505
  URL access to network
        protocols, 502

B

bag (see defaultdict type)
base classes, 82–83
base64 module, 561
BaseHTTPServer module, 530
  web server implementation, 558
BaseRequestHandler class (SocketServer
        module), 528
basestring type, 154
benchmarking, 451, 475
Berkeley Database library (see BSD DB)
big-O notation and concepts, 476–479
binaries, downloading and
        installing, 18–19
binary data, encoding as text, 561–563
binary files, 219–220
Binary Large OBjects (see BLOBs)
binary search, 176
binding variables, 46
bisect module, 176
BitmapImage class, 414

blank lines, ignored, 33–34
BLOBs (Binary Large OBjects), 294–295
blocks, indentation and, 34
bool type, 154
Boolean values, 45
Boost Python Library, 645
bound methods, 91
break statement, 68
browsers, 575
BSD DB (Berkeley Database
        library), 287, 289
bsddb module, 288–290
buffer type, 154
buffering, cmd.py and, 357
buffers, file objects, 218
building a list (see list comprehensions)
building a string from pieces, 484
built-in exception classes, 129–132
built-in functions, 158–167
built-in modules, 141
  __import__ function, 147
  loading, 144
built-in types, 155–159
  inheriting from, 83, 98, 103–104
built-in variable __debug__, 138
Button class (Tkinter module), 415
  flash method, 415
bz2 module, 232

C

C compiler, ISO-compliant, installing
        Python and, 14
C library, time module and, 302
C programming language, CPython
        and, 614–646
C++ programming language, extending
        Python with, 645–646
calculator, 25
calendar module, 317–318
call stack, unwinding on
        exceptions, 126
callables, 45
calling functions, 73–74
Canvas class (Tkinter
        module), 436–442
case sensitivity, Windows os.environ
        keys, 354
cdef (in Pyrex), 651–652
CGI (Common Gateway Interface), 545
cgi module, 545–552

CGI scripting, 545
    Content-Type header, 549
    cookies, 553
    error messages, 550
    HTML forms submission, 546
    output, 549
    scripts, 551, 557
CGIHTTPServer module, 530
cgitb module, 551
character sets, 34
Checkbutton class (Tkinter
        module), 415
Cheetah package, 586
CherryPy, 559
child widgets, 420
childNodes attribute (Node object), 600
circular imports, 146
class body, 83–85
class methods, 99
class object, 84–85
class statement, 82
classes, 82–85
    bound and unbound methods, 91–94
    descriptors, 82, 85–86
    inheritance, 94–98
    metaclasses, 116–120
    new-style, 81, 83, 103–104, 117–118
    old-style (classic), 81, 103, 117
Classic Python (see Python)
class-level methods, 99
classmethod type, 99, 154
class-private variables, 85
clauses in compound statements, 38
CLDR (Common Locale Data
        Repository), 276
clients, networking, 493
closure (see nested functions)
cmath module, 365
cmd module, 265–268
code object, 329–332
codecs module, 198–199
CodeWarrior Pro 7 C compiler, 18
coercion (see conversions)
collections module, 173–175
COM, extending Python with, 646
command-line options, 23–24, 179
comments, 33
Common Locale Data Repository
        (CLDR), 278
comparing arrays of numbers, 384
comparing directories, 251–252

comparison operators, 51, 53
    special methods, 104–106
    and unit tests, 460
compiling
    to bytecode, 28, 145
    to code objects, 160, 329
    to EXE or .app files, 675–676
    to Java bytecode, 662–664
complex numbers, 40
complex type, 154
compound statements, 38
compressed files
    bz2 module, 232
    gzip module, 230–232
    tarfile module, 233–235
    zipfile module, 235–239
    zlib module, 239
concatenating many strings into one,
        484
concatenation, sequences, 54
Condition class (threading
        module), 344, 347
conditional operator (see ternary
        operator)
config method, Widget object, 411
Connection object (DBAPI-compliant
        modules), 296
console I/O, 260–265
Console module, 265
constants (see literals)
constructing a list (see list
        comprehensions)
constructing a string from parts, 484
constructor, 86
constructor function, copy_reg
        module, 283
container widgets, 420
containers, special methods
        for, 109–110
    (see also collections module)
ContentHandler class (xml.sax
        package), 594–595
continue statement, 68
control flow statements, 62–69
conversions
    numeric operators, 52
    sequences, 54
converting
    numbers, 155
    strings, 198
cookies, 553

Cooledit program, 27
Coordinated Universal Time
        (UTC), 302
copy module, 172
copy_reg module, pickling
        customization with, 283
cPickle module, 279–281
CPython (Classic Python), 5, 613
    C-coded Python
        extensions, 614–627, 633, 638
    CNRI Open Source GPL-Compatible
        License, 7
    embedding, 647–653
    extending, 614, 645
    installing, 14
    reference counts, 333
CRC checksums, 239
cross-platform portability, 5
cStringIO module, 229
ctypes, 646
currying, 175
curses package, 261
Cursor object (DBAPI), 297–298
custom exceptions, 133
custom metaclasses, 116–119
customization, site and user, 338
cyclic garbage loops, 333
Cygwin, building Python for, 17

D

data types
    Boolean values, 45
    callables, 45
    C-coded, 638
    dictionaries, 44
    None, 45
    numbers, 38
        complex, 40
        floating-point, 39
        integers, 39
    sequences
        iterables, 40
        lists, 43
        strings, 40–42
        tuples, 42
    sets, 43
    user-definable, 81
Database API (see DBAPI)
date/time values, 302–316
    computing moveable feast days, 327
    in ISO 8601 formats, 327
    time-tuple, 302

datetime class, datetime module, 309
DateTime class (mx.DateTime
        module), 319–323
datetime module, 306
DateTimeDelta class (mx.DateTime
        module), 324–326
dateutil module, 313–315
date class, datetime module, 306
DB2 module, 299
DBAPI (Database API) 2.0, 277,
        292–299
dbhash module, 286–287
dbm library, 285
dbm module, 287
DBM modules, 285
    anydbm module, 286
    bsddb module, 288
    dbm/gdbm/dbhash modules, 287
    dumbdbm module, 287
    whichdb module, 287
DCOracle2 module, 299
debugging, 451, 461
    CGI scripts, 531
    HTML, 581
    in IDLE, 470
    inspect module, 462
    pdb module, 466
    race conditions, 351
    traceback module, 466
    warnings module, 471
decimal integer literals, 39
decimal module, 372
declarations
    cdef (in Pyrex), 651–652
    no such thing in Python, 37, 46
decorators, 115
deep copies, 172–173
def statement, 70, 85
default encoding (Unicode), 169, 170,
        298, 338–339
defaultdict type (collections module),
        174–175
defining
    functions, 70
        in class body, 85
    metaclasses, 118
del statement, 49
delimiters, 35, 36
deque type (collections module),
        173–174
descendants, 83
description attribute, 297

descriptors, 85
destructor, 105
development environments, 26
    text editors with Python support, 27
dict type, 154
dictionaries, 44
    exec statement and, 328
    indexing, 60
    membership checking, 60
    methods, 60
    optimizing operations on, 479
DictionaryType attribute (types
        module), 332
DictType attribute (types module), 332
dircmp class, 251
directories (see filesystem operations)
directory paths, distribution
        utilities, 667
dispatcher class (asyncore
        module), 535–536
distributed computing, 516–519
distribution root directory, 667
    setup.py script, 667
distribution utilities (see distutils)
distributions, 667
    root directory of, 667
distutils (distribution utilities), 150, 666
    creating prebuilt distributions, 674
    distribution contents, 669
    distribution root directory, 666
    distutils module, setup function, 667
    distutils package, 151
    providing metadata about
            distribution, 667
    setup.cfg file, 673
    setup.py script, 667
division operators, 52
Django, 559
DLLs (dynamic load libraries), 613
    interoperability of Python release and
            debugging builds, 16
DNS (Domain Name System), 521
docstrings (documentation strings), 72,
        85, 142
doctest module, 454
Document class (minidom
        module), 602–607
Document Object Model (see DOM)
Document Type Definition (DTD), 593
documentation, 10
    embedding/extending Python, 613
documentation strings (see docstrings)

DOM (Document Object Model),
        parsing XML, 599
    minidom module, 599
    pulldom module, 605
    xml.dom package, 599
Domain Name System (DNS), 521
DOMException class (xml.dom
        package), 599
double-ended queue (see deque type)
DTD (Document Type Definition), 593
dumbdbm module, 286–287
dynamic execution, 328
dynamic load libraries (see DLLs)

E

EAFP (easier to ask forgiveness than
        permission), 134
    Queue module and, 343
echo servers
    TCP, 525
    UDP, 527
eGenix GmbH, 306, 319
Element class (minidom
        module), 603–607
ElementTree, 592, 599, 607
ellipsis (...)
    in array slicing, 382–383
    in doctest tracebacks, 456
    prompt in interactive sessions, 25
else clause, loop statements, 69
emacs program, 27
email package, 564
    Encoders module, 570
    functions, 564
    Generator module, 568
    Utils module, 570
email protocols, 503
    poplib module, 503
    smtplib module, 505
embedding/extending
    CPython, 613
    Jython, 655
Encoders module, 570
encoding attribute, 219
encoding binary data as text, 561
    base64 module, 561
    quopri module, 562
    uu module, 563
encodings
    codecs, 198
    default (see default encoding)

Latin-1, 582
network, 561
encodings package, 199
entity references, HTML, 582
Entry class (Tkinter module), 416
enumerate type, 155
environ attribute (os module), 354
environment variables
    process environment, 353
    Python interpreter and, 22
EOFError exception, 165
epoch, 302
equality and inequality, 50, 53
    and hashing, 107
    identity, 162
    special methods, 104–106
    and unit tests, 460
errno module, 240
error handling, 134–138
error messages, 471
    CGI scripting, 550
    file printed to, 127
    traceback messages, 121
escape sequences, strings, 41
etree (see ElementTree)
Event class
    threading module, 344
    Tkinter module, 446
event scheduler, 316
event-driven applications
    GUI applications, 406
    network programs, 533
events, 540
    binding callbacks to, 446
Exception class (built-in), 129
exception classes
    custom, 132
    DBAPI, 293
    standard, 130
exception handling, 121
    exception propagation, 126
    Python 2.5, 124
    try statement, 121–123
exceptions, 121
    C-coded Python extensions, 625
    custom, 133
    exception objects, 129–132
    OSError, 240
    pending, gathering information
        about, 133

raise statement, 128
    standard, hierarchy of, 129
exec statement, 328
    limiting use of, 328, 486
executables, creating, 674–676
execution, 145
    dynamic, 328
exponentiation operators, 53
    ternary exponentiation-and-modulo,
        165, 115
expression statements, 329
expressions, 37, 50
    exec statement and, 329
eXtensible Markup Language (see XML)
extension modules, 5, 153
    C-coded, 615
    portability and, 5
    Python implementations and, 7
    resources for further information, 11
    writing in lower-level languages, 5

F

False, 45
factory functions, 88
FastCGI, 557
Feasts module, 327
FFT (Fast Fourier Transform), 403
FieldStorage class (cgi
        module), 547–548
FIFO (first-in first-out) queue (see deque
        type)
file descriptor operations, 253–256
file extensions, order of, when searching
        filesystem for modules, 145
file objects, 155, 216–221
    file-like objects, polymorphism, 222
    memory-mapped, 360
    tempfile module, 223–224
filecmp module, 250–252
fileinput module, 224–226
files
    compressed, 15
        bz2 module, 232
        gzip module, 230–232
        tarfile module, 233–235
        zipfile module, 235–239
        zlib module, 239
    HTML, getting information
        from, 576
    __init__.py, 667

files *(continued)*
    .jar, Jython and, 6
    jython.jar, 657
    permissions, 242
    .pythonrc.py, 339
    site.py, 338
filesystem operations, 241–256
filesystems, searching for modules, 144
filling text, 197
filters, warnings module, 472
flags argument (compile function), 205
float type, 155
floating-point numbers, 39
    generating pseudorandom, 372
    in string formats, 195
    mathematical functions on, 365
Font class (tkFont module), 433
for statement, 64–68
    else clause, 69
formatter module, 581
formatting strings, 193–195
Fortran, extending Python, 645
Frame class (Tkinter module), 420
from statement
    avoiding from...import, 486
    importing modules from
        packages, 149
    module object, 142
frozenset type, 155
FTP class (ftplib module), 506–509
ftplib module, 493, 507
functional module, 175
functions, 70–80
    built-in, 158–167
    calling and argument passing, 73–74
    C-coded Python extension
        modules, 617
    classes with callable instances,
        93–94, 105
    defining, 70, 85
    function objects, 72–73, 332
    generators, 78–80
    lambda expressions, 78
    nested, 77
    parameters, 71–72
    recursion, 80
__future__, importing, 36, 53

G

gadfly module, 299
garbage collection
    getrefcount function (module sys),
        169
    reference counting (C extensions),
        620
    (see also gc module)
gc module, 333
    disable function, 335
    garbage attribute, 334
gdbm module, 287
generator expressions (genexps), 79–80
Generator module (email package), 568
generators
    functions, 78–80
    generator objects, Python 2.5, 126
genexps (generator expressions), 79–80
getpass module, 258
gettext module, 274–276
GIF (Graphical Interchange
        Format), 414
GIL (global interpreter lock), 341
global statement, 76
global variables, thread synchronization
        and, 346
gmpy module, 373–374
GMT (Greenwich Mean Time),
        retrieving current, 320
GNU, 258
GNU Public License (GPL), 8
GNU Readline Library, 258
GPL (GNU Public License), 8
Graphical Interchange Format (GIF),
        414
graphical user interfaces (see GUIs)
Greenwich Mean Time (GMT),
        retrieving current, 320
Gregorian calendar, 319
GUIs (graphical user interfaces),
        405–450
    other GUI toolkits, 405
    Tkinter package, 405–450
gzip module, 230–232

H

hashing, 43–44, 107, 162
headers, clauses, 38
heapq module, 177

hierarchy of standard exceptions, 129
HTML (HyperText Markup
        Language), 575–590
    forms and CGI scripting, 546
    generating, 586–590
    getting information from (parsing),
        575–585
htmlentitydefs module, 582
htmllib module, 580
HTMLParser class (HTMLParser
        module), 580–585
HTTP protocol, 499, 506
    cookies and, 553
    httplib module, 506
    twisted.protocols package, 540
HTTP servers, 530
HTTPBasicAuthHandler class, 502
HTTPConnection class, 507
HTTPDigestAuthHandler class, 502
httplib module, 493, 506
HTTPPasswordMgrWithDefaultRealm
        class, 502
I ITTPResponse class, 506–507
https protocol, 502, 506
    twisted.protocols package, 540
HTTPSConnection class, 507
HTTPServer class, 530–531
HyperText Markup Language (see
        HTML)

I

IBM DB/2, 299
identifiers, 35
    assignment statements, 47
identity (see is)
IDEs (Integrated Development
        Environments), 22
IDLE (Interactive DeveLopment
        Environment), 26
    debugging in, 470
if statement, 62–63
images, supported by Tkinter
        module, 414
IMAP4 (Internet Message Access
        Protocol version 4), 503
immutable objects, 38
implementations of Python, 5
import statement, 140
in (membership test), 50, 54, 58, 60
    __contains__ special method, 111

indentation, 33
    blocks and, 34
Indexed-Sequential Access Method
        (ISAM), 285
indexing
    assignment statements, 48
    dictionaries, 60
    sequences, 54
industry-specific markup languages, 591
inequality (see equality and inequality)
inheritance
    classic classes, 82, 94–98
    multiple, 133
    new-style object model, 97, 104
    properties and, 101
input/output (see I/O)
inspect module, 332, 462–465
installing, 14
    C-coded Python extensions, 614
    IronPython, 21
    Jython, 20
    Python from binaries, 18
    Python from source code, 14–19
    resident extension modules, 647,
        651, 653
instances, 86–87
    getting and setting attributes, 90–91
    per-instance methods, 103
    pickling, 282–283
int type, 155
integers, 39
    bitwise operations, 53
    converting numbers to, 155
    decimal integer literals, 39
Integrated Development Environments
        (IDEs), 22
interactive command sessions, 265–269
Interactive DeveLopment Environment
        (see IDLE)
interactive sessions, 25
    Python interpreter, 25
    sys.displayhook, 168
internal types, 331
internationalization, 269
    codecs module, 199
    gettext module, 274–276
    locale module, 269–274
    resources, 276
Internet Message Access Protocol
        version 4 (IMAP4), 503
Internet Protocol (IP), 521

Internet servers, 528
interoperability, Python release and
    debugging builds, 16
inter-process communication (see IPC)
introspection, 329–332, 462–466
    dir built-in function, 161
    getattr built-in function, 162
I/O (input/output)
    console, 260–265
    getpass module, 258
    operations, optimizing, 488
    print statement, 256
    readline module, 258–260
    stderr, 256
    stadin, 257
    stdout, 256
IP (Internet Protocol), 521
IPC (inter-process communication), 340
    cross-platform mechanism, 360
    mmap object, using for, 364
IronPython
    installing, 21
    interpreter, 30
is (identity test), 50, 162
ISAM (Indexed-Sequential Access
    Method), 285
ISO 8601 formats, time/date values
    in, 327
ISO-compliant C compiler, installing
    Python and, 14
iterables, 40
iteration, file objects, 221
itertools module, 183–185

J

.jar files, 655, 662–664
jarray module, 658
Java
    classes, subclassing, 659
    compiling Python into, 662–664
    embedding Jython, 659–662
Java Development Kit (JDK), 20
Java Native Interface (JNI), 655
Java packages, 656–659
Java Virtual Machines (see JVMs)
JavaBeans, 659
java.util collection classes, 659
JDK (Java Development Kit), 20
JNI (Java Native Interface), 655
.join, 484
joining many strings into one, 484

JVMs (Java Virtual Machines), 6
    Jython installation and, 20
Jython, 6, 656
    documentation, 10
    embedding in Java, 659–662
    importing Java packages, 656–659
    installing, 20
Jython API, 660—662
jython interpreter, 29
jythonc command, 663
jython.jar file, 656

K

keyboard events (Tkinter), 447
keyboard focus (Tkinter), 411
keyed access, 285
keys (in dictionaries), 44
keywords, 35
Komodo, 27

L

Label class (Tkinter module), 417
lambda expressions, 78
language, lexical structure, 33–38
layout manager, 406
LBYL (look before you leap), 134
Lesser GPL (LGPL), 8
lexical structure of language, 33–38
LGPL (Lesser GPL), 8
LinearAlgebra module, 404
linecache module, 226
lines
    blank lines, 34
    logical lines, 33
    physical lines, 33
Linux
    installing Python from binaries, 19
    Red Hat Linux releases 6.x/7.x, 9
    support for cryptographic-quality
        pseudorandom numbers, 370
list comprehensions, 67–68
Listbox class (Tkinter module), 417
lists, 43
    in-place operations, 56
    maintaining order of, 176–179, 183
    methods, 56
    modifying, 56
    optimizing operations on, 478
    sequence operators, 55–58
literals, 35, 37

loading modules, 144–147
  __import__ function, 159
local variables of functions, 76
locale module, 269–274
locale sensitivity, string module, 192
locks, 341–342
  global interpreter lock (GIL), 341
  re-entrant locks (RLock class), 347
logging errors, 136
logging module, 136–138
logical lines, 33
long type, 156
look before you leap (LBYL), 134
loop statements, else clause, 69
loops, optimizing, 486

M

Macintosh
  internationalization, 199
  Mac OS 9/Mac OS X, 18
  making .app files for, 676
  Python IDE, 26
  Python interpreter on, 23
MacPython, IDE included with, 26
mail protocol, 493
mailing lists, 10
main program, module loading
    and, 145
make utility, installing Python and, 14
mappings, 44
  special methods for, 110
markup, 575
marshal module, 278
marshaling, 278
match object, 210
math module, 365
mbcs codec (Windows), 199
membership testing, sequences, 54
memoization (in deep copies), 172–173
memory
  array type and, 375
  leaks, exposing, 333
  saving, __slots__ attribute, 102
  storing array object, 381
Menu class (Tkinter module), 423–424
Message class (email.Message module),
    564–573
Message module, 564
  Message class, 564

metaclasses, 116–119
methods, 82, 85
  bound and unbound, 91–94
  class-level, 99–100
  of dictionaries, 60
  Java-visible, adding, 663
  of lists, 56–57
  per-instance, 103
  of sets, 58
  special, 104–115
  of strings, 186–191
  superclass, delegating to, 96–97
Microsoft Installer (MSI), 18
Microsoft .NET (see IronPython)
Microsoft SQL Server, 299
Microsoft web servers, installing Python
    CGI scripts on, 552
MIME (Multipurpose Internet Mail
    Extensions), 561, 564
mimetools module, 573
minidom module, 599–609
MLab module, 403
mmap module, 360
mmap object, 360–364
mode attribute, 219
mode string, file objects, 217
mod_python, 558
Modules, 280
modules, 139–152
  DBAPI-compliant, 298
  installing, 647, 651, 653
  loading, 144–147, 159, 617
  module object, 139–142
    attributes, 141–143
  packages and, 149
modulo, ternary exponentiation-and-
    modulo, 165, 115
money-related computations, 372
Morsel class (Cookie module), 555
MSI (Microsoft Installer), 18
mssqldb module, 299
msvcrt module, 264
multiple inheritance, 133
multiple precision arithmetic (see gmpy
    module)
Multipurpose Internet Mail Extensions
    (MIME)
multiset (see defaultdict type)
multithreading (see threads)

mutable objects, 38
    shelve module and, 284
mx package, 306, 319
mx.DateTime module, 319–327
mxODBC module, 298
MySQLdb module, 299

N

name attribute, 219
named arguments in function calls,
        74–75
names (see variables)
namespaces, functions, 76
nested functions, 77
network encodings, 561
Network News Transport Protocol (see
        NNTP)
network protocol modules
    client-side, 493, 503, 506, 511, 515,
        516, 519
    server-side, 520, 528
newsgroups, 10
new-style classes, 104
NIST module, 327
NNTP class, 512–514
NNTP (Network News Transport
        Protocol), 493, 511
nntplib module, 493, 511–512
Node class (minidom
        module), 600–602, 608
None, 45
    returned by functions reaching end of
        body, 73
nonpure distributions, 667
nonsequential access, file objects, 218
numarray module, 378
numbers, 38
    complex, 40
    decimal, 372–373
    floating-point, 39, 365, 372
    integers, 39
    pseudorandom, 370
    returning absolute value of, 159
Numeric module, 378–402
    array object, 378–380
    blitz function, 646
    optional modules supplied by, 403
    ufuncs, 399
numeric operations, 52–53
    operator module, 368–369
    special methods for, 113–115

O

object models, 81
    classic, 82, 94
    new-style, 104
object type, 98, 156
object-oriented Python, 81
objects
    assigning, 172
    first-class, classes as, 82
    immutable, 38
    mutable, 38
    mutable/immutable, 284
    polymorphism, 222
    serializing/deserializing, 278
odbc module, 298
ODBC (Open DataBase
        Connectivity), 298
Open DataBase Connectivity
        (ODBC), 298
OpenDirector class, 502
operations, in-place, with Numeric
        ufuncs, 391
operators, 35, 50–58
    chaining of comparisons, 51
    numeric, 52–53
    operator module, 368–369
    precedence, 51
    on sequences, 54–58
    short-circuiting, 51
optimization, 451, 474
    benchmarking, 475
    developing Python applications, 474
    large-scale, 476, 478
    profiling, 480
    small-scale, 483–488
optional parameters of functions, 71
options, command-line, 23–24, 179
optparse module, 179–182
Oracle RDBMS, 299
org.python.core package, 661
os module, 240
    environ attribute, 354
    functions, 242–246
    path-string attributes, 241
    P_WAIT attribute, 357
    system function, 354
OSError, 240
os.path module, 246–249

P

packages, 149
parameters of functions, 71
parent widgets, 406, 420
parentheses (see ())
Parser module, 564
partial application, 175
pass statement, 69
passing arguments to functions, 74
PATH variable, python interpreter
        and, 22
path-string attributes, os module, 241
pdb module, 466
PEPs (Python Enhancement
        Proposals), 8
performance, 476
    arrays and, 375
    asyncore/asynchat modules, 558
    big-O notation and concepts,
        476–479
    CGI scripts, 557
    DBM modules, 287
    extension modules, special-
        purpose, 5
    generator expressions, 78–79
    pickle/cPickle modules, 279
    slicing array object, 382
    threads, 340, 347
    Twisted package, 558
per-instance methods, 103
permissions of files, 242
persistence, 277
Personal Web Server (PWS), 552
PhotoImage class, 414
physical lines, 33
pickle module, 279–283
PIL (Python Imaging Library), 414
pipes, 340, 355–360
plain assignment statements, 47
polymorphism, 94, 98, 101
    to file objects, 222
    type checking and, 157
POP mailboxes, accessing, 503
POP3 class (poplib module), 504
POP3 (Post Office Protocol version
        3), 503
    twisted.protocols package, 540
poplib module, 493, 503
portability
    distributing Python modules, 672
    extension modules and, 5

positional arguments to functions,
        74–75
    when building dictionaries, 44
Post Office Protocol version 3 (see
        POP3)
PostgreSQL, 299
PowerArchiver,
        uncompressing/unpacking, 15
pprint module, 197
PrettyPrinter class, 197
print statement, 61, 256
printing, complicated data in readable
        format, 197
priority queue, 177
process environment, 353
processes, 340
Profile class, 480
profiling, 451
program termination, 169, 337–338
programming paradigms, ability to mix
        and match in Python, 81
prompt string, Python interactive
        sessions, 25
properties, 100–101, 156
    importance of, 101
    and inheritance, 101
protocol module (Twisted package),
        540–543
pseudorandom numbers, 370
PSF (Python Software Foundation), 8
PSP (Python Server Pages), 559
    embedding Python code in
        HTML, 586
pstats module, 481
psycopg module, 299
PTL (Python Template Language), 560
pulldom module, 605–606
punctuation
    in regular expressions, 201
    in string formatting, 193–196
    in URLs, 494
    (see also Symbols)
pure distributions, 667
PWS (Personal Web Server), 552
.py, .pyc, and .pyo files, 28–29, 145
    __init__.py in packages, 149–150
    .pythonrc.py, 339
    setup.py file, 151, 614, 667, 673–675
py2exe tool, 675
PyApache, 558

Py_CompileString function (Python C
      API), 649
PyException Java exception, 661
PyObject Java object, 662
PyPy, 7
pyrex, 646, 650–654
pysqlite, 300–301
Python, 3, 141, 146, 616, 620
      compiling into Java, 662–664
      development, 8
      development environments, 26
      documentation, 10
      embedding/extending, 613
      extension modules, 5
      extensions, 614
      implementations, 5
      installing, 14
      interpreter, 22–25
      language, 3
      library, 5
      modules, 5
      newsgroups/mailing lists, 10
      object models, 81
      object-orientation, 81
      programming paradigms, 81
      programs, 28, 138
      resources, 9, 11
      SIGs, 11
      upgrades, overwriting
            customizations, 338
      versions, 8, 303, 462
Python 2.5, exception handling, 124
Python C API, extending CPython
      with, 614
      building/installing C-coded Python
            extensions, 614
Python Database API 2.0 standard (see
      DBAPI)
Python Enhancement Proposals
      (PEPs), 8
Python Imaging Library (PIL), 414
Python Server Pages (see PSP)
Python Template Language (PTL), 560
PYTHONHOME environment variable,
      22
PythonInterpreter class (Jython
      API), 660
python.path option, 657
PYTHONPATH environment
      variable, 23, 144

PYTHONSTARTUP environment
      variable, 23, 339
pythonw interpreter, 29
PythonWin, 26
pytz module, 313
PyXML, 591

Q
QP encoding (Quoted Printable
      encoding), 562
Queue module, 342–343
      ideal threaded-program architecture,
            350
Quixote, 560
quopri module, 562
Quoted Printable encoding (QP
      encoding), 562
quoted strings, 40

R
Radiobutton class (Tkinter
      module), 418
raise statement, 69, 128
raising to power (see exponentiation
      operators)
Random class, 370
random module, 370
raw strings, 42
RDBMS (relational database
      management system), 277
RDF (Resource Description
      Framework), 591
re module, 201–212
reactor object (Twisted package),
      540–541
readline module, 258–260
ReadLine package for Windows, 25
rebinding, 46, 74
recursion, 80
RedHat Package Manager (RPM),
      installing Python from
      binaries, 19
references
      reference counting, C-coded
            extension modules, 620
      reference loops, 336
      weak, 336
reflection (see introspection)
regular expression object, 207–210

regular expressions, 201–212
   common idioms, 202
   groups, 204
   match object, 210
   matching versus searching, 206
   pattern-string syntax, 201
relational database management system
      (RDBMS), 277
Remote Procedure Calls (RPCs), 516
repetition, sequences, 54
repr module, 198
Resource Description Framework
      (RDF), 591
resources, 9
   PBF, 11
   print, 12
   Python Cookbook, 11
   Python Journal, 11
   Python on Windows, 292
   Python source code, 11
return statement, 73
reversing a sequence, 57–58, 156
rfc822 module, 573
RLock class (threading module), 344
RPCs (Remote Procedure Calls), 516
RPM (RedHat Package Manager),
      installing Python from
      binaries, 19

S

SAP DB, 299
SAX (Simple API for XML), 593
   parsing XHTML, 598
   parsing XML, 593
SAXException class (xml.sax
      package), 593
saxutils module, 597
Scale class (Tkinter module), 419
sched module, 316
SciTE, 27
scopes (see namespaces)
scripts, 28, 557
   CGI, 550, 557
   GUI, running standalone, 405
   setup.py, 667
Scrollbar class (Tkinter module), 419
SCXX library, 645
search path for modules, 144
searching for a regular expression, 210

security
   cookies and, 553
   cryptographic-quality pseudorandom
         numbers, 370
select module, 533
self parameter, 85, 91
Semaphore class (threading
         module), 344, 349, 358
sentinel, 98
sequences, 40–43, 53–58
   arrays, 375–378
   generators, 78–79
   indexing, 48, 50, 54–56, 380–381
   inserting into, 56–57
   iterables, 40
   iterators, 65–66, 183–185
   list comprehensions, 67
   list methods, 56–58
   slicing, 48, 50, 55–56, 381–383
   sorting, 57
   special methods for, 109
   string methods, 186–191
sequential access, file objects, 218
serialization, 277
   marshal module, 278
   pickle/cPickle modules, 279, 283
   shelve module, 284
ServerProxy class, xmlrpclib module,
         518–519
servers, 493
   Apache, 552, 557
   custom Python, 558
   HTTP, 506, 530
   Internet, 528
   Microsoft web, installing Python CGI
         scripts on, 552
   SMTP, 505
   Telnet, 515
   web, subclassing
         BaseHTTPServer, 558
   Xitami, 553
   XML-RPC, 517
server-side web scripting, 545–560
   CGI, 545–553
   CherryPy, Django, Pylon,
         Turbogears, 559
   cookies, 553–557
   FastCGI, 557
   Quixote, 560
   web.py, 560

server-side web scripting *(continued)*
Webware, 559
WSGI, 558
servlets, Jython, 664
sets, 43, 58, 156
special methods for, 110
setup.cfg file, 673
setup.py script, 151, 667
SGML (Standard General Markup
Language), 575
sgmllib module, 576
SGMLParser class
HTMLParser class, compared
to, 583
sgmllib module, 576
shallow copies, 55, 58, 60, 172
shelve module, 284
short-circuiting operators, 51
shutil module, 252
SIGs (Special Interest Groups), 11
Simple API for XML (see SAX)
Simple Mail Transport Protocol (see
SMTP)
simple statements, 37–38
SimpleHTTPServer module, 530
SimpleXMLRPCServer module, 530
Simplified Wrapper and Interface
Generator (SWIG), 646
site customization, 338
site module, 338
sitecustomize module, 199, 338
site.py file, 338
slicing, 48, 50, 55–56
Numeric arrays, 380–381
slice object, 110, 156
SMTP (Simple Mail Transport
Protocol), 503–505
smtplib module, 493, 505
socket module, 521
functions, 521
socket class, 523
sockets, 520–528
event-driven programming, 533–544
methods, 523–525
TCP and UDP, 525–527
timeout behavior, 528
SocketServer module, 528
source code, installing Python from,
14–19

source files, 139
as modules, 140
Python modules in distribution
utilities, 669
Source Navigator (Red Hat), 26
Special Interest Groups (SIGs), 11
special methods, 104–115
for containers, 109
general-purpose, 104
for number objects, 113
Spyce, Cheetah and, 587
SQL (Structured Query Language), 277
SQLite (see pysqlite)
stack (in debugging), 462–470
propagation of exceptions, 127–129
stack level in warnings, 473–474
stack traces (tracebacks), 125–127,
135–136, 455–456, 466
Standard General Markup Language
(SGML), 575
standard input, error, output 171
(see also stderr; stdin; stdout)
stat module, 249
statements
assignment statements, 47–49
break, 68
compound statements, 38
continue, 68
control flow
break, 68
continue, 68
for, 64–68
if, 62
pass, 69
raise, 69
try, 69
while, 63
with, 69
def, 70
del, 49
expressions, 37
for, 64–68
if, 62
pass, 69
print, 61, 256
raise, 69
return, 73
simple statements, 37
terminating, 34

try, 69
while, 63
with, 69
static methods, 99, 157
stderr, 136, 171, 256
stdin, 171
stdout, 171, 256
str, 157, 186, 273
  (see also strings)
string module, 191–193
  locale sensitivity, 192
StringIO module, 229
strings, 40–42, 186–191
  escape sequences, 41
  formatting, 193–197
  methods, 186–191
  mutable, 178
  optimizing operations on, 478
  raw-string syntax, 42
  regular expressions, 201–212
  as sequences, 53–55
  struct formats, 227
  template strings, 196
  triple-quoted syntax, 41
  Unicode, 198–200
struct module, 227–229
Structured Query Language (SQL), 277
subprocess module, 358–360
summing sequences of numbers, 167
subclass relationships, 83
superclass methods, delegating to, 96
  super type, 97, 157
SWIG (Simplified Wrapper and
    Interface Generator), 646
sys module
  and error handling, 127, 133, 136
  and module loading, 144, 147
  stderr, stdin, stdout, 127, 136, 171
system testing, 452
SystemExit exception, 129

T

tags, HTML, 575–584
tar program, 15
tarfile module, 233–235
TCP echo servers, 525
TCPServer class, 528
Telnet class, 515–516
telnet protocol, 493, 515
telnetlib module, 357, 493, 515
tempfile module, 223

template strings, 196
terminating statements, 34
termination functions, 337
ternary operator, 51
TestCase class (unittest module),
    459–460
test-first development, 452
testing, 451–461
text, filling, 197
Text class (Tkinter module), 426
text editors with Python support, 27
text input/output, 256
text wrapping, 197
Textpad class (curses module), 263
Thread class (threading module), 346
thread module, 341
threaded program
    architecture, 350–353
threading module, 344–349
ThreadingTCPServer class, 528
ThreadingUDPServer class, 528
threads, 341–353
  program architecture, 350–353
  synchronizing, 346–349
  thread safety, DBAPI, 293
timedelta class, datetime module, 312
timeit module, 484
timestamps, 307
  in databases, 295
  in logging, 138
time class, datetime module, 308
time module, 302–306
  time-tuple, 302
time zones, 313
tkFont module, 433
Tkinter events, 446–448
Tkinter module, 406
  attributes, 406
  Button class, 415
  Canvas class, 436
  Checkbutton class, 415
  Entry class, 416
  Event class, 446
  events, 446
  Frame class, 420
  geometry management, 442, 445
  Label class, 417
  Listbox class, 417
  Menu class, 423
  Radiobutton class, 418
  Scale class, 419

Tkinter module *(continued)*
    Scrollbar class, 419
    Text class, 426
    Toplevel class, 420
    variable object, 413
    widgets supplied by, 409, 415
tokens, 35–37
toolkits, 405
Toplevel class (Tkinter module), 420
traceback messages, 121
traceback module, 466
tracebacklimit attribute, 171
transport object (Twisted package), 542
troubleshooting
    error-specific information, 129
    memory leaks, 333
    (see also debugging)
True, 45
truncating division, 52
truth values (evaluation), 45
try statement, 69
    exception handling, 121–123, 135
tuples, 42, 157
    in string formatting, 195
    sequence operations, 55
TurboGears, 559
Twisted package, 533–541
    performance characteristics, 558
two's complement, 53
type checking, 157
type codes in arrays, 375
type type, 117, 157, 332
types
    built-in, 154–158
    defining new with C-coded Python
        extensions, 638
    internal, 331
types module, 332

U

UDP echo servers, 527
UDPServer class, 528
ufuncs (universal functions), Numeric
        module, 399–400
unbound methods, 91
Unicode strings, 198–201
    character database, 200
    codecs module, 199
    converting strings to, 198
    literals, 42
    Tkinter and, 406

unicodedata module, 200
Uniform Resource Locators (see URLs)
unittest module, 457–461
    using large amounts of data, 461
universal functions (ufuncs), Numeroc
        module, 399
universal newlines (reading textfiles),
        218
Unix
    dbm module, 287
    installing Python from source, 17
    mmap function, 361
    Python IDEs, 26
    running Python scripts, 29
Unix-to-Unix (UU) encoding, 563
URL-based file-like objects, 497
urllib module, 493–498
urllib2 module, 493, 498–502
urlparse module, 493
URLs (Uniform Resource
        Locators), 493
    access to network protocols, 493
    authentication, 502
    reading data from, 495
Usenet News, 511
user customization, 339
user input, errors depending on, 136
user module, 339
UserDict module, 178
UserList module, 178
UTC (Coordinated Universal
        Time), 302
Utils module (email package), 570
uu module, 563
UU (Unix-to-Unix) encoding, 563

V

variables, 46
    binding, 46
    built-in, 138
    class-private, 85
    global, thread synchronization
        and, 346
    identifiers, 35
    module-private, 142
vim program, 27
Visual C++ (Visual Studio), 15–16, 27
Visual Studio .NET IDE, 27

W

W3C (World Wide Web
  Consortium), 591
warnings module, 471–473
WConio module, 265
weakref module, 333–336
web servers, subclassing
  BaseHTTPServer, 558
web.py, 560
Webware, 559, 586
whichdb module, 287
while statement, 63
  else clause, 69
whitespace
  check is string is all whitespace, 192
  indentation, 34
  separates tokens, 35
  splitting strings, 189
Widget class (Tkinter module), 408,
  411–412, 443–445
widgets, 405, 408
  canvas, 436, 438, 440
  checkboxes, 415
  child/parent, 420
  color options, 409
  container, 420
  length options, 410
  listboxes, 417
  menus, 423, 425
  pushbuttons, 415
  radiobuttons, 418
  scrollbars, 419
  text, 426, 428, 432
  text entry fields, 416
  Tkinter module, 415
win32all package, 646
Windows
  applications, embedding/extending
    Python with COM, 646
  CGI scripting on, 549
  installing Python from binaries, 19
  installing Python from source, 15
  IronPython, 6
  keys into os.environ, 354
  mbcs codec, 199
  mmap function, 361
  py2exe tool, 675
  Python scripts, 29
  resource for further information, 292
Wing IDE, 27
WinZip program, 15

with statement (Python 2.5), 69, 125
World Wide Web Consortium (W3C),
  591
wrapping text, 197
WSGI, 558
wxWindows toolkit, 26

X

XHTML, 575
  changing/outputting with
    minidom, 609
  parsing, 583, 598, 605
Xitami servers, installing Python CGI
  scripts on, 553
XML (eXtensible Markup
  Language), 591
  generating, 606
  parsing, 592, 599
xml package, 591
xml.dom package, 599
XMLGenerator class (saxutils
  module), 597
XML-RPC, 493, 516, 519
  xmlrpclib module, 517
XML-RPC servers, 517, 531
xmlrpclib module, 517
xml.sax package, 593–597
XPath, 591
xrange type, 158
XSLT, 591

Y

yield statement (generators), 76

Z

ZIP files, importing from, 144, 148
zipfile module, 235–239
zlib module, 239
Zope, 557

About the Author

Alex Martelli is a member of the Python Software Foundation and works as Uber Tech Lead for Google, Inc. in Mountain View, California. Before joining Google, Alex spent eight years with IBM Research, winning three Outstanding Technical Achievement Awards. He won 13 as Senior Software Consultant at think3 inc, where he developed libraries, network protocols, GUI engines, event frameworks, and web access frontends. He won three more as a freelance consultant, working mostly for AB Strakt, a Python-centered software house in Göteborg, Sweden. Alex has also taught programming languages, development methods, and numerical computing at Ferrara University and other venues. Alex's proudest achievement is the articles that appeared in *Bridge World* (January/February 2000), which were hailed as giant steps toward solving issues that had haunted contract-bridge theoreticians for decades.

Colophon

The animal on the cover of *Python in a Nutshell*, Second Edition, is an African rock python, one of approximately 18 species of python. Pythons are nonvenomous constrictor snakes that live in tropical regions of Africa, Asia, Australia, and some Pacific Islands. Pythons live mainly on the ground, but they are also excellent swimmers and climbers. Both male and female pythons retain vestiges of their ancestral hind legs. The male python uses these vestiges, or spurs, when courting a female.

The python kills its prey by suffocation. While the snake's sharp teeth grip and hold the prey in place, the python's long body coils around its victim's chest, constricting tighter each time it breathes out. They feed primarily on mammals and birds. Python attacks on humans are extremely rare.

The cover image is a 19th-century engraving from the Dover Pictorial Archive. The cover font is Adobe ITC Garamond. The text font is Linotype Birka; the heading font is Adobe Myriad Condensed; and the code font is LucasFont's TheSans Mono Condensed.

Better than e-books

Buy *Python in a Nutshell*, 2nd Edition,
and access the digital edition FREE on
Safari for 45 days.

Go to www.oreilly.com/go/safarienabled
and type in coupon code 3BG5-EEUE-6XRA-NDEB-Q2UD

Search
thousands of
top tech books

Download
whole chapters

Cut and Paste
code examples

Find
answers fast

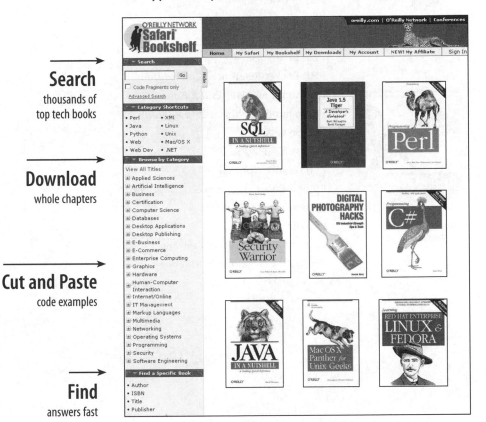

Search Safari! The premier electronic reference
library for programmers and IT professionals.

Related Titles from O'Reilly

Scripting Languages

Essential PHP Security

Exploring Expect

Jython Essentials

Learning Python, *2nd Edition*

PHP 5 Essentials

PHP Cookbook, *2nd Edition*

PHP Hacks

PHP in a Nutshell

PHP Pocket Reference, *2nd Edition*

Programming PHP, *2nd Edition*

Programming Python, *2nd Edition*

Python & XML

Python Cookbook

Python in a Nutshell

Python Pocket Reference, *3rd Edition*

Python Standard Library

Ruby in a Nutshell

Ruby on Rails: Up and Running

Twisted: A Developer's Notebook

Web Database Applications with PHP and MySQL, *2nd Edition*

O'REILLY®

Our books are available at most retail and online bookstores.
To order direct: 1-800-998-9938 • *order@oreilly.com* • *www.oreilly.com*
Online editions of most O'Reilly titles are available by subscription at *safari.oreilly.com*